THE COSTS OF WAR

THE COSTS OF WAR

AMERICA'S
PYRRHIC
VICTORIES

EDITED WITH AN
INTRODUCTION BY
JOHN V.
DENSON

TRANSACTION PUBLISHERS
NEW BRUNSWICK (U.S.A.) AND LONDON (U.K.)

Copyright © 1997 by Transaction Publishers, New Brunswick, New Jersey 08903.

The publisher acknowledges the assistance of the Ludwig von Mises Institute, Auburn, Alabama 36849, in the preparation of this volume.

Library of Congress Catalog Number: 96-51721
ISBN: 1-56000-319-7
Printed in the United States of America

Library of Congress Cataloging-in-Publication Data

The costs of war : America's pyrrhic victories / edited with an introduction by John V. Denson.
    p. cm.
Includes bibliographical references and index.
ISBN 1-56000-319-7 (cloth : alk. paper)
    1. War and society. 2. War, Cost of. I. Denson, John V., 1936–
HM36.5.C66 1997
303.6'6—dc21   96-51721
                                                    CIP

Dedication

Dedicated to the memory of John T. Flynn,
a brilliant writer, a consummate journalist, and
a true American patriot who understood,
far more than almost anyone else, the terrible
costs of war, especially the loss of freedom,
even in a "victory."

Acknowledgements

In addition to its generous members, there are many people with the Ludwig von Mises Institute in Auburn, Alabama, to recognize and thank for their parts in this book. First and foremost, there is Lew Rockwell, president and founder, who selected and recruited all of the speakers for the *Costs of War* conference in Atlanta in May of 1994. Most of these speakers became contributors to this book. Pat Heckman skillfully managed the conference, and Judy Thommesen, a person of immense intelligence and the patience of Job, worked with all of the contributors and all of my last-minute suggested changes and molded this book into its present form. Scott Kjar handled the typesetting responsibilities.

Thank you, as well as many others at the Institute, for all of your hard work.—J.V.D.

TABLE OF CONTENTS

INTRODUCTION*

T he greatest accomplishment of Western civilization has been
the achievement of individual freedom by imposing limits
on the power of the state. Freedom was the prerequisite for
the other great achievements in science, medicine, industry, technology and the arts. The ancient riddle to be solved in this long
process was how to reconcile government with individual freedom, or law with liberty. The riddle stated differently is: How do
we allow government to have enough power to protect freedom
without giving it too much so that it becomes the oppressor of
freedom?

The founding fathers of the United States provided the best
answer to this question by relying upon the lessons of history,
rather than solely upon abstract theories. The ancient Greeks in-
vented democracy in their city-states but it proved faulty when not
administered by virtuous leaders, and the majority proved to be as
tyrannical as a single despot. The early Roman Republic, and their
development of "The Rule of Law," proved to be more influential
on the founders. The Roman structure of government, with its
checks and balances and separation of powers, helped to prevent
the centralization of power. The fact that the Roman Republic began to decline when power became more centralized was an important lesson.

> The Roman experience was mentioned repeatedly in the
> constitutional debates at Philadelphia. The consequences of
> Roman centralization had their part in discouraging
> schemes for a central, rather than a federal, government in
> America.[1]

After the Romans, the next great advance in the cause of liberty which strongly influenced the founders was their own history in
England, especially in the development of England's unwritten
constitution. The colonists relied upon this constitution for their
rights as Englishmen and this gave them the lessons of their own

---

*In 280 B.C., Pyrrhus, king of Epirus, sent his army to invade Italy. In two glorious
victories, at Heraclea (280 B.C.) and at Asculum (279 B.C.), Pyrrhus crushed the
Romans, and sent them into retreat. However, in the course of his victories, Pyrrhus
sustained immense losses. These losses later led to his defeat and death, when he no
longer could call upon an army that had died during his conquests. Thus, a victory
won at such great cost that the losses outweigh the gains is referred to as a pyrrhic
victory.

[1]Russell Kirk, *The Roots of American Order*, 3rd ed. (Washington, D.C.: Regnery
Gateway, 1991), p. 134.

experience in America. The English constitution was developed through experience spanning more than seven centuries, resulting in a mosaic of law and "spontaneous order" created in many thousands of court decisions, known as the common law. Furthermore, the British carved out their rights and limited the power of government, especially of kings, in numerous charters of freedom, such as the Magna Carta, and various Petitions and Bills of Right.

The English Civil War, in the 17th century, occurred primarily because Charles I violated this long tradition and tried to impose taxes on the people without the consent or authorization of their elected representatives in Parliament. The people's extreme displeasure over this usurpation of power was dramatically demonstrated when they cut off the King's head. The Bill of Rights of 1689 firmly established the complete superiority of Parliament over any king or court, and it placed numerous restrictions on all future monarchs.

The unique contribution of the founding fathers was the abolition of monarchy and the establishment of a written Constitution and Bill of Rights which were superior to all three branches of government. Thomas Jefferson captured the spirit of the times in stating, "In questions of power, then, let no more be heard of confidence in man, but bind him down from mischief with the chains of the Constitution."[2]

The Constitution of the United States delegated specific limited powers to the three branches of government, and imposed numerous checks and balances to prevent their consolidation. The price for gaining support from the opponents of the Constitution was the adoption of the Bill of Rights, which made it clear, especially in the ninth and tenth amendments, that most of the powers and duties of government were to remain with the states and the people; and furthermore, other amendments made it clear that even a majority in Congress could not encroach upon certain basic liberties of the people established by both the British and American experience.

Additionally, a foreign policy of non-intervention and neutrality toward other nations was adopted by the first Washington administration, because history demonstrated that war inevitably consolidates immense powers into the central government, thereby jeopardizing individual liberty. The founders wanted to make sure that wars were extremely rare and restricted only to the defense of America against a clear and present danger.

[2]*The Political Writings of Thomas Jefferson* (New York: Liberty Arts Press, 1955), p. 161.

In the war-torn 20th century, we rarely hear that one of the main costs of war is a long-term loss of liberty to winners and losers alike. There are the obvious and direct costs of the number of dead and wounded soldiers, but rarely do we hear about the lifetime struggles of combat veterans to live with their nightmares and injuries. Nor do we hear much about the long-term hidden costs of inflation, debts, and taxes. Other inevitable long-term costs of war which are not immediately obvious are damages caused to our culture, to our morality, and to civilization in general.

Two of the primary methods by which most modern governments conduct wars are conscription and propaganda.[3] The winners have always written the history, and after the war, propaganda is often adopted as "history" and eventually becomes a myth or legend. We need to pierce through the veils of myth and propaganda to see what the true costs of war have been, especially to American liberty.

Many students of Ludwig von Mises know him only as an economist and often fail to consider his political ideas, especially his views on war and foreign policy. For all of the above reasons, the Mises Institute held a three-day conference in Atlanta, Georgia, in May of 1994, entitled "The Costs of War." The speakers at the conference were all invited to submit papers for this book. Many of those who attended the conference remarked afterward that it was a unique experience since it put a very new light on the old subject of war. I think you will also find this book unique, thought provoking and very disturbing because it shows that our nation has paid a terrible price, especially through the loss of liberty, as a result of its victorious wars. During the 20th century, the United States has been, and continues to be, on a disastrous and tragic course because of its foreign policy.

In 1927, Mises explained many of his political views, including those on war and on foreign policy, in a book entitled *Liberalismus* (*Liberalism*). He used the popular word "liberalism" to mean a government which promotes individual freedom, as it was generally understood in the 18th and 19th centuries in Europe. After World War I, however, the word "liberal" took on a completely different meaning and was used by those who actually were its enemies as a

---

[3]John W. Dower, *War Without Mercy* (New York: Pantheon Books, 1986), chap. 2, "Know Your Enemy," pp. 15–32. This explains how Hollywood directors, and especially Frank Capra, were recruited by the United States government to produce propaganda films. See also Bill Kauffman, *America First: Its History, Culture and Politics* (Amherst, N.Y.: Prometheus Books, 1995), pp. 85–99; and Gore Vidal, *Screening History* (Cambridge, Mass.: Harvard University Press, 1992).

description of their own philosophy.[4] First, the English Fabians adopted the word to describe their brand of gradual socialism. Two American magazines, the *New Republic* and the *Nation*, began to use the term liberal to describe New Dealers, central planners and other soft-core socialists. This was a brilliant propaganda coup, similar to that of the "Nationalists" at the time of the debates surrounding the writing and ratification of the United States Constitution.

Nationalists, during the American Revolution, believed in a strong consolidated central government which would control the economy (known as "mercantilism"), rather than believing in a free market. Their opponents believed in a "federal" system of a limited central government which was granted only a few powers by the sovereign states coupled with a free economy. The Nationalists, whose sympathizers also owned most of the newspapers at that time, were successful in calling themselves "Federalists" and branding their opponents as "Anti-Federalist," thereby giving the Nationalists a decided advantage in the battle of ideas by using these confusing labels.

When Mises published the English translation of *Liberalismus* in 1962, the common understanding of the word liberal had become totally transformed and now described the ideas which Mises opposed. Therefore, he used the word "classical" to describe liberalism in its original meaning and put it at the end of the title of this new edition, i.e., *The Free and Prosperous Commonwealth: An Exposition of the Ideas of Classical Liberalism*.[5] Later, in 1985, the attempt was made again to reclaim the word liberalism for Mises's work and the third edition was entitled *Liberalism: In the Classical Tradition*.[6] In chapter three, Mises states some of his main views on war and foreign policy.[7] He attacks imperialism and colonialism and says that war is the greatest enemy of freedom and prosperity. He points out that we will not succeed in achieving peace throughout the world until it is generally understood that the central government of each nation must be very limited in its scope and power. He specifically states:

---

[4]For an excellent analysis and discussion of the metamorphosis of the meaning of the term "liberal," especially in America, see Dwight D. Murphey, *Liberalism in Contemporary America* (McLean, Va.: Council for Social and Economic Studies, 1992).

[5]Ludwig von Mises, *The Free and Prosperous Commonwealth: An Exposition of the Ideas of Classical Liberalism*, Ralph Raico, trans. (Princeton, N.J.: D. Van Nostrand, 1962).

[6]Ludwig von Mises, *Liberalism: In the Classical Tradition* (Irvington-on-Hudson, N.Y.: Foundation for Economic Education, and San Francisco: Cobden Press, 1985).

[7]See also, Mises's viewpoints on war in his major work *Human Action* (New York: Yale University Press, 1949), pp. 817–28.

> The nations must come to realize that the most important
> problem of foreign policy is the establishment of lasting
> peace, and they must understand that this can be assured
> throughout the world only if the field of activity permitted
> to the State is limited to the narrowest range. Only then will
> the size and extent of the territory subject to the sovereignty
> of the State no longer assume such overwhelming impor-
> tance for the life of the individual as to make it seem natural,
> now as in the past, for the rivers of blood to be shed in dis-
> putes of boundaries.[8]

He argues that there must be a free-trade policy (no protective
tariffs), the right to self-determination (through secession if necessary as is now occurring in Eastern Europe and the former Soviet
Union), the complete protection of private property, and the private ownership of the means of production. There must also be a
free flow of capital and labor between the nations. Mises sets out a
further analysis of war and foreign policy in his 1944 work entitled
Omnipotent Government, by stating:

> Durable peace is only possible under perfect capitalism,
> hitherto never and nowhere completely tried or achieved. In
> such a Jeffersonian world of unhampered market economy
> the scope of government activities is limited to the protec-
> tion of the lives, health, and property of individuals against
> violence or fraudulent aggression.[9]

Mises goes on to say that:

> All the oratory of the advocates of government omnipotence
> cannot annul the fact that there is but one system that makes
> for durable peace: a free market economy. Government con-
> trol leads to economic nationalism and thus results in con-
> flict.[10]

The United States of America is the only country founded on
these great principles of "classical liberalism." Mises maintained
throughout his long and productive life that these ideas were
never proven wrong, unworkable or impractical, but were simply
abandoned to the great detriment of liberty in the 20th century.

This present volume, in the spirit of Mises and in furtherance
of his ideas on war and foreign policy, will examine the costs of
war with special emphasis on the loss of freedom to American citizens. "Successful" wars, or those in which military victory was
achieved, have transformed the American government into something completely different from the design of its founders.

[8]Mises, *Liberalism: In the Classical Tradition,* p. 144.
[9]Ludwig von Mises, *Omnipotent Government: The Rise of the Total State and Total War*
(New Rochelle, N.Y.: Arlington House, 1969), p. 284
[10]Ibid., p. 286.

At the Mises Conference held in Atlanta, I gave the introductory remarks which served as an overview and then the remaining speakers addressed various aspects and details of the costs of war as their chapters do in this volume. My introductory remarks made at the conference have been expanded for the purpose of serving as an overview for this book and constitute the first chapter entitled "War and American Freedom." The chapters which follow address the various aspects of the costs of war and, to my knowledge, no other book has covered the subject of war from the same perspective. The contributors were not strictly limited to particular subjects, but they can be placed into certain categories.

The first article following my overview, by Samuel Francis, sets the stage by placing the views of the founding fathers into their historical perspective, tracing the development of their views over several hundred years, and putting particular emphasis on the Anglo–Saxon experience. While the British have forgotten their own history and given up their right to bear arms, Americans should recall English history, as well as their own, and guard this right carefully. The next article, by Justin Raimondo, traces the American anti-interventionist tradition from the days of the revolution up to the 20th century, giving us a look at what has happened to the original foreign policy of the founders, and exploring the arguments used by those who wish to reclaim the wisdom of Washington, Jefferson, Madison, Monroe, and the other brilliant men who originally laid out the idea of America.

Murray Rothbard discusses the meaning of a "just war." The two just American wars, he says, were the American Revolution and the War for Southern Independence. Both were wars against unfair taxation and oppression, and both wars were rooted in the desire to preserve liberty and self-government.

Because the Civil War was such a major turning point in American history—indeed, nearly all subsequent themes in this book stem from actions undertaken then—we have multiple perspectives on it here. Richard Gamble provides details of how Lincoln arrived at his theory of the mystical Union and how he rewrote American history in order to do so. Lincoln's view of the mystical Union is at the heart of the Civil War, for it was this belief that required the North to wage war, rather than simply allowing the South to peacefully secede. Gamble also provides details on how Lincoln abused the power of the presidency, setting the stage for the modern imperial presidency. Thomas Fleming shows how the South's actions were rooted in a deep tradition of honor, that tradition encompassing the ancient Greeks, the Scottish clans, and the American South. Clyde Wilson shows that the Old Republic of our founders died with the American Civil War, and that President Lincoln first brought us the Leviathan state. The hypocrisy of the North in establishing Reconstruction is also examined.

Joseph Stromberg describes the details of the Spanish–American War. A combination of political leaders and the business establishment wanted to establish a coaling station and military base in the Philippines in order to promote their special-interest trade with the Far East. He points out how propaganda was used to convert a public who supported our traditional policy of avoiding empire into one supporting the conquest of foreign lands.

The outstanding article by Murray Rothbard on World War I, which first appeared in the *Journal of Libertarian Studies*, is included regarding his analysis of the effect which the intellectual leaders of the "Progressive Era" had in bringing about the changes in America during World War I. Contrary to the assertion by some historians that World War I ended the progressive reforms of that era, Rothbard conclusively argues that World War I was the fulfillment for these intellectuals and gave them a chance to implement their ideas and to assume positions of power inside the government.

Those writers specifically addressing World War I and beyond include Ralph Raico's analysis of Winston Churchill, the personification of the war-and-welfare state of the 20th century. He shows that Churchill, like Lincoln, has almost been deified, but rethinking Churchill is necessary in order to understand the war and welfare systems of the 20th century and, especially, why the United States entered the two world wars which began in Europe. Eugene Sledge, a veteran of World War II in the Pacific, relates an eyewitness account of the true horrors of actual combat and shows the long-term costs to the individual soldier. His war and post-war memories are moving and disturbing.

Several authors chose to not confine themselves to a single war, and instead examined larger changes brought about over several wars. Robert Higgs tells us that war is the essential crisis which creates the Leviathan state. Contrary to most histories today, it was not the New Deal wherein the federal government first took over personal and economic liberties. Most of the agencies and controls of the New Deal were merely renewals of those same agencies and programs put in place by World War I, and have been built upon for the rest of the 20th century. Allan Carlson demonstrates how the central planners during wartime have used this opportunity to bring about the types of social and cultural changes which probably could not have been imposed during a time of peace. Novelist Bill Kauffman provides a survey of American poets and writers who have opposed the American empire and the garrison state from the 1850s to the present time. Historically, there is a rich tradition of anti-interventionism in the arts and letters of America, but unfortunately few such writers today. Paul Fussell, another survivor of the World War II battles, provides a look at war as a "culture." Like any culture, it has its traditions, its music, and its unifying themes. Of course, as Fussell points outs, this culture is the antithesis of what America itself stands for, and the culture of war necessarily destroys the American culture. Paul Gottfried shows us that democracy has not proven to be peaceful as previously advertised but, in fact, has been extremely war-like. It is big government which, in spite of being democratic, causes coercive egalitarianism at home and fuels imperialism abroad.

Finally, we take a more abstract approach to the topic. Joseph Salerno demonstrates that wars are so objectionable to the population that they must be financed with the less-obvious means of a deficit and inflation rather than raising taxes to cover all of the costs. Monetary depreciation and economic dislocations are the inevitable costs of war. Hans-Hermann Hoppe gives a very original analysis of how wars, and in particular World War I, have changed the course of Western civilization. He compares wars under monarchy with those of democratic nations and shows how much more terrible, costly, and vicious modern wars have been. He does not advocate a return to monarchy but argues that we must recognize that the restraints upon monarchs, which made war more limited, do not apply to the modern democratic state.

Unlike many books on war, this one does not look for its glory or its grandeur. It shares this same purpose with the great American writer Herman Melville who, after the Civil War, published his poetry entitled *Battle-Pieces*. Melville was a sympathizer with the North, and he had close relatives and friends who served in the Union army, but he was not an abolitionist. Stanton Garner, author of *The Civil War World of Herman Melville*, describes Melville's intent in publishing his poetry:

> For too long war had been glorified and thus masked in idylls of kings and visions of knights—lace and feather— and that habit of glorification was still alive among the poets of the newspapers and in the imaginations of the Southern cavaliers. It communicated little sense of the truth, that the vestments of battle are grime and smoke and suffering and that victory is won by those most adept at killing. But now war reveals its true face: the grimy god, Satan, has found his liege knights in these artificers of destruction.[11]

---

[11]Stanton Garner, *The Civil War World of Herman Melville* (Lawrence: University Press of Kansas, 1993), p. 135.

Melville opens his poem "Ball's Bluff: A Reverie" by saying:

> One noonday, at my window in the town,
> I saw a sight—saddest that eyes can see—
> Young soldiers marching lustily
> Unto the wars.[12]

Finally, I refer you to two quotations, the first being a portion of Sydney Smith's letter written to "My dear Lady Grey" on February 19, 1823. Her husband was the Reform Prime Minister of England which was the foremost imperialistic world power in the 18th and 19th centuries and would continue to be so into the 20th century. Most Americans today would probably sympathize with the expressed frustration of Smith:

> For God's sake, do not drag me into another war! I am worn down, and worn out, with crusading and defending Europe, and protecting mankind; I *must* think a little of myself. I am sorry for the Spaniards—I am sorry for the Greeks—I deplore the fate of the Jews; the people of the Sandwich Islands are groaning under the most detestable tyranny; Baghdad is oppressed; I do not like the present state of the Delta; Thibet is not comfortable. Am I to fight for all these people? The world is bursting with sin and sorrow. Am I to be champion of the Decalogue, and to be eternally raising fleets and armies to make all men good and happy? We have just done saving Europe, and I am afraid the consequences will be, that we shall cut each other's throat. No war, dear Lady Grey!—No eloquence; but apathy, selfishness, common sense, arithmetic! I beseech you, secure Lord Grey's swords and pistols, as the housekeeper did Don Quixote's armor. If there is another war, life will not be worth having.
>
> "May the vengeance of Heaven" overtake all the legitimates of Verona! but, in the present state of rent and taxes, they must be *left* to the vengeance of Heaven. I allow fighting in such a cause to be a luxury; but the business of a prudent, sensible man, is to guard against luxury.
>
> There is no such thing as a "just war," or, at least, a *wise* war.[13]

The second quotation is from one of the greatest war novels which relates the reality experienced by soldiers on the front lines in World War I:

> We see men living with their skulls blown open; we see soldiers run with their two feet cut off, they stagger on their splintered stumps into the next shell-hole; a lance corporal crawls a mile and half on his hands dragging his smashed

---

[12]Ibid, p. 118.

[13]Francis Neilson, *The Makers of War* (Appleton, Wis.: C.C. Nelson Publishing, 1950), p. 30; see also *Selected Writings of Sydney Smith*, W. H. Auden, ed. (New York: Farrar, Straus, and Cudahy, 1956), pp. 323–24.

knee after him; another goes to the dressing station and over
his clasped hands bulge his intestines; we see men without
mouths, without jaws, without faces; we find one man who
has held the artery of his arm in his teeth for two hours in
order not to bleed to death.[14]

In looking at the costs of war we must always keep in mind the
reality experienced by soldiers in actual combat. The tallies of the
dead and wounded soldiers cannot carry the full meaning of the
terror of actually experiencing war. Therefore, the costs of war
considered in this book, which are primarily related to those which
are long-term and sometimes not obvious, should not divert our
attention from the very real horror and violence known by those
on the front lines who actually do the fighting.

John V. Denson
Opelika, Alabama
September 1996

[14]Erich M. Remarque, *All Quiet on the Western Front*, A. W. Wheen, trans. (Boston: Little, Brown, 1975), pp. 117–18.

1

WAR AND AMERICAN FREEDOM

John V. Denson

During the Persian Gulf War, President Bush announced that we were approaching the "New World Order." It is becoming clear that part of what is meant by this phrase is that the United States is to become a permanent garrison state and also the world policeman, under the cloak and command of the United Nations or NATO or some other regional alliance. If this New World Order is fully realized, the United States could be at war constantly without a declaration of war by Congress, and our sovereignty will be destroyed. The Constitution states that the president is commander-in-chief of the armed forces, but only Congress can declare war, which it has done only five times: against England in 1812, Mexico in 1846, Spain in 1898, and to launch America's late entries into World Wars I and II. On more than 200 occasions the president has sent armed forces to foreign lands without a congressional declaration of war.[1] Since 1945 over 100,000 U.S. military personnel have died in undeclared wars and over 400,000 have suffered battle injuries.[2] It can be argued that the founders probably did not intend for this constitutional restraint to apply to very short and limited police actions authorized by the president, but it obviously should have applied to the two major wars in Asia, Korea and Vietnam. President Lincoln, however, in the American Civil War, set the first prominent example of abuse of the presidential powers regarding wars.

The danger of ignoring the Constitution was strongly stated by Senator Daniel Webster:

> Miracles do not cluster. Hold on to the Constitution of the United States of America and the Republic for which it stands—what has happened once in six thousand years may never happen again. Hold on to your Constitution, for if the American Constitution shall fail there will be anarchy throughout the world.[3]

---

[1]Forrest McDonald, *The American Presidency: An Intellectual History* (Lawrence: University Press of Kansas, 1994), p. 392; and see, Library of Congress, Congressional Research Service, *Instances of the Use of United States Armed Forces Abroad, 1789–1983*, Ellen C. Collier, ed. (Washington, D.C.: U.S. Government Printing Office, 1983).

[2]*Commanders in Chief: Presidential Leadership in Modern War*, Joseph G. Dawson, III, ed. (Lawrence: University Press of Kansas, 1993), p. 31.

[3]M.E. Bradford, *Original Intentions: On the Making and Ratification of the United States Constitution* (Athens: University of Georgia Press, 1993), p. xiii.

The historian Charles Beard warned that becoming the world policeman would mean "perpetual war for perpetual peace"[4] and, of course, this is the theme of George Orwell's prophetic novel *1984*. We need to understand the "total" costs of war in order to appreciate the true dangers that war in general, and the New World Order in particular, pose to individual liberty.

Albert Jay Nock was a great individualist, a liberal in the classical sense, and one of my favorite writers. In his essay entitled "Isaiah's Job" he tells the story of the Biblical prophet Isaiah who was instructed not to try to convert the masses but instead to speak to the "Remnant"—defined as that small group of people who would understand and appreciate his message and would be there to put things back together when the time was right.[5] Nock wrote to and for that Remnant, which he recognized as a small group that was working to preserve liberty in America. That Remnant has kept the torch of liberty lit since the chaos of World War I forced the philosophy of freedom off center stage and out of the theater. Collectivism, in various forms, took its place. The philosophy of freedom, which was based largely upon the lessons of history, was born in the 17th century and became dominant in the late 18th and early 19th centuries.[6] It represented the political ideas of, or greatly influenced, most of the founders of the United States.

Today, we call this philosophy "classical liberalism," which historian Ralph Raico says is the "signature political philosophy of Western civilization."[7] An important part of the Remnant has preserved much of this philosophy under various labels, including the Old Right, paleo-conservatism, and libertarianism. Non-interventionism in foreign policy has always been a cornerstone of classical liberalism and the philosophy of the Remnant.

Nock recognized that American citizens had far more to fear from the rapidly increasing powers of our own central government than from any threat of a foreign invasion. He further recognized that it is through the abuse of the war powers granted to the president that our freedom is primarily jeopardized. Indeed, since the

[4]*Perpetual War for Perpetual Peace*, Harry Elmer Barnes, ed. (New York: Greenwood Press, 1953), p. viii.

[5]Albert Jay Nock, *The State of the Union: Essays in Social Criticism* (Indianapolis, Ind.: Liberty Press, 1991), p. 124.

[6]Some of the most prominent classical-liberal thinkers from the 17th century up through the 20th century are John Locke, Adam Smith, David Hume, Thomas Jefferson, Thomas Paine, James Madison, Herbert Spencer, Ludwig von Mises and Friedrich Hayek (a student of Mises who won the 1974 Nobel Prize in economics). See *Great Thinkers in Classical Liberalism*, Amy H. Sturgis, ed., vol. 1, *The LockeSmith Review* (Nashville, Tenn.: LockeSmith Institute, 1994).

[7]Ralph Raico, "The Rise, Fall and Renaissance of Classical Liberalism—Part 1," *Freedom Daily* (August 1992), p. 11.

end of World War II, some presidents and their representatives have claimed that the constitutional limitation providing that only Congress can declare war is archaic and no longer applies.

> Under Secretary of State Nicholas Katzenbach informed the Senate Foreign Relations Committee in August 1967 that "the expression of declaring war is one that has become outmoded in the international arena."[8]

When the Senate considered and passed the National Commitments Resolution in 1969, a representative of the Nixon administration informed them that:

> As Commander-in-Chief, the President has the sole authority to command our armed forces, whether they are inside or outside the United States. And although reasonable men may differ as to the circumstances in which he should do so, the President has the constitutional power to send U.S. military forces abroad without specific Congressional approval.[9]

We have now reached a point in our history where it is strongly asserted that the president of the United States claims the power to declare a crisis and then send troops wherever he pleases without Congressional authority or approval. Shakespeare dramatized this same point with Mark Antony in *Julius Caesar* where he states: "Cry 'Havoc!' and let slip the dogs of war."[10]

Nock addressed the long-term aspects of the total costs of war: "I am coming to be much less interested in what war does to people at the time of war, and much more in what it does to them after it is over."[11] The starting point, however, for understanding the total costs of war is the well-known warning from U.S. Senator Hiram Johnson, during the debate over whether or not America should enter World War I: "When war is declared, truth is the first casualty."[12] Another well-known truism was stated by the writer Randolph Bourne who opposed America's entry into World War I: "War is the health of the State,"[13] meaning that the government must grow stronger and necessarily increase its powers and scope in order to engage in war. Alexis de Tocqueville, the astute observer of American democracy, stated the truth about the relationship between war and freedom succinctly: "All those who seek to

[8]Dawson, *Commanders in Chief*, p. 43.

[9]Ibid., p. 44.

[10]William Shakespeare, "Julius Caesar," act 3, sc. 1, *William Shakespeare: The Complete Works*, Peter Alexander, ed. (New York: Random House, 1952), p. 985.

[11]Nock, *The State of the Union*, p. 65.

[12]John Quigley, *The Ruses of War* (New York: Prometheus Books, 1992), p. 27.

[13]*Randolph S. Bourne: War and the Intellectuals; Collected Essays, 1915–1919*, Carl Resek, ed. (New York: Harper and Row Publishers, 1964), p. 71.

destroy the liberties of a democratic nation ought to know that war is the surest and shortest means to accomplish it."[14]

History shows us that even the just war, fought to oppose a clear-and-present danger to life, liberty, and property, still causes a severe loss of freedom. Even in a just and successful war, the result is one step forward in the defense of freedom, and then two steps backward to increase and centralize governmental power in order to engage in the war. This net deficit must be made up after the war in order to have a net gain for freedom. Throughout history, we see taxes raised, governmental powers increased and centralized for purposes of war, and then, when peace arrives, there is no real relinquishment of those burdens on freedom. As one author states, "War is like that cave of bones and carcasses in mythology into which led many tracks, but out of it, none."[15] On the other hand, we are told by official propagandists, or the "Court Historians," and many political leaders like the "Megaphone of Mars," Teddy Roosevelt, that wars are simply the instruments of progress and serve a similar purpose to that of a summer thunderstorm which clears and cools the air. Those who love freedom must never cease to challenge those ideas.

Ludwig von Mises opposed the unjust war, but he was no pacifist. He recognized that there are just wars, rightfully fought for the honorable purposes of protecting our families, our lives, our liberty, and our property. For instance, I think that there is a clear consensus that the American Revolution was a just war fought for the proper purposes.

Liberty is fragile and its defense cannot be left to the pacifist, the advocate of unilateral disarmament, or to the weak or faint of heart. But also, because liberty is so fragile, its true defender recognizes that war is its greatest enemy, and therefore the true patriot is often the courageous individual who opposes a particular war because he recognizes that it is unjust—that it would be fought for the wrong purposes or that the risk for the loss of liberty is greater than any benefit to be gained by the war.

None of this should be construed in any way as an attack upon the American soldier, or any soldier for that matter. One of the great injustices of the Vietnam War was the abuse heaped upon the returning veterans instead of criticism of the politicians who caused that war, America's only military defeat. While I consider World War I the greatest disaster of the 20th century, in no way do I condemn my father who fought in that war with the American

[14]Alexis de Tocqueville, *Democracy in America* (New York: Vintage, 1990), 2, p. 269.
[15]E.A. Pollard, *The Lost Cause* (New York: Bonanza Books, 1867), p. 562.

forces in France, nor do I condemn Ludwig von Mises, who fought on the opposing side with Austria on the Russian front. These men remain two of my heroes and I admire their individual courage demonstrated in that war. We can "toast the soldier without honoring the war."

Likewise, this should not be understood as advocating "Isolationism," that pejorative term used by the Franklin Roosevelt administration to condemn its critics. In fact, one of the arguments made by Mises in advocating a non-interventionist foreign policy is that no nation is entirely self-sufficient; because of the division of labor and the scarcity of resources, we must have worldwide trade, and war is its greatest enemy. Thomas Paine gave a similar economic reason:

> War can never be in the interest of a trading nation any more than quarrelling can be profitable to a man in business. But to make war with those who trade with us is like setting a bulldog upon a customer at the shop-door.[16]

Thomas Jefferson, in his first Inaugural Address, succinctly restated America's foreign policy as first outlined in President Washington's Farewell Address. Jefferson said, "Peace, commerce and honest friendship, with all nations—entangling alliances with none."[17]

Today in America, as we stand at the end of the 20th century, we can look back and see that it has been a century of constant assault on individual freedom. It has been a century of big government and collectivism, under various labels including communism, Nazism, fascism, socialism, the New Deal, and state capitalism; it is the war-and-welfare century. Now we have finally reached the end of the Cold War between the two great superpowers, the Soviet Union and the United States, a war which lasted for more than 40 years.

Mises predicted, soon after communism took over Russia during World War I, that it would eventually collapse, because without market prices you could not accurately calculate supply and demand. This final collapse of the Soviet Union, which would have occurred much sooner without help from the West,[18] leaves the

---

[16]Charles T. Sprading, *Liberty and the Great Libertarians: An Anthology on Liberty* (New York: Arno Press, [1913] 1972), p. 75.

[17]*The Life and Selected Writings of Thomas Jefferson,* Adrienne Koch and William Peden, eds. (New York: Random House, 1993), p. 300.

[18]Werner Keller, *Are the Russians Ten Feet Tall?*, Constantine FitzGibbon, trans. (London: Thames and Hudson, 1961); see also Major George R. Jordan (USAF), *From Major Jordan's Diaries* (New York: Harcourt, Brace, 1952). This tells the story of the secret transfer by the American government of massive amounts of weapons,

United States as a staggering giant, badly wounded from the loss of freedom and weighed down by excessive government.

Many rightfully expected a peace dividend as a result of the end of the Cold War. Instead, taxes have been drastically increased and America is becoming widely recognized as the world police-man, by sending her sons and daughters to police the Persian Gulf and charging rent for the army from other countries. Likewise, we have sent our young people to Somalia in Africa as an armed wel-fare agency. America's armed forces have been stationed in Europe and Asia since the end of World War II and have now become a part of the United Nations and NATO police forces in Bosnia, Haiti, and around the world.

What has become of America in the 20th century? One British historian offered this assessment:

> To most Europeans, I guess, America now looks like the most dangerous country in the world. Since America is un-questionably the most powerful country, the transformation of America's image within the last thirty years is very fright-ening for Europeans. It is probably still more frightening for the great majority of the human race who are neither Euro-peans nor North Americans, but are the Latin Americans, Asians and Africans. They, I imagine, feel even more inse-cure than we feel. They feel, at any moment, America may intervene in their internal affairs, with the same appalling consequences as have followed from the American interven-tion in Southeast Asia.
>
> In today's climate, wherever there is trouble, violence, suffering, tragedy, the rest of us are now quick to suspect that the CIA—the new bogey man—had a hand in it. Our phobia about the CIA is, no doubt, as fantastically excessive as America's phobia about world communism used to be; but in this case, too, there is just enough convincing evidence to make the phobia genuine. In fact, the roles of the United States and Russia have been reversed in the eyes of much of the world. Today, America has become the nightmare.[19]

THE FOUNDING FATHERS AND THE COSTS OF WAR

In order to see how war has transformed the U.S. government and show the danger posed to our freedom by our current foreign policy, we first need to revisit briefly our original principles. I have already alluded to the non-interventionist foreign policy state-ments of Presidents Washington and Jefferson. Consider now the

---

military material (including uranium), and technology to the Soviet Union during World War II.

[19]Arnold Toynbee, *New York Times*, May 7, 1971.

statement of President James Madison, who explained why our non-interventionist policy was necessary in order to preserve freedom at home:

> Of all the enemies to public liberty, war is, perhaps, the most to be dreaded, because it comprises and develops the germ of every other. War is the parent of armies; from these proceed debts and taxes; and armies, and debts, and taxes are the known instruments for bringing the many under the domination of the few. . . . No nation could preserve its freedom in the midst of continual warfare.[20]

Madison addressed the delegates to the Constitutional Convention on the threat of war to liberty:

> Constant apprehension of War has the . . . tendency to render the head too large for the body. A standing military force, with an overgrown Executive will not long be safe companions to liberty. The means of defense agst. Foreign danger, have been always the instruments of tyranny at home.[21]

Madison further addressed the question of why the Constitution attempts to restrain the president's war powers and only allows Congress to declare war:

> War is in fact the true nurse of executive aggrandizement. In war, a physical force is to be created; and it is the executive will, which is to direct it. In war, the public treasuries are to be unlocked; and it is the executive hand which is to dispense them. In war, the honors and emoluments of office are to be multiplied; and it is the executive patronage under which they are to be enjoyed; and it is the executive brow they are to encircle. The strongest passions and most dangerous weaknesses of the human breast; ambition, avarice, vanity, the honorable or venal love of fame, are all in conspiracy against the desire and duty of peace.[22]

President John Quincy Adams, who was from Massachusetts and therefore not a part of the Virginia dynasty, continued the foreign policy which was unique to the United States:

> America goes not abroad in search of monsters to destroy. She is the well wisher to the freedom and independence of

---

[20]James Madison, "Political Observations," *Letters and Other Writings of James Madison* (1795) (Philadelphia: J.B. Lippincott, 1865), 4, pp. 491–92; see also Bruce D. Porter, *War and the Rise of the State* (New York: Free Press, 1994), p. 10.

[21]*The Records of the Federal Convention of 1787*, Max Farrand, ed., 4 vols. (New Haven, Conn: Yale University Press, 1911), p. 465; also Dawson, *Commanders in Chief*, p. 32.

[22]"Letters of Helvidius" (Aug., Sept. 1793), no. 4, *The Writings of James Madison*, Gaillard Hunt, ed. (New York: G.P. Putnam, 1900–1910), 6, pp. 171–72; see also, Robert W. Tucker and David L. Hendrickson, *Empire of Liberty, The Statecraft of Thomas Jefferson* (New York: Oxford University Press, 1990), pp. 39–40.

all. She is the champion and vindicator only of her own. She will recommend the general cause by the countenance of her voice, and the benignant sympathy of her example. She well knows that by once enlisting under other banners than her own, were they even the banners of foreign independence, she would involve herself beyond the power of extrication in all the wars of interest and intrigue, of individual avarice, envy and ambition, which assume the colors and usurp the standards of freedom. The fundamental maxims of her policy would insensibly change from liberty to force.[23]

Before becoming president, Adams served as Secretary of State to President Monroe and thereby played the major role in forming the Monroe Doctrine. This Doctrine told the European nations to keep their military forces out of our hemisphere, and implied that we would keep our military forces out of theirs.

Toward the end of America's Old Republic, in 1852, Henry Clay stated:

By following the policy we have adhered to since the days of Washington we have prospered beyond precedent; we have done more for the cause of liberty in the world than arms could effect; we have shown to other nations the way to greatness and happiness.

But if we should involve ourselves in the web of European politics, in a war which could effect nothing, . . . where, then, would be the last hope of the friends of freedom throughout the world? Far better it is . . . that, adhering to our wise pacific system, and avoiding the distant wars of Europe, we should keep our own lamp burning brightly on this western shore, as a light to all nations, than to hazard its utter extinction amidst the ruins of fallen or falling republics in Europe.[24]

Our founding fathers advocated this non-interventionist foreign policy because they wanted to preserve freedom at home and they understood the clear lessons of history, especially those gained from the long experience of the ancient Greeks and Romans. Forrest McDonald states:

History, to most of the authors of the Constitution, was more valuable than political theory because it was more real; as Bolingbroke put it, history was philosophy teaching by example. Eighteenth-century Americans read widely in history, thought historically, and cited history as authority.[25]

In the same work, McDonald also said:

[23]Barnes, *Perpetual War for Perpetual Peace*, p. ii.
[24]Ibid., p. 555.
[25]McDonald, *The American Presidency*, p. 67.

> John Dickinson expressed a prevailing sentiment when he
> said that "Experience must be our only guide" for "Reason
> may mislead us."[26]

Patrick Henry, both a leader for independence and a critic of
the Constitution because of too much centralization of power,
stated that, "I have but one lamp by which my feet are guided, and
that is the lamp of experience. I know of no other way of judging
the future but by the past."[27]

The founders were familiar with the first historian, Herodotus,
who wrote about the Persian armies invading Greece. He marveled
at the heroic efforts of the Greeks, who were outnumbered by a ratio of ten-to-one, but still defeated their invaders, and then resisted
any impulse toward empire themselves.[28] He was repulsed by the
arrogance of the Persian leader Darius, and his son Xerxes, who
conducted these imperialistic wars. The founders were also familiar with the great historian Thucydides, a warrior himself, who
tells about the infamous Peloponnesian War which destroyed the
fabulous Greek civilization.[29] He teaches us the lesson that the love
of freedom and justice by the Athenians could not survive their
continual warfare with Sparta. He shows that the Athenians,
through their new-found imperialistic tendencies, became as cruel,
arrogant, and tyrannical as had been the invading Persians or their
Grecian enemy Sparta. He taught that through constant war,
Athens lost her soul. Thucydides points out that the turning point
of the Peloponnesian War was the destruction of a major portion of
the great Athenian navy which, at the time, was not defending
Athens, but was lost in the harbor of Syracuse while trying to conquer Sicily. The framers were especially influenced by the rise and
fall of the early Roman Republic, as revealed in the works of such
historians as Polybius and Livy, as well as those of the great
lawyer, statesman, and patriot Cicero. Russell Kirk tells us about
the particular lessons by stating:

> And yet the old Roman society had begun to break up even
> while Polybius praised it. The chief material cause of the
> Republic's decay appears to have been the military success
> of its armies and the expansion of Roman territories and
> power. The three Punic Wars ruined the majority of the

[26]Ibid., p. 38; and see Farrand, *The Records of the Federal Convention of 1787*, p. 278 (Madison's Notes, August 13).

[27]Russell Kirk, *The Roots of American Order*, 3rd ed. (Washington, D.C.: Regnery Gateway, 1991), p. 401.

[28]*The History of Herodotus*, George Rawlinson, trans., *The Great Books*, vol. 6 (Encyclopedia Britannica, 1953).

[29]*Thucydides: The History of the Peloponnesian War*, Richard Crawley, trans., *The Great Books*, vol. 6 (Encyclopedia Britannica, 1953).

Roman peasants, who died valiantly by hundreds of thousands; those who returned after years or decades of campaigning found themselves hopelessly in debt. With the conquest of Carthage and her dependencies, and later of Macedonia, Greece, Asia, Gaul, and other lands, innumerable slaves poured into Italy, further injuring the old economic pattern and forming an alien proletariat in the imperial city itself.[30]

The founders were also familiar with the ancient "trick of the trade" of kings, dictators, and tyrants who used foreign wars to concentrate more power into themselves, to stifle domestic opposition, to silence critics and to otherwise divert attention away from domestic problems and politics. The literature of Great Britain contains Shakespeare's famous example of this old trick in *Henry IV*. In this play, the dying King gives his son, who is heir to the throne, his advice on the Machiavellian use of power. The King admits that his long-planned crusade to the Holy Land was only a political ploy designed to distract his critics and enemies and to keep them from looking too closely into his domestic machinations. The Shakespearean critic Harold Goddard says that, in effect, the King advises his son to "Make war, dear boy, and God grant your reign may be a peaceful one."[31]

Shakespeare's actual language is:

... [a]nd had a purpose now
To lead out many to the Holy Land,
Lest rest and lying still make them look
Too near unto my state. Therefore, my Harry,
Be it thy course to busy giddy minds
With foreign quarrels, that action, hence borne out,
May waste the memory of the former days.[32]

The framers were suspicious that this trick might be used by future presidents in a democracy, and therefore they placed in the Constitution a requirement that only Congress could declare war.

When the Spaniards conquered the ancient civilizations of the Aztecs and the Inca as part of the discovery of the New World, certain important lessons of history became clear to the framers. The rulers of these two ancient civilizations subjugated their respective populations through the war and welfare system. The lesson we learn from the Aztecs and the Inca is that the people exchanged

---

[30]Kirk, *The Roots of American Order*, p. 104.

[31]Harold C. Goddard, *The Meaning of Shakespeare* (Chicago: University of Chicago Press, 1951), 1, p. 197.

[32]William Shakespeare, "Henry IV," part 2, act 4, sc. 5, *William Shakespeare: The Complete Works*, Alexander, ed., p. 544.

their freedom for promises from their rulers that they would be given security from want and from foreign enemies.

> They had nothing they wished to give their subjects, except a measure of security against want and external enemies. But the enemy within—the rulers themselves—were more fearsome than any foreign foe. And the price exacted for freedom from want turned out to be very high.[33]

THE CIVIL WAR

Now, let us look at what happened when we abandoned our original principles. As part of this examination, I will explore certain long-term costs of American wars in general, but of three wars in particular: the American Civil War (or more correctly labeled, the War for Southern Independence),[34] the Spanish–American War, and World War I. The combination of these three wars, all of which the United States government won, repudiated many of the most important principles upon which this nation was founded: first, by completely transforming the design and powers of the central government, especially as to its relationship with the states, and then, by changing the direction of its foreign policy by 180 degrees. The United States could have avoided these wars, if our presidential leadership had desired peace rather than war.

Before addressing the subject of the Civil War, and the legacy of President Lincoln, it is important to state some of my personal views. Many have since learned what Avery Craven learned in 1942 when he first published his book *The Coming of the Civil War*, which is, that if you take issue with the conclusion that the abolition of slavery was the sole cause of the war, and instead present a more balanced view, you will be dismissed as a defender of slavery.[35] I believe that slavery was wrong, as are all statist, involuntary policies of segregation, integration, affirmative action, and quotas, because they are all based upon the concept of unequal group rights which require force, or the threat of force, by the government for implementation. In my opinion, a free society can only be based upon equal individual rights, with the role of government being limited to protecting those rights and to removing barriers which prevent their free exercise.

---

[33]Charles Van Doren, *A History of Knowledge* (New York: Ballantine Books, 1991), p. 12.
[34]Carl N. Degler, "The United States and National Unification," in *Lincoln, The War President: The Gettysburg Lectures*, Gabor S. Boritt, ed. (New York: Oxford University Press, 1992), p. 101.
[35]Avery O. Craven, *The Coming of the Civil War* (Chicago: University of Chicago Press, 1966), see in particular the three prefaces in the 1966 edition, p. vii.

The abolition of slavery, which occurred after the Civil War, was a great step forward for individual freedom, but the abolition of slavery was not the true purpose or fundamental cause of the war. In fact, President Lincoln demonstrated that he would support slavery where it already existed when he required that each member of his cabinet pledge in writing that they would fully support the controversial Fugitive Slave provision of the Constitution which required that all the states of the North return fugitive slaves to the South.[36] Also, early in the war, Lincoln rescinded the military order of General Fremont to free the slaves in Missouri; Lincoln then dismissed Fremont from his command. The argument is made that since the Emancipation Proclamation was made during the war, and the 13th Amendment, which abolished slavery, was passed after the war, then it must follow that the abolition of slavery was the purpose and cause of the war. However, if the facts are studied objectively, it will be found that the conclusion is untrue. The question relating to slavery which existed between the North and the South before the war was whether slavery would be extended into new states and territories under the Kansas–Nebraska Act of 1854, and was not whether slavery would be abolished in the states where it already existed.

Before the war, some moderate Northerners, such as Daniel Webster, argued that had it not been for the Northern assault on slavery, a Southern abolitionist movement would have arisen. Anti-slavery sentiment was by no means unknown in the antebellum years, particularly in the upper South, and there were those who would have welcomed gradual emancipation under Southern control. As Lee wrote to his wife late in 1856, "In this enlightened age, there are few, I believe, but what will acknowledge, that slavery as an institution, is a moral and political evil in any country." As did many of his class in the border and upper South, he believed that emancipation would "sooner result from the mild and melting influence of Christianity, than the storms and tempests of fiery controversy."[37]

Slavery had already reached its real potential boundaries in America and was not likely to spread to the new territories or states.[38] The United States was one of the few remaining countries

[36]John Niven, *Gideon Welles: Lincoln's Secretary of the Navy* (Baton Rouge: Louisiana State University Press, 1994), p. 311.

[37]Ludwell H. Johnson, *North Against South: The American Iliad 1848–1877*, (Columbia, S.C.: Foundation for American Education, 1993), p. 179.

[38]Charles W. Ramsdell, "The Natural Limits of Slavery Expansion," *Mississippi Valley Historical Review* 16 (1929): 151–71; also see extracts in Kenneth M. Stampp, *The Causes of the Civil War* (New York: Simon and Schuster, 1991), pp. 115–21.

in the West in 1860 where slavery remained legal, the others being Cuba and Brazil.[39] Slavery was being abandoned throughout the world in the 19th century, and probably would have died a natural death in America, too. Leaders from both regions realized before the war that the days of slavery were numbered.

The South, with its political position as a numerical minority,[40] had attempted to restrain the centralization of power into the federal government by an alliance with the Northern Democrats and by asserting the theories of states' rights, nullification, and concurrent majority. The South had become a tax slave to the North through the protective tariff (which was extracted mostly from the South and then used for internal improvements, almost entirely in the North) under the general welfare clause of the Constitution, over the protest of the South.[41]

Lincoln began his political career as a Whig by campaigning on the three economic issues which later became the main platform of the new Republican Party and which had always been three of the main objections of the South to the union:

> I presume you all know who I am. I am humble Abraham Lincoln. I have been solicited by my many friends to become a candidate for the Legislature. My politics are short and sweet, like the old woman's dance. I am in favor of a national bank . . . in favor of the internal improvement system and a high protective tariff.[42]

In President Lincoln's first Inaugural Address, he guaranteed the South that his administration would leave the question of slavery alone in the states where it already existed, and soon thereafter, in July 1861, both houses of Congress resolved overwhelmingly that slavery would be fully protected, and even proposed to pass a thirteenth amendment to do so.[43] In this first address, Lincoln also

[39]Harry T. Williams, *The History of American Wars from 1745 to 1918* (Baton Rouge: Louisiana State University Press, 1981), p. 205.

[40]In 1860, the North outnumbered the South by two and one–half to one in population, had three times its railroad capacity and nine times its industrial production. See Gabor S. Boritt, *Why the Confederacy Lost* (New York: Oxford University Press, 1992), p. 20.

[41]Charles Adams, *For Good and Evil: The Impact of Taxes on the Course of Civilization* (New York: Madison Books, 1993), pp. 323–37; also see Richard Hofstadter, "The Tariff Issue and the Civil War," *American Historical Review* (October 1938); see generally "John Taylor (of Caroline)," in *Tyranny Unmasked*, F. Thornton Miller, ed. (Indianapolis, Ind.: Liberty Fund, 1992), especially the excellent introduction by Miller.

[42]Lord Charnwood *Abraham Lincoln* (New York: Henry Holt, 1917), pp. 65–66; see also M. E. Bradford, *The Reactionary Imperative* (Peru, Ill.: Sherwood Sugden, 1990), pp. 221–22.

[43]Kenneth M. Stampp, "The United States and National Self-Determination," in *Lincoln, The War President*, Boritt, ed., p. 135.

restated his campaign promise: "I have no purpose, directly or indirectly, to interfere with the institution of slavery in the states where it exists. I believe I have no lawful right to do so, and I have no inclination to do so."[44] The tariff, and taxes generally, were another matter, and force was threatened against the South in the same speech when he stated that he would: "*Collect the duties and imposts,* but beyond *what may be necessary for these objects,* there will be no invasion, no using of force against or among people anywhere."[45]

The charge by the South concerning Northern oppression had been constant since the "Tariff of Abomination" in 1828. John C. Calhoun had carried the battle flag on this issue until his death in 1850.

> Federal import tax laws were, in Calhoun's view, class legislation against the South. Heavy taxation on the South raised funds that were spent in the North. This was unfair. Calhoun argued further that high import taxes forced Southerners to pay either excessive prices for Northern goods or excessive taxes. Competition from Europe was crushed, thereby giving Northerners a monopoly over Southern markets. Federal taxation had the economic effect of shifting wealth from the South to the North.[46]

The author, Charles Adams, in his sweeping survey of the effect of taxes throughout the course of Western civilization, documents why economic and taxation policies, rather than abolition of slavery, were the primary causes of the American Civil War.

> By 1832 the national debt was paid and there was no justification for the import taxes at high rates, except to promote a monopoly in the hands of Northern industrialists to raise prices for Southern consumers. The South exported about three quarters of its goods and in turn used the money to buy European goods, which carried the high import tax. This means that the South paid about three quarters of all federal taxes, most of which were spent in the North. If the South did not buy foreign goods and pay high taxes, the alternative was to buy Northern manufactured products at excessively high prices. Either way Southern money ended up in the North.[47]

Adams continues with what happened after Lincoln's election, when the South's nightmare became reality with the passage of the Morrill Tariff:

[44]Adams, *For Good and Evil,* p. 324.
[45]Ibid., p. 334, emphasis supplied.
[46]Ibid., p. 326.
[47]Ibid., p. 327.

The rebellion in South Carolina in 1832 was a prelude to greater and more violent things. It was the South's first try at rebellion; 1861 was its last try. Lincoln was supported in his bid for the presidency by rich industrialists of the North. He was their man and he had been their lawyer. At the heart of his platform was a return to high import taxes, reminiscent of the "tariff of abomination" of 1832 [Sic]. No sooner had Congress assembled in 1861 than the high tariff was passed [on March 2, 1861] and signed into law by Lincoln. The Morrill Tariff, as it was called, was the highest tariff in U.S. history. It doubled the rates of the 1857 tariff to about 47 percent of the value of the imported products. This was Lincoln's big victory. His supporters were jubilant. He had fulfilled his campaign [promise] and IOUs to Northern industrialists. By this act he had closed the door for any reconciliation with the South. In his inaugural address he had also committed himself to collect customs in the South, even if there were a secession. With slavery, he was conciliatory; with the import taxes, he was threatening. Fort Sumter was at the entrance to the Charleston Harbor, filled with Federal troops to support U.S. Customs officers. It wasn't too difficult for angry South Carolinians to fire the first shot.[48]

Therefore, to understand more clearly the real causes of the war, the most important question to answer is not, "Why did the South secede?" but rather, "Why did the North refuse to let the South go?" If the South had been allowed to secede, it would have deprived the North of most of its tax revenue, as well as the principal market for its high-priced manufactured goods. A separate Southern nation, based upon a policy of free trade without tariffs, was an ominous economic threat to the North. Adams concludes his analysis of the cause of the Civil War by stating: "Secession was unquestionably the cause of the Civil War. . . . Southern slavery was to be tolerated by the North; Southern free ports were not."[49]

The Confederate Constitution adopted in Montgomery, Alabama, in March of 1861, was not a radical document, but rather was an attempt to improve upon the U.S. Constitution, demonstrating that the South was trying to preserve the ideas of the American Revolution. Among the changes were the elimination of the general welfare clause, which had been used to expand the power of the central government, and a limitation was placed on the tenure of the president to a single six-year term, but he was to have a line-item veto. Most importantly however, it prohibited a protective tariff, as well as prohibiting the use of federal funds for

[48]Ibid., p. 330.
[49]Ibid., p. 337; see also Robert L. Dabney, "Memoir of Colonel John D. Baldwin Touching the Origin of the War" and "The True Purpose of the War," *Discussions* (Harrisburg, Va.: Sprinkle Publications, 1994), 4, pp. 87–107.

internal improvements, except for rivers and harbors.[50] Alexander
H. Stephens, Vice President of the Confederacy, commented on the
tariff and internal improvement provision:

> The question of building up class interests, of fostering one
> branch of industry to the prejudice of another under the ex-
> ercise of the revenue power, which gave us so much trouble
> under the old constitution, is put at rest forever under the
> new law.[51]

We can get another perspective on the causes of the Civil War,
and the issues confronting those who had to choose sides, by examining the memoirs of one of the most famous Southern participants, naval commander Raphael Semmes. Semmes was a high-
ranking career U.S. naval officer who had no interest in slavery
whatsoever. When he chose to resign his commission and offer his
services to the Confederacy, his wife, who did not believe in the
right of secession or the Southern cause, took their daughters to
Ohio to live with her family. Their three sons fought with the Confederacy, but Semmes's only brother was a unionist, and his
cousin, Alexander Semmes, was a flag officer in the federal navy.
Semmes became the Commander of two warships, the first being
the *Sumter* and then the famous *Alabama*. He disrupted the union
supply lines and severely damaged the Northern merchant fleet by
capturing 82 ships. A recent biography reviews the post-war memoirs of Semmes regarding the reasons that he believed the Confederate cause to be just and worth defending. John M. Taylor summarizes Semmes's views:

> Since the Mexican War, Semmes had come to identify more
> with the South and less with the United States. His was
> much more than the sectional loyalty of a newcomer to Ala-
> bama; rather, it grew out of his study of economic trends
> and constitutional doctrine. An avid reader, Semmes was
> convinced that the South was a victim of economic oppres-
> sion by the North—that policies determined in Washington
> had resulted in a transfer of wealth from the South to the
> North. He placed much of the blame on the recently depart-
> ed Henry Clay. Clay's "American System" had provided for
> tariffs to protect fledgling New England industries. Yet the
> effect of tariff legislation, Semmes concluded, was to stifle
> foreign competition and compel the Southern consumer to
> pay artificially high prices for manufactured goods. [52]

[50]George C. Rable, *The Confederate Republic* (Chapel Hill: University of North Carolina Press, 1994), pp. 39–63.
[51]Henry Cleveland, *Alexander H. Stephens, in Public and Private* (Philadelphia: National Publishing, 1866), p. 719; and see Rable, *The Confederate Republic*, p. 56.
[52]John M. Taylor, *Confederate Raider* (Washington, D.C.: Brassey's, 1994), p. 42.

In Semmes's view the problem went beyond economic policy. He saw the North and the South as inherently antagonistic. Thinking in the North was dominated by the New England intelligentsia, which in turn was drawn from intolerant descendants of the Puritans. From religious intolerance it was but a short step to constitutional obstructionism. Recalling New England's opposition to the War of 1812, Semmes concluded, "As long as they were in a minority . . . [the New England states] stood strictly on their state rights, in resisting such measures as were unpalatable to them, even to the extremity of threatening secession."[53] It was only when they found themselves in the majority that New Englanders had abandoned their States' rights doctrine.

Thus Semmes saw the United States as composed of incompatible societies; the result could only be disastrous for the Southern minority. He quoted with approval the French writer Alexis de Tocqueville, who two decades earlier had compared the states to hostile nations under one government. The tyranny of the majority, of which de Tocqueville had warned, was at hand. One of Semmes's heroes was Patrick Henry, who had opposed ratification of the Constitution on the ground that the more populous North would eventually come to dominate the South.

As for the volatile issue of slavery, Semmes dismissed anti-slavery agitation as a red herring, an issue that Northern politicians exploited in order to isolate and weaken the South. Those who opposed the spread of slavery were not humanitarians; rather, they feared the political repercussions from the formation of new slave states. "The fat Southern goose could not resist being plucked as things stood, but it was feared that if slavery was permitted to go into the Territories, the goose might become strong enough to resist being plucked."[54]

The noted Civil War scholar James McPherson recently published his study of the letters and diaries written during the war by union and Southern soldiers, many from the battlefield setting. Regarding his sources he states:

> Of 374 Confederate soldiers whose letters and diaries I have read, two-thirds express patriotic motives. The proportion that discoursed in more depth on ideological issues such as liberty, constitutional rights, resistance to tyranny, and so on was smaller—40 percent.[55]

[53]Ibid.

[54]Ibid., p. 43.

[55]James M. McPherson, *What They Fought For, 1861–1865* (Baton Rouge: Louisiana State University Press, 1994), pp. 13–14.

A sampling of the Southern soldiers' letters contains one from a young Virginia officer to his mother wherein he compares the North's "war of subjugation against the South" to "England's war upon the colonies." He was confident that the Confederacy would win this "second war for American Independence" because "Tyranny cannot prosper in the nineteenth century" against "a people fighting for their liberties."[56] A captain in the 5th Alabama Infantry wrote to his mother: "How trifling were the wrongs complained of by our Revolutionary forefathers, in comparison with ours! If the mere imposition of a tax could raise such a tumult what should be the result of the terrible system of oppression instituted by the Yankees?"[57] The son of a rich Baltimore merchant defied the wishes of his unionist father and enlisted in the 44th Virginia. He wrote to his father three months before he was killed at Chancellorsville that he considered the war "a struggle between liberty on one side, and Tyranny on the other." He explained that is why "I determined to . . . espouse the holy cause of Southern freedom."[58] A Texas private wrote in 1864 that "We are fighting for matters real and tangible . . . our property and our homes . . . they for matters abstract and intangible."[59] A union officer from Illinois wrote to his wife in the same year on the same point:

> They are fighting from different motives from us. We are fighting for the Union . . . a high and noble sentiment, but after all a sentiment. They are fighting for independence and are animated by passion and hatred against invaders. . . . It makes no difference whether the cause is just or not. You can get up an amount of enthusiasm that nothing else will excite.[60]

Historian Ludwell H. Johnson concludes:

> The reasons for seceding were not at all obscure to Southerners at the time. Many saw themselves fighting a second War for Independence. For example, the South Carolina convention made an explicit comparison between 1776 and 1861 and charged that the Northern majority, by arrogating more and more power to the central government, had imposed the same unjust burdens on Southern commerce as the British had attempted to levy on the colonies. "No man can, for a moment, believe that our ancestors intended to establish over their posterity, exactly the same sort of Government they had overthrown."[61]

[56]Ibid., p. 9.
[57]Ibid.
[58]Ibid., p. 11.
[59]Ibid., p. 18.
[60]Ibid., p. 19.
[61]Johnson, *North Against South*, p. 71.

Nearly 100 years after the Civil War, conservative writer Russell Kirk addressed the role of the New England intellectuals in helping to cause the war:

> Despite all the conservative threads in the Yankee tapestry, New England's intellectual pattern was perplexed by an enduring streak of tinkering. Rather as Cotton Mather could not resist whittling behind the church door, so New England was incessantly tempted to improve and purify—particularly to improve and purify other people. A Puritanical legacy, this; and prodigiously diluted though the heritage of Puritanism had become in Transcendentalism and Unitarianism, that optimistic meddling-urge remained in full strength. The impulse was responsible in appreciable measure for the outbreak of the Civil War and for the fiasco of Reconstruction.[62]

The principal competing forces in the protracted English Civil War during the 17th century were labeled the "Puritans" and the "Cavaliers." Large numbers from both sides created the first colonies in America, with the Puritans locating in Massachusetts and the Cavaliers in Virginia. Their contrasting cultures and their political and religious ideas dominated their respective regions up through the 19th century and were important factors in causing the American Civil War.[63] The authoritarian New England intelligentsia, who wanted to reform the "evil and sinful" Southerners by force, were the intellectual heirs of the Puritans, as well as the intellectual ancestors to the Progressives who would come to power in the first two decades of the 20th century.[64]

---

[62]Russell Kirk, *The Conservative Mind: From Burke to Santayana*, 7th ed. (Chicago: Regnery Gateway, [1953] 1987), p. 240; see also Otto Scott, *The Secret Six: John Brown and the Abolitionist Movement* (New York: Times Books, 1979). The "Secret Six" were prominent New England intellectuals who supported John Brown, both morally and financially before and after his terrorist activities in Kansas, as well as his attack on Harper's Ferry. There were several prominent Unitarian ministers connected with this group who replaced religion in their pulpits with social reform, to be accomplished through force if necessary. Also see George M. Fredrickson, *The Inner Civil War: Northern Intellectuals and the Crisis of the Union* (New York: Harper and Row, 1965).

[63]See David Hackett Fischer, *Albion's Seed: Four British Folkways in America* (New York: Oxford University Press, 1989), espe. chaps. 1 and 2, pp. 13–418 and portions of the conclusion, pp. 859–63. The other two folkways or cultures were the Quakers in the North and those who came from the outer borders of Scotland, Ireland, and England who located in the South. Lincoln was a combination of both northern cultures, Thomas Jefferson and Robert E. Lee were representative of the Cavaliers, and Andrew Jackson and Patrick Henry were representative of the Scotch–Irish–English borderland immigrants. See also Lewis P. Simpson, *Mind and the American Civil War: A Meditation on Lost Causes* (Baton Rouge: Louisiana State University Press, 1989).

[64]See Murray N. Rothbard, "World War I as Fulfillment: Power and the Intellectuals," *Journal of Libertarian Studies* 9, no. 1 (Winter 1989): also included in this volume. In addition, see Paul Kleppner, *The Cross of Culture* (New York: Free Press, 1970); and also, Ernest L. Tuveson, *Redeemer Nation: The Idea of America's Millennial Role* (Chicago: University of Chicago Press, 1968).

Historian Frank Owsley commented upon the South's attempt to gain its independence from Northern oppression with the following observation:

> The war for Southern independence was and remains unique: It is the only war ever fought upon the principle of the right of a people to choose their own government, for the purpose of separating from a government founded upon this principle.[65]

Confederate President Jefferson Davis stated at the very beginning of the conflict: "We seek no conquest, no aggrandizement, no concession of any kind. . . . All we ask is to be let alone."[66] The South offered to assume its share of the national debt and to pay for any union property located in the South, which included Fort Sumter.

The great British historian of liberty, Lord Acton, is best known because of his famous phrase that "All power tends to corrupt; absolute power corrupts absolutely." He is less widely known as a strong, contemporary supporter of the Confederate cause. He saw the issues of this struggle from a long historical perspective and he considered the secession of the South as the Second American Revolution. The colonists had rebelled against England's tariff and Southerners now rebelled against the North's tariff. Acton stated that, "Slavery was not the cause of secession, but the reason of its failure."[67] He determined that the political ideals of the South represented the preservation of the original purpose of the Constitution, which basically was to promote liberty by preventing a strong centralized national government. Acton wrote at the time of the War, "But it seems clear to me that if slavery had never existed, a community divided by principles so opposite as those of Jefferson and Hamilton will be distracted by their antagonism until one of them shall prevail."[68] Acton was no defender of slavery and lamented the compromise reached with slavery in the Constitution. But he saw slavery in the context of historical, religious, and ethical developments—an institution rooted in the ideas and circumstances of a particular era in time and destined for early extinction. Acton realized that the question involving slavery between the North and the South prior to the Civil War related to its

[65]Frank Owsley, "The Fundamental Cause of the Civil War: Egocentric Sectionalism," in *A Vanderbilt Miscellany, 1919–1944*, Richmond Croom Beatty, ed. (Nashville, Tenn.: Vanderbilt University Press, 1944), p. 235.
[66]William C. Davis, *A Government of Our Own* (New York: Free Press, 1994), pp. 340–41.
[67]*Essays in the History of Liberty: Selected Writings of Lord Acton*, J. Rufus Fears, ed., (Indianapolis, Ind.: Liberty Classics, 1985), 1, p. 277.
[68]Ibid., p. 270.

expansion into the new territories and new states, which was a matter of political balance in Congress, especially in the Senate where each state got two senators regardless of population.

One of the main compromises in the Constitution was the attempt to equalize the voting strength of the less-populous South with that of the North. Article 1, section 2, clause 3, provided that each state could count five slaves as three additional people in calculating the population in order to arrive at the number of Congressmen to represent the state in the House of Representatives. This was known as the "federal ratio." However, the tremendous increase in population in the North from about 1820 had allowed it to dominate the South in the House of Representatives for several years before 1860. The South's only political hope was to have an equal number of states as the North, and therefore equal strength in the Senate, to protect them from punitive legislation, mainly regarding the protective tariff and the distribution of funds for internal improvements. The North did not have enough strength to amend the Constitution to prohibit slavery and the U.S. Supreme Court had upheld slavery in the *Dred Scott* decision in 1857. Therefore, the main threat to the South was from Congressional action, especially as to the protective tariff, which is exactly what happened in early 1861, when the Republicans came to power without having received any electoral votes in the South.

In August of 1862, more than one year *after* the war began, publisher Horace Greeley of the *New York Tribune* advised Lincoln in an editorial to declare that the purpose of the war was to abolish slavery in order to make it a campaign of high moral purpose. Lincoln sent back a letter published in the same paper on August 25, 1862, to make it clear once and for all that the purpose of the Civil War was to preserve the union and not to abolish slavery. His words in the published letter were:

> My paramount object in this struggle is to save the Union, and is not either to save or destroy slavery. If I could save the Union without freeing any slave I would do it, and if I could save it by freeing all the slaves I would do it; and if I could save it by freeing some and leaving others alone I would also do that.[69]

One of the first thorough studies of American history was written by Charles and Mary Beard. Their study carefully examined the question of whether the issue of the abolition of slavery caused the Civil War, concluding:

[69]Howard Jones, *Union in Peril: The Crisis Over British Intervention in the Civil War*, (Chapel Hill: University of North Carolina Press, 1992), p. 153.

> Since, therefore, the abolition of slavery never appeared in
> the platform of any great political party, since the only ap-
> peal ever made to the electorate on that issue was scornfully
> repulsed, since the spokesman of the Republicans [Lincoln]
> emphatically declared that his party never intended to inter-
> fere with slavery in any shape or form, it seems reasonable
> to assume that the institution of slavery was not a funda-
> mental issue during the epoch preceding the bombardment
> of Fort Sumter.[70]

The writings of Lord Acton, among other influences, had convinced the Chancellor of the Exchequer, William Gladstone, that
Britain should intervene to support the Confederacy. Britain needed Southern cotton and the South needed Britain's manufactured
goods. They both suffered from the North's protective tariff and its
wartime blockade of the South. Just as America probably could not
have achieved its independence without French intervention in the
cause of 1776, the South probably could not have achieved its independence without Britain's intervention in the Southern cause of
1861. The British led the world in both the Industrial Revolution
and the abolition of slavery, which went hand in hand. Machines
replaced many people and industry replaced most agriculture as
the primary source of wealth. When slavery began to become obsolete and less practical it also seemed immoral to an increasing
number of people. Lincoln knew that he must prevent Britain's intervention and his trump card was the Emancipation Proclamation. The British did not want to be on the side of the South if the
war was perceived as a battle over slavery. When Lincoln issued
the Emancipation Proclamation, which was to become effective on
January 1, 1863, the possibility of Britain's intervention was precluded. This is the main reason that Lord Acton thought that the
"slavery question" was the reason secession failed even though it
was not the cause of secession. Historian Howard Jones also believes that the Emancipation Proclamation was the key factor in the
defeat of the South:

> The British decision to stay out of the war proved crucial to
> the collapse of the Confederacy. Before 1863, when talk of in-
> tervention was at its highest, the verdict of the war hung in
> the balance. Had the British chosen to intervene, the South
> would doubtless have won recognition and dissident groups
> in the North would have been strengthened in their opposi-
> tion to the War. The British would have felt called upon to
> challenge the blockade, assuring confrontations with Union
> vessels and a virtual certainty of war. In the meantime, the
> Confederacy would have secured enough outside military

[70]Charles A. and Mary R. Beard, *The Rise of American Civilization* (New York:
Macmillan, 1927), 2, pp. 39–40; see also Adams, *Good and Evil*, p. 336.

and commercial aid to have prolonged its resistance and perhaps to have won independence.[71]

The Proclamation had the effect of suddenly diverting the war from the North's original and stated purpose (preserving the Union) to a new and entirely different purpose (eliminating slavery). While the Emancipation Proclamation was intended primarily to keep Britain out of the war, and secondarily, to cause a slave rebellion in the Confederacy, its immediate effect did not help the war effort of the North. Civil War scholar, James McPherson, points out that,

> Confederate prospects for victory appeared brightest during the months after the Emancipation Proclamation, partly because the measure divided the northern people and intensified a morale crisis in the Union armies.[72]

Lincoln's Proclamation, by its specific terms, only purported to free the slaves in the rebelling states and did not apply to the four slave states which remained in the union, i.e., Maryland, Delaware, Kentucky, and Missouri. Also, the Proclamation specifically exempted certain counties in the rebelling states which were still loyal to the union. Slaveholders in these four states and these loyal counties could continue to keep their slaves.[73] Furthermore, the Proclamation stated that it would not take effect and no slave would be free on the proposed date of January 1, 1863 if the seceded states returned to the union prior to that time.[74]

The Proclamation was made, admittedly by Lincoln, strictly for military and propaganda purposes.[75] After issuing the Proclamation, Lincoln admitted that: "the character of the war will be changed. It will be one of subjugation. . . . The [old] South is to be destroyed and replaced by new propositions and ideas."[76] Lincoln defended himself against the charge that his act was unconstitutional by stating that the Proclamation was a military necessity and within the war powers of the president as commander-in-chief to

---

[71]Jones, *Union in Peril*, p. 229.

[72]McPherson, *What They Fought For, 1861–1865*, pp. 48–49; Stanton Garner, *The Civil War of Herman Melville* (Lawrence: University Press of Kansas, 1993), p. 198.

[73]Frederickson, *The Inner Civil War*, pp. 113–29.

[74]Niven, *Gideon Welles: Lincoln's Secretary of the Navy*, p. 422.

[75]Gore Vidal, *United States Essays: 1952–1992* (New York: Random House, 1993), p. 690; and see Arthur M. Schlesinger, Jr., "Arbaham Lincoln and Franklin D. Roosevelt," in *Lincoln, The War President*, Boritt, ed., p. 157; also see Jones, *Union in Peril*, pp. 139–41, 143.

[76]Lincoln, quoted in a letter from T. J. Barnett to Samuel L. M. Barlow, Sept. 25, 1862, cited in James M. McPherson, *Battle Cry of Freedom: The Civil War Era* (New York: Oxford University Press, 1988), p. 558; see also Jones, *Union in Peril*, pp. 174–75.

do whatever is required to win the war.[77] Lincoln further explained the Proclamation by stating:

> Things had gone from bad to worse, until I felt that we had reached the end of our rope on the plan we were pursuing; that we had about played our last card, and must change our tactics or lose the game. I now determined upon the adoption of the emancipation policy.[78]

The outspoken abolitionist and constitutional lawyer Lysander Spooner, wrote in 1867 that it was a well-established fact that slavery had been abolished "not from any love of liberty in general—not as an act of justice to the black himself, but only 'as a war measure.'"[79] Russell Kirk, who has much praise for Lincoln as a president, states that Lincoln "never was an Abolitionist, and the act for which he is most celebrated, the Emancipation Proclamation, he undertook as a measure of military expediency, not as a moral judgment. If he could have preserved the Union, short of war, by tolerating slavery, he would have done so"[80]

Gore Vidal, in his study of the American Civil War, and of Lincoln in particular, concluded that Lincoln was America's first dictator.[81] He says that, "The memory of Lincoln was—and is—a constant stimulus to the ambitious chief magistrate who knows that once the nation is at war his powers are truly unlimited, while the possibilities of personal glory are immeasurable."[82] Historian Forrest McDonald cites numerous sources, both by Lincoln's contemporaries and from current historians, all of whom agree with Vidal's assessment:

> Many people, then and later, criticized Lincoln's conduct as excessive. The abolitionist Wendell Phillips called Lincoln an "unlimited despot," and Justice Benjamin R. Curtis wrote that he had established "a military despotism." When William Whiting, solicitor of the War Department, published a book called *War Powers under the Constitution* in which he maintained that in wartime the president's actions are subject to no constitutional restraints whatever, Sen. Charles Sumner thundered that that doctrine (and Lincoln's behavior under it) was "a pretension so irrational and unconstitutional, so absurd and tyrannical" as to deserve no respect. The doctrine when followed changed the federal authority

---

[77]Ibid., p. 173.

[78]Lincoln quoted in *The Lincoln Reader*, Paul M. Angle, ed. (New Brunswick, N.J.: Rutgers University Press, 1947), p. 407; and see Adams, *Good and Evil*, p. 324.

[79]Lysander Spooner, *No Treason*, no. 6 (Boston, 1870), p. 57. Pamphlet in the Harvard University library.

[80]Kirk, *The Roots of American Order*, p. 455.

[81]Gore Vidal, *Lincoln* (New York: Ballantine Books, 1984), p. 460.

[82]Vidal, *United States Essays*, p. 970.

"from a government of law to that of a military dictator."
Twentieth-century historians and political scientists routinely characterized Lincoln's presidency as a "dictatorship" or
as a "constitutional dictatorship"—sometimes using the
word in the benign Roman sense, sometimes in a sinister
modern sense.[83]

Lincoln's Secretary of State William Henry Seward, and his top
military advisor General Winfield Scott, both strongly advised the
president to abandon Fort Sumter, rather than reinforce the federal
troops in the Charleston harbor.[84] He was advised that such reinforcement could serve no military purpose and would be a useless
act that would probably provoke an unnecessary war. Lincoln's act
of reinforcing Fort Sumter and thereby provoking the South into
firing the first shot,[85] set an example for later presidents to follow
in order to involve America in a war, such as Wilson concerning
the events surrounding the sinking of the *Lusitania*,[86] and Roosevelt
and the bombing of Pearl Harbor.[87] Seward's advice to avoid a war
with the South was based partly upon his concern that it would
disrupt the South's economy thereby adversely affecting the
North.[88] In a written memorandum to Lincoln dated April 1, 1861,
prior to the firing on Fort Sumter on April 12, 1861, Seward, who
knew the old political trick, "to busy giddy minds with foreign
quarrels," recommended that Lincoln provoke a war with either
France or Spain.[89] However, Lincoln, who also knew the benefits of
war to presidential power, considered a war with the Confederacy
less risky. Seward also indicated privately to Lincoln, and implied
publicly, that a war with England should take place, which would

[83]McDonald, *The American Presidency*, p. 400.

[84]Carl M. Dengler, "The United States and National Unification," in *Lincoln, The War President*, Boritt, ed., pp. 108 and 135; Kenneth M. Stammp, "The United States and National Self-determination," in ibid., p 135; also see Ludwell H. Johnson, *Division and Reunion: America 1848–1887* (New York: Wiley, 1978) pp. 78–79.

[85]John Shipley Tilley, *Lincoln Takes Command* (Nashville, Tenn.: Bill Coats, 1991), chap. 15, p. 262; see also, Charles W. Ramsdell, "Lincoln and Fort Sumter," *Journal of Southern History* 3 (1937): 259–288. He argues that Lincoln intentionally provoked the firing on Fort Sumter so that he could unify the Radical and Conservative wings of his party and attract Northern Democrats, thereby consolidating the north for his war of aggression to preserve the Union; see also Johnson, *Division and Reunion: America 1848–1877*, pp. 78–79.

[86]Colin Simpson, *The Lusitania* (New York: Ballantine Books, 1972); also see Charles C. Tansil, *America Goes to War* (Gloucester, Mass.: Peter Smith, [1938] 1963).

[87]Robert A. Theobald, *The Final Secret of Pearl Harbor* (Old Greenwich, Conn.: Devin-Adair, 1971); Harry Elmer Barnes, *Pearl Harbor After a Quarter of a Century* (New York: Arno Press, 1972).

[88]Jones, *Union in Peril*, p. 15.

[89]Ibid., pp. 7, 15, and 223 n. 5 and 6; for original documents see *Collected Works of Abraham Lincoln*, Roy P. Basler, ed. (New Brunswick, N.J.: Rutgers University Press, 1953–55), 4, pp. 316–18, 136–37, 153–55; see Howard K. Beale, *Diary of Gideon Welles: Secretary of Navy Under Lincoln and Johnson* (New York: Norton, 1960), 1, p. 37.

be the third attempt to take Canada.[90] Seward understood the desirability of a foreign war for the new administration since Lincoln had only received 40 percent of the popular vote and he was the leader of a new and radical party. By following Seward's advice, Lincoln could have silenced his opponents, diverted attention away from domestic problems, consolidated his presidential powers, united the country and avoided fratricide. Ironically, it was Congressman Lincoln who had publicly condemned President Polk for provoking the Mexican War, which Lincoln denounced as both unnecessary and unconstitutional.[91] Although Congressman Lincoln was probably correct that the president intentionally provoked Mexico into firing the first shot by ordering U.S. troops into an area of the disputed boundary, Polk did request and get a declaration of war from Congress on May 13, 1846.

Others, such as Dwight Anderson, have labeled Lincoln as "America's Robespierre," not primarily for the conduct of the war toward the South, but rather for his unconstitutional and tyrannical treatment of American citizens in the North.[92] Lincoln's repressive policy in the North was a major issue in the 1864 presidential election.[93] In areas far removed from the war zone, such as in New York, Ohio and Illinois, where the court systems were fully operable, Lincoln allowed martial law to be declared and thousands of American citizens to be arrested without warrants, tried before military judges without a jury or counsel and convicted and sentenced without an appeal, some merely upon suspicion of disloyalty to his cause. He unconstitutionally suspended the writ of *habeas corpus*, a time-honored, basic right in Anglo–American jurisprudence. In a recent book, Mark Neely, Director of the Lincoln Museum, makes a full study of the question of civil liberties at the hands of President Lincoln. Neely carefully reviewed the records of over 13,000 of these unconstitutional trials and concludes that while he is unable to refute the charge that the president became a

[90]Jones, *Union in Peril*, pp. 84 and 90.

[91]Arthur M. Schlesinger, Jr., "Abraham Lincoln and Franklin D. Roosevelt," pp. 155, 190–91; also Gabor S. Boritt, "War Opponent and War President," in *Lincoln, The War President*, Boritt, ed., pp. 190–91.

[92]Dwight G. Anderson, *Abraham Lincoln: The Quest for Immortality* (New York: Alfred A. Knopf, 1982), pp. 5, 61 and 193; see also Mark E. Neely, Jr., *The Fate of Liberty, Abraham Lincoln and Civil Liberties* (New York: Oxford University Press, 1991), p. 232; and, James G. Randall, *Constitutional Problems Under Lincoln*, rev. ed. (Gloucester, Mass.: Peter Smith, 1963), pp. 378, 513–14.

[93]Historian Ludwell Johnson states, "It seems plain that without the use of military force and other extraordinary means in 1864, the Republicans . . . quite possibly would have lost the election. A shift of only 38,111 votes in the right places, less than 1 percent of the 4,015,902 votes cast, would have given the election to McClellan." *North Against South*, p. 127.

dictator, nevertheless he states that the president should and will be absolved of blame by history because the ends justified the means, that is, that slavery was abolished. However, he concludes his book with this true statement: "War and its effect on civil liberties remain a frightening unknown."[94]

It is doubtful that the abolitionists of the North or the fire-eaters of the South, both small groups who were unrepresentative of their respective regions, fully appreciated the risk to liberty posed by the war that they both so emotionally demanded.[95] However, Lord Acton, writing to General Lee after Appomattox, demonstrated his understanding of the costs of the war:

> I saw in State Rights the only availing check upon the absolutism of the sovereign will, and secession filled me with hope, not as the destruction but as the redemption of Democracy. . . . Therefore I deemed that you were fighting the battles of our liberty, our progress, and our civilization; and I mourn for the stake which was lost at Richmond more deeply than I rejoice over that which was saved at Waterloo.[96]

Beginning with the modern civil-rights movement in the 1950s, it became popular and "politically correct" to proclaim that the Civil War was fought for the purpose of abolishing slavery and therefore was a just and great war. This gave the civil-rights movement much of its momentum, but it also served to injure race relations severely, and further, to mask the immense and disastrous costs of the Civil War, which included the deaths of 620,000 soldiers. The destruction of the South and its Jeffersonian Ideals of a free market, a non-interventionist foreign policy, and a limited central government were replaced by the ideals of Hamilton, thereby completely transforming the American government created by its founders. The Civil War was, in effect, a new constitutional convention held on the battlefield, and the original document was drastically amended by force in order to have a strong centralized federal government, which was closely allied with industry in the North. Foreign policy would now become heavily influenced by the economic interests of big business rather than by any concern for the freedom of the individual. Domestic policies of regulation, subsidy and tariff would now benefit big business at the expense of small business and the general population. Beginning with the end of the Civil War, the American mind and policy

[94]Neely, *The Fate of Liberty*, p. 235.
[95]Eric H. Walther, *The Fire-Eaters* (Baton Rouge: Louisiana State University Press, 1992); see also Scott, *The Secret Six*.
[96]Fears, *Essays in the History of Liberty*, p. 363.

would become molded into the image of Hamilton rather than Jefferson.[97]

Russell Kirk observed part of the tragic costs of the war by stating in 1953 that the Civil War and the suppression of the South so injured the ideas of a limited central government and free-market economics that it took nearly 100 years for these ideas to begin to make a recovery, and even then not in the popular mind.[98] He also stated that "The influence of the Virginia mind upon American politics expired in the Civil War."[99] Herman Melville, the great American novelist, had many close relatives and friends who served in the union army. After the Civil War he published his collection of poems entitled *Battle-Pieces* with one of the primary purposes to be that war should not be glorified. In these poems he recognized the tremendous costs, especially through the loss of freedom and the end of the founders' dream for America as a result of the North's victory. He viewed the construction of the new iron dome on the Capitol in Washington, D.C., which replaced the wooden one, as a symbol for America's future. In one of his poems entitled "The Conflict of Convictions" Melville states:

> Power unanointed may come –
> Dominion (unsought by the free)
> And the Iron Dome,
> Stronger for stress and strain,
> Fling her huge shadow athwart the main;
> But the Founders' dream shall flee.[100]

Bruce Porter's well-documented study relates some of the drastic economic costs of the Civil War:

> In connection with the war the Lincoln administration attempted to intervene in areas of the national life and economy that the federal government had never touched before. . . .
>
> Prior to 1861, the national government had been a minor purchaser in the American economy. During the war, it became the largest single purchaser in the country, a catalyst of rapid growth in key industries such as iron, textiles, shoe manufacturing, and meat packing. . . .

[97]Merrill D. Peterson, *The Jefferson Image in the American Mind* (New York: Oxford University Press, 1960); see also Samuel Fowler, "The Political Opinions of Thomas Jefferson," *North American Review* (October 1865): 313–34; Frederickson, *The Inner Civil War*, pp. 183–89; and, Hugh Ruppersburg, *Robert Penn Warren and the American Imagination* (Athens: University of Georgia Press, 1990), pp. 1–37 and 161–78.

[98]Kirk, *The Conservative Mind*, p. 239.

[99]Ibid., p. 348.

[100]Robert Penn Warren, *The Essential Melville* (New York: Echo Press, 1987), pp. 3–4; see also Stanton Garner, *The Civil War World of Herman Melville* (Lawrence: University of Kansas Press, 1993), pp. 77–78.

The Civil War spawned a revolution in taxation that permanently altered the structure of American federalism and the relationship of the central government to the national economy. Prior to the war, over 80 percent of federal revenue had come from customs duties, but despite numerous upward revisions of the tariffs during the war, those could provide only a fraction of what was needed to sustain the union armies. On August 5, 1861, the first income tax in U.S. history came into effect, followed by the Internal Revenue Act of 1862, which levied a whole series of new taxes: stamp taxes, excise taxes, luxury taxes, gross receipts taxes, an inheritance tax, and value-added taxes on manufactured goods. The latter Act also created the Bureau of Internal Revenue, perhaps the single most effective vehicle of federal power ever created. . . .

The formation of an internal revenue system was part of a larger Civil War revolution in the nation's financial structure. In February 1862, Congress enacted the Legal Tender Act, authorizing the Treasury to issue $150 million in notes, "Greenback Dollars" not covered by hard specie. The creation of a national currency forever altered the monetary structure of the United States. . . .

Neither taxes nor paper dollars, however, came close to covering the enormous costs of the war. Dire fiscal straits forced the federal government to borrow over 80 percent of its cost, or more than $2.6 billion. Here, too, a dual metamorphosis occurred, with important long-term implications. First, the Lincoln administration created a captive source of credit by granting a monopoly on issuance of the new national currency to banks that agreed to purchase large quantities of federal bonds. The National Banking Acts of 1863 and 1864 also imposed a 10 percent tax on certificates issued by state-chartered banks, thus virtually compelling the large Eastern banks to purchase federal bonds in order to obtain the new greenback currency. But to qualify to purchase the federal bonds, the banks had to agree to accept federal regulation and federal charters. Thus, almost overnight, a national banking system came into being.

The second component of the government's deficit financing was the sale to the public of $1.2 billion of war bonds in denominations as low as 50 dollars, payable in monthly installments. . . . Eric Foner writes that the fiscal measures represented in their "unprecedented expansion of federal power . . . what might be called the birth of the modern American state. . . . "

Another component of state-building during the Civil War that facilitated societal penetration by the federal government was the creation of new administrative institutions. In addition to the Bureau of Internal Revenue, the war saw the founding of the Department of Agriculture, the Bureau of Immigration, and the National Academy of Sciences, founded in 1863 in the hope of harnessing science for the war effort. . . . It also established the Union Pacific and Central Pacific Railroad companies as federally-chartered corporations. All these measures had some link to the war effort—it was vital to retain Western support against the South, to protect industry from competition, and to obtain cheap labor from abroad—but their long-term thrust was to favor industrial growth, westward expansion, and the interests of Eastern urban capital over those of agriculture. Appomattox thus represented not just the defeat of the South, but the defeat of the whole Southern economic and political system, and the triumph of a state-fostered industrial and financial complex in the North.[101]

This was the birth in America of a government–industrial partnership which would later evolve into the "Military–Industrial Complex" about which President Eisenhower warned us in 1961. It was also the birth of the first national Conscription which occurred with the Enrollment Act of March 3, 1863. Furthermore, widespread seizure of private property took place especially after Congress authorized Lincoln to seize any railroad line that public safety required.[102]

After the Civil War, local and state governments became ineffective and weak while the central government began to become all-powerful. It was as though the American ship of state, without rudder or anchor, set sail with the winds of centralized power, and after the winds built up to storm proportions over the next three-and-a-half decades, she shipwrecked upon the rocky shoals of big government at the beginning of the 20th century. The foundation was now being laid for the war-and-welfare century of America to begin. First, however, one last attempt was made to revive the Jeffersonian–Jacksonian ideals with the election of Grover Cleveland to the presidency in 1884. He received solid Southern support and was the only Democrat elected to the presidency since before the Civil War when James Buchanan was elected in 1856 and up until 1912 when Woodrow Wilson was elected. Cleveland directed his main efforts toward reducing the high protective tariff which "had become entrenched in United States politics ever since the Morrill Tariff of 1861."[103] He attempted to retain a sound money system and prevent inflation by protecting the gold standard from the

---

[101]Porter, *War and the Rise of the State*, pp. 259–62.

[102]Ibid., pp. 262–63.

[103]Robert E. Welch, Jr., *The Presidencies of Grover Cleveland* (Lawrence: University Press of Kansas, 1988), p. 88; see also Robert Higgs, *Crisis and Leviathan: Critical Episodes in the Growth of American Government* (New York: Oxford University Press, 1987), pp. 77–106.

silver money advocates. He was also probably the last president to be personally committed to three of the most important original American principles: a free-market economy, a limited central government, and a non-interventionist foreign policy.[104]

THE SPANISH–AMERICAN WAR

The next huge lurch towards a centralized federal government was the period euphemistically called the "Progressive Era" with America's first two foreign wars as its bookends. Arthur Ekirch clearly demonstrates in his excellent study of this period that "progressivism and war were not unrelated."[105] America's first foreign military venture was the Spanish–American War which had its genesis with the election of President McKinley in 1896. His domestic policy was to bolster the basic Republican platform of the protective tariff and, "quite simply, was to encourage the concentration of economic power into the hands of the few."[106] His foreign policy, however, was his defining legacy and this was to expand American possessions and influence throughout the world; it was called the "Republican large policy." Walter Karp, contributing editor of *Harper's*, summarizes McKinley's purpose:

> What McKinley envisioned for the American Republic was a genuine new order of things, a modern centralized order, elitist in every way, profoundly alien to the spirit of the Republic. . . . Of necessity, therefore, the key to McKinley's grand design for national unity and cohesion was the Republican large policy. It was the only way to supplant the republican spirit with the spirit of nationalism, to replace love of liberty with love of the flag, and to make the Nation a political presence strong enough to overwhelm the Republic and supplant it in popular affections. Only by transforming America into an active world power "in contact with considerable foreign powers at as many points as possible" could the Nation (which exists only in relation to other nations) become the unifying force that McKinley and the Republican oligarchy intended to make of it.[107]

McKinley's Spanish–American War began in 1898 and lasted for only 229 days, with the costs in lives and taxes being relatively

[104]Walter Karp, *The Politics of War*, (New York: Harper and Rowe, 1979), pp. 28–48. Here, Karp argues that Cleveland abandoned his non–interventionist views in the dispute with Britain over the Venezuelan boundary. However, Cleveland later opposed the Spanish–American War.

[105]Arthur A. Ekirch, Jr., *Progressivism in America* (New York: New Viewpoints, 1974), p. 260; see also Rothbard, "World War I as Fulfillment: Power and the Intellectuals."

[106]Karp, *Politics of War*, p. 73.

[107]Ibid., pp. 73–74.

small. Karp gives an excellent analysis of both the causes and the results of the war and describes the legacy of the war for America as follows:

> It had been, as McKinley's Secretary of State John Hay put it, "a splendid little war." Yet that little war against a fifth-rate power marked one of the major turning points in American history. At its end, the United States supplanted the broken Spanish Empire as the colonial overlord of Puerto Rico and the Philippine Islands, thus making a radical break with one of America's oldest republican traditions—its repudiation of empire and colonial hegemony. At the war's end America became for the first time a recognized world power, thus marking a break in yet another venerated republican tradition—America's deliberate self-isolation from the perilous international arena and its rejection of what John Quincy Adams had called "the murky radiance of dominion and power."[108]

The Spanish–American War repudiated the non-intervention-ist foreign policy which had served America well for over 100 years.[109] This change in foreign policy is illustrated by a few lines in Robert Frost's famous poem:

> Two roads diverged in a wood, and I—
> I took the one less traveled by,
> And that has made all the difference.[110]

The founders had taken the less-traveled road of non-interven-tionism to avoid an empire and to protect American freedom at home, which had truly made America unique, because most Euro-pean nations, which had always been prone to war, had obtained extensive colonial markets and possessions.

The 1890 census revealed that the western frontier of America had been closed and no new territory existed to be developed. In 1893 Frederick Jackson Turner wrote his famous essay from which he and his disciples argued that since there were no new frontiers on our continent that new colonies, like those of Europe, may become necessary for America if it was to continue its economic growth.[111] This was explicit Marxist dogma to argue that capitalism, in order to survive, must use force to acquire new markets. However, throughout the works of Ludwig von Mises, he shows

---

[108]Ibid., p. 3.

[109]See Robert L. Beisner, *Twelve Against Empire* (Chicago: University of Chicago Press, 1985); and see William Graham Sumner, *The Conquest of the United States by Spain, and Other Essays* (Chicago: Regnery, 1965).

[110]*Robert Frost's Poems*, Louis Untermeyer, ed. (New York: Washington Square Press, 1964), p. 223.

[111]Ekirch, *Progressivism in America*, pp. 4 and 13.

that free-market capitalism believes in international trade, but not in forced exploitation of foreign nations; and he shows that there is nothing inherent in a free market which requires force or war to acquire new possessions, colonies or markets in order to prosper.

In addition to the economic argument for the war, Teddy Roosevelt, the self-proclaimed military hero of the Spanish–American War, substituted the flag and the martial arts, rather than love of liberty, as the appropriate signs of patriotism. He told the students at the Naval War College in 1897:

> All great masterful races have been fighting races and the minute that a race loses the hard fighting virtues, then . . . no matter how skilled in commerce and finance, in science or art, it has lost its proud right to stand as the equal of the best. . . . No triumph of peace is quite so great as the supreme triumphs of war.[112]

At a later time, President Taft wrote to Secretary of State Knox and said that Teddy Roosevelt

> is obsessed with his love of war and the glory of it. That is the secret of his present attitude. . . . He would think it a real injury to mankind if we would not have a war.[113]

The famous small-town editor of the Emporia *Gazette*, William Allen White, also tried to glorify the Spanish–American War with the following rationale:

> It is the Anglo–Saxon's destiny to go forth as a world conqueror. He will take possession of all the islands of the sea. He will exterminate the peoples he cannot subjugate. This is what fate holds for the chosen people. It is so written. Those who would protest will find their objections overruled. It is to be.[114]

When America finally succumbed to the temptation of this more-traveled road of empire by launching a completely unnecessary war without any provocation from Spain, or any clear or present danger to America, she ceased to be an example of freedom to the world. The war with Spain was also completely unnecessary because Spain had agreed to all of the essential terms proposed by McKinley for settlement of the issues two days *before* the president's war speech to Congress, a small detail that the president failed to disclose.[115] Furthermore, the credible evidence now seems conclusive that the explosion which sank the *Maine* in Havana's

[112]Ibid., p. 200.
[113]Ibid., p. 216.
[114]Ibid., p. 189.
[115]Karp, *Politics of War*, pp. 92–93.

harbor came from inside the ship, and can no longer be blamed on Spain.[116] The slogan "Remember the *Maine*" was pure war propaganda perpetrated by the Hearst and Pulitzer newspapers to deceive the American people into believing that Spain had fired the first shot, thereby clearly violating what Supreme Court Justice Hugo Black later said was the highest duty of a free press:

> The Government's power to censor the press was abolished so that the press would remain forever free to censure the Government. The press was protected so that it could bare the secrets of government and inform the people. Only a free and unrestrained press can effectively expose deception in government. And paramount among the responsibilities of a free press is the duty to prevent any part of the government from deceiving the people and sending them off to distant lands to die of foreign fevers and foreign shot and shell.[117]

McKinley deceitfully promised the Philippine rebels freedom from Spain and joined them in their quest. When this goal was accomplished, he turned his guns upon the rebels, killing 3,000 of them and then claimed the islands for the United States. This war gave America its first taste of an imperialistic world power aimed at the perceived unlimited markets of China, which was the true purpose of the war. It established a foothold in Asia by acquiring the Philippines, thereby violating our own implied promise in the Monroe Doctrine not to send our military forces beyond our own hemisphere. Mark Twain saw at the time the full significance of this drastic change in policy and recognized the ominous threat to freedom when he wrote, "We cannot maintain an empire in the Orient and maintain a republic in America."[118] McKinley became the first imperialist American president by conquering foreign lands, and

> His conduct of the war expanded the possibilities of what presidents could do as the leader of the nation's armed forces. By 1900, for example, the president was using the war powers as a rationale for sending American troops into China at the time of the Boxer Rebellion, even though the United States was not at war with the Chinese or any other foreign power.[119]

He sent 5,000 soldiers and marines to China while Congress was not in session and claimed that he was acting pursuant to the war powers of the president. He cited the same war powers for his

[116]H. D. Rickover, *How the Battleship Maine was Destroyed* (Washington, D.C.: U.S. Department of Navy, 1976), p. 91.
[117]*New York Times Company* v. *United States*, 403 US 713, 717 (1971).
[118]Vidal, *United States Essays*, p. 1012.
[119]Dawson, *Commanders in Chief*, p. 51.

right to rule Puerto Rico, Cuba, and the Philippines for several years after the war with Spain had ended. A scholar of military government stated in 1904 that "In America we were supposed to have started out with an Executive with carefully defined powers, but we are now developing one with prerogatives which must be the envy of crowned heads."[120]

The mislabeled "Progressive Era" is praised by most historians as a "reform era" which is proclaimed to have attacked the rich and powerful in order to bring power back to the people. But, in fact, almost every "reform" worked to achieve the opposite effect. Between the Spanish–American War and World War I, during this "reform era," three of the most drastic changes in domestic policy occurred, all becoming effective in 1913. Two of these were actual amendments to the Constitution, the first being the 16th Amendment which allowed a direct tax upon the income of the people, which was temporarily only a tax on the rich. The second alleged reform was the 17th Amendment, which changed the method of selecting U.S. Senators from being elected by the state legislatures to a direct vote of the people. This was supposed to give the people more power, but the real effect was to destroy the last true restraint possessed by the states on the growth of the federal government.[121] The U.S. Senate was originally designed to represent the state governments in order to restrain the growth and power of the central government. The third change was to establish the Federal Reserve System which, in reality, was essentially the same national-bank idea which was fought so long and successfully by Jefferson and Jackson. This "reform" placed the complete control of the nation's monetary and credit policies into the hands of a few non-elected insiders and, to this day, there has been no audit of this agency and there is no accountability to the American people or to any other government agency or official.[122] Ekirch, in his book *Progressivism in America*, quotes from one of Teddy Roosevelt's professors from Columbia University Law School (who obviously had little influence upon Roosevelt) which sums up the effect of the Spanish–American War and the "reforms" that followed:

> In his *Reminiscences of an American Scholar*, the political scientist John W. Burgess deplored the evil effect of the Spanish–American War on the national character. "We started then

---

[120]David Yancy Thomas, *A History of Military Government in New Acquired Territories of the United States* (New York: Columbia University Press, 1904), p. 320; see also Dawson, *Commanders in Chief*, p. 63.

[121]Isabel Paterson, *The God of the Machine* (Caldwell, Idaho: Caxton Printers, 1964), pp. 165–72.

[122]Murray N. Rothbard, *The Case Against the Fed* (Auburn, Ala.: Ludwig von Mises Institute, 1994).

on the road of imperialism and we have not turned back. The exaggeration of government at the expense of liberty made a mightier spring forward than at any preceding period in our history. . . ." Burgess . . . believed that the United States, in its adoption of imperialism, and income tax, and direct democracy, was aping Europe. America, he feared, was moving steadily away from liberty of the individual toward despotic government at home as well as abroad.[123]

WORLD WAR I

The Spanish–American War was a break in the dike of America's foreign policy of non-interventionism, but this became a flood with World War I. Under the misguided leadership of President Wilson, the United States, without a just cause or real provocation, jumped into the European cauldron of constant conflict. The entangling alliances of the European nations had served as trip wires to allow the assassinations of Crown Prince Ferdinand and his wife, the Countess of Hohenberg, to erupt into a world war, thereby demonstrating the wisdom of the advice of the American founding fathers to avoid such alliances. This event, which occurred in the remote city of Sarajevo, Bosnia, was hardly a clear-and-present danger to American interests. America's late entry into the war completely tipped the scales to the side of the Allies, thus causing Germany to lay down its arms when the Allies promised that a peace treaty would be based upon the 14 points proposed by President Wilson. Instead, a Carthaginian peace treaty was fraudulently forced upon Germany at Versailles which led directly to the rise of Nazism, partly because the Nazis advocated a repudiation of this treaty. This *peace* treaty played the most important role in bringing about the next world war. Albert Jay Nock, writing about World War I, stated:

> The war immensely fortified a universal faith in violence; it set in motion endless adventures in imperialism, endless nationalistic ambition. Every war does this to a degree roughly corresponding to its magnitude. The final settlement at Versailles, therefore, was a mere scramble for loot.[124]

World War I is like a continental divide for Western civilization and may turn out to be the Peloponnesian War of modern times. It brought communism to Russia, Nazism to Germany, fascism to Italy and socialism to England. As a result of America's entry into World War I, state capitalism was reinforced here,[125] kept

[123]Ekirch, *Progressivism in America*, pp. 186–87.

[124]Nock, *The State of the Union*, p. 89.

[125]Ronald Schaffer, *America in the Great War: The Rise of the War Welfare State* (New York: Oxford University Press, 1991), pp. 31–63, 225–28.

alive by the New Deal, and then cemented into place by World War II. World War I further demonstrated to the politically-powerful business interests the financial benefits of a war economy. Ronald Schaeffer, in his study of the war, states:

> Potentially the most important result of all was a lesson deposited in the historical record: overseas wars can be beneficial to American business—for the profits they generate and for the security and stability a war welfare state affords to those in a position to take advantage of it.[126]

One of the foremost authorities on the history of war, John Keegan, sees World War I as a turning point in Western civilization with tremendous detrimental and long-range costs. He states:

> The First World War, fought almost exclusively between European states, terminated European dominance of the world and, through the suffering it inflicted on the participant populations, corrupted what was best in their civilization—its liberalism and hopefulness—and conferred on militarists and totalitarians the role of proclaiming the future. The future they [militarists and totalitarians] wanted brought about the Second World War which completed the ruin initiated by the First. It also brought about the development of nuclear weapons, the logical culmination of the technological trend in the Western way of warfare.[127]

Winston Churchill built his entire political career upon Great Britain's wars. His strategy in both World Wars was to bring America in on their side in order to win conclusively without a negotiated peace which might still leave Germany as the dominant power in Europe. Churchill perceived that a strong Germany would upset the balance of power in Europe and constitute an economic threat to the British Empire. While Churchill's role in the sinking of the *Lusitania* as a method of bringing the United States into World War I still remains somewhat cloudy, we now have the details of how the British, and Churchill in particular, worked to involve America in World War II. Churchill's close associate, William Stephenson, set up a secret office in New York City a year-and-a-half before Pearl Harbor. Stephenson's main purpose was to work secretly with President Roosevelt to defeat the America First Committee and to get America into the war eventually.[128] After World War I, Churchill found much to admire in the Italian Fascist dictator, Mussolini. Churchill praised him publicly beginning in

---

[126]Ibid., p. 63.

[127]John Keegan, *A History of Warfare* (New York: Alfred A. Knopf, 1993), p. 391.

[128]William Stevenson, *A Man Called Intrepid: The Secret War* (New York: Ballantine Books, 1976).

1927, and as late as 1940 referred to him as a "great man." Mussolini captured and expressed the prevailing political spirit of the 20th century after World War I:

> Fascism . . . believes neither in the possibility nor the utility of perpetual peace. . . . War alone brings up to its highest tension all human energy and puts the stamp of nobility upon the peoples who have the courage to meet it. . . . It may be expected that this will be a century of authority, a century of the Left, a century of Fascism. For if the nineteenth century was a century of individualism (Liberalism always signifying individualism), it may be expected that this will be the century of collectivism, and hence the century of the State. . . . For Fascism, the growth of Empire, that is to say, the expansion of the nation, is an essential manifestation of vitality, and its opposite is a sign of decay and death.[129]

If President Wilson had been truthful with the American people about the real facts surrounding the sinking of the British liner, the *Lusitania*, he would have lacked his *causus belli*. He failed to warn and prevent American citizens from making the voyage after receiving official notice from the German embassy that the ship contained illegal contraband thereby making it a lawful target for German submarines. Wilson's deceitful conduct in this matter led to the resignation of his Secretary of State, William Jennings Bryan.[130] Without this loss of over 100 American lives in an alleged "illegal and unprovoked attack" on a passenger ship, Wilson would have lacked any apparent strong reason or emotional basis for his request made later for Congress to declare war so that he could "Make the world safe for Democracy."

Wilson campaigned for reelection in 1916 on the platform that "He kept us out of war," but almost immediately after being sworn in he asked Congress to declare war. The most compelling reason why Wilson and his close adviser, Colonel House, wanted America to enter the European war was that they perceived a "New Order" was going to be created in Europe as a result of the war, and unless America was a significant participant, Wilson would have little if any influence in the formation of this structure.[131]

Walter Karp carefully analyzed how Wilson maneuvered the United States into World War I, concluding that the president, "In the name of 'permanent peace' and an 'association of nations,' . . .

---

[129]Benito Mussolini, "The Political and Social Doctrine of Fascism," in *Fascism: An Anthology*, Nathanael Greene, ed. (New York: Thomas Y. Crowell, 1968), pp. 41 and 43–44.

[130]Simpson, *The Lusitania*, pp. 90 and 185.

[131]Karp, *The Politics of War*, pp. 174–75; see also Charles Seymour, *The Intimate Papers of Colonel House* (New York: Houghton, 1926), 2, p. 92.

had deceived and betrayed his countrymen, had falsely maneuvered them into war, had robbed them of their peace, their hopes and lives of 116,708 of their sons."[132]

During the war, President Wilson followed Lincoln's example and ruthlessly crushed the civil liberties of those Americans who opposed his war, by subjecting them to prosecutions and persecutions under the Espionage Act of 1917 and the Sedition Act of 1918.[133] In order to control what Americans thought and said about the war, President Wilson, by an executive order issued on April 13, 1917, created the Committee on Public Information which was funded with executive funds without Congressional approval. One of the main functions of this Committee was to disseminate false propaganda to aid in the war effort.[134] Ronald Schaeffer states that:

> To manage a divided nation in a total war, Wilson felt compelled to follow Lincoln and John Adams and limit the freedom of ordinary Americans to dissent. A time of war the president said "must be regarded as wholly exceptional" and it was legitimate to regard things "which would in ordinary circumstances be innocent as very dangerous to the public welfare."[135]

One example among the thousands of individuals who were prosecuted and persecuted for their "unpatriotic" statements was the case of Rose Pastor Stokes who wrote a letter published in the Kansas City *Star* which stated: "No government which is for profiteers can also be for the people, and I am for the people while the Government is for the profiteers."[136] Judge Valkenburgh sentenced her to 10 years in the penitentiary and stated that the only protected free speech was that which is "friendly to the government, friendly to the war, friendly to the policies of the government."[137]

President Wilson encouraged the Attorney General to institute treason proceedings against any publication critical of him or his war policies and in the case of Ms. Stokes asked that the publisher of the newspaper also be charged with treason.[138] Wilson also favored a peacetime sedition act and even as late as 1920 he vetoed a bill which would have abolished the Espionage and Sedition Acts.[139] Bruce Porter's detailed study of the war concludes that:

[132]Karp, "The Old America That was Free and is Now Dead," in *Politics of War*, pp. 331–32.
[133]Schaffer, *America in the Great War*, pp. 3–30, 218–21.
[134]Ibid., pp. 4, 223–25.
[135]Ibid., p. 29.
[136]Ibid., p. 16.
[137]Ibid., pp. 16–17.
[138]Ibid., p. 28.
[139]Ibid.

Among the more egregious abuses were the hundreds of prosecutions brought under the Espionage Act of June 1917 and the Sedition Act of May 1918, which made even verbal opposition to the war illegal. A Wisconsin official received a thirty-month sentence for criticizing a Red Cross fund-raising drive; a Hollywood producer, a ten-year sentence for a film that portrayed atrocities committed by British troops during the Revolutionary War. All told, as many as 8,000 to 10,000 Americans faced imprisonment, official suppression, deportation, or mob violence during the war.

Though much of the apparatus of wartime repression was dismantled after 1918, World War I left an altered balance of power between state and society that made future assertions of state sovereignty more feasible—beginning with the New Deal.[140]

In Porter's sweeping survey of how war has created the Leviathan state, he shows some of the economic costs of World War I in America:

In virtually all cases of state-building since the Renaissance, war-induced taxation was the wedge by which state power advanced. The United States in World War I conformed to the historical pattern, despite the fact that over three-fourths of the cost of the war was funded by borrowing. The Income Tax Amendment ratified in 1913 had been a minor source of federal revenue until Congress passed the Wartime Revenue Act of October 1917. . . . Never before had federal taxation affected so many Americans so directly. The Revenue Act of 1918 went further, increasing the total income-tax load on American citizens by nearly 250 percent over the 1917 Act. The top bracket reached 77 percent, while the "normal" tax bracket rose to 6 percent. The burgeoning tax burden also included corporate income taxes, a war estate tax, excise and import taxes, and an excess-profits tax.

The tax legislation of World War I permanently altered the structure of American taxation. Not only did this legislation greatly elevate the importance of the income tax, but it made the principle of progression a permanent fixture of the nation's tax system. On the eve of entry into the war, personal and corporate income taxes constituted only 24 percent of internal revenue. This figure rose sharply during the war and remained high afterward, averaging 75 percent throughout the 1920s. Federal tax receipts never again dropped lower than five times the prewar level. World War I thus catalyzed the transformation of the income tax—the most direct and intrusive of all forms of revenue extraction—into becoming the mainstay of American federal financing.

---

[140]Porter, *War and the Rise of the State*, pp. 273–74.

The bureaucratic growth that resulted from World War I was of obvious long-term import for the structure of the U.S. government. But the enhancement of the power of the Presidency that accompanied the expansion was even more significant. A series of legislative measures passed in 1916 and 1917 gave the Wilson administration unprecedented authority to intervene in the national economy. The National Defense Act compelled factories to sell their products to the government on a priority basis at prices determined by the Secretary of War. The Army Appropriations Act authorized the seizure of transportation. (Taking a page from Lincoln, Wilson used this to take control of all U.S. railroads in December 1917.)[141]

Arthur Ekirch concludes his analysis of "Progressivism" and World War I in his book, *Progressivism in America*:

> The war made partners of government and business, and the individual caught up in the rising tide of nationalism and patriotism could offer only feeble protest. Because the new role of the state was subjected to less criticism in wartime, the Progressives and reformers could indulge themselves in the illusion of success and power. War offered the supreme example of the classless national state, with country above party and all particular or individual loyalties. Thus the Progressive exhortations of sacrifice and duty, of social justice at home, were easily translated into a crusade to make democracy and peace, and indeed all desired values, open to the rest of the world.
>
> In arguing the case for a more positive national state and government, American Progressives, like the social democrats in Europe, confused ends and means and were reduced finally to accepting war as the best way to institute social change and reform. From their original revolt against corporate power and the old formalistic absolutisms in thought, the Progressives now had turned to the new Leviathan of the modern warfare state. It was ironic, perhaps, that the final example of European social democracy to American Progressivism should have been this common experience of a world war. But the war, it must be remembered, merely exaggerated the nationalism and statism already implicit in both American Progressivism and European social democracy. Thus the irony of Progressivism swallowed up in the fact of war was a paradox only for the more naive and uninitiated children of America's past.[142]

WORLD WAR II TO THE PRESENT

Following the war, President Wilson's ultimate goal of having the United States join the League of Nations was defeated by the

[141]Ibid., pp. 270–71.
[142]Ekirch, *Progressivism in America*, pp. 274–75.

U.S. Senate when it asserted America's traditional policy against entangling alliances. In fact, after the alliance with France to fight the American Revolution, the United States did not enter into another formal military alliance until the North Atlantic Treaty, creating NATO, was signed after World War II.[143] Since then, the United States government has engaged in many entangling alliances, thus setting traps and trip wires for American wars throughout the world. The last plank of the founders' foreign-policy platform has now been completely destroyed.

Even though the president does not have the constitutional power to declare war, the war powers which are granted have become the Achilles heel of American liberty. A good example of this power is demonstrated in the dissenting opinion of U.S. Supreme Court Justice Jackson in the *Korematsu* case, where he warned us about the abuse of these war powers. In this case, a loyal American citizen was arrested, convicted and placed in a concentration camp during World War II primarily because of his Japanese ancestry. A military order to arrest him was based upon President Roosevelt's executive order, issued pursuant to his war powers, which later resulted in 120,000 loyal American citizens of Japanese ancestry being placed in concentration camps during the war.[144] Justice Jackson stated in the *Korematsu* case that:

> If the people ever let command of the war power fall into irresponsible and unscrupulous hands, the courts wield no power equal to its restraint. The chief restraint upon those who command the physical forces of the country, in the future as in the past, must be their responsibility to the political judgments of their contemporaries and to the moral judgments of history.[145]

Another example is when President Truman completely bypassed Congress and merely issued an executive order committing American troops to the Korean War by ostensibly relying upon a resolution of the United Nations, which we know today was actually passed after the president's order, as Congressman Howard Buffet pointed out at that time.[146] Senator Robert Taft vigorously opposed Truman's Korean War as "a complete usurpation by the President of authority to use the Armed Forces of this country"

---

[143]Robert Higgs, *Arms, Politics and the Economy: Historical and Contemporary Perspectives* (New York: Holmes and Meier, 1990), p. xviii.

[144]*Justice Delayed: The Record of the Japanese American Internment Cases*, Peter Irons, ed. (Middletown, Conn.: Wesleyan University Press, 1989).

[145]*Korematsu v. U.S.*, 323 US 214, 248 (1944); and see Schlesinger, "Abraham Lincoln and Franklin D. Roosevelt, p. 178.

[146]*Commanders in Chief*, Dawson, ed., p. 38; and Quigley, *The Ruses of War*, p. 41.

and furthermore, he said, Truman made "no pretense of consulting the Congress."[147]

President Johnson used the specious and contrived Tonkin Gulf Resolution, instead of a declaration of war by Congress, as his authority to issue an executive order committing American armed forces to Vietnam, another ill-advised land war in Asia. The Tonkin Gulf Resolution authorized the president to retaliate against North Vietnam, but not to launch a war. It was based upon a false representation by President Johnson that the destroyer *USS Maddox* had been the target of North Vietnamese torpedo boats on the night of August 3, 1964. Johnson stated that although the torpedoes missed, the intent expressed by North Vietnam justified reprisal strikes by the U.S. forces. Johnson knew at the time that the report was false and was based upon an erroneous reading of the radar screen on board the *Maddox*. The error was confirmed the day after the incident by the commander of the *Maddox* and by another destroyer in the same area, the *USS C. Turner Joy*, which had more sophisticated radar equipment. There had been no attempt to torpedo the *Maddox*.[148] Truth was clearly the first American casualty of the Vietnam War. Presidents Truman and Johnson stated that these two wars were merely "police actions" and therefore the Constitutional requirement of a declaration of war by Congress did not apply.

It was also President Truman who started America down the tragic road of becoming the world policeman with the CIA as the president's secret police force. Forrest McDonald states:

> He [Truman] called Congress into special session and requested $400 million in emergency aid to Greece and Turkey. On March 12 [1947] he announced to Congress what became known as the Truman Doctrine or policy of containment: "I believe that it should be the policy of the United States to support free peoples that are resisting attempted subjugation by armed minorities or by outside pressures." Congress voted the funds. That was an awesome commitment, amounting to nothing less than declaring the United States policeman to the world and the president chief of police.
>
> The Central Intelligence Agency, charged with worldwide espionage and covert operations, was organized on a basis so secret that Congress voted it funds without being allowed to ask what it was doing. Soon, the United

---

[147]*Congressional Record*, 96, pp. 9320, 9323, June 28, 1950; and Quigley, *The Ruses of War*, p. 39.

[148]Ibid., pp. 108–18; see also Kathy Wilhelm, "McNamara Meets Enemy Strategist," *Montgomery Advertiser*, November 10, 1995.

States negotiated collective security arrangements—the North Atlantic Treaty Organization (NATO) and later the Southeast Asia Treaty Organization (SEATO)—that created permanent alliances in opposition to the Soviet Union and its satellites. These steps were departures from American tradition, and as a whole they redefined the president's role in directing foreign relations.[149]

Over the last 40 years the United States government, under the guise of the CIA, has secretly intervened into the internal politics of numerous foreign governments, mostly in Latin America and other Third World countries. The usual reason given after the fact has been to prevent the spread of Communism, but the practical effect is that the U.S. gets access to their natural resources and a market for our products. The CIA is under the direct control of the president and his National Security Council with little, if any, control by Congress.[150] It has often been the case that the new ruler installed by the CIA was loyal to the United States, even though he was a tyrant to his own people. The CIA has its own worldwide media empire for propaganda purposes, as well as its own airline and armed forces. Congress, through a committee, only learns of the covert activities after the fact in most cases. A recent study of the CIA's activities over its entire history was made by an ex-marine, now a law professor, who was an eyewitness to many of these secret activities. He shows how the United States, through the CIA, has become a menace to the internal affairs of others, often leading to direct American intervention of our armed forces and thereby jeopardizing our own freedom, as was demonstrated in the Vietnam War.[151]

Frederick J.P. Veale, a British attorney, wrote a book[152] about the history of warfare which reveals the return to barbaric methods of killing used first in the American Civil War, and reaching an even more horrible level in World War I. Veale recounts the optimistic faith of Western civilization during the 19th century wherein it appeared that the industrial revolution and the outstanding achievements in science and technology would bring unlimited progress to the world. This optimistic dream was shattered when the concept of "total warfare" was adopted with all of its new weapons of mass slaughter.

---

[149]McDonald, *The American Presidency*, pp. 412–13.

[150]John Prados, *Keeper of the Keys: A History of the National Security Council from Truman to Bush* (New York: Wilbur Morrow, 1991).

[151]Quigley, *The Ruses of War*.

[152]F.J.P. Veale, *Advance to Barbarism* (Old Greenwich, Conn.: Devin-Adair, 1968); see also Charles Royster, *The Destructive War* (New York: Vintage Books, 1991). This book covers the total war concept of the American Civil War.

When we look at the rampant violence in America today we are, I believe, also looking at one element of the costs of war. The world is still haunted by the use of atomic weapons by the United States in World War II.[153] This controversial bombing of Japanese civilians is made much more disturbing by the evidence from reliable sources reported in several press releases, articles, and books which allege that seven months before the atom bombs were dropped on the two cities of Nagasaki and Hiroshima, the Japanese government had offered to surrender on virtually the identical terms which were accepted one month after the bombings.[154] These sources have alleged that the surrender terms of the Japanese government were specified in a 40-page memorandum from General MacArthur to President Roosevelt dated January 20, 1945, which has never been made public, acknowledged, or denied by the American government. It is reported that the information in the memo was secretly delivered by the Chairman of the Joint Chiefs of Staff, Admiral William D. Leahy, to journalist Walter Trohan of the *Chicago Tribune* because the Admiral rightfully feared that the offer would be ignored by the president and he wanted history to record the truth. Furthermore, President Truman, who assumed office after Roosevelt's death in April, 1945, is reported to have later admitted to former President Herbert Hoover that by early May, 1945, he was aware of the peace offer and that further fighting was unnecessary, yet he still authorized the bombing.[155] It is further alleged that President Truman also discussed the specific terms of the peace offer with Stalin at Bebelsberg prior to the bombing; and finally, that General MacArthur confirmed the existence of this memo and its contents after the war.[156]

Trohan first published this information about the Japanese peace offer in the *Chicago Tribune* on August 19, 1945, after the bombs were dropped earlier that month causing the deaths of approximately 210,000 civilians. Harry Elmer Barnes revealed more about this story in *National Review* on May 10, 1958. Trohan updated this story in the *Chicago Tribune* on August 14, 1965.

---

[153]John W. Dower, *War Without Mercy* (New York: Pantheon Books, 1986), pp. 37–38, 316, 324 n. 13, and 325 n. 21.

[154]Henry M. Adams, "Harry Elmer Barnes as a World War II Revisionist," in *Harry Elmer Barnes, Learned Crusader: The New History in Action*, Arthur Goddard, ed. (Colorado Springs, Colo.: Ralph Myles, 1968), p. 306; and Murray N. Rothbard, "Harry Elmer Barnes as Revisionist of the Cold War," in *Harry Elmer Barnes, Learned Crusader*, Goddard, ed., pp. 327–28.

[155]Ibid., p. 328.

[156]Ibid., p. 327.

It is time that the United States government be open and candid with its citizens about why the bombs were dropped. The government should either produce or deny the MacArthur memorandum. The only explanation for the bombing given by the government to this point is that it ended the war earlier and saved the lives of American soldiers. If peace offers were proposed by Japan before the bombing, then the government needs to tell us why the peace terms were not accepted and why the bombs were used instead.

Stanford University history professor Barton J. Bernstein wrote an article in which he quoted the highest-ranking military officers who were the leaders at the time the decision was made by the president to drop the bombs on the two Japanese cities. These military leaders strongly opposed the bombing, saying it was both unnecessary as a military measure and ill-advised as a policy measure. Some of these quotations were to be part of the Smithsonian Institute's exhibit relating to the bombing which, after intense political pressure, was canceled. The article states in part:

> Neither the atomic bombing nor the entry of the Soviet Union into the war forced Japan's unconditional surrender. She was defeated before either of these events took place.[157]

That kind of "revisionist" statement—implying that the atomic bombing of Japan was unnecessary—has so angered veterans' organizations that they forced the Smithsonian Institution to gut its controversial exhibit on the B-29 that dropped the bomb on Hiroshima in August 1945. Yet, the words were written not by some revisionist historian, nor by someone who knew little about the brutality of World War II in the Pacific. They were written shortly after V-J Day by Brigadier General Bonnie Fellers for use by General Douglas MacArthur, the Army's triumphant commander in the Pacific.

Other high-ranking military men expressed similar sentiments. "It is my opinion that the use of this barbarous weapon at Hiroshima and Nagasaki was no material success in our war against Japan" wrote Admiral William Leahy, the wartime Chairman of the Joint Chiefs of Staff, in 1950. "The Japanese were already defeated and ready to surrender because of the effective sea blockade and the successful bombing with conventional weapons. . . . My own feeling was that in being the first to use it, we had adopted an ethical standard common to the barbarians of the Dark Ages."[158]

---

[157]Barton J. Bernstein, "Hiroshima Rewritten," *New York Times,* Jan. 31, 1995.
[158]Ibid.

After his White House years, President Dwight D. Eisenhower, looking back on his earlier service as a five-star general, also said he considered the bombing both unnecessary and morally dubious. In 1963, he said: "The Japanese were ready to surrender and it wasn't necessary to hit them with that awful thing. . . . I hated to see our country be the first to use such a weapon."[159] (Ike's objections, like Leahy's, were purged from the Smithsonian script even before the exhibition was cut back.)

In May, 1945, 10 weeks before Hiroshima, General George C. Marshall, the Army's Chief of Staff, said an atomic bomb should be dropped only on a "straight military objective such as a large military installation," and then, if necessary, on a manufacturing center—but only after civilians were adequately warned so they could flee.[160] He did not want to break the old moral code against killing noncombatants. This counsel was, of course, rejected.

It should be noted that President Truman, during the Korean War, "indicated we might have to use the atomic bomb against China, a statement that prompted an international furor."[161]

It may come as some dubious consolation to Americans to be able to point to Winston Churchill's "splendid decision" in May of 1940 as being the first modern instance of terrorist bombings of civilian populations, rather than military targets. The stated purpose was to break the German morale and public will to continue the war.[162] The British attack against the civilian populations of several cities in western Germany occurred on May 11, 1940, which was the first violation of the European practice known as the "Rules of Civilized Warfare."

These rules grew out of a tacit understanding in Europe at the end of the 17th century to restrain the savagery of warfare. Later, this understanding was reflected in the codes adopted at the Geneva Convention and at The Hague.[163] The main principle was

[159]Ibid.

[160]Ibid.

[161]Quigley, *The Ruses of War*, p. 61; also see, "Statement by the President," November 30, 1950, and "President Clarifies Position on Use of Atom Bomb in Warfare," November 30, 1950, *United States, Department of State Bulletin* 23 (1950): 925.

[162]For a detailed analysis of this subject see the following: James M. Spaight, *Bombing Vindicated* (London: G. Bles, 1944); Sir Charles Snow, *Science and Government* (Cambridge, Mass.: Harvard University, 1961); *The Strategic Air Offensive Against Germany, 1939–1945* (London: H. M. Stationery Office, 1961); Air Marshall Sir Arthur Harris, *Bomber Offensive* (London: Collins, 1947); David Irving, *The Destruction of Dresden* (London: Kimber, 1963); Veale, "The Splendid Decision," in *Advance to Barbarism*, p. 163.

[163]*Restraints on War: Studies in the Limitation of Armed Conflict*, Michael Howard, ed. (New York: Oxford University Press, 1979).

that all hostilities should be restricted to the armed and uniformed forces of the combatants, thereby leaving the civilian population entirely outside the scope of military operations. The barbaric practices of Attila the Hun and Genghis Kahn were to seek out the civilian population of their enemies, especially the women and children, and to slaughter them in order to demoralize the enemy and to win the war without significant casualties to their own armed forces. It was the intent of these rules to remove this barbarity from modern wars.

This British bombing in May, 1940, was followed by extensive efforts on the part of Germany to negotiate a peace treaty with Great Britain, but these were summarily rejected by Churchill. It was not until November 14, 1940, that Germany retaliated by bombing the civilian population of the English town of Coventry. Allied war propaganda at the time stated that Germany started the air war on civilians. Churchill's terrorist methods finally culminated on February 13, 1945 with the bombing of the ancient city of Dresden, with American planes participating on the following two days. Hundreds of thousands of refugees had fled to this city of culture and art because it had no important military targets. It is estimated that between 35,000 and 135,000 civilians, mostly women and children, were killed. The bodies were too numerous to bury so they were stacked in high piles and burned by the survivors to prevent the spread of disease.

There can be little doubt that this dreadful violence, or advance to barbarism, by the United States and Great Britain during the wars of the 20th century has had an adverse impact upon our culture, as well as on the standard of morality for all mankind. There should be little mystery today as to why our cities, our entire culture, and especially our movies, television, and print media, are dominated by horrible violence, and that we live in a new age of decreased morality at the end of the 20th century. We have witnessed on television the recent killings of innocent children in Waco, Texas, by agents of the federal government; and the deliberate shooting which killed the wife and child of Randy Weaver, as they were standing in the doorway to their home in Idaho, again being accomplished by agents of the federal government. These two horrible killings were followed by an even more terrible event, an apparent retaliation against the federal government, resulting in the massacre of innocent people, including many children, by an American terrorist who bombed the federal government building in Oklahoma City. The massive killing of innocent people became prevalent in World War II and has now become part of our American domestic culture. The barbarians are no longer at the gate, but are now within. As the fictional character Pogo said, "We have met the enemy and he is us." America has forfeited its original claim to serve as the beacon for justice and peace throughout the world.

CONCLUSIONS

We had over 100 years of experience with our original non-interventionist foreign policy and have now had nearly 100 years of experience with our present policy. I believe that the empirical evidence clearly shows which policy should be adopted for the future. In deciding this question, one should recall the answer of James Russell Lowell when he was asked how long the United States would endure: "So long as the ideas of its founders remain dominant."[164] It will do little good, however, to change our foreign policy unless we also follow Mises's advice to reduce the scope and power of our central government drastically and adopt a true free-market economy so that the economic interests of certain businesses do not determine that policy.

It has been the pyrrhic victories resulting from American wars which have been the principal causes of the loss of our liberty, mainly because of the centralization of power into the federal government. Our political leaders have proclaimed in each and every war that we were fighting to protect our liberties, which has usually proven to be false, and the end result has been just the opposite. Bruce Porter, who surveyed the detrimental effects of war on Western civilization since the time of the Renaissance, agrees and says:

> Throughout the history of the United States, war has been the primary impetus behind the growth and development of the central state. It has been the lever by which presidents and other national officials have bolstered the power of the state in the face of tenacious popular resistance. It has been a wellspring of American nationalism and a spur to political and social change.[165]

In conclusion, I remind you of the speech Ludwig von Mises gave at Princeton University in 1958.[166] The main beneficiaries of a true free market, he said, are the consumers or general population,

---

[164]Beisner, *Twelve Against Empire*, p. 15; also see quote in David Starr Jordan, *The Question of the Philippines. An Address Delivered Before the Graduate Club of Leland Stanford Junior University on February 14, 1899* (Palo Alto, Calif.: John J. Valentine, 1899), p. 42.

[165]Porter, *War and the Rise of the State*, p. 291.

[166]This speech is now in a pamphlet entitled *Liberty and Property* (Auburn, Ala.: Ludwig von Mises Institute, 1988).

and they, rather than businessmen, should be its champion. He pointed out that many powerful business interests oppose the free market and prefer a government-regulated market wherein they can avoid competition and are able to charge excessive prices and reap massive profits through their political influence.

The same is true in regard to the issues of war and peace. It is the broad general population who lose their lives, their wealth, their property, and their liberty, and who pay the total costs of war. History proves that certain powerful economic interests, the "merchants of death," promote and support most wars in order to gain unjust and immense profits which they could not obtain through a true free market. The roll call of those who oppose the free market, as well as those who oppose peace often contain the same names.

President Eisenhower, who was no stranger to the military, in a rare moment of candor for modern American presidents, lifted the curtain of deception slightly in his January 17, 1961, Farewell Address to the nation and warned us about the Military–Industrial complex:

> We must never let the weight of this combination endanger our liberties or democratic processes. We should take nothing for granted. Only an alert and knowledgeable citizenry can compel the proper meshing of the huge industrial and military machinery of defense with our peaceful methods and goals, so that security and liberty may prosper together.[167]

Unfortunately, these special interests, along with certain power-seeking politicians and sycophantic intellectuals, all working together, often outside of the public view, have been the principal impetus for involving America in needless and disastrous wars.

The ending of the Cold War, which left the United States without a threat from any superpower, coupled with our non-involvement in a major war at the present time, creates a window of opportunity to open the debate on how to recapture the unique American design of a limited central government with a free-market economy and a non-interventionist foreign policy. The damage caused to liberty by prior wars must be recognized and repaired,

---

[167]Arthur A. Ekirch, Jr., *The Civilian and the Military: A History of the American Antimilitaristic Tradition* (Colorado Springs, Colo.: Ralph Myles, 1972), p. x; see also L. Fletcher Prouty, *JFK: The CIA, Vietnam, and the Plot to Assassinate John F. Kennedy* (New York: Carol Publishing Group, 1992), pp. 150, 314–15, 286; and Higgs, *Arms, Politics and Economy*, pp. 1–19, 22–35.

while future unnecessary wars and damages must be avoided. The key point is that the total costs of war must be fully and widely understood so that liberty can be safely protected.[168]

When armed with knowledge of the problem as well as the solution, the will of the American people is strong, even irresistible. To reclaim the American dream for our future, we should look back to our beginnings to see what made America great and its people free.

---

[168]For an excellent study of the number of deaths caused by governments throughout the world, see R.J. Rummel, *Death By Government* (New Brunswick, N.J.: Transaction, 1995). Rummel not only analyzes the deaths caused to foreign enemies during wars, but also the deaths of citizens caused by their own governments. Stalin, who was America's ally in World War II and referred to by President Roosevelt as "Uncle Joe," clearly emerges as the greatest murderer and tyrant in all history. Rummel concludes: "In any case, the empirical and theoretical conclusion is this: The way to end war and virtually eliminate democide appears to be through restricting and checking Power, i.e., through *fostering democratic freedom*." (p. 27)

2

CLASSICAL REPUBLICANISM AND THE RIGHT TO BEAR ARMS

Samuel Francis

One of the incredibly bizarre ironies of the Clinton administration seems to be that at the same time it has been waging war or straining to wage war all over the planet, from
Somalia to the Balkans and from Korea to Haiti, it also is in the
process of trying to disarm American citizens at home through the
most ambitious program of gun control in American history. Of
course, the Clinton administration did not originate this seemingly
inconsistent policy. The military interventionism that has now become almost a routine and unremarkable constant of American life
originated, at least in recent times, under President Bush in the
Gulf War. Indeed, it enjoyed the enthusiastic support of most of
the Republicans in Congress, an enthusiasm somewhat muted today only because the Democrats now manage our global adventures.

Nor are the Democrats the only ones who bear responsibility
for the disarmament of the citizens. Here too Republicans have
played major roles in popularizing the war against guns—not only
through the efforts of Sarah Brady and her husband, but also by
the endorsement of the recent congressional assault weapons ban,
a measure sponsored and supported by left-wing Democrats. Both
former Presidents Reagan and Ford also endorsed the assault
weapons ban shortly before the House vote, and two Republican
congressmen who usually oppose gun control legislation, Henry
Hyde and Robert Michel, actually voted for the bill on the floor,
thereby ensuring its passage by their two votes. This alone ought
to show that it is really the Republicans, the Stupid Party, perhaps
even more than the Democrats whom we have to thank for whatever successes the Clinton administration will enjoy in conquering
both other nations as well as this one.

Of course, a foreign policy of military interventionism combined with a domestic policy of disarming and pacifying the citizenry at home is perhaps not as ironic or as paradoxical as it may
at first seem. It is a combination that would not have surprised,
though it would have deeply alarmed, the exponents of the tradition of political thought which is known today as "classical republicanism." This tradition of classical republicanism exerted a very

profound influence on those 18th-century Americans who formed the American Republic. To a very large extent, the combination of a militarily-aggressive foreign policy with an internal policy of disarmament and pacification constituted the essence of tyranny to the classical republicans as their thought developed in Great Britain and as it was transmitted to America in the generations before the revolution, and it was precisely to avoid and prevent the evolution of such tyranny that the American republicans established certain institutions and principles in the Constitution, the main one of course being the Second Amendment itself, under which "the right of the people to keep and bear arms shall not be infringed." The legacy of the classical republicans is thus not only particularly relevant to Americans but also has important implications for the meaning of what is happening in our own society today, and what classical republicanism has to tell us about power and its strategies of social conquest is well worth examining.

Classical Republicanism refers to a body of thought that evolved in Britain and Western Europe from the 16th through the 18th centuries,[1] a body of thought that in modern times largely developed from the ideas of Niccolò Machiavellió and centered on various political movements in various countries aimed at restricting or doing away with the power of the dynastic monarchies that ruled in those states.

If there was any defining principle to classical republicanism it was its insistence on the restraint of power, and the favorite mechanism by which power was to be restrained was what came to be called "mixed government." In this, Machiavelli followed classical writers such as Aristotle, Cicero, and Polybius in grouping all forms of government into those of the rule of the one (monarchy), the few (aristocracy or its degenerate cousin oligarchy), and the many (democracy). Machiavelli, like some classical theorists, saw

---

[1]Examples of British classical republican thinkers include James Harrington, John Milton, Algernon Sidney, and (in part) John Locke in the 17th century. Two 18th-century republicans, John Trenchard and Walter Moyle, are discussed below. The classical modern study of classical republicanism is Zera S. Fink, *The Classical Republicans: An Essay in the Recovery of a Pattern of Thought in Seventeenth-Century England* (Evanston, Ill.: Northwestern University Press, 1945). More recent studies include Caroline Robbins, *The Eighteenth-Century Commonwealthman: Studies in the Transmission, Development and Circumstance of English Liberal Thought from the Restoration of Charles II until the War with the Thirteen Colonies* (Cambridge, Mass.: Harvard University Press, 1959); J.G.A. Pocock, *The Machiavellian Moment: Florentine Political Thought and the Atlantic Republican Tradition* (Princeton, N.J.: Princeton University Press, 1975); and Paul A. Rahe, *Republicans Ancient and Modern: Classical Republicanism and the American Revolution* (Chapel Hill: University of North Carolina Press, 1992). For a discussion of the influence of classical republicanism on recent American political thought, see Christopher Lasch, *The True and Only Heaven: Progress and Its Critics* (New York: W.W. Norton, 1991), esp. pp. 172–76.

in a mixture of these pure forms the most effective means of ensuring both political stability and institutionalizing liberty.[2] In this preference for a mixed government, the classical republicans challenged the prevailing monarchies of Europe and England, and their theories played an important role in developing resistance to the Stuart monarchy of the 17th century, eventually resulting in its overthrow in the English civil wars, the execution of King Charles I, and the republican experiments under the Commonwealth and later the effective dictatorship of Oliver Cromwell. But the ideal of mixed government, through Locke and Montesquieu, also eventually came to influence the Framers of the Constitution of the United States, and is the ultimate source of our own principle of the separation of powers, under which executive, legislative, and judicial functions check and balance each other.

But while the original republican ideal of mixed government meant that no single social element of society should be dominant in the state, it also meant that all such elements should actively participate in government and public life, and thereby it introduced what was really a subversive idea in the hierarchical and deferential societies of early modern Europe. The republican ideal of an active political life essentially introduced a new political psychology and a new political sociology. Machiavelli argued that while some republics such as Venice and Sparta could flourish and remain stable with essentially oligarchical governments, this was not the safest way for republics to organize themselves. A better way was that of the ancient Roman republic, in which the plebeians played an active part, and while the admission of the plebeians to political power led to internal civil conflicts, it also enabled the Roman state to draw upon the plebeians for military purposes and thereby to overcome its enemies, survive, and flourish as an empire. What Rome lost in internal tranquillity, then, in Machiavelli's view, it gained in its capacity to survive militarily, and the key to its survival, expansion, and success lay in its reliance on its plebeian citizenry for its army. Reliance on a citizen army meant also that the Romans had to admit its plebeians to a share of political power; hence the plebeians were supposed to participate in public life and government no less than the patricians and so the Roman government evolved into a mixed government that combined elements of democracy, aristocracy, and monarchy. In

[2]See Niccolò Machiavelli, *Discourses on the First Ten Books of Titus Livius*, especially Book 1, chapters 2–6; see also Neal Wood, "The Value of Asocial Sociability: Contributions of Machiavelli, Sidney, and Montesquieu," in *Machiavelli and the Nature of Political Thought*, Martin Fleischman, ed. (London: Croom Helm, 1972), pp. 282–307.

Machiavelli's theory, the connection between political and military participation was crucial to the very nature of the republic.[3]

Machiavelli developed this connection between the citizen and the soldier at more length in his book *The Art of War*, which is more than merely a military cookbook. He is commonly faulted because he rejected the use of mercenaries and criticized reliance on artillery, and the use of both was indeed important in the rise of the absolute monarchies of his age. But Machiavelli's point was that he was not trying to develop an absolute monarchy but a republic, and it was his constant teaching that the use of mercenaries and high-tech gadgetry like artillery was dangerous and corruptive to republics.[4] They were dangerous because they placed independent military power in the hands of the state and those who controlled the state and allowed them to circumvent the restraints imposed by an armed people, and they were corruptive because reliance on professional soldiers and military technology meant that the people would have no reason to bear arms in their own defense; if they did not bear arms, they could not expect to have a share of public power, and the whole concept of a republican mixed government and an active public life withered.

Moreover, it was the heart of Machiavelli's theory that citizens who bore arms would necessarily retain the ethic of personal and political independence that would ensure the survival of the republic. As historian J.G.A. Pocock puts it in recounting what he calls Machiavelli's "doctrine of arms,"

> The analysis of the *Arte* [*Art of War*] defines both the moral and the economic characteristics of the citizen warrior. In order to have a proper regard for the public good, he must have a home and an occupation of his own, other than the camp. . . . The mercenary soldier is a mere instrument in another man's hand; but the citizen warrior is more than an instrument in the public hand, since his *virtù* is his own and he fights out of knowledge of what it is he fights for. . . . [But when a city ceased to use its own citizens in its armies and employed mercenaries] The citizens would be corrupted because they permitted inferiors to do for them what should be done for the public good; the mercenaries would be agents of that corruption because they performed a public function without regard for the public good.[5]

[3]Pocock, *Machiavellian Moment*, pp. 197–204; in addition to the chapter of Book 1 of Machiavelli's *Discourses* cited above, similar ideas are developed in Niccolò Machiavelli, *The Art of War*, Ellis Farnsworth, trans. (Indianapolis, Ind.: Bobbs-Merrill, 1965), pp. 17–20.

[4]See Pocock, *Machiavellian Moment*, pp. 204–11; see also Neal Wood, "Introduction," in Machiavelli, *Art of War*, pp. xxxi–xxxiv.

[5]Pocock, *Machiavellian Moment*, pp. 203–4.

In other words, for Machiavelli and for almost all classical republicans after him, it is the essential independence or autonomy of the citizen—as citizen and as warrior—that makes republican life possible. The republican citizen, unlike the passive subject of a monarchy, took an active part in both war and government, and he was able to take an active part precisely because of his personal independence—economically, morally, politically, and militarily. It was Machiavelli's emphasis on the role of arms in the civic life of the republic that accounts for the long classical republican tradition of popular militias, and in the Second Amendment of our own Constitution we find the descendant of Machiavelli's doctrine of arms—that "a well-regulated militia, being necessary to the security of a Free State, the right of the people to keep and bear arms shall not be infringed."

Many of the framers of our own Constitution and Bill of Rights no doubt knew Machiavelli's works directly and could have gotten the idea of a citizens' militia from him, but there was a good deal of intervening experience and theory between Machiavelli and the late 18th century that reinforced his teaching, and it was mainly from the British experience in the late 17th and 18th centuries that American republicans drew their immediate lessons about a citizens' militia and what it meant for the preservation of political freedom.

England had a militia since Anglo–Saxon times, and throughout most of English history, the monarchs had actually encouraged and supported the militia, on the reasoning that well-armed subjects were useful supports for internal peace and external defense. Beginning in the mid 17th century, however, when various social reforms of the Stuart dynasty began to meet resistance from popular elements well schooled in the use of weapons, the monarchy began a policy of trying to disarm the English people and to rely instead on a standing army. During the English Revolution of the 1640s, this policy of the Stuart monarchs was actually continued and enhanced by Oliver Cromwell and his military dictatorship, which relied on a standing army. After the restoration of the monarchy in 1660, Charles II also sought to build up the military power of his government, and in fact this policy was part of a general transformation of the English state and society in that period.

What was happening in England was essentially the creation of the modern state, with a monopoly of the means of violence and the financial resources to support the monopoly. Between 1660 and approximately 1720, the monarchy developed and institutionalized a standing army and the bureaucratic machinery to tax and borrow

sufficient money to finance it, and under William III these state institutions were used for the explicit purposes of waging war on a
global scale. But even under the last Stuart kings, Charles II and his
brother James II, the same trends were apparent. In order for the
state, in the person of whatever king of whatever dynasty sat on
the throne, to transform the society to the point that it was possible
for the state to raise money and wage war without internal resistance, it was necessary to disarm the English people.

The later Stuarts tried to do just that. The Militia Act of 1662
thus gave the officers of the militia, appointed by the crown, the
power to disarm any subject at the officer's discretion, a power
unprecedented in English history. A few years later, in 1671, the
first of a long series of laws known as the Game Laws was passed
which actually forbade hunting by persons who lacked sufficient
property and which authorized the confiscation of guns and other
sporting equipment in the possession of people not qualified to
hunt. Once the Catholic James II came to the throne in 1685, he
consciously sought to disarm Irish Protestants and doubled the
standing army that he had inherited from his brother, Charles II,
the first standing army under the monarchy in English history. As
the historian J.R. Western writes,

> there are signs that the disarming of the people for good was
> an integral part of the crown's measures for destroying whig
> powers of resistance. . . . The disarming of the people was
> accompanied and intensified by the decline of the militia. . . .
> Under James II the militia was steadily superseded by the
> standing army.[6]

A military force independent of his control than the Stuart
kings he had replaced. He refused to repeal the Militia Act and at
the end of the Nine Years War in 1697 refused to demobilize the
standing army, now far larger than anything the later Stuarts had
planned. It was his insistence on retaining a standing army, which
soon was involved in yet another continental dynastic war, the
War of the Spanish Succession, that led to the first explicit defense
of a popular militia in English political thought by the classical republican pamphleteers John Trenchard and Walter Moyle.[7]

Trenchard and Moyle, along with several other theorists, argued that the "ancient constitution" of England inherited from the
Anglo–Saxon times had been overthrown by the monarchs using

---

[6]J.R. Western, *Evolution: The English State in the* 1680s (London: Blanford Press,
1972), pp. 144–46.

[7]Trenchard and Moyle collaborated on their main work on militias and standing
armies, *An Argument against a Standing Army*, in Walter Moyle, *Whole Works*, 2 vols.
(London, 1726).

mercenary soldiers and that the way to restore the ancient constitution and the freedom that went with it was to rebuild the militia. They laid out rather elaborate plans by which all male free-holders were to join in the militia, with each parish to provide its own stock of arms and ammunition. As historian Caroline Robbins describes the republican discussion of militia reform,

> The emphasis . . . was upon the danger to internal security from royal power rather than upon necessary protection against external attacks. Over and over again the connection between absolutism and mercenaries was pointed out. . . . All deduced the same moral: "He that is armed is always master of the purse of him that is unarmed."[8]

Unfortunately, the classical republicans who urged militia re-form and opposed a standing army were defeated, in large part by the defection of what came to be known as the "Court Whigs," led by Lord John Somers, who sided with the monarchy and used popular fear of Catholic absolutist France to justify constructing a large standing army and all the paraphernalia of the modern state, including the financial, administrative, and diplomatic machinery to support the armed forces. But even though the supporters of the militia lost the political battle, there are two significant implications of this episode of English history.

The first is that the Whig and classical republican debate over militia reform had a profound effect on American colonists in the 18th century, and it is largely from the works of such men as Trenchard and his colleagues that the Americans formed their own theoretical ideas about owning and bearing arms and maintaining a citizens' militia.

The second implication is that the state's attack on the militia and the effort to disarm the English people was accompanied by the state's efforts to expand its military power and to use its military power for external interventionism and war. The conjunction is not accidental. The English monarchs, of whatever dynasty, understood that they could not mobilize the financial resources for war from their subjects or indeed exercise political domination of their subjects at all if those subjects retained the means of military resistance, and therefore the disarmament of the people through legal restrictions on the possession of guns was a constant theme of the early history of the modern state and modern imperialism.

But despite the late-17th-century efforts at disarmament, Englishmen retained the right to bear arms and even confirmed and

[8]Robbins, *The Eighteenth-Century Commonwealthman*, p. 105.

expanded it in the course of the 18th century. In the Convention summoned to sit in place of a parliament at the time of the Revolution of 1688, the Whigs and classical republicans exerted considerable influence on the English Bill of Rights that the Convention adopted, and one of these rights was "that the subjects which are protestants may have arms for their defence suitable to their conditions and as allowed by law." This was the direct ancestor of our own Second Amendment, and in fact the original language of the right was even more radical and asserted or implied an actual duty of subjects to keep arms. Probably due to the influence of William III himself, this language was altered to express a right rather than a duty to keep arms since the clear rationale of a duty was to resist royal authority. The recognition of the right to keep arms in the English Bill of Rights was the foundation of this right in Great Britain down to the 20th century. Although the English Bill of Rights restricted the right to keep arms to Protestants, the only restrictions on Roman Catholics were that Catholics were legally forbidden to store arms that could be used for rebellious purposes; they were explicitly assured of the right to keep arms for their personal defense in laws adopted in the 18th century. Moreover, in 1692, 21 years after the passage of the Game Law restricting the right to bear arms, the law was amended so as to continue to protect game animals against hunting but not to restrict ownership or possession of firearms.

The great English jurist of the 18th century, Sir William Blackstone, was emphatic about the right to keep arms and the central importance of that right to a free people. In his *Commentaries on the Laws of England*, after enumerating the rights of Englishmen, Blackstone writes,

> But in vain would these rights be declared, ascertained, and protected by the dead letter of the laws, if the constitution had provided no other method to secure their actual enjoyment. It has therefore established certain other auxiliary rights of the subject, which serve principally as outworks or barriers, to protect and maintain inviolate the three great and primary rights, of personal security, personal liberty, and private property.[9]

There were five such "auxiliary rights" in Blackstone's view,

> The fifth and last auxiliary right of the subject, that I shall at present mention, is that of having arms for their defence, suitable to their condition and degree, and such as are allowed by law . . . and is, indeed, a publick allowance under due restrictions, of the natural right of resistance and self

[9]William Blackstone, *Commentaries on the Laws of England* (Chicago: University of Chicago Press, 1979), 1, p. 136.

> preservation, when the sanctions of society and laws are
> found insufficient to restrain the violence of oppression.[10]

Despite the qualifying language Blackstone used about the right to keep arms, his view also deeply influenced the American Framers who took a less qualified and indeed more egalitarian view of who might keep arms, regardless of what was "suitable to their condition and degree." And in fact there was in Great Britain throughout the 18th and 19th centuries very little dispute about the right to keep arms. The only exception was an act passed in 1819 as one of what came to be called the Six Acts, which were six laws enacted in the wake of the Napoleonic wars to control internal security. One of these, known as the Seizure of Arms Act, allowed for magistrates to seize weapons from subjects under certain circumstances, but it is notable that even the government spokesman who sponsored the Seizure of Arms Act in the House of Commons, Lord Castlereagh, acknowledged that it violated the constitutional right to keep arms. Castlereagh stated the "principle of the bill was not congenial with the constitution, that it was an infringement upon the rights and duties of the people, and that it could only be defended upon the necessity of the case."[11] Despite strenuous opposition to the bill, it passed, but only because it was supposed to expire in two years, which it did. From that time until a century later there was virtually no serious attempt to enact gun control in England; there was certainly no successful attempt. Indeed, Lord Macaulay in the middle of the 19th century defended the right to keep arms as "the security without which every other is insufficient."[12]

Toward the end of the 19th century, there were certain laws adopted that imposed minor legal restrictions on the right to keep arms. In 1870 there was a Gun Licence Act that required those who wanted to carry firearms outdoors to buy a 10-shilling license at the post office; it was intended simply as a revenue device. In 1893 and 1895 the House of Commons considered more rigorous pistol control bills but rejected them as "grandmotherly, unnecessary and futile." In 1903 the Commons passed a Pistols Act that prohibited the sale of pistols to minors and felons. As late as 1920 then, the British people enjoyed virtually as much right to own, buy, sell, keep, and bear firearms as Americans did.

In 1920, however, the Coalition government of David Lloyd George introduced what became known as the Firearms Control

[10]Ibid., p. 139.
[11]Quoted in Joyce Lee Malcolm, *To Keep and Bear Arms: The Origins of an Anglo-American Right* (Cambridge, Mass.: Harvard University Press, 1994), p. 169.
[12]Quoted in ibid.

Act, which effectively repealed the right to bear arms by requiring
a certificate for anyone wishing to "purchase, possess, use, or carry
any description of firearm or ammunition for the weapon." The local chief of police was supposed to decide who was and who was
not to have firearms and could exclude anyone based on "intem-
perate habits, unsound mind or for any reason unfitted to be trusted," a condition that today would certainly disqualify most members of Parliament. The applicant had to convince the police that he
had "a good reason for requiring such a certificate," and the government spokesman in the House of Lords conceded that "good
reason" would be "determined by practice"—in other words, that
good reason would mean what the police decided it meant. Under
the bill Englishmen could appeal refusal of a certificate to a court,
but Irishmen were explicitly denied such a right of appeal.[13]

While the 1819 Seizure of Arms Act, introduced in an undemocratic House of Commons in a period of severe social instability
and revolutionary activity, was met with strong opposition, the
Firearms Control Act of 1920 encountered little resistance. One
member of the Commons, a Col. Kenworthy, did object and
pointed out that the right to keep arms had been important historically if only in order to keep and acquire other political rights that
all Englishmen now enjoyed precisely because keeping arms enabled the people to resist the state. He was at once denounced by a
Major Winterton, who sneered that his colleague's

> idea is that the State is an aggressive body, which is endeav-
> ouring to deprive the private individual of the weapons
> which Heaven has given into his hands to fight against the
> State. . . . There are other people who hold those views in
> this country, and it is because of the existence of people of
> that type that the Government has introduced this Bill.[14]

Apparently, the government of 1920 would have considered that it
had every reason to seize the weapons found on the persons or in
the homes of John Trenchard, Sir William Blackstone, Lord Macaulay and other "people of that type" who had defended the right to
keep arms precisely as a security against the state.

But in fact Major Winterton was probably right. The main reason for the bill seems to have been fear of the Bolshevik revolution
by the government, even though the official reason offered by the
government was that armed crime had increased. In fact, in the
years 1915 to 1917, the average number of crimes in which firearms

[13]Ibid., pp. 170–71.
[14]Ibid., p. 174.

were used fell from 45 to 15.[15] Not only Bolshevism but also labor unrest in general as well as Irish violence may have contributed to the decision of the government to sponsor this law, and it is significant that this gun control measure too, like those of the late 17th century, was driven not by a desire to curb crime but by a fear of popular resistance—in other words, by fear of the government's own people and of the very thing the right to keep arms was intended to ensure.

But what is also significant is that the 1920 bill passed in the House of Commons by a vote of 254 to 6. Thus, by an overwhelming majority did the British Parliament toss away a fundamental right the defense of which had helped inspire the Revolution of 1688 and which had been defended as central to English liberty by the country's greatest jurist and one of its foremost historians. As Major Winterton's stupid remarks make clear, by the time of the debate on the Firearms Control Act, the English ruling class had forgotten what the right to keep arms meant, how it had developed, or why it was important, and there is no evidence to this day that Englishmen understand it any better now than they did when they stripped themselves of the right to keep arms in 1920. The act has been progressively toughened several times, each time with little objection, and today *The Economist* magazine loves to publish factually inaccurate editorials sneering at the backward Americans' insistence on their Second Amendment rights. The editorials are as inaccurate in their understanding of contemporary America as they are ignorant of the history of Great Britain itself.

The immediate reason for the British government's desire to pass gun control and abolish the right of Englishmen to keep arms may have been fear of revolution and unrest, but in a larger sense, the passage of the 1920 act was certainly related to the major enlargement of state power that was then beginning in Great Britain and the United States, where the first federal firearms act was passed in 1934. I do not suggest that either the British or the American governments consciously sought to disarm their citizens as a preparatory move to depriving them of further liberties through superior force, though that possibility cannot be excluded. What I do say is that the curtailment of the right to bear arms makes perfect sense in a society in which statism has triumphed, in which the central state as opposed to the people who compose it is the real source of authority, and that it makes no sense at all for such a society to permit or recognize a right to keep arms on the part of the subjects of the state.

[15]Ibid., p. 171.

Those classical republicans who first expressed and defended a right to keep arms understood that the kind of society they envisioned would be one in which authority came from the bottom up, that the democratic element of the mixed constitution, often in league with the aristocratic element, would through the right to keep arms prevent the state from transgressing on liberty, property, and personal security. They also knew that an institution like the militia would establish the right to keep arms and ensure its effectiveness against an aggressive state, and the economically independent citizens who would serve in the militia with their own arms would ensure the success of republican self-government.

It can hardly be surprising that a society that has forgotten the teaching of classical republicanism, that personal and social independence is the precondition of free government, has also forgotten the meaning of the right to keep arms, which it so gaily pitches away, and the integral relationship of that right to the very nature of a self-governing republic. The alternative to the kind of mixed regime the classical republicans supported is precisely the kind of autocratic one they often gave their lives to resist, the kind that James II and William III tried to build by first ensuring that their own subjects were too disarmed to raise a hand against their schemes. In the republic as the classical theorists conceived it, as in the American Republic that owes so much to their conception, the authority of the state is supposed to come from the people, from the social elements of which the mixed constitution is composed, and so it is the state that must persuade us, the citizens, and prove things to us, whether to enact a law that criminalizes otherwise law-abiding gun-owners or go to war in Rwanda. In the autocracy envisioned by James II and William III, not to mention their spiritual descendants in the shapes of David Lloyd George and John Major, George Bush and Bill Clinton, it is the citizen who must convince the state that he should be allowed to have a gun, and the state and its agents may deny his plea for whatever it considers to be "good reason."

What is involved in the current craze for gun control, then, is a bit more than just a drive for law and order or a crackdown on hunters and gun collectors. It is implicitly a revolution against our fundamental conception of the state, an implicit transformation of the American republic from its republican character to an essentially autocratic character, because the right to keep and bear arms, either as a militia or as individuals, is an essential characteristic of a republic and a free people. It is meaningless to say that we have a republic unless we also have the right to keep arms, since the capacity of the people to protect and defend themselves—against criminals, foreign aggressors, or their own government—is also a condition of their capacity to rule themselves and to prevent others from ruling them. And the denial of the right to keep arms is equally characteristic of an autocracy and of a people that is essentially enslaved, regardless of how much money it makes or how often it votes, because a people stripped of the capacity to protect and defend themselves is certainly not the stuff of which a *res publica* is made—and indeed, it is not even a people.

3

DEFENDERS OF THE REPUBLIC: THE ANTI-INTERVENTIONIST TRADITION IN AMERICAN POLITICS

Justin Raimondo

What is today reviled as Isolationism is deeply rooted in American history. As the anti-isolationist historian Selig Adler pointed out, "The American Revolution was in itself an act of isolation, for it cut the umbilical cord to the mother country."[1] The American Revolution was, as Garet Garrett put it,

> a pilot flame that leaped the Atlantic and lighted holocaust in the Old World. But its character was misunderstood and could not have been reproduced by any other people. It was a revolution exemplary.[2]

THE FOREIGN POLICY OF THE FOUNDERS: ENTANGLING ALLIANCES WITH NONE

This "revolution exemplary" gave birth to a New World, bereft of the encrusted evils, the ancient hatreds, and the convoluted obsessions of the Old. This sense of the unique American character permeates the revolutionary propaganda of the American patriots; freedom from European militarism was one of the great benefits of independence touted in Thomas Paine's *Common Sense*. In 1783, at the end of the Revolutionary War, Congress passed a resolution rejecting American entry into the European League of Armed Neutrality, declaring that the 13 states "should be as little as possible entangled in the politics and controversies of European nations."

The classic statement of the founders' foreign policy is, of course, to be found in George Washington's *Farewell Address*. Caught in the crossfire of radical Jeffersonians and the pro-British Federalists led by Alexander Hamilton, and having decided to drop out of the increasingly-bitter political fray, the father of his country was desperately concerned about two big problems facing the young American republic: internal factional strife, and the threat of attack from the European great powers. While Federalist propaganda depicted Jefferson and his party as the agents of France, the Anti-Federalists saw Hamilton as the agent of another

[1] Adler, Selig, *The Isolationist Impulse: Its Twentieth Century Reaction* (New York: Collier Books, 1961), p. 16.

[2] Garet Garrett, *The American Story* (Chicago: Regnery, 1955), p. 19.

foreign power, namely Britain. Deftly balancing between these two parties, outgoing-President Washington warned against "permanent, inveterate antipathies against particular nations and passionate attachment for others." A nation so entangled "is in some degree a slave. It is a slave to its animosity or to its affection, either of which is sufficient to lead it astray from its duty and its interest."[3]

Reading the *Farewell Address* today, one is struck by its modernity. Washington might have been describing the pro-NAFTA crowd when he explained that these passionate antipathies and attachments give

> to ambitious, corrupted, or deluded citizens (who devote themselves to the favorite nation) facility to betray or sacrifice the interests of their own country without odium, sometimes even with popularity, gilding with the appearances of a virtuous sense of obligation, a commendable deference for pubic opinion, or a laudable zeal for public good the base or foolish compliances of ambition, corruption, or infatuation.[4]

Surrounded on every side by the vultures of Europe, Washington sought to steer his country between the Scylla of France and the Charybdis of the British Empire. He was alarmed by the growth of foreign partisanship as a factor in American politics, and the growing rivalry between the two camps. Thus he warned

> against the insidious wiles of foreign influence (I conjure you to believe me, fellow-citizens) the jealousy of a free people ought to be *constantly* awake, since history and experience prove that foreign influence is one of the most baneful foes of republican government.[5]

While proponents of non-interventionism have traditionally invoked Washington's words to support their position, the interventionists have put their own peculiar spin on the *Farewell Address*. We are informed that the *Farewell Address* was a reaction to specific historical circumstances, and that non-interventionists take Washington's words out of context. We are even told that, far from warning against entangling alliances, Washington was an "apostle of empire!"[6] For a long time, the interventionists were content to say Washington's policy was merely outmoded. Now, however, in the modern fashion, Washington's words are inverted, "deconstructed," and perverted into a rationale for Empire.

---

[3]*Washington's Farewell Address: The View From the Twentieth Century,* Burton Ira Kaufman, ed. (Chicago: Quadrangle Books, 1969), pp. 26–27.
[4]Ibid.
[5]Ibid.
[6]See Burton Ira Kaufman, "Washington's Farewell Address: A Statement of Empire," ibid., pp. 169–91, wherein the author proffers a single quotation from the alleged object of his analysis—a few vague phrases about America's coming greatness—and then ignores the rest of the text.

To the charge that non-interventionists take the *Farewell Address* out of its historical context, one can only admit that, yes, Washington's words were indeed spoken at a time when he was concerned about foreign intrigues fostering internal disunity. But to maintain that this is *all* Washington was concerned about is to ignore large sections of the text. A few examples will suffice:

> Europe has a set of primary interests which to us have none or a very remote relation. Hence, she must be engaged in frequent controversies, the causes of which are *essentially* foreign to our concerns.[7]

Referring to "our detached and distant situation," which enables us to pursue "a different course," Washington declares that

> it is *our true policy* to steer clear of permanent alliances with any portion of the foreign world.[8]

And again:

> Taking care *always* to keep ourselves by suitable establishments on a respectable defensive posture, we may safely trust to temporary alliances for extraordinary emergencies.[9]

These key words—*essentially* foreign, *true* policy, taking care *always*—are those of a man quite well aware that he was addressing posterity. And the message he meant to leave is clear enough:

> The great rule of conduct for us in regard to foreign nations is, in extending our commercial relations to have with them as little *political* connection as possible. So far as we have already formed engagements let them be fulfilled with perfect good faith. Here let us stop.[10]

And we *did* stop. After the Treaty of Alliance with France that aided and speeded the victory of the American revolutionaries, the American government did not enter into another formal alliance with a foreign power until World War II.[11]

JEFFERSON, ADAMS, AND CONTINENTALISM

Although George Washington is often credited with calling for "peace, commerce, and honest friendship with all nations,

---

[7]Ibid. , p. 27; emphasis added.
[8]Ibid.; emphasis added.
[9]Ibid., p. 28; emphasis added.
[10]Ibid., p. 27.
[11]During World War I, official documents referred to the "Allies and Associated Powers."

entangling alliances with none," it was in fact Jefferson who said it in his first inaugural address.[12] In any event it neatly sums up the predominant view of nearly all of the original American revolutionary leaders, Federalist or Anti-Federalist. Bounded by the British in the northern outposts, and the Spanish to the Southwest, the fledgling American republic could not afford another war, and was desperately attempting to avoid encirclement by the predatory European powers. With Europe aflame, American shipping and sailors were prey to both sides, and it was all John Adams could do—amid cries of "Millions for defense, not one cent for tribute!"—to stay out of a war with France that might have sounded the death knell of the Republic. Jefferson continued this policy of isolation—that is, isolation from the wars and militarism that were decimating Europe and threatening the Americas. If the first principle of Jeffersonian foreign policy was the avoidance of war, this was not due just to American military weakness, but also to Jefferson's dedication to limited constitutional government. He knew that war would lead to the centralization of power, and, perhaps, the restoration of monarchy to America. War would mean the defeat of Jeffersonian political goals; it would mean debt, onerous taxes, and a standing army that would in itself constitute a threat to the republican form of government. As Madison put it:

> war is in fact the true nurse of executive aggrandizement. In war, a physical force is to be created; and it is the executive will, which is to direct it. In war, the public treasuries are to be unlocked; and it is the executive hand which is to dispose them. In war, the honours and emoluments of office are to be multiplied; and it is the executive patronage under which they are to be enjoyed. It is in war, finally, that laurels are to be gathered; and is the executive brow they are to encircle.[13]

This theme—that the violence done to republican institutions by war is as irreparable (and fatal) as the violence inflicted on men—is echoed down through the years by virtually all the critics of an American imperial policy. From the New England mugwumps who opposed the annexation of Hawaii, Cuba, Puerto Rico, and the Philippines, to the Western progressive Republicans and populist Democrats who opposed Wilson's "war to end all wars," to the America First movement of John T. Flynn, Senator Gerald Nye, and Colonel Robert Rutherford McCormick: as we

---

[12]*The Chief Executive: Inaugural Addresses of the Presidents of the United States*, Fred L. Israel, ed. (New York: Crown Publishers, 1965), p. 16.

[13]James Madison, *Letters of Helvidius*, no. 4. Cited in *The Writings of James Madison*, Gaillard Hunt, ed., 4, p. 174. Cited in Robert W. Tucker and David C. Hendrickson, *Empire of Liberty: The Statecraft of Thomas Jefferson* (New York: Oxford University Press, 1990), pp. 39–40.

carry out the tasks of war we do violence to our Republic, to our nature as Americans, and to ourselves.

While the threat from France loomed large for a while, the great enemy, Jefferson knew, was England. Perfidious Albion was merely biding its time, conspiring with the more extreme Federalists to restore British economic and political hegemony in the former colonies. Jefferson's strategy was to delay the inevitable as long as possible, to play the great powers off against each other, and maintain the peace, however precarious. Given a breathing spell, a chance to consolidate the gains of the Revolution, the young Republic would have the chance to expand Westward. When war broke out in 1812, and the Federalists rose in open support of their British paymasters, Jefferson's bitter evaluation of the Hamiltonians as traitors was proved correct. Britain was the main external enemy, but the main long-term threat, Jefferson believed, was internal: a Federalist counterrevolution that would centralize all power, political and financial, in the hands of a new aristocracy.

The Jeffersonian foreign policy was continued and expanded by President James Monroe, and guided under the expert hand of Secretary of State John Quincy Adams. From 1814 to 1828, Adams led the drive to establish a continental Republic strong enough to stand up to the kings of Europe; he was the true author of what is called the Monroe Doctrine, which gave diplomatic and political form to the old revolutionary doctrine of American exceptionalism. This vision of a New World exempt from the arbitrary terrors of the Old had been the motive power behind the American Revolution—and now the European powers were forced to acknowledge it. By the terms of the Treaty of Ghent, negotiated by Adams, British warships were cleared from the Great Lakes, and U.S. fishing rights were extended northward. It was Adams who made possible the establishment of a secure border with Canada from the Great Lakes to the Rockies. It was under the initiative of this most energetic secretary of state that the first American claims on the Pacific Coast were established.

The Jeffersonian strategy had succeeded not only in preserving the Republic, but also in pushing back the Western frontier of freedom. Expansion, Adams believed, was inevitable; in his *Memoirs*, Adams relates a Cabinet meeting in which reports of European concerns over an "ambitious and encroaching" America were discussed. Adams dismissed the idea that we ought to be "guarded and moderate" so as not to offend or provoke the Europeans. "Nothing that we could say or do would remove this impression," said Adams,

> until the world shall be familiared with the idea of consider-
> ing our proper dominion to be the continent of North Amer-
> ica. From the time when we became an independent people
> it was as much a law of nature that this should become our
> pretension as that the Mississippi should flow to the sea.[14]

For Adams, and others who shared the Jeffersonian vision of a
continental Republic, American expansion was a force as natural as
the flowing of a river. But the river must not be allowed to over-
flow its banks. American dominion beyond the nation's natural
boundaries, Adams believed, would be a mistake. He opposed
schemes to incorporate Cuba into the Union, argued against getting involved in Latin America's revolution against Spain, and
talked President Monroe out of threatening to directly interfere to
help revolutionaries in Greece. His famous July 4th *Address* is the
manifesto of a distinctively American foreign policy, the policy of a
free American Republic before it began the long process of degeneration into a bloated and flaccid empire. This country, he said,
"has invariably, though often fruitlessly, held forth to other countries the hand of honest friendship, of equal freedom, of generous
reciprocity." For 50 years, America had

> respected the independence of other nations while asserting
> and maintaining her own. She has abstained from interfer-
> ence in the concerns of others, even when conflict has been
> for principles to which she clings, as to the last vital drop
> that visits the heart. She has seen that probably for centuries
> to come, all the contests of . . . the European world will be
> contests of inveterate power, and emerging right. Wherever
> the standard of freedom and independence has been or shall
> be unfurled, there will her heart, her benedictions and her
> prayers be. But she does not go abroad, in search of mon-
> sters to destroy. She is the well-wisher to the freedom and
> independence of all. She is the champion and vindicator
> only of her own.[15]

Like Jefferson, Adams believed that the victory over monarchism and absolutism would come as a result of America's role as
the great exemplar of liberty. Liberty could not be exported at the
point of a bayonet; the attempt would come at the cost of betraying
not only her national interest but the cause of liberty itself. America had wisely followed a policy of non-intervention, Adams said,
because

> She well knows that by once enlisting under other banners
> than her own, were they even the banners of foreign inde-
> pendence, she would involve herself beyond the power of

[14]*Memoirs of John Quincy Adams*, 4, pp. 437–39; cited in Tucker and Hendrickson,
Empire of Liberty.
[15]Ibid., pp. 44–45.

extrication, in all the wars of interest and intrigue, of individual avarice, envy, and ambition, which assume the colors
and usurp the standard of freedom.[16]

Once embarked upon this course,

The fundamental maxims of her policy would insensibly
change from *liberty* to *force*. . . . She might become the dicta-
tress of the world. She would be no longer the ruler of her
own spirit.[17]

One hundred and seventy-three years after Adams warned
against "enlisting under other banners than her own,"
blue-helmeted American "peacekeepers" have enlisted under the
banner of an international organization that claims sovereignty
over the whole of the earth. Sent to police "all the wars of interest
and intrigue," from Somalia to Macedonia to Korea, Americans are
now fighting and sometimes dying for a cause that has assumed
the colors and usurped the standard of freedom. This is the cause
of internationalism, which has dragged us into two catastrophic
European wars and now threatens to dragoon us into a third, and
to which the elite—in government, the media, and academia—has
pledged allegiance. As the creator and enforcer of a New World
Order, America is no longer the ruler of her own spirit, and the
prophetic warnings of the founding fathers are forgotten. But they
were still fresh in the national memory until the late 1800s, in spite
of conflict and internal dissent over the Mexican–American War.

The completion and consolidation of the continental project,
and then the tumult over slavery, occupied Americans for a good
quarter century, during which the nation enjoyed a blessed hiatus
from foreign crises and entanglements. When newly-elected President Grover Cleveland addressed the nation, on March 4, 1885, he
declared that "the genius of our institutions" dictates

the scrupulous avoidance of any departure from that foreign
policy commended by the history, the traditions, and the
prosperity of our Republic. It is the policy of independence,
favored by our position and defended by our known love of
justice and by our power. . . . It is the policy of neutrality,
rejecting any share in foreign broils and ambitions upon
other continents and repelling their intrusion here. It is the
policy of Monroe and of Washington and Jefferson—"Peace,
commerce, and honest friendship with all nations, entangling alliance with none."[18]

This was not the policy of a particular party or of the anti-
imperialist movement, but was in fact the settled policy of a nation;

[16]Ibid.
[17]Ibid.
[18]Israel, *The Chief Executive*, p. 167.

Cleveland's sentiments represented not only the unbroken tradition of American policymakers, but also the general consensus in
this country regarding America's relation with the world. We were
different; unlike the Europeans, we did not go marauding abroad in
search of trouble, treasure, and trade concessions.

AGAINST THE EMPIRE OF THE PACIFIC:
THE RISE OF THE ANTI-IMPERIALIST MOVEMENT

On February 3, 1893, a curious delegation appeared in San
Francisco. Arriving on the steamer *Claudine*, the five men represented a conspiracy of white settlers who had seized the island of
Hawaii, deposed Queen Liliuokalani, and now sought to incorporate the islands into the first American outpost. What one Congressional opponent of annexation would later call "the bacillus of imperialism" had finally touched U.S. soil.

The conspirators, who claimed to represent the provisional
government of Hawaii, had overthrown the Hawaiian monarchy
with the connivance of the American Minister to that once peaceful
island nation, John L. Stevens. The success of this so-called "revolution" was ensured by U.S. military forces from the *USS Boston*, a
key fact undoubtedly known to President Harrison and his secretary of state but not yet generally known. Stevens had unilaterally
proclaimed a U.S. protectorate over Hawaii, and this delegation of
haolie sugar planters was asking the United States government to
ratify this conquest by making a treaty of annexation with the so-
called provisional government. In San Francisco, the delegation
met with Claus Spreckels, the leader of the sugar trust, who declared his support for annexation and offered the delegates the use
of his private railway car on their way to petition the federal government in Washington. Declining the invitation, the delegates
then proceeded on to Washington, where they asked for and immediately received an appointment with John W. Foster, Secretary
of State under President Benjamin Harrison.

After talking the planters out of a two-cents-per-pound sugar
bounty, to be paid to them, and talking President Harrison out of
asking for a plebiscite of the Hawaiian people, the Secretary of
State submitted the annexation treaty to the Senate. The treaty
caused hardly a ripple, and was little noticed; at any rate, passage
seemed certain until the arrival in Washington of Paul Neumann,
Queen Liliuokalani's personal attorney, bearing a personal letter to
President-elect Grover Cleveland, which told the true story of the
haolie predators and their collusion with Stevens and others in stag-
ing their fake revolution. Horrified by this sordid tale, Cleveland

interceded with Senate Democrats to stop action on the treaty. Upon taking office, he determined to get to the truth of the matter by sending over an investigator; in the meantime, President Harrison withdrew the treaty. This did not stop the annexationists from pressing their case, which was couched in terms of the alleged economic and military benefits to American business; Hawaii, it was said, is the gateway to the markets of the Orient. Opponents of annexation, Southern Democrats and Northern mugwumps, saw the conquest of the Hawaiian kingdom as the first breach in the walls of the American Republic. The country, in possession for the first time of a colonial empire, was on the way to becoming an imperial power, no different from the monarchical powers of Europe.

One such anti-imperialist was the mugwump Carl Schurz who, at the time of the annexationist agitation, was the editor of the prominent *Harper's Weekly*. Born in Germany in 1829, the son of a schoolmaster, Schurz took part in the Prussian Revolution of 1848. The next year he went into exile, only to return in order to take part in the dramatic escape of one of his fellow revolutionaries from a German jail. He came to the United States in 1852, where he plunged into abolitionist activities, became a force among Midwestern German voters and in the Republican party. After the Civil War, Schurz served as a United States Senator, and as secretary of the interior under Rutherford B. Hayes. His subsequent journalistic career included a stint with E.L. Godkin on the *New York Evening Post* and, in the 1890s, he took on the editorship of *Harper's Weekly*.

He had always been a severe critic of expansionism, and made the same arguments against the annexation of Hawaii as he had made against President Grant's ill-fated attempt to grab Santo Domingo. Schurz argued that we could not absorb Santo Domingo and survive as a Republic. For the United States could never rule other peoples by sheer force without doing violence to itself and fundamentally altering its own nature. It followed, therefore, that if Santo Domingo were to be annexed, then it must be admitted as a State, a full-fledged part of the Union right up there with Massachusetts. But this, he averred, was impossible, since no republic had ever flourished beneath a tropical sun. To annex the American tropics would be to acquire no end of trouble. "Have you thought of what this means?" he asked:

> Fancy ten or twelve tropical States added to the Southern
> states we already possess; fancy the Senators and Represen-
> tatives of ten or twelve millions of tropical people . . . fancy
> them sitting in the Halls of Congress, throwing the weight of
> their intelligence, their morality, their political notions and

> habits, their prejudices and passions, into the scale of the
> destinies of this Republic; and, what is more, fancy the Gov-
> ernment of this Republic making itself responsible for order
> and security and republican institutions in such States, in-
> habited by such people; fancy this, and then tell me, does
> not your imagination recoil from the picture?[19]

Cleveland rejected the entreaties of the annexationists, and instead sought to undo the wrong done by American power by demanding that the provisional government dissolve itself, and hand
power back to the Queen.

The would-be empire-builders had better luck under President
McKinley, and an attempt was made to approve the annexation of
Hawaii in 1897; it failed by a few votes. When the Spanish–American War broke out, and the nation suffered its first real bout of
hysterical jingoism, the sugar trust finally succeeded in its colonialist crusade, and the debate over the fate of Cuba, Puerto Rico, and
the Philippines was in full swing.

The views of Carl Schurz regarding the ability of the United
States to assimilate the peoples of the Pacific was shared by Southern Democrats. Senator Ben Tillman, speaking against America's
imperial course, recited Kipling's poem on "The White Man's Burden," there on the Senate floor, up to the part that reads:

> Your new-caught sullen peoples,
> Half devil and half child.

"I will pause here," said Tillman,

> I intend to read more, but I wish to call attention to a fact
> which may have escaped the attention of Senators thus far.
> We of the South have born this white man's burden of a col-
> ored race in our midst since their emancipation and before.
> It was a burden upon our manhood and our ideas of liberty
> before they were emancipated. It is still a burden, although
> they have been granted the franchise. It clings to us like the
> shirt of Nessus, and we are not responsible because we in-
> herited it, and your fathers, as well as ours, are responsible
> for the presence amongst us of that people. Why do we as a
> people want to incorporate into our citizenship ten millions
> more of different or differing races, three or four of them?[20]

This argument against imperialism was not limited to the
South. The analysis of Carl Schurz and other opponents of annexation was that if Hawaii were annexed, and even made a state, it
would always retain a colonial character—a prediction the accuracy of which the native people of Hawaii can sadly affirm.

[19]Robert L. Bleisner, *Twelve Against Empire: The Anti-Imperialists, 1898–1900* (New
York: McGraw-Hill, 1968), p. 24.
[20]*Pictorial History of America's New Possessions* (Chicago: Dominion, 1899), pp. 603–4.

However much many Southern newspapers liked to play this ethnic angle up, the central argument of the anti-imperialists was, as Schurz put it,

> if we take these new regions, we shall be well entangled in that contest for territorial aggrandizement which distracts other nations and drives them far beyond their original design. So it will be inevitably with us. We shall want new conquests to protect that which we already possess. The greed of speculators working upon our government will push us from one point to another, and we shall have new conflicts upon our hands, almost without knowing how we got into them. . . . This means more and more soldiers, ships, and guns.[21]

Schurz goes on to denounce

> a singular delusion [that] has taken hold of the minds of otherwise clearheaded men. It is that our new friendship with England will serve firmly to secure the world's peace.[22]

This suspicion of Britain's baneful influence is a theme that started in Jefferson's day, and resurfaced during the debate over what to do with the spoils of the Spanish–American War. Speaking against the annexation bill, Senator Bland declared that "the secret reason for this bill" was due to "pressure on the part of Great Britain."[23] While one of the arguments of the annexationists was that if we didn't grab the Spanish possessions, then England would, in fact the British ambassador had urged the annexation of Hawaii and encouraged the Americans to take up the white man's burden in the Caribbean and the Philippines. "The diplomacy of Great Britain," said Bland, "has always been marvelous."[24] Isolated, yet possessed of a vast empire, Great Britain needed allies, subordinates really, to do her bidding, and had settled on the United States to play this role in a campaign to assure the world hegemony of Anglo–Saxons. Dependent upon England to hold our Asiatic territory, the Democratic Senator feared we would be pulled into the dispute over the division of the Chinese spoils. In Bland's opinion, the schemes of the annexationists he could not

> but regard it as a deep-laid scheme to enslave the American people under the present domination of plutocracy. . . . The power of the Bank of England, the wealth of that country, over the banks and moneyed institutions of this country has brought to bear the combined power of the capitalists of England and America to control our financial system. The

[21]Ibid., p. 553.
[22]Ibid.
[23]Ibid., p. 601.
[24]Ibid.

> next move is to put our army and navy at the service of Eng-
> land in the prosecution of Asiatic conquest, the end of which
> no man can see.[25]

And so we have a number of Anti-Imperialist, or non-interventionist, themes that sprang up at this time.

(1) *The ideological argument.* In this view, imperialism is seen as a direct threat to republican institutions. The idea that we could rule a people without their consent violated our own anti-colonialist heritage. Furthermore, the decision to set a course for Empire would inevitably mean a huge standing army, huge public debts, and the threat to American liberties represented by both of these dire prospects. In the process of acquiring an Empire, we would lose our distinctively American character, and wind up just like the decadent empires of Europe.

(2) *The cultural argument,* which condemned imperialism as a threat to the cultural homogeneity of American society. We had already fought one civil war over the question of race; the addition of yet more cultural diversity would add the possibility of yet more racial strife. Apart from the racial angle, however, there was a more significant point to be made: that the policy of imperialism would so degrade and contaminate American culture that the very character of the people would be altered, corrupted almost beyond redemption.

(3) *The conspiratorial argument,* couched in populist rhetoric, that imperialism was the policy of a plutocratic elite, of the munitions-makers and the bankers with their foreign loans, who made money off the human slaughter. Furthermore, so went the argument, this plutocracy was so enamored of Great Britain that it was willing to sacrifice our republican heritage and the national interest in playing out the role assigned to us by London. In this view, imperialism was the device of a murderous cabal to wring monstrous profits out of the blood of patriots.

These three themes of non-interventionism had their roots in the old Jeffersonian view of foreign policy, and were revived in the popular imagination just in time to witness the imminent demise of that policy. Under the guidance of a U.S. State Department which saw itself as the junior partner of Great Britain in a quest for world order, an American empire began to take shape. Presided over by an Anglophilic elite, financed by international bankers, and armed to the teeth by the profiteers of mass murder, this empire was, by the standards of the day, rather pitiful, and of no real

---

[25]Ibid., pp. 601–2.

use, either economic or military. It was an albatross hung round our necks, and an expensive one, but its meaning, even if purely symbolic, was still significant. For the great principle of continentalism, enunciated by John Quincy Adams, had been overthrown. The vital importance of this precedent went unnoticed, except to a few, such as Carl Schurz, and they were not listened to. America's acquisition of overseas colonial possessions planted the seeds that would later sprout a crop of Myrmidons.

There are those who argue that the acquisition of the Philippines, Hawaii, and Puerto Rico was just the natural evolution of the expansionist movement, the logical outcome of the frontier spirit. Such people, unburdened by a sense of natural limits or order, are in the rather odd position of saying that the American frontier extends three thousand miles out into the Pacific Ocean. How such an unnatural concept, so obviously a symptom of megalomania, could have become so widespread is a fascinating subject for another essay.

In a broad sense, however, what made possible the overthrow of the old Jeffersonian mindset—at least among the urban intellectuals and the policymaking elite—was the political culture of progressivism: intent on reform, the goal of the progressives was nothing less than reforming the entire human race. These were the purveyors of cultural uplift, riding their various hobbyhorses into the glorious future: abolitionists, feminists, prohibitionists, millenarian fundamentalists, militant vegetarians, and (of course) professional intellectuals of every size, shape, and description, eager to try out their endless schemes for the "improvement" and uplifting of mankind. It was only natural that these people, having set their sights on saving the nation, would feel compelled to take on the rest of the world.

The isolationist reaction to this departure from the wisdom of the founders was profoundly conservative. Yet the opposition to the new internationalism did not divide neatly along left–right, liberal–conservative lines, and included elements of both parties. Both major factions of the Democratic party—Bryanites and Cleveland Democrats—were generally opposed to the policy of imperialism, with the Bryanites more fervent in their anti-militarism. On the Republican side, the Taft Republicans (as in William Howard Taft) and the Roosevelt Bull-Moosers were generally jingoists, while the so-called mugwumps, many of whom were among the founders of the Republican party (along with others such as Speaker of the House Thomas Bracket Reed, of Maine), made up an important part of the emerging anti-imperialist coalition.

The fight over the annexation issue also brought out regional divisions, and these were exacerbated by the debate; opposition to imperialism was centered in the South and the Midwest, with important pockets of organized anti-imperialist activity throughout New England, that bastion of mugwumpery. In the Midwest, this regionalism was associated with a healthy Jeffersonian hatred of the Eastern financial establishment.

THE GREAT WAR AND THE RISE OF
THE PROGRESSIVE REPUBLICAN ISOLATIONISTS

After the annexationists triumphed in Congress, and the great debate ended, foreign policy once again receded into the background. Anti-imperialism was not an issue in the election of 1900. As the horror-ridden 20th century dawned on an unsuspecting American people, however, the battle lines were already being drawn. While the European pot boiled and churned, Americans went blithely about their business—and what happened to a foreign prince in the far-off city of Sarajevo might just as well have happened on the moon, for all any ordinary American knew or cared.

This, of course, is how it should be; how it *was* until we had CNN broadcasting carefully selected images of the world's woes 24 hours a day. In 1900, the American people were still, and indeed always had been, isolationists. This was due not to the absence of CNN, but to the abiding presence of the founders' sense of separateness, a belief that America (for all her cultural ties to the old world) had taken a different and far better path.

The coming of World War I was like "lightning out of a clear sky," as at least two members of Congress put it at the time.[26] The press was well nigh unanimous in its assumption that the U.S. would stay out, and American officials echoed popular opinion. "Thank God for the Atlantic Ocean," wrote the American ambassador to the Court of Saint James, a sentiment shared by the overwhelming majority of Americans.[27]

The official U.S. government position was one of strict neutrality: President Wilson urged the nation to be impartial "in thought as well as deed," and declared that "it is entirely within our own choice what its [the war's] effects on us will be."[28]

[26]John Milton Cooper, Jr., *The Vanity of Power* (Westport, Conn.: Greenwood, 1969), p. 19.
[27]Ibid.
[28]Ibid.

The revulsion against the European catastrophe was broad based and bipartisan; leaders of every faction and subfaction in American politics scrambled to put distance between themselves and even the hint that the United States might become involved in the conflict. One indication of the popular mood of isolationism was the fate of the Republicans' preparedness campaign. As Europe sank into a chaos of blood-drenched darkness, Teddy Roosevelt, Henry Cabot Lodge, and former Secretary of War Henry L. Stimson launched a campaign to reunite the Republicans and the Progressives over the preparedness issue. To that end, Representative Augustus Peabody Gardner, Republican of Massachusetts, demanded a Congressional investigation of the nation's lack of military defenses, declaring that "bullets cannot be stopped by bombast nor powder vanquished by platitudes."[29] Defending the increase in military expenditures proposed by his administration, President Wilson said that an inordinate increase would indicate "that we had been thrown off course by a war with which we have nothing to do."[30]

The preparedness campaign was given a setback from which it never really recovered when Congress nearly succeeded in eliminating the ambitious program of the Navy Department to increase the number of battleships. An amendment to cut the naval appropriation in half failed by a mere 16 votes. Of the 155 votes cast in favor, the majority were Southern and Midwestern Democrats, who represented a point of view expressed by Congressman Martin Dies, of Texas, who asked Congressman Gardner during the debate: "Can you point to a nation of militarism that maintained the liberty of the people?"[31] "The enemies we have to dread in the future are not" abroad, said Tom Watson, the Georgia Populist, but are embodied in "class legislation," "overgrown and insolent corporations," and "the greed of monopolies here at home."[32]

The Democratic party platform of 1900 attacked militarism as

> the strong arm which has ever been fatal to free institutions.
> It is what millions of our citizens have fled from in Europe.[33]

These largely agrarian Democrats were staunch Jeffersonians not only in domestic politics, but also in their view of foreign affairs. They abhorred the rise of a professional military caste, fearing that it would threaten democracy and Prussianize the republic.

[29]Ibid., p. 22.
[30]Ibid., pp. 22–23.
[31]Ibid., p. 25.
[32]Ibid., p. 26.
[33]Ibid.

Midwestern Democrats like Rep. Clyde Tavenner of Illinois denounced the "war trust," which had cornered the market in international strife.

On the Republican side, 15 had voted for the amendment, including 13 Midwesterners, most of whom were progressives, like
Rep. Silas Barton of Nebraska, who warned against "the siren
songs of the interests who sell guns." Rep. James Manahan of Minnesota wanted to know what all this "preparedness" was prepar-
ing us *for*:

> Shall we . . . yield to that same base avarice that has wrecked
> the civilization of Europe and brought hopeless woe upon
> her helpless millions.[34]

This Republican insurgency represented a significant shift. For
years, many of these same people had gone along with imperialism and voted for a greatly expanded army and navy, especially
during the Roosevelt era. Over time, however, many leading progressive Republican legislators, under the pressure of events, came
around to the opposite point of view. Such an event was the sinking of the *Lusitania*, which shocked the nation not only with its
savagery, but with the sudden realization that America might become involved in the war. For the first time, this arose as a distinct
and ominous possibility.

It was nowhere seriously suggested that the sinking of "a
British ship flying the British flag"[35] was cause for America to go to
war, as the chairman of the Senate Foreign Relations Committee
observed. Senator John D. Works, progressive Republican of California, held the United States "morally responsible" for the sinking
of the *Lusitania*: we had allowed the munitions makers to ply their
trade with impunity, hadn't we? The Democratic leadership in
Congress passed the word on to Wilson: they wanted nothing to
do with the European war. Wilson obligingly gave them what they
wanted in a series of speeches, wherein he declared:

> our whole duty, for the present at any rate, is summed up in
> this motto, "America First." Let us think of America before
> we think of Europe, in order that we may be fit to be Eu-
> rope's friend when the day of tested friendship comes.[36]

Less than two years after that Presidential utterance, "the day
of tested friendship" dawned in a declaration of war.

Until then, however, anti-interventionism dominated the
scene: it was simply unimaginable that the United States would get

[34]Ibid., p. 27.
[35]Ibid., p. 35.
[36]Ibid., p. 36.

involved in the war. In Congress, there was opposition to the President's military appropriations bill; Wilson had switched his position, and was now calling for a greatly expanded army and navy. Although the President insisted that this military buildup was "not for war" but to carry out "essentially a mission of peace and good will among men,"[37] he failed to convince Congressman Tavenner, who said that "war trafficking firms" were intent on making their profits by putting "the peace of 100,000,000 people in jeopardy."[38]

A working alliance of William Jennings Bryan, Southern and Midwestern congressional Democrats, and Oswald Garrison Villard, editor of the *Nation*, launched a campaign against the President's preparedness bill. They recruited Henry Ford, who denounced Wilson's war preparations and gave substantial amounts of money to the anti-war forces to purchase magazine and newspaper advertisements.[39]

It was most embarrassing for the President that much of the opposition to his program was coming from within the ranks of his own party. "Militarism and imperialism are a couplet of devious devils that will carry the American people on the down grade speedily,"[40] declared Rep. James Sherwood, Democrat of Ohio. James H. "Cyclone" Davis, of Texas—so-called because of the rapid-fire gesturing that punctuated his orations—announced that the "millionaire magi" were

> forming cabals to force upon the country a stupendous program of military preparedness, hoping to put in the White House a dictator to execute it.[41]

This sounds remarkably like the critique a later generation of progressive Republican isolationists would make of FDR's drive to war: that war preparations were a prelude to the dictatorship of the New Deal. As to the fate of what Davis called "the unhappy nations of Europe":

> "The wages of sin is death" applies to nations the same as to individuals. The nations, now drunk on blood, rioting in ruinous war, are paying the death penalty because their sins have found them out. Given over to ravenous greed, with a riotous aristocracy living in luxury and lust, ruling in rapacity . . . they are now reaping the harvest of their sowing.[42]

[37]Ibid., p. 90.
[38]Ibid.
[39]Ibid., p. 93.
[40]Ibid.
[41]Ibid.
[42]Ibid., pp. 93–94.

Rep. James L. Slayden, a Texas Democrat, declared that he suspected "a conspiracy to force our country into a war with Germany." He attacked the "great and influential lobby operating about the halls of Congress and in the press" whose purpose was not only to feed the maw of the munitions makers but also to deploy "our enlarged forces in Europe."[43] Here Slayden is expressing the main theme of anti-imperialism, first raised in the battle against annexation, now amplified and applied to Wilson's military buildup and his handling of the submarine crisis: A warmongering and profiteering elite, motivated by greed and a treasonous devotion to Great Britain, was conspiring to involve us in the intrigues of Europe and get us into the war. This concept, first articulated by the anti-imperialist movement of the 1890s, was a favorite populist theme that developed and grew stronger with the years carrying over into the isolationist resistance to World War I and permeating the rhetoric of noninterventionist factions within both parties. Slayden reminded his audience of "the sound advice of George Washington"[44] and wondered if they had forgotten the timeless wisdom of the founders. It seemed to Slayden that they *had* forgotten, otherwise they would have resisted the efforts of the "enemies of peace" with their "exhaustless resources" to militarize the country. The people, he contended, must be mobilized "against the majority of the newspapers and great commercial interests."[45]

Traditional Democratic opposition to militarism and big military budgets was muted by the fact that they were the party in power, and thus reluctant to oppose the President's armaments program. While there was a hard core of anti-preparedness Democrats in the House and Senate, their numbers dwindled as the diplomatic situation momentarily cooled down, and the pressures of party politics were brought to bear.

Among the Republicans, opposition to Wilson's preparedness campaign fell to a small but influential and vocal band of Midwesterners. Senator Works, the California progressive who had held the "war trust" responsible for the sinking of the *Lusitania*, attacked the arms buildup as indicative of a "sentiment foreign to the free institutions of our government." A combination of "army and navy officers and big business engaged in furnishing war materials"[46] was intent on militarizing the country and destroying democracy. Works declared that the current struggle of the

[43]Ibid., p. 94.
[44]Ibid.
[45]Ibid., pp. 94–95.
[46]Ibid., p. 99.

European empires was but "a war of kings against kings"[47] in which the U.S. could have no possible interest. Other progressive Republicans now began to shift toward the anti-militarist, anti-war position: La Follette attacked Wilson's proposals to expand military expenditures as the result of the influence of "the glorious group of millionaires who are making such enormous profits out of the European war."[48] Outstripping the Democrats in their opposition to the arms race, progressive Republicans voted solidly against Wilson's proposals on three key occasions: increasing the size of army reserve units, new battleship construction, and the greatly expanded naval appropriation bill.

At about this time there came into existence the first internationalist organization in American history, with the rather ominous name of the League to Enforce Peace. William Howard Taft, chairman of the League, asserted that "We have got to depart from the traditional policy of this country." This was true not only because "we have to assume certain obligations to the interest of the world"[49] but also because of the looming threat of war. As to whether these obligations included getting into the war, the League did not explicitly say. But it was implicit in their program, which envisioned ambitious multi-lateral "peacekeeping" operations of the sort that, if applied to the conflict in Europe, meant massive intervention by the U.S.

Founded on June 17, 1915, at a conference held in Philadelphia's Independence Hall, the League was the creature of the internationally-minded Taft Republicans (that is, the party of Eastern finance capital): it was not some fringe group of fuzzy-minded radical pacifists, but the big business establishment itself that was sponsoring and propagandizing the most wide-ranging scheme of international organization yet devised. The League wanted to set up an international Council of Conciliation which would hear all disputes between nations. Force would be used against "outlaw" nations who refused to submit. An exception was made for the big imperialist powers: if the Council could not reach a decision, then a war could be "legalized."

On May 27, 1916, Wilson addressed the leaders and members of the League to Enforce Peace, and endorsed the group's collective security plan. While the forces behind this latest addition to the "peace" movement were the most pro-British in the country, it was necessary for the moment to dress up the League's true

[47]Ibid., p. 100.
[48]Ibid., p. 103.
[49]Ibid., p. 44

allegiance in the snow-white robes of semi-pacifist international-ism. William Jennings Bryan denounced the League plan as a part-nership not of peace but of war; an "international police force which will *compel* peace, and *compel it by the use of force.*"[50] Such a paradoxical foreign policy would surely betray the principles laid down by the founders, and also the spirit and letter of the Monroe Doctrine. Randolph Bourne, the young hunchbacked radical and literary apotheosis of pre-war liberalism, denounced the League to Enforce Peace as "an alliance of all against each" that "practically ensures that every war within the system would be a world war." The League, he said, advocated "international order founded on universal militarism."[51]

This debate over the merits of internationalism had absolutely no effect on the 1916 election. In spite of Wilson's sudden reversal of the traditional Democratic opposition to big arms spending and foreign interventionism, there was little resistance to the Presi-dent's insistence on putting the demand for a League of Nations in the party platform. As happens so often in U.S. history, it was a bi-partisan internationalism that faced the voters that presidential election year. The Republican nominee, Charles Evans Hughes, sounding very much like his friends in the League to Enforce Peace, also endorsed "the development of international organiza-tion" and remarked (with characteristic profundity) that "there is no national isolation in the world of the 20th century."[52] Foreign policy played almost no role in the campaign, except for Wilson's slogan "He kept us out of war." Foreign policy was not much of an issue that year for two reasons: first, as we have noted, there weren't many disagreements in this area between the candidates, so there was little occasion to debate. Second, the two parties were badly split on the issue, and debate was stifled in the name of party unity.

It wasn't until after Wilson's election victory that the contro-versy started to heat up again. At a banquet given by the Demo-cratic National Committee, William Jennings Bryan denounced any thought of "our being an international policeman," and called for a constitutional amendment requiring the submission of "every declaration of war to a referendum of the people, except in case of actual invasion of the country."[53]

In his note to the belligerents, asking them to state their peace terms, Wilson declared the necessity of "a league of nations to

[50]Ibid., p. 56
[51]Ibid., pp. 72 and 75.
[52]Ibid., p. 74.
[53]Ibid., p. 123.

insure peace and justice throughout the world."[54] This made little impression until Secretary of State Lansing—in an effort to reassure the pro-British faction that this was not a pro-German maneuver—told reporters that the new policy would entail the abandonment of our traditional policy of isolation: "I mean by that," he said, "that we are drawing nearer to the verge of war ourselves."[55]

A rush of denials immediately poured forth from the White House and the State Department: neutrality was upheld, the Monroe Doctrine reaffirmed, and the plan of the League to Enforce Peace was disavowed. But it was too late: the cat was out of the bag. That same day, Senator William E. Borah, Republican of Idaho, who had sometimes gone along with the preparedness campaign, but had recently begun moving in the opposite direction, declared that this slip of the tongue on Lansing's part was the last straw. When a resolution approving Wilson's appeal to the belligerents came up in the Senate, Borah blocked it until after the Christmas recess. He then charged that the President's League of Nations would represent "an entire change of policy in regard to our foreign affairs."[56] The new policy, he said, was indeed that of the League to Enforce Peace, a scheme that would not only drag this country into endless foreign wars, but also would

> authorize other nations to make war upon the United States
> if we refuse to submit some vital issue of ours to the decision
> of some European or Asiatic nations. This approaches, to my
> mind, moral treason.[57]

We were headed, warned the Senator, into "the storm center of European politics," and would rue the day we "abandoned the policy of nearly a century and a half." Shortly after giving this speech, Borah told a friend that Wilson's internationalist schemes "would be practically the end of the Republic."[58]

The League of Nations proposal solidified the progressive Republican response to Wilsonian internationalism, and portended a shift in the alignment of the two parties in the realm of foreign policy. From this time until the Cold War, the Republicans moved toward isolationism and the Democrats moved increasingly toward interventionism, reversing their historic roles. There were, of course, exceptions: Taft and his followers remained internationalists, and Roosevelt and Lodge also were in favor of maintaining

[54]Ibid., pp. 133–34.
[55]Ibid., p. 134.
[56]Ibid., p. 135.
[57]Ibid., p. 136.
[58]Ibid., pp. 136–37.

our international alliances. But these leaders came more and more to be in a minority. As a *New Republic* editorial put it, what had been the party of jingoism and imperial overstretch was now proposing

> to crouch at its own fireside, build a high tariff wall, arm against the whole world, cultivate no friendships, take no steps to forestall another great war, and then let things rip. The party which was inspired by the American union is becoming a party of secession and states' rights as against world union.[59]

Among the Democrats, the party regulars were forsaking their traditional fealty to the foreign policy of Thomas Jefferson and uniting around President Wilson's internationalist program. While some Democrats spoke out in defense of the old program, opposition from the Bryan wing was muted, as was Bryan himself.

The real test came in February of 1917, when the question of war was posed pointblank. The crisis culminated in intensified German submarine warfare, the breaking of diplomatic relations between the two countries, the arming of American merchant ships, and, finally, the declaration of war in April, 1917. At each step along the road to war, Wilson spoke in terms of peace and internationalism—and his critics, especially among the progressive Republicans, responded in terms of an unabashed and increasingly acerbic Americanism.

Senator Works denounced the severing of diplomatic relations as "a long step toward war,"[60] while William Kirby, Democrat of Arkansas, said the President's action was "a preliminary declaration of war."[61] The resolution to approve the severing of relations passed the Senate, 78 to 6, with three Bryanite Democrats and three Midwestern progressive Republicans among the dissenters. As the crisis deepened, the House took up the debate, where the isolationist themes were reiterated with renewed vigor: in entering the war, we would hand the victory to the money-mad profiteers who trafficked in arms; in spreading democracy and peace abroad, we would lose it at home; in saving the Europeans, we would lose our own souls.

In the vote on a bill that armed merchant ships, Senator La Follette expressed the essence of Midwestern populist–progressive opposition to intervention.

> Shall we hind up our future with foreign powers and hazard the peace of this nation for all time by linking the destiny of

[59]Ibid., p. 157.
[60]Ibid., pp. 169–70.
[61]Ibid., p. 170.

American democracy with the ever menacing antagonisms
of foreign monarchies?[62]

Europe, said La Follette, is

Cursed with a contagious, deadly plague, whose spread
threatens to devastate the civilized world.[63]

This fear of contamination, of the irreparable loss of innocence,
was the leitmotif of the developing isolationist coalition, the
linchpin of the anti-interventionist argument, and it had the power
to move the public. The congressional opposition was a reflection
of popular feeling that ran deep. Mass rallies were held in several
cities to mobilize the people against the now greatly increased
prospect of intervention. What everyone, from the President on
down, had once claimed was unthinkable—America's entry into
the war—had become all too probable.

The sinking of yet more British ships carrying American pas-
sengers and the infamous Zimmerman message intercepted by the
British and handed over to the United States—in which the Kaiser
offered to Mexico the American Southwest in exchange for a military alliance with Germany—caused a wave of indignation to
sweep across the country. When Wilson finally made the decision
to go to war, the anti-interventionist opposition in Congress was
considerably reduced but still defiant. Senator Stone called intervention "the biggest national blunder of history," La Follette
blamed the moguls of big business, and Senator Norris made similar accusations against the men of the trusts:

concealed in their palatial offices on Wall Street, sitting behind mahogany desks, covered up with clipped coupons . . .
coupons stained with mothers' tears, coupons dyed in the
lifeblood of their fellow men.[64]

Those who voted in the House of Representatives against the
war resolution reflected the politics of the emerging isolationist
coalition, which would retain its essential character for the next 40
years. Fifty-four congressmen voted against Wilson's war; 35 Republicans, 18 Democrats, and one Socialist. Although there were a
few conservative Republicans who voted no, most were left-wing
populists of the La Follette variety, midwesterners who hated bigness, the eastern establishment, and the government–business
partnership that was the basis of the state capitalist order. Most of
the Democratic opponents of the war resolution were Bryanites,

[62]Ibid., p. 183.
[63]Ibid.
[64]Ibid., p. 197.

mostly from the South, who shared this populist sentiment and remembered the Democratic party's historical antipathy to war, militarism, and overseas adventurism.

The wave of war hysteria, government repression, and official propaganda that followed the declaration of war made the expression of anti-interventionist sentiments dangerous. Anti-war newspapers (the Socialist and German presses) were banned from the U.S. mails. *Seven Arts*, which Randolph Bourne wrote for, was suppressed. Rep. Charles Lindbergh's (father of the famous aviator) anti-war tract[65] was confiscated and burned by federal authorities. Senator Robert M. La Follette, Senior, was burned in effigy, almost run out of the Senate, and his magazine harassed by postal authorities. Burton K. Wheeler, then a Montana district attorney, was smeared as a "Red" for refusing to prosecute opponents of Wilson's Great Crusade. The teaching of German in the schools was forbidden, books by German authors (such as Goethe and Kant) were pulled off library shelves; and a propoganda campaign of incredible proportions, sponsored and funded by the government, was loosened upon the American people, one that rivaled in scope and mendacity even the one to be unleashed on the country during the second great war for democracy.

THE GREAT DISILLUSIONMENT: LIBERALISM, REVISIONISM, AND THE ANTI-INTERVENTIONIST BACKLASH

The battle against Wilsonian internationalism and the League to Enforce Peace, although lost in the short run, continued after the war in the form of the struggle against American membership in the League of Nations. The victory of the anti-interventionists in this case was made possible by the widespread feeling of revulsion against the war—and, more importantly, against the peace.

It was supposed to have been an idealist's war: that is, a war for democracy, for national self-determination, for collective security and peace among nations. A war, as Wilson declared, to end all war. When it was over, the liberal and progressive politicians and intellectuals who had followed Wilson into battle were thoroughly sickened by what they had wrought.

Aside from the sheer bloody savagery, the toll in lives and the physical devastation of Europe, it was the Treaty of Versailles that was at the root of the liberal defection from the interventionist coalition. As the imperialist powers of Europe set out to divide up

---

[65]Rep. Charles Lindbergh, *Why Your Country is At War and What Happens to Your Country After a War, and Related Subjects* (Washington: National Capital Press, 1917).

the spoils of war, the scramble was on for German colonies, pieces of the Turkish Empire, and whatever reparations could be squeezed out of the Germans. When the Soviet government, under Lenin, disclosed the secret pre-war treaties made by the Allies, it was clear that the failure to achieve Wilson's new millennium of peace and international cooperation had been doomed from the start. As Selig Adler puts it, liberals rejected "both the treaty and its Siamese twin the League [of Nations]."[66]

The elements of a new isolationist coalition that would hold sway until the outbreak of World War II now began to take shape. To the left-isolationists, such as Herbert Croly, editor of the *New Republic*, what Wilson had created was simply a league of illiberal governments. The old-fashioned liberals, such as Oswald Garrison Villard, saw the League as something more akin to the Holy Alliance, the exact opposite of the benign vision originally upheld by the President. The liberal wing of the isolationist coalition was further buoyed up and swelled by the rise of the revisionist school of the history of World War I. In the summer of 1920, the first of Professor Sidney Bradshaw Fay's "New Light" articles appeared in the *American Historical Review*, in which the myth of German war guilt—encoded in the Versailles Treaty—was shattered.[67] Instead of plotting war with the Austrians, it turned out that the Kaiser had foolishly given his allies *carte blanche* in dealing with Serbia, and then blithely gone off on a vacation cruise. The influence of this article was to prove immense, and perhaps it had the biggest effect on the historian who was to embody the ideas of the revisionist school, Harry Elmer Barnes. In a series of articles and in two books,[68] Barnes exploded the mythology of the angelic Allies, led by the saintly President Wilson, that the court historians passed off as historical truth. Barnes fixed the blame for the outbreak of war on France and Russia. We had been led into war because Wilson had surrounded himself with incompetent and pro-British advisors, such as the U.S. ambassador to England, Page Hines, and the enigmatic Colonel House.

The Barnes critique of U.S. intervention in World War I was preceded by, and quite similar in terms of theme, to the work of Judge Frederick Bausman.[69] A power in Democratic party politics

---

[66]Adler, *The Isolationist Impulse*, p. 57.

[67]Sidney B. Fay, "New Light on the Origins of the World War," *American Historical Review* (July 1920, October 1920, January 1921). Cited in *Harry Elmer Barnes, Learned Crusader*, Arthur Goddard, ed. (Colorado Springs, Colo.: Ralph Myles, 1968), p. 263.

[68]Harry Elmer Barnes, *Genesis of the War* (New York: Alfred A. Knopf, 1926); idem, *In Quest of Truth and Justice* (Chicago: National Historical Society, 1928).

[69]Judge Frederick Bausman, *Let France Explain* (London: Allen and Unwin, 1922).

in the state of Washington, Bausman had retired from the State Supreme Court and devoted himself to writing the first American book to take on the myth of German war guilt. Citing the work of English revisionists such as Frances Neilson, Bausman was convinced that the Allies were as guilty as the Central Powers in dragging Europe into the maelstrom of war. We had been tricked by the Europeans, and by Wilsonian rhetoric, into entering a war that was none of our business. A popularization of revisionist views was published in Albert J. Nock's *Myth of a Guilty Nation*.[70]

Another precursor to Barnes, who went further than Bausman, was John Kenneth Turner, whose book, prophetically titled *Shall It Be Again?*,[71] traces the degeneration of Wilsonian internationalism into warmongering of the more traditional kind, debunks the idea that America was itself ever in any danger from the Central Powers, and mocks the idea that this was ever a "war to end wars":

> even were a government to be found unselfish enough to assume the fearful cost of war, simply for the sake of extending democracy, the very attempt to impose democracy upon another nation would constitute a violation of sovereignty.

The great myth of the world war was Wilson's alleged idealism: the man, said Turner, was a hypocrite. Behind the war drive were certain financial interests who got us involved in a war that was essentially an effort to prop up decadent British imperialism. The Great War was not unlike

> all wars fought by England within the present generation, as well as by every other great power . . . [it was] a war for business.[72]

In Turner's view, Wilson's record in the Dominican Republic, Haiti, Nicaragua, and China had prefigured U.S. entry into the European arena: our Latin American policy had been no better than any conceived in London, Paris, Berlin, Vienna, or Moscow. The Great War had been a war to ensure overseas markets for American big business, and, therefore, said Turner,

> the real enemy of America is not autocracy abroad. It is not kings or kaisers or czars. The real enemy of America is our rich fellow citizen who is willing to plunge our country into war for his own selfish purposes—his political servant without whose voluntary cooperation public war for private profit would be impossible—his intellectual henchman, of

---

[70]Albert J. Nock, *The Myth of a Guilty Nation* (New York: B.W. Huebsch, 1922).
[71]John Kenneth Turner, *Shall It Be Again?* (Chicago: C. H. Kerr, 1922).
[72]Cited in Warren I. Cohen, *The American Revisionists: The Lessons of Intervention in World War I* (Chicago: University of Chicago Press, 1967), p. 50.

> the press, the pulpit, and the college, whose function is to
> identify the national honor with the business ambitions of a
> small but powerful minority.[73]

The solution, said Turner, was a hemispheric isolationism, a
kind of Pan-Americanism, of the sort advocated many years later
by Louis Bromfield,[74] and a constitutional amendment requiring a
popular referendum before any decision to send U.S. troops outside the territorial waters of the United States.

Writing in H. L. Mencken's *American Mercury*, Bausman asked

> Was ever a country so deviled as ours? Has there ever been
> one in all history in which the class most powerful in con-
> trolling government and public opinion was determinedly
> bent on giving away enourmous sums of the country's mon-
> ey to nations already heavily armed and openly expressing
> contempt for [our] sacrifice which they would accept only as
> their due. . . . It is an actual fact that in many circles of
> wealth and fashion in this country one who takes his coun-
> try's side in these debates is put to shame at dinner tables.[75]

It all depended on *whose* dinner table you ate at. In the East,
among the Tory-loving would-be aristocrats of American society,
attended by liveried servants in their fake-Tudor mansions, this
was no doubt true. But in the Midwest, a new Americanism was
brewing. The general disillusionment that follows any war, combined with popular resentment against British wartime propaganda, and their attempt to get out of paying their war debts to the
United States, reached the boiling point in the late 1920s. A wave
of anti-British feeling swept the country. A coalition of groups,
such as the Veterans of Foreign Wars, and the Patriotic League for
the Preservation of American History, joined forces to get rid of the
Anglophilic bias in the nation's school textbooks. The VFW declared that

> The heroic history of a nation is the drum-and-fife music to
> which it marches. It makes a mighty difference whether
> America continues to quick-step to "Yankee Doodle" or
> takes to marking time to "God Save the King."[76]

In October, 1927, Bausman testified in the celebrated case of
William McAndrew, the superintendent of schools in Chicago,
who had been suspended for authorizing blatantly pro-British
textbooks with an explicitly internationalist bias. Initiated by
Chicago Mayor "Big Bill" Thompson, and his advisor, pro-Ameri-
can journalist and author Charles Grant Miller, the campaign to

[73]Ibid., p. 52.
[74]See Louis Broomfield, *A New Pattern for a Tired World* (New York: Harper, 1954).
[75]Cited in Cohen. *The American Revisionists*, p. 95.
[76]Adler, *The Isolationist Impulse*, p. 87.

decolonize and reclaim the history of this country was given voice in Bausman's testimony. England, he said, had "beguiled us into war, took all the spoils of it, and did not want to pay her debts."[77] The inculcation of American youth with a treasonous reverence for the so-called Mother Country was the

> deliberate work of human kinds, aided by financiers of England, who seek, first, the full cancellation of England's war debt to the United States and, second, the placing of the Union Jack wherever now flies the Stars and Stripes.[78]

The trumpet of this Midwestern isolationism of the right was Colonel Robert Rutherford McCormick's *Chicago Tribune*, the flagship of the McCormick–Medill–Paterson newspaper chain. McCormick regularly excoriated our deadbeat "Allies" for welching on their war debts, and castigated the state department for toadying up to the British. Another editorial voice raised against Wilsonian internationalism was that of George Horace Lorimer, founding editor of the *Saturday Evening Post*. An implacable enemy of internationalism and Bolshevism, he used his popular magazine to crusade against the forces that were slowly gathering to drag us into yet another European war. In a series of *Post* articles on the war debt question, the great old right polemicist Garet Garrett exemplified this right–isolationist view of the 1920s as the seedbed of World War II. The Allies had imposed a harsh peace, demanded reparations from the Germans—and then lent them the money to pay, earning a high rate of interest in the process. The German response—inflation of its currency beyond anything ever seen before—was blackmail, and behind it was the threat to go Bolshevist. The debt structure created by the Allies was in danger of imminent collapse; such an event, said Garrett, would drag down the American economy as well. Why had we done it? Garrett thought that

> beyond all considerations of an economic or financial character, there is pressing upon us all the time that sense of obligation to save Europe. [That same motive] seized us deeply during the war. It carried us into the war. We were going to save Europe from Germany, the German people from the Hohenzollerns, little nations from big ones, all the people from the curse of war forever.[79]

What came of the Wilsonian crusade, said Garrett, was the hatred of our ex-Allies, who told the Germans that they must be squeezed in order to pay off Uncle Sam. In saving Europe from the

---

[77]Cited in Cohen, *The American Revisionists*, p. 95.
[78]Ibid., pp. 95–96.
[79]Garrett's series in the *Saturday Evening Post* was published in pamphlet form; see *Other People's Money* (New York: Chemical Foundation, 1931), p. 39.

threat of bankruptcy with periodic injections of cash, we were setting her up for a far grislier fate.

The war had also ushered in the threat of socialism: not from
Bolshevist agents, but because the war had

> Profoundly altered the significance and status of American
> industry. . . . During and after the war, industry came to be
> regarded as an attribute of state power, almost as clearly
> such as the military establishment. And why not? Security,
> independence, national welfare, economic advantage,
> diplomatic prestige—were not all as dependent upon effi-
> cient machine industry as upon an army or navy? . . . The
> new way of thinking about industry, therefore, was basically
> political. A factory thereafter would be like a ship—a thing
> to be privately owned and privately enjoyed only in time of
> peace, always subject to mobilization for war.[80]

Perhaps the most dynamic force in the new isolationist coalition was the progressive–populist tendency in the United States
Senate, headed up by the indomitable William E. Borah and centered in the Midwest. The once-vacillating Borah had now moved
fully into the isolationist camp, and become the leader of the so-
called Irreconcilables, the 15 mostly Republican Senators who saw
U.S. entry into the League of Nations as nothing short of treason.
Unlike the liberals who were in theory internationalists, the progressives were natural isolationists who emphasized war as the inevitable consequence of a foreign policy put in the service of big
business. They spoke of the "war trust," and the responsibility of
the bankers, whose European investments had been the real cause
of the Great War; it was, they said, a war for markets. On the domestic front, the progressives were for farm relief, public power,
and direct democracy by means of public referendums. To stop the
warmongerers from enriching themselves through the further
spilling of blood, the progressives demanded that future wars be
declared only after a plebiscite, except in case of foreign invasion.

This new isolationist coalition—made up of disaffected liberals, conservative nationalists, and Midwestern populists–progressive rebels—faced opposition from two powerful groups. First,
there were what Selig Adler calls "the spiritual heirs of Theodore
Roosevelt," who, "in league with the generals and admirals, fought
for large military budgets."[81] These Eastern internationalist Republicans, such as Lodge, had opposed or obstructed the League because they favored their own even more far-reaching brand of

---

[80]Cited in Justin Raimondo, *Reclaiming the American Right* (Burlingame, Calif.: Center for Libertarian Studies, 1993), p. 62.
[81]Adler, *The Isolationist Impulse*, p. 169.

interventionism, one which relied exclusively on U.S. military power. Then there were the unreconstructed Wilsonians, who tirelessly acted as the agents of Geneva within the United States, propagandizing the idea of collective security and an international organization, while subtly but effectively chipping away at the concept of American sovereignty. The chief journalistic banner of this treasonous crusade was the *New York Times* of Adolph Ochs. The *New York Herald Tribune*, owned by Ogden M. Reid, represented the Republican wing of the internationalist press. In the Democratic party, there was the still-active Wilsonian wing, and even a national federation of Woodrow Wilson clubs. Franklin Roosevelt was a prominent figure in the movement to canonize Wilson, the author of a plan to construct some sort of monument to the interventionist icon; but when Wilson heard about it, he objected because the project seemed far too much like a premature burial. In the end, Wilson consented to the creation of an endowment, the Woodrow Wilson Foundation.

The key role of the professional intellectuals in the propaganda campaign on behalf of internationalism is pointed out by Selig Adler. The Wilson Foundation, says Adler,

> turned to the promotion of essay contests with cash awards to the winners. . . . While the money might have been spent to better advantage in a country that was tiring of such contests, the competition was publicized in the schools, thus affording teachers an opportunity to lay special stress upon the Wilson story.[82]

Bankers and certain industrialists, whose economic interests intersected neatly with internationalist dogma, bankrolled the pro-League forces, sponsoring an array of organizations, manifestos, and other educational activities, downplaying their ultimate goals (the elimination of American sovereignty and the rise of world government) and, following Wilson's advice, patiently boring from within. The focus was on institutions dominated by the elite: the universities, the media, and the intellectual class.

Among ordinary folk, however, the isolationist tide swept everything before it. All over the country, groups formed spontaneously to defeat the League of Nations and support the Irreconcilables; the League for the Preservation of American Independence; local groups, including the American Club, in Minneapolis, and a similar group in Buffalo. A Committee of American Business Men, based in New York City, was organized to save the Republic. The

[82]Ibid., p. 183.

American eagle, said Committee leader Otto H. Kahn, was in danger of being turned "into an international nondescript."[83]

The election of 1920, which Wilson himself had declared to be "a great and solemn referendum"[84] on the League, delivered a smashing defeat to the Wilsonians. The defeat of the treaty in the Senate, on two occasions, and the presidential victory of Warren G. Harding, signaled the triumph of the new isolationist coalition. The popular feeling toward all things foreign, and especially all things European, was summed up by Will Rogers, who wrote:

> Why if they had Niagara Falls, they would have had eighty-five wars over it at various times to see who would be allowed to charge admission to see it.[85]

Undaunted by their defeat, the internationalists rallied for the counterattack. Local groups under the sponsorship of the International Good Will Commission of the Federal Council of Churches, merged to form the League of Nations Nonpartisan Association (now the American Association for the United Nations); concentrated in New York City, the internationalist nerve center, the Association branched out in a network of university-centered local chapters. What they lacked in numbers they more than made up for in tenacity: in just nine months during 1925 they managed to distribute 1,000,000 pieces of literature. The ranks of the internationalists, although thin, and somewhat chastened by the isolationist backlash, were filled with some of the ablest, most influential people in the country: educators, lawyers, philanthropists, many of them clergymen and professional uplifters who, as Selig Adler says, "more often than not . . . . were the descendants of old-stock, affluent families."[86] Prominent among the troops were the new generation of college-educated women, such as "Mrs. Franklin D. Roosevelt and some of her socially prominent friends [who] supplied verve and energy for the Women's Pro-League Council."[87]

Through the administrations of Warren G. Harding and Calvin Coolidge, the Republican establishment tried to pursue a moderate course somewhere between the Irreconcilables and the League enthusiasts. While Harding listed a bit to the isolationist side, Coolidge was more internationally minded, and his World Court proposal engendered bitter opposition from the Irreconcilables. He was supported by a bipartisan coalition consisting primarily of

[83]Ibid., p. 102.
[84]Ibid., p. 104.
[85]Ibid., p. 136.
[86]Ibid., p. 176.
[87]Ibid.

pro-League Democrats, reservationist Republicans, and left-wing-pacifist internationalists. Secretary of State Charles Evans Hughes had endorsed the Court in his 1916 presidential campaign, and pursued his goal shortly after Harding took office. But as the storm broke, the new President began to backtrack; just before he died, Harding was saying that he wanted a World Court that would, somehow, not be affiliated with the League. When Coolidge took office, one of his first decisions was whether to back up Hughes, or beat a hasty retreat. He chose to stick with the Court, and the battle was on: the issue would bedevil American politics for the next decade.

Once again, the church groups, women's groups, and legions of uplifters and do-gooders went into action: a blizzard of petitions, leaflets, pamphlets, proclamations, and resolutions bombarded Congress, all with essentially the same message: only the World Court could save humanity from the horror of another world war.

On the other side, the congressional opponents of the World Court did not have a national organization dedicated to propagating the isolationist point of view. As the vote drew near, the Irreconcilables took to the hustings with their warning that the World Court was the back-door entrance to the League. There was an open revolt in the rank-and-file of the Republican party, in spite of the overwhelming vote in the House for the measure; the Senate Irreconcilables were ready to filibuster this latest threat to American sovereignty.

The party chieftains managed to push the resolution through, finally, by a vote of 76 to 17, only on the condition that they attach numerous qualifying reservations.

But the Republican internationalists would pay the political price in the primary elections of 1926. In both Wisconsin and Illinois, Republican Senators who had voted for the Court were defeated by staunch isolationists. With the defeat of Coolidge protégé William M. Butler, of Massachusetts, by isolationist Democrat David I. Walsh, the trend was clear. Once again, the American people had reaffirmed the isolationist consensus, just as they always have on those rare occasions when they are presented with a clear choice.

The presidential election of 1928 offered the electorate no such opportunity. Al Smith managed to capture the Democratic nomination, against the isolationist Senator James A. Reed, of Missouri. Between Smith and Herbert Hoover, his Republican opponent, there was no dissent from the noninterventionist consensus: both eschewed foreign entanglements, and, this time around, the Democratic platform made no mention of either the League or the Treaty of Versailles, as if both had happened in a dream, and the dreamer had suddenly awakened.

Hoover was a moderate internationalist, whose foreign policy of cautious cooperation with the League precluded any involvement in the quarrels of Europe, and his victory did not portend any great change in the foreign policy of the United States. As a happy and placid decade came to an end, a decade of prosperity and self-preoccupation, of unprecedented industrialization and a fantastic rise in the national standard of living, the American people went about the everyday business of enjoying life, utterly unaware of the horror that loomed not far in the future.

THE THIRTIES: INTO THE INFERNO

The stock market collapse of October, 1929, and the worldwide depression that followed, set off a chain of events that would challenge and finally overthrow the isolationist consensus in America. The victory of internationalism was made possible by a profound change in the political culture. The leitmotif of that culture *had* been its sense of uniqueness. America was the great exception; it would avoid the tyranny of monarchy, the pitfalls of imperialism, the corrupting influence of militarism which plagued the war-torn Europeans. It was not just a political but a moral contrast that was drawn between the New World and the Old. Up until the 1930s, this American exceptionalism permeated the popular consciousness, guided American foreign policy, and reined in the internationalists. America would have a separate destiny, because ours had been, as Garet Garrett put it, "a revolution exemplary."[88] This assumption had been shared by virtually all Americans, except eccentrics and outright foreign agents, until the rise of Wilsonian internationalism and the coming of the Great War. Even Teddy Roosevelt and the would-be empire-builders of the late 1800s shared, with the isolationists, this American separatism. But, as we have seen, the seed of internationalist ideology was planted not only by Wilson but also by the Russian Revolution, and by the flowering of radicalism in Western Europe and the United States. It lay dormant during the interwar years, waiting for the right season, the right weather, the right domestic and international conditions. With the coming of the great stock market crash, the seed sprouted, and grew.

---

[88]Garret, *The American Story*, p. 19.

Garet Garrett had sounded the warning about the insupportable debt structure that characterized the post-war period, and his fears proved uncannily accurate. The chain of Allied war debts, American loans to Germany, and reparations payments snapped when the French demanded payment of $300,000,000 in short-term loans from German and Austrian banks. Panic swept through the financial centers of Europe, as Weimar Germany teetered on the brink of economic chaos. England suspended the gold standard, and put up tariff walls, as did the British dominions. To meet this sudden insolvency, Europeans called in their gold deposits from American banks, and dumped their securities on the New York Stock Exchange—while their governments repudiated their wartime debts to the United States.

This action by the "Allied" ingrates did much to buttress isolationist sentiment, and reinforced the idea of the moral contrast between America and Europe. Those European welchers who took the spilling of American blood as their due were deserving of nothing but contempt, and the less we had to do with them the better.

A variety of other factors gave rise to the illusion that the isolationist consensus was impregnable. First and foremost was the natural preoccupation with events on the home front, precipitated by the Crash and its aftermath. Facing economic disaster, not many Americans were overly concerned with the fate of far-off Manchuria when it was invaded by the Japanese in September of 1931. In the presidential election year of 1932, the electorate was focused on events at home, and so was Franklin Delano Roosevelt. The Midwestern progressives who would be the greatest opponents of his drive to war supported his domestic policies; indeed, initially, they often felt that FDR did not go far enough. They had toyed with the idea of running a third party candidate, but this was not feasible and would have delivered the election to the Republicans. Most of the progressives were nominally Republicans, but in fact were completely alienated from the national GOP, which they considered the instrument of big business and eastern interests. Typical of the Progressive mentality was Senator Hiram Johnson, who dominated California politics from 1910, when he was elected Governor, until 1940, when he was reelected to the Senate with the endorsement of both major parties and swept into office with a record 1.1 million votes. His credo, and that of his fellow Western and Midwestern progressives, was best expressed in his 1911 inaugural address: "In some form or another, nearly every governmental problem . . . has arisen because some private interest has intervened or has sought for its own gain to exploit either the resources or the politics of the state." He fought against the

Southern Pacific railroad, which used the power of the state legislature to create and enforce its monopoly. Battling the bosses and machine politics, Johnson broke the hold of Southern Pacific over state politics. He ran as the vice presidential candidate of the "Bull Moose" Progressives in 1912, and was elected to the Senate in 1916 with an overwhelming 70 percent of the vote.[89]

Johnson, like the other progressives, supported FDR initially. In a letter to his son, Johnson wrote:

> The one thing that draws to Roosevelt those of us who be-lieve in real democracy is the character of the opposition to him. This opposition embraces all of those who believe in the right to exploit government for their own selfish advan-tage. Al Smith has become the mouthpiece of these people.[90]

A staunch isolationist, Johnson saw war and preparations for war as beneficial to the big business interests he had been fighting all his political life. During a meeting with FDR shortly after the new President's inauguration, Johnson pressed home the point that:

> the most important position he had to fill was that of Secre-tary of State. . . . Since 1920 the personnel of the State De-partment has been drawn from three sources, and always visaed by one. It came either from [Charles Evans] Hughes's office, or [Elihu] Root's office, or the Morgan House in New York City, and had to be approved by Morgan and Com-pany. During these past twelve years, our foreign affairs have been manipulated, operated, managed, directed and controlled by Morgan and Company and until the fourth of March this would be the undoubted fact.[91]

The "war trust," the weapons cartel, the international bankers, and their bought-and-paid-for front men in the leadership of both major parties: this greedy and exploitive elite not only fed on war, but provoked it. This insight informed the foreign policy views of both the Midwestern Republican mavericks and the La Follette–Progressive–Farmer–Labor Party bloc.

FDR was a committed internationalist and worshipper at the shrine of Wilson, although he was careful not to reveal his hand too soon. In a speech to the New York State Grange in February of 1932, he opposed participation in the League of Nations, and there-after avoided any mention of foreign policy during the campaign.

---

[89]He arrived in Washington too late to cast the vote against U.S. entry into World War I.

[90]Wayne G. Cole, *Roosevelt and the Isolationists, 1932–45* (Lincoln: University of Ne-braska Press, 1983), p. 22.

[91]Ibid., p. 35.

The voters were interested in how and when the country could get back on its feet, and the progressive isolationists supported Roosevelt in '32, hopeful that he could accomplish the task.

Their first clash with the new President was over the National Industrial Recovery Act (NRA), passed in June 1933, which set the New Deal on the road to the corporate state. The NRA was the progressive's worst nightmare. It was the embodiment of bigness, a celebration of economic and political centralization and, as such, represented a sharp betrayal of the old liberalism that had once stood up for small business, farmers, the workingman, and all those who wanted to "make it" in a capitalist society. Although they were advocates of public power, such so-called reforms as workman's compensation, child labor laws, etc., they were most emphatically not socialists. They had been the most implacable foes of the trusts, and for this reason had opposed FDR's corporatist industry-wide codes of "fair" competition. The New Deal was sold to the voters as the revolution of the little guy, but the NRA revealed its true character as the dictatorship of big business. In comments that reflect the individualistic, pro-small business spirit of the Western progressives, Senator William E. Borah expressed the values behind growing progressive isolationist resistance to the New Deal:

> I look upon the fight for the preservation of the "little man," for the small, independent producer and manufacturer, as a fight for a sound, wholesome, economic national life. It is more than that. It is a fight for clean politics and for free government. When you have destroyed small business, you have destroyed our towns, and our country life, and you have guaranteed and made permanent the concentration of economic power. . . . The concentration of wealth always leads, and always has led, to the concentration of political power. Monopoly and bureaucracy are twin whelps from the same kennel.[92]

The NRA came under increasing criticism, and was finally declared unconstitutional by the Supreme Court. While generally supportive of New Deal relief measures, especially for farmers, the progressive isolationists, as Wayne G. Cole puts it,

> preferred antitrust policies, inflation, and tax reforms rather than the government regulation and controls that were more attractive to urban liberals. Those patterns were to project themselves into foreign affairs; the big government, big military, federal regulation, large government expenditures, and huge deficits that came with American participation in World War II were as much a defeat for the western

[92]Ibid., p. 46.

progressive domestic programs as they were a defeat for
their programs in foreign affairs.[93]

The progressive isolationist critique of the policy of interventionism, and what is today called the "Military–Industrial Complex," reached its highest expression in the great Nye Committee
hearings on the munitions industry. From 1934–36, the Senate
committee, under the leadership of Gerald P. Nye, Republican
from North Dakota, investigated the causes of war, exposed the
role of weapons manufacturers in stirring it up, and explored a
possible legislative solution to the problem of war profiteering. For
18 months, the revelations of the Nye Committee shocked the nation—and shook the "war trust" to its very foundations. The hearings generated miles of newsprint, and the American people read
about the machinations of the DuPonts, J. P. Morgan, and their
agents inside the U.S. government who acted as virtual salesmen
for the arms cartel.

FDR had endorsed the creation of the Nye Committee, although not without some trepidation on the part of the State Department. In the political atmosphere that prevailed at the time,
there was no other course open to the President. As preparations
for the hearings were being made, that year saw a spate of books
and articles detailing the central role of the munitions makers in international power politics.[94] As Nye told a reporter:

> I suppose nothing [in the munitions investigation] has aston-
> ished me so much as to discover the large amounts of evi-
> dence which indicate that, instead of munitions makers
> promoting the military activities of governments, govern-
> ments—especially our own war and navy departments—
> have been actively promoting the munitions makers for
> years. . . . Certain departments in our government are co-de-
> fendants with the munitions industry and its profiteers in
> this great "trial."[95]

The populist–progressive assault on Wall Street and heartless
bankers was becoming an increasingly sophisticated critique of
international state capitalism, of the interplay between economy
and state projected on the wide screen of international affairs. The
device of putting militarism on trial was a masterful one: it heightened the mood of disillusionment with the broken promises of the
Wilsonians, and solidified the isolationist consensus.

[93]Ibid., p. 140.
[94]Frank Hanighen and Helmuth Engelbrecht, *Merchants of Death: A Study of the International Armament Industry* (New York: Dodd, Mead, 1934) named names and
verified a key point made in the hearings: the cozy interplay of government and the
arms industry.
[95]Cited in Cole, *Roosevelt and the Isolationists*, p. 152.

The most sensational revelation of the hearings concerned the sainted Woodrow Wilson, and raised a question that is often asked of modern Presidents: what did he know, and when did he know it? On January 15, 1936, as the Nye Committee prepared for the final phase of its deliberations, Senator Champ Clark entered a document in evidence which showed that Wilson and his advisors were fully informed as to the existence and content of the "secret" treaties struck by the Allied powers of Europe. The document was a memorandum from British Foreign Secretary Arthur J. Balfour to Wilson's Secretary of State, Robert J. Lansing, which the U.S. and British governments refused to make public, but which was made available to the committee.

In other words, Wilson was a liar.

As Wayne G. Cole puts it, "Senator Nye's statement about Wilson was factually correct, and none of his critics cited any evidence to disprove it."[96] Nye's critics were many, and vociferous: the attack on Wilson had made the hearings into a partisan issue. This is why no legislation was ever passed on the basis of the work done by the Nye Committee. If it had, FDR's campaign to drag us into World War II might never have succeeded. If anything could have avoided that terrible catastrophe, then it might have been something very like the proposal conceived by Nye Committee advisor John T. Flynn, which would not only have disallowed any wartime profits over 3 percent, but would also have taxed all income over $10,000 *one-hundred percent*! As John Edward Wiltz relates in his account of the Nye Committee hearings:

> Nye questioned Flynn about the effect of such taxation upon persons accustomed to high incomes. How would they care for their families and estates on $10,000 per year?[97]

Flynn's answer underscored the premise on which the committee based its work: war was the result of a conspiracy of the rich and powerful against the long-suffering middle and lower classes:

> I rather think that the existence of taxes like this would make war a very unpopular thing. I rather think that the man who is disposed to be very sensitive if some Japanese lieutenant fails to take his hat off in the presence of the American flag some place in Manchukuo, will not be so sensitive and will be more reasonable in his patriotism.[98]

As war clouds darkened the horizon in Asia, and the Italians tried to recreate the ancient Roman Empire in the wilderness of

[96]Ibid., p. 159.
[97]John Edward Wiltz, *In Search of Peace: The Senate Munitions Inquiry, 1934–36* (Baton Rouge: Louisiana State University Press, 1963), p. 134.
[98]Cited in Ibid.

Ethiopia, the isolationist consensus in America broadened and deepened. The Nye Committee, the revelations of the revisionist historians, the acute economic crisis, and the rise of European totalitarianism all reinforced the moral contrast between the United States and the rest of the world, strengthened the resolve of the isolationists in Congress to steer clear of foreign entanglements, and made possible the enactment of neutrality laws. These laws embargoed trade in weaponry and vital materials with warring nations, and forbade Americans to travel on the vessels of combatants. This brought the isolationist bloc into increasing conflict with Roosevelt, a battle that would climax in the great debate over U.S. entry into World War II.

On the domestic front, too, the isolationist contingent in Congress increasingly opposed the President's initiatives. Up until this point, in spite of the conflict over the NRA, the Midwestern progressive isolationists were generally sympathetic to the announced aims of the New Deal. This changed dramatically, in February of 1937, when the President's infamous court-packing scheme became the number one political issue. Hostile to the centralization of economic and political power, and fearful of a presidential dictatorship, the progressive isolationists were bitterly opposed to this blatant power-grab. In this they were merely applying the same arguments they had used in the battle to pass meaningful neutrality laws. FDR had wanted the power to enforce such laws at his discretion; under his proposed legislation, the president would have had the sole discretion to determine when and if (and in what manner) to impose an embargo. The isolationists insisted on a mandatory embargo that would be automatically triggered once hostilities commenced. Roosevelt argued that a distinction ought to be made between aggressors and victims of aggression—and that he would do the distinguishing. The isolationists feared—correctly—that discretionary trade sanctions would in effect give the President the power to create a situation in which war was inevitable. This centralization of power (and blatant disregard for the Constitution), they thought, would create an imperial presidency, one which had the power to declare war without bothering to consult Congress. After a long, drawn-out legislative wrangle, the result was a compromise weighted in favor of the isolationists: the Neutrality Act of 1937 imposed a mandatory arms embargo, a prohibition on the arming of merchant ships, a ban on travel by Americans on the ships of warring nations, and, most important of all, loans and credits to the belligerents were cut off.[99]

---

[99]The law did not abrogate the Monroe Doctrine; it was not applicable to those cases in which an American republic is under attack from, say, a European power.

The passage of neutrality legislation was a victory for the isolationists, yet still they were not satisfied. The international situation was heating up: the Spanish Civil War was in full swing, with Stalin's legions, the so-called Loyalists, slaughtering Roman Catholic priests, raping nuns, burning churches to the ground—and thereby gaining the sympathy and material support of American leftists. As the Japanese incorporated China into their Far Eastern Co-Prosperity Sphere, prominent internationalists—including Secretary of State Cordell Hull, Interior Secretary Harold Ickes, and Clark Eichelberger, of the League of Nations Association—urged the President to make a strong statement. With the New Deal stalled, and opposition to his domestic policies reaching a dangerous level, the President took this opportunity to shift his emphasis to the foreign-policy realm—and divert the nation's attention from the failure of his domestic policies. It was Ickes who suggested the "quarantine" motif of the President's famous speech, in which he likened the rise of the Axis powers to the appearance of a deadly epidemic: they must, he maintained, be quarantined. If the Axis was allowed to carry out its policy of aggression unchallenged, "let no one imagine that America will escape, that it may expect mercy, that this Western Hemisphere will not be attacked."[100]

Up until this point, the President had gone along with popular isolationist sentiment. His stealthy attempts to expand his own discretionary power in the foreign-policy realm, and efforts to abrogate the neutrality laws, had always been couched in isolationist rhetoric, disavowing any vital American interests outside the Western Hemisphere. Now, for the first time, he overtly challenged the isolationist consensus previously dominant in both parties.

The President had thrown down the gauntlet, and the isolationists did not hesitate to pick it up. Against a backdrop of international treachery and looming danger—the Italian–Ethiopian war, the Sino–Japanese conflict, the rise of Hitler and the rearmament of Germany—the isolationists sought to build a bulwark high enough to stem the floodtide of the European "isms": militarism, aggressive nationalism, and international Bolshevism. But neutrality legislation alone could not guarantee against a repeat of what happened in 1917, and so another method was attempted: this was the proposed Ludlow Amendment to the Constitution. Introduced by Congressman Louis L. Ludlow, a Democrat from Indiana and a staunch Jeffersonian, the amendment would have required that a declaration of war passed by Congress be

[100]Cited in Cole, *Roosevelt and the Isolationist*, p. 245.

subject to a national referendum. Aside from a direct attack on the United States, the only other exception to the strictures of the Amendment would be in case of a violation of the Monroe Doctrine. This measure was barely defeated in the House of Representatives, 209–188, and only after a furious campaign by the Administration.

The campaign for the Ludlow Amendment split the pacifist–liberal wing of the anti-war forces, with Clark Eichelberger and Eleanor Roosevelt opposing, and Dorothy Detzer of the Women's International League for Peace and Freedom (a key figure in the Nye Committee hearings) and Frederick J. Libby, of the National Council for the Prevention of War, in support. The split reflected the liberal-left stampede to abandon their old principles of anti-militarism, and forget the bitter lessons of the Great War. On the left, the twin impulses of pacifism and internationalism diverged and fought it out for hegemony, with the latter winning out in record time.[101]

In the Ludlow Amendment we see the formal programmatic merger of the three major elements that cohered into the highly organized and fiercely ideological movement opposing U.S. entry into World War II, the movement known today as the old right. This movement was drawn from two major sources:

(1) *Populism*—Direct democracy, embodied in legislation allowing statewide referendums in California and much of the West, was a key element of progressivism. An enraged and newly empowered people rise up to smite a warmongering business and political elite—it was an image that set the populist imagination ablaze with possibilities, such as the Ludlow Amendment. The key point to remember is that the isolationists were confident that any referendum would result in a victory for nonintervention and peace. Polls recorded that 73 percent of the American people supported the Ludlow Amendment; an even bigger majority opposed U.S. entry into another European war.

(2) *Anti-Statism*—The merger of what was left of the populist and progressive movements with the emerging conservative Republican opposition to FDR and the New Deal was a complex and drawn-out process, which ultimately culminated in the organization of the America First Committee, a mass anti-war movement where progressive Republican Senator Burton K. Wheeler could find common cause with the conservative General Robert E. Wood,

---

[101]For a blow-by-blow analysis of the liberal transition from principled noninterventionism to rabid militarism, see James J. Martin, *American Liberalism and World Politics* (New York: Devin–Adair, 1964).

of Sears and Roebuck, and urban liberals such as John T. Flynn, formerly of the *New Republic*. The same people who opposed the President's court-packing bill, and called for abolition of the NRA, wound up opposing Roosevelt's drive to war. In the heat of battle, the differences between progressive isolationists and their conservative brethren melted away, as they embraced a common critique of centralism, internationalism, and rampant militarism.

TURNING POINT

As the prelude to the outbreak of World War II—the collapse of the Munich Pact, the German invasion of Czechoslovakia, and the crisis over the Danzig Corridor—was played out on the European chessboard, FDR began to undermine the neutrality laws. At first, he had little success, but, as Hitler's legions marched into Poland, the President succeeded in repealing the embargo and substituting a policy of "cash-and-carry." Bowing to the political winds, the President still vowed that he was a man of peace, and that the United States had no business intervening in the battle for Europe, but Senator Nye knew better: "If we make it a cash-and-carry proposition," he said,

> it will be only a matter of weeks until they ask us to repeal the "cash" part. The next step will be to throw the "carry" part out the window. . . . The last step will be a declaration of war.[102]

The great turning point, where one can say that the isolationist consensus was broken and reversed, came in the latter half of 1940, as Hitler's armies blitzed Denmark and Poland, Belgium, Holland, Luxembourg, and France. That summer, the Battle of Britain lit up the international landscape, as the British pleaded for American help. The mother country would hold out, said newly-installed British Prime Minister Winston Churchill,

> until, in God's good time, the New World, with all its power and might, steps forth to the rescue and the liberation of the Old.[103]

The call to arms had been sounded, and America's Anglophiles responded, as did the other elements in the interventionist coalition, who Selig Adler describes as:

> veteran internationalists, educators, Protestant or Jewish clergymen, cosmopolitan businessmen, and journalists. Usually the national and community leaders were old-stock

[102]Cited in Cole, *Roosevelt and the Isolationists*, p. 328.
[103]Cited in ibid., p. 362.

> Americans who, because of racial descent or cultural affinity,
> were specially sympathetic to the fighting Britons.[104]

Aside from the covert political operations carried out by British intelligence, interventionist activities were centered in a number of homegrown groups, the biggest of which was the Committee to Defend America by Aiding the Allies. Headed by William Allen White, editor of the Kansas City *Emporia Gazette*, the Committee advocated aid to the Allies "short of war." The group eventually split into two factions, with the more militant interventionists organizing the Fight For Freedom Committee, which demanded an immediate declaration of war on the Axis powers. The White Committee served as a virtual propaganda arm of the U.S. government, working openly and closely with the White House. After the Nazis betrayed their Communist allies, and Hitler invaded the Soviet Union, the number and militance of the interventionist groups would grow: the League Against War and Fascism, the "Friends of Democracy," the Century Club (an Anglophile outpost) and a host of others, all busily engaged full-time in a single activity: smearing the isolationist opposition.

It is no exaggeration to say that, during the heyday of the Popular Front, an entire mini-industry grew up around the Communist campaign to link the peace movement with Hitler. This was the strategy of Roosevelt and his far-left allies, as the battle for the soul of a nation commenced, and it is why the great isolationist leader and writer John T. Flynn called them the Smear Bund. Certainly the most odious of this unsavory bunch was "John Roy Carlson," professional sneak and *agent provocateur*, whose real name was Avedis Derounian. His book[105] quoted obscure cranks, anti-Semites, and Nazi sympathizers as if they represented the isolationist movement. Carlson's chief target was the largest and most effective anti-interventionist organization, the America First Committee. Juxtaposing the rantings of (for example) the almost completely unknown George Deatherage—whose American Nationalist Confederation had only one member, himself—with a mention of some well-known legitimate isolationist leader, such as General Wood or John T. Flynn, the Carlson technique was unsubtle but effective. Carlson was in the employ of the Friends of Democracy, a fellow-traveling front organization headed up by the Reverend Leon Birkhead; he also worked for the Federal Bureau of Investigation, when Roosevelt's secret political police were ordered by the White House to find something—anything—on the America First Committee.

[104]Adler, *The Isolationist Impulse*, p. 262.
[105]John Roy Carlson, *Under Cover* (New York: Dutton, 1943).

The America First Committee was the response of the isolationist movement to the President's war drive; it was founded on September 4, 1940, 15 months before the Japanese attack on Pearl Harbor. The AFC grew out of a student anti-war organization, led by R. Douglas Stuart, Jr., son of the first vice president of the Quaker Oats Company. After linking up with General Robert E. Wood, chairman of the board of Sears, Roebuck & Co., the AFC went national, set up a Chicago headquarters, and began running newspaper ads attacking the interventionist policies of the Administration. With a speakers bureau, a variety of publications, local chapters, and rallies in cities and towns all across America, America First eventually grew to 850,000 members organized in 450 chapters.[106]

It was a grand coalition, encompassing conservative Republicans such as William R. Castle, Undersecretary of State in the Hoover administration, the liberal Chester Bowles, and the populist progressives Phillip La Follette and Senator Burton K. Wheeler. Conservatives saw Roosevelt's determination to get us into the war as part of his domestic strategy to impose socialism on American industry. With war would come wage and price controls, the militarization of the economy, and compulsory unionism. Liberals saw the prospect of war as the prelude to an all-out attack on civil liberties. The result would be censorship, and political repression that would make Woodrow Wilson's fairly draconian crackdown on the anti-war opposition seem mild in comparison. Both left- and right-isolationists argued in favor of maintaining America's traditional foreign policy of nonintervention, creating an impregnable defense, and ensuring the integrity of the Western Hemisphere.

I will not here attempt a comprehensive account of the history and activities of the AFC,[107] but merely underscore its significance as the final stage in the development of the progressive isolationists in their journey to the right side of the political spectrum. In the course of a struggle against war and militarism, their views on domestic matters underwent a transformation; or, perhaps, one could say their views matured under the pressure of events. For the populist–progressive critique of bigness and centralization was in no way incompatible with the conservative critique of the New Deal: it was the fight against the warmongers that convinced them

---

[106]Adler, *The Isolationist Impulse*, p. 381.

[107]Such an account has already been written. See Wayne G. Cole, *America First: The Battle Against Intervention, 1940–41* (Madison: University of Wisconsin Press, 1953); see also *In Danger Undaunted: The Anti-Interventionist Movement of 1940–41, As Revealed in the Papers of the America First Committee,* Justus D. Doenecke, ed. (Stanford, Calif.: Hoover Institution Press, 1990).

that, while big business (the "war trust") often manipulated the state to its own advantage, big government was the source of the problem and the real threat to our liberties.

The career of John T. Flynn, head of the AFC's vitally important New York chapter, and a member of its national committee, is dramatic evidence of this political evolution. As a columnist for that paragon of enlightened liberalism, the *New Republic*, Flynn backed FDR in 1932, and devoted his journalistic energies to exposing fraud and abuses in the financial markets. Like many progressives, he was shocked at the corporatist initiatives that came out of the Administration, especially the National Recovery Act. The blizzard of alphabet-soup agencies created by unprecedented government spending led him to the conclusion that the New Deal would have to culminate in war. It would be politically impossible to maintain the level of spending the President required, and he would need conservatives—the internationalist wing of the Republican party—to get his program through Congress. By combining national defense with the need to employ and otherwise subsidize large numbers of people, the President could solve his political and economic troubles in one blow. Flynn charged that

> There is not the slightest doubt that the only thing that now prevents his active entry on the side of the Allies is his knowledge that he cannot take the American people in yet.[108]

As the liberals gave up their noninterventionist principles and joined with the Stalinists in the Popular Front drive to war, Flynn's *New Republic* column became controversial and was eventually discontinued. In an article for the *Yale Review*, Flynn attacked the President and his aide, Harry Hopkins; FDR responded with a note to the editor in which he declared that Flynn had become "a destructive rather than a constructive force." The President went on to say that, in his opinion, Flynn

> should be barred hereafter from the columns of any presentable daily paper, monthly magazine or national quarterly, such as the *Yale Review*.[109]

This is precisely what happened, not only to Flynn but to a whole generation of old-fashioned liberals, assorted progressives, and old rightists who were victimized by the Smear Bund, their careers ruined or else seriously compromised. Garet Garrett, who blazed away at the President's policies, both foreign and domestic,

[108]John T. Flynn, *Country Squire in the White House* (New York: Doubleday, 1940), p. 113.
[109]Cited in Raimondo, *Reclaiming the American Right*, p. 102.

in the pages of the *Saturday Evening Post*, met a similar fate, along with Albert J. Nock and Oswald Garrison Villard.

We often hear of the alleged terrors of the McCarthy period, especially in Hollywood; a veritable army of second-rate actors, screenwriters, and movie colony sycophants has for years been whining about the persecution of red subversives during the 1950s. But the treatment they had to endure was a Sunday School picnic compared to the blacklisting of isolationist writers, journalists, politicians, and, yes, actors, during the previous decade. A good example is the actress Lillian Gish, who was a member of the national committee of America First and a frequent speaker at their rallies. As Wayne G. Cole tells it,

> in August, 1941, [Gish] privately told General Wood that because of her active role in America First she had been blacklisted by movie studios in Hollywood and by legitimate theater and had been unable to find employment acting. Her agent finally got her a movie contract offer, but it was made on the condition that she first resign from America First and refrain from stating that reason for her resignation. She needed the work. Consequently (though still opposed to American involvement in World War II), Miss Gish resigned from the committee, gave no more speeches at America First meetings, and never made public the reason for her action.[110]

Flynn suffered much, both financially and professionally, from the blacklisting. On the other hand, persecution only seemed to clarify his thought. His best book, *As We Go Marching*,[111] written during the war, integrates the progressive abhorrence of war and militarism with the conservative analysis of the dangers of socialism and economic centralization. Flynn saw the growth of state power under FDR and the President's war drive as dual aspects of a unitary system; war and preparations for war fueled the economic engine of the emerging welfare state, and provided the political backing from conservatives who were willing to countenance socialism in the pursuit of preparedness.

The postwar phase of Flynn's career was as a staunch old right radio commentator and the author of many books attacking socialism and all its works. Unlike many on the right, he remained a noninterventionist during the Cold War years, opposing the Korean war, warning against the Vietnam quagmire, and predicting that the Communist empire would ultimately be impaled on its own sword. He ended his public career in 1960, at the age of 79.

---

[110]Cole, *Roosevelt and the Isolationists*, p. 474.
[111]John T. Flynn, *As We Go Marching* (New York: Doubleday, 1944).

When he died in 1964, his work was largely forgotten, and the legacy of America First ignored or disdained by the new right of William F. Buckley, Jr., and the ex-Communist intellectuals grouped around *National Review* magazine, who were embarked on an interventionist crusade of their own.

The course of Flynn's development as a writer and ideologue illustrates perfectly the primacy of foreign-policy views in determining the ultimate political stance of a given individual or movement. From the time he served as an advisor to the Nye Committee, to his radio broadcast of July 30, 1950, when he warned against defending French colonialism in Indochina, his views on domestic matters changed while noninterventionism was a constant. So it was also with most of the Midwestern progressive isolationists in Congress, such as Senators Wheeler, Nye, and Johnson.

I have covered much of this territory in my 1993 book, *Reclaiming the American Right*. There I tell the story of the old right—its rise and fall, and its extension into the 1950s and right up until our own time—and I will only give a brief summary of that story here.

U.S. entry into World War II destroyed the isolationist movement as a major force in American politics. After Pearl Harbor, the America First Committee shut down, and isolationists went underground for the duration. While there was a brief postwar revival of noninterventionism, this was soon suffocated by the rise of Cold War conservatism and the "new" right of William F. Buckley, Jr., and the rabidly interventionist *National Review*.

The isolationist consensus, developed over 150 years, had unraveled: as the postwar era dawned, both liberals and conservatives were united in their fervent interventionism. Both parties gloried in the imperial pretensions of Henry Luce and associates, who proclaimed the "American Century" as the slogan and credo of the rising American Empire. The noninterventionist movement was relegated to the margins of American politics, confined to pacifists and extreme leftists, on the one hand, and extreme rightists, including libertarians as well as members of the John Birch Society,[112] on the other.

Today, as we face an economic and cultural crisis similar in some important ways to the one that gripped the United States during the 1930s, a new isolationist coalition is developing, and the

---

[112] Aside from denouncing the Vietnam war as a Communist plot to drag us into an unwinnable land war in Asia, Robert Welch, the Society's founder, expressed his isolationism in a 1961 speech, "Through All the Days to Be," reprinted in Robert Welch, *The New Americanism* (Belmont, Mass.: Western Islands, 1966), pp. 56–88.

noninterventionist consensus is making a comeback. With the fall of Communism, this new movement is making real inroads on the right, and the old slogan "America First!" is once again heard in the land.

It is therefore relevant, especially to those of us who consider ourselves part of this new movement on the right, to ask: why did the old right fail? Why did the America First Committee, at one time the largest, the most articulate and active anti-war movement in American history, meet defeat at the hands of Roosevelt and the war party?

There were three major reasons for the defeat of the noninterventionists, three areas of weakness in a movement which otherwise had the resources to win.

(1) *The isolationists failed to gain control of the Republican party.* The analysis of the Midwestern progressives—that the "war trust" was an Anglophilic cabal of bankers and mandarins of high finance—was proven by the victory of Wendell Wilkie at the 1939 Republican national convention, when Wall Street packed the convention with their bought-and-paid-for delegates. The defeat of the isolationist Senator Robert A. Taft meant that the anti-war forces had lost their last chance to stop the drive to war. Americans still wanted to stay out of the war, if it was at all possible, but there was no way for them to express this sentiment politically, faced as they were with two internationalist presidential candidates. The America First Committee, at one of its last national committee meetings before Pearl Harbor, had planned to enter candidates in the upcoming primary elections of both parties, but the turn toward major party electoral politics came too late.

(2) *The isolationists failed to guard the "back door to war."*[113] Even if the America First Committee had turned to electoral politics earlier, the method by which Roosevelt dragged us into the war against the Axis powers was a strategy the isolationists were woefully unprepared for. That strategy entailed provoking the Japanese into attacking the United States in response to an American economic blockade. As Wayne G. Cole points out:

> Isolationism took shape as Americans looked across the Atlantic toward Europe; those patterns blurred a bit when they looked westward across the Pacific toward Hawaii, the Philippines, Japan, and China.[114]

---

[113]See Charles Callan Tansill, *Back Door to War* (Chicago: Regnery, 1952).

[114]Cole, *Roosevelt and the Isolationists*, p. 239.

While isolationists in Congress opposed any attempt to get us into war on behalf of China during the Sino–Japanese conflict, some isolationists

> unintentionally played into the hands of those whose hard-line approaches eventually provoked Japan into striking at the United States. Some nationalistic isolationists, particularly from the Far West, took hard-line views in opposition to the Japanese. That was the case with Senator Hiram Johnson in California.[115]

The populist movement from which Johnson built his political base was openly anti-Japanese. Prominent among Johnson's California supporters were members of the Asian Exclusion League, which advocated legislation keeping Japanese out of the state and forbidding them to own property. Anti-Japanese racism was undoubtedly a major factor in the isolationist lack of response to the President's war moves in Asia.

Another factor in the isolationist neglect of the Pacific front was the precedent set by the imperialist policy of the 1890s: we already had colonial possessions in the Pacific, and it was therefore necessary to defend them against the rising influence of Japan. A few isolationists called for granting independence to the Philippines, but found themselves virtually alone. As the prospect of war with Japan loomed large, the America First Committee turned to the task of applying a noninterventionist analysis to events on the Pacific front—but, again, it was too late.

(3) *The isolationists fell victim to the Smear Bund and government repression.* The campaign against the isolationist movement, coordinated out of the White House and conducted by a plethora of government agencies and private groups working in close cooperation, was an exercise in character assassination unparalleled in the history of this country. At the head of this Smear Bund was the President himself, who did not lose any opportunity to link the isolationists, and especially the America First Committee, with the Nazis and their agents and sympathizers in the United States. Before Pearl Harbor, this campaign was conducted by professional smear-mongers, such as John Roy Carlson, columnist Walter Winchell, the pro-Communist front groups such as the "Friends of Democracy" and the Nonsectarian Anti-Nazi League, along with the interventionist organizations such as Fight for Freedom. Supplementing these efforts were covert operations carried out by British intelligence against the activities of the America First

---

[115]Ibid., pp. 240–41.

Committee and designed to aid the interventionists.[116] The President was eager to get something on the America First Committee, and he badgered J. Edgar Hoover to investigate the AFC's income in an attempt to tie them to the Nazis. FBI agents infiltrated the AFC, attended meetings, examined Committee records—and came up with nothing, much to the President's chagrin.

After Pearl Harbor, the federal government was even less concerned with legal niceties. A sedition trial was launched, in the waning days of the war: the America First Committee was named, along with most of the other anti-interventionist groups, in the first two indictments. Also named was Lawrence Dennis, author of *The Dynamics of War and Revolution, Is Capitalism Doomed?*, and *The Coming American Fascism*,[117] whose great crime was to write books similar in theme (and style) to James Burnham's *The Managerial Revolution*,[118] which was just then receiving much acclaim in left-wing intellectual circles. A vicious propaganda campaign was conducted in the press, smearing isolationists as Nazi agents and focusing on members of Congress who had done their best to keep us out of the slaughter.

THE LESSONS OF HISTORY

A history of the anti-interventionist movement is essentially an examination of the interplay between domestic and foreign policy issues in American politics, a study that immediately poses the question: which is primary? Do domestic political considerations drive foreign policy, or is it the other way around? One could take refuge in taking the safe middle-of-the-road position that each influences the other, but this denies the nature of war as the essence and chief organizing principle of the State. It therefore follows that the war party, if the logic of its position is followed through to the end, will become (if it is not already) the party of increased State power and centralized government. The history of the anti-interventionist movement in American politics bears this out. The transformation of the previously anti-interventionist, staunchly Jeffersonian Democratic Party into the party of internationalism and big government was driven by the party's support of Wilson's policies

[116]See ibid., p. 487; see also Mark Lincoln Chadwin, *Hawks of World War II* (Chapel Hill: University of North Carolina Press, 1968), pp. 138–39, 186–87, 245; H. Montgomery Hyde, *Room 3603: The Story of the British Intelligence Center in New York During World War II* (New York: Farrar, Straus, 1962), pp. 2–5, 26–27, 72–74.

[117]Lawrence Dennis, *The Coming American Fascism* (New York: Harper, 1936); idem, *Is Capitalism Doomed?* (New York: Harper, 1932); idem, *The Dynamics of War and Revolution* (New York: Weekly Foreign Letter, 1940).

[118]James Burnham, *The Managerial Revolution* (New York: John Day, 1941).

that led to World War I. Conversely, the political evolution of the Midwestern progressives into the staunchest opponents of the New Deal demonstrates the same principle in reverse. The lesson of history is that of the mix of issues which confront us, from race relations to economic concerns, foreign policy is primary. It is primary in the moral sense, because it involves the question of war and peace: the question of whether many of thousands of people may live or die. What is not so obvious is that it is also primary in the ideological and political sense: that the attitudes of individuals, movements, and party organizations on the question of America's role in the world is decisive in determining their political evolution on the domestic scene. This goes beyond the old right idea, revived among today's paleo-conservatives, that an interventionist foreign policy was the key factor in the growth and development of the modern welfare–warfare state. It means that foreign policy is crucial in a *teleological* sense, that is, in the sense that the issue is intimately bound up with the ultimate destiny of the American Republic.

Now, the opponents of Franklin Roosevelt's drive to establish a wartime dictatorship, the heroic men and women of the old right, certainly knew this; what they didn't and couldn't know was how their own struggle, even their defeats, would one day culminate in a chance to take back what had been lost. The old rightists, with the exception of Rose Wilder Lane and, perhaps, Louis Bromfield, were all pessimists of the darkest hue. They were libertarians who mourned the passing of liberty; nationalists who spoke of a nation betrayed; Americans who wanted their Old Republic back, and knew that the celebration of that victory would have to be left to some future generation. In the old right view, the country was being taken over by One-Worlders, Communists, and what John T. Flynn called "radical aristocrats,"[119] and there wasn't much anyone could do about it. "We have passed the boundary that lies between Republic and Empire,"[120] wrote Garet Garrett in *Rise of Empire*, and one gets the feeling, reading Garrett's 1952 pamphlet, that there is no going back.

The pessimism of the old right is understandable. They faced an unprecedented campaign of vilification, blacklisting, and even legal sanctions as World War II broke out. They watched as the wave of collectivism hit American shores in the form of the New Deal, eroding and almost washing away the foundations of the Republic. Caught up as they were in the enormity of their own defeat and the triumph of the modern managerial state, they could

[119]Flynn, *As We Go Marching*, p. 254.
[120]Garet Garrett, *Rise of Empire* (Caldwell, Idaho: Caxton, 1952), p. 5.

not see that their movement, although it failed to achieve its political objectives, was part of a larger and recurring pattern in American politics—one that seems to get stronger and more defined as time goes on and the nation departs even further from the foreign policy of the founding fathers. The history of the anti-interventionist movement in America—rooted as it is in the traditions and ideology of the American revolutionaries—is the story of a developing Americanism, of an American ideology that encompasses not only foreign but domestic policy, of a libertarian nationalism that extols America as the fatherland of liberty.

Those who opposed the transformation of our American Republic into an Empire hailed from both ends of the political spectrum, from right to left and virtually all points in between. From the free-silver populism of William Jennings Bryan to the old right laissez-fairism of Garet Garrett, the various strands of non-interventionist thought are made of distinct and diverse fibers. These disparate threads of agrarian progressivism and right-wing populism, of nationalism and libertarianism, have been slowly woven together over time until, in the 20th century, certain distinct patterns began to emerge. The evolution of these patterns, or common themes, is an ongoing process that shows every sign of some day culminating in the birth of an authentic and fully-matured American nationalism.

4
AMERICA'S TWO JUST WARS: 1775 AND 1861

Murray N. Rothbard[*]

Much of "classical international law" theory, developed by the Catholic Scholastics, notably the 16th-century Spanish Scholastics such as Vitoria and Suarez, and then the Dutch Protestant Scholastic Grotius and by 18th- and 19th-century jurists, was an explanation of the criteria for a just war. For war, as a grave act of killing, needs to be justified.

My own view of war can be put simply: a *just* war exists when a people tries to ward off the threat of coercive domination by another people, or to overthrow an already-existing domination. A war is *unjust*, on the other hand, when a people try to impose domination on another people, or try to retain an already existing coercive rule over them.

During my lifetime, my ideological and political activism has focused on opposition to America's wars, first because I have believed our waging them to be unjust, and, second, because war, in the penetrating phrase of the libertarian Randolph Bourne in World War I, has always been "the health of the State," an instrument for the aggrandizement of State power over the health, the lives, and the prosperity, of their subject citizens and social institutions. Even a just war cannot be entered into lightly; an unjust one must therefore be anathema.

There have been only two wars in American history that were, in my view, assuredly and unquestionably proper and just; not only that, the opposing side waged a war that was clearly and notably unjust. Why? Because we did not have to question whether a threat against our liberty and property was clear or present; in both of these wars, Americans were trying to rid themselves of an unwanted domination by another people. And in both cases, the other side ferociously tried to maintain their coercive rule over Americans. In each case, one side—"our side" if you will—was notably just, the other side—"their side"—unjust.

To be specific, the two just wars in American history were the American Revolution, and the War for Southern Independence.

[*This article is composed from notes used by the author in his presentation at the Mises Institute's "Costs of War" conference in Atlanta, May 20–22, 1994.]

I would like to mention a few vital features of the treatment of war by the classical international natural lawyers, and to contrast this great tradition with the very different "international law" that has been dominant since 1914, by the dominant partisans of the League of Nations and the United Nations.

The classical international lawyers from the 16th through the 19th centuries were trying to cope with the implications of the rise and dominance of the modern nation–state. They did not seek to "abolish war," the very notion of which they would have considered absurd and Utopian. Wars will always exist among groups, peoples, nations; the *desideratum*, in addition to trying to persuade them to stay within the compass of "just wars," was to curb and limit the impact of existing wars as much as possible. Not to try to "abolish war," but to constrain war with limitations imposed by civilization.

Specifically, the classical international lawyers developed two ideas, which they were broadly successful in getting nations to adopt: (1) above all, don't target civilians. If you must fight, let the rulers and their loyal or hired retainers slug it out, but keep civilians on both sides out of it, as much as possible. The growth of democracy, the identification of citizens with the State, conscription, and the idea of a "nation in arms," all whittled away this excellent tenet of international law.

(2) Preserve the rights of neutral states and nations. In the modern corruption of international law that has prevailed since 1914, "neutrality" has been treated as somehow deeply immoral. Nowadays, if countries A and B get into a fight, it becomes every nation's moral obligation to figure out, quickly, which country is the "bad guy," and then if, say, A is condemned as the bad guy, to rush in and pummel A in defense of the alleged good guy B.

Classical international law, which should be brought back as quickly as possible, was virtually the opposite. In a theory which tried to limit war, neutrality was considered not only justifiable but a positive virtue. In the old days, "he kept us out of war" was high tribute to a president or political leader; but now, all the pundits and professors condemn any president who "stands idly by" while "people are being killed" in Bosnia, Somalia, Rwanda, or the hot spot of the day. In the old days, "standing idly by" was considered a mark of high statesmanship. Not only that: neutral states had "rights" which were mainly upheld, since every warring country knew that someday it too would be neutral. A warring state could not interfere with neutral shipping to an enemy state; neutrals could ship to such an enemy with impunity all goods except

"contraband," which was strictly defined as arms and ammunition, period. Wars were kept limited in those days, and neutrality
was extolled.

In modern international law, where "bad-guy" nations must
be identified quickly and then fought by all, there are two rationales for such world-wide action, both developed by Woodrow Wilson, whose foreign policy and vision of international affairs has
been adopted by every President since. The first is "collective security against aggression." The notion is that every war, no matter
what, must have one "aggressor" and one or more "victims," so
that naming the aggressor becomes a prelude to a defense of
"heroic little" victims. The analogy is with the cop-on-the-corner.
A policeman sees A mugging B; he rushes after the aggressor, and
the rest of the citizens join in the pursuit. In the same way, supposedly, nations, as they band together in "collective security" arrangements, whether they be the League, the United Nations, or
NATO, identify the "aggressor" nation and then join together as an
"international police force," like the cop-on-the-corner, to zap the
criminal.

In real life, however, it's not so easy to identify one warring
"aggressor." Causes become tangled, and history intervenes. Above all, a nation's current border cannot be considered as evidently
just as a person's life and property. Therein lies the problem. How
about the very different borders ten years, twenty years, or even
centuries ago? How about wars where claims of all sides are
plausible? But any complication of this sort messes up the plans of
our professional war crowd. To get Americans stirred up about
intervening in a war thousands of miles away about which they
know nothing and care less, one side must be depicted as the clear-
cut bad guy, and the other side pure and good; otherwise,
Americans will not be moved to intervene in a war that is really
none of their business. Thus, feverish attempts by American pundits and alleged foreign-policy "experts" to get us to intervene
against the demonized Serbs ran aground when the public began
to realize that *all three* sides in the Bosnian war were engaging in
"ethnic cleansing" whenever they got the chance. This is even forgetting the fatuity of the propaganda about the "territorial integrity" of a so-called "Bosnian state" which has never existed even
formally until a year or two ago, and of course in actuality does not
exist at all.

If classical international law limited and checked warfare, and
kept it from spreading, modern international law, in an attempt to
stamp out "aggression" and to abolish war, only insures, as the

great historian Charles Beard put it, a futile policy of "perpetual war for perpetual peace."

The second Wilsonian excuse for perpetual war, particularly relevant to the "Civil War," is even more Utopian: the idea that it is the moral obligation of America and of all other nations to impose "democracy" and "human rights" throughout the globe. In short, in a world where "democracy" is generally meaningless, and "human rights" of any genuine sort virtually non-existent, that we are obligated to take up the sword and wage a perpetual war to force Utopia on the entire world by guns, tanks, and bombs.

The Somalian intervention was a perfect case study in the workings of this Wilsonian dream. We began the intervention by extolling a "new kind of army" (a new model army if you will) engaged in a new kind of high moral intervention: the U.S. soldier with a CARE package in one hand, and a gun in the other. The new "humanitarian" army, bringing food, peace, democracy, and human rights to the benighted peoples of Somalia, and doing it all the more nobly and altruistically because there was not a scrap of national interest in it for Americans. It was this prospect of a purely altruistic intervention—of universal love imposed by the bayonet—that swung almost the entire "anti-war" Left into the military intervention camp. Well, it did not take long for our actions to have consequences, and the end of the brief Somalian intervention provided a great lesson if we only heed it: the objects of our "humanitarianism" being shot down by American guns, and striking back by highly effective guerrilla war against American troops, culminating in savaging the bodies of American soldiers. So much for "humanitarianism," for a war to impose democracy and human rights; so much for the new model army.

In both of these cases, the modern interventionists have won by seizing the moral high ground; *theirs* is the cosmic "humanitarian" path of moral principle; those of us who favor American neutrality are now derided as "selfish," "narrow," and "immoral." In the old days, however, interventionists were more correctly considered propagandists for despotism, mass murder, and perpetual war, if not spokesmen for special interest groups, or agents of the "merchants of death." Scarcely a high ground.

The cause of "human rights" is precisely the critical argument by which, in retrospect, Abraham Lincoln's War of Northern Aggression against the South is justified and even glorified. The "humanitarian" goes forth and rights the wrong of slavery, doing so through mass murder, the destruction of institutions and property, and the wreaking of havoc which has still not disappeared.

Isabel Paterson, in *The God of the Machine*, one of the great books on political philosophy of this century, zeroed in on what she aptly called "The Humanitarian with the Guillotine." "The humanitarian," Mrs. Paterson wrote, "wishes to be a prime mover in the lives of others. He cannot admit either the divine or the natural order, by which men have the power to help themselves. The humanitarian puts himself in the place of God." But, Mrs. Paterson notes, the humanitarian is "confronted by two awkward facts: first, that the competent do not need his assistance; and second, that the majority of people, if unperverted, positively do not want to be 'done good' by the humanitarian." Having considered what the "good" of others might be, and who is to decide on the good and on what to do about it, Mrs. Paterson points out: "Of course what the humanitarian actually proposes is that *he* shall do what he thinks is good for everybody. It is at this point that the humanitarian sets up the guillotine." Hence, she concludes, "the humanitarian in theory is the terrorist in action."

There is an important point about old-fashioned, or classical, international law which applies to any sort of war, even a just one: Even if country A is waging a clearly just war against country B, and B's cause is unjust, this fact by no means imposes any sort of moral obligation on any other nation, including those who wish to abide by just policies, to intervene in that war. On the contrary, in the old days neutrality was always considered a more noble course. If a nation had no overriding interest of its own in the fray, there was no moral obligation whatever to intervene. A nation's highest and most moral course was to remain neutral; its citizens might cheer in their heart for A's just cause, or, if someone were overcome by passion for A's cause he could rush off on his own to the front to fight, but generally citizens of nation C were expected to cleave to their own nation's interests over the cause of a more abstract justice. Certainly, they were expected not to form a propaganda pressure group to try to bulldoze their nation into intervening; if champions of country A were sufficiently ardent, they could go off on their own to fight, but they could not commit their fellow countrymen to do the same.

Many of my friends and colleagues are hesitant to concede the existence of universal natural rights, lest they find themselves forced to support American, or world-wide intervention, to try to enforce them. But for classical natural law international jurists, that consequence did not follow at all. If, for example, Tutsis are slaughtering Hutus in Rwanda or Burundi, or *vice versa*, these natural lawyers would indeed consider such acts as violations of the natural rights of the slaughtered; but that fact in no way implies any moral or natural-law obligation for any other people in the world to rush in to try to enforce such rights. We might encapsulate this position into a slogan: "Rights may be universal, but their enforcement must be local" or, to adopt the motto of the Irish rebels: *Sinn Fein*, "ourselves alone." A group of people may have rights, but it is *their* responsibility, and theirs alone, to defend or safeguard such rights.

To put it another way, I have always believed that when the left claims that all sorts of entities—animals, alligators, trees, plants, rocks, beaches, the earth, or "the ecology"—have "rights," the proper response is this: when those entities act like the Americans who set forth their declaration of rights, when they speak for themselves and take up arms to enforce them, then and only then can we take such claims seriously.

I want to now return to America's two just wars. It is plainly evident that the American Revolution, using my definition, was a just war, a war of peoples forming an independent nation and casting off the bonds of another people insisting on perpetuating their rule over them. Obviously, the Americans, while welcoming French or other support, were prepared to take on the daunting task of overthrowing the rule of the most powerful empire on earth, and to do it alone if necessary.

What I want to focus on here is not the grievances that led the American rebels to the view that it had become "necessary for One People to dissolve the political bonds which have connected them with another." What I want to stress here is the ground on which the Americans stood for this solemn and fateful act of separation. The Americans were steeped in the natural-law philosophy of John Locke and the Scholastics, and in the classical republicanism of Greece and Rome. There were two major political theories in Britain and in Europe during this time. One was the older, but by this time obsolete, absolutist view: the king was the father of his nation, and absolute obedience was owed to the king by the lesser orders; any rebellion against the king was equivalent to Satan's rebellion against God.

The other, natural law, view countered that sovereignty originated not in the king but in the people, but that the people had delegated their powers and rights to the king. Hugo Grotius and conservative natural lawyers believed that the delegation of sovereignty, once transferred, was irrevocable, so that sovereignty must reside permanently in the king. The more radical libertarian theorists, such as Father Mariana, and John Locke and his followers, believed, quite sensibly, that since the original delegation was voluntary and contractual, the people had the right to take back that sovereignty should the king grossly violate his trust.

The American revolutionaries, in separating themselves from Great Britain and forming their new nation, adopted the Lockean doctrine. In fact, if they *hadn't* done so, they would not have been able to form their new nation. It is well known that the biggest moral and psychological problem the Americans had, and could only bring themselves to overcome after a full year of bloody war, was to violate their oaths of allegiance to the British king. Breaking with the British Parliament, their *de facto* ruler, posed no problem; Parliament they didn't care about. But the king was their inherited sovereign lord, the person to whom they had all sworn fealty. It was the king to whom they owed allegiance; thus, the list of grievances in the Declaration of Independence mentioned only the king, even though Parliament was in reality the major culprit.

Hence, the crucial psychological importance, to the American revolutionaries, of Thomas Paine's *Common Sense*, which not only adopted the Lockean view of a justified reclaiming of sovereignty by the American people, but also particularly zeroed in on the office of the king. In the words of the New Left, Paine delegitimized and desanctified the king in American eyes. The king of Great Britain, Paine wrote, is only the descendent of "nothing better than the principal ruffian of some restless gang; whose savage manner or preeminence in subtlety obtained him the title of chief among plunderers." And now the kings, including the "Royal Brute of Great Britain," are but "crowned ruffians."

In making their revolution, then, the Americans cast their lot, permanently, with a contractual theory or justification for government. Government is not something imposed from above, by some divine act of conferring sovereignty; but contractual, from below, by "consent of the governed." That means that American polities inevitably become republics, not monarchies. What happened, in fact, is that the American Revolution resulted in something new on earth. The people of each of the 13 colonies formed new, separate, contractual, republican governments. Based on libertarian doctrines and on republican models, the people of the 13 colonies each set up independent sovereign states: with powers of each government strictly limited, with most rights and powers reserved to the people, and with checks, balances, and written constitutions severely limiting state power.

These 13 separate republics, in order to wage their common war against the British Empire, each sent representatives to the Continental Congress, and then later formed a Confederation, again with severely limited central powers, to help fight the British. The hotly contested decision to scrap the Articles of Confederation and to craft a new Constitution demonstrates conclusively that the central government was not supposed to be perpetual, not to be the sort of permanent one-way trap that Grotius had claimed turned popular sovereignty over to the king forevermore. In fact, it would be very peculiar to hold that the American Revolutionaries had repudiated the idea that a pledge of allegiance to the king was contractual and revocable, and break their vows to the king, only to turn around a few short years later to enter a compact that turned out to be an irrevocable one-way ticket for a permanent central government power. Revocable and contractual to a king, but irrevocable to some piece of paper!

And finally, does anyone seriously believe for one minute that any of the 13 states would have ratified the Constitution had they believed that it was a perpetual one-way Venus fly trap—a one-way ticket to sovereign suicide? The Constitution was barely ratified as it is!

So, if the Articles of Confederation could be treated as a scrap of paper, if delegation to the confederate government in the 1780s was revocable, how could the central government set up under the Constitution, less than a decade later, claim that *its* powers were permanent and irrevocable? Sheer logic insists that: if a state could enter a confederation it could later withdraw from it; the same must be true for a state adopting the Constitution.

And yet, of course, that monstrous illogic is precisely the doctrine proclaimed by the North, by the Union, during the War Between the States.

In 1861, the Southern states, believing correctly that their cherished institutions were under grave threat and assault from the federal government, decided to exercise their natural, contractual, and constitutional right to withdraw, to "secede" from that Union. The separate Southern states then exercised their contractual right as sovereign republics to come together in another confederation, the Confederate States of America. If the American Revolutionary War was just, then it follows as the night the day that the Southern cause, the War for Southern Independence, was just, and for the same reason: casting off the "political bonds" that connected the two peoples. In neither case was this decision made for "light or transient causes." And in both cases, the courageous seceders pledged to each other "their lives, their fortunes, and their sacred honor."

What of the grievances of the two sets of seceders? Were they comparable? The central grievance of the American rebels was the taxing power: the systematic plunder of their property by the British government. Whether it was the tax on stamps, or the tax on imports, or finally the tax on imported tea, taxation was central. The slogan "no taxation without representation" was misleading; in the last analysis, we didn't want "representation" in Parliament; we wanted not to be taxed by Great Britain. The other grievances, such as opposition to general search warrants, or to overriding of the ancient Anglo-Saxon principle of trial by jury, were critical because they involved the power to search merchants' properties for goods that had avoided payment of the customs taxes, that is for "smuggled" goods, and trial by jury was vital because no American jury would ever convict such smugglers.

One of the central grievances of the South, too, was the tariff that Northerners imposed on Southerners whose major income came from exporting cotton abroad. The tariff at one and the same time drove up prices of manufactured goods, forced Southerners and other Americans to pay more for such goods, and threatened to cut down Southern exports. The first great constitutional crisis with the South came when South Carolina battled against the well named Tariff of Abomination of 1828. As a result of South Carolina's resistance, the North was forced to reduce the tariff, and finally, the Polk administration adopted a two-decade long policy of virtual free trade.

John C. Calhoun, the great intellectual leader of South Carolina, and indeed of the entire South, pointed out the importance of a very low level of taxation. All taxes, by their very nature, are paid, on net, by one set of people, the "taxpayers," and the proceeds go to another set of people, what Calhoun justly called the "tax-consumers." Among the net tax-consumers, of course, are the politicians and bureaucrats who live full-time off the proceeds. The higher the level of taxation, the higher the percentage which the country's producers have to give the parasitic ruling class that enforces and lives off of taxes. In zeroing in on the tariff, Calhoun pointed out that "the North has adopted a system of revenue and disbursements, in which an undue proportion of the burden of taxation has been imposed on the South, and an undue proportion appropriated to the North, and for the monopolization of Northern industry."

What of the opposition to these two just wars? Both were unjust, since in both the case of the British and of the North, they were waging fierce war to maintain their coercive and unwanted rule over another people. But if the British wanted to hold on and expand their empire, what were the motivations of the North? Why, in the famous words of the abolitionist William Lloyd Garrison, at least early in the struggle, didn't the North "let their erring sisters go in peace?"

The North, in particular the North's driving force, the "Yankees"—that ethnocultural group who either lived in New England or migrated from there to upstate New York, northern and eastern Ohio, northern Indiana, and northern Illinois—had been swept by a new form of Protestantism. This was a fanatical and emotional neo-Puritanism driven by a fervent "postmillenialism" which held that, as a precondition for the Second Advent of Jesus Christ, man must set up a thousand-year Kingdom of God on Earth.

The Kingdom is to be a perfect society. In order to be perfect, of course, this Kingdom must be free of sin; sin, therefore, must be stamped out, and as quickly as possible. Moreover, if you didn't try your darndest to stamp out sin by force you yourself would not be saved. It was very clear to these neo-Puritans that in order to stamp out sin, government, in the service of the saints, is the essential coercive instrument to perform this purgative task. As historians have summed up the views of all the most prominent of these millennialists, "government is God's major instrument of salvation."

Sin was very broadly defined by the Yankee neo-Puritans as anything which might interfere with a person's free will to embrace salvation, anything which, in the words of the old Shadow radio serial, "which might cloud men's minds." The particular cloud-forming occasions of sin, for these millennialists, were liquor ("demon rum"), any activity on the Sabbath except reading the Bible and going to Church, slavery, and the Roman Catholic Church.

If anti-slavery, prohibitionism, and anti-Catholicism were grounded in fanatical post-millennial Protestantism, the paternalistic big government required for this social program on the state and local levels led logically to a big government paternalism in national economic affairs. Whereas the Democratic Party in the 19th century was known as the "party of personal liberty," of states' rights, of minimal government, of free markets and free trade, the Republican Party was known as the "party of great moral ideas," which amounted to the stamping-out of sin. On the economic level, the Republicans adopted the Whig program of statism and big government: protective tariffs, subsidies to big business, strong central government, large-scale public works, and cheap credit spurred by government.

The Northern war against slavery partook of fanatical millennialist fervor, of a cheerful willingness to uproot institutions, to commit mayhem and mass murder, to plunder and loot and destroy, all in the name of high moral principle and the birth of a perfect world. The Yankee fanatics were veritable Patersonian humanitarians with the guillotine: the Anabaptists, the Jacobins, the Bolsheviks of their era. This fanatical spirit of Northern aggression for an allegedly redeeming cause is summed up in the pseudo-Biblical and truly blasphemous verses of that quintessential Yankee Julia Ward Howe, in her so-called "Battle Hymn of the Republic."

Modern left-liberal historians of course put this case in a slightly different way. Take for example, the eminent abolitionist historian of the Civil War James McPherson. Here's the way McPherson revealingly puts it: "Negative liberty [he means "liberty"] was the dominant theme in early American history—freedom *from* constraints on individual rights imposed by a powerful state." "The Bill of Rights," McPherson goes on, "is the classic expression of negative liberty, or Jeffersonian humanistic liberalism. These first ten amendments to the Constitution protect individual liberties by placing a straitjacket of 'shall not' on the federal government." "In 1861," McPherson continues, "Southern states invoked the negative liberties of state sovereignty and individual rights of property [i.e., slaves] to break up the United States."

What was McPherson's hero Abraham Lincoln's response? Lincoln, he writes, "thereby gained an opportunity to invoke the positive liberty [he means "statist tyranny"] of reform liberalism, exercised through the power of the army and the state, to overthrow the negative liberties of disunion and ownership of slaves." Another New Model Army at work! McPherson calls for a "blend" of positive and negative liberties, but as we have seen, any such "blend" is nonsense, for statism and liberty are always at odds. The more that "reform liberalism" "empowers" one set of people, the less "negative liberty" there is for everyone else. It should be mentioned that the southern United States was the only place in the 19th century where slavery was abolished by fire and by "terrible swift sword." In every other part of the New World, slavery was peacefully bought out by agreement with the slaveholders. But in these other countries, in the West Indies or Brazil, for example, there were no Puritan millennialists to do their bloody work, armed with gun in one hand and hymn book in the other.

In the Republican Party, the "party of great moral ideas," different men and different factions emphasized different aspects of this integrated despotic world-outlook. In the fateful Republican convention of 1860, the major candidates for president were two veteran abolitionists: William Seward, of New York, and Salmon P. Chase of Ohio. Seward, however, was distrusted by the anti-Catholic hotheads because he somehow did not care about the alleged Catholic menace; on the other hand, while Chase was happy to play along with the former Know-Nothings, who stressed the anti-Catholic part of the coalition, he was distrusted by Sewardites and others who were indifferent to the Catholic question. Abraham Lincoln of Illinois was a dark horse who was able to successfully finesse the Catholic question. *His* major emphasis was on Whig economic statism: high tariffs, huge subsidies to railroads, public works. As one of the nation's leading lawyers for Illinois Central and other big railroads, indeed, Lincoln was virtually the candidate from Illinois Central and the other large railroads.

One reason for Lincoln's victory at the convention was that Iowa railroad entrepreneur Grenville M. Dodge helped swing the Iowa delegation to Lincoln. In return, early in the Civil War, Lincoln appointed Dodge to army general. Dodge's task was to clear the Indians from the designated path of the country's first heavily subsidized federally chartered trans-continental railroad, the Union Pacific. In this way, conscripted Union troops and hapless taxpayers were coerced into socializing the costs on constructing and operating the Union Pacific. This sort of action is now called euphemistically "the cooperation of government and industry."

But Lincoln's major focus was on raising taxes, in particular raising and enforcing the tariff. His convention victory was particularly made possible by support from the Pennsylvania delegation. Pennsylvania had long been the home and the political focus of the nation's iron and steel industry which, ever since its inception during the War of 1812, had been chronically inefficient, and had therefore constantly been bawling for high tariffs and, later, import quotas. Virtually the first act of the Lincoln administration was to pass the Morrill protective tariff act, doubling existing tariff rates, and creating the highest tariff rates in American history.

In his First Inaugural, Lincoln was conciliatory about maintaining slavery; what he was hard-line about toward the South was insistence on collecting all the customs tariffs in that region. As Lincoln put it, the federal government would "collect the duties and imposts, but beyond what may be necessary for these objects, there will be no invasion, no using of force against . . . people anywhere." The significance of the federal forts is that they provided the soldiers to enforce the customs tariffs; thus, Fort Sumter was at the entrance to Charleston Harbor, the major port, apart from New Orleans, in the entire South. The federal troops at Sumter were needed to enforce the tariffs that were supposed to be levied at Charleston Harbor.

Of course, Abraham Lincoln's conciliatory words on slavery cannot be taken at face value. Lincoln was a master politician, which means that he was a consummate conniver, manipulator, and liar. The federal forts were the key to his successful prosecution of the war. Lying to South Carolina, Abraham Lincoln managed to do what Franklin D. Roosevelt and Henry Stimson did at Pearl Harbor 80 years later—maneuvered the Southerners into firing the first shot. In this way, by manipulating the South into firing first against a federal fort, Lincoln made the South appear to be "aggressors" in the eyes of the numerous waverers and moderates in the North.

Outside of New England and territories populated by transplanted New Englanders, the idea of forcing the South to stay in the Union was highly unpopular. In many middle-tier states, including Maryland, New Jersey, and Pennsylvania, there was a considerable sentiment to mimic the South by forming a middle Confederacy to isolate the pesky and fanatical Yankees. Even after the war began, the Mayor of New York City and many other dignitaries of the city proposed that the city secede from the Union and make peace and engage in free trade with the South. Indeed, Jefferson Davis's lawyer after the war was what we would now call the "paleo-libertarian" leader of the New York City bar, Irish–Catholic Charles O'Conor, who ran for President in 1878 on the Straight Democrat ticket, in protest that his beloved Democratic Party's nominee for President was the abolitionist, protectionist, socialist, and fool Horace Greeley.

The Lincoln Administration and the Republican Party took advantage of the overwhelmingly Republican Congress after the secession of the South to push through almost the entire Whig economic program. Lincoln signed no less than ten tariff-raising bills during his administration. Heavy "sin" taxes were levied on alcohol and tobacco, the income tax was levied for the first time in American history, huge land grants and monetary subsidies were handed out to transcontinental railroads (accompanied by a vast amount of attendant corruption), and the government went off the gold standard and virtually nationalized the banking system to establish a machine for printing new money and to provide cheap credit for the business elite. And furthermore, the New Model

Army and the war effort rested on a vast and unprecedented amount of federal coercion against Northerners as well as the South; a huge army was conscripted, dissenters and advocates of a negotiated peace with the South were jailed, and the precious Anglo-Saxon right of *habeas corpus* was abolished for the duration.

While it is true that Lincoln himself was not particularly religious, that did not really matter because he adopted all the attitudes and temperament of his evangelical allies. He was stern and sober, he was personally opposed to alcohol and tobacco, and he was opposed to the private carrying of guns. An ambitious seeker of the main chance from early adulthood, Lincoln acted viciously toward his own humble frontier family in Kentucky. He abandoned his fiancee in order to marry a wealthier Mary Todd, whose family were friends of the eminent Henry Clay, he repudiated his brother, and he refused to attend his dying father or his father's funeral, monstrously declaring that such an experience "would be more painful than pleasant." No doubt!

Lincoln, too, was a typical example of a humanitarian with the guillotine in another dimension: a familiar modern "reform liberal" type whose heart bleeds for and yearns to "uplift" remote mankind, while he lies to and treats abominably actual people whom he knew. And so Abraham Lincoln, in a phrase prefiguring our own beloved Mario Cuomo, declared that the Union was really "a family, bound indissolubly together by the most intimate organic bonds." Kick your own family, and then transmute familial spiritual feelings toward a hypostatized and mythical entity, "The Union," which then must be kept intact regardless of concrete human cost or sacrifice.

Indeed, there is a vital critical difference between the two unjust causes we have described: the British and the North. The British, at least, were fighting on behalf of a cause which, even if wrong and unjust, was coherent and intelligible: that is, the sovereignty of a hereditary monarch. What was the North's excuse for their monstrous war of plunder and mass murder against their fellow Americans? Not allegiance to an actual, real person, the king, but allegiance to a non-existent, mystical, quasi-divine alleged entity, "the Union." The King was at least a real person, and the merits or demerits of a particular king or the monarchy in general can be argued. But where is "the Union" located? How are we to gauge the Union's deeds? To whom is this Union accountable?

The Union was taken, by its Northern worshipers, from a contractual institution that can either be cleaved to or scrapped, and turned into a divinized entity, which must be worshipped, and which must be permanent, unquestioned, all-powerful. There is no heresy greater, nor political theory more pernicious, than sacralizing the secular. But this monstrous process is precisely what happened when Abraham Lincoln and his northern colleagues made a god out of the Union. If the British forces fought for bad King George, the Union armies pillaged and murdered on behalf of this pagan idol, this "Union," this Moloch that demanded terrible human sacrifice to sustain its power and its glory.

For in this War Between the States, the South may have fought for its sacred honor, but the Northern war was the very opposite of honorable. We remember the care with which the civilized nations had developed classical international law. Above all, civilians must not be targeted; wars must be limited. But the North insisted on creating a conscript army, a nation in arms, and broke the 19th-century rules of war by specifically plundering and slaughtering civilians, by destroying civilian life and institutions so as to reduce the South to submission. Sherman's infamous March through Georgia was one of the great war crimes, and crimes against humanity, of the past century-and-a-half. Because by targeting and butchering civilians, Lincoln and Grant and Sherman paved the way for all the genocidal horrors of the monstrous 20th century. There has been a lot of talk in recent years about memory, about never forgetting about history as retroactive punishment for crimes of war and mass murder. As Lord Acton, the great libertarian historian, put it, the historian, in the last analysis, must be a moral judge. The muse of the historian, he wrote, is not Clio, but Rhadamanthus, the legendary avenger of innocent blood. In that spirit, we must always remember, we must never forget, we must put in the dock and hang higher than Haman, those who, in modern times, opened the Pandora's Box of genocide and the extermination of civilians: Sherman, Grant, and Lincoln.

Perhaps, some day, *their* statues, like Lenin's in Russia, will be toppled and melted down; their insignias and battle flags will be desecrated, their war songs tossed into the fire. And then Davis and Lee and Jackson and Forrest, and all the heroes of the South, "Dixie" and the Stars and Bars, will once again be truly honored and remembered. The classic comment on that meretricious TV series *The Civil War* was made by that marvelous and feisty Southern writer Florence King. Asked her views on the series, she replied: "I didn't have time to watch *The Civil War*. I'm too busy getting ready for the next one." In that spirit, I am sure that one day, aided and abetted by Northerners like myself in the glorious "copperhead" tradition, the South shall rise again.

5
RETHINKING LINCOLN

Richard Gamble

I n the years since his extraordinary death at the close of the Civil War, Abraham Lincoln has been transfigured into an unassailable icon of the American union. Widely unpopular in his own day, and, like any politician, the object of caricature, scorn and ridicule,[1] Lincoln's reputation since as the savior of the Union has been secured. Now, along the river that for four years divided the nation, he is enshrined in his own marble temple, surrounded by his sacred texts and gazing serenely past the Washington Monument toward the imperial Capitol dome erected during his tenure.

Befitting his place among the gods, his mortal deeds have become redemptive works of national righteousness; to doubt their wisdom, or prudence, or legacy is to entertain heresy. Lincoln's means of saving the union have been locked away, removed from scrutiny as the relics of a national saint and martyr. As M.E. Bradford observed, Lincoln has been "placed beyond the reach of ordinary historical inquiry and assessment."[2] Fashionable academics and politicians, from the ideological Left and Right, are still busy "getting right with Lincoln," still at the mourners' bench confessing their faith in the Deliverer. And in their minds, to question Lincoln's method of preserving an American union is to doubt the value of salvaging the union at all, or, worse, to hold some perverse wish that the United States had collapsed into anarchy in 1861 or even to harbor a secret regret that slavery ever ended. Admittedly, to tamper with his reputation seems reckless, a thoughtless or even malicious attempt to pull down one of the few remaining sacred symbols in a cynical and iconoclastic age. But despite his enduring presence in the American pantheon, the immortality of his words carved in stone, and the consuming fire of his principles, his behavior as Chief Magistrate must be open to examination. The legacy of his ideas and conduct, no matter how noble or virtuous his intentions, must be evaluated. We must confront Lincoln's cost to the character of our union, to the integrity of the Presidency as an institution, and to the nation's subsequent domestic and foreign policy.

---

[1] See David Donald's two essays "Getting Right With Lincoln" and "Abraham Lincoln and the American Pragmatic Tradition" in *Lincoln Reconsidered: Essays on the Civil War Era*, 2nd ed., enlarged (New York: Vintage Books, 1961), pp. 3–18, 128–43.
[2] M. E. Bradford, "The Lincoln Legacy: A Long View," *Modern Age* (Fall 1980): 355.

Lincoln began his administration in 1861 on a note of irony. In his inaugural address, coming after four months of disconcerting silence since his election concerning how he would handle the seceded states, he promised good will and prudential restraint on the part of the North. He also warned of perpetual union and firm resolve. But near the end of his speech, Lincoln inserted an odd word of comfort to the distressed South. He offered this ironic reassurance: "While the people retain their virtue, and vigilence [sic], no administration, by any extreme of wickedness or folly, can very seriously injure the government, in the short space of four years." His Presidency posed no threat to the old Republic as embodied in the Constitution, he promised. And surely, even if it did, the good people of the United States would see to it that he was kept in line, and in four years they would have the opportunity to remove him from office.[3] What injury could this humble rail-splitter possibly inflict on the country in so short a time? The tremendous physical injury of Lincoln's war against his own people, the cost in lives and property, is well known: More than 600,000 soldiers dead and perhaps 20 billion dollars in wealth destroyed. But beyond this immediate and visible cost reaches the enduring legacy of Abraham Lincoln's reasoning and conduct as President, his harm to the limited, constitutional government of the founders' design. In the course of saving the union, he destroyed two confederacies: the one born in 1861 and the one born in 1789.

Lincoln undermined the old Republic in part by substituting for the actual early history of the union his own version of the American founding. Understanding Lincoln the historian is fundamental to understanding his behavior in the crisis of 1861 and his role in "refounding" a consolidated nation. Relying on a selective, and ultimately misleading, version of the founding, Lincoln proposed in his First Inaugural that the union dated from at least the moment Britain's North American colonies had entered into association in 1774 and that it had then been "matured" by both the Declaration of Independence and the Articles of Confederation, only to emerge "more perfect" in the Constitution. The preexisting union had in fact created the Constitution, and not the Constitution the union. This sequence was foundational to Lincoln's argument against disunion and to his subsequent prosecution of the war, for he used this reading of history to reject the legality of secession and to declare any action to secure independence to be "insurrectionary" and "revolutionary."[4]

[3]President Abraham Lincoln, "First Inaugural," March 4, 1861, in *The Collected Works of Abraham Lincoln*, Roy P. Basler, ed. (New Brunswick, N.J.: Rutgers University Press, 1953), 4, p. 270.
[4]Ibid., 264–65.

Lincoln reiterated and developed this point further in his address to a special session of Congress in early July, 1861. At that
time he argued that the states retained only those powers reserved
to them by the Constitution, as if the Constitution were the authority granting power to the several states instead of the other way
around. He repeated his conviction that the union pre-dated even
the War for Independence and that therefore it was an organic,
perpetual, indivisible whole. "The States," he told Congress, "have
their *status* IN the Union, and they have no other *legal status*." Furthermore, he continued, "the Union gave each of them, whatever
of independence, and liberty, it has. The Union is older than any of
the States; and, in fact, it created them as States."[5] This interpretation naturally found no sympathy among the seceding states on
the other side of the Potomac. Confederate President Jefferson
Davis responded directly to Lincoln's version of the Founding
when he reminded the Confederate Congress that the Constitution
ratified in 1789 had been "a *compact between* independent States."
The union was not "over" or "above" the states; it was among
them and was their creation. As the Tenth Amendment to the Constitution made explicit, any powers the federal government enjoyed were delegated; the rest were reserved to the states and the
people. And now the seceding sovereign states had simply withdrawn those delegated powers.[6]

In Lincoln's mind, the union was not only perpetual, ante-
cedent to the Constitution, and the creator of the very states that
now sought to leave, it was also a spiritual entity, the mystical expression of a People. In so arguing, Lincoln held to a progressive
view of history, of history as the inevitable development and un-
folding of a redemptive plan. He and his fellow Unionists transformed the old federation from a practical association of states intended for their mutual defense, order, and prosperity into the
embodiment of an ideal, into the vehicle of an abstract principle
outside human experience and beyond human capacity. In his Gettysburg Address—in which he significantly dated the founding
from 1776, that is, before the Constitution—Lincoln claimed that
the American union had emerged in history to achieve a transcendent purpose; the nation was dedicated to an idea, "to the proposition that all men are created equal." As historian Charles Royster
notes, to the Unionist mind the single People had been made a

[5]President Abraham Lincoln, "Message to Congress in Special Session," July 4,
1861, *Collected Works*, 4, pp. 432–34.
[6]President Jefferson Davis, "Message to the Confederate Congress," April 29, 1861,
in *Democracy on Trial: 1845–1877*, Robert W. Johannsen, ed., in *A Documentary
History of American Life*, David Donald, ed. (New York: McGraw–Hill, 1966), 4,
pp. 191–96.

nation by their devotion to an overpowering idea. The seceding states betrayed the nation's mystical purpose.[7] A divided union could not fulfill its divinely-appointed role in world history.

Lincoln's progressive view of history and his devotion to America's transcendent mission was evident throughout his political career. As a young lawyer in 1842, Lincoln prophesied that the irrepressible advance of political freedom, initiated with the American Revolution, would one day "grow and expand into the universal liberty of mankind."[8] Later, in 1857, in response to Stephen A. Douglas's more constrained view of equality, Lincoln contended that the Declaration of Independence, a veritable manifesto of universal equality in his skillful hands, had "contemplated the progressive improvement in the condition of all men everywhere."[9] After being elected president, on a visit to Independence Hall, he again proclaimed that the United States was founded on an idea. He testified to his political faith, saying, "I have never had a feeling politically that did not spring from the sentiments embodied in the Declaration of Independence." The Declaration was a document not limited to these shores but one that promised to lift the burden "from the shoulders of all men" and that gave, as he phrased it, "hope to the world for all future time."[10] In his Annual Message to Congress in 1862, he warned that history had placed an inescapable burden on the people of the United States to preserve liberty not just for themselves and their posterity, but also for a watching world. In Lincoln's expansive vision, the Union side was compelled by the heavy hand of history to extend freedom's dominion and, for the sake of that mission, to preserve the immortal union, "the last best hope of earth."[11]

By his selective use of the American past, his devotion of the nation to an abstract proposition, and his expansive vision of America's role in the world, Lincoln undermined the old federated Republic. He rewrote the history of the founding, and then waged total war to see his version of the past vindicated by success. But in the course of subjugating the "insurrectionary" and "revolutionary" combination in the South, and in creating a unitary nation, he

[7]Charles Royster, *The Destructive War: William Tecumseh Sherman, Stonewall Jackson, and the Americans* (New York: Vintage Books, [1991] 1993), p. 151.

[8]Abraham Lincoln, "Temperance Address to the Springfield Washington Temperance Society," February 22, 1842, *Collected Works*, 1, p. 278.

[9]Abraham Lincoln, "Speech at Springfield, Illinois," June 26, 1857, *Collected Works*, 2, p. 407.

[10]Abraham Lincoln, "Speech in Independence Hall," Philadelphia, February 22, 1861, *Collected Works*, 4, p. 240.

[11]President Abraham Lincoln, "Annual Message to Congress," December 1, 1862, *Collected Works*, 5, p. 537.

also compromised the integrity of the Presidency as a Constitutional office, first by invading the powers of the other two branches
and then by assuming further powers nowhere mentioned in the
Constitution. He may have claimed that in the midst of an unprecedented national crisis necessity knew no law, but the Constitution
in fact recognized the possibility of emergencies and delegated
necessary and appropriate powers to the President and Congress.
As historian Clinton Rossiter wrote, "The Constitution looks to the
maintenance of the pattern of regular government in even the
most stringent of crises."[12]

But Lincoln acted alone. From the fall of Fort Sumter in April,
1861, to the convening of a special session of Congress in July of
that year, President Lincoln ruled by decree, and on his own initiative and authority he commenced hostilities against the Confederacy. For 11 weeks that spring and early summer, Lincoln exercised
dictatorial power, combining within his person the executive, legislative, and judicial powers of the national government in Washington.[13] In his inaugural speech in March he had announced that
the union had the right and the will to preserve itself. He promised
to secure federal property in the seceding states, to collect all duties and to deliver the mails—all steps short of invasion but intended nevertheless to subjugate the South.[14] He assumed so-called
"war powers"—a familiar feature of the modern Presidency, but
then a novelty—and proceeded to wage war without a declaration
from Congress. The oft-raised concern that Lincoln could not have
proceeded otherwise and still have preserved the Union should
not obscure the problem of the means he resorted to. The Consti-
tutionality of his acts cannot be, as one historian claimed, "a rather
minor issue," for at stake was the integrity of free institutions.[15]

Upon the loss of Fort Sumter in Charleston harbor, Lincoln issued a proclamation calling out a militia of 75,000 troops "in order
to suppress . . . combinations" and to enforce the laws, as he said,
careful to use Constitutional language and to frame the decree as

---

[12]Clinton Rossiter, *Constitutional Dictatorship: Crisis Government in the Modern Democracies* (New York: Harcourt, Brace and World, [1948] 1963), p. 215.

[13]William A. Dunning concluded that "In the interval between April 12 and July 4, 1861, a new principle . . . appeared in the constitutional system of the United States, namely, that of a temporary dictatorship. All the powers of government were virtually concentrated in a single department, and that the department whose energies were directed by the will of a single man." *Essays on the Civil War and Reconstruction and Related Topics* (New York, 1898), pp. 20f, quoted in Gottfried Dietze, *America's Political Dilemma* (Baltimore, Maryland: Johns Hopkins Press, 1968), p. 34.

[14]Lincoln, "First Inaugural," p. 266.

[15]Rossiter, *Constitutional Dictatorship*, p. 224.

an urgent measure against an insurrection.[16] Jefferson Davis interpreted this call for troops as a declaration of war, noting also that it was manifestly unconstitutional, the exercise by the executive of an expressly legislative power. And President Davis's understanding of the issue was consistent with a narrow reading of the Constitution. The Constitution lists among the powers of Congress the authority "to provide for calling forth the militia to execute the laws of the union, suppress insurrections and repel invasions."[17] Even though Lincoln defined secession as an insurrection and as an obstruction of the laws, the Constitution still stood in his way.

Lincoln followed this call four days later with a blockade of Southern ports, expanding it within a week to include Virginia and North Carolina.[18] Again, Lincoln justified his action as an attempt to enforce the laws and collect the revenues. Reasoning according to his logic that the South was still in the union, he again appealed to article I, section 8 of the Constitution, which states that duties had to be "uniform throughout the United States." No section of the union could be exempt from the tariffs. The blockade was a visible declaration of federal sovereignty; it was also an act of war. Within days, Lincoln issued another proclamation, this time calling for more than 40,000 volunteers and substantially increasing the size of the army and the navy.[19] Again, this was a usurpation of Congress's Constitutional powers under article I. Lincoln further infringed on Congressional prerogatives by permitting the military to suspend *habeas corpus* in order to protect "lives, liberty and property."[20] To be sure, the Constitution allows in "cases of rebellion or invasion" for the suspension of the *writ of habeas corpus* for the sake of "public safety."[21] But this extraordinary power is grouped under the responsibilities of the legislative branch. Lincoln even expanded the suspension despite the objections of Supreme Court Chief Justice Roger Taney.[22]

When Lincoln at last convened Congress on July 4, 1861, he reviewed his actions to date and sought formal legislative recognition of the executive decrees he had issued and the broad powers

[16]President Abraham Lincoln, Proclamation of April 15, 1861, *Collected Works*, 4, pp. 331–33.
[17]*U.S. Constitution*, art. I, sec. 8.
[18]President Abraham Lincoln, Proclamations of April 19, 1861 and April 27, 1861, *Collected Works*, 4, pp. 338–39, 346–47.
[19]President Abraham Lincoln, Proclamation of May 3, 1861, *Collected Works*, 4, pp. 353–54.
[20]President Abraham Lincoln, Proclamation of May 10, 1861, *Collected Works*, 4, pp. 364–65.
[21]*U.S. Constitution*, art. I, sec. 9.
[22]Rossiter, *Constitutional Dictatorship*, p. 227.

he had assumed, never acknowledging, however, that he needed such approval.[23] He admitted that his proclamations calling out the militia, blockading Southern ports and increasing the armed forces had been of dubious legality. He explained, however, that he knew Congress would have approved these measures had it been in session and that he had not ventured "beyond the constitutional competency of *Congress*"—a peculiar defense of his behavior that conceded his guilt. He also finessed his suspension of *habeas corpus* by noting that it had been used "very sparingly" and claimed that, after all, the Constitution was unclear in the first place as to who had the power to suspend the privilege. He made a compelling pragmatic argument as well: should he have scrupulously observed the details of the Constitution while a rebellion destroyed the union? Were, he demanded, "all the laws, *but one*, to go unexecuted, and the government itself go to pieces, lest that one be violated?"[24] In a sense, he was asking if the Constitution had any real meaning apart from the union. But the corollary question for the nation's future was whether the union had any meaning apart from the Constitution.

For the moment, Lincoln had operated largely within the bounds of the Constitution; he had not exercised authority beyond the delegated powers of the federal government as a whole. But over the next four years, in his capacity as commander-in-chief, Lincoln exercised powers not delegated by the Constitution to any branch of government, powers that can properly be called "dictatorial." The list of "irregularities" is long. Lincoln imposed martial law and confiscated property, conscripted the railroads and telegraph lines, spent funds from the Treasury without the benefit of Congressional appropriation, personally arranged for a $250,000,000 loan, imprisoned 20,000 to 30,000 civilians without due process, arrested and even banished troublesome political foes, restrained speech and assembly, and suppressed more than 300 newspapers. Lincoln also by executive decree initiated conscription and instituted rules of warfare in violation of the delegated powers of the Constitution.[25] Moreover, as the problem of governing conquered territory presented itself, Lincoln outlined a detailed scheme for Reconstruction, created provisional courts, invented the office of military governor, and issued the Emancipation

[23]Dietze, *America's Political Dilemma*, pp. 36–37.

[24]President Abraham Lincoln, "Message to Congress in Special Session," July 4, 1861, *Collected Works*, 4, pp. 429–31 (emphasis added).

[25]*U.S. Constitution*, art. I, sec. 8. On Lincoln's wartime powers, see Dietze, *America's Political Dilemma*, pp. 34–36; Rossiter, *Constitutional Dictatorship*, pp. 223–39; J.G. Randall, *Constitutional Problems Under Lincoln* (Urbana: University of Illinois Press, 1951).

Proclamation. Whatever its merits as a war measure and as a tool of international diplomacy, the Emancipation Proclamation achieved by executive decree what had never been understood to be within the capacity of the central government in any of its branches. This act of immediate, uncompensated emancipation amounted to an extraordinary exercise of arbitrary executive power.[26] Lincoln later acknowledged that the proclamation had "no constitutional or legal justification, except as a military measure."[27]

Beyond this abuse of executive power, Lincoln also helped clear the way for the triumph of national consolidation, the kind of unitary government that had been feared by the Anti-Federalists, John C. Calhoun, and the secessionists. This accumulation of power was to be a further enduring cost of Abraham Lincoln and his party to the American Republic. The long and complicated debate over the nature of the union, the struggle between localism and consolidation, was decided by force of arms. Lincoln thereby ended meaningful state sovereignty and removed the states as an effective check on national power and potential tyranny. With the impediment of states' rights overcome, the old Hamiltonian dream of an activist central government would be fulfilled. From his days as a Whig in the Illinois Legislature in the 1830s, Lincoln was on record as an advocate of costly internal improvements.[28] He was a loyal disciple of Whig leader Henry Clay and his so-called "American System" of national banking, internal improvements, and protective tariffs.[29] As President he explained his vision of an America that would serve the needs of the people. In his address to Congress in July 1861, he proclaimed that the union was fighting a "People's contest" for the survival of "that form, and substance of government, whose leading object is, to elevate the condition of men," to remove barriers to success, and to extend equal opportunity.[30] His Whig vision of an energetic central government is clear in his later recommendation of ambitious internal improvements and of a national banking system complete with an inflationary paper currency.[31] Under the political and social opportunities

---

[26]Dietze, *America's Political Dilemma*, p. 39.

[27]Rossiter, *Constitutional Dictatorship*, pp. 226–27 and 237; Donald, *Lincoln Reconsidered*, pp. 188–91 and 203.

[28]Randall, *Constitutional Problems under Lincoln*, p. xxi.

[29]Robert W. Johannsen, *Lincoln, the South, and Slavery: The Political Dimension* (Baton Rouge: Louisiana State University Press, 1991), pp. 14 and 45.

[30]President Abraham Lincoln, "Message to Congress in Special Session," July 4, 1861, *Collected Works*, 4, p. 438.

[31]President Abraham Lincoln, "Annual Message to Congress," December 1, 1862, *Collected Works*, 5, pp. 522–23.

afforded by the war, the Republicans crafted, and Lincoln approved, a raft of nationalist legislation, including a large public debt, an income tax, subsidies to railroads, the bureaucratic Department of Agriculture, and protective tariffs for American business nearing 48 percent.[32] The 20th-century Southern novelist Andrew Lytle aptly summarized Lincoln's consolidationist ambitions when he wrote, "Lincoln, who had always been a Hamiltonian, saw that Hamilton's principles finally triumphed."[33]

In an unsympathetic biography of Lincoln written in 1931, the noted Illinois poet Edgar Lee Masters recognized the wartime President's Hamiltonian disposition and identified one further cost of Abraham Lincoln to our Republic, one that has more to do with his legacy than with his conduct as president, although the precedent was clearly there. Masters observed that Lincoln's name has been used ever since his death as one of the "words of magic." The incantatory power of his name has been used to "perpetuate and strengthen" the kind of nation he forged, a nation of "monopoly and privilege" and of imperialist appetite.[34] Masters, a Midwestern Jeffersonian, charged that Lincoln at heart had been an imperialist. While fondly quoting the Declaration's sacred words about the equality of mankind, "he had ignored and trampled its principles that governments derive their just powers from the consent of the governed." The Gettysburg Address would have been impossible, the irony of it too absurd, if Lincoln had chosen to quote the embarrassing phrase about the consent of the governed rather than the honeyed words about equality. As Masters continued, "Lincoln at Gettysburg could not celebrate such a philosophy, for with all his original, if not perverted, view of things, he knew that it was on this field where the right to set up a new government had received its first deadly blow." The right of self-government—not in the sense of plebiscitary democracy, but rather of local autonomy— had indeed perished on the battlefield of Gettysburg. Contrary to his claim, Lincoln had not fulfilled the promise of the American founding; he had betrayed it.[35]

But conquest did not end with the South. The precedent of subjugation, as Masters sensed, had corrupted the Republic in some essential way. Indeed, Masters even charged that Lincoln's

---

[32]Randall, *Constitutional Problems under Lincoln*, p. xxi; Bradford, "The Lincoln Legacy: A Long View," pp. 357–58; Donald, *Lincoln Reconsidered*, pp. 191–94. Donald interprets Lincoln as occupying a minor and passive role in much of this legislation.

[33]Andrew Lytle, "The Lincoln Myth," *The Virginia Quarterly Review* 7 (October 1931): 622.

[34]Edgar Lee Masters, *Lincoln the Man* (New York: Dodd, Mead, 1931), p. 2.

[35]Ibid., pp. 3 and 478.

imperialist spirit had been behind the United States' conquest of the Philippines:

> The abolitionists, the Charles Sumners and the Thaddeus Stevenses, who had no conception of liberty, and the conscious imperialists, who had no regard for it, were historically triumphant when McKinley, who was a major in Lincoln's army, by a military order took over the entire Philippine Islands, and its execution resulted in the slaughter of three thousand Filipinos near the walls of Manila.

Following Lincoln's lead, the imperialists of the 1890s launched "America upon the ways of world adventure and conquest."[36]

General Robert E. Lee's foreboding in 1866 that the victorious Union was "sure to be aggressive abroad and despotic at home" soon came true.[37] While some reformers at the turn of the century, even some who admired Lincoln, condemned America's overseas adventures, most of the "uplifters" embraced Lincoln as their model for pious interventionism. Theodore Roosevelt, Woodrow Wilson, and their Progressive army invoked Lincoln's name and sang the *Battle Hymn of the Republic* as they forged a consolidated nation and waged their "war for righteousness" at home and abroad, first in Latin America and then in Europe. Moreover, as Robert Penn Warren reminds us, it was not the image of Washington or Jefferson that the government used to rally the American people during World War II, but that of the beatified Lincoln.[38]

Generations since the War Between the States have suffered the costs of Lincoln's destruction of the old Republic, a more modest federation with a regard for localism and states' rights, a sense of limits, and a relative freedom from foreign entanglement. While the tragedy of the war must be measured as it was experienced, in the loss of homes and sons, in unfathomable heartache, humiliation and spiritual anguish, it must also be measured in its consequences for true liberty. Lincoln often described his task as the effort to salvage for the world at large the American experiment in majoritarianism, opportunity, and egalitarian democracy. But what about the other American experiment, the losing side of Lincoln's progressive history, the original experiment in localism, federalism, and self-rule, the noble attempt at a manageable, constrained, and decentralized government? Surely this was the tradition worth preserving, the tradition to be reclaimed for ourselves and our posterity.

[36]Ibid., pp. 4–5.
[37]Lee stated this concern in reply to a letter from the future Lord Acton. Quoted in Charles Bracelen Flood, *Lee: The Last Years* (Boston: Houghton Mifflin, 1981), p. 143.
[38]Robert Penn Warren, *The Legacy of the Civil War: Meditations on the Centennial* (New York: Random House, 1961), p. 79.

6
DID THE SOUTH HAVE TO FIGHT?

Thomas Fleming[*]

I n September of 1876, a band of eight men rode into Northfield, Minnesota, and proceeded to rob the First National Bank. From the first everything seemed to go wrong. A teller escaped from the bank to warn the town, and his shooting only alarmed more of the townspeople. The men posted as guards outside the bank were attempting to clear the street, but this was Minnesota, and Nicholas Gustavson, who did not understand English, was shot for refusing to get out of the way. Since the robbers were from Missouri, they probably did not regard the killing of squareheads as murder, but with every such incident, the robbers lost time and alarmed the citizenry.

When the shooting was ended, two of the bank robbers—Clell Miller and William Stiles, otherwise known as Bill Chadwell—lay dead. In the manhunt that followed, the trackers killed Samuel Wells, alias Charley Pitts, and captured three others: Cole, Bob, and Jim Younger. As the prisoners were being transported to Stillwater State Prison, a reporter asked Cole why he had come all this way to rob a bank. "We are rough men," replied the veteran of Quantrill's raiders, "and used to violent ways."

Near the end of his life, Cole explained that life had become too difficult for the Youngers back in Missouri, and they had decided to pull one last job to get a stake. They picked Northfield because they had heard that the bank held the assets of General Benjamin Butler—an infamous reconstruction politician also known as Spoons Butler from his propensity to relieve Southerners of their silverware.

Two gang members who got away, Frank and Jesse James, are said to have planned the Northfield raid as a means of carrying the war into the North. Whatever the truth of the legend, it indicates the sentiment of many Missourians 11 years after the end of the War between the States. But that war, which for the rest of the country—or rather countries—began in Charleston Harbor in 1861, had erupted on the Kansas–Missouri border in 1855, and if the war in general may be accurately described as the first modern war, because of the use of advanced weaponry, trenchwar tactics, and

[*This article is composed from notes used by the author in his presentation at the Mises Institute's "Costs of War" conference in Atlanta, May 20–22, 1994.]

ideological propaganda, the war in Missouri is more like the feuding and raiding described in the Scottish border ballads and ancient Greek epics.

Historians have had a hard time coming to grips with the rough men who rode with Captain William Clarke Quantrill and Bill Anderson in defense of Southern liberties. Typically they are described as savage outlaws who took to banditry at the first opportunity. At the time, however, there were Missouri newspapermen, like John Newman Edwards, who viewed such bandits as mythical heroes. Writing in the *Kansas City Times* (27 September 1872), Edwards described the men who robbed the Kansas City Fair in 1872 as "three bandits . . . come to us from the storied Odenwald, with the halo of medieval chivalry upon their garments."

As much as I hate to admit it, there were no haloes on Frank and Jesse James, but to understand their character and behavior during the long war against the Yankees—a war that only ended with Frank's acquittal in 1884—requires a historical imagination that is not fettered by the Victorian prejudices of the 1870s or the postmodern sentimentality of the 1990s. The proper historical and cultural context for the Jameses and Youngers is not the Kansas–Missouri border in 19th-century America so much as the Scottish–English border in the age of the ballads—"'Fight on, fight on, my merry men all,' cries the outlaw Johnnie Armstrong with his dying breath," and this spirit was if anything even more ferocious in the more purely Celtic areas of Scotland and Ireland.

The clansman's loyalty was to his people rather than to someone so distant as a king, much less to something so impersonal as the state. In 1575 Sorley Boy McDonnell watched as Elizabeth's commander, the Earl of Essex, slaughtered the McDonnell women and children who had been left on Rathlin Island. Writing to his bloody mistress, Essex gloated: "Sorley . . . was likely to run mad for sorrow, tearing and tormenting himself . . . and saying that he then lost all he ever had."

But this spirit of rough heroism and loyalty to clan—especially the women of the clan—is not at all limited to the Scots. At the very beginning of our civilization, we meet a race of warriors who might well have joined the Missourians on their ill-fated expedition to Minnesota. The cliché that the Greeks had a word for it actually works in the case of the exultation that animates the hero: Homer uses *Charme*, a word that from its derivation ought to mean something like happiness or well-being, to signify the joy of battle.

From the very beginning, Greek attitudes to war are ambiguous. They knew the horrors of war all too well: the losers faced the looting and destruction of their entire world, and while a man might die in battle, a harder lot was imposed on his wife and children taken as slaves. A large part of the most familiar Greek literature are plays written in Athens in the fifth century, a period of unremitting warfare, and the plays of Aeschylus, Sophocles, Euripides, and Aristophanes are filled with denunciations of war, which, in the words of Sophocles, takes the best and spares the cowards.

No one has done a better job than Euripides of portraying the horrors and immorality of imperial conquest. Hecuba, Queen of Troy, had been supremely happy in her husband and children: "I saw my sons fall beneath the Greek spear and cut my hair at their tombs. Their father Priam, I did not mourn him after hearing the rumor of his death, but with my own eyes I saw him butchered and my city captured. The virgin daughters I had brought up for princely marriages, I nursed for the aliens who tore them from my arms." But if the price of defeat is so terrible, then it must be glorious to stand up and fight for family and friends. In the same play (*The Trojan Women*) Hecuba's daughter tells the Greeks' messenger that the subjugated Trojans are better-off than the conquering Greeks, who "when they came to the banks of the Scamander, died, not defending their frontiers nor their high-towered homeland. Whom Ares killed, they did not see their children and were not laid out for burial by their wives. They lie in alien earth." The Trojans, on the other hand, "died, first of all, for their native land, the best thing that can be said of anyone, and their friends buried them in the bosom of their ancestral earth."

Herodotus tells a story of Solon the Athenian visiting the court of Croesus. When the wealthy king of Lydia asks Solon who the happiest man on earth is, obviously thinking the answer is Croesus, the Athenian tells him Tellus of Athens, who lived at a time when his city was flourishing, had two fine sons, and after a prosperous life he died fighting for his country.

Herodotus was writing in the generation after the wars with Persia, in which the Athenians and the Spartans showed that small numbers of free men, in defending their cities, could fend off even the greatest military power that world had ever known. One veteran of the Persian wars puts these words into the Greeks at Salamis as they face the massive Persian fleet: "Sons of the Greeks, go and free your fatherland, and free your children, and the shrines of your ancestral gods, and the graves of your forefathers.

Now the contest is for everything." Notice how in every clause the emphasis is on the kinship. These men at Salamis are not merely Greeks but are also sons of the Greeks, because they are links in a chain that binds them with their forefathers and with their own children as well as with the gods of their ancestors.

Why a contest? Because for ancient Greeks, war was the ultimate sport and all the lesser sports—running, riding, wrestling, javelin-throwing—were merely training exercises in preparation for the real thing. When the Persian king sent spies to find out what the Spartans at the pass of Thermopylae were doing, he reported that some were engaged in gymnastic exercises, while others were combing out their hair. The Spartans always comb their hair when they are about to face death, it is explained, but the Persians do not find out about the gymnastic exercises until later, when Arcadian deserters tell him that the Greeks—threatened with total war—are celebrating the Olympic games in which the only prize is a wreath of wild olive. "Good heavens," exclaims one of the Persians, "what kind of men have you brought us to fight against—men who contend with each other not for money but for honor."

Like all great sportsmen, Greek fighters took pride in their gear. The Lesbian troublemaker Alcaeus takes aesthetic delight in depicting weapons of destruction: "The great hall is gleaming in bronze and the rafters are decked out with shining helmets, their horse-hair plumes nodding down . . . bronze greaves cover the pegs they are hanging from . . . fresh linen corslets and hollow shields are strewn about the floor, and by them are swords from Chalcis and many belts and tunics." The scene—and the whole mood of the piece—resembles a locker room before a championship game.

The Spartan poet Tyrtaeus, in urging his fellow citizens to fight, might be describing a football game: "Let the soldier set his feet apart and dig both heels into the ground, biting his lip with his teeth. . . . Let him fight against the man opposing him, with foot against foot, shield braced against shield, helmet against helmet."

The fighter he is describing here is the heavy-armored infantryman known as the hoplite. In earlier ages, what had counted most were the individual noble warriors described by Homer, and the introduction of hoplite warfare represents more than a military revolution, because it meant that the middling classes—men who could afford their own weapons—were now the essential core of the city's defense and of the city's social and political structure. Hoplites were a conservative force, because as land owners they knew that the sort of reckless imperialism in which the Athenian democracy engaged resulted in massive destruction of their agricultural property.

The Greek ambivalence toward war is symbolized by the two gods of war: Ares, who stands for reckless carnage, and Athena, the defender of cities. Ares is portrayed in the *Iliad* as a bloodthirsty but ultimately unreliable warrior capable of shifting sides, while Athena is steadfast, inspiring her champions with the courage to defend their comrades, their families, and their cities. Homer's prince of Troy, Hector, shows both sides of war. When the fighting spirit is on him, Hector—like Achilles and Ajax—can be a force of nature; in his reflective moments, however, Hector knows that he will die in a futile struggle, but his code of honor does not allow him to quit: "I dread the rebuke of the Trojans, if like a coward I should shirk from the war, nor does my heart bid me to do so, since I know how to be brave and always to fight in the front ranks, gaining glory for my father and for myself."

Southerners were to learn the horrors of war and the miseries of subjection almost as well as Homer's Trojans or the very real victims of Athenian imperialism, but in the early stages of the war, many of them went lighthearted into the army and toward battle. All across the South, there were parades and patriotic ceremonies, with orators promising a glorious but easy victory over the timorous Yankees.

Some Southern men went to war as eagerly as they would fight a duel; both were affairs of honor. The duel still flourished in the South before and after the war, and the Southern cause could be regarded as a duel writ large. As Bertram Wyatt-Brown observes, "If honor had meant nothing to men and women . . . there would have been no Civil War." Many Southerners resented conscription not because they were unwilling to fight but because they wanted the honor of fighting as volunteers.

While sober heads like those of Jefferson Davis and Col. Lee might warn against a long and bloody conflict, many young men were afraid the war would be over before they could even get into it. In his reminiscences, General John B. Gordon describes the rebellion that broke out when the governor of Georgia sent a telegram telling the "Raccoon Roughs" to go home: "These rugged mountaineers resolved that they would not go home; that they had a right to go to the war, had started for the war, and were not going to be trifled with by the governor or anyone else."

Civil war diaries and letters can make melancholy reading, but they are also enlivened by accounts of high jinks and practical jokes. Col. Leonidas Lafayette Polk writes home, "You can excuse this bad writing and the matter, too, when I assure you that about 100 boys are frolicking and playing hotjacket all around me." This is more high spirits than Greek athleticism, but if you will read the accounts of cavalry raids staged by Stuart, Mosby, and Morgan (to say nothing of the wild exploits of Quantrill's young pistol shooters), you will come away with the impression that some of the men were having the time of their lives.

When Southerners tried to explain the reasons for the war, they often fell back on the parallels with the first war for American independence. The history of that war was not some ancient record of legendary events; it had been passed down from father to son. American independence was a family legacy rather than an abstract set of rights. Lighthorse Harry Lee, the father of Robert E. Lee, was the most famous cavalryman to serve under George Washington, and it was his son who edited his war memoirs for publication. Throughout Robert E. Lee's career, General Washington served as the model for his own character and as a guide for his critical decisions. His letter of resignation from the U.S. Army echoes Washington, and in making Lee commander of the Virginia forces, the President of the Virginia State Convention closed with a quotation about Washington that echoed the sentiments of most Confederates: "When the Father of his country made his last will and testament, he gave his swords to his nephews with an injunction that they should never be drawn from their scabbards, except in self-defense, or in defense of the rights and liberties of their country."

This high-minded comparison between the War for Southern Independence and the nation's founding was not confined to the leaders of the Confederacy. James McPherson, in a very recent book, found such patriotic motives in two-thirds of the soldiers whose diaries and letters he consulted. An Alabama corporal captured at Gettysburg said he fought for "the same principles which fired the hearts of our ancestors in the revolutionary struggle" and a Missouri lieutenant wounded at Pea Ridge wrote that if he were killed, he would die "fighting gloriously for the undying principles of Constitutional liberty and self-government."

Both sides in the war professed lofty motives, but there was a grand difference: the South was fighting on its own ground in defense of its people, while the North—however noble its ultimate goal—was waging a war of aggression. McPherson quotes a Texas private in 1864, who makes the distinction: "We are fighting for matters real and tangible . . . our property and our homes . . . they for matters abstract and intangible." Even some in the north agreed, as an Illinois officer explained to his wife, "They are fighting from different motives from us. We are fighting for the Union . . . a high and noble sentiment, but after all a sentiment. They are fighting for independence and are animated by passion and hatred against invaders."

As slogans, the cause of the union and the holy crusade to end slavery had a decidedly Jacobin ring that we can detect in American war propaganda ever since. We have fought wars to end all wars, wars to defend democracy, wars to contain communism, and even a war to restore the legitimate monarch to the throne of Kuwait. What we have not heard, however, is the ancient call of Salamis, to defend our homes, our churches, and our graves from an invader. No matter how a Southerner felt about secession or slavery, the army of locusts that descended upon his country enlightened all but the most stubborn unionists.

In the Shenandoah Valley, Col. John Singleton Mosby caught up with a group of 30 Yankee soldiers who had been engaged in plundering and burning down the houses of loyal Virginians. Mosby's men killed 29 of them—the one survivor was an oversight. The North was shocked: making war upon civilians is a just and enlightened practice of civilization; it is only killing soldiers that is immoral.

Euripides, in his war plays, had dwelt upon the sufferings of women, impoverished, humiliated, widowed, and raped by an invading army. Modern men, who look upon women either as economic competitors or impossibly desirable centerfolds, will find it difficult to understand a chivalrous concern for women that endured until very recently in the South. In accepting a battle flag from a group of ladies, a company of Mississippi College Rifles declared, "We prize this flag, ladies, not so much for its intrinsic worth, but for the sake of those who gave it . . . its every fold shall tell . . . of the fair form that bent over it and the bright eyes that followed the fingers as they plied the very stitch; and its every thread shall be a tongue to chant the praise of woman's virtue and woman's worth." The same Texas private who said he was fighting for something tangible, after meeting two beautiful women who put flowers in the barrel of his musket, wrote his parents that he had finally solved the mystery of what they were fighting for: "By George we are fighting for the women."

Many Yankee officers and men, who shared these chivalrous sentiments, treated southern women with honor and respect; however, the exceptions were so common as to give the Union Army an evil reputation. Sherman's bummers, unleashed upon the defenseless women and children of Georgia and South Carolina, stole whatever they did not eat on the spot and burned whatever they could not carry away. If the women irritated the Yankees by complaining about the theft of the family silver, they were paid back with the sight of their burning house. When a Russian Cossack colonel (one of those immigrants who have contributed so much to our civilization) took offense at the contempt displayed by the people of Athens, Alabama, he turned over the town to be sacked by his soldiers who burned, pillaged, and raped to their heart's content. Despite his conviction in a court martial headed by James Garfield, Col. Turchin was reinstated by President Lincoln.

Perhaps the most notorious abuser of Southern womanhood was General Benjamin Butler—known as Picayune Butler for his size, alias Beast Butler for his general order directing "that hereafter when any female shall, by word, gesture or movement, insult or show contempt for any officer or soldier of the United States, she shall be regarded and held liable to be treated as a woman of the town plying her avocation." Hearing of this order, Lord Palmerston observed, "An Englishman must blush to think that such an act has been committed by one belonging to the Anglo–Saxon race." In Baton Rouge, 20-year-old Sarah Morgan, hearing the rumor of Palmerston's reaction, wondered what kind of men these Yankees were: "O Free America! You who uphold free people, free speech, free everything, what a foul blot of despotism rests on a once spotless name! A nation of brave men, who wage war on women, and lock them up in prisons for using their woman weapon, the tongue." In excoriating a "nation of free people who advocate despotism" young Sarah also noted "the extraordinary care they take to suppress all news excepting what they themselves manufacture."

Much of the North's manufactured news were the atrocity stories of rebel soldiers stabbing doctors trying to save their lives, massacres of civilians, etc. The big atrocity story of the war was the so-called "massacre" that took place when Bedford Forrest stormed Ft. Pillow. According to an editorial in the *New York Tribune* that was echoed repeatedly in the Congressional hearings, Forrest was accused of egging his men on to slaughter women and children, burned wounded men alive, buried the living with the dead.

The kernel of truth in all these tales is that many of Forrest's soldiers were from families that had been forced to endure the arrogance of Union soldiers, both former slaves and the local unionists they called "homemade Yankees." The Yankee defenders, who had been drinking heavily, taunted the rebels who, in their moment of victory, took the opportunity for private vengeance. When Gen. Forrest, arriving late on the scene, realized what was happening, he did his best to put a stop to it.

The other notorious tale of Southern atrocities was the raid on Lawrence, Kansas. The horrors were real enough. Quantrill told his men: "Kill every man big enough to hold a gun," which meant in practice anyone 14 years old and up. But why? In the first place, Quantrill's men were forced to fight under the black flag, neither taking nor giving quarter, because the Union army had declared them outlaws rather than soldiers. (The same treatment was given to Mosby.) More specifically, Lawrence was home to the worst Kansas Jayhawkers, men like Congressman Jim Lane who had led expeditions of plunder and slaughter across the border into Missouri. But most important had been Brigadier General Thomas Ewing's decision to round up and intern the female relatives of men thought to be Confederate guerrillas. Taken to Kansas City, many of the women were herded into a dilapidated building that Ewing had been told was unsafe. When the building collapsed, killing four women, and maiming many others, Quantrill and his lieutenants decided upon revenge. John McCorkle, whose sister was one of the four women killed in Kansas City, spoke for Quantrill's men, when he recalled: "We could stand no more."

Captain Bill Anderson was unhinged by the event, in which one of his sisters had been killed and another injured, and it was at Lawrence he earned the sobriquet "Bloody Bill," but neither Anderson nor the other guerrillas laid a hand upon the women of Kansas. Instead of learning humanity from his mistakes, Ewing issued his famous General Order 11 forcing the immediate evacuation of all Missouri families from the border area, where their homes were pillaged and burned by the Kansas troops. For years afterward, it was known as the "the Burnt District."

Frank James and Cole Younger had been at Lawrence, and when the war was over, the Youngers and Jameses found it hard to resume normal life. If the stories are true, Frank's brother Jesse was seriously wounded while trying to surrender to the Yankees. During the war years, Quantrill and Anderson had taken to robbing Yankee banks as a means of financing their operations, and some of the boys saw no reason to quit practicing a profession they were just getting good at. They even took to robbing trains, a habit frowned upon by the Yankee-owned railroads who hired the Pinkerton Detective Agency to track down and kill the outlaws. The detectives did not succeed in getting the James brothers, but they did attack their mother's house on January 26th, 1875, hurling some kind of incendiary device through the window. The result was an explosion that killed Frank and Jesse's nine-year-old half-brother and blew off most of their mother's right hand. There were those at the time who called it murder; some even complained when the Governor of Missouri bribed one of Jesse's men to kill him. Living quietly under the name of Howard, the outlaw was shot by Robert Ford, "the dirty little coward that shot Mr. Howard and laid poor Jesse in his grave."

What does all this banditry have to do with war, much less with war as understood by Homer and Euripides? Everything. Odysseus, returning to Ithaca after 20 years, finds his wife besieged by men who would stop at nothing to get at her person and property—they even plot to kill her son. Odysseus, in the most beautiful scene in all literature, mercilessly kills every one of them, knowing full well he faces a feud with their families. The only war worth fighting is a war in defense of your wife, your children, your parents, and your home: "For how can man die better than facing fearful odds, for the ashes of his fathers and the altars of his gods?"

We Americans, as subjects of a metastasizing world empire, know all too well that war is indeed "the health of the state," and that every display of muscle in Bosnia, Iraq, and Somalia, is being matched by similar displays against the American people. In 1875, a corrupt state government refused to punish Pinkerton agents for firebombing a home in the name of law and order. In 1994 the highest legal official of the United States is the person who sent in the tanks against the followers of David Koresh. When the Pinkertons own and operate the country, it is high time for the rest of us to realize that a virtual state of war exists between the government and the people of the United States. If this be paranoia, then let us make the most of it.

7

WAR, RECONSTRUCTION, AND THE END OF THE OLD REPUBLIC

Clyde Wilson

There is not a more perilous or immoral habit of mind than
the sanctifying of success.
                              —Lord Acton

A distinguished American historian of two generations ago
once remarked that the historical knowledge of a great
many people consists of an enthusiastic belief in a few
things that are not so; he had in mind such stories as George
Washington and the cherry tree. This is certainly the case today in
regard to the War Between the States—still the most important
event in American history in the scale of mobilization, casualties,
and revolutionary change, and the most definitive event in terms
of long-range consequences. A great deal of what passes for
common knowledge about this great war in public discourse and
government-subsidized television propaganda is simply not true.

I have in mind the image of the victorious side marching into
battle singing hymns with noble hearts intent on freeing the poor
suffering black man from his chains. Or a little less fantastic—to
preserve the sacred Union (though why the Union is so sacred remains a little vague). The triumph in 1861–65 of the Republican
Party over the will of the American people and the invasion, destruction, and conquest of the Southern States like a foreign territory has somehow, strangely, gotten mixed up with the idea of
government of, by, and for the people.

Lest this appear just the ruminations of a nostalgic Confederate, I intend to use mostly Northern and European authorities in
my discussion of the War between the States and its costs.

In 1920, H. L. Mencken wrote a little essay on the Gettysburg
Address. He praised its "gemlike perfection" and commented that
there is nothing else like it in literature:

> It is genuinely stupendous. But let us not forget that it is po-
> etry, not logic; beauty, not sense. Think of the argument in it.
> Put it into the cold words of everyday. The doctrine is simp-
> ly this: that the Union soldiers who died at Gettysburg sacri-
> ficed their lives to the cause of self-determination—"that
> government of the people, by the people, for the people,"
> should not perish from the earth. It is difficult to imagine

anything more untrue. The Union soldiers in that battle actually fought against self-determination; it was the Confederates who fought for the right of their people to govern themselves. What was the practical effect of the battle of Gettysburg? What else than the destruction of the old sovereignty of the States, i.e., of the people of the States.[1]

Edgar Lee Masters, the distinguished Illinois poet, wrote in 1931:

> Lincoln carefully avoided one half of the American story. . . .
> The Gettysburg oration, therefore, remains a prose poem,
> but in the inferior sense that one must not inquire into its
> truth. One must read it apart from the facts. . . . Lincoln
> dared not face the facts at Gettysburg. . . . He was unable to
> deal realistically with the history of his country, even if the
> occasion had been one when the truth was acceptable to the
> audience. Thus we have in the Gettysburg Address that re-
> fusal of the truth which is written all over the American
> character and its expressions. The war then being waged
> was not glorious, it was brutal and hateful and mean
> minded. It had been initiated by radicals and fanatics.[2]

A different-from-the-official view of what was at stake at Gettysburg is given by the great Alexis de Tocqueville, writing in the antebellum period:

> The Union was formed by the voluntary agreement of the
> states; and these, in uniting together, have not forfeited their
> sovereignty, nor have they been reduced to the condition of
> one and the same people. If one of the states chose to with-
> draw its name from the contract, it would be difficult to dis-
> prove its right of doing so, and the Federal government
> would have no means of maintaining its claims directly,
> either by force or by right.[3]

To spell it out a little further: the Union was transformed, in the Gettysburg Address and in the actions which it celebrated, from the rational device of self-government and social comity established by the founders into a mystical, self-justifying goal. The use of Biblical language, as M. E. Bradford showed so skillfully, transfers us from political tradition and reason to pseudo-religious faith—refounding the American polity by sacred mythology.[4] In his first message to Congress Lincoln used the traditional term

[1]H.L. Mencken, *The Vintage Mencken*, Alistair Cooke, ed. (New York: Vintage Books, 1958), pp. 79–80.

[2]Edgar Lee Masters, *Lincoln, The Man* (New York: Dodd, Mead, 1931), pp. 478–79.

[3]Alexis de Tocqueville, *Democracy in America* (New York: Vintage Books, 1990), 1, pp. 387–88.

[4]M.E. Bradford, *A Better Guide than Reason: Studies in the American Revolution* (LaSalle, Ill.: Sherwood Sugden, 1979), pp. 29–57, 185–203; and idem, *Remembering Who We Are: Observations of a Southern Conservative* (Athens: University of Georgia Press, 1985), pp. 143–56.

"Union," implying a confederacy of States, 32 times and "nation" three times. In the Gettysburg Address the word "Union" is not used. There and in the second inaugural we are told that the war is fought to preserve the "nation"—though how that reconciles with destroying a good part of the "nation" is not made clear.

The historian John Lukacs, among others, has written about the important distinction between patriotism and nationalism. Patriotism is the wholesome, constructive love of one's land and people. Nationalism is the unhealthy love of one's government, accompanied by the aggressive desire to put down others—which becomes in deracinated modern men a substitute for religious faith. Patriotism is an appropriate, indeed necessary, sentiment for people who wish to preserve their freedom; nationalism is not, as the history of this century demonstrates fully. What we have with the Gettysburg Address is the creation of a nationalist mythology—one under which we still live. What it celebrates is not the American republican Union established by our forefathers, which was—unlike the authoritarian governments of the Old World—based on the consent of the people.

The "Union" was preserved, but it was not the Union established by the founders. The real union was described by John C. Calhoun, with his usual prophetic power, in his last speech in 1850:

> But, surely, that can, with no propriety of language, be called a union, when the only means by which the weaker is held connected with the stronger portion is *force*. It may, indeed, keep them connected; but the connection will partake much more of the character of subjugation, on the part of the weaker to the stronger, than the union of free, independent, and sovereign States. . . . The cry of "Union, Union, the glorious Union!" can no more prevent disunion than the cry of "health, health, glorious health!" on the part of the physician, can save a patient lying dangerously ill. . . . Besides, this cry of Union comes commonly from those whom we cannot believe to be sincere. . . . For, if they loved the Union, they would necessarily be devoted to the Constitution. It made the Union, and to destroy the Constitution would be to destroy the Union.[5]

James Madison, the "Father of the Constitution," tells us that the meaning of the Constitution is to be sought only in the opinions and intentions of the "State conventions where it received all . . . Authority which it possesses."[6] That is, the sovereignty of

[5]John C. Calhoun, *The Works of John C. Calhoun*, Richard K. Crallé, ed. (Columbia, S.C.: A. S. Johnston, and New York: D. Appleton, 1851–1857), 4, pp. 558–59.

[6]James Madison to Thomas Ritchie, September 15, 1821, in *Writings of James Madison*, Gaillard Hunt, ed. (New York: G.P. Putnam, 1900–1910), 9, p. 372.

the people means purely and simply, and can mean nothing else in the American system, the people of each State acting in their sovereign constitution-making capacity—as they did in the American Revolution and in forming their own and the federal constitutions, and as the Southern States did in 1861 in rescinding their participation in the federal Constitution. The sovereignty of the people was ended by the outcome of The War Between the States, so that the real sovereign is now not the people but the nine black-robed deities in Washington who at will decree what our Constitution means.

The greatest cost of the war, then, was the end of the old Union and the substitution of one of force—the end of the American ideal of consent of the people and the substitution of the Old World idea of obedience to those in power by whatever means.

Let us recall that Lincoln in 1860 received the suffrages of only 39.9 percent of the American electorate, that his public statements were deliberately ambiguous, that he was by a large measure the most unknown and undistinguished man who had ever entered the White House, and the first entirely sectional candidate. And that the vote against him in the North increased by 10 percent in 1864. Lincoln only carried that election by engaging in the arbitrary warrantless arrests of political opponents, suppression of hundreds of newspapers, conducting the count at bayonet point in the border states, New York City and other places, and the hasty admission of several new States. We need to examine closely what Lincoln meant by government of, by, and for the people.

The Republican Party, even after having won the war, maintained its power only by force and fraud, known as Reconstruction. The war had been fought on the basis that the States could not leave the Union, but were only temporarily under the control of a conspiracy of rebels. But, when the "rebellion" was ended, rather than restoring the States, the Republicans declared that the States had committed suicide and were now "conquered provinces." Reconstruction was built on an utterly dishonest reversal of ground. The Constitution has never recovered from these lies.

It would have been far better to allow the American Union to dissolve at the will of the people into two or more confederacies. There is nothing whatever in the legacy of the founders or in the theory of self-government to prevent this, or that argues against it. In fact, Jefferson rather expected it. The point for him was to preserve the principle of the consent of the governed, not the Union as an end in itself, which might or might not be conducive to the consent of the governed.

But it might not have been necessary to destroy the Union had there been in 1861 an honest government in Washington—one really interested in preserving the real Union and Constitution rather than carrying through a revolutionary party platform. Given Lincoln's minority status, he would have been sustained by much Northern and all border-state and upper-South opinion had he sought compromise. Instead he kept silent except for disingenuous statements that did not meet the occasion. That is, he put himself and party above country and exhibited the most conspicuous failure of statesmanship that any American President has ever shown.

Though it is not widely known, the Confederacy had commissioners in Washington ready to make honorable arrangements—to pay for the federal property in the South, assume their share of the national debt, and negotiate all other questions. Lincoln would not deal with these delegates directly. Instead, he deceived them into thinking that Fort Sumter would not be reinforced—thus precipitating reaction when reinforcement was attempted. Even so, the bombardment of Sumter was largely symbolic. There were no casualties, and, remember, all the other forts in the South had already peacefully been handed over. Sumter in itself did not necessarily justify all-out civil war; it was simply the occasion Lincoln was waiting for. /

Even after the war had progressed it would have been possible, with a Northern government on traditional principles, to have made a peace short of the destruction that ensued. Or it would have been possible, as millions of Northerners wanted, to have sustained a war for the Union, a gentleman's disagreement over the matter of secession, that was far less destructive and revolutionary than the war turned out to be. Many, many Northerners favored this and supported the war reluctantly and only on such grounds—a suppressed part of American history. A great deal of death and destruction, as well as the maiming of the Constitution, might have been avoided by this approach.

This did not happen. Why? Because, in fact, for Lincoln and his party, it was the revolution that was the point. Throughout the war and Reconstruction, the Republican Party behaved as a revolutionary party—though sometimes using conservative rhetoric—a Jacobin party, bent on ruling no matter what, on maintaining its own power at any cost. At times they even hampered the Northern war effort for party advantage. It is very hard to doubt this for anyone who has actually closely studied the behavior of the Republicans. during this period rather than simply picking out a few of Lincoln's prettier speeches to quote.

Lord Acton, the great English historian of liberty, wrote: "The calamity ... was brought on ... by the rise of the republican party—a party in its aims and principles quite revolutionary." And when it was all over, Acton remarked that Appomattox had been a greater setback for the cause of constitutional liberty than Waterloo had been a victory.[7] James McPherson, the leading contemporary historian of the Civil War, though he approves rather than deplores the revolution that was carried out, agrees that it was a revolution.

Our rubric is the costs of war. We are interested because war is inseparable from the growth of the leviathan state and the shrinking of liberty—the greatest problem of our time. By liberty I mean self-government of the individual and of the community; what our founders understood as liberty—freedom from rule by exploitive minorities against the sense of the people. The growth of total war is inseparable from the growth of the leviathan state. They rise or fall together.

It has been said that the only thing worse than fighting a war is losing a war. But winning a war has its costs also. I would like to address the costs of winning the war for the Union—costs moral and economic. The subject is worthy of a book and my treatment will necessarily be summary. Everything that I have to say is well known, long known, and well documented by historians. There is nothing new or surprising or very controversial about any of these observations. They are usually ignored, explained away, or simply not put together logically. Historians who are well aware of the corruption that followed the war, for instance, seem to imply that it mysteriously appeared after Lincoln's death, and somehow miss the obvious conclusion that it was implicit in the goals of the Lincoln war party. This is to abandon fact and reason for the mysticism of Union and emancipation, a pseudo-religious appeal inappropriate to the discourse of free men.

In our day, it is easy to overlook the extent and unprecedented nature of Lincoln's actions—organizing armies and spending money, suspending the writ of *habeas corpus*, declaring blockades, confiscating property without legislative sanction until after the fact and often in the teeth of court rulings. The precedent for the "Imperial Presidency" is obvious.

James G. Randall, who was a great Lincoln scholar and a great excuser of Lincoln's conduct, which he portrays as reluctant, unavoidable, and moderate (compared to the Radicals), yet writes:

[7]Lord Acton, *Selected Writings of Lord Acton*, J. Rufus Fears, ed. (Indianapolis, Ind.: Liberty Press, 1985), 1, pp. 256, 363.

> When the government of Lincoln is set over against this standard [of the rule of law], its irregular and extra-legal characteristics become conspicuous. . . . Lincoln, who stands forth in the popular conception as a great democrat, was driven by circumstances to the use of more arbitrary power than perhaps any other president has seized. . . . While greatly enlarging his executive powers he also seized legislative and judicial functions as well.[8]

If Lincoln did these things from "necessity," the evidence is abundant that many of his supporters did them with glee. They deliberately smashed economic liberty and abandoned the republican virtue the fathers had considered essential, because they considered that these stood in the way of their profit and power.[9]

Indeed, it is in the economic program that we find the real reason for the war, and not in the sacred bonds of Union nor the welfare of the suffering blacks. The exit of the South from Congress led to the immediate enactment of a host of economic measures which the South had previously been able to block or ameliorate.

Foremost among these, of course, was the tariff. The movement of influential segments of Northern opinion toward a policy of coercion, from an original stance of "let them go in peace," as is well documented, was based on a realization within big business that if the South was independent there would be, to them, an intolerably immense free-trade zone along the Atlantic and Gulf.[10] Though Republicans liked to allege that Southerners were lazy and unproductive (a lie), they knew perfectly well that their economy was dependent upon Southern productivity both for its markets and its government revenue.

More than half the export of the country was made up of cotton and other Southern staple crops, of which the North got the benefit of the finance and transport. This cotton made possible much of the domestic trade and nearly all the foreign trade, which in turn made possible the tariff which protected Northern manufactures and provided most of the revenue for the Northern political class, revenue which had been consistently spent on building up the Northern infrastructure.

The high tariff became permanent policy after 1861—at great cost to the American consumer, to agriculture, and to American

[8]James G. Randall, *Constitutional Problems under Lincoln*, rev. ed. (Gloucester, Mass: Peter Smith, 1963), pp. 513–14.

[9]See T. Harry Williams, *Lincoln and the Radicals* (Madison: University of Wisconsin Press, 1965).

[10]This point was recently made by Charles Adams, *For Good and Evil: The Impact of Taxes Upon the Course of Civilization* (New York: Madison Books, 1992). See also Kenneth M. Stampp, *And The War Came: The North and the Secession Crisis, 1860–1861* (Baton Rouge: Louisiana State University Press, 1950).

development. It was accompanied by contract laws by which millions of immigrant labor gangs were brought to Republican sweat shops, thus depressing the wages of native American labor—a system implemented at the same time as emancipation of the blacks. And to the record of Republican "progressive" economic measures we must add a national banking system that was so partisan and corrupt that the Federal Reserve was actually an improvement, the first income tax, and the first federally-induced inflation.

Then there is the vaunted Homestead Act—the giving away of the public domain which was the country's greatest resource. The policy had been to sell off the lands gradually at moderate price to encourage legitimate settlement. This also provided revenue for the government which obviated the need for other taxes, like the tariff. This was the wise policy designed by the Southern statesmen who had acquired most of these lands.

Of course, the public lands should have gotten into private hands for settlement and development. But that is not what the Homestead Act was really about. In fact, less than 20 percent of the lands given away went to *bona fide* settlers, and many of them were foreigners lured here for that purpose. The rest went to railroad and mining corporations amidst vast corruption and at the expense of the taxpayer.[11] Here we have the origins of the widespread American folk prejudice against business corporations, of which demagogues have made such good use.

Then we have the arbitrary arrest by military authorities, in the North where there was no "rebellion," of some 30,000 persons, as well as the suppression of 300 newspapers. In most cases this was not for overt acts but for merely criticizing the Lincoln government and no judicial charges were ever brought. (The 30,000 refers only to federal arrests, and does not include those by Republican state and local authorities and vigilantes.)[12] Let's put a human face on these acts of destruction of the old Republic. They included the arrest of the son of Francis Scott Key, author of the "Star Spangled Banner," the seizure of the Washington family property at Arlington, and the herding of women into concentration camps in Missouri.

Secretary of State William Henry Seward is said to have bragged to the British ambassador: "I can touch a bell on my right hand

[11]Ludwell H. Johnson, *Division and Reunion: America, 1848–1877* (New York: John Wiley and Sons, 1978), pp. 110–12.

[12]Dean Sprague, *Freedom Under Lincoln* (Boston: Houghton Mifflin, 1965). See also Harold Frederic's classic novel, *The Copperhead* (1893), arising out of the real experiences of a family of Democratic farmers in New York who were persecuted for declining to join the war frenzy of their Republican neighbors.

and order the arrest of a citizen of Ohio. I can touch the bell again and order the arrest of a citizen of New York. Can Queen Victoria do as much?" She could not, nor could the Emperor of France or the King of Prussia. And Seward was one of the mildest of the Republicans, an easy-going Hermann Goering compared to Secretary of War Edwin M. Stanton's Heinrich Himmler.

Then there was the immense corruption involved in the financing of the war and the vast favoritism and fraud in the letting of war contracts. The wise Orestes Brownson wrote some years after the war:

> Nothing was more striking during the late civil war than the very general absence of loyalty or feeling of duty, on the part of the adherents of the Union, to support the government because it was the legal government of the country, and every citizen owed it the sacrifice of his life, if needed. The administration never dared confide in the loyalty of the federal people. The appeals were made to interest, to the democracy of the North against the aristocracy of the South; to anti-slavery fanaticism, or to the value and utility of the Union, rarely to the obligation in conscience to support the legitimate or legal authority; prominent civilians were bribed by high military commissions; others, by advantageous contracts for themselves or their friends for supplies to the army; and the rank and file, by large bounties and high wages. There were exceptions, but such was the rule.[13]

All of which involved a fall of ethical standards and ideas of liberty from which we have never recovered. Indeed, Brownson was describing the way politicians ever since have led Americans to war. It was then that we began to take such abuses for granted; we have become used to them. We fail to recognize how revolutionary this was for Americans who had prided themselves on their individual liberty, rule of law, and republican virtue and patriotism compared to the corrupt and arbitrary regimes of the Old World.

Another great moral cost of the war, as Richard Weaver pointed out, was inauguration by the Republicans of the total war concept, reversing several centuries of Western progress in restraining warfare to rules. General Sherman himself estimated that in his march across Georgia and the Carolinas only 20 per cent of the destruction had any military value. The rest was sheer wanton terrorism against civilians—theft and destruction of their food, housing, and tools.[14] One egregious example was the burning and sack of Columbia—a city which had already surrendered and was

[13]Orestes Brownson, "The Democratic Principle," in *Orestes Brownson: Selected Political Essays*, Russell Kirk, ed. (New Brunswick, N.J.: Transaction, 1989), pp. 204–5.

[14]Johnson, *Division and Reunion*, p. 187.

full of women and children and wounded soldiers—a looting which marked the emancipation of black women by their wholesale rape.

The assessed value of wealth in the South in 1870 was 59 percent of what it had been in 1860, not including slave property. If we count the loss of slave property, the wealth of the South in 1870 was 37 percent of its prewar value. In the same period the wealth of the North increased by 150 percent—though this wealth was much more unevenly distributed than before the war.[15] The war was carried out on the backs of Northern farmers and workingmen. Read Herman Melville's poem on the New York City draft riots in his *Battle-Pieces*.

Along with destruction went immense confiscation and theft, much of it under cover of a Confiscation Act which was enforced without ever being legally passed. The Republican Speaker of the House of Representatives simply declared the bill passed and adjourned. This high-handed legislative practice continued throughout the war and Reconstruction. The Republican Governor of Indiana suspended the legislature and acted as dictator for two years. Republicans continually agitated for an open dictatorship under Fremont or some other trustworthy Radical; all of this is known but seldom acknowledged.[16]

In addition to the Confiscation Act for rebel property there was a mechanism for the government to collect taxes in the occupied regions of the South to finance the war. At least $100,000,000 in cotton (the most valuable commodity in North America) was seized—$30,000,000 more or less legally under the confiscation and tax acts, the rest sheer theft. Of the $30,000,000 only about 10 percent ever reached the Treasury. The rest was stolen by Republican appointees. A Secretary of the Treasury commented that he was sure a few of the tax agents he sent South were honest, but none remained so very long. We know, for instance, of that great hero Admiral Porter, who with General Banks was badly beaten by vastly inferior Confederate forces in the Red River campaign, yet emerged from that campaign with $60,000 worth of stolen cotton for his personal profit. The confiscation and theft continued in full force until at least 1868—they did not end with the hostilities.[17]

But, you say, did we not free the slaves? I have had the argument a hundred times, and this is what the defenders of Lincoln always come back to when cornered. Set aside that emancipation

[15]Ibid., pp. 189–90.
[16]Williams, *Lincoln and the Radicals.*
[17]Johnson, *Division and Reunion*, pp. 115–18, 188–89.

was not the declared purpose for which the war was initiated against the South. It became a war aim 18 months into hostilities. As the letters of Northern soldiers reveal, a great many of them were opposed to emancipation as a war aim and felt betrayed. Set aside that in the British and French Empires and elsewhere slavery was ended gradually, peacefully, and with compensation, while in the United States it cost the life of every fourth Southern and every tenth Northern white man. The implied premise is that the freeing of the slaves was justified at any cost.

And of what did freeing the slaves consist? At the Hampton Roads conference, Alexander Stephens asked Lincoln what the freedmen would do, without education or property. Lincoln's answer: "Root, hog, or die."[18] Not the slightest recognition of the immense social crisis presented to American society by millions of freedmen. The staple agriculture of the South, the livelihood of the blacks as well as the whites, was destroyed. While the federal government had millions of acres of land in the West to give away to corporations and foreigners, there was none for the ex-slaves. That would have brought the blacks into Northern territory. Let them stay in the South, give them the vote to sustain the Republican party, and organize them to keep down Southern whites. This was the sum total of the Republican freeing of the slaves.

In fact, social statistics indicate that the black people were in many respects worse off in 1900 than they had been under slavery—in work skills, family stability, health and mortality, crime.[19] Our brilliant pundits have, curiously, blamed the Southern antebellum regime for all the current problems of Northern cities. But in fact, the further away from the plantation we get in both time and space, the worse the problems become. Not slavery, but the way it was ended are to blame.

We have only scratched the surface of the damage done to the Old Republic in the winning of the war. It saw our first government propagandizing of the citizens. Then there were the soldiers' pensions. Pensions under the old Union had been regarded as a reward for the disabled and the extremely meritorious. After the war this was turned into a vast entitlement for anyone who had

[18]Alexander H. Stephens, *A Constitutional View of the Late War between the States* (Philadelphia: National Publishing, 1870), 2, p. 615. "Root, hog, or die," was the refrain of a popular minstrel tune. On April 16, 1863, Lincoln wrote on a War Department document, in regard to the blacks, "They had better be set to digging their subsistence out of the ground." Cited in *Freedom: A Documentary History of Emancipation,* Ira Berlin, et al., eds. (Cambridge: Cambridge University Press, 1987), 1, p. 306.

[19]C. Vann Woodward, *Origins of the New South, 1877–1913* (Baton Rouge: Louisiana State University Press, 1951), pp. 205–21, 360–68.

ever worn the blue uniform for five minutes—the first of the great entitlement programs. And, of course, there was the 14th Amendment—illegally adopted and a source of endless mischief.

Our greatest constitutional historian, Forrest McDonald, has recently called our attention once again to the fraud and coercion in the adoption of the 14th Amendment. But the problem was not conferring basic citizenship rights on the freedman, which was necessary and inevitable, but the debasement of the concept of citizenship that ensued. Citizenship had been a state matter, subject only to the federal power of uniform rules of naturalization. Immigrants became citizens by being accepted into existing communities as members in good standing. The wholesale granting of citizenship by the federal government, not only to the freedmen but to the vast numbers of Irish and Germans who filled up the ranks of the Union armies, rendered citizenship a federal entitlement rather than an earned privilege and led us to the present situation where the government forces vast numbers of immigrants on American communities whether they want them or need them.

Did the war leave America a full-fledged Empire? No, but not from lack of trying. Reconstruction was ended, finally, by Northern exhaustion and Southern resistance.[20] The courts, not then completely corrupted, invalidated many of the acts of the Lincoln government. It was after the fact, but at least kept them from being repeated for a time. The fabric of self-government was too strong in the American people to be destroyed all at once in normal times. But all the precedents were set—the precedents that the Progressives were able to adopt in the following decades, culminating in our intervention into World War I in Europe, a purely Lincolnian exercise.

One of our greatest artists summed up the costs of the war for the Union. The thoughtful Northerner Herman Melville, in the midst of the conflict, wrote:

> Power unannointed may come—
> Dominion unsought by the free
> . . .
> The Founders' dream shall flee.[21]

[20]A great deal of historiographical effort has been devoted in the last three decades to redeeming the besmirched reputation of Reconstruction, a hopeless task for any but the blindest ideologues. There is no question that the carpetbagger regimes were made up of criminals and opportunists who did not have even the respect of decent Northerners, who looted, and who betrayed the black people they had supposedly come to help. Reconstruction certainly involved corruption, lawlessness, tyranny, and a deceitful violation of the terms under which Lee and Johnston had laid down their arms.

[21]Herman Melville, "The House-top: A Night Piece (July 1863)," in *Battle-Pieces and Aspects of the War* (Amherst: University of Massachusetts Press, 1972).

The Republican Party victory was a Jacobin Revolution. What are the signs of Jacobinism? A power grab by a minority leading to a centralized state, an egalitarian ideology masking the will to power of one-party rule, a great transfer of wealth, a ruthless disregard for tradition and law, an overturning of organic social relations, a tendency toward a totalitarian state. The revolution was not perfected because 19th-century America did not have the instruments for totalitarianism, but it was not from lack of trying.

So I suggest that we are living with a tainted inheritance. If our desire is to restore the principle of liberty as it was originally understood by Americans, if that is possible, we need to rid ourselves, intellectually and morally, of the superstitions of unionism and emancipation which are the fountain of all the other statist superstitions and all the other statist usurpations from which we have suffered and by which we have been cursed in this century. It seems a very unlikely thing to happen, I admit, although recently the French people celebrated their Revolution and a great many of them rethought the heritage of Jacobinism which they had been taught was a great tradition. There was a real revulsion of opinion about that, rejection of what had been regarded as a great accomplishment. Americans will have to do no less if they wish to recover genuine self-government.

8

THE SPANISH–AMERICAN WAR AS TRIAL RUN, OR EMPIRE AS ITS OWN JUSTIFICATION

Joseph R. Stromberg

Viewed through the dim mists of time, the Spanish–American War seems an unqualified success story. It was a popular war, a war to liberate the Cuban people from the oppression of wicked Spanish feudalists; it seemed a morally supportable war. In addition, it was brief and cheap—especially in terms of casualties. At the end of the conflict, John Hay, U.S. Ambassador to Great Britain, wrote, "It has been a splendid little war; begun with the highest motives, carried on with magnificent intelligence and spirit, favored by that fortune which loves the brave."[1]

Historians have tended to treat the war as a sort of youthful fling, a lost weekend of American history, the last war of a more innocent age. As a result, the war is sometimes denied its full historical significance and treated as the "great aberration" of American diplomatic and military history. The war's bloody sequel, the savage counterinsurgency campaign necessary to secure U.S. colonial power in the Philippines, disappeared into an Orwellian memory hole not to be heard from again until the war in Vietnam, to which it bore a certain resemblance.

This aberrationist approach has done the Spanish–American War grave injustice, for the war was less an exception than the beginning of a new, active, interventionist foreign policy to which succeeding American governments have shown continuing fealty. It was what Theodore Roosevelt and his cohorts called the "large policy." Set against the economic distress and political discontent of the 1890s—the national "psychic crisis" of which Richard Hofstadter wrote[2]—the war was a stunning success: first in terms of U.S. policymakers' goals in Asia and the Caribbean, and second as a distraction from American domestic affairs.

The war created an independent Cuban Republic—which was subject, of course, to American intervention under the Platt Amendment—and brought to an inglorious end the long career of the

---

[1]Walter Millis, *The Martial Spirit* (Boston: Literary Guild of America, 1931), p. 340.

[2]Richard Hofstadter, "Depression and Psychic Crisis," in *American Expansion in the Late Nineteenth Century: Colonialist or Anticolonialist?*, J. Rogers Hollingsworth, ed. (New York: Holt, Rinehart and Winston, 1968), pp. 25–28.

Spanish Empire. With Spanish cession to the victors of Puerto Rico, Guam, and the Philippine Islands, the United States consolidated its power in the western hemisphere and gained a forward position in Asia. This was especially important to those who saw the Chinese markets as America's economic destiny.

The war had important consequences for American government and society. The logistical failures of the war revealed weaknesses in U.S. military organization whose reform was soon undertaken. The war also had a "unifying" aspect to which I will return later. Acquisition of the Philippines—complicated by the resistance of Filipino patriots led by Emilio Aguinaldo—unleashed a national debate over the "large policy" itself.

At a less cosmic level, the war contributed to American folklore and legend. New heroes, sayings, and ideas entered American life. The romance of the tropics—tempered somewhat by the notion that white people tend to deteriorate when deprived of the challenge of a Teutonic winter—combined with the unreflecting sense of innate superiority of Anglo-Saxons in the popular appreciation of the war. Finally, this was America's last war fought without conscription, a fact that may have contributed subtly to the war's happy aura.

The war was, however, a departure. Up to 1898 most Americans had been happy with continental "isolation." An empire of contiguous land had come into being over the objections of separatist elements (Confederates, Mormons, Indians). To most Americans this process merely extended the area of republican liberty and self-government. The Northwest Ordinances had symbolized the American experience with colonization. The territories brought into political being were next door to existing communities, and unassimilable elements (as they were regarded at the time) did not participate. Republican government had indeed followed Americans across a moving land frontier and appeared entirely compatible with continental expansion.

Overseas, or "saltwater," imperialism as practised by the major European powers was another matter. Americans had not yet governed foreign subject peoples across an ocean. Up to 1898 they could view their career of Indian wars, annexations, and gargantuan real–estate deals as consistent with the ideals of self-government, republicanism, and even anti-colonialism. In their eyes, at least, the Monroe Doctrine was an anti-colonial and anti-imperialist document.[3]

---

[3]On the career of the Monroe Doctrine, see Dexter Perkins, *A History of the Monroe Doctrine* (Boston: Little, Brown, 1941). For an even more caustic treatment see T. D.

THE EXPANSIONIST FORMULA

To all intents, then, most Americans were satisfied with their continental domain at the end of the 19th century. Many of them (perhaps most) eschewed and even condemned the overseas imperialism of the British, French, Spanish, and Belgians. So little interest was there in overseas expansion that the U.S. army virtually demobilized following the War for Southern Independence, save for the blue-clad cavalry still subduing America's "internal dependent nations" west of the Mississippi. In 1867 Secretary of State William Seward was barely able to pry money out of Congress for the purchase of Russian Alaska. Despite the apparent satisfaction of the American majority, an active minority began by the 1880s to preach and agitate for an expanded U.S. world role. They naturally argued as well for the military spending necessary to make such a policy effective. Politicians, professors, clergymen, publicists and other would-be statesmen cried up a New Manifest Destiny of American world power.

Already in the second Cleveland administration Secretary of State Richard Olney gave the Monroe Doctrine a new emphasis when he said, "Today, the United States is practically sovereign on this continent, and its fiat is law upon the subjects to which it confines its interposition."[4] But the New Manifest Destiny was broader and more ambitious than renewed pursuit of U.S. dominance in the western hemisphere. Several themes emerged as the expansionists presented their case.

One of these was, of course, destiny itself. Captain Alfred Thayer Mahan (United States Navy), navalist and influential author,[5] wrote in 1890, "Whether they like it or not, Americans must now look outward. The growing production of the country demands it. An increasing volume of public sentiment demands it."[6]

Four years later, Senator Henry Cabot Lodge of Massachusetts, an ardent imperialist and close friend of Theodore Roosevelt, suggested in the *Forum* that success was its own justification:

Allman, *Unmanifest Destiny: Mayhem and Illusion in American Foreign Policy* (Garden City, N.Y.: Doubleday, 1984), esp. pp. 98–160.

[4]Quoted in Philip S. Foner, *The Spanish–Cuban–American War and the Birth of American Imperialism [1895–1898]* (New York: Monthly Review, 1972), 1, p. 154.

[5]Alfred Thayer Mahan, *The Influence of Sea Power upon History, 1660–1783* (New York: Hill and Wang, [1890] 1957).

[6]Alfred Thayer Mahan, "The United States Looking Outward," *Atlantic Monthly* 66 (December 1890), as reprinted in *Builders of American Institutions: Readings in United States History*, Frank Freidel and Norman Pollack, eds. (Chicago: Rand McNally, 1963), pp. 368–72; quotation on p. 371.

We have a record of conquest, colonization and expansion unequaled by any people in the Nineteenth Century. We are not to be curbed now by the doctrines of the Manchester School, which . . . as an importation are even more absurdly out of place than in their native land.[7]

In 1898, Brooks Adams, brother of Henry and a leading light of the expansionist *literati*, gave in to some sort of alliterative instinct (in a passage awaiting deconstruction, no doubt):

It is in vain that men talk of keeping free from entanglements. Nature is omnipotent; and nations must float with the tide. Whither the exchanges flow, they must follow; and they will follow as long as their vitality endures.[8]

Although a torrent of rhetoric about destiny was filling the air, a few scoffed at the whole thing. Morrison Swift commented that "Never was such a scurvy thing as this destiny running around the universe. Signs should be erected everywhere—Shoot it at sight."[9]

The racial destiny of the Anglo-Saxons, a second theme of the expansionists, ran together with the "civilizing mission" proclaimed as their own by European imperial powers. The Reverend Josiah Strong, bringing a postmillenialist Protestant perspective to bear on the question, asked, "Is there room for reasonable doubt that this race, unless devitalized by alcohol and tobacco, is destined to dispossess many weaker races, assimilate others, and mold the remainder, until, in a very true and important sense, it has Anglo–Saxonized mankind?"[10]

Theodore Roosevelt agreed:

Of course, our whole national history has been one of expansion. . . . That the barbarians recede or are conquered, with the attendant fact that peace follows their retrogression or conquest, is due solely to the power of the mighty civilized races which have not lost the fighting instinct, and which by their expansion are gradually bringing peace into the red wastes where the barbarian peoples of the world hold sway.[11]

A third major theme by which the expansionists stressed was the supposed need for ever-expanding foreign markets for the

[7]Millis, *The Martial Spirit*, p. 27.

[8]Quoted in Albert K. Weinberg, *Manifest Destiny: A Study of Nationalist Expansion in American History* (Chicago: Quadrangle Books, 1963), p. 275.

[9]Ibid, p. 254.

[10]Quoted in *Major Crises in American History*, Merrill D. Peterson and Leonard W. Levy, eds. (New York: Harcourt, Brace and World, 1962), 2, p. 139.

[11]Quoted in Richard Drinnon, *Facing West: The Metaphysics of Indian-Hating and Empire-Building* (New York: New American Library, 1980), p. 232.

American economy. This, in turn, rested in part on the interpretation of American history put forward by Frederick Jackson Turner in July, 1893. With the closing of the contiguous land frontier in the late 19th century, concern shifted to foreign commerce as a new frontier. Turner, Brooks Adams, and other "frontier-expansionist" theorists—as William Appleman Williams calls them[12]—believed that the moving land frontier had been the *key* to America's freedom, republican institutions, and prosperity. As Turner put it in 1896: "For really three centuries the dominant fact of American life has been expansion."[13]

The lesson seemed clear. A substitute frontier *must* be found, or republican institutions would fail and American prosperity would come to a grinding halt. With the "psychic crisis" of the 1890s came a pervasive fear of disorder; after the Panic of 1893 (caused, one might well argue, by *monetary* factors), businessmen and policymakers turned increasingly to the expansion of overseas trade as the solution to America's ills. Foreign markets would be the way out of the supposed dilemma of a frontier-less democracy; they would solve America's supposed problem of overproduction.[14]

World markets—the fabled China market above all—would cure the economic and social crisis which America's *fin de siècle* elites were feeling so acutely. Unfortunately, to guarantee foreign markets to American traders and investors, the military power of the United States would have to be exerted here and there due to certain intractable world realities. This fundamentally *mercantilist* conception of trade, presented as an improvement upon classical-liberal commercial policy, led directly to opening markets by force and keeping them open by force, as necessary, to sustain American prosperity. This led logically to the expansionists' enthusiasm for a modernized U.S. military, especially a modern Navy, if we were to follow in Great Britain's footsteps, or even supplant Britain, as the center of world commercial empire.

A chorus rose calling for overseas trade. Economist Charles A. Conant wrote in 1900:

---

[12]William Appleman Williams, *The Contours of American History* (New York: New Viewpoints, 1973), esp. pp 363–70 and 452–65.

[13]Quoted in Stephen Kern, *The Culture of Time and Space, 1880–1918* (Cambridge, Mass.: Harvard University Press, 1983), pp. 239–40.

[14]See especially William Appleman Williams, *The Tragedy of American Diplomacy* (New York: Dell Publishing, 1962); Walter LaFeber, *The New Empire: An Interpretation of American Expansion, 1860–1898* (Ithaca, N.Y.: Cornell University Press, 1967), esp. pp. 150–96; and Thomas McCormick, *The China Market: America's Quest for Informal Empire, 1893–1901* (Chicago: Quadrangle Books, 1967).

> The United States have actually reached, or are approaching, the economic state where . . . outlets are required outside their own boundaries, in order to prevent business depression, idleness, and suffering at home. Such outlets might be found without the exercise of political and military power, if commercial freedom was the policy of all nations. As such a policy has not been adopted by more than one important power of western Europe, . . . the United States are compelled, by the instinct of self-preservation, to enter, however reluctantly, upon the field of international politics.[15]

Henry Cabot Lodge stated that "For the sake of our commercial supremacy in the Pacific we should control the Hawaiian Islands and maintain our influence in Samoa."[16] In *America's Economic Supremacy* (1900), Brooks Adams wrote: "All the energetic races have been plunged into a contest for the possession of the only markets left open capable of absorbing surplus manufactures, since all are forced to encourage exports to maintain themselves."[17]

The kernel of truth in the expansionists' analysis probably lay in protectionism. Behind America's tariff walls cartelization proceeded apace. The tariffs made possible domestic prices well above world market prices; but to realize lower unit costs manufacturers had to produce larger quantities of goods than could be sold in the home market at those prices. The result was artificially created "surpluses" whose producers wished to sell them overseas at world-market or lower prices. Hence the turn to the political engrossment of overseas markets.[18]

With some expansionists, like Theodore Roosevelt, simple bellicosity co-existed with their reasoned strategic arguments. By the 1890s, a whole generation had grown up on tales of Civil-War

---

[15]Weinberg, *Manifest Destiny*, p. 395.

[16]Millis, *The Martial Spirit*, p. 27.

[17]Quoted in Kern, *The Culture of Time and Space*, p. 240.

[18]On this point see Ludwig von Mises, "Autarky and Its Consequences," in *Money, Method, and the Market Process: Essays by Ludwig von Mises*, Richard M. Ebeling, ed. (Norwell, Mass.: Kluwer Academic Publishers, 1990), pp. 146–49; Ludwig von Mises, *Omnipotent Government* (New Haven, Conn.: Yale University Press, 1944), pp. 69–72; and idem, *Human Action* (Chicago: Henry Regnery, 1966), pp. 364–39. Mises is concerned with the German case in which the government sponsored domestic cartelization to make possible an ambitious *Sozialpolitik*, but observes that export subsidies became necessary to sustain the whole operation. Without discussing any Anglo–Saxon imperialisms, Joseph Schumpeter describes the pattern of "export imperialism" in *Imperialism and Social Classes* (New York: Meridian Books, 1955), pp. 79–80ff. See also William L. Langer, "A Critique of Imperialism," in *American Imperialism in 1898*, Theodore P. Greene, ed. (Boston: D.C. Heath, 1955), pp. 15–16. The drive for legislative rationalization of the U.S. political economy, as described in the works of Gabriel Kolko, Robert H. Wiebe, William Appleman Williams, Murray N. Rothbard, and others, suggests that tariffs alone were insufficient to achieve full cartelization.

heroism and in the shadow of Civil-War heroes still active in national life. This generation had heard the glories of war without witnessing its grim realities, and many were eager for a war of their own. Still others feared domestic social revolution, viewing war, almost any war, as a welcome distraction from internal upheaval. "Marse" Henry Watterson, editor of the Louisville *Courier-Journal*, announced the advent of American empire in these terms:

> From a nation of shopkeepers we become a nation of warriors. We escape the menace and peril of socialism and agrarianism, as England has escaped them, by a policy of colonialism and conquest. From a provincial huddle of petty sovereignties held together by a rope of sand we rise to the dignity and prowess of an imperial republic incomparably greater than Rome. . . . We risk Caesarism, certainly; but even Caesarism is preferable to anarchism. We risk wars; but a man has but one time to die, and either in peace or war, he is not likely to die until his time comes.[19]

Watterson's bombast was an echo of the pro-war rhetoric that was being heard in England, Germany, and France at the turn of the century. Some have suggested that this rhetoric reflected a general cultural malaise which beset western civilization and which took the form of a loud rejection of the "unheroic" economic outlook of the 19th century. Ludwig von Mises rather caustically observed that much of the pseudo-Homeric prattle about the virtues of war came from the pens of weak and neurasthenic individuals like Friedrich Nietzsche. Watterson's very contrast between shopkeepers and warriors reappeared in the title of the 1915 manifesto of German social imperialism, *Haendler und Helden* by Werner Sombart.[20]

TEMPTATIONS AND OPPORTUNITIES

During the same years that the New Manifest Destiny came into being, several developments overseas gave impetus to a more aggressive American world role. The first of these developments was the Hawaiian "revolution" of January 1893 in which a Revolutionary Committee of Safety, which was dominated by American

[19]Leon Wolff, *Little Brown Brother* (Garden City, N.Y.: Doubleday, 1961), pp. 269–70.
[20]On Nietzschean neurasthenia, see Mises, *Human Action*, p. 172. On Sombart and his ilk, see Friedrich A. Hayek, *The Road to Serfdom* (Chicago: University of Chicago Press, 1944), pp. 167–80. For the convergence of social reformers and imperialists in the U.S., Britain, and Europe, which ultimately yielded national socialism, see Arthur A. Ekirch, Jr., *Progressivism in America* (New York: New Viewpoints, 1974); idem, "The Reform Mentality, War, Peace, and the National State: From the Progressives to Vietnam," *Journal of Libertarian Studies* 3, no. 1 (1979): 55–72; and Bernard Semmel, *Imperialism and Social Reform: English Social-Imperial Thought, 1895–1914* (Garden City, N.Y.: Anchor Books, 1968).

businessmen, deposed Queen Liliuokalani. This coup d'etat was made possible by the landing of U.S. marines—an instance, as Walter Millis put it, of the "admirable device of preserving order before it had been endangered."[21] In mid-January President Harrison sent the Senate an annexation treaty, which languished there until 1898. Captain Mahan, meanwhile, was drumming up the naval advantages of owning Hawaii. The incoming Cleveland administration effectively buried the treaty.

Another crisis came in 1894–1895—a dispute between Britain and Venezuela over the Venezuelan boundary with British Guyana. Consistent with the new British policy of cultivating the Americans as possible junior partners in the empire game, Britain submitted the dispute to peaceful arbitration, but not before the naturally belligerent Theodore Roosevelt had called (at least in private) for the tonic of a little bloodshed (and *this* from an ardent Anglophile).

The third crisis was so opportune as to seem made-to-order. In February, 1895, Cuban rebels rose against the colonial rule of the decrepit Spanish Empire. Cubans had rebelled before with little success. From 1868 to 1878, a protracted war (naturally enough called the Ten Years War) ended with Spain still in control of Cuba and with the rebel leaders in exile. Cuba had long been on the agenda of American expansionists, and Americans had long dabbled in Cuban revolutions; the 1895 Cuban revolt was no exception. Moreover, the Cuban revolutionaries were based in the United States—in the Cuban communities in New York, Tampa, Ocala, New Orleans, and Key West. From New York, the Cuban Revolutionary Party, founded there in 1892, sought to coordinate and plan another Cuban revolt under the leadership of such exiles as Jose Marti, romantic nationalist, writer and poet, and General Maximo Gomez, the Junta's chief military leader and a veteran of the Ten Years War.[22]

In March and April 1895, exiled Cuban leaders sailed to Cuba to link up with the insurgents in the field. Within weeks of the landing, Marti was killed in battle. General Gomez adopted a strategy of random destruction of sugar plantations—his slogan was "Blessed be the torch"—designed to completely disrupt the economic life of the island. As war once again engulfed Cuba, Americans were both sympathetic to the rebels and apprehensive about the danger to American lives and property. The American

[21]Millis, *The Martial Spirit*, p. 20.
[22]See generally Louis Perez, Jr., *Cuba: Between Reform and Revolution* (New York: Oxford University Press, 1988).

presidential election of 1896 intervened and brought to power new men who would ultimately deal with the Cuban problem.

Finally, the development from the 1880s of a significant American blue-water navy conditioned the responses and aspirations of U.S. statesmen. Advocates of the "forward" American policy naturally called for the naval forces to make it possible. As presented by Captain Mahan, the case for the enlarged, modern navy was that only with such a force at their command could American leaders secure the foreign markets, raw materials, and even colonies now deemed necessary to U.S. safety and prosperity. Under the administration of Benjamin Harrison, Naval Secretary Benjamin F. Tracy, a firm believer in Mahan's neo-mercantilism, oversaw the building of steam-powered steel battleships to replace the wooden antiques still in service. Tracy enjoyed the support of Lodge and Roosevelt in his efforts (and Roosevelt would later become undersecretary of the navy). In the expansionists' scheme of things, the long-discussed isthmian canal through Nicaragua or Panama would be essential as well to secure and protect American commercial empire.

The scene now shifts to the election of 1896. The 1890s had witnessed serious threats to the two-party system of politics which had prevailed since 1865; the most significant challenge came from populists. According to these partisans of agrarian America, unlimited ("free") coinage of silver would solve the farmers' problems and help U.S. farm exports penetrate foreign markets. (Farmers, too, had come to see overseas trade as the key to U.S. prosperity.[23]) The Depression of 1893 and the violent Pullman strike in the summer of 1894 testified to the existence of politicized discontent. The new rebellion in Cuba presented a serious problem for U.S. leaders as well, a problem well inside America's sphere of influence. Already in February 1896, the Senate Foreign Relations Committee had called on President Cleveland to recognize the Cuban rebels as belligerents under international law. The American press was denouncing the cruelty of Spain's policy of *reconcentracion*, a forerunner of 20th-century concentration camps and strategic hamlets.

Reconcentracion was the attempt of Spanish General Valeriano Weyler y Nicolau—an admirer of William Tecumseh Sherman—to divide the guerrillas from their popular supporters. The U.S. press unceasingly excoriated "Butcher" Weyler for his conduct toward the Cuban people.

---

[23]See William Appleman Williams, *The Roots of the Modern American Empire* (New York: Random House, 1969).

THE EXPANSIONISTS TAKE CHARGE

Against the backdrop of these issues, the Republican Party met in convention in June 1896 at St. Louis, nominating two-term Ohio Governor William McKinley. McKinley's almost self-effacing dullness as a leader made him an enigma even to his contemporaries. Many assumed, given his friendship with industrialist Mark Hanna, that McKinley would simply be a front man for Big Business. Roosevelt's famous remark that McKinley had "no more backbone than a chocolate eclair!"[24] gives credence to the conventional view that yellow journalists and an aroused public pushed a weak and vacillating McKinley into war in 1898.

Some of McKinley's associates saw him more clearly. The celebrated Henry Adams wrote privately that "[t]he major is an uncommonly dangerous politician." John Hay, who would serve as Secretary of State under McKinley and Roosevelt, wrote to Adams in late 1896: "I was more struck than ever by his mask. It is a genuine Italian ecclesiastical face of the 15th century. And there are idiots who think Mark Hanna will run him." Perhaps most perceptive was Elihu Root, who would serve as Secretary of War under McKinley and achieve fame for the administrative reform of the army. According to Root, McKinley "had a way of handling men, so that they thought his ideas were their own." Further: "He was a man of great power, because he was absolutely indifferent to credit. His great desire was 'to get it done.' He cared nothing about the credit, but McKinley *always had his way.*"[25]

The GOP platform of 1896 stressed high tariffs combined with reciprocity treaties to open up export markets. At the same time, it clearly adumbrated the large policy: "The Hawaiian Islands should be controlled by the United States, and no foreign power should be permitted to interfere with them. The Nicaraguan Canal should be built, owned and operated by the United States. And, by the purchase of the Danish Islands, we should secure a much needed Naval station in the West Indies."[26]

The Democratic Party met the next month. The high point of their convention was the famous "Cross of Gold" speech by William Jennings Bryan, a former Nebraska Congressman, whose nomination—it was hoped—would attract disaffected voters away

[24]Thomas A. Bailey, *A Diplomatic History of the American People* (Englewood Cliffs, N.J.: Prentice-Hall, 1974), p. 460.
[25]Walter Karp, *The Politics of War* (New York: Harper and Row, 1979), pp. 69–70; Lewis Gould, *The Presidency of William McKinley* (Lawrence: Regents Press of Kansas, 1980), p. 9.
[26]*Documents of American History,* Henry Steele Commager, ed. (New York: Appleton-Century-Crofts, 1963), 1, p. 624.

from the Populists and into the Democratic fold. Calling for the monetization of silver, the Bryan Democrats entered upon one of the most bitter campaigns in U.S. history. For eastern establishment figures of both parties, the semi-populist Bryan was a dangerous radical to be tarred with the brush of socialism and other foreign ideas. McKinley, easily elected, took office squarely faced with the possibility of war over Cuba.

For an administration committed to neo-mercantilist expansion, the Cuban struggle was both obstacle and opportunity. First, there were the threats to American investments and lives in Cuba. These required pacification, and cooperation with Spain would not have been out of the question. But U.S. popular opinion favored the Cuban rebels' cause. A war to liberate Cuba and put it under American protection would be popular and would further consolidate U.S. dominance in the Caribbean. Interestingly, the Northeastern business community, many of whom were hard-money ("gold bug") Democrats, opposed war over Cuba up to the last possible moment, causing Roosevelt to shout at Hanna that "[w]e will have this war for the freedom of Cuba in spite of the timidity of the commercial interests."[27]

In Congress, ardent expansionists and spread-eagle imperialists expatiated on the themes of America's duty to drive non-republican regimes from the hemisphere alongside America's selfless concern for the freedom of the Cuban people. The press kept up a constant barrage of sensationalist stories. The Cuban revolutionary junta in America, knowing that only U.S. intervention could guarantee Cuban independence, adroitly exploited American popular feeling in favor of the underdogs and against the arrogant, haughty Spanish.

For the administration, the constant agitation of the Cuban matter in Congress and the press was becoming a distraction from bigger issues. These statesmen, after all, were committed to an integrated neo-mercantilist program to extend American commerce *as a political-economic system*. On this scheme, the markets of China, Pacific coaling stations on the way to Asian markets, and an isthmian canal in Central America loomed much larger than existing investments in Cuba. As historian William Appleman Williams has suggested, the administration ultimately put itself in charge of events in Cuba precisely so it could go on to the more important goals of the large policy. At the same time, U.S. policymakers could anticipate that war with Spain would lead to Spain's cession of its Pacific possessions to the United States, which would neatly

[27]Wolff, *Little Brown Brother*, p. 41.

put America's new commercial frontiers well into Asia. Theodore Roosevelt, now serving as Assistant Secretary of the Navy, was especially aware of the Asian dimension of the Cuban crisis.

MANEUVERING THE SPANIARDS

In May, 1897, McKinley requested from Congress $50 million for the relief of American citizens in Cuba. In June, he resubmitted the Hawaiian annexation treaty. By now the administration had taken to lecturing Madrid on the injury to U.S. interests and ideals which continued disorder in Cuba was inflicting. Caught in a Cuban impasse, Spain probably recalled that the U.S. seizure of Florida in 1819 had rested on the "derelict province" argument, i.e., that if Spain could not govern a territory contiguous to the United States, American intervention was rightful to restore peace and order. A new Liberal ministry in Spain, in power from October 4, sought to conciliate the Cuban rebels and the United States. The new ministers offered Cuban autonomy short of independence and recalled "Butcher" Weyler. The Spanish government called on the United States to restrict the activities of the pro-Cubans on its soil.

Partly in response to the alarmist reports of Fitzhugh Lee, a former Confederate officer and U.S. consul at Havana, about imperiled Americans in Cuba, the administration dispatched the battleship *Maine* to Key West, sending her on to Havana to keep up pressure on the Spanish authorities. The *Maine* arrived in Havana on January 25, 1898, on an ostensibly friendly visit. After the *Maine* arrived, two unexpected events made war more likely. The first was a diplomatic incident: the Spanish minister in Washington, Enrique DeLôme, wrote a private letter critical of McKinley (calling him "weak and a bidder for the admiration of the crowd").[28] Cuban revolutionary agents stole the letter, which soon appeared in nearly every American newspaper. DeLôme was recalled by his government. On February 15, 1898, even before the furor over DeLôme had died down, the *Maine* exploded in Havana harbor with the loss of 260 American lives. U.S. outrage was immediate, with the jingo press flatly blaming Spain. A U.S. naval board concluded in March that persons unknown had planted a submarine mine to destroy the *Maine*. A Spanish naval board blamed spontaneous combustion. (The most recent investigation, completed in 1976, substantially confirmed the Spanish theory.[29]) The American

[28]DeLôme Letter in Commager, *Documents of American History*, 1, p. 632.

[29]Results of U.S. naval enquiry led by Admiral Hyman Rickover as reported in G.J.A. O'Toole, *The Spanish War: An American Epic–1898* (New York: W.W. Norton, 1984), p. 400.

public blamed Spain and the slogan "Remember the *Maine!*" became the rallying cry of the war party.

The events of 1898 kept pace behind the scenes as well. On February 25, with Secretary of the Navy John D. Long out of the office for a day, his assistant, the inimitable Roosevelt, cabled Commodore George Dewey to get ready to engage the Spanish navy in the Pacific. Roosevelt had handpicked Dewey back in October and ordered him to Asia to command America's Pacific fleet.[30] By now, the rush to war was well advanced. On March 17 Senator Redfield Proctor of Vermont rose to report on his mission to Cuba. He stated that "It is practically the entire Cuban population on one side and the Spanish army and Spanish citizens on the other." He said that half of the *reconcentrados* had died of malnutrition or disease with more deaths expected, and he called for prompt American action.[31]

A SPLENDID WAR

On March 26, 1898, the U.S. government demanded, in effect, that Spain negotiate with the Cubans with a view to Cuban independence. While that would have been too much for Spanish pride, Spain agreed on March 31 to end *reconcentracion* and make a truce with the Cuban insurgents. In a manner that would become characteristic of American diplomacy (compare, for example, the Bush administration's mysteriously self-sabotaged talks with the Iraqis in the count-down to Desert Storm) these concessions were no longer enough for the U.S. On April 11, McKinley asked Congress "to empower the President to take measures to secure a full and final termination of hostilities between the Government of Spain and the people of Cuba" including military force.[32]

Congress responded with a four-point joint declaration on April 19. It called for Cuban independence, and Spanish withdrawal from Cuba, and authorized the President to use the armed forces to implement these goals. The fourth point, the Teller Amendment (named for Senator Henry M. Teller of Colorado), declared that the United States did not want sovereignty over Cuba and promised "to leave the government and control of the island to its people."[33] Spain recalled its ambassador. McKinley called for volunteers. On April 24, Naval Secretary Long cabled Dewey to

[30]Millis, *The Martial Spirit*, pp. 85–87, 112.
[31]See speech in Peterson and Levy, *Major Crises*, 2, pp. 174–76.
[32]*Sources in American Diplomacy*, Armin Rappaport, ed. (New York: Macmillan, 1966), p. 135.
[33]Joint declaration quoted in Peterson and Levy, *Major Crises*, pp. 191–92.

commence operations in the Pacific. A Declaration of War by Congress on April 25 began America's advance to empire.

The outbreak of war found the American military establishment unprepared for even a minor campaign. The difficulties encountered on the Cuban front take on an almost comic-opera aspect in today's perspective; at the time, things were not so amusing. Nonetheless, Peter Finley Dunne's Mr. Dooley remarked that the U.S. fought the war in a dream, but fortunately the Spaniards had been in a trance.[34]

While matters proceeded apace on the Asian front, the Caribbean theater suffered from many tribulations. There was the matter of logistics. Overseas invasions were not at this time an American *forte* (or habit). Chaos and confusion attended the massing of men and materiel at Port Tampa, the debarkation site for Cuba. The logistical problems that plagued the army at Tampa continued aboard ship and all through the land campaign in Cuba. War Secretary Russell A. Alger observed that "[t]he army had not been mobilized since the Civil War."[35] There were far too many volunteers to process; McKinley had asked for 25,000 men—a million presented themselves. In addition, Congress authorized special volunteer units, such as the famous Rough Riders (the only special unit that actually served).

As the army began its fitful mobilization and men and supplies piled up at Port Tampa, waiting on a strategy, the naval war got under way. The U.S. North Atlantic Squadron had blockaded Cuba since April 22, and in the Far East, the U.S. Asiatic Squadron under Dewey had sailed from Hong Kong on April 25. Dewey's one-sided defeat of the Spanish fleet at Manila on May 1 came before the first American soldier landed in Cuba. Spanish naval forces in Cuba fatalistically accepted their inevitable defeat at the hands of the aggressive Yankees. Meanwhile, uncertainty as to the location of the Spanish fleet helped delay departure of the U.S. invasion forces from Florida.

On June 22, 1898, 6,000 U.S. soldiers landed in Cuba at Daiquiri, led by 300-pound General Rufus Shafter. First blood was drawn by the Americans at Las Guasimas near Siboney. Seeing the Spaniards in retreat, General "Fighting Joe" Wheeler, an ex-Confederate brigadier, forgot himself and shouted, "we've got the damn' Yankees on the run!"[36] (Wheeler himself laughed about the

[34] As paraphrased by T. Harry Williams, *Americans at War* (New York: Collier Books, 1962), p. 105.

[35] O'Toole, *The Spanish War*, p. 230.

[36] Quoted in Page Smith, *The Rise of Industrial America* (New York: MacGraw-Hill, 1984), p. 875.

incident later.) The main American objective was the city of Santiago with its fortifications and port. Between the U.S. forces and their goal lay the San Juan Hills and the small Spanish fortress at El Caney. With the arrival of 4,000 more U.S. troops on June 26, the American commanders decided to attack El Caney and the San Juan Hills simultaneously. The Cuban rainy season was almost due and, with it, yellow fever and malaria. Shafter was well aware of the toll tropical disease had taken on the British forces in a similar campaign in 1762.

The attacks, launched on July 1, cost some 1,000 U.S. wounded. At San Juan the heights were finally taken in the famous frontal assaults undertaken by the Negro 9th Cavalry, the Negro 10th Cavalry (whose white officer was Lt. John J. Pershing), some of the 1st Cavalry, and of course Teddy Roosevelt and the Rough Riders (who actually took Kettle Hill as it came to be known). Interestingly, many of the black soldiers at San Juan Hill were veterans of the last Indian wars, the so-called Buffalo Soldiers.

On July 3, 1898, Admiral Cervera attempted to run the U.S. blockade and leave Santiago harbor. The Spanish fleet was completely destroyed, with 323 Spanish deaths as against one U.S. death. U.S. commanders now undertook to negotiate with the Spanish for the surrender of Santiago. The U.S. generals sought a face-saving surrender for the enemy, while Secretary Alger, reasonably safe in Washington, D.C., breathed fire about "unconditional surrender."[37] The surrender took place on July 17, effectively ending the war in Cuba. Shafter excluded the rebel Cuban generals, showing that Cuban independence was an American operation. The Cubans, to be sure, as guerrilla warriors, had contributed little to the campaign.

Halfway across the world, the initial American success was even more stunning. Admiral Dewey's forces met and destroyed the antiquated Spanish fleet at Manila on May 1. Again the death toll was uneven: Spain 400, U.S. 0. Like Roosevelt, Dewey became one of the popular heroes of the war. His words to the commander of the *Olympia*, "You may fire when you are ready, Gridley," were quoted often.

For the next several months, Dewey's squadron kept up the blockade of Manila, while American soldiers arrived for a combined operation against the city itself. It was assumed that the Filipino insurgent forces—whose revolt, begun in 1896, had been on hold until America went to war with Spain—would be of importance to the success of the campaign. These forces had occupied

[37]O'Toole, *The Spanish War*, p. 346.

the surrounding province of Cavite and were placed all around Manila. Relations between the Americans and Filipinos were already a problem.

When word of war between the United States and Spain reached the exiled Filipino rebel leaders at Hong Kong, they issued an optimistic appeal to their countrymen:

> Compatriots! Divine Providence is about to place independence within our reach, and in a way the most free and independent nation could hardly wish for. The Americans, not from mercenary motives, but for the sake of humanity and the lamentations of so many persecuted people, have considered it opportune to extend their protecting mantle to our beloved country.[38]

But that was in April of 1898. In the first burst of enthusiasm, Commodore Dewey brought Emilio Aguinaldo, the chief rebel commander, and his associates from Hong Kong to Manila with him. By June 16, Secretary of State William R. Day was having misgivings:

> To obtain the unconditional personal assistance of General Aguinaldo . . . was proper, if in so doing he was not induced to form hopes which it might not be practicable to gratify. This Government has known the Philippine insurgents only as discontented and rebellious subjects of Spain, and is not acquainted with their purposes. . . . The United States, in entering upon the occupation of the islands as a result of military operations in that quarter, will do so in the exercise of the rights which the state of war confers, and will expect from the inhabitants . . . that obedience which will be lawfully due from them.[39]

None of this boded well for future Philippine–American cooperation. With only 10,000 or so American soldiers to take on 20,000 Spaniards, the 14,000 insurgents under Aguinaldo were a necessary evil for the time being. When the Battle of Manila finally came on August 13, 1898, it was largely a sham, an orchestrated performance designed to save face for the Spanish officers at a minimal cost to both sides. After the surrender, the Americans and Filipinos eyed one another warily from their completely separate positions.

As the Philippine events played themselves out, other pieces had fallen together in the expansionists' jigsaw puzzle. On June 20, American forces occupied Guam in the Ladrones (now the Marianas). The Hawaiian annexation treaty was dusted off and presented as a war measure. The *Cincinnati Enquirer* editorialized that

---

[38]Millis, *The Martial Spirit*, p. 183.
[39]Ibid., p. 252.

"there suddenly comes upon us the necessity for a half-way station to the Philippine Islands. A scheme of empire has come upon the country in spite of our extraordinary conservatism. Opposition to the annexation of the Hawaiian group is merely another fight against destiny."[40] In due course Congress annexed Hawaii by joint resolution.

As for the Battle of Manila, it—like the Battle of New Orleans in 1814—had been unnecessary. America and Spain had signed a protocol ending the hostilities the day before, on August 12. The war was over. As Ambassador Hay wrote Roosevelt, it had indeed been "a splendid little war" with many interesting and amusing episodes. Lt. Andrew S. Rowan's intelligence mission early in the Cuban campaign became the basis of Elbert Hubbard's famous short story "The Message to Garcia." In those days of rudimentary intelligence activities and few covert actions, it is interesting that the Cuban telegraph clerk working for the Spanish Governor General in Havana was dutifully relaying summaries of Madrid's communiques to Key West, thence to the White House. With a view to the future Anglo–Saxon détente, British foreign service officers quietly aided American intelligence throughout the crisis and war with Spain.

The war had lasted a grand total of 113 days. Three hundred and sixty-nine American soldiers, 10 sailors and 6 marines had died in battle. Some 2,000 others perished variously from tropical diseases or the food provided the army. As wars go, this was pretty inexpensive. It remained to be seen what America had gained.

CLAIMING THE SPOILS LEADS TO A COUNTERINSURGENCY

At the end of July, the McKinley administration proposed the independence of Cuba and the cession of Puerto Rico and Manila to the United States as the basis of peace with Spain. For the Spanish, the sticking point was in the Philippines. After the August 12 protocol ended the fighting, U.S. demands escalated. President McKinley wrote to his peace commissioners on September 16, "[T]he United States cannot accept less than the cession in full right and sovereignty of the island of Luzon."[41]

In November, McKinley raised the ante, telling his negotiators, "We are clearly entitled to indemnity to the cost of the war. . . . It

[40]Weinberg, *Manifest Destiny*, p. 263.
[41]Rappaport, *Sources in American Diplomacy*, p. 138.

would probably be difficult for Spain to pay money. All she has are the . . . Philippines and the Carolinas."[42]

McKinley later explained his changing positions on the Philippines to a delegation of Methodist clergymen:

> I walked the floor of the White House night after night until midnight; and I am not ashamed to tell you, gentlemen, that I went down on my knees and prayed Almighty God for light and guidance. . . . And one night late it came to me this way. . . . (1) That we could not give them back to Spain—that would be cowardly and dishonorable; (2) that we could not turn them over to France or Germany—our commercial rivals in the Orient—that would be bad business and discreditable; (3) that we could not leave them to themselves—they were unfit for self-government—and they would soon have anarchy and misrule over there worse than Spain's was; and (4) that there was nothing left for us to do but take them all and educate the Filipinos, and uplift and Christianize them, and by God's grace do the very best we could by them, as our fellowmen for whom Christ also died.[43]

Whether the largely Roman Catholic Filipinos were in quite the need of Christianizing that McKinley suggested, cession of the island chain became a firm U.S. demand. The final agreement met all the American specifications. By the Treaty of Paris, signed on December 10, 1898, Spain relinquished sovereignty over Cuba, ceded to the United States Puerto Rico, Guam, and the Philippine Islands. The U.S. would pay Spain $20 million. The United States was now a colonialist power in the full salt-water imperialist sense of the term, poised to engross the markets of Asia, barring unforeseen developments.

One such development of immediate consequence was the unexpected determination of the Filipino insurgents and populace not to exchange their Spanish overlords for new American ones. On February 4, 1899, the uneasy truce between the American forces and the Filipino rebels gave way to actual fighting. From then until July 4, 1902—and later in some outlying islands—the United States government waged a colonial war whose "marked severities" eventually surpassed those of the Spanish in Cuba. This war—officially known by the somewhat inappropriate title of the Philippine Insurrection—served to intensify the domestic debate in America over the whole policy of expansion.

As hostilities began, Aguinaldo announced: "My nation cannot remain indifferent in view of such a violent and aggressive seizure

[42]Frederick Merk, *Manifest Destiny and Mission in American History* (New York: Vintage Books, 1963), p. 253.

[43]Bailey, *A Diplomatic History of the American People*, pp. 473–74.

of a portion of its territory by a nation which has arrogated to itself the title: champion of oppressed nations. Thus it is that my government is disposed to open hostilities if the American troops attempt to take forcible possession. Upon their heads will be all the blood which may be shed."[44]

Early in the war, Rounceville Wildman, American Consul at Hong Kong, had warned the State Department:

> I wish to put myself on record as stating that the insurgent government of the Philippine Islands cannot be dealt with as though they were North American Indians, willing to be removed from one reservation to another at the whim of their masters. . . . The attempt of any foreign nation to obtain territory or coaling stations will be resisted with the same spirit with which they fought the Spaniards.[45]

Unfortunately, the American authorities did choose to view the Philippine insurgents as though they were North American Indians. Their previous experience with counterinsurgency warfare, after all, had been the wars against tribal peoples at home; these wars offered the nearest analogy to the Philippine insurgency. General Ewell S. Otis, as well as other American officers and fighting men in the Philippines, was a veteran of the late 19th-century Indian wars. The ingrained racism of the white officers and men came to the fore in fighting the Filipinos, who were called "niggers," "goo-goos," and other unflattering names. One American Negro soldier, David Fagen, defected and became a captain with the Filipino insurgents; a price was put on his head.

Like any colonial war where the occupying forces can no longer distinguish friend from foe and "good natives" from the guerrillas who pop up at night to raid and harass, this war soon became one against the general Philippine population. "There are no more amigos," said the rank-and-file American troops, who came to regard all Filipinos as enemies. Soon the very policy of reconcentration, which had been so evil when practised by General Weyler in Cuba, was instituted and was the basis of American success. General J. Franklin Bell had his officers in Batangas province inform the people "of the danger of remaining outside these limits, and that unless they move by December 25 from outlying barrios and districts with all their movable food supplies, including rice, palany, chicken, live stock, etc., to within the limits of the zone established at their own or nearest town, their property (found outside of said zone at said date) will become liable to confiscation and destruction."[46]

[44]O'Toole, The Spanish War, p. 388.
[45]Wolff, Little Brown Brother, p. 112.
[46]O'Toole, The Spanish War, p. 395.

In a letter to the pro-administration *Philadelphia Ledger* on November 11, 1901, an American officer admitted that "Our men have been relentless, have killed to exterminate men, women, and children, prisoners and captives, active insurgents and suspected people, from lads of ten up, an idea prevailing that the Filipino was little better than a dog."

Another officer who had served in the Philippine War wrote to a reporter: "There is no use in mincing words. . . . If we decide to stay, we must bury all qualms and scruples about Weylerian cruelty, the consent of the governed, etc., and stay. We exterminated the American Indians, and I guess most of us are proud of it, or, at least, believe the end justified the means; and we must have no scruples about exterminating this other race standing in the way of progress and enlightenment, if it is necessary."[47]

As of July 4, 1902, the official end of the Philippine–American War (by mere arbitrary proclamation of Theodore Roosevelt), 4,200 Americans were dead, as were 20,000 insurgents. In addition, 200,000 Filipinos, possibly more, had died of malnutrition, disease, and other results of the war (e.g., massacres and burial in mass graves). U.S. forces destroyed property and put villages to the torch. Brigadier General J. Franklin Bell "compared such tactics to those of General Sherman in Georgia during the War Between the States." This put the U.S. in the same league as the wicked feudal–absolutist Spaniards in Cuba, where even by official Spanish estimates some 400,000 Cuban civilians died in the "reconcentration" camps.[48]

Mr. Dooley explained the water torture to Henessy:

> A Filipino . . . nivver heerd iv th' histhry of this counthry. He is met be wan iv our sturdy boys in black an' blue. . . . who asts him to cheer f'r Abraham Lincoln. He rayfuses. He is thin placed upon th' grass an' given a dhrink, a baynit bein' fixed in his mouth so he cannot rejict th' hospitality. Undher th' inflooence iv th' hose that cheers but does not inebriate, he soon warrums or perhaps I might say swells up to a ralization iv th' granjoor iv his adoptive counthry. One gallon makes him give three groans f'r th' constitchoochion. At four gallons, he will ask to be wrapped in th' flag. At th' dew pint he sings Yankee Doodle.[49]

[47]Drinnon, *Facing West*, pp. 314–15.

[48]O'Toole, *The Spanish War*, pp. 57–58; and see generally Stuart Creighton Miller, *Benevolent Assimilation: American Conquest of the Philippines, 1899–1903* (New Haven, Conn.: Yale University Press, 1982), p. 208.

[49]Quoted by Samuel F. Wells, Jr., "The Challenge of Power: American Diplomacy, 1900–1921," in *The Unfinished Century: America Since 1900*, William E. Leuchtenberg, ed. (Boston: Little, Brown, 1973), p. 121.

THE ANTI-IMPERIALIST REACTION

Reports of such practices had helped to bring into being the American Anti-Imperialist League, formed to combat the policies of overseas imperialism and expansion. Ideologically, the anti-imperialists were for the most part consistent classical liberals who believed in *laissez faire*, free-market economics, and the republicanism of the constitution. This led them to oppose the use of government to secure foreign markets, while at the same time they espoused the right of all peoples to self-government. Lenin later derided them as "the last of the Mohicans of bourgeois democracy"—a title they certainly deserve as opponents of empire and neo-mercantilism.[50]

Many—like Boston textile magnate Edward F. Atkinson and former Ohio Senator Carl Schurz—were veterans of the antislavery campaign and other 19th-century liberal causes. Other prominent members of the League were former Secretary of the Treasury George S. Boutwell, industrialist Andrew Carnegie, author Mark Twain, and philosopher William James.

Edward Atkinson, perhaps the most active and radical figure in the League, stirred up a hornet's nest when he mailed anti-war pamphlets to American troops in the Philippines. The War Department denounced this as sedition and seized the material in transit. Some of the press defended Atkinson's right to print and mail his pamphlets.

Possibly due to the overwhelmingly upper-middle-class character of the League, no mass-based anti-imperialist movement was created. Skepticism about overseas empire existed outside the League among old-fashioned Republicans, Democrats, and Populists. But in the election of 1900, the supposedly anti-imperialist Democratic candidate, William Jennings Bryan, handled the issue with little real interest. As a result, the Republican team of President McKinley and his running mate, the ineffable Theodore Roosevelt, won easily on the economic issues. Hence, the race was no mandate for empire, which hardly figured as an issue in the campaign.

Even if Bryan played down the question of empire in 1900, the essential issues were being debated in the press and in Congress with considerable heat. Senator Albert J. Beveridge of Indiana, an

[50]"Imperialism, the Highest Stage of Capitalism" in *Essential Works of Lenin*, Henry M. Christman, ed. (New York: Bantam Books, 1966), p. 255. On the Anti-Imperialist League, see William F. Marina, "Opponents of Empire" (Ph.D. diss., University of Denver, 1968); and Robert L. Beisner, *Twelve Against Empire: The Anti-Imperialists, 1898–1900* (New York: MacGraw-Hill, 1968).

ardent expansionist, tied together all the major arguments for overseas involvement in a remarkable speech in January 1900. Following a "fact-finding mission" to the Philippines, he said:

> Mr. President, the times call for candor. The Philippines are ours forever. . . . And just beyond the Philippines are China's illimitable markets. We will not retreat from either. We will not repudiate our duty in the Orient: We will not renounce our part in the mission of our race, trustee, under God, of civilization of the world. And we will move forward to our work, not howling out regrets like slaves whipped to their burdens, but with gratitude for a task of our strength, . . . henceforth to lead in the regeneration of the world.
>
> But, Senators, it would be better to abandon this combined garden and Gibraltar of the Pacific, and count our blood and treasure already spent a profitable loss, than to apply any academic arrangement of self-government to these children. They are not capable of self-government. How could they be? They are not of a self-governing race. They are Orientals, Malays, instructed by Spaniards in the latters' worst estate.
>
> Mr. President, this question is deeper than any question of party politics. . . . It is elemental. It is racial. God has not been preparing the English-speaking and Teutonic peoples for a thousand years for nothing but vain and idle self-contemplation and self-admiration! No! He has given us the spirit of progress to overwhelm the forces of reaction throughout the earth. He has made us adepts in government that we may administer government among savage and senile peoples. . . . And of all our race He has marked the American people as His chosen nation to finally lead in the regeneration of the world.[51]

This was a hard act to follow, but the strongly anti-imperialist Senator George F. Hoar of Massachusetts rose in reply, saying:

> I could think as this brave young republic of ours listened to what the senator had to say of but one sentence: "And the Devil taketh Him up into an exceeding high mountain and showeth Him all the kingdoms of the world and the glory of them. And the Devil said unto Him, 'All these things will I give thee if thou wilt fall down and worship me.'"[52]

Rudyard Kipling, unofficial poet laureate of British imperialism, entered the fray in 1899 with "The White Man's Burden." The poem lent itself to innumerable parodies by the anti-imperialists. One such effort went as follows: "We've taken up the white man's

[51]Freidel and Pollack, *Builders of American Institutions*, pp. 374–47.

[52]Quoted in John T. Flynn, *As We Go Marching* (Garden City, N.Y.: Doubleday, 1944), p. 219.

burden, Of ebony and brown; Now will you tell us, Rudyard, How we may put it down?"[53] The editor of a black American newspaper opined that it was "a sinful extravagance to waste our civilizing influence upon the unappreciative Filipinos when it is so badly needed right here in Arkansas!"[54]

The Anti-Imperialist League complained that "it has become necessary in the land of Washington and Lincoln to reaffirm that all men, of whatever race or color, are entitled to life, liberty, and the pursuit of happiness. We maintain that governments derive their just powers from the consent of the governed. We insist that the subjugation of any people is 'criminal aggression' and open disloyalty to the distinctive principles of our Government."[55]

Anti-imperialist Moorfield Storey expressed the major concerns of the anti-empire men. Some of the highlights are these:

> The citizen of Porto Rico today has no American citizenship, no constitutional rights, no representation in the legislature which imposes the important taxes that he pays, no voice in the selection of his executive or judicial officers, no effective voice in his own legislature. He is governed by a foreign nation under law which he had no part whatever in framing, and the Republican party offers the island no hope either of independence or of statehood. This is government without the consent of the governed. This is what is meant by "imperialism."[56]

With respect to the Philippines, Storey writes:

> To impose our sway upon them against their will, to conquer a nation of Asiatics by fire and sword, was the abandonment of every principle for which this country had stood. It was "criminal aggression."[57]

The American people were not consulted regarding this momentous change of national policy, nor was Congress, nor were the people of the Philippines.

> It was one man, and that man the President, who insisted upon taking the Philippine Islands against the will of their people, and who, to do it, departed from all the traditions of our country."

---

[53]Wolff, *Little Brown Brother*, p. 271.

[54]Richard O'Connor, *Pacific Destiny* (Boston: Little, Brown, 1969), p. 282.

[55]O'Toole, *The Spanish War*, p. 386.

[56]Moorfield Storey, *Our New Departure* (Boston, 1901), excerpted in *Late Nineteenth-Century American Liberalism: Representative Selections, 1880–1900*, Louis D. Filler, ed. (New York: Bobbs-Merrill, 1962), p. 234.

[57]Ibid., p. 237

And:

> The President alone assumed "that absolute authority over the Philippines" which Secretary Long praised him for refusing.[58]

McKinley, in effect, declared war on a functioning, popular Filipino government before the matter had come before Congress and before effective American sovereignty extended beyond Manila Bay.

The celebrated Mark Twain bitterly satirized western claims that empire advanced the cause of "civilization." Characterizing official accounts of the war in the Philippines as mendacious and the war itself as atrociously cruel, Twain wrote:

> Everything is prosperous, now; everything is just as we should wish it. We have got the Archipelago, and we shall never give it up. Also, we have every reason to hope that we shall have an opportunity before very long to slip out of our congressional contract with Cuba and give her something better in the place of it.[59]

Alluding to the misgivings of some Americans about the Cuban and Philippine affairs, Twain suggested a program of national self-rehabilitation to rid ourselves of such feelings, including a new flag with black stripes replacing the white ones and the skull and crossbones replacing the stars.[60]

The anti-imperialists sometimes used arguments involving race, arguments which would be considered politically incorrect today. In this they followed the accepted wisdom that republican forms of government presupposed representation of ethnically homogeneous regions at the same level of civilization. German-born Carl Schurz brought this inherited idea to bear on the problem of empire under the American form of government:

> The prospect of the consequences which would follow the admission of the Spanish creoles and the negroes of the West India islands and of the Malays and Tagals of the Philippines to participation in the conduct of our government is so alarming that you instinctively pause before taking the step.

Of the Philippines, Schurz said:

> They are . . . situated in the tropics, where people of the northern races, such as Anglo-Saxons, or generally speaking, people of Germanic blood, have never migrated in mass to

[58]Ibid., pp. 238 and 240.
[59]Mark Twain, "To the Person Sitting in Darkness" (1901), in *The Complete Essays of Mark Twain*, Charles Neider, ed. (Garden City, N.Y.: Doubleday, 1963), p. 295–96.
[60]Ibid., p. 296.

stay; and they are more or less densely populated. . . . Their population consisting almost exclusively of races to whom the tropical climate is congenial— . . . Malays, Tagals, Filipinos, Chinese, Japanese, Negritos, and various more or less barbarous tribes.[61]

In the *Arena* of January 1900, Mrs. Jefferson Davis, widow of the Confederate President, wrote in part:

If to have a modest opinion contrary to that of the Administration concerning the Philippines is to be an anti-imperialist—if to see no good reason for adding the Philippines to our possessions is to be an anti-expansionist—then I presume I am both of these. . . . For my own part, however, I cannot see why we should add several millions of negroes to our population when we already have eight millions of negroes in the United States. The problem of how best to govern *these* and promote their welfare we have not yet solved.

She continued:

The question is, What are we going to do with these additional millions of negroes? Civilize them? . . . I see only one solution to the problem. Give the Filipinos the right to govern themselves under certain restrictions, commercial and otherwise, and refuse to burden the United States with fresh millions of foreign negroes whose standards are different and whose language is alien—at least until we have solved the race problem here at home.[62]

Despite the eloquence and occasional bitterness of the anti-imperialists, they never received a full hearing from the American people. The League broke up and only a few die-hards like Storey and Erving Winslow kept up the fight after the first few years of the 1900s; the expansionists had won.[63] A little chastened by the costs of suppressing the Filipinos, they resolved upon the pursuit of informal, rather than colonial, empire. They presented informal empire as mere U.S. support for the broad ideal of the Open Door. The Open Door, however, was not simply *laissez passer*, or free trade, but depended for its success on unrelenting U.S. pressure to make the world safe for U.S. exporters and investors. As Harold Baron wrote, "The free trade concept of developing international

[61]Quoted in Christopher Lasch, "The Anti-Imperialists and the Inequality of Man," in *American Expansion*, Hollingsworth, ed., pp. 93–94.

[62]Mrs. Jefferson Davis, "Why We Do Not Want the Philippines," in *The Anti-Imperialist Reader*, Philip S. Foner and Richard C. Winchester, eds. (New York: Holmes and Meier, 1984), 1, pp. 235–36.

[63]Bailey, *Diplomatic History of the American People*, p. 479, denies that the election of 1900 was fought on the issue of empire; it was *not* a mandate for imperialism. This is probably true, although, as an establishment aberrationist historian, he is interested in playing down imperialism as an American phenomenon generally.

trade had nothing in common with the neo-mercantilist governmental policy that prevailed in the United States."[64] Free trade it
was not, but the course of U.S. foreign policy was now set for the
next century.

CONCRETE COSTS: U.S., PHILIPPINE, AND CUBAN

The immediate costs of the Spanish–American War, what we
might term the concrete costs, were modest by later standards.
American deaths in the war were 2,900, of which only 385 occurred
in battle. There were another 1,662 Americans wounded. The war
cost some $250 million (presumably including the $20 million
given to Spain in the big real-estate deal at the peace settlement).
However, adding the costs of suppressing the Filipinos raises the
price somewhat. In the Philippine Insurrection, American casualties were 4,200 dead and 2,800 wounded. The Philippine war cost
some $600 million to prosecute.[65]

Costs to Filipinos were greater. Fifteen thousand Filipinos died
in combat, while as many as 220,000 Filipino civilians perished
from "gunfire, starvation, and the effects of concentration camps."
As if to prove what I call Stromberg's First Law (which states that
there is virtually no situation anywhere in the world that can't be
made worse by U.S. intervention), American rule in the Philippines
led to massive acquisition of Philippine resources by U.S. companies by political means. U.S. rule reinforced the power of local feudal elements, landlords, and bureaucrat–capitalists. Political instability, dictatorship, and revolutionary outbreaks characterized the
American-trained Philippine nation after independence following
World War II.[66]

The Spanish–American War also imposed costs on the Cuban
people. One was the aborting and derailing of the Cuban Revolution. As Perez puts it, "[t]he intervention changed everything,
as it was meant to. A Cuban war of liberation was transformed into

[64]Harold Baron, "Commentary on John W. Rollins, 'The Anti-Imperialists and
Twentieth Century American Foreign Policy,'" *Studies on the Left* 3, no. 1 (1962): 26.

[65]Walter LaFeber, *The American Age: United States Foreign Policy at Home and Abroad
Since 1750* (New York: W.W. Norton, 1989), pp. 195–96; and T.D. Allman,
Unmanifest Destiny, p. 326.

[66]LaFeber, *The American Age*, p. 202; Allman, *Unmanifest Destiny*, p. 326, says that
220,000 Filipinos perished. On "democracy" as practiced in the Philippine Republic,
see Edgar E. Escultura, "The Roots of Backwardness: An Analysis of the Philippine
Condition," *Science and Society* 38, no. 1 (Spring 1974): 49–76; Benedict Anderson,
"Cacique Democracy in the Philippines: Origins and Dreams," *New Left Review* 169
(May–June 1988): 3–31; and Robert B. Stauffer, "The Political Economy of
Refeudalization" in *Marcos and Martial Law in the Philippines*, David A. Rosenberg,
ed. (Ithaca, N.Y.: Cornell University Press, 1979), pp. 180–218.

a U.S. war of conquest."[67] Revolution and war had devastated the island. Policies of the U.S. military occupation government—especially Civil Order No. 62, which reorganized Cuban landholding practices—brought about a virtual Scottish "clearance" in the countryside, most notably in Oriente province. Civil Order No. 62 eliminated thousands of small landholders as teams of lawyers retained by foreign (mostly U.S.) land syndicates exploited the Order's implementation.

U.S. authorities prevented attempts to establish credit institutions controlled by Cubans. Their chief concern was to oversee transfer of Cuban resources and opportunities to U.S. enterprisers. General Leonard Wood, chief of the occupation, said, "When people ask me what I mean by stable government, I tell them 'money at six percent.'" Perez sums up the outcome:

> The net effects of the production practices before the war, of the destruction caused during the war, and of the practices of the occupation after the war were to facilitate land transfer, foster land concentration, and favor foreign ownership.[68]

The longer-run consequences were sugar monoculture conducted on great latifundia and perpetual political instability complicated by repeated U.S. intervention.

The Americans forced the Cuban Republic to incorporate into its very constitution the Platt Amendment, which allowed U.S. intervention in Cuban affairs at the Americans' discretion. Texas Congressman James L. Slayden commented, on his return from Cuba, that the provision was adopted in the same way that "the citizen yields his purse to the robber who has him covered with a pistol." General Wood wrote to Elihu Root in October 1901 that "with the control which we have over Cuba, a control which will soon undoubtedly become possession, combined with other sugar producing lands which we now own, we shall soon practically control the sugar trade of the world."[69]

American interference in Cuban politics, which continued even after the abrogation of the Platt Amendment in 1934, contributed to instability and a distorted development of the Cuban economy. By preventing Cubans from resolving Cuban problems by revolution in the 1890s and by reform under the Grau San Martin government in 1933–1934, the United States made possible, perhaps

---

[67]Perez, *Cuba*, p. 178.

[68]Louis A. Perez, "Insurrection, Intervention, and the Transformation of Land Tenure Systems in Cuba, 1895–1902," *Hispanic American Historical Review* 65, no. 2 (May 1985): 229–54; Leonard Wood quoted, p. 239.

[69]Foner, *Spanish–Cuban–American War*, 2, pp. 612, 635.

inevitable, the radical revolution captured by Fidel Castro's cadre. Interestingly, Castro's movement found its initial mass base among the *precaristas*, or squatters, displaced marginal farmers descended from those who lost their lands in Oriente at the turn of the century. All of this made possible the 1962 Cuban Missile Crisis.[70] This suggests a corollary to my first Law, namely, the more U.S. interference and "help" a country receives, the bigger the anti-American explosion down the line (e.g., Cuba, the Philippines, Nicaragua, Iran).

COSTS AT HOME I: REUNIFICATION AND THE NEW SOUTH

Before turning to the effects of the Spanish–American War on the United States as a whole, I wish to break with tradition and count as part of the war's costs the reunification of North and South to which the war contributed. President McKinley deliberately used ex-Confederate officers in the war effort. The press, North and South, celebrated the fight against a common foe and, with it, the end of sectional strife.[71]

But Southern co-operation was not assumed. As Donald Davidson put it, the "North, it is true, watched for a moment with bated breath in 1898 to see whether the South would actually be loyal in a time of foreign war."[72] Edward P. Lawton, a Southerner and retired U.S. foreign service officer, commented in 1963 that the nature of the enemy had been crucial: "Had the situation been reversed, had, for instance, England been the enemy in 1898 because of issues of concern chiefly to New England, there is little doubt that large numbers of Southerners would have happily put on their old Confederate uniforms to fight as allies of Britain."[73]

Southerners, for their part, were happy enough to participate and be praised for their participation. Only a small number were to be found in the anti-war and anti-imperialist camp. In this minority we find the remarkable Georgia Jeffersonian–populist politician

[70]See Perez, "Insurrection" and *Cuba*; see also Robert B. Hoernel, "Sugar and Social Change in Oriente, Cuba, 1898–1946," *Journal of Latin American Studies* 8, no. 2 (1976): 215–49. For the analysis of the Castroism as a classically fascist movement with a veneer of Marxist rhetoric, see A. James Gregor, *The Fascist Persuasion in Radical Politics* (Princeton, N.J.: Princeton University Press, 1974), pp. 260–319.

[71]For the conventional view, see Paul H. Buck, *The Road to Reunion* (Boston: Little, Brown, 1937), pp. 304–7. For Northern appreciation of Southern military abilities in the war, see Nina Silber, *The Romance of Reunion: Northerners and the South, 1865–1900* (Chapel Hill: University of North Carolina Press, 1993), pp. 178–85.

[72]Donald Davidson, *Southern Writers in the Modern World* (Athens: University of Georgia Press, 1958), p. 31.

[73]Edward P. Lawton, *The South and the Nation* (Fort Myers Beach, Fla.: Island Press, 1963), p. 15.

and writer Tom Watson, who pointed out that "Republics cannot go into the conquering business and remain republics. Militarism leads to military domination, military despotism."[74]

A few Southerners drew an analogy between the treatment of the Filipinos and that accorded the South 30 years earlier. James H. Berry, Senator for Arkansas, stated that if "the doctrine that 'all just powers of government are derived from the consent of the governed,' was true in 1861, it is true in 1898. . . . I, for one, will never vote to force upon an unwilling people principles and policies against which Lee fought and to protect which Jackson died." Senator Edward W. Carmack of Tennessee said that if U.S. rule in the Philippines was "not ten thousand times better" than carpetbag rule in the South, "may the Lord God have mercy upon the Philippine Islands." One Confederate expatriate, living in Oregon, derided Joe Wheeler and Fitzhugh Lee for "turn[ing] out to help a lot of d----d Yankee jamizaries [*sic*] hunt down other 'rebels' in far off lands—'rebels' not against *us* or *our government*, but against Spain and Russia and The Emperor of China."[75]

The chorus of New South propagandists, however, joined in the general clamor in favor of the war and the large policy. One result, as Davidson writes with evident regret, was that by the next war, "Blue and gray had merged in undistinguished khaki, and we were going to cross the Atlantic Ocean in the first world war of our century to fight an alleged enemy for reasons that we had to take on faith."[76] Richard M. Weaver likewise expressed more than a little doubt about the whole process of national unification and expansion. With clear insight into the logic of the whole process Weaver wrote:

> One cannot feign surprise, therefore, that thirty years after the great struggle to consolidate and unionize American power, the nation embarked on its career of imperialism. The new nationalism enabled Theodore Roosevelt, than whom there was no more staunch advocate of union, to strut and bluster and intimidate our weaker neighbors. Ultimately it launched America upon its career of world imperialism, whose results are now being seen in indefinite military conscription, mountainous debt, restriction of dissent, and other abridgments of classical liberty.[77]

[74]Quoted in C. Vann Woodward, *Tom Watson: Agrarian Rebel* (New York: Oxford University Press, 1979), p. 335.
[75]Gaines M. Foster, *Ghosts of the Confederacy: Defeat, the Lost Cause, and the Emergence of the New South, 1865 to 1913* (New York: Oxford University Press, 1987), pp. 150–52.
[76]Davidson, *Southern Writers in the Modern World*, p. 34.
[77]Richard M. Weaver, "The South and the American Union," in *The Southern Essays of Richard M. Weaver*, George M. Curtis, III, and James J. Thompson, Jr., eds. (Indianapolis, Ind.: Liberty Press, 1987), p. 247. Weaver continues: "And with the

COSTS AT HOME II: THE LARGE COSTS OF THE LARGE POLICY

The splendid little war was indeed a major turning point in American life. Classical liberal sociologist William Graham Sumner wrote in 1900 that "[t]he political history of the United States for the next fifty years will date from the Spanish war of 1898."[78] No longer content to develop their large continental territories, American policymakers took their fellow countrymen into the midst of global imperial competition. The Open Door Notes of 1899 and 1900 proclaimed Americans' right to trade anywhere in the world and pledged U.S. support for the territorial integrity of China. In so doing they paved the way for all manner of future armed conflict and intervention.

Increased American co-operation with the British Empire made sense under these conditions,[79] but embraced the danger of involving the U.S. in wars with Britain's enemies. After the assassination of President McKinley in 1901, his successor, the arch-imperialist Teddy Roosevelt, sought to increase U.S. political and commercial influence in Asia, Latin America, and even the Mediterranean. Roosevelt's "corollary" to the Monroe Doctrine contemplated constant U.S. intervention in its hemisphere to "keep order." Roosevelt's mediation of the Russo–Japanese War helped to establish Japan as a major power—a counterweight to Tsarist Russia—something a later Roosevelt, among others, would one day regret. Roosevelt's support for the Panamanian revolutionaries' secession from Colombia in order to secure an isthmian canal on better terms reflected his aggressive conception of U.S. power and interests (an interesting position for a government unequivocally opposed to secession in 1861).

Theodore Roosevelt's somewhat plodding successor, William Howard Taft, pursued much the same policies. Woodrow Wilson, coming into office in 1912 as a beneficiary of a GOP split, believed firmly in the substitute frontier of foreign markets.[80] In addition, Wilson brought with him a sense of moral rightness that led him to intervene militarily in Mexico, allegedly to teach the Mexicans to elect good men to office. Given the policymakers' determination

---

United States insisting on independence for this and that country halfway around the world . . . it has certainly been handsome of the South not to raise the question of its own independence again" (p. 254).

[78]William Graham Sumner, *War and Other Essays* (New Haven, Conn.: Yale University Press, 1914), p. 337.

[79]Secretary Hay, author of the Open Door Notes, conducted an openly anti-Boer, pro-British foreign policy during the Boer War. See Kenton J. Clymer, *John Hay: The Gentleman as Diplomat* (Ann Arbor: University of Michigan Press, 1975), pp. 158–61.

[80]Williams, *The Tragedy of American Diplomacy*, pp. 61–67.

that America must be an active world power, the outbreak of the European war in 1914 created a dangerous situation. The first decades of the 20th century witnessed U.S. interventions in such places as Nicaragua, Haiti, and Cuba. (The Nicaraguan episode, certainly, deserves to be considered a proto-quagmire, the model for so many other unedifying American overseas adventures in this century.)

In addition to the fairly obvious costs in blood and treasure attendant on an ambitious imperial world role there were, of course, the more subtle, but no less real, institutional, moral, and ideological costs. This, of course, was the central theme of the anti-imperialists. For Sumner, the United States—victorious militarily—had been conquered morally by Spain and had adopted the values of arbitrary rule, militarism, and empire. The original American design had been quite different:

> This confederated state of ours was never planned for indefinite expansion or for an imperial policy. . . . The fathers of the Republic planned a confederation of free and peaceful industrial commonwealths, shielded by their geographical position from the jealousies, rivalries, and traditional policies of the Old World and bringing all the resources of civilization to bear for the happiness of the population only.[81]

The new policy threatened fundamentally to undermine the republican and libertarian foundations of American life:

> The evil of imperialism is in its reaction upon our own national character and institutions, on our political ideas and creed, on our way of managing our public affairs, on our temper in political discussion.[82]

A later republican scholar, Felix Morley, said of the Spanish–American War that

> the deeper result was to make Washington for the first time classifiable as a world capital, governing millions of people as subjects rather than as citizens. The private enslavement of Negroes was ended. The public control of alien populations had begun.[83]

The English classical liberal Goldwin Smith noted in 1902, from the relative safety of Canada, that "the President of the United States has, over the subject Filipinos, powers from the assumption of which Washington would have recoiled, and which would have filled Jefferson with dismay." An element of irresponsible, arbitrary executive power introduced in overseas possessions

[81]Sumner, *War and Other Essays*, pp. 291–92.
[82]Ibid., p. 347.
[83]Felix Morley, *Freedom and Federalism* (Chicago: Henry Regnery, 1959), p. 104.

would in time yield a liberticide and anti-republican harvest in American life. Already the Insular Cases had revealed the theoretical chasm dividing republic from empire. Like the Southern critics of empire, Smith wondered if U.S. imperialism might not—especially if directed towards Latin America—usher in intensified racial strife in the United States tending towards "either a radical change in the character of the nation and in the spirit, if not in the form of its institutions, or a second disruption" [of the Union].[84] As Secretary of War Elihu Root put it, "as near as I can make out the Constitution follows the flag—but doesn't quite catch up with it."[85]

Bonapartism in the executive branch, bureaucratization at home and abroad, reduction of the sovereign states to mere satrapies, militarism, regimentation, control—this was the syndrome of empire as sketched out by critics of the large policy. Another cost of empire is the decline of public honesty. Like the leaders of any Gnostic Church, the makers of U.S. foreign policy use the Two Doctrines. The outer doctrine, proclaimed to the less adept, stresses U.S. benevolence and adherence to international law. This exoteric doctrine is a horrible amalgam of American exceptionalism, political messianism, and retail Puritanism summed up in Wilsonianism. The Redleg officer in the movie *The Outlaw Josie Wales* expresses its essential point when he says, "Doin' right ain't got no end." The inner doctrine, known to the elect, takes in the frontier-expansionist view of history, Open Door empire, and neo-mercantilism, and deals in statism and power. The exoteric doctrine calls to mind the words of Adam Smith:

> To found a great Empire for the sole purpose of raising up a people of customers, may, at first sight, appear a project fit only for a nation of shopkeepers. It is, however, a project altogether unfit for a nation of shopkeepers, but extremely fit for a nation whose government is influenced by shopkeepers. Such statesmen, and such statesmen only, are capable of fancying that they will find some advantage in employing the blood and treasure of their fellow-citizens to found and maintain such an empire.[86]

The costs to Americans of empire, all told, have been enormous. As the trial run of what became policy and unreflecting habit, the Spanish–American War warrants serious consideration despite its modest costs to Americans in lives and money. I leave the final word on the large policy to the great William Graham Sumner:

[84]Goldwin Smith, *Commonwealth or Empire: A Bystander's View of the Question* (London: Macmillan, 1902), pp. 33 and 45.
[85]Philip C. Jessup, *Elihu Root* (Hamden, Conn.: Archon Books, 1964), p. 348.
[86]Quoted in Smith, *Commonwealth or Empire*, p. 39.

We were told that we needed Hawaii in order to secure California. What shall we now take in order to secure the Philippines? No wonder that some expansionists do not want to "scuttle out of China." We shall need to take China, Japan, and the East Indies, according to the doctrine, in order to "secure" what we have. Of course this means that, on the doctrine, we must take the whole earth in order to be safe on any part of it, and the fallacy stands exposed. If, then, safety and prosperity do not lie in this direction, the place to look for them is in the other direction: in domestic development, peace, industry, free trade with everybody, low taxes, industrial power.[87]

---

[87]Sumner, *War and Other Essays*, p. 351.

9

WORLD WAR I AS FULFILLMENT: POWER AND THE INTELLECTUALS

Murray N. Rothbard*

I n contrast to older historians who regarded World War I as the destruction of progressive reform, I am convinced that the war came to the United States as the "fulfillment," the culmination, the veritable apotheosis of progressivism in American life.[1] I regard progressivism as basically a movement on behalf of big government in all walks of the economy and society, in a fusion or coalition between various groups of big businessmen, led by the House of Morgan, and rising groups of technocratic and statist intellectuals. In this fusion, the values and interests of both groups would be pursued through government. Big business would be able to use the government to cartelize the economy, restrict competition, and regulate production and prices, and also to be able to wield a militaristic and imperialist foreign policy to force open markets abroad and apply the sword of the state to protect foreign investments. Intellectuals would be able to use the government to restrict entry into their professions and to assume jobs in big government to apologize for, and to help plan and staff, government operations. Both groups also believed that, in this fusion, the big state could be used to harmonize and interpret the national interest and thereby provide a middle way between the extremes of dog-eat-dog laissez faire and the bitter conflicts of proletarian Marxism. Also animating both groups of progressives was a postmillennial pietist Protestantism that had conquered Yankee areas of northern Protestantism by the 1830s, and had impelled the pietists to use local, state, and finally federal governments to stamp out sin, to make America and eventually the world holy, and thereby to bring about the Kingdom of God on Earth. The victory of the Bryanite forces at the Democratic national convention of 1896 destroyed the Democratic Party as the vehicle of liturgical Roman Catholics and German Lutherans devoted to personal liberty and laissez faire, and created the roughly homogenized and relatively non-ideological party system we have today. After the turn of the century, this

[*This chapter first appeared as an article in *Journal of Libertarian Studies* 9, no. 1 (Winter 1984): 81–125, and is reprinted here with permission.]

[1]The title of this paper is borrowed from the pioneering last chapter of James Weinstein's excellent work, *The Corporate Ideal in the Liberal State, 1900–1918* (Boston: Beacon Press, 1968). The last chapter is entitled, "War as Fulfillment."

development created an ideological and power vacuum for the expanding number of progressive technocrats and administrators to fill. In that way, the locus of government shifted from the legislature, at least partially subject to democratic check, to the oligarchic and technocratic executive branch.

World War I brought the fulfillment of all these progressive trends. Militarism, conscription, massive intervention at home and abroad, a collectivized war economy, all came about during the war and created a mighty cartelized system that most of its leaders spent the rest of their lives trying to recreate, in peace as well as war. In the World War I chapter of his outstanding work *Crisis and Leviathan*, Professor Robert Higgs concentrates on the war economy and illuminates the interconnections with conscription. In this paper, I would like to concentrate on an area that Professor Higgs relatively neglects: the coming to power during the war of the various groups of progressive intellectuals.[2] I use the term "intellectual" in the broad sense penetratingly described by F. A. Hayek: that is, not merely theorists and academicians, but also all manner of opinion-molders in society—writers, journalists, preachers, scientists, activists of all sorts—what Hayek calls "secondhand dealers in ideas."[3] Most of these intellectuals, of whatever strand or occupation, were either dedicated, messianic postmillennial pietists, or else former pietists born in a deeply-pietist home, who, though now secularized, still possessed an intense messianic belief in national and world salvation through big government. But, in addition, oddly but characteristically, most combined in their thought and agitation a messianic moral or religious fervor with an empirical, allegedly *value-free* and strictly *scientific* devotion to social science. Whether it be the medical profession's combined scientific and moralistic devotion to stamping out sin or a similar position among economists or philosophers, this blend is typical of progressive intellectuals.

I will be dealing with various groups of progressive intellectuals, as well as with some noteworthy individuals, exulting in the triumph of their creed and their own place in it, as a result of America's entry into World War I. Unfortunately, limitations of both space and time preclude dealing with every facet of the wartime

[2]Robert Higgs, *Crisis and Leviathan: Critical Episodes in the Growth of American Government* (New York: Oxford University Press, 1987), pp. 123–58. For my own account of the collectivized war economy of World War I, see Murray N. Rothbard, "War Collectivism in World War I," in *A New History of Leviathan: Essays on the Rise of the American Corporate State*, Ronald Radosh and Murray Rothbard, eds. (New York: Dutton, 1972), pp. 66–110.

[3]F.A. Hayek, "The Intellectuals and Socialism," in *Studies in Philosophy, Politics and Economics* (Chicago: University of Chicago Press, 1967), pp. 178ff.

activity of progressive intellectuals; in particular, I regret having to omit treatment of the conscription movement, a fascinating example of the creed of the "therapy of discipline" led by upper-class intellectuals and businessmen in the J. P. Morgan ambit.[4] I shall also have to omit both the highly significant trooping to the war colors of the nation's preachers, and the wartime impetus toward the permanent centralization of scientific research.[5]

There is no better epigraph for the remainder of this paper than a congratulatory note sent to President Wilson after the delivery of his war message on April 2, 1917. The note was sent by Wilson's son-in-law and fellow Southern pietist and progressive, Secretary of the Treasury William Gibbs McAdoo, a man who had spent his entire life as an industrialist in New York City, solidly in the J.P. Morgan ambit. McAdoo wrote to Wilson: "You have done a great thing nobly! I firmly believe that it is God's will that America should do this transcendent service for humanity throughout the world and that you are His chosen instrument."[6] It was not a sentiment with which the president could disagree.

PIETISM AND PROHIBITION

One of the few important omissions in Professor Higgs's book is the crucial role of postmillennial pietist Protestantism in the drive toward statism in the United States. Dominant in the Yankee areas of the North from the 1830s on, the aggressive evangelical form of pietism conquered Southern Protestantism by the 1890s and played a crucial role in progressivism after the turn of the century and through World War I. Evangelical pietism held that requisite to any man's salvation is that he do his best to see to it that everyone else is saved, and doing one's best inevitably meant that the state must become a crucial instrument in maximizing

[4]On the conscription movement, see in particular Michael Pearlman, *To Make Democracy Safe for America: Patricians and Preparedness in the Progressive Era* (Urbana: University of Illinois Press, 1984). See also John W. Chambers II, "Conscripting for Colossus: The Adoption of the Draft in the United States in World War I," Ph.D. diss., Columbia University, 1973; John Patrick Finnegan, *Against the Specter of a Dragon: the Campaign for American Military Preparedness, 1914–1917* (Westport, Conn.: Greenwood Press, 1974); and John Garry Clifford, *The Citizen Soldiers: The Plattsburg Training Camp Movement* (Lexington: University Press of Kentucky, 1972).

[5]On ministers and the war, see Ray H. Abrams, *Preachers Present Arms* (New York: Round Table Press, 1933). On the mobilization of science, see David F. Noble, *America By Design: Science, Technology and the Rise of Corporate Capitalism* (New York: Oxford University Press, 1977); and Ronald C. Tobey, *The American Ideology of National Science, 1919–1930* (Pittsburgh, Penn.: University of Pittsburgh Press, 1971).

[6]Cited in Gerald Edward Markowitz, "Progressive Imperialism: Consensus and Conflict in the Progressive Movement on Foreign Policy, 1898–1917" (Ph.D. diss., University of Wisconsin, 1971), p. 375, an unfortunately neglected work on a highly important topic.

people's chances for salvation. In particular, the state plays a pivotal role in stamping out sin, and in "making America holy." To the pietists, sin was very broadly defined as any force that might cloud men's minds so that they could not exercise their theological free will to achieve salvation. Of particular importance were slavery (until the Civil War), Demon Rum, and the Roman Catholic Church, headed by the Antichrist in Rome. For decades after the Civil War, rebellion took the place of slavery in the pietist charges against their great political enemy, the Democratic Party.[7] Then in 1896, with the evangelical conversion of Southern Protestantism and the admission to the Union of the sparsely populated and pietist Mountain states, William Jennings Bryan was able to put together a coalition that transformed the Democrats into a pietist party and ended forever that party's once proud role as the champion of *liturgical* (Catholic and High German Lutheran) Christianity and of personal liberty and laissez faire.[8]

The pietists of the 19th and early 20th centuries were all postmillennialist: They believed that the Second Advent of Christ will occur only *after* the millennium—a thousand years of the establishment of the Kingdom of God on Earth—has been brought about by human effort. Postmillennialists have therefore tended to be statists, with the state becoming an important instrument of stamping out sin and Christianizing the social order so as to speed Jesus's return.[9]

---

[7]Hence the famous imprecation, hurled at the end of the 1884 campaign that brought the Democrats into the presidency for the first time since the Civil War, that the Democratic Party was the party of "Rum, Romanism and Rebellion." In that one phrase, the New York Protestant minister was able to sum up the political concerns of the pietist movement.

[8]German Lutherans were largely "high" or liturgical and confessional Lutherans who placed emphasis on the Church and its creed or sacraments rather than on a pietist, "born-again," emotional conversion experience. Scandinavian-Americans, on the other hand, were mainly pietist Lutherans. For an introduction to the growing literature of "ethno-religious" political history in the United States, see Paul Kleppner, *The Cross of Culture* (New York: Free Press, 1970); and idem, *The Third Electoral System, 1853–1892* (Chapel Hill: University of North Carolina Press, 1979). For the latest research on the formation of the Republican Party as a pietist party, reflecting the interconnected triad of pietist concerns—antislavery, prohibition, and anti-Catholicism—see William E. Gienapp, "Nativism and the Creation of a Republican Majority in the North before the Civil War," *Journal of American History* 72 (December 1985): 529–59.

[9]Orthodox Augustinian Christianity, as followed by the liturgicals, is "a-millennialist," i.e., it believes that the millennium is simply a metaphor for the emergence of the Christian Church, and that Jesus will return without human aid and at his own unspecified time. Modern fundamentalists, as they have been called since the early years of the 20th century, are "premillennialists," i.e., they believe that Jesus will return to usher in 1000 years of the Kingdom of God on Earth, a time marked by various tribulations and by Armageddon, until history is finally ended. Premillennialists, or millenarians, do not have the statist drive of the postmillennialists; instead, they tend to focus on predictions and signs of Armageddon and of Jesus's advent.

Professor Timberlake neatly sums up this politico-religious conflict:

> Unlike those extremist and apocalyptic sects that rejected and withdrew from the world as hopelessly corrupt, and unlike the more conservative churches, such as the Roman Catholic, Protestant Episcopal, and Lutheran, that tended to assume a more relaxed attitude toward the influence of religion in culture, evangelical Protestantism sought to overcome the corruption of the world in a dynamic manner, not only by converting men to belief in Christ but also by Christianizing the social order through the power and force of law. According to this view, the Christian's duty was to use the secular power of the state to transform culture so that the community of the faithful might be kept pure and the work of saving the unregenerate might be made easier. Thus the function of law was not simply to restrain evil but to educate and uplift. [10]

Both prohibition and progressive reforms were pietistic, and as both movements expanded after 1900 they became increasingly intertwined. The Prohibition Party, once confined—at least in its platform—to a single issue, became increasingly and frankly progressive after 1904. The Anti-Saloon League, the major vehicle for prohibitionist agitation after 1900, was also markedly devoted to progressive reform. Thus, at the League's annual convention in 1905, Rev. Howard H. Russell rejoiced in the growing movement for progressive reform, and he particularly hailed Theodore Roosevelt as that "leader of heroic mould, of absolute honesty of character and purity of life, that foremost man of this world." [11] At the Anti-Saloon League's convention of 1909, Rev. Purley A. Baker lauded the labor-union movement as a holy crusade for justice and a square deal. The League's 1915 convention, which attracted 10,000 people, was noted for the same blend of statism, social service, and combative Christianity that had marked the national convention of the Progressive Party in 1912. [12] And at the League's June

---

[10]James H. Timberlake, *Prohibition and the Progressive Movement, 1900–1920* (New York: Atheneum, 1970), pp. 7–8.

[11]Quoted in Timberlake, *Prohibition and the Progressive Movement, 1900–1920*, p. 33.

[12]The Progressive Party convention was a mighty fusion of all the major trends in the progressive movement: statist economists, technocrats, social engineers, social workers, professional pietists, and partners of J. P. Morgan and Company. Social Gospel leaders Lyman Abbott, the Rev. R. Heber Newton, and the Rev. Washington Gladden were leading Progressive Party delegates. The Progressive Party proclaimed itself as the "recrudescence of the religious spirit in American political life. " Theodore Roosevelt's acceptance speech was significantly entitled "A Confession of Faith," and his words were punctuated by "amens" and by a continual singing of pietist Christian hymns by the assembled delegates. They sang "Onward Christian Soldiers," "The Battle Hymn of the Republic," and especially the revivalist hymn, "Follow, Follow, We Will Follow Jesus," with the word "Roosevelt" replacing the

1916 convention, Bishop Luther B. Wilson stated, without contradiction, that everyone present would undoubtedly hail the progressive reforms then being proposed.

During the Progressive years, the Social Gospel became part of the mainstream of pietist Protestantism. Most of the evangelical churches created commissions on social service to promulgate the Social Gospel, and virtually all of the denominations adopted the Social Creed drawn up in 1912 by the Commission of the Church and Social Service of the Federal Council of Churches. The creed called for the abolition of child labor, the regulation of female labor, the right of labor to organize (i.e., compulsory collective bargaining), the elimination of poverty, and an equitable division of the national product. And right up there as a matter of social concern was the liquor problem. The creed maintained that liquor was a grave hindrance toward the establishment of the Kingdom of God on Earth, and it advocated the "protection of the individual and society from the social, economic, and moral waste of the liquor traffic."[13]

The Social Gospel leaders were fervent advocates of statism and of prohibition. These included Rev. Walter Rauschenbusch and Rev. Charles Stelzle, whose tract *Why Prohibition!* (1918) was distributed by the Commission on Temperance of the Federal Council of Churches, after the United States' entry into World War I, to labor leaders, members of Congress, and important government officials. A particularly important Social Gospel leader was Rev. Josiah Strong, whose monthly journal, *The Gospel of the Kingdom*, was published by Strong's American Institute of Social Service. In an article supporting prohibition in the July 1914 issue, *The Gospel of the Kingdom* hailed the progressive spirit that was at last putting an end to personal liberty:

> "Personal Liberty" is at last an uncrowned, dethroned king, with no one to do him reverence. The social consciousness is so far developed, and is becoming so autocratic, that institutions and governments must give heed to its mandate and share their life accordingly. We are no longer frightened by that ancient bogy—"paternalism in government." We affirm boldly, it is the business of government to be just that—

---

word "Jesus" at every turn. The horrified *New York Times* summed up the unusual experience by calling the Progressive grouping "a convention of fanatics." And it added, "It was not a convention at all. It was an assemblage of religious enthusiasts. It was such a convention as Peter the Hermit held. It was a Methodist camp following done over into political terms." Cited in John Allen Gable, *The Bull Moose Years: Theodore Roosevelt and the Progressive Party* (Port Washington, N.Y.: Kennikat Press, 1978), p. 75.

[13]Timberlake, *Prohibition and the Progressive Movement*, p. 24.

> paternal. . . . *Nothing human can be foreign to a true govern-
> ment.*[14]

As true crusaders, the pietists were not content to stop with the stamping out of sin in the United States alone. If American pietism was convinced that Americans were God's chosen people, destined to establish a Kingdom of God within the United States, surely the pietists' religious and moral duty could not stop there. In a sense, the world was America's oyster. As Professor Timberlake put it, once the Kingdom of God was in the course of being established in the United States,

> it was therefore America's mission to spread these ideals
> and institutions abroad so that the Kingdom could be
> established throughout the world. American Protestants
> were accordingly not content merely to work for the
> Kingdom of God in America, but felt compelled to assist in
> the reformation of the rest of the world also.[15]

American entry into World War I provided the fulfillment of prohibitionist dreams. In the first place, all food production was placed under the control of Herbert Hoover, Food Administration czar. But if the U.S. government was to control and allocate food resources, shall it permit the precious scarce supply of grain to be siphoned off into the waste, if not the sin, of the manufacture of liquor? Even though less than two percent of American cereal production went into the manufacture of alcohol, think of the starving children of the world who might otherwise be fed. As the progressive weekly the *Independent* demagogically phrased it, "Shall the many have food, or the few have drink?"

For the ostensible purpose of conserving grain, Congress wrote an amendment into the Lever Food and Fuel Control Act of August 10, 1917, that absolutely prohibited the use of foodstuffs, hence grain, in the production of alcohol. Congress would have added a prohibition on the manufacture of wine or beer, but President Wilson persuaded the Anti-Saloon League that he could accomplish the same goal more slowly and thereby avoid a delaying filibuster by the wets in Congress. However, Herbert Hoover, a progressive and a prohibitionist, persuaded Wilson to issue an order, on December 8, both greatly reducing the alcoholic

---

[14]Quoted in Timberlake, *Prohibition and the Progressive Movement,* p. 27, italics in the article. Or, as the Rev. Stelzle put it in *Why Prohibition!* "There is no such thing as an absolute individual right to do any particular thing, or to eat or drink any particular thing, or to enjoy the association of one's own family or even to live, if that thing is in conflict with the law of public necessity." Quoted in David E. Kyvig, *Repealing National Prohibition* (Chicago: University of Chicago Press, 1979), p. 9.

[15]Timberlake, *Prohibition and the Progressive Movement,* pp. 37–38.

content of beer and limiting the amount of foodstuffs that could be used in its manufacture.[16]

The prohibitionists were able to use the Lever Act and war patriotism to good effect. Thus, Mrs. W. E. Lindsey, wife of the governor of New Mexico, delivered a speech in November, 1917, that noted the Lever Act, and declared:

> Aside from the long list of awful tragedies following in the wake of the liquor traffic, the economic waste is too great to be tolerated at this time. With so many people of the allied nations near to the door of starvation, it would be criminal ingratitude for us to continue the manufacture of whiskey.[17]

Another rationale for prohibition during the war was the alleged necessity to protect American soldiers from the dangers of alcohol to their health, their morals, and their immortal souls. As a result, in the Selective Service Act of May 18, 1917, Congress provided that dry zones must be established around every army base, and it was made illegal to sell or even to give liquor to any member of the military establishment within those zones, even in one's private home. Any inebriated servicemen were subject to courts-martial.

But the most severe thrust toward national prohibition was the Anti-Saloon League's proposed 18th constitutional amendment, outlawing the manufacture, sale, transportation, import or export of all intoxicating liquors. It was passed by Congress and submitted to the states at the end of December 1917. Wet arguments that prohibition would prove unenforceable were met with the usual dry appeal to high principle: should laws against murder and robbery be repealed simply because they cannot be completely enforced? And arguments that private property would be unjustly confiscated were also brushed aside with the contention that property injurious to the health, morals, and safety of the people had always been subject to confiscation without compensation.

When the Lever Act made a distinction between hard liquor (forbidden) and beer and wine (limited), the brewing industry tried to save their skins by cutting themselves loose from the taint of distilled spirits. "The true relationship with beer," insisted the

---

[16]See David Burner, *Herbert Hoover: A Public Life* (New York: Alfred A. Knopf, 1979), p. 107.

[17]James A. Burran, "Prohibition in New Mexico, 1917," *New Mexico Historical Quarterly* 48 (April 1973): 140–41. Mrs. Lindsey of course showed no concern whatever for the German, allied, and neutral countries of Europe being subjected to starvation by the British naval blockade. The only areas of New Mexico that resisted the prohibition crusade in the referendum in the November, 1917, elections were the heavily Hispanic–Catholic districts.

United States Brewers Association, "is with light wines and soft drinks—not with hard liquors." The brewers affirmed their desire to "sever, once and for all, the shackles that bound our wholesome productions . . . to ardent spirits." But this craven attitude would do the brewers no good. After all, one of the major objectives of the drys was to smash the brewers, once and for all, they whose product was the very embodiment of the drinking habits of the hated German–American masses both Catholic and Lutheran, liturgicals and beer drinkers all. German–Americans were now fair game. Were they not all agents of the satanic Kaiser, bent on conquering the world? Were they not conscious agents of the dreaded Hun *Kultur*, out to destroy American civilization? And were not most brewers German?

And so the Anti-Saloon League thundered that "German brewers in this country have rendered thousands of men inefficient and are thus crippling the Republic in its war on Prussian militarism." Apparently, the Anti-Saloon League took no heed of the work of German brewers in Germany, who were presumably performing the estimable service of rendering Prussian militarism helpless. The brewers were accused of being pro-German, and of subsidizing the press (apparently it was all right to be pro-English or to subsidize the press if one were not a brewer). The acme of the accusations came from one prohibitionist: "We have German enemies," he warned, "in this country too. And the worst of all our German enemies, the most treacherous, the most menacing are Pabst, Schlitz, Blatz, and Miller."[18]

In this sort of atmosphere, the brewers didn't have a chance, and the 18th Amendment went to the states, outlawing all forms of liquor. Since 27 states had already outlawed liquor, this meant that only nine more were needed to ratify this remarkable amendment, which directly involved the federal constitution in what had always been, at most, a matter of police power of the states. The 36th state ratified the 18th Amendment on January 16, 1919, and by the end of February all but three states (New Jersey, Rhode Island, and Connecticut) had made liquor unconstitutional as well as illegal. Technically, the amendment went into force the following January, but Congress speeded matters up by passing the War Prohibition Act of November 11, 1918, which banned the manufacture of beer and wine after the following May and outlawed the sale of all intoxicating beverages after June 30, 1919, a ban to continue in effect until the end of demobilization. Thus total national prohibition really began on July 1, 1919, with the 18th Amendment taking over

[18]Timberlake, *Prohibition and the Progressive Movement*, p. 179.

six months later. The constitutional amendment needed a congressional enforcing act, which Congress supplied with the Volstead (or National Prohibition) Act, passed over Wilson's veto at the end of October, 1919.

With the battle against Demon Rum won at home, the restless advocates of pietist prohibitionism looked for new lands to conquer. Today America, tomorrow the world. In June, 1919, the triumphant Anti-Saloon League called an international prohibition conference in Washington and created a World League Against Alcoholism. World prohibition, after all, was needed to finish the job of making the world safe for democracy. The prohibitionists' goals were fervently expressed by Rev. A. C. Bane at the Anti-Saloon League's 1917 convention, when victory in America was already in sight. To a wildly cheering throng, Bane thundered:

> America will "go over the top" in humanity's greatest battle [against liquor] and plant the victorious white standard of Prohibition upon the nation's loftiest eminence. Then catching sight of the beckoning hands of our sister nations across the sea, struggling with the same age-long foe, we will go forth with the spirit of the missionary and the crusader to help drive the demon of drink from all civilization. With America leading the way, with faith in Omnipotent God, and bearing with patriotic hands our stainless flag, the emblem of civic purity, we will soon . . . bestow upon mankind the priceless gift of World Prohibition. [19]

Fortunately, the prohibitionists found the reluctant world a tougher nut to crack.

WOMEN AT WAR AND AT THE POLLS

Another direct outgrowth of World War I, coming in tandem with prohibition but lasting more permanently, was the 19th Amendment, submitted by Congress in 1919 and ratified by the following year, which allowed women to vote. Women's suffrage had long been a movement directly allied with prohibition. Desperate to combat a demographic trend that seemed to be going against them, the evangelical pietists called for women's suffrage (and enacted it in many Western states). They did so because they knew that while pietist women were socially and politically active, ethnic or liturgical women tended to be culturally bound to hearth and home and therefore far less likely to vote. Hence, women's suffrage would greatly increase pietist voting power. In 1869, the Prohibition Party became the first party to endorse women's suffrage,

[19]Quoted in ibid., pp. 180–81.

which it continued to do. The Progressive Party was equally enthusiastic about female suffrage; it was the first major national Party to permit women delegates at its conventions. A leading women's suffrage organization, the Women's Christian Temperance Union, reached an enormous membership of 300,000 by 1900. And three successive presidents of the major women's suffrage group, the National American Woman Suffrage Association—Susan B. Anthony, Mrs. Carrie Chapman Catt, and Dr. Anna Howard Shaw—all began their activist careers as prohibitionists. Susan B. Anthony put the issue clearly:

> There is an enemy of the homes of this nation and that enemy is drunkenness. Everyone connected with the gambling house, the brothel and the saloon works and votes solidly against the enfranchisement of women, and, I say, if you believe in chastity, if you believe in honesty and integrity, then . . . take the necessary steps to put the ballot in the hands of women.[20]

For its part, the German–American Alliance of Nebraska sent out an appeal during the unsuccessful referendum in November 1914 on women suffrage. Written in German, the appeal declared, "Our German women do not want the right to vote, and since our opponents desire the right of suffrage mainly for the purpose of saddling the yoke of prohibition on our necks, we should oppose it with all our might."[21]

America's entry into World War I provided the impetus for overcoming the substantial opposition to woman suffrage, as a corollary to the success of prohibition and as a reward for the vigorous activity by organized women on behalf of the war effort. To close the loop, much of that activity consisted in stamping out vice and alcohol as well as instilling "patriotic" education into the minds of often-suspect immigrant groups.

Shortly after the U.S. declaration of war, the Council of National Defense created an Advisory Committee on Women's Defense Work, known as the Woman's Committee. The purpose of the committee, writes a celebratory contemporary account, was "to coordinate the activities and the resources of the organized and unorganized women of the country, that their power may be immediately utilized in time of need, and to supply a new and direct channel of cooperation between women and governmental departments."[22] The Chairman of the Woman's Committee, who

[20]Quoted in Alan P. Grimes, *The Puritan Ethic and Woman Suffrage* (New York: Oxford University Press, 1967), p. 78.
[21]Ibid., p. 116.
[22]Ida Clyde Clarke, *American Women and the World War* (New York: D. Appleton, 1918), p. 19.

worked energetically and full time, was the former president of The National American Woman Suffrage Association, Dr. Anna Howard Shaw, and another leading member was the suffrage group's current chairman and an equally-prominent suffragette, Mrs. Carrie Chapman Catt.

The Woman's Committee promptly set up organizations in cities and states across the country, and on June 19, 1917, convened a conference of over 50 national women's organizations to coordinate their efforts. It was at this conference that "the first definite task was imposed upon American women" by the indefatigable Food Czar, Herbert Hoover.[23] Hoover enlisted the cooperation of the nation's women in his ambitious campaign for controlling, restricting, and cartelizing the food industry in the name of conservation and elimination of waste. Celebrating this coming together of women was one of the Woman's Committee members, the Progressive writer and muckraker Mrs. Ida M. Tarbell. Mrs. Tarbell lauded the "growing consciousness everywhere that this great enterprise for democracy which we are launching [the U.S. entry into the war] is a national affair, and if an individual or a society is going to do its bit it must act with and under the government at Washington." "Nothing else," Mrs. Tarbell gushed, "can explain the action of the women of the country in coming together as they are doing today under one centralized direction."[24]

Mrs. Tarbell's enthusiasm might have been heightened by the fact that she was one of the *directing* rather than the *directed*. Herbert Hoover came to the women's conference with the proposal that each of the women sign and distribute a "food pledge card" on behalf of food conservation. While support for the food pledge among the public was narrower than anticipated, educational efforts to promote the pledge became the basis of the remainder of the women's conservation campaign. The Woman's Committee appointed Mrs. Tarbell as chairman of its committee on Food Administration, and she not only tirelessly organized the campaign but also wrote many letters and newspaper and magazine articles on its behalf.

In addition to food control, another important and immediate function of the Woman's Committee was the attempt to register every woman in the country for possible volunteer or paid work in support of the war effort. Every woman aged 16 or over was asked to sign and submit a registration card that included all pertinent

[23]Ibid., p. 27.

[24]Ibid., p. 31. Actually Mrs. Tarbell's muckraking activities were pretty much confined to Rockefeller and Standard Oil. She was highly favorable to business leaders in the Morgan ambit, as witness her laudatory biographies of Judge Elbert H. Gary, of U.S. Steel (1925), and Owen D. Young, of General Electric (1932).

information, including training, experience, and the sort of work desired. In that way the government would know the whereabouts and training of every woman, and government and women could then serve each other best. In many states, especially Ohio and Illinois, state governments set up schools to train the registrars. And even though the Woman's Committee kept insisting that the registration was completely voluntary, the state of Louisiana, as Ida Clarke puts it, developed a "novel and clever" idea to facilitate the program: women's registration was made compulsory.

Louisiana's Governor Ruffin G. Pleasant decreed October 17, 1917, compulsory registration day, and a host of state officials collaborated in its operation. The State Food Commission made sure that food pledges were also signed by all, and the State School Board granted a holiday on October 17 so that teachers could assist in the compulsory registration, especially in the rural districts. Six thousand women were officially commissioned by the state of Louisiana to conduct the registration, and they worked in tandem with state Food Conservation officials and parish Demonstration Agents. In the French areas of the state, the Catholic priests rendered valuable aid in personally appealing to all their female parishioners to perform their registration duties. Handbills were circulated in French, house-to-house canvasses were made, and speeches urging registration were made by women activists in movie theaters, schools, churches, and courthouses. We are informed that all responses were eager and cordial; there is no mention of any resistance. We are also advised that "even the negroes were quite alive to the situation, meeting sometimes with the white people and sometimes at the call of their own pastors."[25]

Also helping out in women's registration and food control was another, smaller, but slightly more sinister women's organization that had been launched by Congress as a sort of prewar wartime group at a large Congress for Constructive Patriotism, held in Washington, D.C., in late January, 1917. This was the National League for Woman's Service (NLWS), which established a nationwide organization later overshadowed and overlapped by the larger Woman's Committee. The difference was that the NLWS was set up on quite frankly military lines. Each local working unit was called a detachment under a detachment commander, districtwide and statewide detachments met in annual encampments, and every woman member was to wear a uniform with an organization badge and insignia. In particular, "the basis of training for all detachments is standardized, physical drill."[26]

[25]Ibid., p. 277, 275–79, and 58.
[26]Ibid., p. 183.

A vital part of the Woman's Committee work was engaging in patriotic education. The government and the Woman's Committee recognized that immigrant ethnic women were most in need of such vital instruction, and so it set up a committee on education, headed by the energetic Mrs. Carrie Chapman Catt. Mrs. Catt stated the problem well to the Woman's Committee: millions of people in the United States were unclear on why we were at war, and why, as Ida Clarke paraphrases Mrs. Catt, there is "the imperative necessity of winning the war if future generations were to be protected from the menace of an unscrupulous militarism."[27] Presumably, U.S. militarism, being "scrupulous," posed no problem.

Apathy and ignorance abounded, Mrs. Catt went on, and she proposed to mobilize 20 million American women, the "greatest sentiment makers of any community," to begin a "vast educational movement" to get the women "fervently enlisted to push the war to victory as rapidly as possible." As Mrs. Catt continued, however, the clarity of war aims she called for really amounted to pointing out that we were in the war "whether the nation likes it or does not like it," and that therefore the "sacrifices" needed to win the war "willingly or unwillingly must be made." These statements are reminiscent of arguments supporting recent military actions by Ronald Reagan ("He had to do what he had to do"). In the end, Mrs. Catt could come up with only one reasoned argument for the war, apart from this alleged necessity, that it must be won to make it "the war to end wars."[28]

The "patriotic education" campaign of the organized women was largely to "Americanize" immigrant women by energetically persuading them (a) to become naturalized American citizens and (b) to learn "Mother English." In the campaign, dubbed "America First," national unity was promoted through getting immigrants to learn English and trying to get female immigrants into afternoon or evening English classes. The organized patriot women were also worried about preserving the family structure of the immigrants. If the children learn English and their parents remain ignorant, children will scorn their elders, "parental discipline and control are dissipated, and the whole family fabric becomes weakened. Thus one of the great conservative forces in the community becomes inoperative." To preserve "maternal control of the young," then, "Americanization of the foreign women through language becomes imperative." In Erie, Pennsylvania, women's clubs appointed Block Matrons, whose job it was to get to know the foreign

[27]Ibid., p. 103.
[28]Ibid., pp. 104–5.

families of the neighborhood and to back up school authorities in urging the immigrants to learn English, and who would, in the rather naive words of Ida Clarke, "become neighbors, friends, and veritable mother confessors to the foreign women of the block." One would like to have heard some comments from recipients of the attentions of the Block Matrons.

All in all, as a result of the Americanization campaign, Ida Clarke concludes, "the organized women of this country can play an important part in making ours a country with a common language, a common purpose, a common set of ideals—a unified America."[29]

Neither did the government and its organized women neglect progressive economic reforms. At the organizing June, 1917, conference of the Woman's Committee, Mrs. Carrie Chapman Catt emphasized that the greatest problem of the war was to assure that women receive "equal pay for equal work." The conference suggested that vigilance committees be established to guard against the violation of "ethical laws" governing labor and also that all laws restricting ("protecting") the labor of women and children be rigorously enforced. Apparently, there were some values to which maximizing production for the war effort had to take second place. Mrs. Margaret Dreier Robins, president of the National Women's Trade Unions League, hailed the fact that the Woman's Committee was organizing committees in every state to protect minimum standards for women's and children's labor in industry and demanded minimum wages and shorter hours for women. Mrs. Robins particularly warned that "not only are unorganized women workers in vast numbers used as underbidders in the labor market for lowering industrial standards, but they are related to those groups in industrial centers of our country that are least Americanized and most alien to our institutions and ideals." And so Americanization and cartelization of female labor went hand in hand.[30]

[29]Ibid., p. 101.

[30]Ibid., p. 129, Margaret Dreier Robins and her husband Raymond were virtually a paradigmatic progressive couple. Raymond was a Florida-born wanderer and successful gold prospector who underwent a mystical conversion experience in the Alaska wilds and became a pietist preacher. He moved to Chicago, where he became a leader in Chicago settlement house work and municipal reform. Margaret Dreier and her sister Mary were daughters of a wealthy and socially-prominent New York family who worked for and financed the emergent National Women's Trade Union League. Margaret married Raymond Robins in 1905 and moved to Chicago, soon becoming long-time president of the League. In Chicago, the Robinses led and organized progressive political causes for over two decades, becoming top leaders of the Progressive Party from 1912 to 1916. During the war, Raymond Robins engaged in considerable diplomatic activity as head of a Red Cross mission to Russia. On the Robinses, see Allen F. Davis, *Spearhead for Reform:*

SAVING OUR BOYS FROM ALCOHOL AND VICE

One of organized womanhood's major contributions to the war effort was to collaborate in an attempt to save American soldiers from vice and Demon Rum. In addition to establishing rigorous dry zones around every military camp in the United States, the Selective Service Act of May, 1917, also outlawed prostitution in wide zones around the military camps. To enforce these provisions, the War Department had ready at hand a Commission on Training Camp Activities, an agency soon imitated by the Department of the Navy. Both commissions were headed by a man tailor-made for the job, the progressive New York settlement-house worker, municipal political reformer, and former student and disciple of Woodrow Wilson, Raymond Blaine Fosdick.

Fosdick's background, life, and career were paradigmatic for progressive intellectuals and activists of that era. His ancestors were Yankees from Massachusetts and Connecticut, and Fosdick's great-grandfather pioneered westward in a covered wagon to become a frontier farmer in the heart of the Burned-Over District of transplanted Yankees, Buffalo, New York. Fosdick's grandfather, a pietist lay preacher born again in a Baptist revival, was a prohibitionist who married a preacher's daughter and became a lifelong public school teacher in Buffalo. Grandfather Fosdick rose to become Superintendent of Education in Buffalo and a battler for an expanded and strengthened public school system.

Fosdick's immediate ancestry continued in the same vein. His father was a public school teacher in Buffalo who rose to become principal of a high school. His mother was deeply pietist and a staunch advocate of prohibition and women's suffrage. Fosdick's father was a devout pietist Protestant and a fanatical Republican who gave his son Raymond the middle name of his hero, the veteran Maine Republican James G. Blaine. The three Fosdick children, elder brother Harry Emerson, Raymond, and Raymond's

---

The Social Settlements and the Progressive Movement 1890–1914 (New York: Oxford University Press, 1967).

For more on women's war work and woman suffrage, see the standard history of the suffrage movement, Eleanor Flexner, Century of Struggle: The Woman's Rights Movement in the United States (New York: Atheneum, 1968), pp. 288–89. Interestingly, The National War Labor Board (NWLB) frankly adopted the concept of "equal pay for equal work" in order to limit the employment of women workers by imposing higher costs on the employer. The "only check" on excessive employment of women, affirmed the NWLB, "is to make it no more profitable to employ women than men." Quoted in Valerie J. Conner, "'The Mothers of the Race' in World War I: The National War Labor Board and Women in Industry," Labor History 21 (Winter 1979–80): 34.

twin sister, Edith, on emerging from this atmosphere, all forged lifetime careers of pietism and social service.

While active in New York reform administration, Fosdick made a fateful friendship. In 1910, John D. Rockefeller, Jr., like his father a pietist Baptist, was chairman of a special grand jury to investigate and to try to stamp out prostitution in New York City. For Rockefeller, the elimination of prostitution was to become an ardent and lifelong crusade. He believed that sin, such as prostitution, must be criminated, quarantined, and driven underground through rigorous suppression. In 1911, Rockefeller began his crusade by setting up the Bureau of Social Hygiene, into which he poured $5 million in the next quarter century. Two years later he enlisted Fosdick, already a speaker at the annual dinner of Rockefeller's Baptist Bible class, to study police systems in Europe in conjunction with activities to end the great "social vice." Surveying American police after his stint in Europe at Rockefeller's behest, Fosdick was appalled that police work in the United States was not considered a science and that it was subject to sordid political influences.[31]

At that point, the new Secretary of War, the progressive former mayor of Cleveland, Newton D. Baker, became disturbed at reports that areas near the army camps in Texas on the Mexican border, where troops were mobilized to combat the Mexican revolutionary Pancho Villa, were honeycombed with saloons and prostitution. Baker sent Fosdick on a fact-finding tour in the summer of 1916. Fosdick, scoffed at by tough army officers as the "Reverend," was horrified to find saloons and brothels seemingly everywhere in the vicinity of the military camps. He reported his consternation to Baker, and, at Fosdick's suggestion, Baker cracked down on the army commanders and their lax attitude toward alcohol and vice. But Fosdick was beginning to get the glimmer of another idea. Couldn't the suppression of the bad be accompanied by a positive encouragement of the good, of wholesome recreational alternatives to sin and liquor that our boys could enjoy? When war was declared, Baker quickly appointed Fosdick to be chairman of the Commission on Training Camp Activities.

Armed with the coercive resources of the federal government and rapidly building his personal bureaucratic empire from merely one secretary to a staff of thousands, Raymond Fosdick set out

[31]See Raymond B. Fosdick, *Chronicle of a Generation: An Autobiography* (New York: Harper and Bros., 1958), p. 133. Fosdick was particularly appalled that American patrolmen on street duty actually smoked cigars! (p. 135). Also see Peter Collier and David Horowitz, *The Rockefellers: An American Dynasty* (New York: New American Library, 1976), pp. 103–5.

with determination on his two-fold task: stamping out alcohol and sin in and around every military camp, and filling the void for American soldiers and sailors by providing them with wholesome recreation. For the positions of head of the Law Enforcement Division of the Training Camp Commission, Fosdick selected Bascom Johnson, attorney for the American Social Hygiene Association.[32] Johnson was commissioned a major, and his staff of 40 aggressive attorneys became second lieutenants.

Employing the argument of health and military necessity, Fosdick set up a Social Hygiene Division of his commission, which promulgated the slogan "Fit to Fight." Using a mixture of force and threats to remove federal troops from the bases if recalcitrant cities did not comply, Fosdick managed to bludgeon his way into suppressing, if not prostitution in general, then at least every major red light district in the country. In doing so, Fosdick and Baker, employing local police and the federal Military Police, far exceeded their legal authority. The law authorized the president to

[32]The American Social Hygiene Association, with its influential journal *Social Hygiene*, was the major organization in what was known as the "purity crusade." The association was launched when the New York physician Dr. Prince A. Morrow, inspired by the agitation against venereal disease and in favor of the continence urged by the French syphilographer, Jean-Alfred Foumier, formed in 1905 the American Society for Sanitary and Moral Prophylaxis (ASSMP). Soon, the terms proposed by the Chicago branch of ASSMP, "social hygiene" and "sex hygiene," became widely used for their medical and scientific patina, and in 1910 ASSMP changed its name to the American Federation for Sex Hygiene (AFSH). Finally, in late 1913, AFSH, an organization of physicians, combined with the National Vigilance Association (formerly the American Purity Alliance), a group of clergymen and social workers, to form the all-embracing American Social Hygiene Association (ASHA).

In this social hygiene movement, the moral and the medical went hand in hand. Thus, Dr. Morrow welcomed the new knowledge about venereal disease because it demonstrated that "punishment for sexual sin" no longer had to be "reserved for the hereafter."

The first president of ASHA was the president of Harvard University, Charles W. Eliot. In his address to the first meeting, Eliot made clear that total abstinence from alcohol, tobacco, and even spices was part and parcel of the anti-prostitution and purity crusade.

On physicians, the purity crusade, and the formation of ASHA, see Ronald Hamowy, "Medicine and the Crimination of Sin: 'Self-Abuse' in 19th-Century America," *Journal of Libertarian Studies* 1 (Summer 1972): 247–59; James Wunsch, "Prostitution and Public Policy: From Regulation to Suppression, 1858–1920" (Ph.D. diss., University of Chicago, 1976); and Roland R. Wagner, "Virtue Against Vice: A Study of Moral Reformers and Prostitution in the Progressive Era" (Ph.D. diss., University of Wisconsin, 1971). On Morrow, also see John C. Burnham, "The Progressive Era Revolution in American Attitudes Toward Sex," *Journal of American History* 59 (March 1973): 899; and Paul Boyer, *Urban Masses and Moral Order in America, 1820–1920* (Cambridge, Mass.: Harvard University Press, 1978), p. 201. Also see Burnham, "Medical Specialists and Movements Toward Social Control in the Progressive Era: Three Examples," in *Building the Organizational Society: Essays in Associational Activities in Modern America*, J. Israel, ed. (New York: Free Press, 1972), pp. 24–26.

shut down every red light district in a five-mile zone around each military camp or base. Of the 110 red light districts shut down by military force, however, only 35 were included in the prohibited zone. Suppression of the other 75 was an illegal extension of the law. Nevertheless, Fosdick was triumphant: "Through the efforts of this Commission [on Training Camp Activities] the red light district has practically ceased to be a feature of American city life."[33] The result of this permanent destruction of the red light district, of course, was to drive prostitution onto the streets, where consumers would be deprived of the protection of either an open market or of regulation.

In some cases, the federal anti-vice crusade met considerable resistance. Secretary of the Navy Josephus Daniels, a progressive from North Carolina, had to call out the marines to patrol the streets of resistant Philadelphia, and naval troops, over the strenuous objections of the mayor, were used to crush the fabled red light district of Storyville, in New Orleans, in November, 1917.[34]

In its hubris, the U.S. Army decided to extend its anti-vice crusade to foreign shores. General John J. Pershing issued an official bulletin to members of the American Expeditionary Force in France urging that "sexual continence is the plain duty of members of the A.E.F., both for the vigorous conduct of the war, and for the clean health of the American people after the war." Pershing and the American military tried to close all the French brothels in areas where American troops were located, but the move was unsuccessful because the French objected bitterly. Premier Georges Clemenceau pointed out that the result of the "total prohibition of regulated prostitution in the vicinity of American troops" was only to increase "venereal diseases among the civilian population of the neighborhood." Finally, the United States had to rest content with declaring French civilian areas off limits to the troops.[35]

[33]In Daniel R. Beaver, *Newton D. Baker and the American War Effort 1917–1919* (Lincoln: University of Nebraska Press, 1966), p. 222. Also see ibid., pp. 221–24; and C. H. Cramer, *Newton D. Baker: A Biography* (Cleveland, Ohio: World Publishing, 1961), pp. 99–102.
[34]Fosdick, *Chronicle of a Generation*, pp. 145–47. While prostitution was indeed banned in Storyville after 1917, Storyville, contrary to legend, never "closed," the saloons and dance halls remained open, and contrary to orthodox accounts, jazz was never really shut down in Storyville or New Orleans, and it was therefore never forced up river. For a revisionist view of the impact of the closure of Storyville on the history of jazz, see Tom Bethell, *George Lewis: A Jazzman from New Orleans* (Berkeley: University of California Press, 1977), pp. 6–7; and Al Rose, *Storyville, New Orleans* (Montgomery: University of Alabama Press, 1974). Also, on later Storyville, see Boyer, *Urban Masses*, p. 218.
[35]See Hamowy, "Medicine and the Crimination of Sin," p. 226n. The quote from Clemenceau is in Fosdick, *Chronicle of a Generation*, p. 171. Newton Baker's loyal biographer declared that Clemenceau, in this response, showed "his animal proclivities as the 'Tiger of France.'" Cramer, *Newton D. Baker*, p. 101.

The more positive part of Raymond Fosdick's task during the war was supplying the soldiers and sailors with a constructive substitute for sin and alcohol, "healthful amusements and whole-some company." As might be expected, the Woman's Committee and organized womanhood collaborated enthusiastically. They followed the injunction of Secretary of War Baker that the gov-ernment "cannot allow these young men . . . to be surrounded by a vicious and demoralizing environment, nor can we leave anything undone which will protect them from unhealthy influences and crude forms of temptation." The Woman's Committee found, how-ever, that in the great undertaking of safeguarding the health and morals of our boys, their most challenging problem proved to be guarding the morals of their mobilized young girls. For unfor-tunately, "where soldiers are stationed . . . the problem of pre-venting girls from being misled by the glamour and romance of war and beguiling uniforms looms large." Fortunately, perhaps, the Maryland Committee proposed the establishment of a "Patriotic League of Honor which will inspire girls to adopt the highest standards of womanliness and loyalty to their country."[36]

No group was more delighted with the achievements of Fos-dick and his Military Training Camp Commission than the bur-geoning profession of social work. Surrounded by hand-picked aides from the Playground and Recreation Association and the Russell Sage Foundation, Fosdick and the others "in effect tried to create a massive settlement house around each camp. No army had ever seen anything like it before, but it was an outgrowth of the recreation and community organization movement, and a victory for those who had been arguing for the creative use of leisure time."[37] The social work profession pronounced the program an enormous success. The influential *Survey* magazine summed up the result as "the most stupendous piece of social work in modern times."[38]

[36]Clarke, *American Women and the World War*, pp. 90, 87, 93. In some cases, organ-ized women took the offensive to help stamp out vice and liquor in their commu-nity. Thus, in Texas in 1917, the Texas Women's Anti-Vice Committee led in the cre-ation of a "White Zone" around all the military bases. By autumn, the Committee expanded into the Texas Social Hygiene Association to coordinate the work of erad-icating prostitution and saloons. San Antonio proved to be its biggest problem. Lewis L. Gould, *Progressives and Prohibitionists: Texas Democrats in the Wilson Era* (Austin: University of Texas Press, 1973), p. 227.

[37]Davis, *Spearheads for Reform*, p. 225.

[38]Fosdick, *Chronicle of a Generation*, p. 144. After the War, Raymond Fosdick went on to fame and fortune, first as Under Secretary General of the League of Nations, and then for the rest of his life as a member of the small inner circle close to John D. Rockefeller, Jr. In that capacity, Fosdick rose to become head of the Rockefeller Foundation and Rockefeller's official biographer. Meanwhile, Fosdick's brother, Rev. Harry Emerson Fosdick, became Rockefeller's hand-picked parish minister, first at Park Avenue Presbyterian Church and then at the new interdenominational

Social workers were also exultant about prohibition. In 1917, the National Conference of Charities and Corrections (which changed its name around the same time to the National Conference of Social Work) was emboldened to drop whatever value-free pose it might have had and come out squarely for prohibition. On returning from Russia in 1917, Edward T. Devine of the Charity Organization Society of New York exclaimed that "the social revolution which followed the prohibition of vodka was more profoundly important . . . than the political revolution which abolished autocracy." And Robert A. Woods of Boston, the Grand Old Man of the settlement-house movement and a veteran advocate of prohibition, predicted in 1919 that the 18th Amendment, "one of the greatest and best events in history," would reduce poverty, wipe out prostitution and crime, and liberate "vast suppressed human potentialities."[39]

Woods, president of the National Conference of Social Work during 1917–18, had long denounced alcohol as "an abominable evil." A postmillennial pietist, he believed in "Christian statesmanship" that would, in a "propaganda of the deed," Christianize the social order in a corporate, communal route to the glorification of God. Like many pietists, Woods cared not for creeds or dogmas but only for advancing Christianity in a communal way; though an active Episcopalian, his parish was the community at large. In his settlement work, Woods had long favored the isolation or segregation of the unfit, in particular "the tramp, the drunkard, the pauper, the imbecile," with the settlement house as the nucleus of this reform. Woods was particularly eager to isolate and punish the drunkard and the tramp. "Inveterate drunkards" were to receive increasing levels of punishment, with ever-lengthier jail terms. The "tramp evil" was to be gotten rid of by rounding up and jailing vagrants, who would be placed in tramp workhouses and put to forced labor.

For Woods, the world war was a momentous event. It advanced the process of Americanization, a "great humanizing process through which all loyalties, all beliefs must be wrought together in a better order."[40] The war had wonderfully released the energies of

Riverside Church, built with Rockefeller funds. Harry Emerson Fosdick was Rockefeller's principal aide in battling, within the Protestant Church, in favor of postmillennial, statist, "liberal" Protestantism and against the rising tide of premillennial Christianity, known as "fundamentalist" since the years before World War I. See Collier and Horowitz, *The Rockefellers, An American Dynasty*, pp. 140–42, 151–53.

[39]Davis, *Spearheads for Reform*, p. 226; Timberlake, *Prohibition and the Progressive Movement*, p. 66; Boyer, *Urban Masses*, p. 156.

[40]Eleanor H. Woods, *Robert A. Woods: Champion of Democracy* (Boston: Houghton Mifflin, 1929), p. 316. Also see ibid., pp. 201–2, 250ff, 268ff.

the American people. Now, however, it was important to carry the wartime momentum into the postwar world. Lauding the war-collectivist society during the spring of 1918, Robert Woods asked the crucial question, "Why should it not always be so? Why not continue in the years of peace this close, vast, wholesome organism of service, of fellowship, of constructive creative power?"[41]

THE *NEW REPUBLIC* COLLECTIVISTS

The *New Republic* magazine, founded in 1914 as the leading intellectual organ of progressivism, was a living embodiment of the burgeoning alliance between big business interests, in particular the House of Morgan, and the growing legion of collectivist intellectuals. The founder and publisher of the *New Republic* was Willard W. Straight, partner of J. P. Morgan and Company, and its financier was Straight's wife, the heiress Dorothy Whitney. Major editor of the influential new weekly was the veteran collectivist and theoretician of Teddy Roosevelt's New Nationalism, Herbert David Croly. Croly's two coeditors were Walter Edward Weyl, another theoretician of the New Nationalism, and the young, ambitious former official of the Intercollegiate Socialist Society, the future pundit Walter Lippmann. As Woodrow Wilson began to take America into World War I, the *New Republic*, though originally Rooseveltian, became an enthusiastic supporter of the war, and a virtual spokesman for the Wilson war effort, the wartime collectivist economy, and the new society molded by war.

On the higher levels of ratiocination, unquestionably the leading progressive intellectual before, during, and after World War I was the champion of pragmatism, Professor John Dewey of Columbia University. Dewey wrote frequently for the *New Republic* in this period and was clearly its leading theoretician. A Yankee born in 1859, Dewey was, as Mencken put it, "of indestructible Vermont stock and a man of the highest bearable sobriety." John Dewey was the son of a small town Vermont grocer.[42] Although he was a pragmatist and a secular humanist most of his life, it is not as well known that Dewey, in the years before 1900, was a postmillennial pietist, seeking the gradual development of a Christianized social order and Kingdom of God on Earth via the expansion of science, community, and the state. During the 1890s, Dewey, while a professor of philosophy at the University of Michigan, expounded his vision of postmillennial pietism in a series of

[41]Davis, *Spearheads for Reform*, p. 227.
[42]H. L. Mencken, "Professor Veblen," in *A Mencken Chrestomathy* (New York: Alfred A. Knopf, 1949), p. 267.

lectures before the Students' Christian Association. Dewey argued that the growth of modern science now makes it possible for man to establish the biblical idea of the Kingdom of God on Earth. Once humans had broken free of the restraints of orthodox Christianity, a truly religious Kingdom of God could be realized in "the common incarnate Life, the purpose . . . animating all men and binding them together into one harmonious whole of sympathy."[43] Religion would thus work in tandem with science and democracy, all of which would break down the barriers between men and establish the Kingdom. After 1900, it was easy for John Dewey, along with most other postmillennial intellectuals of the period, to shift gradually but decisively from postmillennial progressive Christian statism to progressive secular statism. The path, the expansion of statism, social control and planning, remained the same. And even though the Christian creed dropped out of the picture, the intellectuals and activists continued to possess the same evangelical zeal for the salvation of the world that their parents and they themselves had once possessed. The world would, and must still, be saved through progress and statism.[44]

A pacifist while in the midst of peace, John Dewey prepared himself to lead the parade for war as America drew nearer to armed intervention in the European struggle. First, in January, 1916, in the *New Republic*, Dewey attacked the "professional pacifist's" outright condemnation of war as a "sentimental phantasy," a confusion of means and ends. Force, he declared, was simply "a means of getting results," and therefore could neither be lauded or condemned per se. Next, in April, Dewey signed a pro-Allied manifesto, not only cheering for an Allied victory but also proclaiming that the Allies were "struggling to preserve the liberties of the world and the highest ideals of civilization." And though Dewey supported U.S. entry into the war so that Germany could be defeated, "a hard job, but one which had to be done," he was far more interested in the wonderful changes that the war would surely bring about in the domestic American polity. War, in particular, offered a golden opportunity to bring about collectivist social control in the interest of social justice. As one historian put it,

[43]Quoted in the important article by Jean B. Quandt, "Religion and Social Thought: The Secularization of Postmillenialism," *American Quarterly* 25 (October 1973): 404. Also see John Blewett, S.J., "Democracy as Religion: Unity in Human Relations," in *John Dewey: His Thought and Influence*, idem, ed. (New York: Fordham University Press, 1960), pp. 33–58; and *John Dewey: The Early Works, 1882–1989*, J. Boydston, et al., eds. (Carbondale: Southern Illinois University Press, 1969–71).

[44]On the general secularization of postmillennial pietism after 1900, see Quandt, "Religion and Social Thought," pp. 390–409; and James H. Moorhead, "The Erosion of Postmillenialism in American Religious Thought, 1865–1925," *Church History* 53 (March 1984): 61–77.

because war demanded paramount commitment to the national interest and necessitated an unprecedented degree of
government planning and economic regulation in that
interest, Dewey saw the prospect of permanent socialization,
permanent replacement of private and possessive interest by
public and social interest, both within and among nations.[45]

In an interview with the *New York World* a few months after
U.S. entry into the war, Dewey exulted that "this war may easily
be the beginning of the end of business." For out of the needs of
the war, "we are beginning to produce for use, not for sale, and the
capitalist is not a capitalist . . . [in the face of] the war." Capitalist
conditions of production and sale are now under government
control, and "there is no reason to believe that the old principle
will ever be resumed. . . . Private property had already lost its
sanctity . . . industrial democracy is on the way."[46] In short, intelligence is at last being used to tackle social problems, and this
practice is destroying the old order and creating a new social order
of "democratic integrated control." Labor is acquiring more power,
science is at last being socially mobilized, and massive government
controls are socializing industry. These developments, Dewey
proclaimed, were precisely what we are fighting for.[47]

Furthermore, John Dewey saw great possibilities opened by
the war for the advent of worldwide collectivism. To Dewey,
America's entrance into the war created a "plastic juncture" in the
world, a world marked by a "world organization and the beginnings of a public control which crosses nationalistic boundaries
and interests," and which would also "outlaw war."[48]

The editors of the *New Republic* took a position similar to
Dewey's, except that they arrived at it even earlier. In his editorial
in the magazine's first issue in November, 1914, Herbert Croly
cheerily prophesied that the war would stimulate America's spirit
of nationalism and therefore bring it closer to democracy. At first
hesitant about the collectivist war economies in Europe, the *New*

[45]Carol S. Gruber, *Mars and Minerva: World War I and the Uses of the Higher Learning
in America* (Baton Rouge: Louisiana State University Press, 1975), p. 92.
[46]Quoted in Gruber, *Mars and Minerva*, pp. 92–93. Also see William E.
Leuchtenburg, "The New Deal and the Analogue of War," in *Change and Continuity
in Twentieth-Century America*, J. Braeman, R. Bremner, and E. Walters, eds. (New
York: Harper and Row, 1966), p. 89. For similar reasons, Thorstein Veblen, prophet
of the alleged dichotomy of production for profit vs. production for use,
championed the war and began to come out openly for socialism in an article in the
New Republic in 1918, later reprinted in his *The Vested Interests and the State of the
Industrial Arts* (1919). See Charles Hirschfeld, "Nationalist Progressivism and World
War I," *Mid-America* 45 (July 1963), p. 150. Also see David Riesman, *Thorstein Veblen:
A Critical Interpretation* (New York: Charles Scribner's Sons, 1960), pp. 30–31.
[47]Hirschfeld, "Nationalist Progressivism," p. 150.
[48]Gruber, *Mars and Minerva*, p. 92.

Republic soon began to cheer and urged the United States to follow the lead of the warring European nations and socialize its economy and expand the powers of the state. As America prepared to enter the war, the *New Republic*, examining war collectivism in Europe, rejoiced that "on its administrative side socialism [had] won a victory that [was] superb and compelling." True, European war collectivism was a bit grim and autocratic, but never fear, America could use the selfsame means for democratic goals.

The *New Republic* intellectuals also delighted in the war spirit in America, for that spirit meant "the substitution of national and social and organic forces for the more or less mechanical private forces operative in peace." The purposes of war and social reform might be a bit different, but, after all, "they are both purposes, and luckily for mankind a social organization which is efficient is as useful for the one as for the other."[49] Lucky indeed.

As America prepared to enter the war, the *New Republic* eagerly looked forward to imminent collectivization, sure that it would bring "immense gains in national efficiency and happiness." After war was declared, the magazine urged that the war be used as "an aggressive tool of democracy." "Why should not the war serve," the magazine asked, "as a pretext to be used to foist innovations upon the country?" In that way, progressive intellectuals could lead the way in abolishing "the typical evils of the sprawling half-educated competitive capitalism."

Convinced that the United States would attain socialism through war, Walter Lippmann, in a public address shortly after American entry, trumpeted his apocalyptic vision of the future:

> We who have gone to war to insure democracy in the world will have raised an aspiration here that will not end with the overthrow of the Prussian autocracy. We shall turn with fresh interests to our own tyrannies—to our Colorado mines, our autocratic steel industries, sweatshops, and our slums. A force is loose in America. . . . Our own reactionaries will not assuage it. . . . We shall know how to deal with them.[50]

[49]Hirschfeld, "Nationalist Progressivism," p. 142. It is intriguing that for the *New Republic* intellectuals, actually existent private individuals are dismissed as "mechanical," whereas nonexistent entities such as "national and social" forces are hailed as being "organic."

[50]Quoted in Hirschfeld, "Nationalist Progressivism," p. 147. A minority of pro-war Socialists broke off from the antiwar Socialist Party to form the Social Democratic League, and to join a pro-war front organized and financed by the Wilson administration, the American Alliance for Labor and Democracy. The pro-war socialists welcomed the war as providing "startling progress in collectivism," and opined that after the war, the existent state socialism could be advanced toward "democratic collectivism." The pro-war socialists included John Spargo, Algie Simons, W. J. Ghent, Robert R. LaMonte, Charles Edward Russell, J. G. Phelps Stokes, Upton Sinclair, and William English Walling. Walling so succumbed to war

Walter Lippmann, indeed, had been the foremost hawk among the *New Republic* intellectuals. He had pushed Croly into backing Wilson and into supporting intervention, and then had collaborated with Colonel House in pushing Wilson into entering the war. Soon Lippmann, an enthusiast for conscription, had to confront the fact that he himself was only 27 years old and in fine health, and therefore was eminently eligible for the draft. Somehow, though, Lippmann failed to unite theory and praxis. Young Felix Frankfurter, progressive Harvard Law Professor and a close associate of the *New Republic* editorial staff, had just been selected as a special assistant to Secretary of War Baker. Lippmann somehow felt that his own inestimable services could be better used planning the postwar world than battling in the trenches. And so he wrote to Frankfurter asking for a job in Baker's office. "What I want to do," Lippman pleaded, "is to devote all my time to studying and speculating on the approaches to peace and the reaction from the peace. Do you think you can get me an exemption on such high-falutin grounds?" Lippman then rushed to reassure Frankfurter that there was nothing personal in this request. After all, he explained, "the things that need to be thought out, are so big that there must be no personal element mixed up with this." Frankfurter having paved the way, Lippmann wrote to Secretary Baker. He assured Baker that he was only applying for a job and draft exemption on the pleading of others and in stern submission to the national interest. As Lippmann put it in a remarkable demonstration of cant:

> I have consulted all the people whose advice I value and they urge me to apply for exemption. You can well understand that this is not a pleasant thing to do, and yet, after searching my soul as candidly as I know how, I am convinced that I can serve my bit much more effectively than as a private in the new armies.

No doubt.

As icing on the cake, Lippmann added an important bit of disinformation. For, he piteously wrote to Baker, the fact is "that my father is dying and my mother is absolutely alone in the world. She does not know what his condition is, and I cannot tell anyone for fear it would become known." Apparently, no one else knew his father's condition either, including the medical profession and his

---

fever that he denounced the Socialist Party as a conscious tool of the Kaiser and advocated the suppression of freedom of speech for pacifists and for antiwar socialists. See Hirschfeld, "Nationalist Progressivism," p. 143. On Walling, see James Gilbert, *Designing the Industrial State: The Intellectual Pursuit of Collectivism in America, 1880–1940* (Chicago: Quadrangle Books, 1972), pp. 232–33. On the American Alliance for Labor and Democracy and its role in the war effort, see Ronald Radosh, *American Labor and United States Foreign Policy* (New York: Random House, 1969), pp. 58–71.

father, for the elder Lippmann managed to peg along successfully for the next ten years.[51]

Secure in his draft exemption, Walter Lippmann hied off in high excitement to Washington, there to help run the war and, a few months later, to help direct Colonel House's secret conclave of historians and social scientists setting out to plan the shape of the future peace treaty and the postwar world. Let others fight and die in the trenches; Walter Lippmann had the satisfaction of knowing that his talents, at least, would be put to their best use by the newly-emerging collectivist state.

As the war went on, Croly and the other editors, having lost Lippmann to the great world beyond, cheered every new development of the massively-controlled war economy. The nationalization of railroads and shipping, the priorities and allocation system, the total domination of all parts of the food industry achieved by Herbert Hoover and the Food Administration, the pro-union policy, the high taxes, and the draft were all hailed by the *New Republic* as an expansion of democracy's power to plan for the general good. As the Armistice ushered in the postwar world, the *New Republic* looked back on the handiwork of the war and found it good: "We revolutionized our society." All that remained was to organize a new constitutional convention to complete the job of reconstructing America.[52]

But the revolution had not been fully completed. Despite the objections of Bernard Baruch and the other wartime planners, the federal government decided not to make permanent most of the war collectivist machinery. From then on, the fondest ambition of Baruch and the others was to make the World War I system a permanent institution of American life. The most trenchant epitaph on the World War I polity was delivered by Rexford Guy Tugwell in 1927. Tugwell, the most frankly collectivist of the Brain Trusters of

[51]In fact, Jacob Lippmann was to contract cancer in 1925 and die two years later. Moreover, Lippmann, before and after Jacob's death, was supremely indifferent to his father. Ronald Steel, *Walter Lippmann and the American Century* (New York: Random House, 1981), pp. 5, 116–17. On Walter Lippmann's enthusiasm for conscription, at least for others, see Beaver, *Newton D. Baker*, pp. 26–27.

[52]Hirschfeld, "Nationalist Progressivism, " pp. 148–50. On the *New Republic* and the war, and particularly on John Dewey, also see Christopher Lasch, *The New Radicalism in America, 1889–1963: The Intellectual as A Social Type* (New York: Vintage Books, 1965), pp. 181–224, esp. pp. 202–4. On the three *New Republic* editors, see Charles Forcey, *The Crossroads of Liberalism: Croly, Weyl, Lippmann and the Progressive Era, 1900–1925* (New York: Oxford University Press, 1961). Also see David W. Noble, "The *New Republic* and the Idea of Progress, 1914–1920," *Mississippi Valley Historical Review* 38 (December 1951): 387–402. In a book titled *The End of the War* (1918), *New Republic*-editor Walter Weyl assured his readers that "the new economic solidarity once gained, can never again be surrendered." Cited in Leuchtenburg, "New Deal," p. 90.

Franklin Roosevelt's New Deal, looked back on "America's war-time socialism" and lamented that if only the war had lasted long-er, that great "experiment" could have been completed. "We were on the verge of having an international industrial machine when peace broke," Tugwell mourned. "Only the Armistice prevented a great experiment in control of production, control of prices, and control of consumption."[53] Tugwell need not have been troubled; there would be other emergencies, other wars.

At the end of the war, Lippmann was to go on to become America's foremost journalistic pundit. Croly, having broken with the Wilson Administration on the harshness of the Versailles Tre-aty, was bereft to find the *New Republic* no longer the spokesman for some great political leader. During the late 1920s he was to dis-cover an exemplary national collectivist leader abroad—in Benito Mussolini.[54] That Croly ended his years as an admirer of Mussolini comes as no surprise when we realize that from early childhood he had been steeped by a doting father in the authoritarian socialist doctrines of Auguste Comte's positivism. These views were to mark Croly throughout his life. Thus, Herbert's father, David, the founder of positivism in the United States, advocated the establish-ment of vast powers of government over everyone's life. David Croly favored the growth of trusts and monopolies as a means both to that end and also to eliminate the evils of individual com-petition and selfishness. Like his son, David Croly railed at the Jeffersonian "fear of government" in America, and looked to Ham-ilton as an example to counter that trend.[55]

---

[53]Rexford Guy Tugwell, "America's War-Time Socialism," the *Nation* (1927), pp. 364–65. Quoted in Leuchtenburg, "The New Deal," pp. 90–91.

[54]In January, 1927, Croly wrote a *New Republic* editorial, "An Apology for Fascism," endorsing an accompanying article, "Fascism for the Italians," written by the distin-guished philosopher Horace M. Kallen, a disciple of John Dewey and an exponent of progressive pragmatism. Kallen praised Mussolini for his pragmatic approach, and in particular for the *élan vital* that Mussolini had infused into Italian life. True, Professor Kallen conceded, fascism is coercive, but surely this is only a temporary expedient. Noting fascism's excellent achievements in economics, education, and administrative reform, Kallen added that "in this respect the Fascist revolution is not unlike the Communist revolution. Each is the application by force . . . of an ide-ology to a condition. Each should have the freest opportunity once it has made a start." The accompanying *New Republic* editorial endorsed Kallen's thesis and added that "alien critics should beware of outlawing a political experiment which aroused in a whole nation an increased moral energy and dignified its activities by subordinating them to a deeply felt common purpose." *New Republic* 49 (January 12, 1927): 207–13. Cited in John Patrick Diggins, "Mussolini's Italy: The View from America" (Ph.D. diss., University of Southern California, 1964), pp. 214–17.

[55]Born in Ireland, David Croly became a distinguished journalist in New York City and rose to the editorship of the New York *World*. He organized the first Positivist Circle in the United States and financed an American speaking tour for the Comtian Henry Edgar. The Positivist Circle met at Croly's home, and in 1871, David Croly published *A Positivist Primer*. When Herbert was born in 1869, he was consecrated

And what of Professor Dewey, the doyen of the pacifist intel-lectuals-turned drumbeaters for war? In a little-known period of his life, John Dewey spent the immediate postwar years, 1919–21, teaching at Peking University and traveling in the Far East. China was then in a period of turmoil over the clauses of the Versailles Treaty that transferred the rights of dominance in Shantung from Germany to Japan. Japan had been promised this reward by the British and French in secret treaties in return for entering the war against Germany. The Wilson Administration was torn between the two camps. On the one hand were those who wished to stand by the Allied decision and who envisioned using Japan as a club against Bolshevik–Russian Asia. On the other were those who had already begun to sound the alarm about a Japanese menace and who were committed to China, often because of connections with the American Protestant missionaries who wished to defend and expand their extraterritorial powers of governance in China. The Wilson Administration, which had originally taken a pro-Chinese stand, reversed itself in the spring of 1919 and endorsed the Versailles provisions.

Into this complex situation John Dewey plunged, seeing no complexity and of course considering it unthinkable for either him or the United States to stay out of the entire fray. Dewey leaped into total support of the Chinese-nationalist position, hailing the aggressive Young China movement and even endorsing the pro-missionary YMCA in China as "social workers." Dewey thundered that while "I didn't expect to be a jingo," Japan must be called to account, and that Japan is the great menace in Asia. Thus, scarcely had Dewey ceased being a champion of one terrible world war than he began to pave the way for an even greater one.[56]

ECONOMICS IN SERVICE OF THE STATE: THE EMPIRICISM OF RICHARD T. ELY

World War I was the apotheosis of the growing notion of in-tellectuals as servants of the state and junior partners in state rule. In the new fusion of intellectuals and state, each was of powerful aid to the other. Intellectuals could serve the state by apologizing for and supplying rationales for its deeds. Intellectuals were also needed to staff important positions as planners and controllers of the society and economy. The state could also serve intellectuals by

---

by his father to the Goddess Humanity, the symbol of Comte's Religion of Hu-manity. See the illuminating recent biography of Herbert Croly by David W. Levy, *Herbert Croly of the New Republic* (Princeton, N.J.: Princeton University Press, 1985).
[56]See Jerry Israel, *Progressivism and the Open Door: America and China, 1905–1921* (Pittsburgh, Penn.: University of Pittsburgh Press, 1971).

restricting entry into, and thereby raising the income and the prestige of, the various occupations and professions. During World War I, historians were of particular importance in supplying the government with war propaganda, convincing the public of the unique evil of Germans throughout history and of the satanic designs of the Kaiser. Economists, particularly empirical economists and statisticians, were of great importance in the planning and control of the nation's wartime economy. Historians playing preeminent roles in the war propaganda machine have been studied fairly extensively; economists and statisticians, playing a less blatant and allegedly value-free role, have received far less attention.[57]

Although it is an outworn generalization to say that 19th-century economists were stalwart champions of laissez faire, it is still true that deductive economic theory proved to be a mighty bulwark against government intervention. For, basically, economic theory showed the harmony and order inherent in the free market, as well as the counterproductive distortions and economic shackles imposed by state intervention. In order for statism to dominate the economics profession, then, it was important to discredit deductive theory. One of the most important ways of doing so was to advance the notion that, to be genuinely scientific, economics had to eschew generalization and deductive laws and simply engage in empirical inquiry into the facts of history and historical institutions, hoping that somehow laws would eventually arise from these detailed investigations. Thus the German Historical School, which managed to seize control of the economics discipline in Germany, fiercely proclaimed not only its devotion to statism and government control, but also its opposition to the abstract deductive laws of political economy. This was the first major group within the economics profession to champion what Ludwig von Mises was later to call antieconomics. Gustav Schmoller, the leader of the Historical School, proudly declared that his and his colleagues' major task at the University of Berlin was to form "the intellectual bodyguard of the House of Hohenzollern."

During the 1880s and 1890s, bright young graduate students in history and the social sciences went to Germany, the home of the

---

[57]For a refreshingly acidulous portrayal of the actions of the historians in World War I, see C. Hartley Grattan, "The Historians Cut Loose," *American Mercury* (August 1927), reprinted in Harry Elmer Barnes, *In Quest of Truth and Justice*, 2nd ed. (Colorado Springs, Colo.: Ralph Myles, 1972), pp. 142–64. A more extended account is George T. Blakey, *Historians on the Homefront: American Propagandists for the Great War* (Lexington: University Press of Kentucky, 1970). Gruber, *Mars and Minerva*, deals with academia and social scientists, but concentrates on historians. James R. Mock and Cedric Larson, *Words that Won the War* (Princeton, N.J.: Princeton University Press, 1939), presents the story of the "Creel Committee," the Committee on Public Information, the official propaganda ministry during the war.

Ph.D. degree, to obtain their doctorates. Almost to a man, they returned to the United States to teach in colleges and in the newly-created graduate schools, imbued with the excitement of the new economics and political science. It was a new social science that lauded the German and Bismarckian development of a powerful welfare–warfare state, a state seemingly above all social classes, that fused the nation into an integrated and allegedly harmonious whole. The new society and polity was to be run by a powerful central government, cartelizing, dictating, arbitrating, and controlling, thereby eliminating competitive laissez-faire capitalism on the one hand and the threat of proletarian socialism on the other. And at or near the head of the new dispensation was to be the new breed of intellectuals, technocrats, and planners, directing, staffing, propagandizing, and selflessly promoting the common good while ruling and lording over the rest of society. In short, doing well by doing good. To the new breed of progressive and statist intellectuals, in America, this was a heady vision indeed.

Richard T. Ely, virtually the founder of this new breed, was the leading progressive economist and also the teacher of most of the others. As an ardent postmillennialist pietist, Ely was convinced that he was serving God and Christ as well. Like so many pietists, Ely was born (in 1854) of solid Yankee and old Puritan stock, again in the midst of the fanatical Burned-Over District of western New York. Ely's father, Ezra, was an extreme Sabbatarian, preventing his family from playing games or reading books on Sunday, and so ardent a prohibitionist that, even though an impoverished, marginal farmer, he refused to grow barley, a crop uniquely suitable to his soil, because it would have been used to make that monstrously sinful product, beer.[58] Having been graduated from Columbia College in 1876, Ely went to Germany and received his Ph.D. from Heidelberg in 1879. In several decades of teaching at Johns Hopkins and then at Wisconsin, the energetic and empire-building Ely became enormously influential in American thought and politics. At Johns Hopkins he turned out a gallery of influential students and statist disciples in all fields of the social sciences as well as economics. These disciples were headed by the pro-union institutionalist economist John R. Commons, and included the social-control sociologists Edward Alsworth Ross and Albion W. Small; John H. Finlay, President of City College of New York; Dr. Albert Shaw, editor of the *Review of Reviews* and influential adviser and theoretician to Theodore Roosevelt; the municipal reformer Frederick C.

---

[58]See the useful biography of Ely, Benjamin G. Rader, *The Academic Mind and Reform: The Influence of Richard T. Ely in American Life* (Lexington: University Press of Kentucky, 1966).

Howe; and the historians Frederick Jackson Turner and J. Franklin Jameson. Newton D. Baker was trained by Ely at Hopkins, and Woodrow Wilson was also his student there, although there is no direct evidence of intellectual influence.

In the mid-1880s, Richard Ely founded the American Economic Association in a conscious attempt to commit the economics profession to statism as against the older laissez-faire economists grouped in the Political Economy Club. Ely continued as secretary-treasurer of the AEA for seven years, until his reformer allies decided to weaken the association's commitment to statism in order to induce the laissez-faire economists to join the organization. At that point, Ely, in high dudgeon, left the AEA.

At Wisconsin in 1892, Ely formed a new School of Economics, Political Science, and History, surrounded himself with former students, and gave birth to the Wisconsin Idea which, with the help of John Commons, succeeded in passing a host of progressive measures for government regulation in Wisconsin. Ely and the others formed an unofficial but powerful braintrust for the progressive regime of Wisconsin Governor Robert M. La Follette, who got his start in Wisconsin politics as an advocate of prohibition. Though never a classroom student of Ely's, La Follette always referred to Ely as his teacher and as the molder of the Wisconsin Idea. And Theodore Roosevelt once declared that Ely "first introduced me to radicalism in economics and then made me sane in my radicalism."[59]

Ely was also one of the most prominent postmillennialist intellectuals of the era. He fervently believed that the state is God's chosen instrument for reforming and Christianizing the social order so that eventually Jesus would arrive and put an end to history. The state, declared Ely, "is religious in its essence," and, furthermore, "God works through the State in carrying out His purposes more universally than through any other institution." The task of the church is to guide the state and utilize it in these needed reforms.[60]

An inveterate activist and organizer, Ely was prominent in the evangelical Chautauqua movement, and he founded there the Christian Sociology summer school, which infused the influential Chautauqua operation with the concepts and the personnel of the Social Gospel movement. Ely was a friend and close associate of

[59]Sidney Fine, *Laissez Faire and the General-Welfare State: A Study of Conflict in American Thought, 1865–1901* (Ann Arbor: University of Michigan Press, 1956), pp. 239–40.

[60]Ibid., pp. 180–81.

Social Gospel leaders Reverends Washington Gladden, Walter Rauschenbusch, and Josiah Strong. With Strong and Commons, Ely organized the Institute of Christian Sociology.[61] Ely also founded and became the secretary of the Christian Social Union of the Episcopal Church, along with Christian Socialist W.D.P. Bliss.

All of these activities were infused with postmillennial statism. Thus, the Institute of Christian Sociology was pledged to present God's "kingdom as the complete ideal of human society to be realized on earth." Moreover,

> Ely viewed the state as the greatest redemptive force in society. . . . In Ely's eyes, government was the God-given instrument through which we had to work. Its preeminence as a divine instrument was based on the post-Reformation abolition of the division between the sacred and the secular and on the state's power to implement ethical solutions to public problems. The same identification of sacred and secular which took place among liberal clergy enabled Ely to both divinize the state and socialize Christianity: he thought of government as God's main instrument of redemption.[62]

When war came, Richard Ely was for some reason (perhaps because he was in his 60s) left out of the excitement of war work and economic planning in Washington. He bitterly regretted that "I have not had a more active part then I have had in this greatest war in the world's history."[63] But Ely made up for his lack as best he could; virtually from the start of the European war, he whooped it up for militarism, war, the discipline of conscription, and the suppression of dissent and disloyalty at home. A lifelong militarist, Ely had tried to volunteer for war service in the Spanish–American War, had called for the suppression of the Philippine insurrection, and was particularly eager for conscription and for forced labor for

[61]John Rogers Commons was of old Yankee stock, descendant of John Rogers, Puritan martyr in England, and born in the Yankee area of the Western Reserve in Ohio and reared in Indiana. His Vermont mother was a graduate of the hotbed of pietism, Oberlin College, and she sent John to Oberlin in the hopes that he would become a minister. While he was in college, Commons and his mother launched a prohibitionist publication at the request of the Anti-Saloon League. After graduation, Commons went to Johns Hopkins to study under Ely, but flunked out of graduate school. See John R. Commons, *Myself* (Madison: University of Wisconsin Press, 1964). Also see Joseph Dorfman, *The Economic Mind in American Civilization* (New York: Viking, 1949), 3, pp. 276–77; Mary O. Furner, *Advocacy and Objectivity: A Crisis in the Professionalization of American Social Science, 1865–1905* (Lexington: University Press of Kentucky, 1975), pp. 198–204.

[62]Quandt, "Religion and Social Thought," pp. 402–3. Ely did not expect the millennial Kingdom to be far off. He believed that it was the task of the universities and of the social sciences "to teach the complexities of the Christian duty of brotherhood" in order to arrive at the New Jerusalem "which we are all eagerly awaiting." The church's mission was to attack every evil institution, "until the earth becomes a new earth, and all its cities, cities of God."

[63]Gruber, *Mars and Minerva*, p. 114.

loafers during World War I. By 1915, Ely was agitating for immediate compulsory military service, and the following year he joined the ardently pro-war and heavily big-business-influenced National Security League, where he called for the liberation of the German people from "autocracy."[64] In his advocacy of conscription, Ely was neatly able to combine moral, economic, and prohibitionist arguments for the draft: "The moral effect of taking boys off street corners and out of saloons and drilling them is excellent, and the economic effects are likewise beneficial."[65] Indeed, conscription for Ely served almost as a panacea for all ills. So enthusiastic was he about the World War I experience that Ely again prescribed his favorite cure-all to alleviate the 1929 depression. He proposed a permanent peacetime industrial army engaged in public works and manned by conscripting youth for strenuous physical labor. This conscription would instill into America's youth the essential "military ideals of hardihood and discipline," a discipline once provided by life on the farm but unavailable to the bulk of the populace now growing up in the effete cities. This small, standing conscript army could then speedily absorb the unemployed during depressions. Under the command of "an economic general staff," the industrial army would "go to work to relieve distress with all the vigor and resources of brain and brawn that we employed in the World War."[66]

Deprived of a position in Washington, Ely made the stamping out of disloyalty at home his major contribution to the war effort. He called for the total suspension of academic freedom for the duration. Any professor, he declared, who stated "opinions which hinder us in this awful struggle" should be fired if not indeed "shot." The particular focus of Ely's formidable energy was a zealous campaign to try to get his old ally in Wisconsin politics, Robert

---

[64]See Rader, *The Academic Mind and Reform*, pp. 181–91. On the big business affiliations of National Security League leaders, especially J. P. Morgan and others in the Morgan ambit, see C. Hartley Grattan, *Why We Fought* (New York: Vanguard Press, 1929) pp. 117–18, and Robert D. Ward, "The Origin and Activities of the National Security League, 1914–1919," *Mississippi Valley Historical Review* 47 (June 1960): 51–65.

[65]The Chamber of Commerce of the United States spelled out the long-run economic benefit of conscription, that for America's youth it would "substitute a period of helpful discipline for a period of demoralizing freedom from restraint. " John Patrick Finnegan, *Against the Specter of a Dragon: The Campaign for American Military Preparedness, 1914–1917* (Westport, Conn.: Greenwood Press, 1974), p. 110. On the broad and enthusiastic support given to the draft by the Chamber of Commerce, see Chase C. Mooney and Martha E. Layman, "Some Phases of the Compulsory Military Training Movement, 1914–1920," *Mississippi Valley Historical Review* 38 (March 1952): 640.

[66]Richard T. Ely, *Hard Times: The Way In and the Way Out* (1931), cited in Dorfman, *The Economic Mind in American Civilization*, 5, p. 671; and in Leuchtenburg, "The New Deal," p. 94.

M. La Follette, expelled from the U.S. Senate for continuing to oppose America's participation in the war. Ely declared that his "blood boils" at La Follette's "treason" and attacks on war profiteering. Throwing himself into the battle, Ely founded and became president of the Madison chapter of the Wisconsin Loyalty Legion and mounted a campaign to expel La Follette.[67] The campaign was meant to mobilize the Wisconsin faculty and to support the ultra-patriotic and ultra-hawkish activities of Theodore Roosevelt. Ely wrote to Roosevelt that "we must crush La Follettism." In his unremitting campaign against the Wisconsin Senator, Ely thundered that La Follette "has been of more help to the Kaiser than a quarter of a million troops."[68] Empiricism rampant.

The faculty of the University of Wisconsin was stung by charges throughout the state and the country that its failure to denounce La Follette was proof that the university—long affiliated with La Follette in state politics—supported his disloyal antiwar policies. Prodded by Ely, Commons, and others, the university's War Committee drew up and circulated a petition, signed by the university president, all the deans, and over 90 percent of the faculty, that provided one of the more striking examples in United States history of academic truckling to the state apparatus. None too subtly using the constitutional verbiage for treason, the petition protested "against those utterances and actions of Senator La Follette which have given aid and comfort to Germany and her allies in the present war; we deplore his failure loyally to support the government in the prosecution of the war."[69]

Behind the scenes, Ely tried his best to mobilize America's historians against La Follette, to demonstrate that he had given aid and comfort to the enemy. Ely was able to enlist the services of the National Board of Historical Service, the propaganda agency established by professional historians for the duration of the war, and of the government's own propaganda arm, the Committee on Public Information. Warning that the effort must remain secret, Ely mobilized historians under the aegis of these organizations to research German and Austrian newspapers and journals to try to build a record of La Follette's alleged influence, "indicating the encouragement he has given Germany." The historian E. Merton Coulter revealed the objective spirit animating these researches: "I

---

[67]Ely drew up a super-patriotic pledge for the Madison chapter of the Loyalty Legion, pledging its members to "stamp out disloyalty." The pledge also expressed unqualified support for the Espionage Act and vowed to "work against La Follettism in all its anti-war forms." Rader, *The Academic Mind and Reform*, pp. 183ff.

[68]Gruber, *Mars and Minerva*, p. 207.

[69]Ibid., p. 207.

understand it is to be an unbiased and candid account of the Senator's [La Follette's] course and its effect—but we all know it can lead but to one conclusion—something little short of treason."[70]

Professor Gruber well notes that this campaign to get La Follette was "a remarkable example of the uses of scholarship for espionage. It was a far cry from the disinterested search for truth for a group of professors to mobilize a secret research campaign to find ammunition to destroy the political career of a United States senator who did not share their view of the war."[71] In any event, no evidence was turned up, the movement failed, and the Wisconsin professoriat began to move away in distrust from the Loyalty Legion.[72]

After the menace of the Kaiser had been extirpated, the Armistice found Professor Ely, along with his compatriots in the National Security League, ready to segue into the next round of patriotic repression. During Ely's anti-La Follette research campaign he had urged investigation of "the kind of influence which he [La Follette] has exerted against our country in Russia." Ely pointed out that modern democracy requires a "high degree of conformity" and that therefore the "most serious menace" of Bolshevism, which Ely depicted as "social disease germs," must be fought "with repressive measures."

By 1924, however, Richard T. Ely's career of repression was over, and what is more, in a rare instance of the workings of poetic justice, he was hoist with his own petard. In 1922, the much traduced Robert La Follette was reelected to the Senate and also swept the Progressives back into power in the state of Wisconsin. By 1924, the Progressives had gained control of the Board of Regents, and they moved to cut off the water of their former academic ally and empire builder. Ely then felt it prudent to move out of Wisconsin together with his Institute, and while he lingered for some years at Northwestern University, the heyday of Ely's fame and fortune was over.

---

[70]Ibid., pp. 208, 208n.

[71]Ibid., pp. 209–10. In his autobiography, written in 1938, Richard Ely rewrote history to cover up his ignominious role in the get-La Follette campaign. He acknowledged signing the faculty petition, but then had the temerity to claim that he "was not one of the ring-leaders, as La Follette thought, in circulating this petition." There is no mention of his secret research campaign against La Follette.

[72]For more on the anti-La Follette campaign, see C. Peterson and Gilbert C. Fite, *Opponents of War: 1917–1918* (Madison: University of Wisconsin Press, 1957), pp. 68–72; Paul L. Murphy, *World War I and the Origin of Civil Liberties in the United States* (New York: W. W. Norton, 1979), p. 120; and Belle Case La Follette and Fola La Follette, *Robert M. La Follette* (New York: Macmillan, 1953).

ECONOMICS IN SERVICE OF THE STATE:
GOVERNMENT AND STATISTICS

Statistics is a vital, though much underplayed, requisite of modern government. Government could not even presume to control, regulate, or plan any portion of the economy without the service of its statistical bureaus and agencies. Deprive government of its statistics and it would be a blind and helpless giant, with no idea whatever of what to do or where to do it. It might be replied that business firms, too, need statistics in order to function. But business needs for statistics are far less in quantity and also different in quality. Business may need statistics in its own micro area of the economy, but only on its prices and costs; it has little need for broad collections of data or for sweeping, holistic aggregates. Business could perhaps rely on its own privately-collected and unshared data. Furthermore, much entrepreneurial knowledge is qualitative, not enshrined in quantitative data, and of a particular time, area, and location. But government bureaucracy could do nothing if forced to be confined to qualitative data. Deprived of profit-and-loss tests for efficiency, or the need to serve consumers efficiently, conscripting both capital and operating costs from taxpayers, and forced to abide by fixed, bureaucratic rules, modern government shorn of masses of statistics could do virtually nothing.[73]

Hence the enormous importance of World War I, not only in providing the power and the precedent for a collectivized economy, but also in greatly accelerating the advent of statisticians and statistical agencies of government, many of which (and whom) remained in government, ready for the next leap forward of power.

Richard T. Ely, of course, championed the new empirical look-and-see approach, with the aim of fact-gathering to "mold the forces at work in society and to improve existing conditions."[74] More importantly, one of the leading authorities on the growth of government expenditure has linked it with statistics and empirical data: "Advance in economic science and statistics . . . strengthened belief in the possibilities of dealing with social problems by collective action. It made for increase in the statistical and other

---

[73]Thus, Terence W. Hutchison, from a very different perspective, notes the contrast between Carl Menger's stress on the beneficent, unplanned phenomena of society, such as the free market, and the growth of "social self-consciousness" and government planning. Hutchison recognizes that a crucial component of that social self-consciousness is government statistics. Terence W. Hutchison, *A Review of Economic Doctrines, 1870–1929* (Oxford: Clarendon Press, 1953), pp. 150–51, 427.

[74]Fine, *Laissez Faire and the General-Welfare State*, p. 207.

fact-finding activities of government."[75] As early as 1863, Samuel B. Ruggles, American delegate to the International Statistical Congress in Berlin, proclaimed that "statistics are the very eyes of the statesman, enabling him to survey and scan with clear and comprehensive vision the whole structure and economy of the body politic."[76]

Conversely, this means that without these means of vision, the statesman would no longer be able to meddle, control, and plan.

Moreover, government statistics are clearly needed for specific types of intervention. Government could not intervene to alleviate unemployment unless unemployment statistics were collected and so the impetus for such collection. Carroll Wright, Bostonian, progressive reformer, and one of the first Commissioners of Labor in the United States, was greatly influenced by the famous statistician and German Historical School member, Ernst Engel, head of the Royal Statistical Bureau of Prussia. Wright sought the collection of unemployment statistics for that reason, and in general, for "the amelioration of unfortunate industrial and social relations." Henry Carter Adams, a former student of Engel's, and, like Ely, a statist and progressive new economist, established the Statistical Bureau of the Interstate Commerce Commission, believing that "ever increasing statistical activity by the government was essential—for the sake of controlling naturally monopolistic industries." And Professor Irving Fisher of Yale, eager for government to stabilize the price level, conceded that he wrote *The Making of Index Numbers* to solve the problem of the unreliability of index numbers. "Until this difficulty could be met, stabilization could scarcely be expected to become a reality."

[75]Solomon Fabricant, *The Trend of Government Activity in the United States since 1900* (New York: National Bureau of Economic Research, 1952), p. 143. Similarly, an authoritative work on the growth of government in England puts it this way: "The accumulation of factual information about social conditions and the development of economics and the social sciences increased the pressure for government intervention. . . . As statistics improved and students of social conditions multiplied, the continued existence of such conditions was kept before the public. Increasing knowledge of them aroused influential circles and furnished working-class movements with factual weapons." Moses Abramovitz and Vera F. Eliasberg, *The Growth of Public Employment in Great Britain* (Princeton, N.J.: National Bureau of Economic Research, 1957), pp. 22–23, 30. Also see M. J. Cullen, *The Statistical Movement in Early Victorian Britain: The Foundations of Empirical Social Research* (New York: Barnes and Noble, 1975).

[76]See Joseph Dorfman, "The Role of the German Historical School in American Economic Thought," *American Economic Review, Papers and Proceedings* 45 (May 1955): 18. George Hildebrand remarked on the inductive emphasis of the German Historical School that "perhaps there is, then, some connection between this kind of teaching and the popularity of crude ideas of physical planning in more recent times." George H. Hildebrand, "International Flow of Economic Ideas-Discussion," ibid., p. 37.

Henry Carter Adams, the son of a New England pietist Congregationalist preacher on missionary duty in Iowa, studied for the ministry at his father's alma mater, Andover Theological Seminary, but soon abandoned this path. Adams devised the accounting system of the Statistical Bureau of the Interstate Commerce Commission. This system "served as a model for the regulation of public utilities here and throughout the world."[77]

Irving Fisher was the son of a Rhode Island Congregationalist pietist preacher, and his parents were both of old Yankee stock, his mother a strict Sabbatarian. As befitted what his son and biographer called his "crusading spirit," Fisher was an inveterate reformer, urging the imposition of numerous progressive measures including Esperanto, simplified spelling, and calendar reform. He was particularly enthusiastic about purging the world of "such iniquities of civilization as alcohol, tea, coffee, tobacco, refined sugar, and bleached white flour."[78] During the 1920s, Fisher was the leading prophet of that so-called New Era in economics and in society. He wrote three books during the 1920s, praising the noble experiment of prohibition, and he lauded Governor Benjamin Strong and the Federal Reserve System for following his advice and expanding money and credit so as to keep the wholesale price level virtually constant. Because of the Fed's success in imposing Fisherine price stabilization, Fisher was so sure that there could be no depression that as late as 1930 he wrote a book claiming that there was and could be no stock crash and that stock prices would quickly rebound. Throughout the 1920s, Fisher insisted that since wholesale prices remained constant, there was nothing amiss about the wild boom in stocks. Meanwhile, he put his theories into practice by heavily investing his heiress wife's considerable fortune in the stock market. After the crash, he frittered away his sister-in-law's money when his wife's fortune was depleted, at the same time calling frantically on the federal government to inflate money and credit and to reinflate stock prices to their 1929 levels. Despite his dissipation of two family fortunes, Fisher managed to blame almost everyone except himself for the debacle.[79]

[77]Dorfman, "The Role of the German Historical School in American Economic Thought," p. 23. On Wright and Adams, see Dorfman, *The Economic Mind in American Civilization*, 3, pp. 164–74, 123; and Boyer, *Urban Masses*, p. 163. Furthee, the first professor of statistics in the United States, Roland P. Falkner, was a devoted student of Engel's and a translator of the works of Engel's assistant, August Meitzen.

[78]Irving Norton Fisher, *My Father Irving Fisher* (New York: Comet Press, 1956), pp. 146–47. Also for Fisher, see Irving Fisher, *Stabilised Money* (London: Allen and Unwin, 1935), p. 383.

[79]Fisher, *My Father Irving Fisher*, pp. 264–67. On Fisher's role and influence during this period, see Murray N. Rothbard, *America's Great Depression*, 4th ed. (New York: Richardson and Snyder, 1983). Also see Joseph S. Davis, *The World Between the Wars*,

As we shall see, in light of the growing importance of Wesley Clair Mitchell in the burgeoning of government statistics in World War I, Mitchell's view on statistics are of particular importance.[80] Mitchell, an institutionalist and student of Thorstein Veblen, was one of the prime founders of modern statistical inquiry in economics and clearly aspired to lay the basis for so-called scientific government planning. As Professor Dorfman, friend and student of Mitchell's, put it, quoting Mitchell:

> "clearly the type of social invention most needed today is one that offers definite techniques through which the social system can be controlled and operated to the optimum advantage of its members." To this end he constantly sought to extend, improve and refine the gathering and compilation of data. . . . Mitchell believed that business-cycle analysis . . . might indicate the means to the achievement of orderly social control of business activity.[81]

Or, as Mitchell's wife and collaborator stated in her memoirs:

> He [Mitchell] envisaged the great contribution that government could make to the understanding of economic and social problems if the statistical data gathered independently by various Federal agencies were systematized and planned so that the interrelationships among them could be studied. The idea of developing social statistics, *not merely as a record but as a basis for planning,* emerged early in his own work.[82]

Particularly important in the expansion of statistics in World War I was the growing insistence, by progressive intellectuals and corporate liberal businessmen alike, that democratic decision-making must be increasingly replaced by the administrative and technocratic. Democratic or legislative decisions were messy, inefficient, and might lead to a significant curbing of statism, as had happened in the heyday of the Democratic party during the 19th century. But if decisions were largely administrative and technocratic, the burgeoning of state power could continue unchecked. The collapse of the laissez-faire creed of the Democrats in 1896 left

---

1919–39: An Economist's View (Baltimore, Maryland: Johns Hopkins University Press, 1975), p. 194; and Melchior Palyi, *The Twilight of Gold, 1914–1936: Myths and Realities* (Chicago: Henry Regnery, 1972), pp. 240, 249.

[80]Wesley C. Mitchell was of old Yankee pietist stock. His grandparents were farmers in Maine and then in Western New York. His mother followed the path of many Yankees in migrating to a farm in northern Illinois. Mitchell attended the University of Chicago, where he was strongly influenced by Veblen and John Dewey. Dorfman, *The Economic Mind in American Civilization*, 3, p. 456.

[81]Dorfman, *The Economic Mind in American Civilization*, 4, pp. 376, 361.

[82]Emphasis added. Lucy Sprague Mitchell, *Two Lives* (New York: Simon and Schuster, 1953), p. 363. For more on this entire topic, see Murray N. Rothbard, "The Politics of Political Economists: Comment," *Quarterly Journal of Economics* 74 (November 1960): 659–65.

a power vacuum in government that administrative and corporatist types were eager to fill. Increasingly, then, such powerful corporatist big business groups as the National Civic Federation disseminated the idea that governmental decisions should be in the hands of the efficient technician, the allegedly value-free expert. In short, government, in virtually all of its aspects, should be "taken out of politics." And statistical research, with its aura of empiricism, quantitative precision, and non-political value-freedom, was in the forefront of such emphasis. In the municipalities, an increasingly powerful progressive reform movement shifted decisions from elections in neighborhood wards to citywide professional managers and school superintendents. As a corollary, political power was increasingly shifted from working class and ethnic-German Lutheran and Catholic wards to upper-class pietist business groups.[83]

By the time World War I arrived in Europe, a coalition of progressive intellectuals and corporatist business men was ready to go national in sponsoring allegedly objective statistical research institutes and think tanks. Their views have been aptly summed up by David Eakins:

> The conclusion being drawn by these people by 1915 was that fact-finding and policymaking had to be isolated from class struggle and freed from political pressure groups. The reforms that would lead to industrial peace and social order, these experts were coming to believe, could only be derived from data determined by objective fact-finders (such as themselves) and under the auspices of sober and respectable organizations (such as only they could construct). The capitalist system could be improved only by a single-minded reliance upon experts detached from the hurly-burly of democratic policymaking. The emphasis was upon efficiency—and democratic policymaking was inefficient. An approach to the making of national economic and social policy outside traditional democratic political processes was thus emerging before the United States formally entered World War I.[84]

Several corporatist businessmen and intellectuals moved at about the same time toward founding such statistical research institutes. In 1906–07, Jerome D. Greene, secretary of the Harvard University Corporation, helped found an elite Tuesday Evening

---

[83]See in particular Weinstein, *The Corporate Ideal in the Liberal State*; and Samuel P. Hays, "The Politics of Reform in Municipal Government in the Progressive Era," *Pacific Northwest Quarterly* 59 (October 1964), pp. 157–69.

[84]David Eakins, "The Origins of Corporate Liberal Policy Research, 1916–1922: The Political-Economic Expert and the Decline of Public Debate," in *Building the Organizational Society*, Israel, ed., p. 164.

Club at Harvard to explore important issues in economics and the social sciences. In 1910, Greene rose to an even more-powerful post as general manager of the new Rockefeller Institute for Medical Research, and three years later Greene became secretary and CEO of the powerful philanthropic organization, the Rockefeller Foundation. Greene immediately began to move toward establishing a Rockefeller-funded institute for economic research, and in March, 1914, he called an exploratory group together in New York, chaired by his friend and mentor in economics, the first Dean of the Harvard Graduate School of Business, Edwin F. Gay. The developing idea was that Gay would become head of a new, scientific and impartial organization, The Institute of Economic Research, which would gather statistical facts, and that Wesley Mitchell would be its director.[85]

However, opposing advisers to John D. Rockefeller, Jr., won out over Greene, and the Institute plan was scuttled.[86] Mitchell and Gay pressed on, with the lead now taken by Mitchell's long-time friend, chief statistician and vice-president of AT&T, Malcolm C. Rorty. Rorty proceeded to line up support for the idea from a large number of progressive statisticians and prominent businessmen, including Chicago publisher of business books and magazines, Arch W. Shaw; E. H. Goodwin of the U.S. Chamber of Commerce; Magnus Alexander, statistician and assistant to the president of General Electric, like AT&T, a Morgan-oriented concern; John R. Commons, economist and aide-de-camp to Richard T. Ely at Wisconsin; and Nahum I. Stone, statistician, former Marxist, a leader in the scientific management movement, and labor manager for the Hickey Freeman clothing company. This group was in the

[85]Herbert Heaton, *Edwin F. Gay, A Scholar in Action* (Cambridge, Mass.: Harvard University Press, 1952). Edwin Gay was born in Detroit of old New England stock. His father had been born in Boston and went into his father-in-law's lumber business in Michigan. Gay's mother was the daughter of a wealthy preacher and lumberman. Gay entered the University of Michigan, was heavily influenced by the teaching of John Dewey, and then stayed in graduate school in Germany for over a dozen years, finally obtaining his Ph.D. in economic history at the University of Berlin. The major German influences on Gay were Gustav Schmoller, head of the German Historical School, who emphasized that economics must be an "inductive science," and Adolf Wagner, also at the University of Berlin, who favored large-scale government intervention in the economy in behalf of Christian ethics. Back at Harvard, Gay was the major single force, in collaboration with the Boston Chamber of Commerce, in pushing through a factory-inspection act in Massachusetts, and in early 1911, Gay became president of the Massachusetts branch of the American Association for Labor Legislation, an organization founded by Richard T. Ely and dedicated to agitating for government intervention in the area of labor unions, minimum wage rates, unemployment, public works, and welfare.

[86]On the pulling and hauling among Rockefeller advisers on the Institute, see David M. Grossman, "American Foundations and the Support of Economic Research, 1913–29," *Minerva* 22 (Spring–Summer 1982): 62–72.

process of forming a Committee on National Income when the United States entered the war, and they were forced to shelve their plans temporarily.[87] After the war, however, the group set up the National Bureau of Economic Research, in 1920.[88]

While the National Bureau was not to take final shape until after the war, another organization, created on similar lines, successfully won Greene's and Rockefeller's support. In 1916, they were persuaded by Raymond B. Fosdick to found the Institute for Government Research (IGR).[89] The IGR was slightly different in focus from the National Bureau group, as it grew directly out of municipal progressive reform and the political-science profession. One of the important devices used by the municipal reformers was the private bureau of municipal research, which tried to seize decision-making from allegedly-corrupt democratic bodies on behalf of efficient, nonpartisan organizations headed by progressive technocrats and social scientists. In 1910, President William Howard Taft, intrigued with the potential for centralizing power in a chief executive inherent in the idea of the executive budget, appointed the "father of the budget idea," the political scientist Frederick D. Cleveland, who was the director of the New York Bureau of Municipal Research, as head of a Commission on Economy and Efficiency (the "Cleveland Commission"). The Cleveland Commission also included political scientist and municipal reformer Frank Goodnow, professor of public law at Columbia University, first president of the American Political Science Association and president of Johns Hopkins; and William Franklin Willoughby, a former student of Ely and Assistant Director of the Bureau of Census, who later became President of the American Association for Labor Legislation.[90] The Cleveland Commission was delighted to tell President Taft precisely what he wanted to hear. The Commission recommended sweeping administrative changes that would provide a Bureau of Central Administrative Control to form a "consolidated information and statistical arm of the entire national government." And at the heart of the new Bureau would be the Budget Division which, at the behest of the president, was to develop and then

[87]See Eakins, "The Origins of Corporate Liberal Policy Research," pp. 166–67; Grossman, "American Foundations," pp. 75–78; Heaton, *Edwin F. Gay*. On Stone, see Dorfman, *The Economic Mind in American Civilization*, 4, pp. 42, 60–61; and Samuel Haber, *Efficiency and Uplift: Scientific Management in the Progressive Era 1890–1920* (Chicago: University of Chicago Press, 1964), pp. 152, 165. During his Marxist period, Stone had translated Marx's *Poverty of Philosophy*.

[88]See Guy Alchon, *The Invisible Hand of Planning: Capitalism, Social Science, and the State in the 1920s* (Princeton, N.J.: Princeton University Press, 1985), pp. 54ff.

[89]Collier and Horowitz, *The Rockefellers*, p. 140.

[90]Eakins, "The Origins of Corporate Liberal Policy Research," p. 168. Also see Furner, *Advocacy and Objectivity*, pp. 282–86.

present "an annual program of business for the Federal Government to be financed by Congress."[91]

When Congress balked at the Cleveland Commission's recommendations, the disgruntled technocrats decided to establish an Institute for Government Research in Washington to battle for these and similar reforms. With funding secured from the Rockefeller Foundation, the IGR was chaired by Goodnow, with Willoughby as its director.[92] Soon, Robert S. Brookings assumed responsibility for the financing.

When America entered the war, present and future NBER and IGR leaders were all over Washington, key figures and statisticians in the collectivized war economy.

By far the most powerful of the growing number of economists and statisticians involved in World War I was Edwin F. Gay. As soon as America entered the war, Arch W. Shaw, an enthusiast for rigid wartime planning of economic resources, was made head of the new Commercial Economy Board by the Council for National Defense.[93] Shaw, who had taught at and served on the administrative board of Harvard Business School, staffed the Board with Harvard Business people; the secretary was Harvard economist Melvin T. Copeland, and other members included Dean Gay. The Board, which later became the powerful Conservation Division of the War Industries Board, focused on restricting competition in industry by eliminating the number and variety of products and by imposing compulsory uniformity, all in the name of aiding the war effort through the conservation of resources. For example, garment firms had complained loudly of severe competition because of the number and variety of styles, and so Gay urged the garment firms to

[91]Stephen Skowronek, *Building a New American State: The Expansion of National Administrative Capacities, 1877–1920* (Cambridge: Cambridge University Press, 1982), pp. 187–88.

[92]Vice-chairman of the IGR was retired St. Louis merchant and lumberman and former president of Washington University of St. Louis, Robert S. Brookings. Secretary of the IGR was James F. Curtis, formerly Assistant Secretary of the Treasury under Taft and now secretary and deputy governor of the New York Federal Reserve Bank. Others on the board of the IGR were ex-President Taft; railroad executive Frederick A. Delano, uncle of Franklin D. Roosevelt and member of the Federal Reserve Board; Arthur T. Hadley, economist and president of Yale; Charles C. Van Hise, progressive president of the University of Wisconsin, and ally of Ely; reformer and influential young Harvard Law professor, Felix Frankfurter; Theodore N. Vail, chairman of AT&T; progressive engineer and businessman, Herbert C. Hoover; and financier R. Fulton Cutting, an officer of the New York Bureau of Municipal Research. Eakins, "The Origins of Corporate Liberal Policy Research," pp. 168–69.

[93]On the Commercial Economy Board, see Grosvenor B. Clarkson, *Industrial America in the World War: The Strategy Behind the Line, 1917–1918* (Boston: Houghton Mifflin, 1923), pp. 211ff.

form a trade association to work with the government in curbing the surfeit of competition. Gay also tried to organize the bakers so that they would not follow the usual custom of taking back stale and unsold bread from retail outlets. By the end of 1917, Gay was tired of using voluntary persuasion, and was urging the government to use compulsory measures.

Gay's major power came in early 1918 when the Shipping Board, which had officially nationalized all ocean shipping, determined to restrict drastically the use of ships for civilian trade and to use the bulk of shipping for transport of American troops to France. Appointed in early January, 1918, as merely a special expert by the Shipping Board, Gay in a brief time became the key figure in redirecting shipping from civilian to military use. Soon Edwin Gay had become a member of the War Trade Board and head of its statistical department, which issued restrictive licenses for permitted imports; head of the statistical department of the Shipping Board; representative of the Shipping Board on the War Trade Board; head of the statistical committee of the Department of Labor; head of the Division of Planning and Statistics of the War Industries Board (WIB); and, above all, head of the new Central Bureau of Planning and Statistics. The Central Bureau was organized in the fall of 1918, when President Wilson asked WIB chairman Bernard Baruch to produce a monthly survey of all the government's war activities. This "conspectus" evolved into the Central Bureau, responsible directly to the President. The importance of the Bureau is noted by a recent historian:

> The new Bureau represented the "peak" statistical division of the mobilization, becoming its "seer and prophet" for the duration, coordinating over a thousand employees engaged in research and, as the agency responsible for giving the president a concise picture of the entire economy, becoming the closest approximation to a "central statistical commission." During the latter stages of the war it set up a clearinghouse of statistical work, organized liaisons with the statistical staff of all the war boards, and centralized the data production process for the entire war bureaucracy. By the war's end, Wesley Mitchell recalled, "we were in a fair way to develop for the first time a systematic organization of federal statistics."[94]

Within a year, Edwin Gay had risen from a special expert to the unquestioned czar of a giant network of federal statistical agencies, with over 1,000 researchers and statisticians working under his direct control.

[94] Alchon, *The Invisible Hand of Puffing*, p. 29. Mitchell headed the price statistics section of the Price-Fixing Committee of the War Industries Board.

It is no wonder then that Gay, instead of being enthusiastic about the American victory he had worked so hard to secure, saw the Armistice as "almost . . . a personal blow" that plunged him "into the slough of despond." All of his empire of statistics and control had just been coming together and developing into a mighty machine when suddenly "came that wretched Armistice."[95] Truly a tragedy of peace.

Gay tried valiantly to keep the war machinery going, continually complaining because many of his aides were leaving and bitterly denouncing the "hungry pack" who, for some odd reason, were clamoring for an immediate end to all wartime controls, including those closest to his heart, foreign trade and shipping. But one by one, despite the best efforts of Baruch and many of the wartime planners, the WIB and other war agencies disappeared.[96] For a while, Gay pinned his hopes on his Central Bureau of Planning and Statistics (CBPS), which, in a fierce bout of bureaucratic infighting, he attempted to make the key economic and statistical group advising the American negotiators at the Versailles peace conference, thereby displacing the team of historians and social scientists assembled by Colonel House in the inquiry. Despite an official victory, and an eight-volume report of the CBPS delivered to Versailles by the head of CBPS European team, John Foster Dulles of the War Trade Board, the bureau had little influence over the final treaty.[97]

Peace having finally and irrevocably arrived, Edwin Gay, backed by Mitchell, tried his best to have the CBPS kept as a permanent, peacetime organization. Gay argued that the agency—with himself of course remaining as its head—could provide continuing data to the League of Nations, and above all could serve as the president's own eyes and ears, and mold the sort of executive budget envisioned by the old Taft Commission. CBPS staff member and Harvard economist Edmund E. Day contributed a memorandum outlining specific tasks for the bureau to aid in demobilization and reconstruction, as well as a rationale for the bureau becoming a permanent part of government. One thing it could do was to make a "continuing canvass" of business conditions in the United States. As Gay put it to President Wilson, using an organicist analogy, a permanent Board would act "as a nervous system to the vast and complex organization of the government, furnishing

[95]Heaton, *Edwin Gay*, p. 129.

[96]See Rothbard, "War Collectivism," pp. 100–12.

[97]See Heaton, *Edwin Gay*, pp. 129ff; and the excellent book on the inquiry, Lawrence E. Gelfand, *The Inquiry: American Preparations for Peace, 1917–1919* (New Haven, Conn.: Yale University Press, 1963), pp. 166–68, 177–78.

to the controlling brain [the President] the information necessary for directing the efficient operation of the various members."[98] Although the President was "very cordial" to Gay's plan, Congress refused to agree, and on June 30, 1919, the Central Bureau of Planning and Statistics was finally terminated, along with the War Trade Board. Edwin Gay would now have to seek employment in, if not the private, at least the quasi-independent, sector.

But Gay and Mitchell were not to be denied. Nor would the Brookings–Willoughby group. Their objective would be met more gradually and by slightly different means. Gay became editor of the *New York Evening Post* under the aegis of its new owner and Gay's friend, J.P. Morgan partner Thomas W. Lamont. Gay also helped to form and become first president of the National Bureau of Economic Research in 1920, with Wesley C. Mitchell as research director. The Institute for Government Research achieved its major objective, establishing a Budget Bureau in the Treasury Department in 1921, with the director of the IGR, William F. Willoughby, helping to draft the bill that established the bureau.[99] The IGR people soon expanded their role to include economics, establishing an Institute of Economics which was headed by Robert Brookings and Arthur T. Hadley of Yale, with economist Harold G. Moulton as director.[100] The Institute, funded by the Carnegie Corporation, would be later merged, along with the IGR, into the Brookings Institution. Edwin Gay also moved into the foreign-policy field by becoming secretary-treasurer and head of the Research Committee of the new and extremely influential organization, the Council on Foreign Relations (CFR).[101]

And finally, in the field of government statistics, Gay and Mitchell found a more gradual but longer-range route to power via collaboration with Herbert Hoover, soon to be Secretary of Commerce. No sooner had Hoover assumed the post in early 1921

[98]Heaton, *Edwin Gay*, p. 135. Also Alchon, *The Invisible Hand of Puffing*, pp. 35–36.

[99]In 1939, the Bureau of the Budget would be transferred to the Executive Office, thus completing the IGR objective.

[100]Moulton was a professor of economics at the University of Chicago, and vice-president of the Chicago Association of Commerce. See Eakins, "The Origins of Corporate Liberal Policy Research," pp. 172–77; Dorfman, *The Economic Mind in American Civilization*, 4, pp. 11, 195–97.

[101]Gay had been recommended to the group by one of its founders, Thomas W. Lamont. It was Gay's suggestion that the CFR begin its major project by establishing an "authoritative" journal, *Foreign Affairs*. And it was Gay who selected his Harvard historian colleague Archibald Cary Coolidge as the first editor and the New York *Post* reporter Hamilton Fish Armstrong as assistant editor and executive director of the CFR. See Lawrence H. Shoup and William Minter, *Imperial Brain Trust: The Council on Foreign Relations and United States Foreign Policy* (New York: Monthly Review Press, 1977), pp. 16–19, 105, 110.

when he expanded the Advisory Committee on the Census to include Gay, Mitchell, and other economists and then launched the monthly *Survey of Current Business*. The *Survey* was designed to supplement the informational activities of cooperating trade associations and, by supplying business information, aid these associations in Hoover's aim of cartelizing their respective industries. Secrecy in business operations is a crucial weapon of competition, and conversely, publicity and sharing of information is an important tool of cartels in policing their members. The *Survey of Current Business* made available the current production, sales, and inventory data supplied by cooperating industries and technical journals. Hoover also hoped that by building on these services, eventually "the statistical program could provide the knowledge and foresight necessary to combat panic or speculative conditions, prevent the development of diseased industries, and guide decision-making so as to iron out rather than accentuate the business cycle."[102] In promoting his cartelization doctrine, Hoover met resistance both from some businessmen who resisted prying questionnaires and sharing competitive secrets, and from the Justice Department. But, a formidable empire-builder, Herbert Hoover managed to grab statistical services from the Treasury Department and to establish a waste-elimination division to organize businesses and trade associations to continue and expand the wartime "conservation program of compulsory uniformity and restriction of the number and variety of competitive products. For the position of assistant secretary to head up this program, Hoover secured engineer and publicist Frederick Feiker, an associate of Arch Shaw's business-publication empire. Hoover also found a top assistant and lifelong disciple in Brigadier General Julius Klein, a protégé of Edwin Gay's, who had headed the Latin American division of the Bureau of Foreign and Domestic Commerce. As the new head of the bureau, Klein organized 17 new export commodity divisions—reminiscent of commodity sections during wartime collectivism—each with experts drawn from the respective industries and each organizing regular cooperation with parallel industrial advisory committees. And through it all, Herbert Hoover made a series of well-publicized speeches during 1921, spelling out how a well-designed government trade program, as well as a program in the domestic economy, could act both as a stimulant to recovery and as a permanent stabilizer, while avoiding such unfortunate measures as abolishing tariffs or cutting wage rates. The most effective weapon, both in foreign and domestic trade, Hoover said,

[102]Ellis W. Hawley, "Herbert Hoover and Economic Stabilization, 1921–22," in *Herbert Hoover as Secretary of Commerce: Studies in New Era Thought and Practice*, Ellis Hawley, ed. (Iowa City: University of Iowa Press, 1981), p. 52.

was to eliminate waste by a cooperative mobilization of government and industry.[103]

A month after the Armistice, the American Economic Association and the American Statistical Association met jointly in Richmond, Virginia. The presidential addresses were delivered by men in the forefront of the exciting new world of government planning, aided by social science, that seemed to loom ahead. In his address to the American Statistical Association, Wesley Clair Mitchell proclaimed that the war had "led to the use of statistics, not only as a record of what had happened, but also as a vital factor in planning what should be done." As Mitchell had said in his final lecture at Columbia University the previous spring, the war had shown that when the community desires to attain a great goal "then within a short period far-reaching social changes can be achieved." "The need for scientific planning of social change," he added, "has never been greater, the chance of making those changes in an intelligent fashion . . . has never been so good." The peace will bring new problems, he opined, but "it seems impossible" that the various countries will "attempt to solve them without utilizing the same sort of centralized directing now employed to kill their enemies abroad for the new purpose of reconstructing their own life at home."

But the careful empiricist and statistician also provided a caveat. Broad social planning requires "a precise comprehension of social processes" and that can be provided only by the patient research of social science. As he had written to his wife eight years earlier, Mitchell stressed that what is needed for government intervention and planning is the application of the methods of physical science and industry, particularly precise quantitative research and measurement. In contrast to the quantitative physical sciences, Mitchell told the assembled statisticians, the social sciences are "immature, speculative, filled with controversy" and class struggle. But quantitative knowledge could replace such struggle and conflict by commonly accepted precise knowledge, objective knowledge "amenable to mathematical formulation" and "capable of forecasting group phenomena." A statistician, Mitchell opined, is "either right or wrong," and it is easy to demonstrate which. As a result of precise knowledge of facts, Mitchell envisioned, we can achieve "intelligent experimenting and detailed planning rather than . . . agitation and class struggle."

To achieve these vital goals none other than economists and statisticians would provide the crucial element, for we would have

---

[103]Ibid., pp. 53 and 42–54. On the continuing collaboration between Hoover, Gay, and Mitchell throughout the 1920s see Alchon, *The Invisible Hand of Puffing*.

to be "relying more and more on trained people to plan changes for us, to follow them up, to suggest alterations."[104]

In a similar vein, the assembled economists in 1918 were regaled with the visionary presidential address of Yale economist Irving Fisher. Fisher looked forward to a reconstruction of the economic world that would provide glorious opportunities for economists to satisfy their constructive impulses. A class struggle, Fisher noted, would surely be continuing over distribution of the nation's wealth. But by devising a mechanism of readjustment, the nation's economists could occupy an enviable role as the independent and impartial arbiters of the class struggle, these disinterested social scientists making the crucial decisions for the public good.

In short, both Mitchell and Fisher were, subtly and perhaps half-consciously, advancing the case for a post-war world in which their own allegedly impartial and scientific professions could levitate above the narrow struggles of classes for the social product, and thus emerge as a commonly accepted, objective new ruling class, a 20th-century version of the philosopher-kings.

It might not be amiss to see how these social scientists, prominent in their own fields and spokesmen in different ways for the New Era of the 1920s, fared in their disquisitions and guidance for the society and the economy. Irving Fisher, as we have seen, wrote several works celebrating the alleged success of prohibition, and insisted even after 1929 that since the price level had been kept stable, there could be no depression or stock market crash. For his part, Mitchell culminated a decade of snug alliance with Herbert Hoover by directing, along with Gay and the National Bureau, a massive and hastily-written work on the American economy. Published in 1929 on the accession of Hoover to the presidency, with all the resources of scientific and quantitative economics and statistics brought to bear, there is not so much as a hint in *Recent Economic Changes in the United States* that there might be a crash and depression in the offing.

The *Recent Economic Changes* study was originated and organized by Herbert Hoover, and it was Hoover who secured the financing from the Carnegie Corporation. The object was to celebrate the years of prosperity presumably produced by Secretary of Commerce Hoover's corporatist planning and to find out how the possibly-future President Hoover could maintain that prosperity by absorbing its lessons and making them a permanent part of the

---

[104]Alchon, *The Invisible Hand of Puffing*, pp. 39–42; Dorfman, *The Economic Mind in American Civilization*, 3, p. 490.

American political structure. The volume duly declared that to maintain the current prosperity, economists, statisticians, engineers, and enlightened managers would have to work out "a technique of balance" to be installed in the economy.

Recent Economic Changes, that monument to scientific and political folly, went through three quick printings and was widely publicized and warmly received on all sides.[105] Edward Eyre Hunt, Hoover's long-time aide in organizing his planning activities, was so enthusiastic that he continued celebrating the book and its paean to American prosperity throughout 1929 and 1930.[106]

It is appropriate to close by noting an unsophisticated yet perceptive cry from the heart. In 1945, the Bureau of Labor Statistics approached Congress for yet another in a long line of increases in appropriations for government statistics. In the process of questioning Dr. A. Ford Hinrichs, head of the BLS, Representative Frank B. Keefe, a conservative Republican Congressman from Oshkosh, Wisconsin, put forth an eternal question that has not yet been fully and satisfactorily answered:

> There is no doubt but what it would be nice to have a whole lot of statistics. . . . I am just wondering whether we are not embarking on a program that is dangerous when we keep adding and adding and adding to this thing. . . . We have been planning and getting statistics ever since 1932 to try to meet a situation that was domestic in character, but were never able to even meet that question. . . . Now we are involved in an international question. . . . It looks to me as though we spend a tremendous amount of time with graphs and charts and statistics and planning. What my people are interested in is what is it all about? Where are we going, and where are you going?[107]

---

[105]One exception was the critical review in the *Commercial and Financial Chronicle* (May 18, 1929), which derided the impression given the reader that the capacity of the United States "for continued prosperity is well-nigh unlimited." Quoted in Davis, *World Between the Wars,* p. 144. Also on *Recent Economic Changes* and economists' opinions at the time, see ibid., pp. 136–51, 400–17; David W. Eakins, "The Development of Corporate Liberal Policy Research in the United States, 1885–1965" (Ph.D. diss., University of Wisconsin, 1966), pp. 166–69, 205; and *Oh Yeah?,* Edward Angly, comp. (New York: Viking Press, 1931).

[106]In 1930, Hunt published a book-length, popularizing summary, *An Audit of America: A Summary of Recent Economic Changes in the United States* (New York: McGraw Hill, 1930). On *Recent Economic Changes,* also see Alchon, *The Invisible Hand of Puffing,* pp. 129–33, 135–42, 145–51, 213.

[107]Department of Labor—FSA Appropriation Bill for 1945. Hearings Before the Subcommittee on Appropriations. 78th Cong., 2d Session, Pt. 1 (Washington, D.C.:1945), pp. 258f., 276f. Quoted in Rothbard, "Politics of Political Economists," p. 665. On the growth of economists and statisticians in government, especially during wartime, see also Herbert Stein, "The Washington Economics Industry," *American Economic Association Papers and Proceedings* 76 (May 1986): 2–3.

10
RETHINKING CHURCHILL

Ralph Raico

CHURCHILL AS ICON

When, in a very few years, the pundits start to pontificate on the great question: "Who was the Man of the Century?" there is little doubt that they will reach virtually instant consensus. Inevitably, the answer will be: Winston Churchill. Indeed, Professor Harry Jaffa has already informed us that Churchill was not only the Man of the Twentieth Century, but the Man of Many Centuries.[1]

In a way, Churchill as Man of the Century will be appropriate. This has been the century of the State—of the rise and hypertrophic growth of the welfare–warfare state—and Churchill was from first to last a Man of the State, of the welfare state and of the warfare state. War, of course, was his lifelong passion; and, as an admiring historian has written: "Among his other claims to fame, Winston Churchill ranks as one of the founders of the welfare state."[2] Thus, while Churchill never had a principle he did not in the end betray,[3] this does not mean that there was no slant to his actions, no systematic bias. There was, and that bias was towards lowering the barriers to state power.

To gain any understanding of Churchill, we must go beyond the heroic images propagated for over half a century. The conventional picture of Churchill, especially of his role in World War II, was first of all the work of Churchill himself, through the distorted histories he composed and rushed into print as soon as the war

---

This essay is respectfully dedicated to the memory of Henry Regnery, who was, of course, not responsible for its content.

[1]Harry V. Jaffa, "In Defense of Churchill," *Modern Age* 34, no. 3 (Spring 1992): 281. For what it is worth, Henry Kissinger, "With Faint Praise," *New York Times Book Review*, July 16, 1995, p. 7, has gone so far as to call Churchill "the quintessential hero."

[2]Paul Addison, "Churchill and Social Reform," in *Churchill*, Robert Blake and William Roger Louis, eds. (New York: Norton, 1993), p. 57.

[3]A sympathetic historian, Paul Addison, *Churchill on the Home Front 1900–1955* (London: Pimlico, 1993), p. 438, phrases the same point this way: "Since [Churchill] never allowed himself to be hampered by a fixed programme or a rigid ideology, his ideas evolved as he adapted himself to the times." Oddly enough, Churchill himself confessed, in 1898: "I do not care so much for the principles I advocate as for the impression which my words produce and the reputation they give me." Clive Ponting, *Churchill* (London: Sinclair-Stevenson, 1994), p. 32.

was over.[4] In more recent decades, the Churchill legend has been adopted by an internationalist establishment for which it furnishes the perfect symbol and an inexhaustible vein of high-toned blather. Churchill has become, in Christopher Hitchens's phrase, a "totem" of the American establishment, not only the scions of the New Deal, but the neo-conservative apparatus as well—politicians like Newt Gingrich and Dan Quayle, corporate "knights" and other denizens of the Reagan and Bush Cabinets, the editors and writers of the *Wall Street Journal*, and a legion of "conservative" columnists led by William Safire and William Buckley. Churchill was, as Hitchens writes, "the human bridge across which the transition was made" between a noninterventionist and a globalist America.[5] In the next century, it is not impossible that his bulldog likeness will feature in the logo of the New World Order.

Let it be freely conceded that in 1940 Churchill played his role superbly. As the military historian, Major-General J.F.C. Fuller, a sharp critic of Churchill's wartime policies, wrote: "Churchill was a man cast in the heroic mould, a berserker ever ready to lead a forlorn hope or storm a breach, and at his best when things were at their worst. His glamorous rhetoric, his pugnacity, and his insistence on annihilating the enemy appealed to human instincts, and made him an outstanding war leader."[6] History outdid herself when she cast Churchill as the adversary in the duel with Hitler. It matters not at all that in his most famous speech—"we shall fight them on the beaches . . . we shall fight them in the fields and in the streets"—he plagiarized Clemenceau at the time of the Ludendorff offensive that there was little real threat of a German invasion or, that, perhaps, there was no reason for the duel to have occurred in the first place. For a few months in 1940, Churchill played his part magnificently and unforgettably. [7]

---

[4]For some of Churchill's distortions, see Tuvia Ben-Moshe, *Churchill: Strategy and History* (Boulder, Colo.: Lynne Rienner, 1992), pp. 329–33; Dietrich Aigner, "Winston Churchill (1874–1965)," in *Politiker des 20. Jahrhunderts*, 1, *Die Epoche der Weltkriege*, Rolf K. Hocevar, et al., eds. (Munich: Beck, 1970), p. 318, states that Churchill, in his works on World War II, "laid the foundation of a legend that is nothing less than a straightforward travesty of the historical truth. . . . But the Churchill version of World War II and its prehistory remains unshaken, the power of his eloquence extends beyond the grave." Aigner, incidentally, is an informed, scholarly critic of Churchill, and by no means a "right-wing radical."

[5]Christopher Hitchens, *Blood, Class, and Nostalgia: Anglo–American Ironies* (New York: Farrar, Straus, and Giroux, 1990), p. 186.

[6] J.F.C. Fuller, *The Conduct of War 1789–1961* (London: Eyre and Spottiswoode, 1961), p. 253.

[7]For a skeptical account of Churchill in this period, see Clive Ponting, *1940: Myth and Reality* (Chicago: Ivan R. Dee, 1991).

OPPORTUNISM AND RHETORIC

Yet before 1940, the word most closely associated with Churchill was "opportunist."[8] He had twice changed his party affiliation —from Conservative to Liberal, and then back again. His move to the Liberals was allegedly on the issue of free trade. But in 1930, he sold out on free trade as well, even tariffs on food, and proclaimed that he had cast off "Cobdenism" forever.[9] As head of the Board of Trade before World War I, he opposed increased armaments; after he became First Lord of the Admiralty in 1911, he pushed for bigger and bigger budgets, spreading wild rumors of the growing strength of the German Navy, just as he did in the 1930s about the buildup of the German Air Force.[10] He attacked socialism before and after World War I, while during the War he promoted war-socialism, calling for nationalization of the railroads, and declaring in a speech: "Our whole nation must be organized, must be socialized if you like the word."[11] Churchill's opportunism continued to the end. In the 1945 election, he briefly latched on to Hayek's *Road to Serfdom*, and tried to paint the Labour Party as totalitarian, while it was Churchill himself who, in 1943, had accepted the Beveridge plans for the post-war welfare state and Keynesian management of the economy. Throughout his long career his one guiding rule was to climb to power and stay there.

There *were* two principles that for a long while seemed dear to Churchill's heart. One was anti-Communism: he was an early and fervent opponent of Bolshevism. For years, he—very correctly—decried the "bloody baboons" and "foul murderers of Moscow." His deep early admiration of Benito Mussolini was rooted in his shrewd appreciation of what Mussolini had accomplished (or so he thought). In an Italy teetering on the brink of Leninist revolution, *Il Duce* had discovered the one formula that could counteract the Leninist appeal: hyper-nationalism with a social slant. Churchill lauded "Fascismo's triumphant struggle against the bestial appetites and passions of Leninism," claiming that "it proved the necessary antidote to the Communist poison."[12]

[8]Cf. A.J.P. Taylor, "The Statesman," in idem, et al., *Churchill Revised: A Critical Assessment* (New York: Dial Press, 1969), p. 26.
[9]Henry Pelling, *Winston Churchill* (New York: Dutton, 1974), pp. 347–48, 355; and Paul Addison, *Churchill on the Home Front*, pp. 296–99.
[10]Taylor, "The Statesman," p. 31; Robert Rhodes James, "Churchill the Politician," in A.J.P. Taylor, et al., *Churchill Revised*, p. 115, writes of "Churchill's extremely exaggerated claims of German air power."
[11]Emrys Hughes, *Winston Churchill: British Bulldog* (New York: Exposition, 1955), p. 104.
[12]"Churchill Extols Fascismo for Italy," *New York Times*, January 21, 1927. Churchill even had admiring words for Hitler; as late as 1937, he wrote: "one may dislike

Yet the time came when Churchill made his peace with Communism. In 1941, he gave unconditional support to Stalin, welcomed him as an ally, embraced him as a friend. Churchill, as well as Roosevelt, used the affectionate nickname, "Uncle Joe"; as late as the Potsdam conference, he repeatedly announced, of Stalin: "I like that man."[13] In suppressing the evidence that the Polish officers at Katyn had been murdered by the Soviets, he remarked: "There is no use prowling round the three year old graves of Smolensk."[14] Obsessed not only with defeating Hitler, but with destroying Germany, Churchill was oblivious to the danger of a Soviet inundation of Europe until it was far too late. The climax of his infatuation came at the November, 1993, Tehran conference, when Churchill presented Stalin with a Crusader's sword.[15] Those who are concerned to define the word "obscenity" may wish to ponder that episode.

Finally, there was what appeared to be the abiding love of his life, the British Empire. If Churchill stood *for anything at all*, it was the Empire; he famously said that he had not become Prime Minister in order to preside over its liquidation. But that, of course, is precisely what he did, selling out the Empire and everything else for the sake of total victory over Germany.

Besides his opportunism, Churchill was noted for his remarkable rhetorical skill. This talent helped him wield power over men, but it pointed to a fateful failing as well. Throughout his life, many who observed Churchill closely noted a peculiar trait. In 1917, Lord Esher described it in this way:

> He handles great subjects in rhythmical language, and becomes quickly enslaved to his own phrases. He deceives himself into the belief that he takes broad views, when his mind is fixed upon one comparatively small aspect of the question.[16]

During World War II, Robert Menzies, the Prime Minister of Australia, said of Churchill: "His real tyrant is the glittering

---

Hitler's system and yet admire his patriotic achievement. If our country were defeated, I hope we should find a champion as indomitable to restore our courage and lead us back to our place among the nations." James, "Churchill the Politician," p. 118. On the conditions of the Fascist takeover in Italy, see Ralph Raico, "Mises on Fascism and Democracy," *Journal of Libertarian Studies* 12, no 1 (Spring 1996): 1–27.

[13]Robin Edmonds, "Churchill and Stalin," in *Churchill*, Blake and Louis, eds., p. 326.

[14]Norman Rose, *Churchill: The Unruly Giant* (New York: Free Press, 1994), p. 378.

[15]J.F.C. Fuller, *The Second World War 1939–45: A Strategical and Tactical History* (London: Eyre and Spottiswoode, 1954), p. 218.

[16]James, "Churchill the Politician," p. 79. The same quotation from Esher is cited and endorsed by Basil Liddell Hart, "The Military Strategist," in A.J.P. Taylor, et al., *Churchill Revised*, p. 221.

phrase—so attractive to his mind that awkward facts have to give way."[17] Another associate wrote: "He is . . . the slave of the words which his mind forms about ideas. . . . And he can convince himself of almost every truth if it is once allowed thus to start on its wild career through his rhetorical machinery."[18]

But while Winston had no principles, there *was* one constant in his life: the love of war. It began early. As a child, he had a huge collection of toy soldiers, 1500 of them, and he played with them for many years after most boys turn to other things. They were "all British," he tells us, and he fought battles with his brother Jack, who "was only allowed to have colored troops; and they were not allowed to have artillery."[19] He attended Sandhurst, the military academy, instead of the universities, and "from the moment Churchill left Sandhurst . . . he did his utmost to get into a fight, wherever a war was going on."[20] All his life he was most excited— on the evidence, only really excited—by war. He loved war as few modern men ever have[21]—he even "loved the bangs," as he called them, and he was very brave under fire.

In 1925, Churchill wrote: "The story of the human race is war."[22] This, however, is untrue; potentially, it is disastrously untrue. Churchill lacked any grasp of the fundamentals of the social philosophy of classical liberalism. In particular, he never understood that, as Ludwig von Mises explained, the true story of the human race is the extension of social cooperation and the division of labor. Peace, not war, is the father of all things.[23] For Churchill, the years without war offered nothing but "the bland skies of peace and platitude." This was a man, as we shall see, who wished for more wars than *actually happened*.

When he was posted to India and began to read avidly, to make up for lost time, Churchill was profoundly impressed by Darwinism. He lost whatever religious faith he may have had— through reading Gibbon, he said—and took a particular dislike, for some reason, to the Catholic Church, as well as Christian missions.

---

[17]David Irving, *Churchill's War*, vol. 1, *The Struggle for Power* (Bullsbrook, Western Australia: Veritas, 1987), p. 517.

[18]Charles Masterman, cited in James, "Churchill the Politician," p. 71.

[19]Hart, "The Military Strategist," pp. 173–74.

[20]Ibid., p. 174.

[21]Churchill told Asquith's daughter in 1915: "I know this war is smashing and shattering the lives of thousands every moment—and yet—I cannot help it—I love every second I live." Michael Howard, "Churchill and the First World War," in *Churchill*, Blake and Louis, eds., p. 129.

[22]Maurice Ashley, *Churchill as Historian* (New York: Scribner's, 1968), p. 228.

[23]Ludwig von Mises, *Liberalism: A Socio-Economic Exposition*, Ralph Raico, trans. (Kansas City: Sheed Andrews and McMeel, [1927] 1985), pp. 23–27.

He became, in his own words, "a materialist—to the tips of my fingers," and fervently upheld the worldview that human life is a struggle for existence, with the outcome the survival of the fittest.[24] This philosophy of life and history Churchill expressed in his one novel, *Savrola*.[25] That Churchill was a racist goes without saying, yet his racism went deeper than with most of his contemporaries.[26] It is curious how, with his stark Darwinian outlook, his elevation of war to the central place in human history, and his racism, as well as his fixation on "great leaders," Churchill's worldview resembled that of his antagonist, Hitler.

When Churchill was not actually engaged in war, he was reporting on it. He early made a reputation for himself as a war correspondent, in Kitchener's campaign in the Sudan and in the Boer War. In December, 1900, a dinner was given at the Waldorf-Astoria in honor of the young journalist, recently returned from his well-publicized adventures in South Africa. Mark Twain, who introduced him, had already, it seems, caught on to Churchill. In a brief satirical speech, Twain slyly suggested that, with his English father and American mother, Churchill was the perfect representative of Anglo-American cant.[27]

CHURCHILL AND THE "NEW LIBERALISM"

In 1900 Churchill began the career he was evidently fated for. His background—the grandson of a duke and son of a famous Tory politician—got him into the House of Commons as a Conservative. At first he seemed to be distinguished only by his restless ambition, remarkable even in parliamentary ranks. But in 1904, he crossed the floor to the Liberals, supposedly on account of his free-trade convictions. However, one of Churchill's admirers, Robert Rhodes James, writes: "It was believed [at the time], probably rightly, that if Arthur Balfour had given him office in 1902, Churchill would not have developed such a burning interest in free trade and joined the Liberals." Clive Ponting notes that: "as he had already admitted to Rosebery, he was looking for an excuse to

[24]Ponting, *Churchill*, p. 23; Dietrich Aigner, *Winston Churchill: Ruhm und Legende* (Göttingen: Musterschmidt, 1975), p. 31.

[25]Ibid., pp. 40–44.

[26]Andrew Roberts, *Eminent Churchillians* (New York: Simon and Schuster, 1994), pp. 211–15. Roberts finds it ironic that, given Churchill's views on race, it was "he of all Prime Ministers [who] allowed Britain to start to become a multi-racial society" through Commonwealth immigration during his last "Indian Summer" administration, 1951–55.

[27]Mark Twain, *Mark Twain's Weapons of Satire: Anti-Imperialist Writings on the Philippine–American War*, Jim Zwick, ed. (Syracuse, N.Y.: Syracuse University Press, 1992), pp. 9–11.

defect from a party that seemed reluctant to recognise his talents," and the Liberals would not accept a protectionist.[28]

Tossed by the tides of faddish opinion,[29] with no principles of his own and hungry for power, Churchill soon became an adherent of the "New Liberalism," an updated version of his father's "Tory Democracy." The "new" liberalism differed from the "old" only in the small matter of substituting incessant state activism for laissez-faire.

Although his conservative idolators seem blithely unaware of the fact—for them it is always 1940—Churchill was one of the chief architects of the welfare state in Britain. The modern welfare state, successor to the welfare state of 18th-century absolutism, began in the 1880s in Germany, under Bismarck.[30] In England, the legislative turning point came when Asquith succeeded Campbell-Banner-man as Prime Minister in 1908; his reorganized cabinet included David Lloyd George at the Exchequer and Churchill at the Board of Trade.

Of course, "the electoral dimension of social policy was well to the fore in Churchill's thinking," writes a sympathetic historian— meaning that Churchill understood it as the way to win votes.[31] He wrote to a friend:

> No legislation at present in view interests the democracy. All their minds are turning more and more to the social and economic issue. This revolution is irresistible. They will not tolerate the existing system by which wealth is acquired, shared and employed. . . . They will set their faces like flint against the money power—heir of all other powers and tyrannies overthrown—and its obvious injustices. And this theoretical repulsion will ultimately extend to any party associated in maintaining the status quo. . . . Minimum standards of wages and comfort, insurance in some effective form or other against sickness, unemployment, old age, these are the questions and the only questions by which parties are going to live in the future. Woe to Liberalism, if they slip through its fingers.[32]

Churchill "had already announced his conversion to a collectivist social policy" before his move to the Board of Trade.[33] His

[28]Robert Rhodes James, "Churchill the Parliamentarian, Orator, and Statesman," in *Churchill*, Blake and Louis, eds., p. 510; Ponting, *Churchill*, p. 49.

[29]Churchill at this time even spoke out in favor of state-enforced temperance, an amusing bit of hypocrisy in a man whose lifelong love of drink became legendary.

[30]On the history of the German welfare state, absolutist and modern, see Gerd Habermann, *Der Wohlfahrtsstaat: Geschichte eines Irrwegs* (Berlin: Propyläen, 1994).

[31]Addison, "Churchill and Social Reform," p. 60.

[32]Addison, *Churchill on the Home Front, 1900–1955*, p. 59.

[33]Ibid, p. 51.

constant theme became "the just precedence" of public over private interests. He took up the fashionable social-engineering clichés of the time, asserting that: "Science, physical and political alike, revolts at the disorganisation which glares at us in so many aspects of modern life," and that "the nation demands the application of drastic corrective and curative processes." The state was to acquire canals and railroads, develop certain national industries, provide vastly augmented education, introduce the eight-hour work day, levy progressive taxes, and guarantee a national minimum living standard. It is no wonder that Beatrice Webb noted that Churchill was "definitely casting in his lot with the constructive state action."[34]

Following a visit to Germany, Lloyd George and Churchill were both converted to the Bismarckian model of social insurance schemes.[35] As Churchill told his constituents: "My heart was filled with admiration of the patient genius which had added these social bulwarks to the many glories of the German race."[36] He set out, in his words, to "thrust a big slice of Bismarckianism over the whole underside of our industrial system."[37] In 1908, Churchill announced in a speech in Dundee: "I am on the side of those who think that a greater collective sentiment should be introduced into the State and the municipalities. I should like to see the State undertaking new functions." Still, individualism must be respected: "No man can be a collectivist alone or an individualist alone. He must be both an individualist and a collectivist. The nature of man is a dual nature. The character of the organisation of human society is dual."[38] This, by the way, is a good sample of Churchill as political philosopher: it never gets much better.

But while both "collective organisation" and "individual incentive" must be given their due, Churchill was certain which had gained the upper hand:

> The whole tendency of civilisation is, however, towards the multiplication of the collective functions of society. The ever-growing complications of civilisation create for us new

[34]W. H. Greenleaf, *The British Political Tradition*, vol. 2, *The Ideological Heritage* (London: Methuen, 1983), pp. 151–54.

[35]E. P. Hennock, *British Social Reform and German Precedents: The Case of Social Insurance 1880–1914* (Oxford: Clarendon, 1987), pp. 168–69.

[36]Gordon A. Craig, "Churchill and Germany," in *Churchill*, Blake and Louis, eds., p. 24.

[37]E. P. Hennock, "The Origins of British National Insurance and the German Precedent 1880–1914," in *The Emergence of the Welfare State in Britain and Germany*, W.J. Mommsen and Wolfgang Mock, eds. (London: Croom Helm, 1981), p. 88.

[38]Winston Churchill, *Complete Speeches 1897–1963*, vol. 1, *1897–1908*, Robert Rhodes James, ed. (New York: Chelsea House, 1974), pp. 1029–30, 1032.

services which have to be undertaken by the State, and create for us an expansion of existing services. . . . There is a pretty steady determination . . . to intercept all future unearned increment which may arise from the increase in the speculative value of the land. There will be an ever-widening area of municipal enterprise.

The statist trend met with Churchill's complete approval. As he added:

I go farther; I should like to see the State embark on various novel and adventurous experiments. . . . I am very sorry we have not got the railways of this country in our hands. We may do something better with the canals.[39]

This grandson of a duke and glorifier of his ancestor, the arch-corruptionist Marlborough, was not above pandering to lower-class resentments. Churchill claimed that "the cause of the Liberal Party is the cause of the left-out millions," while he attacked the Conservatives as "the Party of the rich against the poor, the classes and their dependents against the masses, of the lucky, the wealthy, the happy, and the strong, against the left-out and the shut-out millions of the weak and poor."[40] Churchill became the perfect hustling political entrepreneur, eager to politicize one area of social life after the other. He berated the Conservatives for lacking even a "single plan of social reform or reconstruction," while boasting that he and his associates intended to propose "a wide, comprehensive, interdependent scheme of social organisation," incorporated in "a massive series of legislative proposals and administrative acts."[41]

At this time, Churchill fell under the influence of Beatrice and Sidney Webb, the leaders of the Fabian Society. At one of her famous strategic dinner parties, Beatrice Webb introduced Churchill to a young protégé, William—later Lord—Beveridge. Churchill brought Beveridge into the Board of Trade as his advisor on social questions, thus starting him on his illustrious career.[42] Besides pushing for a variety of social insurance schemes, Churchill created the system of national labor exchanges: he wrote to Prime Minister Asquith of the need to "spread . . . a sort of Germanized network of state intervention and regulation" over the British labor market.[43] But Churchill entertained much more ambitious goals for the Board of Trade. He proposed a plan whereby:

[39]Winston Churchill, *Liberalism and the Social Problem* (London: Hodder and Stoughton, 1909), pp. 80–81.
[40]Ibid., pp. 78, 226.
[41]Ibid., p. 227.
[42]Hennock, *British Social Reform*, pp. 157–60.
[43]Ibid., p. 161.

> The Board of Trade was to act as the "intelligence depart-
> ment" of the Government, forecasting trade and employ-
> ment in the regions so that the Government could allocate
> contracts to the most deserving areas. At the summit . . .
> would be a Committee of National Organisation, chaired by
> the Chancellor of the Exchequer to supervise the economy.[44]

Finally, well aware of the electoral potential of organized labor, Churchill became a champion of the labor unions. He was a
leading supporter, for instance, of the Trades Disputes Act of
1906.[45] This Act reversed the Taff Vale and other judicial decisions,
which had held unions responsible for torts and wrongs committed on their behalf by their agents. The Act outraged the great liberal legal historian and theorist of the rule of law, A. V. Dicey, who
charged that it

> confers upon a trade union a freedom from civil liability for
> the commission of even the most heinous wrong by the
> union or its servants, and in short confers upon every trade
> union a privilege and protection not possessed by any other
> person or body of persons, whether corporate or unincorpo-
> rate, throughout the United Kingdom. . . . It makes a trade
> union a privileged body exempted from the ordinary law of
> the land. No such privileged body has ever before been de-
> liberately created by an English Parliament. [46]

It is ironic that the immense power of the British labor unions,
the *bête noire* of Margaret Thatcher, was brought into being with
the enthusiastic help of her great hero, Winston Churchill.

WORLD WAR I

In 1911, Churchill became First Lord of the Admiralty, and
now was truly in his element. Naturally, he quickly allied himself
with the war party, and, during the crises that followed, fanned the
flames of war. When the final crisis came, in the summer of 1914,
Churchill was the only member of the cabinet who backed war
from the start, with all of his accustomed energy. Asquith, his own
Prime Minister, wrote of him: "Winston very bellicose and demanding immediate mobilization. . . . Winston, who has got all his
war paint on, is longing for a sea fight in the early hours of the
morning to result in the sinking of the *Goeben*. The whole thing fills
me with sadness."[47] On the afternoon of July 28, three days before

[44]Ponting, *Churchill*, p. 83.

[45]See, for instance, Churchill, *Liberalism and the Social Problem*, pp. 74–75.

[46]A. V. Dicey, *Lectures on the Relation Between Law and Public Opinion in England during the Nineteenth Century*, 2nd. ed. (London: Macmillan, [1914] 1963), pp. xlv–xlvi.

[47]Herbert Henry Asquith, *Memories and Reflections 1852–1927* (London: Cassell,
1928), 2, pp. 7, 21.

the German invasion of Belgium, he mobilized the British Home Fleet, the greatest assemblage of naval power in the history of the world to that time. As Sidney Fay wrote, Churchill ordered that:

> The fleet was to proceed during the night at high speed and without lights through the Straits of Dover from Portland to its fighting base at Scapa Flow. Fearing to bring this order before the Cabinet, lest it should be considered a provocative action likely to damage the chances of peace, Mr. Churchill had only informed Mr. Asquith, who at once gave his approval.[48]

No wonder that, when war with Germany broke out, Churchill, in contrast even to the other chiefs of the war party, was all smiles, filled with a "glowing zest."[49]

From the outset of hostilities, Churchill, as head of the Admiralty, was instrumental in establishing the hunger blockade of Germany. This was probably the most effective weapon employed on either side in the whole conflict. The only problem was that, according to everyone's interpretation of international law except Britain's, it was illegal. The blockade was not "close-in," but depended on scattering mines, and many of the goods deemed contraband—for instance, food for civilians—had never been so classified before.[50] But, throughout his career, international law and the conventions by which men have tried to limit the horrors of war meant nothing to Churchill. As a German historian has dryly commented, Churchill was ready to break the rules whenever the very existence of his country was at stake, and "for him this was very often the case."[51]

The hunger blockade had certain rather unpleasant consequences. About 750,000 German civilians succumbed to hunger and diseases caused by malnutrition. The effect on those who survived was perhaps just as frightful in its own way. A historian of the blockade concluded: "the victimized youth [of World War I] were to become the most radical adherents of National Socialism."[52] It was also complications arising from the British blockade that eventually provided the pretext for Wilson's decision to go to war in 1917.

---

[48]Sidney Fay, *Origins of the World War*, 2nd. rev. ed. (New York: Free Press, [1930] 1966), p. 495.
[49]Lady Violet Asquith, cited in Hart, "The Military Strategist," p. 182.
[50]C. Paul Vincent, *The Politics of Hunger: The Allied Blockade of Germany, 1915–1919* (Athens: Ohio University Press, 1985); see also Ralph Raico, "The Politics of Hunger: A Review," *Review of Austrian Economics* 3 (1988): 253–59.
[51]Aigner, *Winston Churchill (1874–1965)*, pp. 63–4.
[52]Vincent, *Politics of Hunger*, p. 162. See also Peter Loewenberg, "The Psychohistorical Origins of the Nazi Youth Cohort," *American Historical Review* 76, no. 5 (December 1971): 1457–1502.

Whether Churchill actually arranged for the sinking of the *Lusitania* on May 7, 1915, is still unclear.[53] A week before the disaster, he wrote to Walter Runciman, President of the Board of Trade that it was "most important to attract neutral shipping to our shores, in the hopes especially of embroiling the United States with Germany."[54] Many highly-placed persons in Britain and America believed that the German sinking of the *Lusitania* would bring the United States into the war.

The most recent student of the subject is Patrick Beesly, whose *Room 40* is a history of British Naval Intelligence in World War I. Beesly's careful account is all the more persuasive for going against the grain of his own sentiments. He points out that the British Admiralty was aware that German U-boat Command informed U-boat captains at sea of the sailings of the *Lusitania*, and that a U-boat responsible for the sinking of two ships in recent days was present in the vicinity of Queenstown, off the southern coast of Ireland, in the path the *Lusitania* was scheduled to take. There is no surviving record of any specific warning to the *Lusitania*. No destroyer escort was sent to accompany the ship to port, nor were any of the readily available destroyers instructed to hunt for the submarine. In fact, "no effective steps were taken to protect the *Lusitania*." Beesly concludes:

> unless and until fresh information comes to light, I am reluctantly driven to the conclusion that there *was* a conspiracy deliberately to put the *Lusitania* at risk in the hope that even an abortive attack on her would bring the United States into the war. Such a conspiracy could not have been put into effect without Winston Churchill's express permission and approval.[55]

In any case, what is certain is that Churchill's policies made the sinking very likely. The *Lusitania* was a passenger liner loaded with munitions of war; Churchill had given orders to the captains of merchant ships, including liners, to ram German submarines if they encountered them, and the Germans were aware of this. And, as Churchill stressed in his memoirs of World War I, embroiling neutral countries in hostilities with the enemy was a crucial part of warfare: "There are many kinds of maneuvres in war, some only of which take place on the battlefield. . . . The maneuvre which brings

---

[53]See Colin Simpson, *The Lusitania* (London: Penguin, [1972] 1983), who presents the case for Churchill's guilt; and Thomas A. Bailey and Paul B. Ryan, *The Lusitania Disaster: An Episode in Modern Warfare and Diplomacy* (New York: Free Press, 1975), who attempt to exculpate him. See also Hitchens, *Blood, Class, and Nostalgia*, pp. 189–90.

[54]Patrick Beesly, *Room 40: British Naval Intelligence 1914–18* (San Diego: Harcourt, Brace, Jovanovich, 1982), p. 90.

[55]Ibid., p. 122. Emphasis in original.

an ally into the field is as serviceable as that which wins a great
battle."[56]

In the midst of bloody conflict, Churchill was energy personi-
fied, the source of one brainstorm after another. Sometimes his
hunches worked out well—he was the chief promoter of the tank
in World War I—sometimes not so well, as at Gallipoli. The notoriety of that disaster, which blackened his name for years, caused
him to be temporarily dropped from the Cabinet in 1915.[57] His reaction was typical: To one visitor, he said, pointing to the maps on
the wall: "This is what I live for . . . Yes, I am finished in respect of
all I care for—the waging of war, the defeat of the Germans."[58]

BETWEEN THE WARS

For the next few years, Churchill was shuttled from one ministerial post to another. As Minister of War—of Churchill in this position one may say what the revisionist historian Charles Tansill
said of Henry Stimson as Secretary of War: no one ever deserved
the title more—Churchill promoted a crusade to crush Bolshevism
in Russia. As Colonial Secretary, he was ready to involve Britain in
war with Turkey over the Chanak incident, but the British envoy
to Turkey did not deliver Churchill's ultimatum, and in the end
cooler heads prevailed. [59]

In 1924, Churchill rejoined the Conservatives and was made
Chancellor of the Exchequer. His father, in the same office, was
noted for having been puzzled by the decimals: what were "those
damned dots"? Winston's most famous act was to return Britain to
the gold standard at the unrealistic pre-war parity, thus severely
damaging the export trade and ruining the good name of gold, as
was pointed out by Murray N. Rothbard.[60] Hardly anyone today
would disagree with the judgment of A.J.P. Taylor: Churchill "did
not grasp the economic arguments one way or the other. What

[56]Winston Churchill, *The World Crisis* (New York: Scribner's, 1931), p. 300.
[57]On the Dardanelles campaign, cf. Taylor, "The Statesman," pp. 21–22: "Once
Churchill took up the idea, he exaggerated both the ease with which it could be
carried through and the rewards it would bring. There was no enquiry into the
means available. Churchill merely assumed that battleships could force the Straits
unaided. When this failed, he assumed that there was a powerful army available for
Gallipoli and assumed also that this inhospitable peninsula presented no
formidable military obstacles. Beyond this, he assumed also that the fall of
Constantinople would inflict a mortal blow on Germany. All these assumptions
were wrong."
[58]Hughes, *Winston Churchill: British Bulldog*, p. 78.
[59]James, "Churchill the Politician," p. 93.
[60]Murray N. Rothbard, *America's Great Depression* (Princeton, N.J.: Van Nostrand,
1963), pp. 131–37.

determined him was again a devotion to British greatness. The pound would once more 'look the dollar in the face'; the days of Queen Victoria would be restored."[61]

So far Churchill had been engaged in politics for 30 years, with not much to show for it except a certain notoriety. His great claim to fame in the modern mythology begins with his hard line against Hitler in the 1930s. But it is important to realize that Churchill had maintained a hard line against Weimar Germany, as well. He denounced all calls for Allied disarmament, even before Hitler came to power.[62] Like other Allied leaders, Churchill was living a protracted fantasy: that Germany would submit forever to what it viewed as the shackles of Versailles. In the end, what Britain and France refused to grant to a democratic Germany they were forced to concede to Hitler. Moreover, if most did not bother to listen when Churchill fulminated on the impending German threat, they had good reason. He had tried to whip up hysteria too often before: for a crusade against Bolshevik Russia, during the General Strike of 1926, on the mortal dangers of Indian independence, in the abdication crisis. Why pay any heed to his latest delusion?[63]

Churchill had been a strong Zionist practically from the start, holding that Zionism would deflect European Jews from social revolution to partnership with European imperialism in the Arab world.[64] Now, in 1936, he forged links with the informal London pressure group known as The Focus, whose purpose was to open the eyes of the British public to the one great menace, Nazi Germany. "The great bulk of its finance came from rich British Jews such as Sir Robert Mond (a director of several chemical firms) and Sir Robert Waley-Cohn, the managing director of Shell, the latter contributing £50,000."[65] The Focus was to be useful in expanding

[61]Taylor, "The Statesman," p. 27.

[62]Aigner, *Winston Churchill (1874–1965)*, pp. 100–3. In connection with the Geneva disarmament conference 1931–32, Churchill expressed the same anti-German position as later: Germany would rise again. Aigner sees this as stemming from Churchill's social Darwinist philosophy.

[63]Goronwy Rees, "Churchill in der Revision," *Der Monat*, Nr. 207 (Fall 1965): 12.

[64]E.g., in Churchill's essay of February, 1921, "Zionism vs. Bolshevism"; see Aigner, *Winston Churchill (1874–1965)*, p. 79. See also Oskar K. Rabinowicz, *Winston Churchill on Jewish Problems: A Half Century Survey*, published by the World Jewish Congress, British Section (London: Lincolns-Prager, 1956); and N. A. Rose, *The Gentile Zionists: A Study in Anglo–Zionist Diplomacy, 1929–1939* (London: Cass, 1973). Early on, Churchill had shared the view current among many right-wingers of the time, of Bolshevism as a "Jewish" phenomenon: he referred to the Red leaders as "these Semitic conspirators" and "Jew Commissars." Norman Rose, *Churchill: The Unruly Giant*, p. 180.

[65]John Charmley, *Chamberlain and the Lost Peace* (London: Hodder and Stoughton, 1989), p. 55. See also Irving, *Churchill's War*, pp. 54–65, 67–68, and 82–83. The group's full name was the Focus for the Defence of Freedom and Peace. For a history, see Eugen Spier, *Focus. A Footnote to the History of the Thirties* (London:

Churchill's network of contacts and in pushing for his entry into the Cabinet.

Though a Conservative MP, Churchill began berating the Conservative governments, first Baldwin's and then Chamberlain's, for their alleged blindness to the Nazi threat. He vastly exaggerated the extent of German rearmament, formidable as it was, and distorted its purpose by harping on German production of heavy-bombers. This was never a German priority, and Churchill's fabrications were meant to demonstrate a German design to attack Britain, which was never Hitler's intention. At this time, Churchill busily promoted the Grand Alliance[66] that was to include Britain, France, Russia, Poland, and Czechoslovakia. Since the Poles, having nearly been conquered by the Red Army in 1920, rejected any coalition with the Soviet Union, and since the Soviets' only access to Germany was through Poland, Churchill's plan was worthless.

Ironically—considering that it was a pillar of his future fame—his drumbeating about the German danger was yet another position on which Churchill reneged. In the fall of 1937, he stated:

> Three or four years ago I was myself a loud alarmist. . . . In spite of the risks which wait on prophecy, I declare my belief that a major war is not imminent, and I still believe that there is a good chance of no major war taking place in our lifetime. . . . I will not pretend that, if I had to choose between Communism and Nazism, I would choose Communism.[67]

For all the claptrap about Churchill's "far-sightedness" during the 30s in opposing the "appeasers," in the end the policy of the Chamberlain government—to rearm as quickly as possible, while testing the chances for peace with Germany—was more realistic than Churchill's.

The common mythology is so far from historical truth that even an ardent Churchill sympathizer, Gordon Craig, feels obliged to write:

Oswald Wolff, 1963). In March, 1937, after a luncheon meeting with Churchill, Spier came to the conclusion that "destiny had marked him out to become the destroyer of Hitlerism." (Ibid., p. 112) In October, 1937, a representative of the Focus, H. Wickham Steed, toured Canada and the United States. Among those he found "ready to take the Focus line" were Roosevelt, Cordell Hull, and Arthur Sulzberger, owner of the *New York Times*. In New York, Steed addressed the Council on Foreign Relations. Others with whom Steed met included the financiers Bernard Baruch and Felix Warburg. (Ibid., pp. 124–25.) On The Focus as well as other factors influencing British public opinion in regard to Germany in the 1930s, see Dietrich Aigner, *Das Ringen um England. Das deutsch–britische Verhältnis. Die öffentliche Meinung 1933–1939, Tragödie zweier Völker* (Munich/Esslingen: Bechtle, 1969).
[66] Aigner, *Winston Churchill (1874–1965)*, p. 105–6; see also Irving, *Churchill's War*, pp. 38–40, 44–45, 78–79.
[67] Hart, "The Military Strategist," p. 204.

The time is long past when it was possible to see the protracted debate over British foreign policy in the 1930s as a
struggle between Churchill, an angel of light, fighting
against the velleities of uncomprehending and feeble men in
high places. It is reasonably well-known today that Churchill was often ill-informed, that his claims about German
strength were exaggerated and his prescriptions impractical,
that his emphasis on air power was misplaced.[68]

Moreover, as a British historian has recently noted: "For the
record, it is worth recalling that in the 1930s Churchill did not oppose the appeasement of either Italy or Japan."[69] It is also worth recalling that it was the pre-Churchill British governments that furnished the material with which Churchill was able to win the Battle of Britain. Clive Ponting has observed:

> the Baldwin and Chamberlain Governments . . . had ensured
> that Britain was the first country in the world to deploy a
> fully integrated system of air defence based on radar detec-
> tion of incoming aircraft and ground control of fighters . . .
> Churchill's contribution had been to pour scorn on radar
> when he was in opposition in the 1930s.[70]

EMBROILING AMERICA IN WAR—AGAIN

In September, 1939, Britain went to war with Germany, pursuant to the guarantee which Chamberlain had been panicked into
extending to Poland in March. Lloyd George had termed the guarantee "hare-brained," while Churchill had supported it. Nonetheless, in his history of the war Churchill wrote: "Here was decision
at last, taken at the worst possible moment and on the least satisfactory ground which must surely lead to the slaughter of tens of
millions of people."[71] With the war on, Winston was recalled to his
old job as First Lord of the Admiralty. Then, in the first month of
the war, an astonishing thing happened: the President of the
United States initiated a personal correspondence not with the
Prime Minister, but with the head of the British Admiralty, by-
passing all the ordinary diplomatic channels.[72]

[68]Craig, "Churchill and Germany," p. 35.
[69]Donald Cameron Watt, "Churchill and Appeasement," in *Churchill*, Blake and
Louis, eds., p. 214.
[70]Ponting, *Churchill*, p. 464.
[71]Winston Churchill, *The Gathering Storm*, vol. 1, *The Second World War* (Boston:
Houghton Mifflin, 1948), p. 347. Churchill commented that the guarantee was
extended to a Poland "which with hyena appetite had only six months before joined
in the pillage and destruction of the Czechoslovak State." He was referring to the
annexation of the Teschen district, by which Poland had reclaimed the ethnically
Polish areas of that bizarre concoction Churchill was pleased to dignify as "the
Czechoslovak State."
[72]Irving, *Churchill's War*, pp. 193–96.

The messages that passed between the President and the First Lord were surrounded by a frantic secrecy, culminating in the affair of Tyler Kent, the American cipher clerk at the U.S. London embassy who was tried and imprisoned by the British authorities. The problem was that some of the messages contained allusions to Roosevelt's agreement—even before the war began—to a blatantly unneutral cooperation with a belligerent Britain.[73]

On June 10, 1939, George VI and his wife, Queen Mary, visited the Roosevelts at Hyde Park. In private conversations with the King, Roosevelt promised full support for Britain in case of war. He intended to set up a zone in the Atlantic to be patrolled by the U.S. Navy, and, according to the King's notes, the President stated that "if he saw a U boat he would sink her at once & wait for the consequences." The biographer of George VI, Wheeler-Bennett, considered that these conversations "contained the germ of the future Bases-for-Destroyers deal, and also of the Lend-Lease Agreement itself."[74] In communicating with the First Lord of the Admiralty, Roosevelt was aware that he was in touch with the one member of Chamberlain's cabinet whose belligerence matched his own.

In 1940, Churchill at last became Prime Minister, ironically enough when the Chamberlain government resigned because of the Norwegian fiasco—which Churchill, more than anyone else, had helped to bring about.[75] As he had fought against a negotiated peace after the fall of Poland, so he continued to resist any suggestion of negotiations with Hitler. Many of the relevant documents are still sealed—after all these years[76]—but it is clear that a strong peace party existed in the country and the government. It included Lloyd George in the House of Commons, and Halifax, the Foreign Secretary, in the Cabinet. Even after the fall of France, Churchill rejected Hitler's renewed peace overtures. This, more than anything else, is supposed to be the foundation of his greatness. The British historian John Charmley raised a storm of outraged protest when he suggested that a negotiated peace in 1940 might have been to

[73]James Leutze, "The Secret of the Churchill–Roosevelt Correspondence: September 1939–May 1940," *Journal of Contemporary History* 10, no. 3 (July 1975): 465–91; Leutze concludes that this was the real reason the two governments colluded to silence Tyler Kent.

[74]John W. Wheeler-Bennett, *King George VI: His Life and Reign* (New York: St. Martin's, 1958), pp. 390–92. Wheeler-Bennett added: "On his return to London the King communicated the essence of his talks with the President to the proper quarters, and so greatly did he esteem their importance that he carried the original manuscript of his notes about him in his dispatch case throughout the war."

[75]Hart, "The Military Strategist," p. 208.

[76]John Charmley, *Churchill: The End of Glory* (London: Hodder and Stoughton, 1993), p. 423.

the advantage of Britain and Europe.[77] A Yale historian, writing in the *New York Times Book Review*, referred to Charmley's thesis as "morally sickening."[78] Yet Charmley's scholarly and detailed work makes the crucial point that Churchill's adamant refusal even to listen to peace terms in 1940 doomed what he claimed was dearest to him—the Empire and a Britain that was non-socialist and independent in world affairs. One may add that it probably also doomed European Jewry.[79] It is amazing that half a century after the fact, there are critical theses concerning World War II that are off-limits to historical debate.

Lloyd George, Halifax, and the others were open to a compromise peace because they understood that Britain and the Dominions alone could not defeat Germany.[80] After the fall of France, Churchill's aim of total victory could be realized only under one condition: that the United States become embroiled in another world war. No wonder that Churchill put his heart and soul into ensuring precisely that.

After a talk with Churchill, Joseph Kennedy, American ambassador to Britain, noted: "Every hour will be spent by the British in trying to figure out how we can be gotten in." When he left from Lisbon on a ship to New York, Kennedy pleaded with the State Department to announce that if the ship should happen to blow up mysteriously in the mid-Atlantic, the United States would not consider it a cause for war with Germany. In his unpublished memoirs, Kennedy wrote: "I thought that would give me some protection against Churchill's placing a bomb on the ship."[81]

Kennedy's fears were perhaps not exaggerated. For, while it had been important for British policy in World War I, involving

[77]See also Charmley's review of Clive Ponting's work, in the *Times Literary Supplement*, May 13, 1994, p. 8.

[78]Gaddis Smith, "Whose Finest Hour?" *New York Times Book Review*, August 29, 1993, p. 3.

[79]On March 27, 1942, Goebbels commented in his diary on the destruction of the European Jews, which was then underway: "Here, too, the Führer is the undismayed champion of a radical solution necessitated by conditions and therefore inexorable. Fortunately, a whole series of possibilities presents itself for us in wartime that would be denied us in peacetime. We shall have to profit by this." He added: "the fact that Jewry's representatives in England and America are today organizing and sponsoring the war against Germany must be paid for dearly by its representatives in Europe—and that's only right." *The Goebbels Diaries, 1942–1943*, Louis P. Lochner ed. and trans. (Garden City, N.Y.: Doubleday, 1948), p. 148.

[80]Paul Addison, "Lloyd George and Compromise Peace in the Second World War," in *Lloyd George: Twelve Essays*, A.J.P. Taylor, ed. (New York: Atheneum, 1971), pp. 359–84. Churchill himself told Stalin in 1944: "We never thought of making a separate peace even the year when we were all alone and could easily have made one without serious loss to the British Empire and largely at your expense." Ibid., p. 383.

[81]Irving, *Churchill's War*, pp. 193, 207.

America was the *sine qua non* of Churchill's policy in World War II. In Franklin Roosevelt, he found a ready accomplice.

That Roosevelt, through his actions and private words, evinced a clear design for war before December 7, 1941, has never really been in dispute. Arguments have raged over such questions as his possible foreknowledge of the Pearl Harbor attack. In 1948, Thomas A. Bailey, diplomatic historian at Stanford, already put the real pro-Roosevelt case:

> Franklin Roosevelt repeatedly deceived the American people during the period before Pearl Harbor. . . . He was like a physician who must tell the patient lies for the patient's own good. . . . The country was overwhelmingly noninterventionist to the very day of Pearl Harbor, and an overt attempt to lead the people into war would have resulted in certain failure and an almost certain ousting of Roosevelt in 1940, with a complete defeat of his ultimate aims.[82]

Churchill himself never bothered to conceal Roosevelt's role as co-conspirator. In January, 1941, Harry Hopkins visited London. Churchill described him as "the most faithful and perfect channel of communication between the President and me . . . the main prop and animator of Roosevelt himself":

> I soon comprehended [Hopkins's] personal dynamism and the outstanding importance of his mission . . . here was an envoy from the President of supreme importance to our life. With gleaming eye and quiet, constrained passion he said: "The President is determined that we shall win the war together. Make no mistake about it. He has sent me here to tell you that all costs and by all means he will carry you through, no matter what happens to him—there is nothing that he will not do so far as he has human power." There he sat, slim, frail, ill, but absolutely glowing with refined comprehension of the Cause. It was to be the defeat, ruin, and slaughter of Hitler, to the exclusion of all other purposes, loyalties and aims.[83]

---

[82]Thomas A. Bailey, *The Man in the Street: The Impact of American Public Opinion on Foreign Policy* (New York: Macmillan, 1948), p. 13. A recent writer has commented on Bailey's position: "In reality, when Roosevelt and other presidents lied, they did it for their own good, or what they believed to be their own good. But they were often mistaken because they have tended to be at least as shortsighted as the masses . . . Roosevelt's destroyer deal marked a watershed in the use and abuse of presidential power, foreshadowing a series of dangerous and often disastrous adventures abroad." Robert Shogan, *Hard Bargain* (New York: Scribner's, 1995), pp. 271, 278. The classical revisionist case on Roosevelt's war policy was presented in Charles A. Beard, *President Roosevelt and the Coming of War 1941* (New Haven, Conn.: Yale University Press, 1949); and *Perpetual War for Perpetual Peace*, Harry Elmer Barnes, ed. (Caldwell, Idaho: Caxton, 1953), among other works.

[83]Winston S. Churchill, *The Grand Alliance*, vol. 3, *The Second World War* (Boston: Houghton Mifflin, 1950), pp. 23–24.

In 1976, the public finally learned the story of William Stephenson, the British agent code named "Intrepid," sent by Churchill to the United States in 1940.[84] Stephenson set up headquarters in Rockefeller Center, with orders to use any means necessary to help bring the United States into the war. With the full knowledge and cooperation of Roosevelt and the collaboration of federal agencies, Stephenson and his 300 or so agents "intercepted mail, tapped wires, cracked safes, kidnapped, . . . rumor mongered" and incessantly smeared their favorite targets, the "isolationists." Through Stephenson, Churchill was virtually in control of William Donovan's organization, the embryonic U. S. intelligence service.[85]

Churchill even had a hand in the barrage of pro-British, anti-German propaganda that issued from Hollywood in the years before the United States entered the war. Gore Vidal, in *Screening History*, perceptively notes that starting around 1937, Americans were subjected to one film after another glorifying England and the warrior–heroes who built the Empire. As spectators of these productions, Vidal says: "We served neither Lincoln nor Jefferson Davis; we served the Crown."[86] A key Hollywood figure in generating the movies that "were making us all weirdly English" was the Hungarian émigré and friend of Churchill, Alexander Korda.[87] Vidal very aptly writes:

> For those who find disagreeable today's Zionist propaganda, I can only say that gallant little Israel of today must have learned a great deal from the gallant little Englanders of the 1930s. The English kept up a propaganda barrage that was to permeate our entire culture . . . Hollywood was subtly and not so subtly infiltrated by British propagandists.[88]

While the Americans were being worked on, the two confederates consulted on how to arrange for direct hostilities between the United States and Germany. In August, 1941, Roosevelt and Churchill met at the Atlantic conference. Here they produced the Atlantic Charter, with its "four freedoms," including "the freedom from want"—a blank-check to spread Anglo–American *Sozialpolitik* around the globe. When Churchill returned to London, he informed the Cabinet of what had been agreed to. Thirty years later, the British documents were released. Here is how the *New York Times* reported the revelations:

[84]William Stevenson, *A Man Called Intrepid* (New York: Harcourt Brace Jovanovich, 1976).
[85]Irving, *Churchill's War*, pp. 524–27.
[86]Gore Vidal, *Screening History* (Cambridge, Mass.: Harvard University Press, 1992), p. 40.
[87]Ibid., p. 47.
[88]Ibid., p. 33.

> Formerly top secret British Government papers made public today said that President Franklin D. Roosevelt told Prime Minister Winston Churchill in August, 1941, that he was looking for an incident to justify opening hostilities against Nazi Germany. . . . On August 19 Churchill reported to the War Cabinet in London on other aspects of the Newfoundland [Atlantic Charter] meeting that were not made public. . . . "He [Roosevelt] obviously was determined that they should come in. If he were to put the issue of peace and war to Congress, they would debate it for months," the Cabinet minutes added. "The President had said he would wage war but not declare it and that he would become more and more provocative. If the Germans did not like it, they could attack American forces. . . . Everything was to be done to force an incident."[89]

On July 15, 1941, Admiral Little, of the British naval delegation in Washington, wrote to Admiral Pound, the First Sea Lord: "the brightest hope for getting America into the war lies in the escorting arrangements to Iceland, and let us hope the Germans will not be slow in attacking them." Little added, perhaps jokingly: "Otherwise I think it would be best for us to organise an attack by our own submarines and preferably on the escort!" A few weeks earlier, Churchill, looking for a chance to bring America into the war, wrote to Pound regarding the German warship, *Prinz Eugen*: "It would be better for instance that she should be located by a U.S. ship as this might tempt her to fire on that ship, thus providing the incident for which the U.S. government would be so grateful."[90] Incidents in the North Atlantic did occur, increasingly, as the United States approached war with Germany.[91]

But Churchill did not neglect the "back door to war"—embroiling the United States with Japan—as a way of bringing America into the conflict with Hitler. Sir Robert Craigie, the British ambassador to Tokyo, like the American ambassador Joseph Grew, was working feverishly to avoid war. Churchill directed his foreign secretary, Anthony Eden, to whip Craigie into line:

> He should surely be told forthwith that the entry of the United States into war either with Germany and Italy or with Japan, is fully conformable with British interests. Nothing in the munitions sphere can compare with the importance of the British Empire and the United States being co-belligerent.[92]

[89]"War-Entry Plans Laid to Roosevelt," *New York Times*, January 2, 1972.
[90]Beesly, *Room 40*, p. 121 n. 1.
[91]See, for instance, William Henry Chamberlin, *America's Second Crusade* (Chicago: Henry Regnery, 1950), pp. 124–47.
[92]Richard Lamb, *Churchill as War Leader* (New York: Carroll and Graf, 1991), p. 149.

Churchill threw his influence into the balance to harden American policy towards Japan, especially in the last days before the Pearl Harbor attack.[93] A sympathetic critic of Churchill, Richard Lamb, has recently written:

> Was [Churchill] justified in trying to provoke Japan to attack the United States? . . . in 1941 Britain had no prospect of defeating Germany without the aid of the USA as an active ally. Churchill believed Congress would never authorize Roosevelt to declare war on Germany. . . . In war, decisions by national leaders must be made according to their effect on the war effort. There is truth in the old adage: "All's fair in love and war."[94]

No wonder that, in the House of Commons, on February 15, 1942, Churchill declared, of America's entry into the war: "This is what I have dreamed of, aimed at, worked for, and now it has come to pass."[95]

Churchill's devotees by no means hold his role in bringing America into World War II against him. On the contrary, they count it in his favor. Harry Jaffa, in his uninformed and frantic apology, seems to be the last person alive who refuses to believe that the Man of Many Centuries was responsible to any degree for America's entry into the war: after all, wasn't it the Japanese who bombed Pearl Harbor?[96]

But what of the American Republic? What does it mean for us that a President collaborated with a foreign head of government to entangle us in a world war? The question would have mattered little to Churchill. He had no concern with the United States as a sovereign, independent nation, with its own character and place in the

[93]Ibid., pp. 147–62.

[94]Ibid., p. 162.

[95]Chamberlin, *America's Second Crusade*, p. 177. On Churchill's use of the "backdoor to war" for the United States, see John Costello, *Days of Infamy. MacArthur, Roosevelt, Churchill—The Shocking Truth Revealed* (New York: Pocket Books, 1994). On the question of Pearl Harbor, it is interesting to note that even as "mainstream" a historian as Warren F. Kimball, editor of the Churchill–Roosevelt correspondence, writes: "Doubts have not yet been laid to rest concerning still-closed British intelligence files about the Japanese attack on Pearl Harbor: information that Churchill may have chosen not to pass on to the Americans in the hope that such an attack would draw the United States into war." See also Warren F. Kimball, "Wheel Within a Wheel: Churchill, Roosevelt, and the Special Relationship," in *Churchill*, Blake and Louis, eds., p. 298, where Kimball cites James Rusbridger and Eric Nave, *Betrayal at Pearl Harbor: How Churchill Lured Roosevelt into World War II* (New York: Summit, 1991). Kimball complains that, despite written requests from him and other historians, British government files on relations with Japan in late 1941 remain closed. *Churchill*, p. 546 n. 29. Robert Smith Thompson, in *A Time for War: Franklin Delano Roosevelt and the Path to Pearl Harbor* (New York: Prentice Hall, 1991), presents a useful recent account of the coming of the war with Japan.

[96]Jaffa, "In Defense of Churchill," p. 277.

scheme of things. For him, Americans were one of "the English-speaking peoples." He looked forward to a common citizenship for Britons and Americans, a "mixing together," on the road to Anglo–American world hegemony.[97]

But the Churchill–Roosevelt intrigue should, one might think, matter to Americans. Here, however, criticism is halted before it starts. A moral postulate of our time is that in pursuit of the destruction of Hitler, all things were permissible. Yet why is it self-evident that morality required a crusade against Hitler in 1939 and 1940, and not against Stalin? At that point, Hitler had slain his thousands, but Stalin had already slain his millions. In fact, up to June, 1941, the Soviets behaved far more murderously toward the Poles in their zone of occupation than the Nazis did in theirs. Around 1,500,000 Poles were deported to the Gulag, with about half of them dying within the first two years. As Norman Davies writes: "Stalin was outpacing Hitler in his desire to reduce the Poles to the condition of a slave nation."[98] Of course, there were balance-of-power considerations that created distinctions between the two dictators. But it has yet to be explained why there should exist a double standard ordaining that compromise with one dictator would have been "morally sickening," while collaboration with the other was morally irreproachable.[99]

"FIRST CATCH YOUR HARE"

Early in the war, Churchill, declared: "I have only one aim in life, the defeat of Hitler, and this makes things very simple for me."[100] "Victory—victory at all costs," understood literally, was his policy practically to the end. This points to Churchill's fundamental and fatal mistake in World War II: his separation of operational from political strategy. To the first—the planning and direction of military campaigns—he devoted all of his time and energy; after all, he did *so* enjoy it. To the second, the fitting of military operations to the larger and much more significant political aims they were supposed to serve, he devoted no effort at all.

Stalin, on the other hand, understood perfectly that the entire purpose of war is to enforce certain political claims. This is the

---

[97]Charmley, *Churchill: The End of Glory*, p. 538.

[98]Norman Davies, *God's Playground: A History of Poland*, vol. 2, *1795 to the Present* (New York: Columbia University Press, 1982), pp. 447–53.

[99]For a critique of the view that Hitler's aim was to "conquer the world," see Geoffrey Stoakes, *Hitler and the Quest for World Domination* (Leamington Spa, England: Berg, 1986).

[100]Taylor, "The Statesman," p. 43.

meaning of Clausewitz's famous dictum that war is the continuation of policy by other means. On Eden's visit to Moscow in December, 1941, with the Wehrmacht in the Moscow suburbs, Stalin was ready with his demands: British recognition of Soviet rule over the Baltic states and the territories he had just seized from Finland, Poland, and Romania. (They were eventually granted.) Throughout the war he never lost sight of these and other crucial political goals. But Churchill, despite frequent prodding from Eden, never gave a thought to his, whatever they might be.[101] His approach, he explained, was that of Mrs. Glass's recipe for Jugged Hare: "First catch your hare."[102] First beat Hitler, then start thinking of the future of Britain and Europe. Churchill put in so many words: "the defeat, ruin, and slaughter of Hitler, to the exclusion of all other purposes, loyalties and aims."

Tuvia Ben-Moshe has shrewdly pinpointed one of the sources of this grotesque indifference:

> Thirty years earlier, Churchill had told Asquith that . . . his life's ambition was "to command great victorious armies in battle." During World War II he was determined to take nothing less than full advantage of the opportunity given him—the almost unhampered military management of the great conflict. He was prone to ignore or postpone the treatment of matters likely to detract from that pleasure. . . . In so doing, he deferred, or even shelved altogether, treatment of the issues that he should have dealt with in his capacity as Prime Minister.[103]

Churchill's policy of all-out support of Stalin foreclosed other, potentially more favorable approaches. The military expert Hanson Baldwin, for instance, stated:

> There is no doubt whatsoever that it would have been in the interest of Britain, the United States, and the world to have allowed—and indeed, to have encouraged—the world's two great dictatorships to fight each other to a frazzle. Such a struggle, with its resultant weakening of both Communism and Nazism, could not but have aided in the establishment of a more stable peace.[104]

Instead of adopting this approach, or, for example, promoting the overthrow of Hitler by anti-Nazi Germans—instead of even

[101]For instance, in May, 1944, Eden protested to Churchill, regarding the prospect of the "Communization of the Balkans": "We must think of the after-effect of these developments, instead of confining ourselves as hitherto to the short-term view of what will give the best dividends during the war and for the war." Charmley, *Churchill: The End of Glory*, p. 538.

[102]Ben-Moshe, *Churchill: Strategy and History*, pp. 236–37.

[103]Ibid., p. 241.

[104]Hanson W. Baldwin, *Great Mistakes of the War* (New York: Harper, 1949), p. 10.

considering such alternatives—Churchill from the start threw all of his support to Soviet Russia.

Franklin Roosevelt's fatuousness towards Joseph Stalin is well-known. He looked on Stalin as a fellow "progressive" and an invaluable collaborator in creating the future New World Order.[105] But the neo-conservatives and others who counterpose to Roosevelt's inanity in this matter Churchill's Old World cunning and sagacity are sadly in error. Roosevelt's nauseating flattery of Stalin is easily matched by Churchill's. Just like Roosevelt, Churchill heaped fulsome praise on the Communist murderer, and was anxious for Stalin's personal friendship. Moreover, his adulation of Stalin and his version of Communism—so different from the repellent "Trotskyite" kind—was no different in private than in public. In January, 1944, he was still speaking to Eden of the "deep-seated changes which have taken place in the character of the Russian state and government, the new confidence which has grown in our hearts towards Stalin."[106] In a letter to his wife, Clementine, Churchill wrote, following the October, 1944 conference in Moscow: "I have had very nice talks with the old Bear. I like him the more I see him. Now they respect us & I am sure they wish to work with us."[107] Writers like Isaiah Berlin, who try to give the impression that Churchill hated or despised all dictators, including Stalin, are either ignorant or dishonest.[108]

Churchill's supporters often claim that, unlike the Americans, the seasoned and crafty British statesman foresaw the danger from the Soviet Union and worked doggedly to thwart it. Churchill's famous "Mediterranean" strategy—to attack Europe through its "soft underbelly," rather than concentrating on an invasion of

---

[105]Roosevelt's attitude is epitomized in his statement: "If I give him [Stalin] everything I possibly can, and ask nothing of him in return, [then] *noblesse oblige*, he won't try to annex anything and will work with me for a world of peace and democracy." Robert Nisbet, *Roosevelt and Stalin: The Failed Courtship* (Washington, D.C.: Regnery, 1988), p. 6. Joseph Sobran's remarks in his brief essay, "Pal Joey," *Sobran's* 2, no. 8 (August 1995): pp. 5–6, are characteristically insightful.

[106]Ben-Moshe, *Churchill: Strategy and History*, pp. 287–88, 305–6.

[107]Ponting, *Churchill*, p. 665.

[108]Isaiah Berlin, "Winston Churchill," in idem, *Personal Impressions*, Henry Hardy, ed. (New York: Viking, 1980), p. 16, where Churchill is quoted as saying of Stalin that he is "at once a callous, a crafty, and an ill-informed giant." Note, however, that even this quotation shows that Churchill placed Stalin in an entirely different category from the unspeakably evil Hitler. In fact, as the works by Charmley, Ponting, and Ben-Moshe amply demonstrate, until the end of the war Churchill's typical attitude toward Stalin was friendly and admiring. Berlin's essay, with its mawkish infatuation with "the largest human being of our time," has to be read to be believed. An indication of one source of Berlin's passion is his reference to Churchill's sympathy for "the struggle of the Jews for self-determination in Palestine."

northern France—is supposed to be the proof of this.[109] But this was an *ex post facto* defense, concocted by Churchill once the Cold War had started: there is little, if any, contemporary evidence that the desire to beat the Russians to Vienna and Budapest formed any part of Churchill's motivation in advocating the "soft underbelly" strategy. At the time, Churchill gave purely military reasons for it.[110] As Ben-Moshe states: "The official British historians have ascertained that not until the second half of 1944 and after the Channel crossing did Churchill first begin to consider preempting the Russians in southeastern Europe by military means."[111] By then, such a move would have been impossible for several reasons. It was another of Churchill's bizarre military notions, like invading Fortress Europe through Norway, or putting off the invasion of northern France until 1945—by which time the Russians would have reached the Rhine.[112]

Moreover, the American opposition to Churchill's southern strategy did not stem from blindness to the Communist danger. As General Albert C. Wedemeyer, one of the firmest anti-Communists in the American military, wrote:

> if we had invaded the Balkans through the Ljubljana Gap, we might theoretically have beaten the Russians to Vienna and Budapest. But logistics would have been against us there: it would have been next to impossible to supply more than two divisions through the Adriatic ports. . . . The proposal to save the Balkans from communism could never have been made good by a "soft underbelly" invasion, for

[109]Cf. Charmley, *Churchill: The End of Glory*, pp. 572–73, on "Operation Armpit," the extension of the Italian campaign and a thrust towards Vienna; Charmley concludes that, contrary to Churchill's Cold War defenders: "there is little evidence to show that Churchill's support for 'Armpit' was based upon political motives. . . . [He supported it] for the reason which any student of his career will be familiar with—it fired his imagination."

[110]Cf. Taylor, "The Statesman," pp. 56–57: "According to one version, Churchill was alarmed at the growth of Soviet power and tried to take precautions against it, if not in 1942 at least well before the end of the war. . . . It is hard to sustain this view from contemporary records. Churchill never wavered from his determination that Nazi Germany must be utterly defeated. . . . Churchill had no European policy in any wider sense. His outlook was purely negative: the defeat of Germany. . . . With Churchill it was always one thing at a time." See also Ben-Moshe, *Churchill: Strategy and History*, pp. 292–99, on the southern strategy not being aimed at forestalling Soviet gains.

[111]Ibid., p. 287.

[112]An instance of the lengths to which Churchill's apologists will go is provided by John Keegan, in "Churchill's Strategy," in *Churchill*, Blake and Louis, eds., p. 328, where he states of Churchill: "Yet he never espoused any truly unwise strategic course, nor did he contemplate one. His commitment to a campaign in the Balkans was unsound, but such a campaign would not have risked losing the war." Risking losing the war would appear to be an excessively stringent criterion for a truly unwise strategic course.

> Churchill himself had already cleared the way for the suc-
> cess of Tito . . . [who] had been firmly ensconced in Yugosla-
> via with British aid long before Italy itself was conquered.[113]

Wedemeyer's remarks about Yugoslavia were on the mark. On this issue, Churchill rejected the advice of his own Foreign Office, depending instead on information provided especially by the head of the Cairo office of the SOE—the Special Operations branch—headed by a Communist agent named James Klugman. Churchill withdrew British support from the Loyalist guerrilla army of General Mihailovic and threw it to the Communist Partisan leader Tito.[114] What a victory for Tito would mean was no secret to Churchill.[115] When Fitzroy Maclean was interviewed by Churchill before being sent as liaison to Tito, Maclean observed that, under Communist leadership, the Partisans'

> ultimate aim would undoubtedly be to establish in Jugo-
> slavia a Communist regime closely linked to Moscow. How
> did His Majesty's Government view such an eventuality? . . .
> Mr. Churchill's reply left me in no doubt as to the answer to
> my problem. So long, he said, as the whole of Western civili-
> zation was threatened by the Nazi menace, we could not af-
> ford to let our attention be diverted from the immediate is-
> sue by considerations of long-term policy. . . . Politics must
> be a secondary consideration.[116]

It would be difficult to think of a more frivolous attitude to waging war than considering "politics" to be a "secondary consideration." As for the "human costs" of Churchill's policy, when an aide pointed out that Tito intended to transform Yugoslavia into a Communist dictatorship on the Soviet model, Churchill retorted: "Do you intend to live there?"[117]

Churchill's benign view of Stalin and Russia contrasts sharply with his view of Germany. Behind Hitler, Churchill discerned the

---

[113]Albert C. Wedemeyer, *Wedemeyer Reports!* (New York: Holt, 1958), p. 230. Everyone else was against Churchill's plan, including his own military advisors. Brooke pointed out to his chief that, if they followed through with his idea, "we should embark on a campaign through the Alps in winter." Ponting, *Churchill*, p. 625.

[114]Lamb, *Churchill as War Leader*, pp. 250–75.

[115]Churchill's own Foreign Office informed him that: "we would land ourselves with a Communist state closely linked to the USSR after the war who would employ the usual terrorist methods to overcome opposition." Ibid., p. 256. Anthony Eden told the Cabinet in June, 1944: "If anyone is to blame for the present situation in which Communist-led movements are the most powerful elements in Yugoslavia and Greece, it is we ourselves." British agents, according to Eden, had done the work of the Russians for them. Charmley, *Churchill: The End of Glory*, p. 580.

[116]Fitzroy Maclean, *Eastern Approaches* (London: Jonathan Cape, 1949), p. 281.

[117]Lamb, *Churchill as War Leader*, p. 259. Churchill believed Tito's promises of a free election and a plebiscite on the monarchy; above all, he concentrated on a single issue: killing Germans. See also Charmley, *Churchill: The End of Glory*, p. 558.

old specter of Prussianism, which had caused, allegedly, not only the two world wars, but the Franco–Prussian War as well. What he was battling now was "Nazi tyranny and Prussian militarism," the "two main elements in German life which must be absolutely destroyed."[118] In October, 1944, Churchill was still explaining to Stalin that: "The problem was how to prevent Germany getting on her feet in the lifetime of our grandchildren."[119] Churchill harbored a "confusion of mind on the subject of the Prussian aristocracy, Nazism, and the sources of German militarist expansionism . . . [his view] was remarkably similar to that entertained by Sir Robert Vansittart and Sir Warren Fisher; that is to say, it arose from a combination of almost racialist antipathy and balance of power calculations."[120] Churchill's aim was not simply to save world civilization from the Nazis, but, in his words, the "indefinite prevention of their [the Germans'] rising again as an Armed Power."[121]

Little wonder, then, that Churchill refused even to listen to the pleas of the anti-Hitler German opposition, which tried repeatedly to establish liaison with the British government. Instead of making every effort to encourage and assist an anti-Nazi coup in Germany, Churchill responded to the feelers sent out by the German resistance with cold silence.[122] Reiterated warnings from Adam von Trott and other resistance leaders of the impending "bolshevization" of Europe made no impression on the erstwhile anti-Communist.[123] A recent historian has written: "by his intransigence and refusal to countenance talks with dissident Germans, Churchill threw away an opportunity to end the war in July 1944."[124] To add

[118]On September 21, 1943, for instance, Churchill stated: "The twin roots of all our evils, Nazi tyranny and Prussian militarism, must be extirpated. Until this is achieved, there are no sacrifices we will not make and no lengths in violence to which we will not go." Russell Grenfell, *Unconditional Hatred* (New York: Devin-Adair, 1953), p. 92.

[119]Ponting, *Churchill*, p. 675.

[120]Watt, "Churchill and Appeasement," p. 210.

[121]In a memorandum to Alexander Cadogan, of the Foreign Office; Richard Lamb, *The Ghosts of Peace, 1935–1945* (Salisbury, England: Michael Russell, 1987), p. 233.

[122]Peter Hoffmann, *German Resistance to Hitler* (Cambridge, Mass.: Harvard University Press, 1988), pp. 95–105; idem, *The History of the German Resistance*, Richard Barry, trans. (Cambridge, Mass.: MIT Press, 1977), pp. 205–48; and idem, "The Question of Western Allied Co-Operation with the German Anti-Nazi Conspiracy, 1938–1944," *The Historical Journal* 34, no. 2 (1991): 437–64.

[123]Giles MacDonogh, *A Good German: Adam von Trott zu Solz* (Woodstock, N.Y.: Overlook Press, 1992), pp. 236–37.

[124]Lamb, *Churchill as War Leader*, p. 292. Lamb argues this thesis at length and persuasively in his *The Ghosts of Peace, 1935–1945*, pp. 248–320. A less conclusive judgment is reached by Klemens von Klemperer, *German Resistance Against Hitler: The Search for Allies Abroad 1938–1945* (Oxford: Clarendon, 1992), esp. pp. 432–41, who emphasizes the difficulties in the way of any agreement between the British government and the German resistance. These included, in particular, the loyalty of

infamy to stupidity, Churchill and his crowd had only words of scorn for the valiant German officers even as they were being slaughtered by the Gestapo.[125]

In place of help, all Churchill offered Germans looking for a way to end the war before the Red Army flooded into central Europe was the slogan of *unconditional surrender*. Afterwards, Churchill lied in the House of Commons about his role at Casablanca in connection with Roosevelt's announcement of the policy of unconditional surrender, and was forced to retract his statements.[126] Eisenhower, among others, strenuously and persistently objected to the unconditional surrender formula as hampering the war effort by raising the morale of the Wehrmacht.[127] In fact, the slogan was seized on by Goebbels, and contributed to the Germans' holding out to the bitter end.

The pernicious effect of the policy was immeasurably bolstered by the Morgenthau Plan, which gave the Germans a terrifying picture of what "unconditional surrender" would mean.[128] This plan, initialed by Roosevelt and Churchill at Quebec, called for turning Germany into an agricultural and pastoral country; even the coal mines of the Ruhr were to be wrecked. The fact that it would have led to the deaths of tens of millions of Germans made it a perfect analog to Hitler's schemes for dealing with Russia and the Ukraine.

Churchill was initially averse to the plan. However, he was won over by Professor Lindemann, as maniacal a German-hater as Morgenthau himself. Lindemann stated to Lord Moran, Churchill's personal physician: "I explained to Winston that the plan would save Britain from bankruptcy by eliminating a dangerous competitor. . . . Winston had not thought of it in that way, and he said no

---

the former to its Soviet ally and the insistence of the latter on post-war Germany's keeping ethnically German areas, such as Danzig and the Sudetenland.

[125]Marie Vassiltchikov, who was close to the conspirators, in her *Berlin Diaries, 1940–1945* (New York: Knopf, 1987), p. 218, expressed her bafflement at the line taken by the British: "The Allied radio makes no sense to us: they keep naming people who, they claim, took part in the plot. And yet some of these have not yet been officially implicated. I remember warning Adam Trott that this would happen. He kept hoping for Allied support of a 'decent' Germany and I kept saying that at this point they were out to destroy Germany, any Germany, and would not stop at eliminating the 'good' Germans with the 'bad.'"

[126]Ben-Moshe, *Churchill: Strategy and History*, pp. 307–16. See also Anne Armstrong, *Unconditional Surrender* (Westport, Conn.: Greenwood, [1961] 1974); and Lamb, *The Ghosts of Peace, 1935–1945*, pp. 215–35. Among the strongest wartime critics of the unconditional surrender policy, as well as of the bombing of civilians, was the military expert, Liddell Hart; see Brian Bond, *Liddell Hart: A Study of his Military Thought* (New Brunswick, N.J.: Rutgers University Press, 1977), pp. 119–63.

[127]Lamb, *The Ghosts of Peace, 1935–1945*, p. 232.

[128]Ibid., pp. 236–45.

more about a cruel threat to the German people."[129] According to Morgenthau, the wording of the scheme was drafted entirely by Churchill. When Roosevelt returned to Washington, Hull, and Stimson expressed their horror, and quickly disabused the President. Churchill, on the other hand, was unrepentant. When it came time to mention the Morgenthau Plan in his history of the war, he distorted its provisions and, by implication, lied about his role in supporting it.[130]

Beyond the issue of the plan itself, Lord Moran wondered how it had been possible for Churchill to appear at the Quebec conference "without any thought out views on the future of Germany, although she seemed to be on the point of surrender." The answer was that "he had become so engrossed in the conduct of the war that little time was left to plan for the future":

> Military detail had long fascinated him, while he was frankly bored by the kind of problem which might take up the time of the Peace Conference. . . . The P. M. was frittering away his waning strength on matters which rightly belonged to soldiers. My diary in the autumn of 1942 tells how I talked to Sir Stafford Cripps and found that he shared my cares. He wanted the P. M. to concentrate on the broad strategy of the war and on high policy. . . . No one could make [Churchill] see his errors.[131]

WAR CRIMES DISCREETLY VEILED

There are a number of episodes during the war revealing of Churchill's character that deserve to be mentioned. A relatively minor incident was the British attack on the French fleet, at Mers-el-Kebir (Oran), off the coast of Algeria. After the fall of France, Churchill demanded that the French surrender their fleet to Britain. The French declined, promising that they would scuttle the ships before allowing them to fall into German hands. Against the advice of his naval officers, Churchill ordered British ships off the Algerian coast to open fire. About 1500 French sailors were

---

[129]Lord Moran, *Churchill: The Struggle for Survival, 1940–1965* (Boston: Houghton Mifflin, 1966), pp. 190–91. Churchill's ready acceptance of this specious argument casts considerable doubt on the claim of Paul Addison, *Churchill on the Home Front*, p. 437, that Churchill was "schooled" in free-trade doctrines, which were "ingrained" in him. More consistent with the evidence, including his outright rejection of free trade beginning in 1930, is that Churchill used or cast aside the economic theory of the market economy as it suited his political purposes.

[130]Moran, *Churchill: The Struggle for Survival, 1940–1965*, pp. 195–96.

[131]Ibid., p. 193. That the spirit at least of the Morgenthau Plan continued to guide Allied policy in post-war Germany is shown in Freda Utley's *The High Cost of Vengeance* (Chicago: Henry Regnery, 1949).

killed. This was obviously a war crime, by anyone's definition: an unprovoked attack on the forces of an ally without a declaration of war. At Nuremberg, German officers were sentenced to prison for less. Realizing this, Churchill lied about Mers-el-Kebir in his history, and suppressed evidence concerning it in the official British histories of the war.[132] With the attack on the French fleet, Churchill confirmed his position as the prime subverter through two world wars of the system of rules of warfare that had evolved in the West over centuries.

But the great war crime which will be forever linked to Churchill's name is the terror-bombing of the cities of Germany that in the end cost the lives of around 600,000 civilians and left some 800,000 seriously injured.[133] (Compare this to the roughly 70,000 British lives lost to German air attacks. In fact, there were nearly as many Frenchmen killed by Allied air attacks as there were Englishmen killed by Germans.[134]) The plan was conceived mainly by Churchill's friend and scientific advisor, Professor Lindemann, and carried out by the head of Bomber Command, Arthur Harris ("Bomber Harris"). Harris stated: "In Bomber Command we have always worked on the assumption that bombing anything in Germany is better than bombing nothing."[135] Harris and other British airforce leaders boasted that Britain had been the pioneer in the massive use of strategic bombing. J.M. Spaight, former Principal Assistant Secretary of the Air Ministry, noted that while the Germans (and the French) looked on air power as largely an extension of artillery, a support to the armies in the field, the British understood its capacity to destroy the

---

[132]Lamb, *Churchill as War Leader*, pp. 63–73. See also Ponting, *Churchill*, pp. 450–54; and Hart, "The Military Strategist," pp. 210–21.

[133]The "British obsession with heavy bombers" had consequences for the war effort as well; it led, for instance, to the lack of fighter planes at Singapore. Taylor, "The Statesman," p. 54. On the whole issue, see Stephen A. Garrett, *Ethics and Airpower in World War II: The British Bombing of German Cities* (New York: St. Martin's Press, 1993). See also Max Hastings, *Bomber Command* (New York: Dial Press, 1979); David Irving, *The Destruction of Dresden* (New York: Ballantine, 1963); and Benjamin Colby, *'Twas a Famous Victory* (New Rochelle, N.Y.: Arlington House, 1974), pp. 173–202. On the British use of airpower to "pacify" colonial populations, see Charles Townshend, "Civilization and 'Frightfulness': Air Control in the Middle East Between the Wars," in *Warfare, Diplomacy, and Politics: Essays in Honor of A.J.P. Taylor*, Chris Wrigley, ed. (London: Hamish Hamilton, 1986), pp. 142–62.

[134]Ponting, *Churchill*, p. 620.

[135]Hastings, *Bomber Command*, p. 339. In 1945, Harris wrote: "I would not regard the whole of the remaining cities of Germany as worth the bones of one British grenadier." Ibid., p. 344. Harris later wrote: "The Germans had allowed their soldiers to dictate the whole policy of the Luftwaffe, which was designed expressly to assist the army in rapid advances. . . . Much too late in the day they saw the advantage of a strategic bombing force." Hughes, *Winston Churchill: British Bulldog*, p. 189.

enemy's home-base. They built their bombers and established Bomber Command accordingly.[136]

Brazenly lying to the House of Commons and the public, Churchill claimed that only military and industrial installations were targeted. In fact, the aim was to kill as many civilians as possible—thus, "area" bombing, or "carpet" bombing—and in this way to break the morale of the Germans and terrorize them into surrendering.[137]

Harris at least had the courage of his convictions. He urged that the government openly announce that:

> the aim of the Combined Bomber Offensive . . . should be unambiguously stated [as] the destruction of German cities, the killing of German workers, and the disruption of civilized life throughout Germany.[138]

The campaign of murder from the air leveled Germany. A thousand-year-old urban culture was annihilated, as great cities, famed in the annals of science and art, were reduced to heaps of smoldering ruins. There were high points: the bombing of Lübeck, when that ancient Hanseatic town "burned like kindling"; the 1000 bomber raid over Cologne, and the following raids that somehow, miraculously, spared the great Cathedral but destroyed the rest of the city, including thirteen Romanesque churches; the firestorm that consumed Hamburg and killed some 42,000 people. No wonder that, learning of this, a civilized European like Joseph Schumpeter, at Harvard, was driven to telling "anyone who would listen" that Churchill and Roosevelt were destroying more than Genghis Khan.[139]

---

[136]J.M. Spaight, *Bombing Vindicated* (London: Geoffrey Bles, 1944), p. 70–71. Spaight declared that Britons should be proud of the fact that "we began to bomb objectives on the German mainland before the Germans began to bomb objectives on the British mainland." Hitler, while ready enough to use strategic bombing on occasion, "did not want [it] to become the practice. He had done his best to have it banned by international agreement." Ibid., pp. 68, 60. Writing during the war, Spaight, of course, lied to his readers in asserting that German civilians were being killed only incidentally by the British bombing.

[137]On February 14, 1942, Directive No. 22 was issued to Bomber Command, stipulating that efforts were now to be "focused on the morale of the enemy civil population and in particular of the industrial workers." The next day, the chief of the Air Staff added: "Ref the new bombing directive: I suppose it is clear that the aiming points are to be the built-up areas, not, for instance, the dockyards or aircraft factories." Garrett, *Ethics and Air Power in World War II*, p. 11. By lying about the goal of the bombing and attempting a cover-up after the war, Churchill implicitly conceded that Britain had committed breaches of the rules of warfare. Ibid., pp. 36–37.

[138]Ibid., pp. 32–33.

[139]Richard Swedberg, *Schumpeter: A Biography* (Princeton, N.J.: Princeton University Press, 1991), p. 141.

The most infamous act was the destruction of Dresden, in February, 1945. According to the official history of the Royal Air Force: "The destruction of Germany was by then on a scale which might have appalled Attila or Genghis Khan."[140] Dresden, the capital of the old kingdom of Saxony, was an indispensable stop on the Grand Tour, the baroque gem of Europe. The war was practically over, the city filled with masses of helpless refugees escaping the advancing Red Army. Still, for three days and nights, from February 13 to 15, Dresden was pounded with bombs. At least 30,000 people were killed, perhaps as many as 135,000 or more. The Zwinger Palace; Our Lady's Church, die Frauenkirche; the Brühl Terrace overlooking the Elbe where, in Turgenev's *Fathers and Sons*, Uncle Pavel went to spend his last years; the Semper Opera House, where Richard Strauss conducted the premiere of *Rosenkavalier*; and practically everything else was incinerated. Churchill had fomented it. But he was shaken by the outcry that followed. While in Georgetown and Hollywood, few had ever heard of Dresden, the city meant something in Stockholm, Zurich, and the Vatican, and even in London. What did our hero do? He sent a memorandum to the Chiefs of Staff:

> It seems to me that the moment has come when the question of bombing of German cities simply for the sake of increasing the terror, though under other pretexts, should be reviewed. Otherwise, we shall come into control of an utterly ruined land. . . . The destruction of Dresden remains a serious query against the conduct of Allied bombing. . . . I feel the need for more precise concentration upon military objectives . . . rather than on mere acts of terror and wanton destruction, however impressive.[141]

The military chiefs saw through Churchill's contemptible ploy: realizing that they were being set up, they refused to accept the memorandum. After the war, Churchill casually disclaimed any knowledge of the Dresden bombing, saying: "I thought the Americans did it."[142]

And still the bombing continued. On March 16, in a period of 20 minutes, Würzburg was razed to the ground. As late as the middle of April, Berlin and Potsdam were bombed yet again, killing another 5,000 civilians. Finally, it stopped; as Bomber Harris

[140]Garrett, *Ethics and Air Power in World War II*, p. 202.

[141]Hastings, *Bomber Command*, pp. 343–44. In November, 1942, Churchill had proposed that in the Italian campaign: "All the industrial centers should be attacked in an intense fashion, every effort being made to render them uninhabitable and to terrorise and paralyse the population." Ponting, *Churchill*, p. 614.

[142]To a historian who wished to verify some details, Churchill replied: "I cannot recall anything about it. I thought the Americans did it. Air Chief Marshal Harris would be the person to contact." Rose, *Churchill: The Unruly Giant*, p. 338.

noted, there were essentially no more targets to be bombed in Germany.[143] It need hardly be recorded that Churchill supported the atom-bombing of Hiroshima and Nagasaki, which resulted in the deaths of another 100,000, or more, civilians. When Truman fabricated the myth of the "500,000 U.S. lives saved" by avoiding an invasion of the Home Islands—the highest military estimate had been 46,000—Churchill topped his lie: the atom-bombings had saved 1,200,000 lives, including 1,000,000 Americans, he fantasized.[144]

The eagerness with which Churchill directed or applauded the destruction of cities from the air should raise questions for those who still consider him the great "conservative" of his—or perhaps of all—time. They would do well to consider the judgment of an authentic conservative like Erik von Kuehnelt-Leddihn, who wrote: "Non-Britishers did not matter to Mr. Churchill, who sacrificed human beings—their lives, their welfare, their liberty—with the same elegant disdain as his colleague in the White House."[145]

1945: THE DARK SIDE

And so we come to 1945 and the ever-radiant triumph of Absolute Good over Absolute Evil. So potent is the mystique of that year that the insipid welfare states of today's Europe clutch at it at every opportunity, in search of a few much-needed shreds of glory.

The dark side of that triumph, however, has been all but suppressed. It is the story of the crimes and atrocities of the victors and their protégés. Since Winston Churchill played a central role in the Allied victory, it is the story also of the crimes and atrocities in which Churchill was implicated. These include the forced repatriation of some two million Soviet subjects to the Soviet Union.

---

[143]Garrett, *Ethics and Air Power in World War II*, p. 21.

[144]See Barton J. Bernstein, "A postwar myth: 500,000 U.S. lives saved," *Bulletin of the Atomic Scientists* 42, no. 6 (June/July 1986): 38–40; and, idem, "Wrong Numbers," *The Independent Monthly* (July 1995): 41–44. See also, idem, "Seizing the Contested Terrain of Early Nuclear History: Stimson, Conant, and Their Allies Explain the Decision to Use the Atomic Bomb," *Diplomatic History* 17, no. 1 (Winter 1993): 35–72, where the point is made that a major motive in the political elite's early propaganda campaign justifying the use of the atomic bombs was to forestall a feared retreat into "isolationism" by the American people. It is interesting to note that Richard Nixon, sometimes known as the "Mad Bomber" of Indo–China, justified "deliberate attacks on civilians" by citing the atomic bombings of the Japanese cities, as well as the attacks on Hamburg and Dresden. Richard M. Nixon, "Letters to the Editor," *New York Times*, May 15, 1983.

[145]Erik von Kuehnelt-Leddihn, *Leftism Revisited: From de Sade and Marx to Hitler and Pol Pot* (Washington, D.C.: Regnery, 1990), p. 281. This work contains numerous perceptive passages on Churchill, e.g., pp. 261–65, 273, and 280–81, as well as on Roosevelt.

Among these were tens of thousands who had fought with the Germans against Stalin, under the sponsorship of General Vlasov and his "Russian Army of Liberation." This is what Alexander Solzhenitsyn wrote, in *The Gulag Archipelago*:

> In their own country, Roosevelt and Churchill are honored as embodiments of statesmanlike wisdom. To us, in our Russian prison conversations, their consistent shortsightedness and stupidity stood out as astonishingly obvious . . . what was the military or political sense in their surrendering to destruction at Stalin's hands hundreds of thousands of armed Soviet citizens determined not to surrender.[146]

Most shameful of all was the handing over of the Cossacks. They had never been Soviet citizens, since they had fought against the Red Army in the Civil War and then emigrated. Stalin, understandably, was particularly keen to get hold of them, and the British obliged. Solzhenitsyn wrote, of Winston Churchill:

> He turned over to the Soviet command the Cossack corps of 90,000 men. Along with them he also handed over many wagonloads of old people, women, and children. . . . This great hero, monuments to whom will in time cover all England, ordered that they, too, be surrendered to their deaths.[147]

The "purge" of alleged collaborators in France was a bloodbath that claimed more victims than the Reign of Terror in the Great Revolution—and not just among those who in one way or other had aided the Germans: included were any right-wingers the Communist resistance groups wished to liquidate.[148]

The massacres carried out by Churchill's protégé, Tito, must be added to this list: tens of thousands of Croats, not simply the Ustasha, but any "class-enemies," in classical Communist style. There was also the murder of some 20,000 Slovene anti-Communist fighters by Tito and his killing squads. When Tito's Partisans rampaged in Trieste, which he was attempting to grab in 1945, additional thousands of Italian anti-Communists were massacred.[149]

As the troops of Churchill's Soviet ally swept through central Europe and the Balkans, the mass deportations began. Some in the British government had qualms, feeling a certain responsibility.

[146]Aleksandr I. Solzhenitsyn, *The Gulag Archipelago, 1918–1956: An Experiment in Literary Investigation*, Thomas P. Whitney, trans. (New York: Harper and Row, 1973), 1–2, p. 259n.
[147]Ibid., pp. 259–60.
[148]Sisley Huddleston, *France: The Tragic Years, 1939–1947* (New York: Devin-Adair, 1955), pp. 285–324.
[149]See, for instance, Richard West, *Tito and the Rise and Fall of Yugoslavia* (New York: Carroll and Graf, 1995), pp. 192–93.

Churchill would have none of it. In January, 1945, for instance, he noted to the Foreign Office: "Why are we making a fuss about the Russian deportations in Rumania of Saxons [Germans] and others? . . . I cannot see the Russians are wrong in making 100 or 150 thousand of these people work their passage. . . . I cannot myself consider that it is wrong of the Russians to take Rumanians of any origin they like to work in the Russian coal-fields."[150] About 500,000 German civilians were deported to work in Soviet Russia, in accordance with Churchill and Roosevelt's agreement at Yalta that such slave labor constituted a proper form of "reparations."[151]

Worst of all was the expulsion of some 15 million Germans from their ancestral homelands in East and West Prussia, Silesia, Pomerania, and the Sudetenland. This was done pursuant to the agreements at Tehran, where Churchill proposed that Poland be "moved west," and to Churchill's acquiescence in the Czech leader Eduard Benes's plan for the "ethnic cleansing" of Bohemia and Moravia. Around one-and-a-half to two million German civilians died in this process.[152] As the Hungarian liberal Gaspar Tamas wrote, in driving out the Germans of east-central Europe, "whose ancestors built our cathedrals, monasteries, universities, and railroad stations," a whole ancient culture was effaced.[153] But why should that mean anything to the Churchill devotees who call themselves "conservatives" in America today?

Then, to top it all, came the Nuremberg Trials, a travesty of justice condemned by the great Senator Robert Taft, where Stalin's judges and prosecutors—seasoned veterans of the purges of the 30s—participated in another great show-trial.[154]

By 1946, Churchill was complaining in a voice of outrage of the happenings in eastern Europe: "From Stettin in the north to Trieste

---

[150]Ponting, *Churchill*, p. 665.

[151]Herbert Mitzka, *Zur Geschichte der Massendeportationen von Ostdeutschen in die Sowjetunion im Jahre 1945* (Einhausen: Atelier Hübner, 1986). On other crimes against German civilians in the aftermath of the war, see, among other works, Heinz Nawratil, *Die deutschen Nachkriegsverluste unter Vertriebenen, Gefangenen, und Verschleppten* (Munich/Berlin: Herbig, 1986); John Sack, *An Eye for an Eye* (New York: Basic Books, 1993); and James Bacque, *Verschwiegene Schuld: Die alliierte Besatzungspolitik in Deutschland nach 1945*, Hans-Ulrich Seebohm, trans. (Berlin/Frankfurt a. M.: Ullstein, 1995).

[152]Alfred de Zayas, *Nemesis at Potsdam: The Anglo–Americans and the Expulsion of the Germans. Background, Execution, Consequences* (London: Routledge and Kegan Paul, 1977).

[153]Gaspar M. Tamas, "The Vanishing Germans," *The Spectator*, May 6, 1989, p. 15.

[154]Critiques of the Nuremberg Trials are included in Lord Hankey, *Politics, Trials, and Errors* (Chicago: Henry Regnery, 1950), and F. J. P. Veale, *Advance to Barbarism: The Development of Total Warfare from Serajevo to Hiroshima* (New York: Devin-Adair, 1968).

in the south, an iron curtain has descended over Europe." Goebbels had popularized the phrase "iron curtain," but it was accurate
enough.

The European continent now contained a single, hegemonic
power. "As the blinkers of war were removed," John Charmley
writes, "Churchill began to perceive the magnitude of the mistake
which had been made."[155] In fact, Churchill's own expressions of
profound self-doubt consort oddly with his admirers' retrospective
triumphalism. After the war, he told Robert Boothby: "Historians
are apt to judge war ministers less by the victories achieved under
their direction than by the political results which flowed from
them. Judged by that standard, I am not sure that I shall be held to
have done very well."[156] In the preface to the first volume of his
history of World War II, Churchill explained why he was so troubled:

> The human tragedy reaches its climax in the fact that after
> all the exertions and sacrifices of hundreds of millions of
> people and of the victories of the Righteous Cause, we have
> still not found Peace or Security, and that we lie in the grip
> of even worse perils than those we have surmounted.[157]

On V-E Day, he had announced the victory of "the cause of
freedom in every land." But to his private secretary, he mused:
"What will lie between the white snows of Russia and the white
cliffs of Dover?"[158] It was a bit late to raise the question. Really,
what are we to make of a statesman who for years ignored the fact
that the extinction of Germany as a power in Europe entailed . . .
certain consequences? Is this another Bismarck or Metternich we
are dealing with here? Or is it a case of a Woodrow Wilson redi-
vivus—of another Prince of Fools?

With the balance of power in Europe wrecked by his own policy, there was only one recourse open to Churchill: to bring America into Europe permanently. Thus, his anxious expostulations to
the Americans, including his Fulton, Missouri "Iron Curtain"
speech. Having destroyed Germany as the natural balance to Russia on the continent, he was now forced to try to embroil the
United States in yet another war—this time, a Cold War, that
would last 45 years, and change America fundamentally, and perhaps irrevocably.[159]

[155]Charmley, *Churchill: The End of Glory*, p. 622.

[156]Robert Boothy, *Recollections of a Rebel* (London: Hutchison, 1978), pp. 183–84.

[157]Churchill, *The Gathering Storm*, pp. iv–v.

[158]Nisbet, *Roosevelt and Stalin: The Failed Courtship*, p. 106.

[159]Cf. Robert Higgs, "The Cold War Economy: Opportunity Costs, Ideology, and
the Politics of Crisis," *Explorations in Economic History* 31 (1994): 283–312.

THE TRIUMPH OF THE WELFARE STATE

In 1945, general elections were held in Britain, and the Labour Party won a landslide victory. Clement Attlee, and his colleagues took power and created the socialist welfare state. But the socializing of Britain was probably inevitable, given the war. It was a natural outgrowth of the wartime sense of solidarity and collectivist emotion, of the feeling that the experience of war had somehow rendered class structure and hierarchy—normal features of any advanced society—obsolete and indecent. And there was a second factor—British society had already been to a large extent socialized in the war years, under Churchill himself. As Ludwig von Mises wrote:

> Marching ever further on the way of interventionism, first Germany, then Great Britain and many other European countries have adopted central planning, the Hindenburg pattern of socialism. It is noteworthy that in Germany the deciding measures were not resorted to by the Nazis, but some time before Hitler seized power by Brüning . . . and in Great Britain not by the Labour Party but by the Tory Prime Minister, Mr. Churchill.[160]

While Churchill waged war, he allowed Attlee to head various Cabinet committees on domestic policy and devise proposals on health, unemployment, education, etc.[161] Churchill himself had already accepted the master-blueprint for the welfare state, the Beveridge Report. As he put it in a radio speech:

> You must rank me and my colleagues as strong partisans of national compulsory insurance for all classes for all purposes from the cradle to the grave.[162]

[160]Ludwig von Mises, *Human Action* (New Haven, Conn.: Yale University Press, 1949), p. 855.

[161]Charmley, *Churchill: The End of Glory*, p. 610, 618. Cf. Peter Clarke, *Liberals and Social Democrats* (Cambridge: Cambridge University Press, 1978), p. 281: "When the Churchill Coalition was formed in May 1940 it gave progressivism a central political role which it had lacked since 1914. . . . The people's war brought a people's government in which ordinary Labour and good Liberals were the ascendant elements. . . . Anti-appeasement was the dominant myth; it helped displace the Guilty Men of Munich; and it prepared the ground for the overthrow of the Chamberlain consensus in domestic policy too. Keynes suddenly moved to a pivotal position inside the Treasury. Labour's patriotic response to the common cause was symbolised by the massive presence of Ernest Bevan as Minister of Labour."

[162]Addison, "Churchill and Social Reform," p. 73. Addison states: "By the spring of 1945 the Coalition government had prepared draft bills for comprehensive social insurance, family allowances, and a national health service." As Leader of the Opposition for the next six years, "in social policy [Churchill] invariably contested the Labour Party's claim to a monopoly of social concern, and insisted that the credit for devising the post-war welfare state should be given to the wartime Coalition, and not to the Attlee government." For a contrasting view, see Kevin

That Mises was correct in his judgment on Churchill's role is indicated by the conclusion of W. H. Greenleaf, in his monumental study of individualism and collectivism in modern Britain. Greenleaf states that it was Churchill who

> during the war years, instructed R. A. Butler to improve the education of the people and who accepted and sponsored the idea of a four-year plan for national development and the commitment to sustain full employment in the post-war period. As well he approved proposals to establish a national insurance scheme, services for housing and health, and was prepared to accept a broadening field of state enterprises. It was because of this coalition policy that Enoch Powell referred to the veritable social revolution which occurred in the years 1942–4. Aims of this kind were embodied in the Conservative declaration of policy issued by the Premier before the 1945 election.[163]

When the Tories returned to power in 1951, "Churchill chose a Government which was the least recognizably Conservative in history."[164] There was no attempt to roll back the welfare state, and the only industry that was really reprivatized was road haulage.[165] Churchill "left the core of its [the Labour government's] work inviolate."[166] The "Conservative" victory functioned like Republican victories in the United States, from Eisenhower on—to consolidate socialism. Churchill even undertook to make up for "deficiencies" in the welfare programs of the previous Labour government, in housing and public works.[167] Most insidiously of all, he directed his leftist Labour Minister, Walter Monckton, to appease the unions at all costs. Churchill's surrender to the unions, "dictated by sheer political expediency," set the stage for the quagmire in labor relations that prevailed in Britain for the next two decades.[168]

Yet, in truth, Churchill never cared a great deal about domestic affairs, even welfarism, except as a means of attaining and keeping office. What he loved was power, and the opportunities power provided to live a life of drama and struggle and endless war.

***

Jeffreys, *The Churchill Coalition and Wartime Politics, 1940–1945* (Manchester: Manchester University Press, 1991).

[163]Greenleaf, *The British Political Tradition*, pp. 254–55.

[164]Roberts, *Eminent Churchillians*, p. 258.

[165]Ibid., p. 254. Roberts points out that "when the iron and steel industries were denationalized in 1953, they effectively continued to be run via the Iron and Steel Board."

[166]Roy Jenkins, "Churchill: The Government of 1951–1955," in *Churchill*, Blake and Louis, eds., p. 499.

[167]Addison, "Churchill and Social Reform," p. 76.

[168]Roberts, *Eminent Churchillians*, pp. 243–85.

There is a way of looking at Winston Churchill that is very tempting: that he was a deeply flawed creature, who was summoned at a critical moment to do battle with a uniquely appalling evil, and whose very flaws contributed to a glorious victory—in a way, like Merlin, in C.S. Lewis's great Christian novel, *That Hideous Strength*.[169] Such a judgment would, I believe, be superficial. A candid examination of his career, I suggest, yields a different conclusion: that, when all is said and done, Winston Churchill was a man of blood and a politico without principle, whose apotheosis serves to corrupt every standard of honesty and morality in politics and history.

---

[169]C.S. Lewis, *That Hideous Strength: A Modern Fairy-Tale for Grown-Ups* (New York: Collier, [1946] 1965), p. 291.

11
THE OLD BREED AND THE COSTS OF WAR

Eugene B. Sledge*

The first day of boot camp, 1943. (I had been in college for one year, and then had joined the Marine Corps.) The drill instructor set the tone for the next several weeks: "You people are stupid." We hadn't taken any sort of test, or had any type of evaluation, but he said to us, "You people are stupid, and if any of you think you can tell me what to do, step outside and I will whip your ass right now." None of us stepped outside. That was the reality of the Marine Corps I entered, a reality which descended upon you quickly and mercilessly.

One day, early on in boot camp, I got out of step. I usually managed to keep the cadence, but I was just a little off that day. The drill instructor walked up beside me, and in a very quiet menacing voice said, "Boy, you pick up the cadence, or they're gonna have to take us both to sick bay, because it's going to take a major operation to get my foot out of your rear end." You know, I never lost the cadence after that.

I graduated from boot camp on Christmas Eve, 1943. On Christmas Day, most of us in my platoon were assigned to infantry school, Camp Elliott, near Los Angeles. After several weeks of intensive rigorous infantry training, we boarded the U.S.S. President Polk, an old luxury liner converted into a troopship. After 28 days at sea, packed on the Polk like thousands of sardines, we landed in New Caledonia. While there, we trained hard with every infantry weapon from the 7-inch-blade Kabar knife to the bayonet, from the flame thrower to the 37mm antitank cannon. We also became thoroughly familiar with all Japanese weapons. Running up and down high, rugged mountains conditioned us to be as physically tough as possible. Twenty-five mile forced marches and amphibious landings along the coast were frequent. All the instructors were combat veterans who knew what lay ahead of us—and who knew that our survival chances were slim.

In June, we shipped out to an island near the Solomon Islands, where we joined the veteran, elite First Marine Division, nicknamed "The Old Breed." I was assigned to a rifle, or line company

[*This article is composed from notes used by the author in his presentation at the Mises Institute's "Costs of War" conference in Atlanta, May 20–22, 1994.]

(meaning front line), K Company, 3rd Battalion, 5th Marines (Regiment), First Marine Division. K Company became my "home," and the veterans treated us replacements like brothers— with the understanding we had to prove ourselves in combat. They were the best teachers in the world in how to kill Japs because, simply said, that is the infantryman's job, to *kill* the enemy. No euphemisms were needed. We were told frankly that we were expected to uphold the high standards of the 5th Marines, an old distinguished and much decorated Regiment of 3,000 Marines. It was decorated at Belleau Wood in World War I, in the Banana Wars, and recently on Guadalcanal. The Company was made up of young men of very high caliber. I was 20 years old; many others were teenagers, some were veterans, some were college men—all were volunteers. They were the finest, bravest men I ever knew. At Peleliu, K Company suffered 64 percent casualties. On Okinawa we received replacements during the three-month-long ordeal; K Company suffered 153 percent casualties—we actually lost more men than we started with.

Julius Caesar said, "Terror robs men of their power of reason and judgment and impairs their physical capacity." On the battlefield, the primary emotion is sheer, absolute terror. Even the veterans, like my gunnery sergeant, who didn't seem to have a nerve in his body, told me at the first post-war reunion of the First Marine Division I attended, "Sledgehammer, I was as scared as you were, but I just couldn't show it." And he said, "You remember that patrol we went on in that swamp on Peleliu—the 40 of us, who were to hold the advance of 1500 Japs? They were supposed to be on the other side of the swamp, and we were supposed to hold them up long enough to get help." He then said, "That was a *suicide* patrol. I didn't tell anybody that." Well, 40-odd years later, when he told me that, I fell into the nearest chair.

It has been said that the combat veteran has to *live through* the experience and then, if he survives, he has to *live with* it the rest of his life. How you handle yourself and what you make of yourself depends a great deal on your upbringing, your discipline, and things of this sort.

I want to make some remarks about the people we fought, the Japanese soldiers. To us they were "Japs." The Japanese soldier was dedicated to his cause; h. ·ght to the death because that was the way he had been trained. He was loyal to the Emperor, unbelievably physically tough, and well disciplined. When he was inducted into the Japanese army he was brutalized by his superiors. Brutality was institutionalized in the Japanese Army. There are documented cases of the cruelty imposed on Japanese troops in training—the barbarism lasted through the first year. If the soldier even looked at this sergeant without the proper respect (what might be called silent contempt), he was in trouble. I picked up many a rotten coconut on working details when I was in base camp because of silent contempt, i.e. the way I looked at somebody in authority. But a Japanese lieutenant would have his troops stand at attention and then take a hobnail shoe and beat his men in the face until their faces bled. With such cruel treatment from their superior officers, they were conditioned to treat their enemies with utter barbarity. Compassion was something that was totally foreign to them. This is why they could rampage through China and commit rape and murder. The soldier was told that the rape of enemy women was macho. Take Nanking for instance, where thousands of Chinese were murdered and raped over a period of about three or four weeks. The best kept secret of World War II is the truth about Japanese atrocities. But business is good with Japan, so do not embarrass her people, as our liberal news media does the Germans with almost monthly programs about the holocaust. There is not much even written about the Japanese conduct; do not even worry about embarrassing a young Japanese by bringing it up, because the only thing they are taught about World War II is that the U.S. bombed Japan.

In regard to the bombing of Nagasaki and Hiroshima, as Paul Fussell says, "Anybody who thinks it was a bad idea says so because his life wasn't saved by it." But ours were. We were scheduled to invade Japan, and we literally would have had to kill every man, woman, and child. The Japanese had a song that said "100,000,000 souls will die for the Emperor." Despite revisionist claims, if we had invaded Japan, we would have suffered enormous casualties, and the fighting would have lasted for *years*.

War to the infantryman meant killing. If you had any qualms about killing the enemy, you had better get over it in a hurry, because when you made an attack, or they made an attack, it was kill or be killed. I must admit, the first Japs I saw close by, I did not pull the trigger. Three ran out of a pillbox and Snafu Shelton, my foxhole buddy, said, "What the hell's the matter with you, do you want them in the foxhole here with us?" I said, "No." Then seven more ran out of that pillbox with their bayonets fixed, and I was firing at them before he was. Typical of the Japanese, and rarely described, they ran out of the pillbox each holding his bayoneted rifle in the right hand, and unbuttoned britches held up with the left hand. When they got killed, they dropped their britches. There was something in their religion, or the military Code of Bushido, that designated the lower abdomen as the place of manhood, instead of the chest as it is in Western culture. We saw thousands of them killed on Okinawa lying about, practically in their birthday clothes. With their last ounce of strength, they had pulled their trousers down. At this pillbox, a Jap stood up at an opening in the side and tried to throw a grenade at us. I shot him in the chest and the grenade exploded as he fell. I felt no regret.

The front line is a place of passion, terror, and hatred. We hated the Japs with a passion, so I felt no regret when killing them. It has been said by some revisionists that we hated them because we were racist; this is nonsense. The Japanese were hated because they fought with savagery beyond necessity according to the Code of Bushido. This meant you had to kill every last one of them before you could get off an invaded island.

Jap brutality extended to our wounded. We all acted as stretcher bearers, as needed, and had to get the wounded out as fast as possible or both the bearers and the wounded man on the stretcher were apt to get shot. If they could, the Japs shot the wounded man on the stretcher, and then tried to shoot down the stretcher team. I had a good friend, "Doc," who was a medical corpsman. During an attack up a long sloping ridge on Okinawa, he was working on a wounded Marine. Doc almost had this boy fixed up and a sniper shot Doc in the left leg up in the hip region. I ran up there with two stretcher teams to get them down. We got Doc up on the stretcher, and that sniper, son of a bitch, shot Doc in the other hip just as we got him on the stretcher. Now, why didn't he shoot to kill him? Well, he shot him in two places to immobilize him, so that we would have to carry Doc, then he could shoot at us. Well, we out-ran all the Olympic runners getting Doc and the other wounded man down that ridge so all of us could get out of his way. Fortunately, he didn't hit any of the rest of us.

Wild excitement existed on the front line. When you are so close to a Jap you can throw a hand grenade at him, but you know you had better not throw it because he will throw it back at you before it explodes, you have a decision to make!

During an attack, either ours or theirs, the artillery and mortar bombardment was so loud it was thunderous. You couldn't even talk to the Marine next to you, and the ground swayed and shook from concussion as shells erupted all around and steel fragments tore through the air and through men's bodies. On Okinawa, some of the Japanese artillery barrages went on for four and five days. When the shells finally stopped we were all shaking. You couldn't hold your rifle steady. Your nerves had been so knocked about by all that terrific concussion. All the while we were carrying wounded and dead out. We moved them to the rear if we could, but sometimes shells fell so thickly we couldn't move the dead. The violence was inconceivable.

To the infantryman, artillery is one of the worst things you have to put up with—right up there with machine guns, snipers, mortars, hand grenades, and tanks. As for enemy artillery, we were especially unlucky at Okinawa. The Japanese started with a full compliment of artillery there. They had *additional* artillery shipped to the Philippines, but before the ships got to the Philippines, they were rerouted to Okinawa, because the Philippines were going to fall. So that meant those of us who landed on Okinawa got a double dose of shelling. Those terrible shellings shattered the nerves of many front-line Marines.

We got new second lieutenants with each set of replacements. Many were full of bravado and swagger they had learned at Quantico in officer training. One good shelling knocked it out of them, whether they got hit or not. Poor souls, they usually didn't last but a few days before death or wounding.

At Peleliu we had to attack several hundred yards across the open airfield through heavy Jap fire from every type of weapon they had. Machine gun fire was something you could get away from if you could get hunkered down in a foxhole, but if it caught you out in the open, it was terrifying. When I ran across the air field at Peleliu, I could see the bluish-white Jap tracers coming by me just like the railings on a porch, the bullets making a "snapping" sound close by. The big shells were erupting and thundering to such an extent you couldn't even yell to the Marine next to you. The ground swayed back and forth. To be shelled out in the open, on your feet, was nerve-shattering terror. After that was over, a buddy of mine said, "Sledgehammer, did you know that Billy 'cracked up' back there on the airfield, and they had to actually drag him across here under cover?" And I said, "No, I didn't know that, what happened to him?" My buddy looked sick, and said, "Well, you remember Joe, we all went through boot camp together? Joe got hit in the head and it splattered his brains all over Billy's face." I gasped in horror. It was that kind of thing that was apt to happen at any time in infantry combat.

You developed a "close personal" relationship with a sniper, because you could only cringe in your foxhole with your buddy, and my buddy was Snafu Shelton, who was from the swamps of Louisiana. Snafu could cuss a blue streak, and conversation under fire resulted in a very fascinating juxtaposition of emotions—*The Lord's Prayer* and the *Twenty-third Psalm* on my part, and "God damn you son-of-a-bitch," on Snafu's part. We knew that sniper was after us personally, so we would curse him personally. Japanese snipers were crack shots. There were actual records of them hitting Marines on Peleliu at 600 yards. The volume of fire that came at us when the Japanese made an attack was tremendous. When you think of the amount of steel and fragments and bullets that came at a man it is amazing any of us survived. My company suffered 64 percent casualties at Peleliu; it lasted 30 days and 30 nights, because the Japs fought us all night.

I recently received a letter from an Air Force man who had been stationed on Okinawa, and he said he read my book, *With The Old Breed: At Peleliu and Okinawa*. He said he examined the ground on a particular ridge we defended during a Japanese major attack. It was no suicide Bonzai charge, not the stupid kind that allowed John Wayne to mow them down by the thousands. This had been a well-planned counterattack at Okinawa. This airman was just curious as to the volume of fire to which we had been subjected. He measured off a square foot of ground and then he dug just below the surface. He wrote me that he found 30 pieces of shrapnel or bullets in that single square foot. In combat, I thought I was going to catch all 30 every time I took a step. Every man thought that he was the object of the whole, entire Japanese barrage.

The nights were sheer terror in the Pacific. Savage hand-to-hand combat was often the rule rather than the exception. It was terrifying, dirty, sickening and vile. About an hour after darkness fell on the battlefield (anywhere in the Pacific), single or small groups of Japs began creeping toward our foxholes. No Marine moved out of his foxhole after dark. If he had to identify himself he whispered the password. My buddy and I took turns trying to catch a "cat nap" and keeping our eyes and ears concentrated on even the least suspicious sound. Star shells and mortar flare shells were used periodically (each a flare on a small parachute) and brightly illuminated our area. Between these periods of blessed light we crouched in our hole, Kabar knife in one hand and grenade, rifle, or Thompson submachine gun in the other. We strained eyes and ears in the inky blackness to catch the first warning of a Jap creeping in close. The tension was awful. The Japs crept in by ones or twos. If we, or some other Marine, saw them first, the eerie silence in our area exploded with the firing of our weapons—the bang of our firearm and the pop of grenade detonator caps followed by the loud "BANG!" of our grenades. If the Japs came in undetected, there was the pop of a Jap grenade detonator followed by the bang of their grenades, as they tried to throw them into the Marine positions. This was followed by wild, incoherent

Jap screaming as they rushed us swinging Samurai saber, bayonet, or rifle butt. Marine curses and warnings to neighboring foxholes sounded. Amid the sound of the thud of body blows as men yelled, screamed, cursed, and choked back groans of pain, men fought hand-to-hand with the savagery probably typical of Neanderthal man. There were yells for flares, and the hoarse shouts "corpsman" when Marines were wounded. This went on almost every night after the heavy fighting of the day. We were exhausted after each close encounter. We usually lost Marines, killed or wounded, but we always killed the Japs. Strict discipline, complete reliance on other Marines, and cool heads prevented total panic on our part in these terrifying fights. It was war at its most elemental, brutal level as men slashed, stabbed, shot, or brained their enemies. Snafu and I never let a Jap get into our foxhole because of our alertness, but it happened many times in neighboring foxholes and we lost some fine buddies this way. All night, bursts of firing along the lines indicated where these desperate struggles took place, while shells screamed and whistled back and forth overhead.

At night, the Japanese tried to "infiltrate" the lines. At Peleliu, they had a whole battalion to raid the lines in small groups. They would slip up as close as they could to us, throw a grenade into our foxholes, and then come in screaming with a saber or a bayonet. Now, the idea of a saber in a modern war might sound ridiculous, but I had a buddy whose right arm was amputated by a Jap officer who slipped up close and then jumped in his position. I had another buddy who lost two fingers while he was holding onto his rifle parrying a saber thrust. The Jap swung his saber and cut the Marine's hand, and then my buddy hit the Jap just like you hit a baseball, with the butt of his rifle; that ended the fight. The Japs usually got killed in those night attacks but we always had casualties, too.

The typical German soldier was a superb soldier from everything anybody writes or says about them. He wanted to fight as honorably as he could and then get home to his family. The typical Japanese soldier wanted to fight honorably, but instead of wanting to go home, the Japanese soldier wanted to die for the Emperor, so that meant you had to kill him before you could get it over with. Of course, he made that difficult because he wanted to make sure that when he died, he took you with him. If you advanced to a new position and the enemy wounded were lying around there, somebody routinely went around and shot them in the head. Some of the outfits called these men "the 'possum squad." The Japs would resort to any kind of ruse to trick us, such as slipping behind the lines at night and calling for a corpsman and begging for assistance. Often, they would play dead in order to lure us closer until they could kill us with a bayonet or knife. Fortunately, I went into a veteran outfit as a replacement, so I learned many of these tricks from the men who had combat experience. Also, you could distinguish the intonation of the Jap voice and you could learn to recognize them.

The fatigue a combat infantryman is exposed to is absolutely beyond description. Nothing like it in civilian life even approaches the intensity of physical and nervous exhaustion caused by close combat. Sometimes on the news you will see exhausted football players, or exhausted basketball players. But any combat veteran can tell you what real fatigue does to a man. When one goes for two weeks or for 30 days, we were literally shuffling around like zombies. I had weighed about 145 pounds when I went into the Okinawa campaign, and when it was over and we got up North and built a tent camp, I weighed about 120 pounds.

The front-line companies suffered staggering casualties during fierce combat. K company had invaded Peleliu with 235 Marines; only 85 survived death or wounds. Replacements were added to bring the company up to normal stength of 235 Marines to invade Okinawa. During this battle, the company absorbed 250 replacements to make up for the continuous losses. Only 50 Marines remained at the end. Of these, only 26 had made the landing, and only 10 were never wounded.

Everybody lost weight because of the sheer stress and extreme physical exhaustion. You can't imagine the hard labor just in bringing up ammunition through the mud. The 30-caliber ball, which was the standard ammo for the M-1 rifle, was in a wooden box which weighed over a 100 pounds. The "genius" who designed the box placed a little finger groove in each end. You were supposed to put the tips of your fingers in there to lift up a box that weighed over 100 pounds. In the rains, and with mud smeared all over the box, this, of course, just brought forth more creative cursing on the part of the troops. To move each box across rough terrain, often under fire, in driving rain, and through deep mud, required two Marines. Each man firmly gripped the bottom corners of one end— usually slippery with mud. Heavy boxes of grenades fortunately had two rope handles. Machine gun ammo boxes had well-designed folding metal handles.

It has been shown that the longer combat went on, the worse the stress became, and the more exhausted the troops became because the "Fight or Flight Syndrome" physiologically took over.

We were all keyed up, the adrenaline was pumping, and when that goes on for almost three months, one doesn't have much reserve left. When buddies were killed or wounded many of us just simply cried, because we were very closely knit. Even the replacements became absorbed into the "brotherhood" of unit cohesion. We had a great deal of respect for each other, because in the Marine Corps you were taught loyalty. The greatest sin you could commit was to let a buddy down, so we knew we could depend on any man that had on a Marine uniform, whether we knew his name or not.

We generally could not move forward without tanks, because the Japs would simply mow us all down the way infantry was massacred in World War I. By following tanks, the infantry could have some protection, and the tank could be firing its 75 mm gun at the same time. On Okinawa, we went through a period of about 10 days of torrential rain; this meant the tanks could not move. We were right in front of Shuri, the main Japanese defense bastion. The outfit that had tried to take Half Moon Hill before my battalion moved up had very heavy casualties. They could not remove their dead because of the thousands of Jap shells unleashed on the area. The day we moved onto Half Moon, torrential rains began and did not slacken for 10 days. Tanks bogged down and all our attacks had to stop, so we occupied the Hill amid death and heavy shell fire. Almost every shell hole in the area had a dead Marine in it, and they were all infested with maggots. The rain washed the maggots off the dead over the top of the soil into our foxholes. In the foxhole that Snafu and I dug, we had to put boards in the bottom and then dig a sump hole in one end. We frequently bailed it out with an old helmet that a casualty had left. If we hadn't bailed, the foxhole would have flooded. It was just like a colander immersed in water. Water came over the edges of the hole, and water came through the soil of the sides. It looked like spouts—just like turning on the spigot, it was raining so hard. We stayed soaked, cold, and muddy. It must have been 50°F at night, our teeth chattered as we shivered on the wet, cold battlefield.

The Japs were attacking every night, and we were killing them in our lines every night. In the Pacific, decay was rapid. We threw mud on the dead bodies with our entrenching tools to hold down the swarms of big flies and maggots. The next day, or the next few days, shells came in and blew the corpses apart. There were body parts lying all over the place; we called it "Maggot Ridge." If we went down the ridge and slipped and fell, we slid all the way down to the bottom. Then, when we came up to our feet, the maggots were falling out of our dungaree pockets, our cartridge belts and everything else. Many men were nauseated and threw up. The stench was awful; beyond description. Also, the personal filth that the infantryman had to endure was inconceivable. There was one period of three months during which we existed without a bath, just living in the slimy mud. My mouth felt like it was full of mud, but we had no way to brush our teeth. Still, we had to stay alert. We had to be attuned to every tiny sound at night, even amidst the rush of shells and rattle of machine guns. On Half Moon, as else-where, the Japs slipped around at night, and they were experts at it. Of course, you can imagine the odor of the dead. The only way we could eat anything (our stomachs were tied in knots) was to use a little tripod-like device we could put a sterno tablet on and heat a can of ration beans or coffee—always before dark, because any light after dark would draw sniper fire. Once heated, we had to eat the beans quickly or the torrential rain filled the ration can with cold water.

We had tremendous loyalty to our units and this was mainly the cement that kept us together. When we were out there and "the stuff hit the fan," it was a matter of life and death. Sure, we were all fighting for the Constitution, but basically, each man was fighting for his buddy, and he was fighting for you, because that was war at the elemental level. There wasn't anything between us and the Japs except space. Sometimes at night, that space was not more than a few feet. If they got in your foxhole, it was a hell of a lot closer than that.

The aftermath of all of this was that there were widows and there were orphans. Many of our men were very young, and had not married; others were married, and some had children. The one curse that we were all left with from combat, whether we were married or single, was the nightmares. I had them for 25 years. I would wake up in a cold sweat and screaming—having gone through something in a dream that was just as realistic as what I had survived. Some nights I was afraid I would have nightmares and I was afraid to go to sleep, so I would stay up late reading, and hoping the nightmares wouldn't come. But all the survivors hear the memories, like a curse, for the rest of their lives.

The dead we mourn. If he was a buddy, you wept over him. History remembers the wounded men as numbers—often as just statistics. But for some wounded, the physical pain has been with them every day since the war. I have a buddy named John Huber who lives up in Virginia. He is one of the finest men I ever knew. At Okinawa, Huber's hip was terribly damaged by a grenade. Now, 50 years later, he had to have another of numerous surgical operations because his hip had to be replaced. The wound threw his spine out of line. Then, after years of suffering, it threw his right ankle out of line. He has never complained; he is alive. To Huber, to complain would be ridiculous.

Another friend, Jim Kronaizl, whose family lived in the Dakotas on a big wheat farm, had his post-war life altered by his wound. It was his ambition, his dream, to get back and work that wheat farm after the war. He loved the independence of farming and the outdoors. One day, on Okinawa, I was standing right on the front edge of a little ridge. A deep standing foxhole was right in front of me. I was watching the front line through binoculars because we had been pulled off the line. We had made an attack the day before and lost heavily in my company, so the Battalion C.O. pulled us off the line for a few days rest. I had seen mortar shells coming toward us, so I got the binoculars and was watching our front. Six or eight buddies were behind me playing cards around an ammo box. I said, "You guys better look out, that Jap gunner is walking those shells right down this little valley." Well, I got what a Marine usually got in a case like that, "Oh hell, Sledgehammer, you're just nervous in the service." So I said, "Okay I'm telling you, you'd better look out." At that moment, there was a terrific crash as a shell exploded right down in front of me down at ground level. The concussion knocked me off my feet and down into the foxhole—amazingly, I was still standing upright. How in God's name I didn't get my head blown off I'll never know, but poor Kronaizl received a bad wound in the head and was carried to the nearby aid station. After the war, he had a bad seizure and he fell off his tractor. He told me, "When I fell, I luckily kicked the tractor gear lever in neutral, otherwise the tractor would have run over me. I went to my doctor and he said, 'Son you are going to have these seizures all the rest of your life because of that head wound. Get off that farm.'" So, Jim said, "Sledgehammer, I had to give up the farm, and if you can believe it, loving the outdoors like I do, I am now in a damn insurance office."

Another buddy, Jim Day from California, had a horse farm. His dream, when he returned home, was to make it into a horse ranch. At Peleliu, a Japanese machine gun shattered one of Jim's legs. It was a heavy machine gun, and the Jap was so close to us that he just moved the gun a little bit and poor Jim just toppled over. There was his leg shattered, a bloody pulp as he was lying on the ground, blood spurting out of the stump. Later, when Jim came to the First Marine Division reunions (maybe some of you can't conceive of this), we would have to help him go to the bathroom. His wife had to do that at home. The poor man couldn't handle it by himself, because of that stump of a leg cut off at the hip. He died a premature death after years of pain and back trouble.

I had a wonderful friend named Marion Vermeer, who had been a lumberjack from Washington State before enlisting in the Marines. He wanted to be a lumberjack when he went back home. One day on Half Moon Hill on Okinawa, the Japs put some pressure on the Army unit on our left, and the Army line moved to the rear a little distance. That meant there was a bend in our line to the left. The Japs got in close with a 70-millimeter mountain gun and sighted it along our line from the left flank. This artillery piece was on small wheels so they could move it around quickly. But a 70 millimeter is a rather large shell and was a high velocity shell. The Japs fired the first shell, and it went right behind our lines and exploded to our rear where some of our knocked out tanks were. Somebody said, "What the hell was that?" One of the NCO's said, "That was a mountain gun." The next shell came screaming along our front line, no more than a foot over my head, I am not exaggerating. It passed the foxhole next to me with two young Marines who were replacements and exploded in Marion's foxhole. Marion was dug in with Bill Leyden and another Marine. Bill was blown up into the air and Vermeer just fell over. The two boys in the hole next to me were hit. One of them jumped up and was flailing the air with his arms and fell dead. The other one was yelling, "Oh, Jesus Christ, it hurts so bad, make me die, I can't stand it. For Christ's sake, Jesus do something." And then he just toppled over onto the mud dead. I started over to their foxhole and the sergeant said, "Sledgehammer, get back on the mortar." The mortar was right at the base of the ridge, and I had more experience than the gunner that was on the mortar at the time. He said, "If they locate that mountain gun, I'm gonna need you to get on the mortar and shell that Jap gun crew." So, I must admit I was glad to get down below the crest of the ridge. Fortunately, the Jap gun didn't fire anymore. A little later, they brought Vermeer by me on a stretcher, his right leg below the knee was just a bloody bandage. Thrown onto the stretcher was his field shoe with his bloody ankle sticking out of it. He said, "Sledgehammer, you think I'll ever be able to be a lumberjack again?" and I said, "Sure ole buddy you'll make it, you'll be back in all those beautiful trees and doing what you want to do." I felt as though I had been stabbed in the heart. They carried him 20 yards, and then put the stretcher down; he was dead. All of the Marines who were dug in near me, and the four on the stretcher team, all had tears streaming down our muddy, bearded faces. Bill Leyden was seriously wounded, and lost part of his right hand. Since the war, he has been bothered by seizures caused by the concussion that blew him into the air. Both Leyden and Vermeer had been wounded on Peleliu.

Those are some of the tragedies that are called "The Costs of War" to those who actually fight on the front lines. The following applies to every Marine and Soldier who fought up-front:

> And when he goes to Heaven
> To St. Peter he'll tell
> Another Marine reporting, Sir,
> I've served my time in Hell.[1]

---

[1]Written by an anonymous World War II Marine.

For additional readings on World War II in the Pacific, see Gavin Daw, *Prisoners of the Japanese: POWs of World War II in the Pacific* (New York: William Morrow, 1995); George Feifer, *Tennozan: The Battle of Okinawa and the Atomic Bomb* (New York: Ticknor and Fields, 1992); Meirion and Susie Harries, *Soldiers of the Sun: The Rise and Fall of the Imperial Japanese Army* (New York: Random House, 1991); and Eugene B. Sledge, *With The Old Breed: At Peleliu and Okinawa* (Novato, Calif.: Presidio Press, 1981).

12

WAR AND LEVIATHAN IN TWENTIETH-CENTURY AMERICA: CONSCRIPTION AS THE KEYSTONE

Robert Higgs

> Times of danger, when Power takes action for the general safety, are worth much to it in accretions to its armoury; and these, when the crisis has passed, it keeps. . . . It is impossible to exaggerate the part played by war in the distension of Power.
> —Bertrand de Jouvenel[1]

The association of war and the growth of government in the modern era is a commonplace. Randolph Bourne's observation that "war is the health of the state" has become a cliché. Having extensively surveyed the fatal linkage, Bruce Porter concludes that "a government at war is a juggernaut of centralization determined to crush any internal opposition that impedes the mobilization of militarily vital resources. This centralizing tendency of war has made the rise of the state throughout much of history a disaster for human liberty and rights."[2] Porter maintains that much of the history of the West during the past six centuries can be reduced to a simple formula: war made the state, and the state made war. In the process, countless individuals suffered the destruction of their liberties, properties, and lives.

Still, as a cause of the development of big government in the United States, war seldom receives its due. Scholars and laymen alike usually trace the origins of our own Leviathan to the New Deal. In doing so, they attribute too much influence to the New Dealers as such. Franklin D. Roosevelt and friends never would—or could—have done what they did in the 1930s without the state-building precedents of World War I, which in many important cases they reinstituted with little more than a change of name. But if World War I gets insufficient notice from students of the growth of government, World War II gets even less. Too often, it is viewed as a discrete event, an episode when government took on awesome

---

[1]Bertrand de Jouvenel, *On Power: The Natural History of Its Growth* (Indianapolis, Ind.: Liberty Fund, 1993; original French edition 1945), p. 142.

[2]Bruce D. Porter, *War and the Rise of the State: The Military Foundations of Modern Politics* (New York: Free Press, 1994), p. xv.

dimensions but then relinquished the new powers after victory had been won, more or less returning the relations between government and civil society to the prewar status quo. Nothing of the sort happened, or could have happened. A politico-economic undertaking of such enormous magnitude does not just come and go, leaving no trace.

The government's organization of the economy for war, more than anything else, determined how the central government would grow in the United States in the 20th century. And conscription, more than anything else, determined how the government would organize the economy for war. Thus, in a multitude of ways, the military draft shaped not only the contours of the nation at war but the course of its politicoeconomic development throughout the past 80 years.

Notwithstanding the important developments during President Woodrow Wilson's first term, the federal government on the eve of World War I was quite limited. In 1914, federal outlays totaled less than two percent of GNP. The top rate of the recently enacted federal individual income tax was seven percent on income over $500,000 (equivalent to about 10 times that amount in present-day dollars), and 99 percent of the population owed no income tax. The 402,000 federal civilian employees, most of whom worked for the Post Office, made up about one percent of the labor force. Nor did the armed forces amount to much, numbering fewer than 166,000 active duty personnel. The federal government did not regulate securities markets, labor-management relations, or agricultural production. It set no minimum wage rate, collected no social security tax, provided no make-work jobs or make-believe job training for the unemployed. Although the feds did meddle in a few areas of economic life, prescribing railroad rates and prosecuting a handful of unlucky firms under the antitrust laws, the central government was for the most part only a small nuisance. It was not very expensive and did not exert an important direct effect on the daily lives of many citizens. On the positive side, the government maintained the gold standard and suppressed labor disturbances that threatened to obstruct interstate commerce. The U.S. Supreme Court gave fairly strong protection to private property rights and freedom of contract while generally insisting that state governments not deprive citizens of property rights without substantive due process. After World War I, the American people would never again enjoy a government which so closely approximated the Jeffersonian ideal.

With U.S. entry into World War I, the federal government expanded enormously in size, scope, and power. The government

virtually nationalized the ocean shipping industry. It did national-
ize the railroad, telephone, domestic telegraph, and international
telegraphic cable industries. It became deeply engaged in manipulating labor-management relations, securities sales, agricultural
production and marketing, the distribution of coal and oil, international commerce, and the markets for raw materials and manufactured products. Its Liberty Bond drives dominated the financial
capital markets. It turned the newly-created Federal Reserve System into a powerful engine of monetary inflation to help satisfy the
government's voracious appetite for money and credit. In view of
the more than 5,000 mobilization agencies of various sorts—
boards, committees, corporations, and administrations—contemporaries who described the government's creation as "war socialism" were well justified.[3]

During 1917 and 1918 the government built up the armed
forces to a strength of four million officers and men, drawn from a
prewar labor force of 40 million persons. Of those added to the
armed forces after the U.S. declaration of war, more than 2.8 million, or 72 percent, were drafted.[4] By employing the draft, the government got more men into the army and got them quicker than it
could have by recruiting volunteers. Moreover, it got the men's
services at far less expense to the Treasury. As the army leadership
had recommended and President Wilson had accepted—even before the declaration of war—the U.S. government obtained its servicemen by following the Prussian model.[5]

Men alone, however, did not make an army. They required
barracks and training facilities, transportation, food, health care,
and clothing. They had to be equipped with modern arms and
great stocks of ammunition. In short, to be an effective fighting
force, a large soldiery required immense amounts of complementary resources. As the buildup began, the requisite resources were
in the possession of private citizens. Although manpower could be
obtained by conscription, public opinion would not tolerate the
outright confiscation of all the property required to turn the men
into a well-equipped fighting force. Still, ordinary market mechanisms operated too slowly and at too great an expense to facilitate

[3]For details, see Robert Higgs, *Crisis and Leviathan: Critical Episodes in the Growth of
American Government* (New York: Oxford University Press, 1987), pp. 123–58 and
sources cited there; see also James L. Abrahamson, *The American Home Front*
(Washington, D.C.: National Defense University Press, 1983), pp. 101–12.

[4]John Whiteclay Chambers, III, *To Raise An Army: The Draft Comes to Modern America*
(New York: Free Press, 1987), p. 338 n. 68.

[5]Chambers, *To Raise an Army*, pp. 125–51. One is reminded of Bertrand de
Jouvenel's observation (*On Power*, p. 157) that "war is like a sheep-dog harrying the
laggard Powers to catch up their smarter fellows in the totalitarian race."

the government's plans. The Wilson administration therefore resorted to the vast array of interventions mentioned above. All may be seen as devices to hasten the delivery of the requisite resources and diminish the fiscal burden of equipping the huge conscript army for effective service in France. Notwithstanding these contrivances to keep the Treasury's expenses down, enormously increased taxes still had to be levied—federal revenues increased by nearly 400 percent between fiscal 1917 and fiscal 1919—and even greater amounts had to be borrowed. The national debt swelled from $1.2 billion in 1916 to $25.5 billion in 1919.

To insure that the conscription-based mobilization could proceed without obstruction, critics had to be silenced. The Espionage Act of June 15, 1917, penalized those convicted of willfully obstructing the enlistment services with fines as much as $10,000 and imprisonment as long as 20 years. An amendment, the notorious Sedition Act of May 16, 1918, went much further, imposing the same harsh criminal penalties on all forms of expression in any way critical of the government, its symbols, or its mobilization of resources for the war. These suppressions of free speech, subsequently upheld by the Supreme Court, established dangerous precedents that derogated from the rights previously enjoyed by citizens under the First Amendment. The government further subverted the Bill of Rights by censoring all printed materials, peremptorily deporting hundreds of aliens without due process of law, and conducting—and encouraging state and local governments and vigilante groups to conduct—warrantless searches and seizures, blanket arrests of suspected draft evaders, and other outrages too numerous to catalog here. In California the police arrested Upton Sinclair for reading the Bill of Rights at a rally. In New Jersey the police arrested Roger Baldwin for publicly reading the Constitution.[6] The government also employed a massive propaganda machine to whip up what can only be described as public hysteria. The result was countless incidents of intimidation, physical abuse, and even lynching of persons suspected of disloyalty or insufficient enthusiasm for the war. People of German ancestry suffered disproportionately.[7]

The connection of the draft with these official subversions of the Constitution could hardly be considered coincidental; it was direct, intentional, and publicly acknowledged. Consider the words of a contemporary legal authority, Professor John Henry Wigmore:

[6]Michael Linfield, *Freedom Under Fire: U.S. Civil Liberties in Times of War* (Boston: South End Press, 1990), p. 65.
[7]Ronald Schaffer, *America in the Great War: The Rise of the War Welfare State* (New York: Oxford University Press, 1991), pp. 3–30.

> Where a nation has definitely committed itself to a foreign
> war, all principles of normal internal order may be suspend-
> ed. As property may be taken and corporal service may be
> conscripted, so liberty of speech may be limited or suppress-
> ed, so far as deemed needful for the successful conduct of
> the war. . . . All rights of the individual, and all internal civic
> interests, become subordinated to the national right in the
> struggle for national life.[8]

The formula, applied again and again, was quite simple: If it is acceptable to draft men, then it is acceptable to do X, where X is any
government violation of individual rights whatsoever. Once the
draft had been adopted, then, as Justice Louis Brandeis put it, "all
bets are off."[9]

When the war ended, the government abandoned most—but
not all—of its wartime control measures. The draft itself ended
when the armistice took effect on November 11, 1918. By the end of
1920 the bulk of the economic regulatory apparatus had been
scrapped, including the Food Administration, the Fuel Administration, the Railroad Administration, the War Industries Board, and
the War Labor Board. Some emergency powers migrated into regular government departments such as State, Labor, and Treasury,
and continued in force. The Espionage Act and the Trading with
the Enemy Act remained on the statute books. Congressional en-
actments in 1920 preserved much of the federal government's
wartime involvement in the railroad and ocean shipping industries. The War Finance Corporation shifted missions, subsidizing
exporters and farmers until the mid-1920s. Wartime prohibition of
alcoholic beverages, a purported conservation measure, transmo-
grified into the ill-fated 18th Amendment.

Most importantly, the dominant contemporary interpretation
of the war mobilization, including the belief that federal economic
controls had been instrumental in achieving the victory, persisted,
especially among the elites who had played leading roles in the
wartime economic management. Economic czar Bernard Baruch
did much to foster the postwar dissemination of this interpretation
by historians, journalists, and other shapers of public opinion.[10] But
many interest groups, like the farmers, needed no prompting to arrive at a Baruchian conclusion. "By the time the Food Administration dropped its wartime controls, it had weakened farmer resistance to governmental direction of their affairs. Having observed

[8]Quoted in ibid., pp. 49–50.
[9]Quoted in ibid., p. 52.
[10]On the various legacies, see Higgs, *Crisis and Leviathan*, pp. 150–56, and sources
cited there. On Baruch's public relations activities, see Jordan A. Schwarz, *The
Speculator: Bernard M. Baruch in Washington, 1917–1965* (Chapel Hill: University of
North Carolina Press, 1981), pp. 193–206, 212.

how the government could shape wartime food prices, farmers would expect it also to act in peacetime to maintain the prosperity of America's farms."[11] Big businessmen in many industries took a similar lesson away from the war.[12]

In the depths of the Great Depression, the federal government employed the wartime measures as models for dealing with what Franklin Roosevelt called "a crisis in our national life comparable to war."[13] Hence the War Finance Corporation came back to life as the Reconstruction Finance Corporation, the War Industries Board as the National Recovery Administration, the Food Administration as the Agricultural Adjustment Administration, the Capital Issues Committee as the Securities and Exchange Commission, the Fuel Administration as the Connolly Act apparatus for cartelizing the oil industry and the Guffey Act apparatus for cartelizing the bituminous coal industry. The military mobilization of young men came back as the quasi-military Civilian Conservation Corps. The Muscle Shoals hydroelectric munitions facility became the germ of the Tennessee Valley Authority. The wartime U.S. Housing Corporation reappeared first as part of the Public Works Administration in 1933 and then as the U.S. Housing Authority in 1937. The New Deal's federal social security program harked back to the wartime servicemen's life insurance and the payments made to the soldiers' dependents. The temporary wartime abandonment of the gold standard became permanent in 1933–1934, when the government nationalized the monetary gold stock and abrogated all contractual obligations, both public and private, to pay gold. Along with the revived agencies came many of the wartime planners, including Baruch, Felix Frankfurter, George Peek, Hugh Johnson, John Hancock, Leon Henderson, and John Dickinson, not to mention FDR himself, as advisers or administrators. Obviously the wartime precedents were crucial in guiding the New Dealers and helping them to justify and gain acceptance of their policies.[14]

When World War II began in Europe in 1939, the size and the scope of the central government of the United States were much greater than they had been 25 years earlier, owing mainly to World War I and its peacetime offspring, the New Deal. Federal outlays now equaled 10 percent of GNP. Of a labor force of 56 million, the

[11]Abrahamson, *The American Home Front*, p. 103.
[12]Murray N. Rothbard, "War Collectivism in World War I," in *A New History of Leviathan: Essays on the Rise of the American Corporate State*, Ronald Radosh and Murray N. Rothbard, eds. (New York: Dutton, 1972), pp. 66–110.
[13]Quoted by Porter, *War and the Rise of the State*, p. 277.
[14]William E. Leuchtenburg, "The New Deal and the Analogue of War," in *Change and Continuity in Twentieth-Century America*, John Braeman, Robert H. Bremner, and Everett Walters, eds. (Columbus: Ohio State University Press, 1964), pp. 81–143.

federal government employed about 1.3 million persons (2.2 percent) in regular civilian and military jobs plus another 3.3 million (5.9 percent) in emergency work relief programs. The national debt held outside the government had grown to nearly $40 billion. Most importantly, the scope of federal regulation had increased immensely to embrace agricultural production and marketing, labor-management relations, wages, hours, and working conditions, securities markets and investment institutions, petroleum and coal marketing, trucking, radio broadcasting, airline operation, provision for income during retirement or unemployment, and much, much more.[15] Notwithstanding these prodigious developments, during the next six years the federal government would achieve vastly greater dimensions, in many respects its greatest size, scope, and power ever.[16]

Again conscription served as a springboard for the growth of the state. This time the political pressure to adopt the draft mounted long before the United States entered the war. In mid-1940 the armed forces had only 458,000 officers and men on active duty. After the great German advances and the defeat of France in the spring of 1940, proponents of a new draft—including Henry Stimson, Grenville Clark, and others who had led the charge for conscription before and during World War I—gained greater public support. But opponents fought hard, and a national debate raged furiously throughout the summer. Finally, on September 16, 1940, Congress enacted the Selective Training and Service Act, authorizing the conscription of 900,000 men. The law was extended and amended in the fall of 1941 and again several times after the U.S. declaration of war. Eventually the draftees numbered more than 10 million men, or about 63 percent of all those who served in the armed forces at some time during the war.[17] Obviously, many of those who volunteered for military service did so to escape the draft and the consequent likelihood of assignment to the infantry.

As before, a huge conscript-based armed force required enormous amounts of complementary resources to make possible its housing, subsistence, clothing, medical care, transportation, and training, not to mention the special equipment, ammunition, arms, and expensive weapons platforms that now included tanks, fighter and bomber aircraft, and naval aircraft carriers. For the Treasury, World War II was 10 times more expensive than World War I. Many new taxes were levied. Income taxes were raised repeatedly, until the individual income tax rates extended from a low of 23

[15]Higgs, *Crisis and Leviathan*, pp. 159–95 and sources cited there.
[16]Abrahamson, *American Home Front*, pp. 131, 142.
[17]Chambers, *To Raise an Army*, pp. 254–55; Higgs, *Crisis and Leviathan*, pp. 200–2.

percent to a high of 94 percent. The income tax, previously a "class tax," became a "mass tax," as the number of returns grew from 15 million in 1940 to 50 million in 1945.[18] Even though annual federal revenues soared from $7 billion to $50 billion between 1940 and 1945, most war expenses still had to be financed by borrowing. The national debt held by the public went up by $200 billion, or more than five-fold. The Federal Reserve System itself bought some $20 billion of government debt, thereby acting as a *de facto* printing press for the Treasury. Between 1940 and 1948 the money stock (M1) increased by 183 percent, and the dollar lost nearly half its purchasing power.

Had the government relied exclusively on fiscal and market mechanisms to marshal the desired resources, the expense of the war would have been far greater, probably much greater than the government could possibly finance. Accordingly, the authorities resorted to a vast system of controls and market interventions to gain possession of resources without having to bid them away from others in free markets.

Although relatively few resources were simply confiscated or requisitioned, the effect was similar. By fixing prices, directly allocating physical and human resources, establishing official priorities, prohibitions, and set-asides, then rationing the civilian consumer goods in short supply, the war planners steered raw materials, intermediate goods, and finished products into the uses to which they attached greatest importance. Markets no longer functioned freely; in many areas they did not function at all. The economic system was transformed from one in which the market allocated resources, with some peripheral government distortions, to one in which the central government allocated resources, with market (including black market) influences operating only at the fringes of the command economy.[19]

As before, the draft played a key role in justifying the government's imposition of a command economy. The same formula applied: If the draft is acceptable, then X is acceptable, X being any form of government coercion whatsoever. As the eminent economist Wesley Mitchell put it in 1943, "After common consent has been given to that act [conscription], civilians are morally bound to accept the lesser sacrifices war imposes on them."[20] Even the Supreme Court adopted the argument, as Justice Hugo Black evinced

[18]Carolyn C. Jones, "Class Tax To Mass Tax: The Role of Propaganda in the Expansion of the Income Tax during World War II," *Buffalo Law Review* 37 (Fall 1988/89): 685–737.

[19]Higgs, *Crisis and Leviathan*, pp. 196–236 and sources cited there.

[20]Quoted in ibid., p. 202.

in a 1942 decision: "Congress can draft men for battle service. Its power to draft business organizations to support the fighting men who risk their lives can be no less."[21]

World War II witnessed massive violations of human rights in the United States, apart from the involuntary servitude of the military draft. Most egregiously, about 112,000 blameless persons of Japanese ancestry, most of them U.S. citizens, were uprooted from their homes and confined in concentration camps without due process of law. Those who were subsequently released as civilians during the war remained under parole-like surveillance. The government also imprisoned nearly 6,000 conscientious objectors— three-fourths of them Jehovah's Witnesses—who would not comply with the service requirements of the draft laws.[22] Scores of newspapers were denied the privilege of the mails under the authority of the Espionage Act still in effect from World War I. Some newspapers were banned altogether.[23] The Office of Censorship restricted the content of press reports and radio broadcasts and censored personal mail entering or leaving the country. The Office of War Information put the government's spin on whatever it deigned to tell the public, and the military authorities censored news from the battlefields, sometimes for merely political reasons. The government seized more than 60 industrial facilities—sometimes entire industries (e.g., railroads, bituminous coal mines, meatpacking)—most of them in order to impose employment conditions favorable to labor unions engaged in disputes with the management.[24] One indication of the enlarged federal capacity for repression was the increase in the number of FBI special agents from 785 in 1939 to 4,370 in 1945.[25]

At the end of World War II most—but not all—of the economic control agencies shut down. Some powers persisted, either lodged at the local level, like New York City's rent controls, or shifted from emergency agencies to regular departments, like the international trade controls moved from the Foreign Economic Administration to the State Department. The military–industrial complex, which had grown to gargantuan size during the war, shrank but survived, as top military officers and big contractors, especially the aircraft companies, lobbied hard for new procurements to shore up

[21]*United States of America* v. *Bethlehem Steel Corporation*, 315 U.S. 289 (1942) at 305, quoted in Higgs, *Crisis and Leviathan*, p. 221. For similar argument by the Court in other cases, see ibid., pp. 222–25.

[22]Abrahamson, *American Home Front*, p. 159.

[23]Linfield, *Freedom Under Fire*, p. 73.

[24]Ibid., p. 102.

[25]Porter, *War and the Rise of the State*, p. 284.

their bureaucratic clout and financial condition.[26] Federal tax revenues remained very high by prewar standards. In the late 1940s the IRS's annual take averaged four times greater in constant dollars than in the late 1930s. In 1949, federal outlays amounted to 15 percent of GNP, up from 10 percent in 1939. The national debt stood at what would have been an unthinkable figure before the war, $214 billion—in constant dollars this was roughly 100 times the national debt in 1916.

The prevailing interpretation of the wartime experience gave unprecedented ideological support to those who desired a big federal government actively engaged in a wide range of domestic and international tasks. After all, the wartime central planners had just carried out successfully a complex undertaking of enormous dimensions. They had waged a global war, marshaling, organizing, and allocating the requisite resources to defeat two mighty adversaries while leaving American civilian consumers relatively well off, at least by comparison with the suffering populations of the Soviet Union, Japan, Germany, or Great Britain. Surely this great accomplishment testified to the planners' knowledge, abilities, and devotion to the public interest. Surely a central government capable of winning the greatest war in human history could carry out such relatively mundane tasks as stabilizing the business cycle, guaranteeing all citizens a good job and a high standard of living, and regulating the industrial life of the nation to achieve greater fairness than the unfettered market. Surely. In this spirit, Congress enacted in 1946 the Employment Act, pledging the federal government to play a permanent role as macroeconomic savior of the U.S. economy.[27] Thanks to the GI Bill, the Veterans Administration became the overseer of what amounted to a substantial welfare state *within* a welfare state.

Soon after World War II ended, the Cold War began. In 1948 the government reimposed the military draft. Then, over the next 25 years, conscription was repeatedly extended until the Nixon administration, in the face of massive protests, finally allowed it to expire in 1973. Draftees supplied the principal cannon fodder for the U.S. adventures in Korea and Vietnam as well as a large part of the standing forces positioned throughout the world to challenge

[26]Gregory Hooks, *Forging the Military–Industrial Complex: World War II's Battle of the Potomac* (Urbana: University of Illinois Press, 1991), pp. 225–66.

[27]In the words of Abrahamson, *American Home Front*, p, 155, "World War II . . . validated the Keynesian economic theories that liberal governments would subsequently use to maintain full employment and justify welfare programs." For an argument that this "validation" was invalid, see Robert Higgs, "'Wartime Prosperity': A Reassessment of the U.S. Economy in the 1940s," *Journal of Economic History* 52 (March 1992): 41–60.

the Soviets and their surrogates. After 1950 the military–industrial–congressional complex achieved renewed vigor, sapping 7.7 percent of GNP on average during the next four decades—cumulatively more than $10 trillion dollars of 1994 purchasing power.[28] During the Cold War the government's operatives committed crimes against the American people too numerous to catalog here, ranging from surveillance of millions of innocent citizens and mass arrests of political protesters to harassment and even murder of persons considered especially threatening.[29] These actions warrant close examination by students of the relation between war (or the threat of war) and the growth of the state, but for present purposes we need not dwell upon them. So far as the relation between war and the development of America's Leviathan is concerned, the deed had largely been done even before the outbreak of the Korean War.

Within three decades, from the outbreak of World War I in Europe to the end of World War II, the American people endured three great national emergencies, during each of which the federal government imposed unprecedented taxation and economic controls and accumulated enormous debts. By the late 1940s these government actions no longer startled the citizenry; indeed many Americans, including highly regarded intellectuals and top policy makers, had come to regard them as desirable. Even businessmen, many of whom had resisted the encroachments of the New Deal bureaucrats throughout the 1930s, now looked upon the American Leviathan with an approving eye. The wartime experience, said Calvin Hoover, had "conditioned them to accept a degree of governmental intervention and control after the war which they had deeply resented prior to it."[30] As Herbert Stein recognized, American businessmen tended to "regard the regulations they are used to as being freedom."[31] Rather than resisting the government's impositions, they looked for ways to adapt to them, positioning themselves so that the government policies would provide a tax advantage, channel a subsidy their way, or hobble their competitors.[32]

---

[28]Robert Higgs, "Introduction: Fifty Years of Arms, Politics, and the Economy," in *Arms, Politics, and the Economy*, Robert Higgs, ed. (New York: Holmes and Meier, 1990), pp. xv–xxxii; and Higgs, "The Cold War Economy: Opportunity Costs, Ideology, and the Politics of Crisis," *Explorations in Economic History* 31 (July 1994): 292.

[29]Linfield, *Freedom Under Fire*, pp. 113–67.

[30]Calvin B. Hoover, *The Economy, Liberty, and the State* (New York: Twentieth Century Fund, 1959), p. 212.

[31]Herbert Stein, *Presidential Economics: The Making of Economic Policy from Roosevelt to Reagan and Beyond* (New York: Simon and Schuster, 1984), p. 84.

[32]Higgs, *Crisis and Leviathan*, pp. 243–44, and the *Wall Street Journal*, any day of any week of any year since World War II.

If the business class, with its immense financial resources and its considerable political clout, would not strive seriously to over-throw the Leviathan that had come into being by the late 1940s, there was scant chance that anyone else would mount a formidable attack. Reactionaries could hardly expect to succeed in any event, because the post–World War II ideological climate showered an active federal government with public trust and approbation. As Ben Page and Robert Shapiro have documented in their massive survey of public opinion, World War II stands as "the most perva-sive single influence on public opinion" since the mid-1930s. Am-ong other things, it "transformed American public opinion con-cerning virtually all aspects of foreign affairs," opening the way for the imperial presidency and the use of U.S. forces as world police-men.[33] Opponents of global interventionism were smeared as "iso-lationists" and "appeasers" and thereby completely discredited. In 1953 Senator Robert Taft died, and his followers, already a dwin-dling corps, soon abandoned their old beliefs and political commit-ments.[34] Domestically, the people's devotion to the welfare state solidified. No amount of contradictory evidence seemed to dent the prevailing faith in the government's ability to create personal and social security and to remedy the full range of human prob-lems and pathologies.[35]

Nor did the Constitution serve any longer as a bulwark of in-dividual rights. After World War II, as Edward Corwin observed, for the first time in American history after a war the country did not revert to a "peacetime Constitution." Instead, the Supreme Court's wartime surrender to the President combined with the *carte blanche* it had granted to federal economic regulation in the late 1930s to enhance all of the following:

> (1) the attribution to Congress of a legislative power of in-definite scope;
>
> (2) the attribution to the President of the power and duty to stimulate constantly the positive exercise of this indefinite power for enlarged social objectives;

---

[33]Benjamin T. Page and Robert Y. Shapiro, *The Rational Public: Fifty Years of Trends in Americans' Policy Preferences* (Chicago: University of Chicago Press, 1992), p. 332.

[34]Justin Raimondo, *Reclaiming the American Right: The Lost Legacy of the Conservative Movement* (Burlingame, Calif.: Center for Libertarian Studies, 1993), pp. 149–56.

[35]For extensively documented surveys of modern public opinion on a wide range of policy issues, see Herbert McClosky and John Zaller, *The American Ethos: Public Attitudes toward Capitalism and Democracy* (Cambridge, Mass.: Harvard University Press, 1984); see also Linda L. M. Bennett and Stephen Earl Bennett, *Living with Leviathan: Americans Coming to Terms with Big Government* (Lawrence: University of Kansas Press, 1990).

(3) the right of Congress to delegate its powers *ad libitum* to the President for the achievement of such enlarged social objectives;

(4) the attribution to the President of a broad prerogative in the meeting of "emergencies" defined by himself and in the creation of executive agencies to assist him;

(5) a progressively expanding replacement of the judicial process by the administrative process in the enforcement of the law—sometimes even of constitutional law.[36]

Under these conditions the only impediment to the relentless growth of the central government consisted of partisan and interest-group opposition to particular proposals. Time would reveal that such obstructionism, ever-shifting with the winds of partisan politics and immediate interest-group objectives, could do no more than slow the onrushing Leviathan.

"It is not possible," said William Graham Sumner, "to experiment with a society and just drop the experiment whenever we choose. The experiment enters into the life of the society and never can be got out again."[37] World War I, the New Deal, and World War II gave rise to the greatest experiments in collectivization America had ever experienced. These experiments radically transformed the political economy institutionally and ideologically. The political economy of 1948 bore scarcely any resemblance to that of 1912, and the changes gave every indication of being irreversible.

In the process by which this radical transformation occurred, the military draft played a central part. Conscription made possible the creation of a huge armed force in 1917–1918, which in turn required massive amounts of complementary resources. To get these resources the government had to raise taxes enormously, go deeply into debt, and impose a great variety of controls on the market economy; that is, it had to override traditional limitations on government action and to disallow long-standing economic liberties. In light of the apparent success of the policies employed during World War I, the temptation to impose similar policies during the Great Depression proved irresistible. In large part the New Deal consisted of quasi-war policies to deal with a pseudo-war emergency. Participation in World War II, with its global reach and voracious demand for resources, increased every aspect of the process by an order of magnitude: the draft permitted the

---

[36]Edward Corwin, *Total War and the Constitution* (New York: Alfred A. Knopf, 1947), p. 179.
[37]William Graham Sumner, *Essays of William Graham Sumner*, Albert G. Keller and Maurice R. Davie, eds. (New Haven, Conn.: Yale University Press, 1934), 2, p. 473.

creation of a huge army, which gave rise to vast military resource requirements that could be met expeditiously only by imposition of a command-and-control system throughout the economy.

By the late 1940s the three great experiments had entered, institutionally and ideologically, into the life of the society. With all the fundamental barriers to the growth of government having been battered down during war and pseudo-war emergencies, nothing substantial remained to impede the relentless growth of government.[38]

[38]Higgs, *Crisis and Leviathan*, pp. 20–34, 237–57 and sources cited there.

13
THE MILITARY AS AN ENGINE
OF SOCIAL CHANGE

Allan Carlson

D escribing the military—or its object, war—as an engine of
social change is a kind of truism; certainly so in our century. As poet William Butler Yeats wrote, amidst the carnage
of World War I, "All changed, changed utterly. . . . A terrible
beauty is born."[1]

Another English poet, John Masefield, made a government-
sponsored propaganda/lecture tour of the United States in 1918,
offering the same judgment. "Whatever this war is," he stated, "it
is a getting rid of the past. The past has gone into the bonfire. We
are all in the war now," he noted—I suspect—with a certain twin-
kle in his eye, "realizing with more or less surprise and shock and
bitterness, that the old delights, the old ideals, the old way of life,
with its comfortable loves and hatreds are gone. We have to re-
make our lives, forget our old hatreds and learn new ones."[2]

The standard argument among historians is that World War II
also produced vast social consequences. As Richard Polenberg
summarized in his volume, *War and Society*,

> World War II radically altered the character of American so-
> ciety and challenged its most durable values. The war rede-
> fined the relationship of government to the individual and
> of individuals to each other, and it posed questions about
> the relationship between civilians and the military, [and] be-
> tween liberty and security . . . which continue to perplex
> Americans.

He added, "Pearl Harbor marked more than the passing of a
decade; it signified the end of an old era and the beginning of a
new."[3] However, others have argued that the seemingly vast changes brought about by modern war are ephemeral, not durable, and
that society rolls back toward "normalcy" after the crisis has passed. British journalist Michael MacDonagh had that view of 'The

---

[1]Quoted in Morris Eksteins, *Rites of Spring: The Great War and the Birth of the Modern Age* (Boston: Houghton Mifflin, 1989), book jacket.
[2]John Masefield, *St. George and the Dragon* (London: William Heineman, 1919), pp. 49–50.
[3]Richard Polenberg, *War and Society: The United States, 1941–1945* (Philadelphia: J.B. Lippincott, 1972), p. 4.

Great War,' concluding, "I think no permanent change of importance has been made by the war in the character, customs and habits of the [British] people."[4]

Of late, feminist historians have made the same argument,
or—better put in their case—complaint. Dismissing all the stories
about "Rosie the Riveter" and her ilk, these writers argue that neither World War I nor II produced real long-term changes in wom-
en's lives. Women were primarily wives and mothers before each
of these total wars; alas, they were primarily wives and mothers afterward. As a prominent feminist historian recently concluded,
"although government propaganda exhorted women to brave un-
familiar work, these appeals were contained by nationalist and
militarist discourse that reinforced patriarchal, organistic notions
of gender relations."[5]

Indeed, I note as an aside, feminist historians looking at the
early 20th century have had to go to unusual places to find real
heroines. Many are familiar with talk-show host Rush Limbaugh's
term, Femi–Nazis. In truth, there were real Feminist Nazis in the
early German Third Reich, mainly female professors at several
German universities. In 1933, these authentic Femi-Nazis prepared
an anthology, entitled *German Women Address Adolf Hitler*. Among
other novelties, it contained an article by a Nazi Paleoanthropolo-
gist who claimed to have discovered skeletons in an excavation in
Norway, which proved that prehistoric Nordic males and females
had been equal in size and strength. She theorized that Nordic men
had subsequently underfed the women, who shrank in stature.
Nazi culture, she told an undoubtedly perplexed Mr. Hitler, could
equalize Nordic men and women again.[6]

But let us move beyond such ideological exotica. When one
examines the military's role in stimulating government actions or
innovations that later become institutionalized, the effect of war in
driving social revolution grows evident. To choose just a few examples from this century:

— In 1917, the U.S. Navy distributed the first official U.S. government condoms (today, of course, the distribution of condoms to
the citizenry is the primary purpose of government);

— In 1941, the U.S. government opened the first Lanham Act
day-care center, to tend to the children of mothers working in a

---

[4]Quoted in Eksteins, *Rites of Spring*, p. 170.

[5]*Behind the Lines: Gender and the Two World Wars*, Margaret Randolph Higonnet,
et al., eds. (New Haven, Conn.: Yale University Press, 1987), p. 7.

[6]See Claudia Koontz, *Mothers in the Fatherland: Women, the Family, and Nazi Politics*
(New York: St. Martin's Press, 1987), p. 142.

defense plant, marking the first federal intrusion into the care of infants and small children;

— In 1942, the U.S. Army, for the first time, extended military health care services to civilian dependents, arguably the inaugural step in the federalization of American medicine.

And there are other stories to tell. Relative to sexuality, there is little doubt that the world wars of the 20th century accelerated the disintegration of inherited sexual mores. John Costello's so-called "sexual history of World War II," entitled *Virtue Under Fire*, carried this theme: "Amidst the upheaval that uprooted so many lives, [the] cure [for loneliness] was discovered in a changing approach to . . . sexual . . . relations as they adapted to a more dangerous . . . and unorthodox lifestyle."[7]

A more forceful explanation of sexual adventures among the wartime masses is found in a peculiar, but illuminating book from the early 1970s, entitled *The Rape of the A*P*E** (APE being the *American *Puritan *Ethic). Published by the Playboy Press, subtitled "The Official History of the Sex Revolution," and written by humorist Allan Sherman, the book opens with a chapter on "World War II as Sex Education." The author describes the deployment of American soldiers throughout the world as "a fly-opening experience." In Italy, he says, the soldiers found pornography enshrined in stone; in Africa and the South Seas, they viewed bare breasts galore; in Paris, the GIs found "books we hadn't dreamed existed, postcards too marvelous to mail and girls anxious to share their gratitude for being liberated." In the China–Burma theater, the American boys discovered hashish, and a little Oriental guidebook called *The Perfumed Garden;* over in India, they found *The Kama Sutra.* Sherman continues, "We went to Scandinavia and the Low Countries and Germany and Japan. Everywhere there were girls who did things our well-scrubbed sweethearts hadn't yet imagined, and did them for nothing, without a labored seduction routine, without the promise of marriage or eternal love."[8]

When the boys came home, Sherman reports, they pondered their experiences, and some of them began to plot the sexual revolution in a peculiarly militarized way:

> Wherever there was a strawberry church social, they would search and destroy. They would storm every bastion of decency; besmirch and defile the enemy on the beaches, in the

[7]John Costello, *Virtue Under Fire: How World War II Changed our Social and Sexual Attitudes* (Boston: Little, Brown, 1985), p. 9.

[8]Allan Sherman, *The Rape of the A*P*E**. *The Official History of the Sex Revolution, 1945–1973: The Obscening of America* (Chicago: Playboy Press, 1973), pp. 72–73.

homes and in the streets. They would recruit allies among
the corrupt, and despoil the innocent. They would experiment with new sex positions, new sex locations, new sex
kicks. They would open new sex fronts—science, for example; they would give smut respectability by dressing it in the
dignified cloak of science. They would shock, and shock
again.[9]

I think it correct, at least in a symbolic way, that Sherman dates
the beginning of the postwar American "sex revolution" as November 13, 1945, when Bob Hope—that paragon of "World War II
Americanism"—introduced a new joke, to wild laughter, on his
Tuesday night Pepsodent radio show. This veteran of the USO ex-
travaganza had already discovered the crowd-stimulating value of
beefcake. His next innovation, on that fateful evening, was a joke
about Sonny Wisecarver, a 14-year-old Lothario, who had just been
hauled into California juvenile court for sleeping with, and satisfy-
ing, a variety of Los Angeles housewives. Encouraged by the wild
response, Hope made "Sonny Wisecarver" jokes a weekly staple
on his show. We see here the ancestor of David Letterman's contemporary Joey Buttafuoco routine.[10]

The common point of both Costello—a somewhat serious
journalist–historian—and Sherman—a somewhat honest literary
clown—is this: If you find modern sexual ethics at all troubling,
don't blame just the Woodstock crowd of the late 1960s. Also
blame the fallout from the militarized America of World War II,
the so-called "good war."

Among the better known tales of military social engineering
can also be counted:

— Harry Truman's use of the armed forces as a race-relations
laboratory in the late 1940s;

— Gerald Ford's and Jimmy Carter's use of West Point, An-
napolis, and Colorado Springs as experiment stations for gender
role manipulation in the mid–1970s;

— Bill Clinton's contemporary efforts to use the services for a
new kind of sexual experimentation.

But I would rather look today at two less-well-known aspects
of clear wartime aggression against the American social order: the
campaign against American regionalism, and the campaign against
the family.

We have all seen those World War II-era films, where a new
infantry platoon goes into basic training, containing a drunken

[9]Ibid., pp. 73–74.
[10]Ibid., pp. 196–97.

Irishman from Chicago, a sensitive Jew from Manhattan, a cracker from Georgia, a naive farm boy from Iowa, and so on. The essential plot, of course, is the manner in which the military tears down their regional biases and loyalties, and builds instead a common Americanism, which goes out to vanquish the fascist foe.

This is, in fact, an apt metaphor for what took place in America on a larger scale during these years, as "nation-builders" worked to crush the regionalisms still existing on the land. Driven by military actions, social mobility in the United States reached its highest peak. Between December 7, 1941 and March, 1945—less than three-and-one-half years—12 million men and women entered the armed forces while another 15,300,000 American adults left their county of residence, and moved to another location. "Never before in the history of our country," the U.S. Bureau of the Census reports, "has there been so great a shuffling and redistribution of population in so short a time." Adding to this was the deliberate substitution of a militia-based war force by a national army, without local ties and loyalties.

The South was the chief loser in this war-induced migration and leveling. As Dartmouth sociologist Francis Merrill concluded, "The war accelerated the prewar migration of Southerners from the rural areas to rapidly growing industrial areas," with a consequent change in what he called—with a typical New England accent—"the extreme cultural isolation which formerly characterized farm life in this region." He added: "At no time since the Civil War has the South undergone such a tremendous social ferment."[11]

More broadly, by the mid 1940s, a "new America" was being forged to replace the regional diversity of the old. Among the architects of this new American order was Henry Luce, editor-in-chief of *Life, Time*, and *Fortune*. Contemptuous of American regionalism (not coincidentally, he was born and raised in China, the child of missionaries), Luce used his magazines during the war to define and instill a generic Americanism. In 1946–47, at the dawn of the Cold War, he crafted a major promotional campaign for *Life* magazine under the theme, "The New America." Built around a Picturama presentation shown to invited audiences across the country, the campaign subtly denigrated the "isolation" of the old American regions, and celebrated instead the vast expansion of industry, the growing number of middle-class families, the new suburbs, the spirit of unity, and the American military forces stationed around the globe. The script concluded that the America of the 1930s and

[11]Francis E. Merrill, *Social Problems on the Home Front: a Study of War-Time Influences* (New York: Harper and Brothers, 1948), pp. 16–17.

this "New America" forged in World War II were "almost two different countries, so huge are the changes that have increased our
national stature."[12]

The Good War also brought to culmination the federal government's campaign against the family as an autonomous institution, with the military serving as the vehicle for another kind of social engineering.

The effort had been mounting for 30 years. From Theodore
Roosevelt's 1909 White House Conference on Children through
Herbert Hoover's 1930 White House Conference on Child Health
and Protection, Washington bureaucrats had worked to dissolve
parent–child bonds. As participants in the 1930 assembly noted,
the federal government's emphasis had swung from handicapped
children "to all children . . . the whole family of the nation, wherever they lived and whatever their situation." Indeed, one book issuing from Hoover's conference described a new being, called
"Uncle Sam's Child"—in truth, a kind of socialist bastard—but in
the Conference's words, a "new racial experiment," and a citizen
of "a world predestinedly moving toward unity." The same volume attacked the rural home and family—legacies of the old order—as psychologically inadequate for shaping the independent
personality, while praising the state-run schools as "a community
power with more potential influence for orienting the child to his
environment than any other."[13]

But in truth the federal government had so far failed to find a
really effective vehicle to bring this so-called "new racial experiment" to fruition. The breakthrough came in 1940, when Franklin
Roosevelt convened his own White House Conference on Children
in a Democracy. This conference shifted the rhetoric in a new way,
claiming to work for "the security of the family." Indeed, it devoted four of the 11 chapters of its Final Report to saving the family.
In response to the Conference, Roosevelt created a Family Security
Committee within the aptly named Office of Defense, Health, and
Welfare Services, which claimed to be "safeguarding the values of
family life during the period in which the United States engaged in
war."[14]

One must understand, though, what Roosevelt and his
wartime friends meant by "family." They did not have in mind the

[12]See Allan C. Carlson, "Luce, *Life*, and 'The American Way,'" *This World* 13 (Winter 1986): 66–69.

[13]Katharine Glover and Evelyn Dewey, *Children of the New Day* (New York D. Appleton–Century, 1934), pp. 4–12, 183, 195, 200.

[14]Ernest W. Burgess, "The Family," in *American Society in Wartime*, William Fielding
Ogburn, ed. (Chicago: University of Chicago Press, 1943), p. 33.

free-standing, self-reliant, independent household that was integral to the American past. Rather, the New Dealers at war embraced what progressive sociologists called "the companionate family." As practitioners Ernest Burgess and William Ogburn explained in their revealing 1943 book, *American Society in Wartime,*

> The family has lost or is losing its historic functions of economic production for the market and for home consumption, care of health, education of its members, protective activities, recreation, and religious rites in the home.[15]

Indeed, according to Burgess, the family was left only with "the giving and receiving of affection by its members," the bearing of children for service to community and state, and a modest role in personality development. He went on:

> The concept of the family as a companionship embodies *the ideals for the preservation of which we are waging this war*—of democracy as *the* way of life, of the equality of men and women, and of personality as the highest human value.[16]

But of course, as Burgess admitted, "the loss by the family of its historic functions [has] greatly increased its economic insecurity." The companionship family could not feed or clothe itself, build a house, or care for its own young, sick, or aged; it could not provide self-protection, recreation, or even religious worship to its members. The democratic, egalitarian, person-centered "companionate family" needed—you guessed it—a Welfare State to provide the security and services that families once provided themselves. And that, according to Burgess and Ogburn, was what World War II was all about, at least in its social dimensions.[17] Put another way, the companionate family stood as the ideal consort for the emerging national security state.

The hot war of World War II and the Cold War which followed gave Uncle Sam his experimental fodder. Between 1941 and 1972, over half of all American males served in the active-duty armed forces, an unprecedented generation-and-a-half who could be molded, at least to some degree, into the new model social order. Political and military leaders embraced and institutionalized the "companionate family model" for the far-flung American garrisons. For officers' wives, this meant adapting certain unwritten customs for mass guidance and education, chronicled in the military etiquette books that poured out after 1945. Inhaling deeply the spirit of the Cold War, Helen Todd Westpheling's *Army Lady Today* stressed

[15] Ibid., pp. 31–32.
[16] Ibid., p. 39.
[17] Ibid., p. 32.

that just as wives "esteem, respect, and dignify the estate and sanctity of marriage," so they extended these sentiments "to the integrity and justice of the boundless frontier of democracy our country represents."[18] In their book *The Navy Wife*, Anne Briscoe Pye and Nancy Shea endorsed the production of "Navy Juniors," or children, as "the most important job of your life, the one for which you were designed."[19] This vision of the family married to the democratic empire, and in its reproductive service, was just what FDR had in mind.

The socialization of families of enlisted men occurred in a more direct, statist manner. The services crafted a full welfare system, which turned both the man and his family into "military dependents." Pentagon planners reasoned that adequate welfare benefits would usefully insulate personnel from the outside world, provide a sense of security, foster morale, and encourage an attitude of solidarity—all attributes, I must note, of the ideal socialist order. In 1942, a Congressional act extended for the first time special medical benefits to military dependents, including obstetrical care. Post Exchanges and Commissaries enjoying a number of hidden subsidies offered tax-free goods at discounted costs. Full health benefits for all military dependents came through the Dependents Medical Care Act of 1956. On-base housing construction mushroomed in the 1950s. Meanwhile, the Army opened a series of day-care centers designed "to enhance the morale of servicemen and their families." In the mid–1960s, Congress expanded again the availability of government-backed medical care and social services. This uniquely military form of socialism, spurred on by the Cold War, encompassed an ever-growing number of Americans.

But the "companionate family"—in fact, a weak, fragile, and unstable remnant of the institutional family—could not hold together for long, despite the impressive appearance of the Cold War family structure in the 1950s. By the end of that decade, it is true, 85 percent of all military officers were married (compared to 69 percent of male civilians), while the military divorce rate was significantly lower than the civilian figure. Officers wives appeared to be "more traditional" than their civilian counterparts, and their children more numerous. But when a renewed feminist movement hit the military services with full force after 1970, the whole system collapsed like a house of cards. The very independence which was expected of Cold War military wives left them easy marks for the

[18]Helen Todd Westpheling, *Army Lady Today* (Charlotte, N.C.: Heritage House, 1959), p. 7.

[19]Anne Briscoe Pye and Nancy B. Shea, *The Navy Wife*, revised by Barbara Naylor (New York and London: Harper and Row, 1965), p. 114.

new ideology, while the ideologists of the companionate family—such as Ogburn, Burgess, and Harvard's Talcott Parsons—were pushed aside by a more ruthless breed, a modern version of the National Socialist Feminists of lore. By 1980, fewer than 20 percent of Air Force families were "traditional," composed of an Air Force father, a nonworking mother, and at least one child. Single-parent and androgynous families were soaring in prominence, as were demands for more day care, more health care, and more social services. By the mid–1980s, the U.S. Army had shifted its definition of family once again, embracing a collectivist alternative. As one official Army statement explained, enhanced benefits, increased family dependence on the state, and more therapeutic counseling would help merge individual families into the "Total Army Family," a formulation—dare I note—first promulgated in *1984*.[20]

The story here is actually very simple: modern wars—even Cold ones—swell the size and power of the state; and as the state grows, the family declines. And the lesson is also simple: it is time for persons on the political right to cast off lingering delusions about the "conservative traditions" of the military—traditions such as cultivation of the "arts of war," a sense of duty, and manhood, or defense of one's family and inherited way-of-life. Over the last 50 years, these principles have had ever-diminishing influence. Rather, we face in America at the end of the 20th century something closer to Cromwell's "New Model Army," one being used to re-engineer our society to serve a total state, which in turn engages in a perpetual social and moral revolution.

[20]*The Army Family Action Plan II*, pamphlet 608–41 (Washington, D.C.: U.S. Department of the Army, 1985), p. 7.

14
HIS COUNTRY'S OWN HEART'S-BLOOD: AMERICAN WRITERS CONFRONT WAR

Bill Kauffman

> I suppose I am an isolationist. . . . In a time of war any man working in the arts is sunk. His lamps are out. A new and strange ugliness comes into everyone about him. It is for him a time of death.
>
> —Sherwood Anderson[1]

The guiding spirit of this book is John Randolph, so I shall open with a verse written to memorialize the planter–statesman of Roanoke. The author is John Greenleaf Whittier, the militant Quaker from Massachusetts, the "barefoot boy, with cheek of tan . . . kissed by strawberries on the hill."[2] An odd eulogist—or maybe not.

Randolph, poetized Whittier, was

> Too honest or too proud to feign
>   A love he never cherished
> Beyond Virginia's border line
>   His patriotism perished
> While others hailed in distant skies
>   Our eagle's dusky pinion,
> He only saw the mountain bird
>   Stoop o'er his old Dominion![3]

Whittier was of Puritan stock; he came to Boston to edit a Henry Clay newspaper. He was ardent for temperance, the tariff, and later abolition, the cause to which he dedicated much of his antebellum poetry. He ran for Congress on the Liberty Party ticket, was an active Free Soiler, and he cast an electoral vote for Abraham Lincoln.

And yet, in the winter of 1860–61, Whittier broke with the Unionists; he wished to bid the South good riddance. As he wrote in "A Word for the Hour":

> They break the links of Union: shall we light
> The fires of hell to weld anew the chain
> On that red anvil where each blow is pain?

[1]Sherwood Anderson, *Partisan Review* (Summer/Fall 1939): 105.
[2]John Greenleaf Whittier,*The Complete Poetical Works of Whittier* (Boston: Houghton Mifflin, 1894), p. 396.
[3]Ibid., p. 303.

....
Let us press
The golden cluster on our brave old flag
In closer union, and, if numbering less,
Brighter shall shine the stars which still remain.[4]

Just as it is a remarkably unremarked, utterly forgotten fact that numerous American poets and novelists of note were isolationist as late as 1941, so too does it surprise us how many of our finest Northern writers wanted to let the South go. They were rock-ribbed Whigs and doughface Democrats, among them Emerson, Melville, Lowell, and Hawthorne, who opined that "we never were one people, and never really had a country since the Constitution was founded."[5]

In their opposition to Northern conquest they were part of a long and proud American line of literary dissenters from the federal government's periodic fits of expansion and mass murder. I identify four common sources of this dissent, and most of the folks mentioned herein were motivated by any combination of this quartet.

First is localism, the passionate attachment to one's own postage stamp of ground, à la John Randolph. As G.K. Chesterton understood, "the supreme psychological fact about patriotism" is "that the patriot never under any circumstances boasts of the largeness of his country, but always, and of necessity, boasts of the smallness of it."[6]

Second is the time-honored American belief in the principles of limited government—a philosophical libertarianism, even anarchism. Ralph Waldo Emerson, the Concord epigrammatist, told the Kansas Relief Meeting in Cambridge in 1856, "I am glad to see that the terror at disunion and anarchy is disappearing. Massachusetts, in its heroic day, had no government—was an anarchy. Every man stood on his own two feet, was his own governor, and there was no breach of peace from Cape Cod to Mount Hoosac."[7]

The third wellspring of anti-interventionism is the proprietary patriotism often, but not exclusively, evinced by the New England Brahminate and the Hudson Valley patroonage: the sense that this

---

[4]Quoted in Albert Mordell, *Quaker Militant: John Greenleaf Whittier* (Boston: Houghton Mifflin, 1933), p. 333.

[5]Quoted in Lewis Mumford, *Herman Melville* (New York: Harcourt, Brace, 1929), p. 297.

[6]G.K. Chesterton, *The Napoleon of Notting Hill* (Mineola, N.Y.: Dover, [1904] 1991), p. 69.

[7]Ralph Waldo Emerson, *Emerson's Works* (Boston: Houghton Mifflin, 1883), 11, p. 247.

country is theirs, that their ancestors paid for it in blood and toil, and they will not have the johnny-come-latelies sullying this bequest. This grounds the two great literary isolationists of post–republic America, Edmund Wilson and Gore Vidal, and as we shall see, it underlay much of what later came to be dismissed as the racialist opposition to the Spanish–American War and its imperial aftermath.

The fourth reason so many writers have opposed our adventures in empire was expressed by Sherwood Anderson in the epigraph. I will concede that a few fine novels have come from veterans of modern warfare, but I rather doubt that 400,000 American corpses are worth one *Naked and the Dead*.

John Greenleaf Whittier, our improbable chaperone, took up pen, if not sword, to do battle with the granddaddy of our current multi-cultural mess, the Mexican War. Whittier mocked his quondam ally, the political General Caleb Cushing, for "leading off a company of deluded unfortunates thousands of miles to shoot men, with whom THEY at least have no quarrel, or be shot by them; and this too, without the plea that the welfare of the country requires it or its true honor demands it."[8] In "The Crisis" he saw:

> Great spaces yet untravelled,
> > great lakes whose mystic shores
> The Saxon rifle never heard,
> > nor dip of Saxon oars;
> Great herds that wander all unwatched,
> > wild steeds that none have tamed,
> Strange fish in unknown streams,
> > and birds the Saxon never named;
> . . . .
> > all these ye say are ours![9]

As early as March, 1844, Emerson saw the annexation of Texas—indeed, U.S. dominion from ocean to ocean—as inevitable. Yet he deplored the distention of America: "it is quite necessary & true to our New England character," he wrote, "that we should consider the question in its local and temporary bearings, and resist the annexation with tooth & nail." He predicted that "the United States will conquer Mexico, but it will be as the man who swallows the arsenic, which brings him down in turn. Mexico will poison us."[10] This is an uncanny prefiguration of a later New England prophet of individualism, William Graham Sumner, who

[8]Quoted in Mordell, *Quaker Militant*, p. 152.
[9]Whittier, *The Complete Poetical Works of Whittier*, p. 309.
[10]Quoted in Gay Wilson Harden, *Waldo Emerson* (New York: Viking, 1981), pp. 443–44, 446.

titled his most famous anti-imperialist speech, "The Conquest of the United States by Spain."

Emerson's handyman, Henry David Thoreau, understood the Mexican War to be "the work of comparatively a few individuals using the standing government as their tool; for, in the outset, the people would not have consented" to its prosecution.[11] Thoreau's anarchism is a lustrous link in an antinomian chain that stretches out to include, in our day, Norman Mailer and Paul Goodman.

One American poet who gloried in our war against Mexico was a Loco Foco editor, a William Leggett Democrat who signed his name Walter Whitman. "Mexico must be thoroughly chastised!" he declared to readers of the *Brooklyn Eagle*. "America knows how to crush, as well as how to expand!"[12] He explained his bellicosity:

> We pant to see our country and its rule far-reaching, only inasmuch as it will take off the shackles that prevent men the even chance of being happy and good. . . . We have no ambition for the mere physical grandeur of this Republic. Such grandeur is idle and deceptive enough. Or at least it is only desirable as an aid to reach the truer good, the good of the whole body of the people.[13]

This aggrandizing bombast is difficult to reconcile with Whitman's role as a publicist of the laissez-faire wing of the Northern Democracy. His editorials consistently denounced monopoly, the tariff, internal improvements, the national bank, the extension of slavery and sumptuary laws. He averred,

> The true government is much simpler than is supposed, and abstains from much more. Nine tenths of the laws passed every winter at the Federal Capitol, and all the State Capitols, are not only unneeded laws, but positive nuisances, jobs got up for the service of special classes or persons.[14]

Young Whitman was certainly not the last fervent libertarian whose embrace of the "where liberty dwells, there is my country" will-o-the-wisp led him to rhapsodize over mass slaughter.

In his 1856 tract *The Eighteenth Presidency!*, Whitman longed to espy

> some heroic, shrewd, fully-informed, healthy-bodied, middle-aged, beard-faced American blacksmith or boatman

[11]Henry David Thoreau, *Walden and Civil Disobedience* (New York: New American Library, [1848] 1960), p. 222.
[12]Quoted in *The Mexican War: Crisis for American Democracy*, Archie P. McDonald, ed. (Lexington, Mass.: D.C. Heath, 1969), p. 47.
[13]Quoted in ibid., p. 48.
[14]Walt Whitman, *The Eighteenth Presidency!* (Lawrence: University of Kansas Press, [1856] 1956), p. 36.

> come down from the West across the Alleghenies, and walk
> into the presidency, dressed in a clean suit of working attire,
> and with the tan all over his face, breast, and arms.[15]

And then along came Abe, and Walt had all the blinded amputees and gangrenous limbs a nurse could ever hope for.

I tease Whitman—whom I admire, warts and all—but the great and disabling flaw of his Transcendentalism was captured by the Harvard Class Poet of 1838, James Russell Lowell, who in his class poem poked fun at those who "having made a 'universal soul,' forget their own in thinking of the whole."[16]

Lowell, a lawyer by training and a confrere of the literary nationalists of the "Young America" school, composed *The Biglow Papers*, one of the few lasting works of political poetry in the American language. This sometimes sly, sometimes obvious satire, written in dialect, presented the thoughts of a crackerbarrel Yankee philosopher and his supporting cast of fools and sages. Hosea Biglow has no truck with the Mexican War:

> Ez fer war, I call it murder—
> There you hev it plain an' flat;
> I don't want to go no furder
> Than my Testyment fer that; . . .
>
> Wy, it's jest ez clear ez figgers,
> Clear ez one an' one makes two,
> Chaps thet make black slaves o' niggers
> Want to make wite slaves o' you.[17]

Lowell was a Seward man in 1860, but he, too, preferred separation to war. In the interregnum between Lincoln's election and inauguration, he wrote, "even if seceding states should be conquered back again, they would not be worth the conquest."[18] Alas, like Whitman, he stirred to the martial drumbeat, and when in 1862 he penned an inferior sequel to *The Biglow Papers* there was none of that "I call it murder" milquetoastery. "Conciliate?" declaims Hosea. "It jest means *be kicked*."[19]

Lowell was a decent man with a capacious heart, and he came to despise Reconstruction, saying, "We are deliberately trying to make an Ireland of the South, by perpetuating misgovernment

[15]Ibid., p. 21.

[16]Quoted in Martin Duberman, *James Russell Lowell* (Boston: Houghton Mifflin, 1966), p. 28.

[17]James Russell Lowell, *The Complete Poetical Works of James Russell Lowell* (Boston: Houghton Mifflin, 1910), p. 174.

[18]Quoted in Duberman, *James Russell Lowell*, p. 202.

[19]Quoted in ibid., p. 281.

there."[20] He became the Mugwump par excellence, a protester against confiscatory taxes, high tariffs, and the corruption embodied by his nemesis James G. Blaine, the continental liar from the state of Maine. "Office," Lowell rhymed, "means a kind of patent drill/To force an entrance to the Nation's till."[21]

In 1876 he was an elector for Rutherford B. Hayes, and the rumor spread that in a towering act of Mugwump conscience and New England rectitude, the poet was going to cast his decisive 185th electoral vote for someone other than Hayes or Tilden, but the family must be fed, after all, and James Russell Lowell put Rutherford and Lucy Hayes in the White House. After an indecorously short interval, Lowell was appointed Minister to Spain, where he continued to compose witty verse deploring political corruption. (The ministerial post was engineered by Lowell's young and impossibly well-connected friend William Dean Howells, a Hayes in-law. Three years later Lowell was promoted to Minister to England, a position he filled with distinction for five years.)

In denouncing jobbery and patronage while seeking a patronage job, Lowell was the quintessential New Englander. Forty years earlier Nathaniel Hawthorne, Loco Foco Democrat and biographer of his doughface friend Franklin Pierce, had written his Sophia, "I want nothing to do with politicians—they are not men; they cease to be men in becoming politicians. Their hearts wither away, and die out of their bodies."[22]

My great affection for Hawthorne does not prevent me from noting that for the better part of his adult life he sought preferment from this race of sub-men, and his skillful flattery earned him posts from surveyor of the Salem Custom House to the consulship at Liverpool.

Howells, the man who effected Lowell's diplomatic career, was the son of an Ohio editor; he was deservedly proud of his father's polemics against the Mexican War. In his early twenties Howells wrote a campaign biography of candidate Abraham Lincoln; conveniently, he obtained a consulship in Venice when the terrible swift fury of Lincoln's sword hacked other sons of the Buckeye State to bits. A self-described "theoretical socialist and practical aristocrat,"[23] a staunch Republican who defended the

[20]Quoted in ibid., p. 275.
[21]Lowell, *The Complete Poetical Works*, p. 491.
[22]Quoted in Randall Stewart, "Hawthorne and Politics," *New England Quarterly* 5 (1932): 240.
[23]Quoted in Edward Wagenknecht, *William Dean Howells: The Friendly Eye* (New York: Oxford University Press, 1969), p. 271.

Haymarket anarchists, a champion of emerging realist novelists who sniffily dismissed Grover Cleveland because of "that harlot and her bastard,"[24] Howells, by virtue of his "Editor's Easy Chair" at *Harper's Magazine*, became the ringleader of the literary anti-imperialists during the Spanish–American War, which he deemed "the most stupid and causeless war that was ever imagined by a kindly and sensible nation."[25]

Scoffing that "our war for humanity has unmasked itself as a war for coaling stations,"[26] Howells became a vice-president of the Anti-Imperialist League and did his Midwestern best to revive the Anglophobia that so enriched our early politics. An outspoken champion of independence for both Filipinos and Boers, Howells attacked Kipling: "To be a flanneled fool at the wicket or a muddled oaf at the goal is possibly very bad, but it is not so bad as bayoneting a Boer, or helping herd his wife and children from his burning farm into a concentration camp."[27]

"The year 1898 is a great landmark in the history of the United States,"[28] wrote William Graham Sumner, and virtually every American novelist or poet who thought about such matters concurred. Howells worried that the Spanish–American War "has brutalized the popular mind and spoiled the taste," but he buoyed himself with the thought that "we still have a republic and not yet an empire of letters, and no one is obliged to read silly books."[29]

Mark Twain, despite his initial enthusiasm for kicking the Spanish out of Cuba—I have "never enjoyed a war . . . as I am enjoying this one,"[30] he confessed—came to share his friend Howells's sentiments: "I am opposed to having the eagle put its talons on any other land,"[31] he said, and he began to speak balefully of our "dying republic."[32]

American writers flocked to the anti-imperialist cause: Democrat, Republican, Populist, socialist, high Brahmin and low prole, from the roughest frontier humorist to the rarefied Henrys, Adams and James. The latter fretted over the prospect of "remote colonies

[24]Quoted in ibid., p. 153.
[25]Ibid., p. 213.
[26]Ibid.
[27]Ibid.
[28]William Graham Sumner, *On Liberty, Society, and Politics: The Essential Essays of William Graham Sumner* (Indianapolis, Ind.: Liberty Fund, 1992), p. 272.
[29]Quoted in William M. Gibson, "Mark Twain and Howells: Anti-Imperialists," *New England Quarterly* 20 (1947): 448.
[30]Ibid., p. 437.
[31]Ibid., p. 446.
[32]Ibid., p. 468.

run by bosses" and wrote his nephew Harry: "Expansion . . . has educated the English. Will it only demoralise us?"[33]

Opponents of the Spanish–American War were not hauled into kangaroo courts or beheaded, but then as the Ole Miss lawyer said in *Easy Rider*, this used to be a free country, and a Mark Twain could vilipend his country's political class and not be read out of "the community of enlightened discourse," or whatever the cant phrase is. The fever swamps, as Twain knew, are America.

Sherwood Anderson's belief that American participation in foreign wars damped the creative fires was anticipated by Henry Blake Fuller, a Mayflower descendant, the son of prominent Chicagoans whose family fortune was raised in the grubby commercial world of railroads, banking and real estate. His philistine parents warned the bookish Henry that reading would "injure his eyes,"[34] and the boy's rebellion—the sojourn in Europe, the supercilious dismissal of his acquisitive forbears, the dalliance with Bohemia, and the eventual understanding that he was, indissolubly, an American, a Chicagoan, a Fuller—traced a familiar arc.

Henry was apolitical, but his latent patriotism flared when it became clear that in our splendid little war we had, as Sumner put it, been conquered by Spain. Sumner had seen that in Europe "it is militarism which is eating up all the products of science and art, defeating the energy of the population and wasting its savings,"[35] and Fuller watched in horror as the virus crossed the Atlantic.

In 1899, Henry Blake Fuller became a vice president of the Chicago Anti-Imperialist League, and he published, at his own expense, *The New Flag: Satires*, 60 pages of poetic poison darts aimed at McKinley, Dewey, Teddy Roosevelt (whom he memorably dubbed "Megaphone of Mars"), and the other shoulderers of the white man's burden. He proposed that we trade in the stars and stripes for the skull and crossbones, a suggestion later adopted by Mark Twain and Ernest Crosby.

Fuller expatiated on this theme in his 1899 address "Art in America." Imperialism, he argued, would prevent a robust and native American literature from developing:

> We see ourselves—whether too flatteringly or not—as a race
> of rulers and administrators, the Romans of the modern
> world. Our place is on the dais or under the canopy; and art,

[33]Quoted in Leon Edel, *Henry James 1895–1901: The Treacherous Years* (Philadelphia: Lippincott, 1969), pp. 238–39.
[34]Kenneth Scambray, *A Varied Harvest: The Life and Works of Henry Blake Fuller* (Pittsburgh: University of Pittsburgh Press, 1987), p. 31.
[35]Sumner, *On Liberty, Society, and Politics*, p. 290.

as practised by other—and inferior—races, may amuse our leisure and adorn our festivities. The Greeks were privileged to do as much for the Romans of the Empire; let the French, the Germans and the Italians do as much for us. . . . [T]he hallmark of the artist absolute is his wish, as an individual personality, to do and be the thing in its entirety. . . . [H]e desires neither to direct or to be directed in turn. This feeling is, of course, in opposition to the whole trend of modern American civilization.[36]

Imperialism was working a less subtle alteration on American civilization. In the Senate this alloying was foreseen by Missouri's redoubtable Champ Clark: "How can we endure our shame when a Chinese senator from Hawaii, with his pigtail hanging down his back, with his pagan joss in his hand, shall rise from his curule chair and in pidgin English proceed to chop logic with GEORGE FRISBIE HOAR or HENRY CABOT LODGE? O tempora, O mores!"[37] Clark didn't know the half of it: instead of an exotic Chinese logician we ended up with Dan Inouye pawing beauticians.

Even more than the Mexican War, the Spanish–American War brought within the American ambit persons of—however distinguished and venerable their culture—strikingly alien stock. "We regarded the United States as quite large enough for our civilizing activities,"[38] novelist Hamlin Garland later recalled, but the Roosevelts and Beveridges did not. They ignored the wise counsel of William Graham Sumner, who warned against the annexation of Hawaii: if "we could have free trade with Hawaii while somebody else had the jurisdiction, we should gain all the advantages and escape all the burdens."[39]

Moreover, Sumner pointed out,

all extension puts a new strain on the internal cohesion of the pre-existing mass, threatening a new cleavage within. If we had never taken Texas and Northern Mexico we should never have had secession.[40]

Informal strictures on public speech, which are usually far more rigid and confining than legal bans, were fewer in 1899 than today, and American poets had a field day skewering their jingo brethren.

---

[36]Quoted in Bernard Bowron, Jr., *Henry B. Fuller of Chicago* (Westport, Conn.: Greenwood Press, 1974), pp. 185–87.

[37]Quoted in H. Wayne Morgan, *America's Road to Empire: The War with Spain and Overseas Expansion* (New York: Wiley, 1965), p. 107.

[38]Quoted in Fred Harvey Harrington, "Literary Aspects of American Anti–Imperialism, 1898–1902," *New England Quarterly* (December 1937): 667.

[39]Sumner, *On Liberty, Society, and Politics*, p. 268.

[40]Ibid., p. 270.

A favorite of mine is "Expansion" by James T. DuBois. In this dialect poem the narrator relates his encounters with a variety of exotic individuals—"fellers," I should say—wearing "tropic garments," a "somber-e-ro", and speaking a "forren lingo." When asked where they're from, these aliens reply "Porto Rico, U.S.A." "Santiago, U.S.A", "Manila, U.S.A.", and so on, till finally our narrator is exasperated:

> "Hully Gee," says I, "I never heard o'
>   These here cannibals before.
> Air these heathens yere all voters?
>   Will we stan' fur enny more?
> Nex' you know you'll ask a feller
>   Whur he's frum, he'll up an' say
> With a lordly kind o' flourish,
>   'All creation, U.S.A.'"[41]

The theme of betrayal dominates the anti-imperialist literature. Corporal John Mulcahey's "In the Trenches" reads in part:

> Facing death in rice-fields which are shambles,
>   For yellow men who're fighting to be free;
> Here, amid the cactus and the brambles,
>   Old Glory seems ashamed across the sea;
> Dying here before the malarial breezes,
>   That swamp across the camp-ground and the bay,
> Bringing here the fever that seizes
>   And lays the strong man low within a day;
>   This is Empire.
>
> Fighting niggers who themselves are fighting
>   For the same cause our fathers fought to save;
> Fighting in a way that is forever blighting
>   The fairest heritage our fathers gave;
> Fighting in a cause that is forever grabbing,
>   The cause that is the old-time robber's still;
> Fighting in a cause that's only stabbing
>   The one we battled for at Bunker Hill;
>   This is Empire.[42]

Sounding a similar note was William Vaughn Moody, whose "An Ode in the Time of Hesitation" is, with Mark Twain's "The War Prayer," the only anti-imperialist literary work still read. Moody was an Indiana boy, a poet and dramatist who taught English at Harvard and the University of Chicago. Like Fuller, he abjured political action, preferring, he said, to give the world "not a syllogism, but a song."[43] He was mildly pro-Spanish–American

[41]James T. DuBois, "Expansion," in *Liberty Poems: Inspired by the Crisis of 1898–1900* (Boston: James H. West, 1900), pp. 82–83.

[42]Corporal John Mulcahey, "In The Trenches," in ibid., pp. 8–9.

[43]Maurice F. Brown, *Estranging Dawn: The Life and Works of William Vaughn Moody* (Carbondale: Southern Illinois University Press, 1973), p. 112.

War, but our refusal to turn the Philippines over to the Filipinos disgusted him. "We have changed our birthright for a gourd,"[44] he wrote in the "Ode," in which he measured the decay of American ideals by appealing to the example of Robert Gould Shaw, the Boston gentleman, "this delicate and proud New England soul,"[45] who fell on July 18, 1863, while leading the first enlisted Negro regiment, the 54th Massachusetts.

In "On a Soldier Fallen in the Philippines," Moody urges us never to let the deceased know of the rotten cause for which he gave his life. The last two stanzas read:

> Toll! Let the great bells toll
>   Till the clashing air is dim.
> Did we wrong this parted soul?
>   We will make it up to him.
> Toll! Let him never guess
>   What work we sent him to.
> Laurel, laurel, yes;
>   He did what we bade him do.
> Praise, and never a whispered hint
>   but the fight he fought was good;
> Never a word that the blood on his sword
>   was his country's own heart's-blood.
>
> A flag for the soldier's bier
>   Who dies that his land may live;
> O, banners, banners here,
>   That he doubt not nor misgive!
> That he heed not from the tomb
>   The evil days draw near
> When the nation, robed in gloom,
>   With its faithless past shall strive.
> Let him never dream that
>   his bullet's scream went wide of its island mark,
> Home to the heart of his darling land
>   where she stumbled and sinned in the dark. [46]

To his biographer's dismay, Moody upheld "the old conservative positions of laissez-faire government and nonintervention."[47] He rang the death knell for his beloved country when the Megaphone of Mars, the Sissy of Kettle Hill, Theodore Roosevelt, won the presidential election of 1904. Moody wrote despairingly that "the vision in the light of which our country was created and has grown great, will soon fade, and one more world-dream will have been found impossible to live out. . . . Our different destiny may be

---

[44]William Vaughn Moody, *Poems* (Boston: Houghton Mifflin, 1901), p. 18.
[45]Ibid., p. 16.
[46]Ibid., pp. 24–25.
[47]Brown, *Estranging Dawn*, p. 171.

greater, but the America that we have known and passionately believed in, will be no more."[48]

This awareness worked perhaps its greatest miracle on Thomas Bailey Aldrich, the stalwart Republican editor of the Gilded Age *Atlantic Monthly*, who said in 1899 that he'd not "vote for McKinley again. I would sooner vote for Bryan. To be ruined financially is not so bad as to be ruined morally."[49]

I have dwelt on New England writers because I am so profoundly ambivalent about that region, so blessed and so blind. She and the Midwest supplied the passion and wit and brawn and style of the republic's defense, yet her sons were capable of asking, as one poet did, "What Would Lincoln Say?"[50] What, indeed, would Abraham Lincoln say of a large industrial nation's suppression of a smaller country's independence movement?

Poet W.A. Croffut, in "Columbia's Call," invokes the shades of "Grant! Sherman! Sumner! Lincoln!" and claims: "Heroes beloved! Your noble work was foreign/To all the nation's words and deeds to-day!"[51]

Keener observers understood the kinship of the Civil and Spanish–American Wars. William T. Eggleston's "Our New National Hymn" is a burlesque of Julia Ward Howe's wrathful grapy anthem:

> We are robbing Christian churches
>   in our missionary zeal,
> And we carry Christ's own message
>   in our shells and bloody steel.
> By the light of burning roof-trees
>   they may read the Word of Life,
> In the mangled forms of children
>   they may see the Christian strife.
> We are healing with the Gatling,
>   we are blessing with the sword;
> For the Honor of the Nation
>   and the Glory of the Lord.[52]

Just as biting was the antiwar verse of the prolific Ernest Crosby. Born into a socially prominent New York City family, Crosby was a young lawyer who in 1887 succeeded to the State Assembly seat vacated by Theodore Roosevelt. He became a Tolstoyan anarchist, spiked with a healthy dose of Henry George, and

[48]Ibid.

[49]Quoted in Harrington, "Literary Aspects," p. 666.

[50]Howard S. Taylor, "What Would Lincoln Say?" in *Liberty Poems*, p. 98–99.

[51]W. A. Croffut, "Columbia's Call," in ibid., p. 43.

[52]William T. Eggleston, "Our New National Anthem," in ibid., p. 27.

he was the biographer of the great Tolstoyan Mayor of Toledo, Sam "Golden Rule" Jones, who thought if we'd all just follow the Golden Rule we wouldn't have need of nuisances such as police and laws.

Crosby wrote a very broad satire on the expansionist fever that was invaliding the American Republic. *Captain Jinks: Hero* (1902) follows its myrmidon namesake from "East Point," the U.S. military academy, to the Cubapine Islands, where his exploits—burning native temples; censoring Spanish translations of the Declaration of Independence; learning, as one monopolist explains, that "the best way to civilize the Cubapines is to tax them"[53]—are gilded by yellow journalists into the elements of heroism.

Captain Jinks: Hero isn't exactly funny—Crosby was a zealous Tolstoyan, after all, and however congenial we may find those mystical anarchists we must admit they are strangers in the house of mirth. There is a relaxed certitude in Crosby; he understands that imperialism is a rebarbative thing, it doesn't fit America, and once we come to our senses, say by 1905, we'll repair to the old standards of liberty and non-interference in the quarrels of other nations. This is in contrast to the desperation, the panicky realization that the game is up, that our America is destroyed, which one finds in much of the antiwar writing of the 1940s.

Once upon a time in America, wit was not an indictable offense. In the Hosea Biglow tradition, an anti-imperialist poet jested:

> When Jim Monroe paid his respex
>   To them there European kings,
> Requestin' them just not to vex
>   Republics on this side, and things,
> He never thought this country'd go
>   And grab an archypellygo.[54]

Half a century later, the poet Robinson Jeffers, "an old-fashioned Jeffersonian republican . . . defender of the spartan and honest American commonweal against the thickening of empire,"[55] had 10 of his poems censored by Random House when he dared dream of a better world in which FDR and Woodrow Wilson would meet in Hell, and bombers might drop "wreaths of roses"[56]

---

[53]Ernest Crosby, *Captain Jinks: Hero* (Upper Saddle River, N.J.: The Gregg Press, [1902] 1968), p. 87.

[54]W.A.B., "Expansion," in *Liberty Poems*, p. 54.

[55]Robert Hass, Introduction to *Rock and Hawk: A Selection of Shorter Poems by Robinson Jeffers* (New York: Random House, 1987), p. xxxvi.

[56]Robinson Jeffers, *The Double Axe*, restored version (New York: Liveright, 1977), p. 156.

upon a shining city whose boys hang "Hitler and Roosevelt in one tree/Painlessly, in effigy."[57]

I have dealt elsewhere with those American writers who in the period up to December 7, 1941, stood on the tracks and yelled "Stop" at the runaway train carrying American blood and dollars to the European war, and American ideals to the boneyard.[58] Suffice here to say that they were many, they were distinguished, they were honorable, and they were crushed. Their names include Robinson Jeffers, e.e. cummings, Sinclair Lewis, Edmund Wilson, Robert Lowell, William Saroyan, Theodore Dreiser, Henry W. Clune, Edgar Lee Masters, Kathleen Norris, and Samuel Hopkins Adams, among others.

"Everything before the war is out,"[59] says a distraught lady in John P. Marquand's novel of the American metamorphosis, *B.F.'s Daughter* (1946); the world turned topsy-turvy, and all the stuffing fell out of our country. The Taft Republican Jack Kerouac noticed that "America was invested with wild self-believing individuality and this had begun to disappear around the end of World War II with so many great guys dead."[60]

As Robinson Jeffers prophesied, the Spirit of '76 took to the hills and mountains and hinterlands. The beliefs our forefathers held were now identified with remoteness. This is how the iconoclastic editor of the journal *Politics*, Dwight Macdonald, whose isolationism somehow bloomed in the New York Trotskyite hothouse, was attacked in 1946 by his erstwhile allies at *Partisan Review*: "For its crackerbox bluster, wide-eyed idealism, and ingenue dogmatism," *Politics* "might just as well be put out at some tiny whistle-stop in Oklahoma."[61]

Exactly. In a more than metaphorical sense, American politics has been for 60 years about the steady triumph of *Partisan Review* over 10,000 tiny whistle-stops in Oklahoma. Saith the cynical newsman in John Ford's elegiac movie *The Man Who Shot Liberty Valance*, "When the legend becomes fact, print the legend."

Fifty years of smears have so blackened the reputations of the courageous men who fought to preserve the republic that today no libel is too preposterous. One of the only contemporary novels

---

[57]Ibid.

[58]Bill Kauffman, "There are Left the Mountains," *Chronicles* (December 1993): 16–20. See also Bill Kauffman, *America First! Its History, Culture, and Politics* (Amherts, N.Y.: Prometheus Books, 1995).

[59]John P. Marquand, *B.F.'s Daughter* (Boston: Little, Brown, 1946), p. 257.

[60]Jack Kerouac, "The Origins of the Beat Generation," *Playboy* (June 1959): 32.

[61]William Barrett, "The Resistance," *Partisan Review* (September–October 1946): 487.

written about the Great Debate of 1940–41 is *Secret Anniversaries* (1990) by Scott Spencer, best known for the Brooke Shields vehicle *Endless Love*. In Spencer's fantasy, a Hudson Valley debutante takes a job with a barely disguised Congressman Hamilton Fish, and our apple-cheeked heroine descends into the clammy isolationist netherworld—America Firsters were hags and creeps, you know, ugly monsters like Charles Lindbergh and Lillian Gish. Our gal falls under the spell of Fish's adjutant, an insatiable pro-Nazi lesbian. The Nazi dyke routine was done much better in the porn classic *Ilse, She-Wolf of the SS*, but *Secret Anniversaries* is more than just macabre camp: it is, in Spencer's conceit, a rigorously researched historical novel. He credits, as his source on America First, the discredited agit-prop classic *Under Cover* (1943) by John Roy Carlson, alias Avedis Derounian.

But this is America, and there will always be men who can track in the dark. Contemporaneous with *Secret Anniversaries* was Edward Abbey's penultimate novel, *The Fool's Progress* (1988), which gave us the Lightcap family of Stump Creek, West Virginia.

Paw, Joe Lightcap, "thought he was the only Wobbly east of the Mississippi River. The only freethinker in West Virginia. The only isolationist left in Shawnee County."[62] He's a village crank of the kind who kept this country turning. "The majority of Americans never wanted to get into this rotten war," he harangues anyone who'll listen. "And when Roosevelt maneuvered us into it, even after Pearl Harbor, the majority still never wanted to go overseas to fight. That's why the government needs the draft. . . . Because there was no other way they could get our boys into it. They have to force them to fight."[63]

When his son Will enlists, Joe is enraged.

> "You're gonna go git your head blowed off for that damned old windbag Winston Churchill?"
> Will said nothing.
> "For that scheming old sneaky son of a bitch Roosevelt?"
> Will remained silent.
> "For that bloody old communist tyrant Joe Stalin?"
> Will did not reply.
> "I'm disgusted," Paw said. "Absolutely disgusted. That any son of mine would go fight in that rich man's war. Would risk his neck for"—he put on his fake Groton–Harvard accent—"foah thu bullluddy"—rolling the r's—"Buh-ritish . . . Empah!"[64]

---

[62]Edward Abbey, *The Fool's Progress* (New York: Henry Holt, 1988), p. 110.
[63]Ibid., p. 153.
[64]Ibid., p. 108.

Paw later takes enormous pride in Will's soldierly feats, all the while hating the war.

Scott Spencer, by his own account, lived for years via an IV hooked up to the government welfare-culture machine; Edward Abbey, by contrast, was one of the last of the independents. When in 1987 the American Academy of Arts and Letters got around to honoring him, he refused the award and instead ran a river in Idaho. (This reminds me of our pre-eminent America Firster, Gore Vidal, whose senatorial grandfather was a Bryanite foe of the U.S. entrance into World War I. As a boy, Vidal himself was a leader of the America First Committee at Exeter. In 1976 Vidal was extended; with the usual pomp and absurd solemnity, an invitation to join the "200 immortals" of the National Institute of Arts and Letters. He forever earned their enmity by declining the invitation, wiring them, "I cannot accept this election as I already belong to the Diner's Club."[65])

The Mexican War provoked Ralph Waldo Emerson to call democracy a government of bullies tempered by editors, and what do we do when the editors grow fangs? When Thomas Bailey Aldrich and Dwight Macdonald vanish, and we're left with William F. Buckley, Jr. and Abe Rosenthal? When William Dean Howells and the Anti-Imperialist League give way to Susan Sontag and a belligerent legion of Writers-in-Residence—the Breadloaf Brigade—giving public readings demanding that boys from Fargo and Batavia and Harlem be sent to die in Sarajevo? Whittier was wiser than Lincoln and Moody McKinley, and even today it is men of letters, not men of state, who know the way back home.

Consider two quotes, one from the leading organ of the Establishment Right, the other from a poet. A couple of years ago, the *Wall Street Journal* editorial page instructed us that "patriotism" is "fundamentally" about "defense policy": it can be measured in dollars and megatons. This obscenity requires no elaboration, other than to restate Tom Fleming's observation that Official Conservatives seem eager to watch on CNN as American boys in blue helmets die on foreign sands in order to make the world safe for the Fortune 500.

Now, in an American accent, listen to the Kentucky poet–farmer (tobacco farmer, no less) Wendell Berry. At the raucous wake held for Edward Abbey, Berry saluted his friend as a true patriot, remarking: "Patriotism is not the love of air conditioning

---

[65]Barbara Grizzuti Harrison, "Pure Gore," *Los Angeles Times Magazine* (January 28, 1990), p. 13.

or the interstate highway system or the government or the flag or power or money or munitions. It is the love of country."[66]

"Don't yelp with the pack," William James told his students in 1898.[67] Bostonian or Confederate, Quaker or village atheist, the American writers discussed herein have exhibited the cussed ornery independence and willingness to stray that are among our noblest traditions. Whatever else may be said of them, they have loved their country. They have much to teach us.

I began with an epigraph so I'll end with an epilogue. It's from a poem by Ernest Crosby titled "The State."

> They talked much of the State—the State.
> I had never seen the State, and I asked them to picture it to me, as my gross mind could not follow their subtle language when they spake of it.
> Then they told me to think of it as of a beautiful goddess, enthroned and sceptred, benignly caring for her children.
> But for some reason I was not satisfied.
>
> And once upon a time, as I was lying awake at night and thinking, I had as it were a vision,
> And I seemed to see a barren ridge of sand beneath a lurid sky;
> And lo, against the sky stood out in bold relief a black scaffold and gallows-tree, and from the end of its gaunt arm hung, limp and motionless, a shadowy, empty noose.
> And a Voice whispered in my ear, "Behold the State incarnate!"[68]

[66]"Author Edward Abbey is Remembered," *Rochester Democrat and Chronicle* (May 23, 1989), p. C10.

[67]Quoted in Van Wyck Brooks, *New England: Indian Summer* (New York: Dutton, 1940), p. 430.

[68]Ernest Crosby, *Plain Talk in Psalm and Parable* (Boston: Small, Maynard, 1899), p. 182.

15
THE CULTURE OF WAR

Paul Fussell[*]

My friends and I sometimes play a game that you might enjoy; we call it "oxymoron." The object is to come up with phrases which, while superficially plausible, prove on skeptical examination to involve intellectually comical contradictions in terms. Take, for example, creation science, or journalistic ethics, or the Maoist concept of a cultural revolution. How about the term scholar-athlete or, looking toward the university faculty instead of the students, the scholar-activist. That is actually a phrase the *Washington Post* used recently to describe the newly-appointed president of the University of the District of Columbia. Some deeply cynical players of the game "oxymoron," contemplating much of higher education today, might go so far as to propose as the winning oxymoron: college education.

Now I start this way because my title, "The Culture of War," might be regarded as that kind of flagrant oxymoron. And so it would be if I were evoking the term culture in any artistic or intellectual sense, implying within the armed forces a considerable amount of viola playing, classical acting, liberal drawing, painting, modeling, poetry, fiction writing, and difficult reading. But actually it is not these sorts of things that I am trying to suggest by the word culture. I am using it in a quasi–anthropological sense: the way T.S. Eliot used it when he wrote a book called *Notes Towards the Definition of Culture*,[1] a book in which he considered the possibility of a healthy and interesting society based on something like religious principles. In that book, Eliot understands how much, as he puts it, is embraced by the word culture, a term not designating merely artistic or ennobling activities but the general forms and usages and techniques of a given society including military society. To Eliot, culture includes all the characteristic activities and interests of a people. Using the British people and their culture as his examples, he goes on to list as components of British culture these things: Derby Day, the Henley regatta, dog racing, dart boards, boiled cabbage cut into sections (a rather disgusting idea surely),

[*This article is transcribed from the author's presentation at the Mises Institute's "Costs of War" conference in Atlanta, May 20–22, 1994.]

[1]T.S. Eliot, *Notes Towards the Definition of Culture* (New York: Harcourt, Brace, 1949).

19th-century Gothic churches, and the music of Sir Edward Elgar. In the same way, probably any one of us could make a list of things comprising the culture of war. At the outset I should warn you that the items I mention are collected not by any military strategist, theoretician, historian, or scholar. They are the views of a superannuated, badly wounded, former infantry lieutenant, a one-time rifle platoon leader who fought in World War II in Europe, and commanded 40 terrified young Americans, many of whom were killed or cruelly wounded. Thus, if the word "culture" presents some problems, the word "war" will present even more.

The truth is that very few people know anything about war. In an infantry division, for example, fewer than half of the troops actually fight, that is, fight with rifles, mortars, machine guns, grenades, and trench knives. The others, thousands upon thousands of them, are occupied with truck driving, photocopying, cooking and baking, ammunition and ration supplying, and similar housekeeping tasks. Now those things are no doubt necessary, but they are hardly bellicose; they don't provide the sort of experience required to define what the word "war" might mean. This is the reason why most combat veterans tend to smile cynically and sardonically at veterans reunions when those reunions are attended by very large numbers. Very few of those attending, the real veterans know, deserve to be there. For most soldiers participating in World War II, the war meant inconvenience rising sometimes to hardship, enforced travel and residence abroad, unappetizing food, and the absence of table cloths or bed sheets. For those unlucky enough to be in the forward combat units, the war meant death or maiming, usually in extraordinarily dirty and undignified circumstances. At the very least, for most it meant a rapid and shocking metamorphosis from boyhood innocence to adult cynicism and bitterness. It is an experience remembered so vividly even at this distance that it has inducted me into my understanding of the culture of war. It is a culture hard for civilians to understand, because civilians occupy a world, thank God, which is in large part rational and predictable, a world which makes sense in an old-fashioned way.

Now let me illustrate what I mean. A while ago I was telephoned by a lawyer in New York City. He indicated that he was conducting a course for cadets at West Point, a course in the relation between language and violence. This course focused on the deformations of language required for the registration of non-rational violent behavior. He asked me to take part in a class on this topic and I agreed cheerfully. He then specified the subject further. He was going to focus, he said, on the after-action reports from combat units, and he wanted me to indicate what problems I had experienced in writing my after-action reports. What problems had I had adapting normal language to this special use? For example, what euphemisms, if any, were employed in these after-action reports? What were the temptations that I felt to provide rational motives for violent or inexplicable events?

As this phone call went on, I confess that I suffered an outburst of extreme anger, the sort of thing that is common among infantrymen reinstalled in an optimistic and unimaginative civilian culture. With some passion, I asked this lawyer, have you ever been in combat? He answered no. I then explained, with elaborate sarcasm, that I never heard of such things as after-action reports from small assault units. Perhaps they had some existence at battalion or regimental level, but not down where the fighting was. How, after all, could one pull oneself together to compose an after-action report with pencil and paper when you had the following after-action features to attend to: first, the question of what to do with the six German prisoners the assault has just yielded. How can one keep a very angry private who had seen his buddy's eye shot out from doing what he really much wanted to do, to kill all the prisoners? Second, after-action you had to clean up the mess. This meant taking care of the wounded, some of whom are suffering intense, unrelievable pain because the morphine is already exhausted. Third, after-action you had to reposition your soldiers to repel a German counter-attack, and you had to jolly them up to make them work to continue fighting the war in the prescribed manner. Fighting the war after-action is going to be very difficult because your sergeant is over there crying. Fourth, how could a junior officer, like me, write an after-action report when his hand was covered with the blood of one of his men whose wound in the back I had ineffectively tried to bandage while the bullets and shell fragments were flying around? Fifth, given all this, how could such a person have waited a day or so to file his after-action report in a calmer mood, when a third of the men whose testimony would be required were gone, killed, or wounded? Besides, where would he find the quiet to write it? By that time he would be engaged in further violence himself. The point is that producing after-action reports is the privilege of leaders who are non-combatants, and are useful only in works of fiction.

My point is not that we did not write such reports; rather, my point is that the lawyer, a very representative human being, suffered from an extreme naiveté about the facts of war. One would expect a lawyer, in New York City especially, to be quite sophisticated about the facts of life, but here is one who imagined that the conduct of combat was rational. He was a victim of what I call "inappropriate rationalism" mixed in with a bit of inappropriate optimism as well. Those who find it hard to understand how often soldiers kill their own comrades during friendly fire episodes are victims of the same intellectual and emotional error. The culture of war, in short, is not like the culture of ordinary peace-time life. It is a culture dominated by fear, blood, and sadism, by irrational actions and preposterous (and often ironic) results. It has more relation to science fiction or to absurdist theater than to actual life, and that makes it hard to describe. If you like you can regard what I have said about this bizarre and ignorant concern with after-action reports as just another bureaucratic intrusion into a place where such intrusion is entirely inappropriate and, even worse, stupid. It is especially unfortunate because it simply underlines the unpleasant fact of the military class system. On the one hand, there are the remote and privileged staffs and administrators; on the other hand, there are the troops, mostly sad conscripts, that must do the dangerous work.

The distance between serious survivors of war and optimistic onlookers can be measured by a current controversy in Britain between veterans of World War II and the government. The veterans want D-day commemorated with solemnity and sorrow. After all it marked the beginning of a battle in which 37,000 people, most of them pathetically young, were killed. The government, desirous of tourist dollars, takes a different approach. It proposes not a commemoration but a celebration, involving street parties, dances, huge reenactments, band concerts, Glenn Miller impersonators and the like. Well, the quarrel is between those who know the culture of war, and those who think they know it, or who are prepared to profit from a misrepresentation of it. Between these two groups a reconciliation is hardly possible. A spokesman for the veterans has said that the event is being trivialized. Those who actually took part feel it was just a battle, albeit a successful one. Many of their comrades lost their lives in the process and many ladies were widowed. That the allies won World War II does not oblige us to be cheerful about it. Wars are won by distinction in the techniques of mass murder, and that is hardly something for people pretending to civilization to be proud of. Tolstoy's words are worth recalling: war he said, "is not a polite recreation, but the vilest thing in life, and we ought to understand that and not play at war." It will be many years—perhaps decades—before it becomes clear whether the Cold War was really necessary, or was a gratifying and profitable playing at war whose beneficiaries were not the people of the Earth, but the makers of armaments designed to become rapidly obsolete and quickly replaceable. If focusing the economy on armaments bankrupted the Soviet Union, think what it did to the United States.

Thus, if the culture of war solidifies those who fight, it alienates them from those who do not. It has other regrettable aspects, one of which is censorship. War kills people; the culture of war does not, but the culture of war kills something precious and indispensable in a civilized society: freedom of utterance, freedom of curiosity, freedom of knowledge. Recently, an official of the Pentagon explained why the military had censored some TV footage depicting Iraqi soldiers cut in half by automatic fire from U.S. helicopters. He explained, "If we let people see that kind of thing there would never again be any war."[2] Now I got that quotation from a comical gift book titled *The Seven Hundred and Seventy-six Stupidest Things Ever Said*. But that remark is far from stupid; it is very true and its implications spread very far. It is obvious that censorship of that type is a necessity in any modern war. It is usually rationalized by the need to keep the enemy in the dark about our plans; it is also valuable to conceal military blunders and war crimes from a public that, in the absence of censorship, might learn to be critical of the military's actions.

Now my point is simple: if you are trained to be uncritical of the military, you can easily go a little further and learn to be uncritical of government and authority, and even to be uncritical of all established and received institutions. The ultimate result is the death of the mind, the transformation of the higher learning and independent scholarship into a cheering section for whatever popular notions and superstitions prevail at the moment. During wartime, and during the Cold War, we all had to pretend that the military is a force for some kind of social good. I wonder if the habit of unthinking obedience is a good one to instill in young Americans. For one thing, what is clear about the culture of war is that it is necessarily an obedience culture. In armies, as one critic has noticed, where there must be unquestioning obedience, there must necessarily be passive injustice. And not just that—the obedience culture is certain over the long-run to shrivel originality and to constrict thought, to encourage witless adaptation and social dishonesty.

The culture of war is the only culture where the concept of morale is crucial, and that is a significant point. Morale is crucial in the culture of war because at all times the troops are engaging in

[2]*The Seven Hundred and Seventy-six Stupidest Things Ever Said,* Ed Ross and Kathryn Petra, eds. (New York: Doubleday, 1993), p. 213.

activities sure to undermine cheerfulness and hope. They are either being bored picking up cigarette butts, or they are being dehumanized by killing their fellow creatures who, like them, are for the most part helpless conscripts who have done nothing for which they deserve to be blown to bits. In a war-time culture, censorship has the assistance of general euphemism and programmatically inaccurate language. Before long we are calling war "peace-keeping." What used to be designated aerial bombing has been euphemised into air strikes and even surgical strikes, dishonestly implying a degree of accuracy which would make combat veterans laugh out loud. Originally, artillery or mortar shells fired by mistake at our own troops were called terrible mistakes, or tragic errors. Then the euphemism of "incontinent ordinance" was devised, and finally some Pentagon genius hit upon the warmer and cozier term "friendly fire."

During the Gulf War, friendly fire caused a large share of the American casualties. Twenty-three percent of the American dead died from friendly fire. Fifteen percent of the American wounded were wounded by friendly fire. Of course, blunders are the very essence of war, which is why the culture of war is so far removed from the culture of predictability and rationality. Soldiers know that mistakes are the essence of war, because they know what is likely to happen when you arm a lot of frightened boys with deadly weapons. But the public must not be told, lest their simple faith in military authority and rationality be shaken.

Transforming the ugly and shocking into the noble and bright is the business of the most popularly illustrated history of World War II. I am referring to the Time–Life volumes with titles like the *Italian War* or *Across the Rhine*. In those volumes, clear and noble cause and purpose are assigned systematically to events which are really accidental or which are embarrassingly demeaning. Readers of those books are insulted by being presumed to be incapable of confronting the truth. Everything must be transformed into fairy tales of heroism, success, and nobility. The entire series of books attempts to portray catastrophic occurrences in an orderly, wholesome, and optimistic fashion. For example, the shooting down of hundreds of American paratroopers during the invasion of Sicily by frightened and undisciplined American sailors, who were convinced that the large airplanes flying overhead held enemy troops, is presented in a fashion that does not show the complete bungling that occurred. The presentation of war by such dishonest means is a fine way, actually, to encourage a moralistic, nationalistic, and bellicose international politics.

It is customary to maintain that American wars are all fought on behalf of freedom, but few notice that for the sake of freedom millions of young men are enslaved for years, Shanghaied by conscription into a life whose every dimension is at odds with the idea of freedom. Flags, uniforms, bugle calls, band music, and all the trappings of military glory hardly suffice to persuade the hapless conscript that he is involved in the defense of freedom, especially when his weekend pass has just been canceled at the last minute in retribution for a heartfelt satiric remark which his sergeant has just overheard. To invoke a rude term which I hope will offend no one here, the culture of war is hardly separable from the culture of chicken shit.

During World War II, an Australian poet, John Manifold, wrote a poem entitled "Ration Party." It dramatizes the irony of slaves in uniform defending freedom. It adds to the irony by being a sonnet, a kind of poetry normally associated with delicate or beautiful sentiments. Here is his poem "Ration Party":

> Across the mud the line drags on and on;
> Tread slithers, foothold fails, all ardors vanish,
> Rain falls; the barking N.C.O.'s admonish
> The universe more than the lagging man.
>
> Something like an infinity of men
> Plods up the slope; the file will never finish,
> For all their toil serves only to replenish
> Stores for tomorrow's labors to begin.
>
> Absurd to think that Liberty, the splendid
> Nude of our dreams the intercessory saint
> For us to judgment, needs to be defended
>
> By sick fatigue-men brimming with complaint
> And misery, who bear till all is ended
> Every imaginable pattern of constraint.[3]

Now, the final thing I want to point out about the culture of war is that it is necessarily adversarial and dualistic. We are here, the enemy is over there, and a no-mans land, either literal (geography) or figurative (ideology), divides us. The divisiveness at home occasioned by the Vietnam War is an example. That divisiveness almost ruined the United States. You remember how it went —if you opposed the war you were dishonoring the flag and were practically a traitor. If you favored the war you were a true American. You had to be either a dove or a hawk—take your choice.

---

[3]John Manifold, "Ration Party," *Selected Verse* (New York: John Day, 1946), p. 72.

There was no room for compromise, conciliation, or even very subtle discussion. If you were not for the war you must be for communism. It was that attitude that finally brought down the Nixon White House.

Earlier in our history, invasion or physical pressure against American territory were provocations leading to war. During the Nixon era, the U.S. became "Kissingerized." No longer requiring threats to American territory, threats to American "national interest" became a sufficient reason for sending the troops into bloody action. National interest is an interesting term because it is legally meaningless and constitutionally undefinable, hence popular. The term "national interest" is the best gift ever awarded to those Americans who are neurotically bellicose, but who, like Henry Kissinger, always seem to avoid being on the frontline, preferring to serve their country by getting others to drop bombs on people. Of course, the people they drop bombs on, and this is notable, are always more primitive and unfortunate than themselves. They are always smaller in stature. They usually have darker skins. That is what the current culture of war seems to amount to. Clearly, we should abhor it.

16
IS MODERN DEMOCRACY WARLIKE?

Paul Gottfried

The view of democracy as producing peace-loving and stable regimes has become a settled opinion of our time. Almost every day, editorialists and commentators in *The Wall Street Journal*, *New York Times* and in other respected national newspapers stress the correlation between democratic values and perpetual peace. In a January 19, 1994, column in the *Philadelphia Inquirer*, feature writer Trudy Rubin explains that America's choice in dealing with post–communist Russia is either to assist passively in "the triumph of neofascism" or to take energetic steps "on behalf of democrats in Russia and Western Europe." Peace, Ms. Rubin adds, requires a vigorous interventionist policy aimed at spreading democracy. Walter Bernes, Olin Professor at Georgetown University, has insisted that democracies "never fight wars with each other," a problematic statement that has now acquired the status of a truism. R.J. Rummel, a friend of Bernes, has recently altered this assertion to the equally suspect one, that democracies "have fought each other for 150 years." What exactly, one might ask, was a democracy like 150 years ago? There were in fact no governments at that time more democratic, by current egalitarian standards, than was South Africa under apartheid.

Any hostile actions taken by self-described democracies, moreover, are now routinely described as advancing peace by containing or punishing non-democrats. Of course, demanding that the entire world be made to conform to their values is by no means a pacifist stance. In the summer of 1993, self-proclaimed defenders of human rights in France formed the "Appeal to Vigilance Committee" to marginalize their opposition. This committee, which included such progressive celebrities as Bernard-Henri Levy, Jacques Derrida, and Umberto Eco, complained that on the anniversary of the Jacobin ascendancy in revolutionary France the "extreme right" is still being allowed to frolic in the public square. Unnamed rightists are mocking the supposed excesses of the democratic Left's crusade against racists and anti-immigrationists. According to the 40 intellectuals who signed the "Appeal to Vigilance" published in *Le Monde* on July 13, 1993: "Writers, publishers and those responsible for the written and audiovisual press are not sufficiently suspicious of those ruses being used to relegitimate the Right." The media, we are told, provide a forum for the critics of human rights and anti-racist public education, and by this "involuntary complicity threaten both democracy and human lives."

On July 13, 1993, *Le Monde* published its own editorial support for this appeal, lamenting the danger created "by a world of ideas still under the sway of freedom of opinion." The alliance between "militant communists and neo-fascists," *Le Monde* sternly warns, "benefits the chaos that reigns in Russia, the racist murders that are proliferating in Germany, and the unforeseeable consequences of the war in the former Yugoslavia."

Let us keep in mind that there is nothing undemocratic about these calls to democratic intolerance. The Jacobins of the French Revolution muzzled and threatened French citizens while screaming about the enemy at the gates and within their own city. The doctrine of human rights that French intellectuals are now exalting has never been viewed as a purely national patrimony. Its adherents since 1789 have affirmed their universal proselytizing mission; Edmund Burke was correct to perceive a vast gulf between the historical liberties of Englishmen and the "armed doctrines" of the French revolutionaries. Note well that the terror in revolutionary France killed far more than the 30,000 or so who died on the scaffold. Between March, 1793, and July, 1795, over 100,000 peasants from the Vendée and Brittany regions were massacred by revolutionary armies for counterrevolutionary activities, ranging from reluctance to be conscripted into the republican army to alleged support for priests who refused to swear unqualified allegiance to the revolutionary state.[1] The French historians Pierre Chaunu and Reynald Sécher have documented these massacres, which involved the drowning in the Loire River of masses of women and children. While these acts of ideological intolerance were not unprecedented in Western history (certainly one can point back to the sad examples of the Inquisition and the sacking of Jewish and Byzantine settlements in the crusades), what stands out about the Revolution is the wholesale killing of people in the name of democratic ideals.

This democratic potential for destruction was already known in the 18th century. The Scottish philosopher and historian David Hume cited it in making a case against democracy and for British constitutional monarchy. In his revulsion for popular government, Hume might have been following another anti-democratic skeptic, Thomas Hobbes. Neither Hume nor Hobbes was impressed by the Greek democratic experience, and Hobbes—who translated Thucydides's *History of the Peloponnesian War*—attributed the defeat of

---

[1] Pierre Chaunu, *Le grand déclassment* (Paris: Laffant, 1989), pp. 139–95; Reynald Sécher, *La guerre de la Vendée* (Paris: Talladier, 1987); and J.F. Fayard, *La justicé révolutionnaire* (Paris: Laffont, 1986).

Athens in that ancient struggle to its democratic defect, combining instability with relentless imperialism. Certainly the founders of the American Republic were deeply suspicious of a highly centralized state invoking the majority will. Distributed national power, entrusting the franchise to propertied state legislators, dual sovereignty, and the making of the defense of life and property the justification for the Constitution, all pointed not to a democratic but to a conservative–liberal world view. Popular government would be allowed, but with suitable checks on its expressions.

For the radical elements among the founding generation, grouped around Thomas Jefferson, the term democracy had a positive connotation suggesting liberty and localism. No matter how foolishly Jefferson celebrated the French Revolution, it was not the centralized government of the Jacobins, appealing to the general will, on which the Virginia planter based his democratic hopes; it was on communities of craftsmen and yeoman farmers. As late as the 1830s, Alexis de Tocqueville, the French visitor to America, drew a critical distinction between American and European notions of democracy; in the U.S., one saw self-government in practice in small towns run by local gentry and intrusive pecksniffs; in Europe, by contrast, it was the centralizing and often militaristic vision of Jacobin France that held sway. If democracy would triumph as the inevitable wave that de Tocqueville already took it to be in the mid-1830s, the unanswered question became which form would prove stronger: American localism or French Jacobinism.

By now there is no question that the second form of democracy has prevailed, as a globalist, bellicose ideology often representing the ambitions of a well-organized political class and its journalistic adjuncts. There are many reasons for this development: economic, administrative, and geopolitical causes have all played a role in turning de Tocqueville's America as a shrine to local self-government into the aggressive behemoth spouting therapeutic bromides that all of us have come to recognize as the perfected version of American democracy. Real self-government has been supplanted by electoral inclusiveness, so that every deadbeat is urged to vote as a testimony to the expansiveness of our system. Democracy is equated with the extension of special rights—often to fictitious ethnicities like "Hispanics"—as evidence of a public commitment to egalitarianism. A class of public administrators, judges, and career officers decide how we live and die in a society that tax-paying citizens can do less and less to influence. We can no longer even determine who should be allowed to enter the country and become a citizen, since the demand for such a control is by now considered undemocratic. Only neofascists, as journalists tell us, try to restrict immigration—or oppose open borders with Third World countries. As the classicist Paul Veyne makes clear, a self-restricted political community is the mark of ancient and medieval democracies and republics. A government's denial to its citizens of their right to limit citizenship on religious, cultural, or ethnic grounds indicates, according to Veyne, not a democratic but an imperial order, a supranational sovereignty in which the ruler or ruling class allows anyone born or found in that territory to become a subject.[2]

These remarks are not intended as an endorsement of a return to racially-homogeneous ancient politics. Rather I am trying to determine in what sense contemporary America is or is not democratic. The typical neoconservative response to my unseemly questioning would be to say that we are democratic because we place neither gender, nor racial, nor ethnic restrictions on voting, because we redistribute earnings, and finally, because in our truly inspired moments, we work to make the entire world safe for democracy. In any case, the response would continue, America is a *liberal* democracy and as such committed to a rotating party system, human rights, and open citizenship, political features that were unknown in ancient (bigoted and collectivist) democracies.

This particular argument is basic to an 1,100-page study dealing with ancient and modern republics by the Straussian Paul Rahe.[3] I agree with Rahe's distinction up to a point: that is, too much has been made of the fascination of 18th-century republicans with Greek and Roman popular government. Obviously there were liberal, individualist concerns in Thomas Jefferson and James Madison which were lacking in ancient republican rhetoric and practice. Madison's idea of an extended republic balanced by material interests suggests the application of the new science of politics. It seems to me, from a recent reading of Mises's social thought, that for Mises, few words were more disagreeable than "organic" and "communal," except possibly for "socialist." Mises asserts in *Die Gemeinwirtschaft* that to be a liberal, one must be committed to a "scientific" approach to life that maximizes individual prosperity. Societies that have focused on preserving the past or maintaining a cultural heritage, Mises argues, have been unable to achieve that goal.[4]

---

[2]Paul Veyne, *La Pain et le cirque: Sociologie d'un pluralisme politique* (Paris: Seuil, 1976), pp. 87–92 and 106–8.

[3]Paul Rahe, *Republics Ancient and Modern: Classical Republicanism and the American Revolution* (Chapel Hill: University of North Carolina Press, 1992). See also my review of Rahe's book in *Modern Age* 37, no. 3 (Spring 1995): 264–69.

[4]Ludwig von Mises, *Die Gemeinwirtschaft* (Munich: Philosophia Verlag, [1932] 1981), pp. 209–47.

The defense of democracy made by Mises is typical of a certain classical-liberal optimism. Democratic regimes, Mises believed, can minimize internal tensions by allowing the majority to cast votes for its leaders. Once this electoral process occurs, Mises hoped, liberal norms and parliamentary procedures can be counted on to keep society tranquil and economically productive. Though Mises knew that "socialist demagogues draw instant crowds in today's democracies," he found nothing in the "democratic principle" that requires this situation. Democracy means popular elections but not the automatic rights to change liberal rules.[5]

For all of his brilliant economic insights, Mises did not understand the operation of modern liberal democracy, particularly as practiced in the U.S. The democratic principle has indeed led toward social democracy, with the fully bureaucratized society that Mises feared. Democracy has not meant mere electoral procedures combined with 19th-century liberal safeguards of life and property, but a perpetual administrative intrusion into the lives of progressively disempowered citizens. One reason for this problem, I would submit, is that liberal democracy is a dangerous mixed regime, which upholds neither liberal freedom nor democratic self-rule. It is the hegemonic ideology of the American political class, invoked to justify the seizure of power by public administrators, privileged corporate interests, social therapists, and mediacrats. The dissociation of liberalism from property rights and a limited franchise, and the divorce between American democracy and any meaningful exercise of self-rule are not accidental. They belong to the strategy of manipulation practiced by those who have benefited from the reconstruction of liberalism and democracy. And essential to the liberal democratic regime that has developed in America since the Progressive Era is an expansionist imperative fueled by what Burke called "armed doctrine." From the perspective of the interventionist doctrine, it is as insensitive or morally callous for the U.S. government and its subjects not to concern themselves with everyone else's human rights.

By now, human rights have become the rhetorical pretext for governmental inroads at home and abroad. Not everyone, mind you, is equally authorized to distill or apply these rights. Journalists, administrators, "experts," and the spokespersons for designated victims are presumed to have a privileged understanding of governing. Thus American intervention in Somalia took place after the media and black civil rights leaders stressed the urgent need for sending American forces into that troubled area. The President

[5]Ibid., pp. 46–53.

consulted with an undersecretary for human rights before dispatching American lives and treasure to Somalia.

Even now media celebrities and journalists are belaboring the President with demands to expand NATO, to micromanage the internal politics of Russia, and to be even more decisive about Bosnia. Human rights require all these entanglements and more, including the punishment of China for not respecting the political sensibilities of American journalists. Though some of these same journalists had jubilated over the tyranny of Maoist China, today the situation is obviously different. Mao's successors are less brutal than was the leader so long revered in the *New York Times* and *Washington Post*, but also less socialistic, and therein lies the rub. By 1994, all the major TV networks were featuring scenes of unemployed and ill-housed Chinese, who are the supposed victims of China's "rush into capitalism." We are told these people are "angry at the system" because of the lack of a safety net. China then is a country to which the American government is being urged to "send a message." Meanwhile, Ben Wattenberg, among legions of other journalists, insists that "we stand tall for human rights."

Despite this pressure for "democratic" intervention and, yes, despite the Jacobin transformation of American democracy, it may be argued that American foreign entanglements have become fewer and less dramatic since the end of the Cold War. Though not totally resistant to formed "public opinion," Clinton went slower than the journalists would have liked in committing American forces to the Bosnian conflict; he also withdrew armies from Somalia, and did little to meddle in Haiti once the military regime had stepped down and the flow of refugees stopped.

It may be suggested that the Clinton administration bears some of the New Left's isolationist baggage. Bill and Hillary Clinton, longtime anti-war protesters concerned with social reconstruction at home, do not come out of the Cold War liberalism exemplified by Hubert Humphrey, George Will, and Jack Kemp. While Clinton may push Secretary of State Warren Christopher to lecture Chinese leaders on human rights, he has not taken stronger action to express his displeasure at their jailing of dissidents. Threats were made against North Korea for developing atomic weapons, but again the Clinton administration pulled back from doing more. Though appeals to democratic triumphalism have resounded from the Clinton administration, they have not lead, for the most part, to a politics of extensive interventionism. This may change if Bob Dole and the Republicans recapture the presidency in 1996 and allow neo-conservatives to guide their foreign policy. The presence of Daniel Pipes, Michael Ledeen, and other democracy spokesmen among Bob Dole's advisors betokens the likely direction that a Republican administration would take internationally. Such a direction is also in keeping with a basic difference between the American Left and American Right. While one side hopes to impose a more thoroughly Jacobin democracy at home, the other plans to do its missionizing elsewhere. Thus, the Left contrives to bring all social relations within the purview of the state, whereas the respectable Right works to exports *its* version of democracy.

Given this division of concerns, there is certainly no reason to believe that American Jacobin crusades are strictly a thing of the past. Our president is eminently susceptible to media pressures and may push harder, for example, the already-scheduled plan for war trials in Bosnia or the implementation of human rights in China. Though our human-rights crusades are popular with intellectuals, it might be useful to speculate on our probable response to such meddling from others. Would we gladly listen to a reactionary Christian foreign power (assuming one existed) that dared to support anti-abortion activists in the U.S. or to protest the imposition of gays on American Christian communities and business establishments? Though this question is obviously rhetorical, it is being used to underline something equally obvious. Except for the military and economic leverage we can exert and the differing values of our intelligentsia, the interventionism being imagined would be no less defensible than what our democracy boosters try to do to others. The fact that they treat their value-preferences as an absolute good does not give them a right to reconstruct other societies, while violating national sovereignty.

Indeed, the success of value-imposition comes down to a question of power, who is in a position to make others bow to his notion of a highest value or of a human right. One suspects that high-placed policymakers may find the impulse to be belligerently "democratic" hard to resist, and a Republican return to executive control could provide the occasion to vent this impulse as an expression of morality. The current regime has taken activist stances abroad, when it has been pushed. A man of the therapeutic Left, President Clinton has focused on expanding the welfare state and deepening sensitivity at home; and he has generally avoided getting out front as commander-in-chief, a position that calls up unhappy memories of his own past as a draft-dodger. A Dole presidency would not be hampered by such hesitations. A former war-hero, surrounded by neoconservative advisors, would likely find its own Jacobin mission beyond our borders.

17
WAR AND THE MONEY MACHINE: CONCEALING THE COSTS OF WAR BENEATH THE VEIL OF INFLATION

Joseph T. Salerno

In every great war monetary calculation was disrupted by inflation. . . . The economic behavior of the belligerents was thereby led astray; the true consequences of the war were removed from their view. One can say without exaggeration that inflation is an indispensable means of militarism. Without it, the repercussions of war on welfare become obvious much more quickly and penetratingly; war weariness would set in much earlier.[1]

[Governments] know that their young men will readily sacrifice their lives and limbs and that their old men will readily sacrifice the lives and limbs of their sons and grandsons, and that their women will readily sacrifice the lives and limbs of their husbands, their sons, and their brothers in what they believe to be a noble cause, but they have a deadly fear— sometimes, but not always, well founded—that women and old men will shrink from pinching the stomachs of themselves and the young children, so that warlike enthusiasm will decay if it once gets about that the association of war with abundance to eat, drink, and wear is delusive, and that there is still truth in the old motto of "Peace and plenty". . . . True that to be pinched by high prices rather than by small money incomes and large taxes made the people rage in the first place against the persons who were supposed to profit and often did profit—most of them quite innocently—by the rise of prices instead of against Government.[2]

[T]he true costs of the war lie in the goods sphere: the used-up goods, the devastation of parts of the country, the loss of manpower, these are the real costs of war to the economies. . . . Like a huge conflagration the war has devoured a huge part of our national wealth, the economy has become poorer. . . . However, in money terms the economy has not become poorer. How is this possible? Simply . . . claims on the state and money tokens have taken the place of stocks of goods in the private economy.[3]

War, huh, what is it good for? Absolutely nothin' . . .
It ain't nothin' but a heartbreaker.
It's got one friend, that's the undertaker. . . .
War can't give life, it can only take it away.[4]

---

[1]Ludwig von Mises, *Nation, State, and Economy: Contributions to the Politics and History of Our Time*, Leland B. Yeager, trans. (New York: New York University Press, 1983), p. 163.

[2]Edwin Cannan, *An Economist's Protest* (New York: Adelphi, 1928), p. 100; also idem, *Money: Its Connection with Rising and Falling Prices*, 6th ed. (Westminster: P.S. King and Son, 1929), p. 99.

[3]Joseph A. Schumpeter, "The Crisis of the Tax State," in idem, *The Economics and Sociology of Capitalism*, Richard Swedberg, ed. (Princeton, N.J.: Princeton University Press, 1991), pp. 118–19.

[4]N. Whitfield and B. Strong, "War," *War and Peace*, Edwin Starr (Detroit: Motown Record Corporation, 1970), audio recording.

As the above quotations trenchantly indicate, war is enormously costly, and inflation is a means by which governments attempt, more or less successfully, to hide these costs from their citizens. For war not only destroys the lives and limbs of the soldiery, but, by progressively consuming the accumulated capital stock of the belligerent nations, eventually shortens and coarsens the lives and shrivels the limbs of the civilian population. While the enormous destruction of productive wealth that war entails would become immediately evident if governments had no recourse but to raise taxes immediately upon the advent of hostilities, their ability to inflate the money supply at will permits them to conceal such destruction behind a veil of rising prices, profits, and wages, stable interest rates, and a booming stock market.

In the following section I explain how war—completely apart from its physical destructiveness—brings about the economic destruction of capital and a consequent decline in labor productivity, real income, and living standards. The argument in this section draws on the Austrian theory of capital as expounded in the works of Ludwig von Mises and the late Murray N. Rothbard. The middle section analyzes the reasons why different methods of war financing will have different effects on the public's perceptions of the costs attending economic mobilization for war. The analysis developed in this section owes much to the classic interwar discussion of inflationary war financing by Mises.[5] The final section concludes the paper with a brief explanation of how inflation constitutes the first step on the road to the fascist economic planning that is typically foisted upon capitalist economies in the course of a large-scale war.

THE ECONOMICS OF WAR

The conduct of war necessitates that scarce resources, previously allocated to the production of capital or consumer goods, be reallocated to the raising, equipping, and sustaining of the nation's fighting forces. While the newly enlisted or inducted military personnel must abandon their jobs in the private economy, they still require food, clothing, and shelter in addition to weapons and other accouterments of war. In practice this means that "nonspecific" resources, such as labor and "convertible" capital goods (e.g., steel, electrical power, trucks, etc.), which are not specific to a single production process, must be diverted from civilian to military production. Given the reduction in the size of the civilian labor force and

[5]Mises, *Nation, State, and Economy*, pp. 151–71.

the conversion of substantial amounts of the remaining labor and capital to the manufacture of military hardware, the general result is a greater scarcity of consumer goods and a decline of real wages and civilian living standards.

However, the transformation of the economy to a war footing implies much more than merely a "horizontal" reallocation of factors from consumer goods to military production. It also entails a "vertical" shift of resources from the "higher" stages of production to the "lower" stages of production, that is, from the production and maintenance of capital goods temporally remote from the service of the ultimate consumers to the production of war goods for present use. For, as Mises points out, "War can be waged only with present goods."[6] But in substituting the production of tanks, bombs, and small arms destined for immediate use for the replacement and repair of mining and oil drilling equipment intended to maintain the flow of future consumer goods, the economy is shortening its time structure of production and thus "consuming" its capital. Initially, this capital consumption is manifested in the idleness of fixed capital goods that cannot be converted to immediate war production (e.g, plants and equipment producing oil drilling machinery), and the simultaneous overutilization of fixed capital goods that can be so converted (e.g., auto assembly plants now used to produce military vehicles). In the short-run, then, the flow of present goods or "real income," in the form of war goods and consumer goods, may actually rise, even in the face of a loss of part of the labor force to military service. But as years pass, and industrial and agricultural equipment is worn out and not replaced, real income inevitably declines—possibly precipitously—below its previous peacetime level.

Schumpeter has provided a graphic summary of the horizontal and vertical shift of resources caused by the exigencies of a war economy and the deleterious effect of the latter on the capital stock:

> First, "war economy" essentially means switching the economy from production for the needs of a peaceful life to production for the needs of warfare. This means in the first place that the available means of production are used in some part to produce different final goods, chiefly of course war materials, and in the most part to produce the same products as before but for other customers than in peacetime. This means, furthermore, that the available means of production are mainly used to produce as many goods for immediate consumption as possible to the detriment of the production of means of production—particularly machinery

[6]Ibid., p. 168.

and industrial plant—so that part of production that in peacetime takes up so much room, namely the production for the maintenance and expansion of the productive apparatus, decreases more and more. The possibility to do just this, that is to use for immediate consumption goods, labor, and capital which previously had made producer's goods and thus only indirectly contributed to the production of consumer's goods (i.e., which made "future" rather than "present" goods to use the technical terminology), this possibility was our great reserve which has saved us so far and which has prevented the stream of consumer's goods from drying up completely. . . . Our poverty will be brought home to us to its full extent only after the war. Only then will the worn-out machines, the run-down buildings, the neglected land, the decimated livestock, the devastated forests, bear witness to the full depth of the effects of the war.[7]

In commenting upon the effects of World War I on the British economy, Edwin Cannan also drew attention to the crucial fact of the vertical shift of resources and the capital consumption it implies, observing that

during the war addition to material equipment at home and foreign property abroad wholly ceased. The labor thus set free was made available for war-production and for the production of immediately-consumable peace-goods. [Moreover] every one conversant with business knows that renewals, if not repairs, have been very seriously postponed in all branches of production and that stocks of everything have run down enormously. The labor which would in ordinary times have been keeping up the material equipment was diverted to war-production and the production of immediately consumable peace-goods. . . . It was chiefly the tapping of these resources that enabled the country as a whole to get through the war with so little privation.[8]

It may be objected that, empirically, the vertical shift of resources is likely to be trivial, because "investment" constitutes such a small segment of real output and therefore the increase in the output of war goods must come mainly from resources diverted from the consumer goods' industries combined with a reduction of the leisure of the civilian population, i.e., through increased overtime and labor participation rates. But this fallacious consumer belt-tightening theory of war economy is based on the Keynesian national income accounting framework, according to which capital investment constitutes a small fraction of total GDP. For example, during the fourth quarter of 1994, the annual rate of real gross private investment in the U.S. totaled $939.7 billion or slightly more

---

[7]Schumpeter, "The Crisis of the Tax State," p. 127.
[8]Cannan, *An Economist's Protest*, p. 183.

than 17 percent of real GDP while real personal consumption expenditures in the same quarter equaled $3629.6 billion or almost 67 percent of real GDP.[9]

Unfortunately, in this framework, the investment in "intermediate inputs" is netted out to avoid "double counting." These intermediate inputs to a great extent comprise precisely those types of capital goods, namely, stocks of raw materials, semi-finished products, and energy inputs, that can most readily be converted for use in the production of present goods, whether for military or consumption purposes. As Mises observes, this is one form that capital consumption took in Germany during World War I: "The German economy entered the war with an abundant stock of raw materials and semi-finished goods of all kinds. In peacetime, whatever of these stocks were devoted to use or consumption was regularly replaced. During the war the stocks were consumed without being able to be replaced. They disappeared out of the economy; the national wealth was reduced by their value."[10] These future or higher-stage goods permanently "disappeared" because the resources previously invested in their reproduction had been withdrawn in order to augment the production of war materials.

In fact, in a modern, capital-using economy, at any given moment during peacetime, the aggregate value of resources devoted to the production and maintenance of capital goods in the higher stages of production far exceeds the value of resources working to directly serve consumers in the final stage of the production process. As an example, for the U.S. economy in 1982, total business expenditures on intermediate inputs plus gross private investment totaled $3,196.7 billion while personal consumer expenditures totaled $2,046.4 billion. Over 60 percent of the available productive resources, outside the government sector, was therefore devoted to the production of capital or future goods as opposed to consumer or present goods.[11]

THE FINANCING OF WAR

Governments have at their disposal three methods for financing a war: taxation, borrowing from the public, and monetary inflation or the creation of new money. Governments may also resort

[9]Federal Reserve Bank of St. Louis, *National Economic Trends* 4 (May 1995): 18–19.
[10]Mises, *Nation, State, and Economy*, p. 162.
[11]Mark Skousen, *The Structure of Production* (New York: New York University Press, 1990), pp. 191–92. On the critical importance for analyzing the capital structure of a concept of "gross investment" that includes both investment in fixed capital and investment in intermediate inputs in all stages of production, see Murray N. Rothbard, *Man, Economy, and State: A Treatise on Economic Principles*, 2nd ed. (Auburn, Ala: Ludwig von Mises Institute, 1993), pp. 339–45.

to coercive requisitioning, that is, confiscating the material resources and conscripting the labor services they deem necessary for the
war effort without compensation or in exchange for below-market
prices and wage rates. Historically, a combination of these methods has generally been used to effect the transfer of resources from
civilian to military uses during a large-scale war. From the view-
point of technical economic theory, however, the government
could always realize the funds necessary to carry out its war aims
exclusively from increased taxation and non-inflationary borrowing on capital markets. As Schumpeter pointed out with regard to
Austria, immediately after World War I, "It is clear that strictly
speaking we could have squeezed the necessary money out of the
private economy just as the goods were squeezed out of it. This
could have been done by taxes which would have looked stifling,
but which would in fact have been no more oppressive than the
devaluation of money which was their alternative."[12]

Why, then, if strictly fiscal measures are capable of yielding
sufficient revenues to pay market prices for all the resources required to conduct war, have belligerent governments almost always taken recourse to the methods of monetary inflation and the
direct commandeering of commodities and services? The answer
lies in the fact that war is an extremely costly enterprise and the
latter two methods, although in very different ways, operate to
partially conceal these costs from the public's view.[13] When the

[12]Schumpeter, "The Crisis of the Tax State," p. 121. Despite his general stance
against inflationary financing of war, Schumpeter does concede that "it is everywhere impossible completely to cover the cost of war by taxation, from the point of
view both of politics and fiscal technique" (p. 121). Mises and Cannan are even
firmer than Schumpeter in their views that inflation is not technically necessary to
finance a major war. For the latter two, whatever quantity of resources can be extracted from the private economy by inflationary finance can also be appropriated
via taxation and non-inflationary borrowing. See Mises, *Nation, State, and Economy*,
pp. 151–71; and Edwin Cannan, *Money: Its Connection with Rising and Falling Prices*,
pp. 93–102. It should be noted however that Mises maintained that market incentives could never be rendered attractive enough in practice to attract sufficient manpower to serve in the armed forces under war conditions and that, therefore, conscription was a necessary supplement to market transactions financed by taxes and
borrowing (Mises, *Nation, State, and Economy*, p. 165). Mises here not only argues
that the supply curve of enlistees is inelastic but also implicitly assumes that it is
fixed under all circumstances, seemingly ignoring the possibility that a spontaneous
shift to the right in the supply curve will occur in the case of a war fought in defense of hearth and home or for a cause that is widely and passionately believed to
be just.

[13]Not all pre-Keynesian economists acceded to the Mises–Schumpeter–Cannan position that inflation is not theoretically or practically necessary for financing a major
war. Two of their prominent contemporaries, A.C. Pigou and Lionel Robbins, insisted that inflationary finance and direct government controls are an inescapable
part of a war economy. See A.C. Pigou, *The Political Economy of War*, 2nd ed. (New
York: Macmillan, 1941); also Lionel Robbins, *The Economic Problem in Peace and War:
Some Reflections on Objectives and Mechanisms* (London: Macmillan, 1950). Beginning

public is accurately apprised of its full costs, war becomes increasingly unpopular, civilian enthusiasm and labor efforts flag, and unrest and even active resistance may ensue on the homefront and spread to the frontlines. The movement for "revolutionary defeatism" successfully fomented by Russia's Bolsheviks during World War I is just one example of such mass resistance.

As Robert Higgs points out with regard to the tendency of governments to partially substitute a command-and-control economy for the regular fiscal mechanism during wartime and other so-called national emergencies:

> Obviously, citizens will not react to the costs they bear if they are unaware of them. The possibility of driving a wedge between the actual and the publicly perceived costs creates a strong temptation for governments pursuing high-cost policies during national emergencies. Except where lives are being sacrificed, no costs are so easily counted as pecuniary costs. Not only can each individual count them (his own tax bill); they can be easily aggregated for the whole society (the government's total tax revenue). It behooves a government wishing to sustain a policy that entails suddenly heightened costs to find ways of substituting nonpecuniary for pecuniary costs. The substitution may blunt the citizen's realization of how great their sacrifices really are and hence diminish their protests and resistance.[14]

The direct expropriation of resources works best when the resources in question are non-reproducible, as in the case of labor. By legally compelling its citizen-subjects to serve a specified term in military service at wage rates far below market levels, the government significantly reduces the budgetary costs of war and thus the amount by which it must ratchet up taxes. The cost concealment this facilitates explains the widespread use of mass conscription especially by almost all modern mass democracies beginning with

---

in the early post-World War II era, neo-Keynesian economists, who were, like Keynes himself, totally innocent of capital theory, turned the older approach to war economics on its head, arguing that war spending, like any other kind of spending, operates through the multiplier process, automatically generating full employment and, therefore, economic prosperity, and is likely to create an "inflationary gap" in the macro economy. They therefore concluded that the conduct of war is inherently inflationary and necessitates extensive government controls over prices, production, and labor markets to repress inflation and prevent it from undermining the war economy. For examples of the neo-Keynesian approach to "defense" economics, see Albert G. Hart, *Defense without Inflation* (New York: Twentieth Century Fund, 1951); see also Donald H. Wallace, *Economic Controls and Defense* (New York: Twentieth Century Fund, 1953). For a long overdue and superb demolition of the Keynesian claim that World War II brought prosperity to the U.S. economy, see Robert Higgs, "Wartime Prosperity? A Reassessment of the U.S. Economy in the 1940's," *The Journal of Economic History* 52 (March 1992): 41–60.

[14]Robert Higgs, *Crisis and Leviathan: Critical Episodes in the Growth of American Government* (New York: Oxford University Press, 1987), p. 65.

revolutionary France. But uncompensated confiscation of reproducible resources confronts an insuperable difficulty: while it does yield access to existing stocks of resources, it destroys the incentive on the part of private individuals and firms to reproduce these resources.

Continuation of industrial production processes requires pecuniary compensation to the producers as determined by the market, unless the government is willing to completely abolish exchange and implement a totally moneyless (and particularly chaotic) form of socialism, in which resources are allocated and the products distributed by bureaucratic ukase. This was attempted by the Bolsheviks during the period known as War Communism in the U.S.S.R. from 1918 to 1920 and proved a miserable failure. While governments of mass democracies admittedly went a long way toward replacing market incentives and processes with substantial elements of the centrally planned or command-and-control economy during the two great wars of the 20th century, at least at the inception of hostilities, they still required a cost-concealing device that would yield them the money revenues with which to purchase real resources from their still operative money-exchange economies. For this purpose, they consolidated the power to issue money in the hands of their central banks. Thus it was, for example, that within days of the outbreak of World War I each and every one of the belligerent governments suspended the operation of the gold standard, effectively arrogating to itself the monopoly of the supply of money in its own national territory.

To grasp how the issuing of new money obscures and distorts the true costs of war, we first must analyze the case of financing a war exclusively through the imposition of increased taxes supplemented with borrowing from the public. Prior to the increase of taxes and issue of government securities to raise war revenues, the national economy is operating with an aggregate capital structure whose size is determined by the "time preferences" or intertemporal consumption choices of the consumer-savers. The lower the public's time preferences, and therefore the more willing its members are to postpone consumption from the immediate to the more remote future, the greater is the proportion of current income that is saved and invested in building up an integrated structure of capital goods. The greater the stock of capital goods, in turn, the greater the productivity of labor and the higher the real wage rate earned by all classes of workers.[15]

---

[15]For detailed explications of the time-preference theory of interest, see Rothbard, *Man, Economy, and State,* pp. 313–86; and Ludwig von Mises, *Human Action: A Treatise on Economics,* 3rd ed. (Chicago: Henry Regnery, 1966), pp. 479–536. A recent

From the point of view of individual investors in the capital structure—business proprietors, stockholders, bondholders, insurance policyholders—the value of their titles and claims to capital goods are revealed by monetary calculation, specifically, capital accounting, and are therefore conceived as sums of monetary wealth.[16] Thus, the accumulation or consumption of capital, *ceteris paribus*—in particular, assuming the purchasing power of money is roughly stable—will always be readily evident in the changing monetary wealth positions of at least some individuals. This will especially be manifested in movements in the stock and real-estate markets, which are devoted largely to the exchange of titles to aggregates of capital goods.[17] In addition, enlargements or diminutions of the capital stock will be manifested in fluctuations in current incomes—in aggregate pecuniary profits in the economy and in the general levels of salaries and wages.

As pointed out above, large-scale war involves a marked increase in preferences for present goods and necessitates a thoroughgoing reorientation of society's productive apparatus away from future and toward present goods. To effectuate this temporal restructuring of production in a money-exchange economy, there must occur a radical alteration in the flows of money expenditure, with consumption and military spending rising relative to saving-investment. Regardless of what technique is utilized to accomplish this shift in relative expenditure, it must give rise to a "retrogressing economy" during the transition to the war economy. The retrogressing economy is one characterized by a declining capital stock. Its onset is marked by a "crisis" involving aggregate business losses, rising interest rates, plunging stock, bond, and real-estate markets, and a deflation of financial asset values.[18]

---

defense and clarification of the theory is found in Israel M. Kirzner, "The Pure Time-Preference Theory of Interest: An Attempt at Clarification," in *The Meaning of Ludwig von Mises: Contributions in Economics, Sociology, Epistemology, and Political Philosophy*, Jeffrey M. Herbener, ed. (Norwell, Mass.: Kluwer Academic Publishers, 1993), pp. 166–92. An illuminating and concise overview can be found in Roger W. Garrison, "Professor Rothbard and the Theory of Interest," in *Man, Economy, and Liberty: Essays in Honor of Murray N. Rothbard*, Walter Block and Llewellyn H. Rockwell, Jr., eds. (Auburn, Ala.: Ludwig von Mises Institute, 1988), pp. 44–55.

[16]As Mises explains: "Monetary calculation reaches its full perfection in capital accounting. It establishes the money prices of the available means and confronts this total with changes brought about by action and by the operation of other factors. This confrontation shows what changes occurred in the state of the acting men's affairs and the magnitude of those changes; it makes success and failure, profit and loss ascertainable," *Human Action*, p. 230.

[17]Thus, as Rothbard points out, "Stocks . . . are *units of title to masses of capital goods*," and "real estate [conveys] units of title of capital in land," Murray N. Rothbard, *America's Great Depression* (Kansas City: Sheed and Ward, 1975), p. 316 n. 29.

[18]For an explanation of the concept of a retrogressing economy and the accompanying crisis, see Rothbard, *Man, Economy, and State*, pp. 483–86; and Mises, *Human*

When taxes are raised to finance the war, the crisis is immediately evident. In order to pay their increased tax liabilities, citizens retrench on their saving as well as their consumption. In fact, they reduce their saving proportionally more than their consumption, for two reasons. First, assuming an increase in the income tax, the net interest return on investment is lowered, meaning that the investor can now expect less future consumption in exchange for a given amount of saving or abstinence from present consumption. If his time preference remains unchanged, the worsened terms of trade between present and future goods encourages the taxpayer to escape the tax by increasing spending on present consumption and reducing saving and, thereby, his prospects for future consumption. With all saver-investors responding in this manner, the aggregate supply of savings will decrease and the interest rate will be driven up to reflect the increased tax on investment income.

Second, moreover, because the incidence of the increased tax always falls on his *present* income and monetary assets, it leaves the taxpayer less well provided with present goods. As his supply of present goods diminishes toward the bare subsistence level—at which point the premium he attaches to present over future consumption becomes approximately infinite—the individual experiences a progressive rise in his time preference, and the prevailing (after-tax) interest rate no longer suffices as adequate compensation for sustaining his current level of saving-investment. He accordingly further reduces the proportion of his income allocated to saving-investment.[19]

Finally, as a means of quickly generating the enormous revenues typically required at the outset of a large-scale war, the government might seek to tap, in addition to current income, accumulated capital. This most likely would involve a wealth tax that is levied on each household in some proportion to the market value of the property it owns, including and especially its cash balances. The tax, if it were uniformly enforced on all categories of wealth, would force capitalist-entrepreneurs to liquidate or issue debt against their real assets in order to discharge their tax liability. By its very nature, then, a wealth tax results directly in the consumption of capital. Moreover, even though such a tax is levied on net wealth accumulated in the past, it operates to powerfully increase time preferences and reduce savings even further, because it must

---

Action, pp. 250–51, 294–400; and F.A. Hayek, "Capital Consumption," in idem, *Money, Capital and Fluctuations: Early Essays*, Roy McCloughary, ed. (Chicago: University of Chicago Press, 1984), pp. 136–58.

[19]On these two effects of the income tax, see Rothbard, *Man, Economy, and State*, pp. 797–99.

be paid out of present income and monetary assets and the prospect of its recurrence can easily be precluded by completely consuming income as it is received and by consuming whatever privately-owned capital remains.[20]

While the incidence of war taxes falls disproportionately on private saving-investment and wealth, the tax revenues thus appropriated are expended by the belligerent government mainly on present goods in the form of military services and equipment for immediate use. As in the case of an increase in the consumption–saving ratio that would follow from an autonomous increase in the social time-preference rate, the "pure" or "real" interest rate that underlies the structure of risk-adjusted loan rates of return on investment is driven up. The higher loan rates and the attendant fall in the market appraisals of debt and equity securities operate to discourage business borrowing and dampen investment in maintaining and reproducing the existing capital structure. The result is a contraction of the demand for capital goods and the sudden onset of "crisis" conditions.

The consequent decline in the prices of capital goods relative to consumer–military goods reflects the greater discount on future *vis-à-vis* present goods that is revealed in the higher interest rate, and it results in losses for firms in higher stages of the production structure. In the aggregate, the losses of firms producing capital goods exceed the profits gained by the firms favored by the enhanced military expenditures. The appearance of aggregate losses in the capital-consuming or retrogressing economy is ultimately attributable to the fact that the productivity of labor and real income

---

[20]An analysis of taxes on accumulated capital or wealth can be found in Murray N. Rothbard, *Power and Market: Government and the Economy* (Menlo Park, Calif.: Institute for Humane Studies, 1970), pp. 83–84, 87–88. As an important measure of war finance, Pigou advocates a progressive tax on personal wealth, defined broadly to include durable consumer goods and "the capitalized value of a man's mental and manual powers," Pigou, The *Political Economy of War*, p. 84. Mises views short-term government borrowing as a preferable alternative to a tax on personal wealth. Mises, *Nation, State, and Economy*, pp. 166–67. Pigou also considers borrowing as economically substitutable for a wealth tax, but prefers the latter on grounds of equity, viz., it compels "the rich" to bear a greater proportion of the burdens of war. By the way, Pigou misses the point when he claims that "the costs of a war can [not] be paid out of capital. . . . The *source* of the funds raised must be the real income of the country." Pigou, *The Political Economy of War*, p. 84 n. 1. The result of capital consumption induced by the wealth tax is precisely an increase in present real income at the expense of future real income as convertible capital goods and labor are shifted toward the production of present goods. As Hayek pertinently remarks concerning taxes levied on capital: "Even though the production facilities which correspond to these sums of capital do not disappear from the face of the earth, the diversion of these sums for the purpose of consumption (or war) still cannot fail to bring about a corresponding reduction in the stock of capital equipment in the final analysis." Hayek, "Capital Consumption," p. 153.

are declining as resources are bid away from capital goods production by the increased military expenditures. These transitional, though highly visible, losses suffered by business firms are the first step in the process of imputing the decline of marginal productivities attendant upon the dissipation of the capital stock back to the incomes of labor and natural resources.[21]

The capital-decumulation crisis is also manifested in a crash of the stock market because, as noted above, stocks represent titles to *pro rata* shares of ownership in existing complements of capital goods known as "business firms." It is precisely the values of the prospective future outputs of a firm's productive assets, particularly its fixed capital goods, that are suddenly more heavily discounted in appraising the capital value of the firm. This is especially true of firms that are themselves producing durable capital goods or inputs into these goods. The overall decline in the market's estimation of the capitalized value of various business assets that is indicated by the fall in value of equity and debt securities, of course, reflects not only current business losses but is precisely how monetary calculation reveals the fact of capital decumulation. A drop in real-estate markets would also occur at the inception of a tax-financed transition to a war economy, because industrial and commercial construction and land represent particularly durable resources whose capital values are therefore extremely sensitive to a higher rate of discount on future goods. Even if such capital goods may be converted to current military production, their values would still have to be lowered to reflect the waste of capital involved in their construction. Thus, if the exigencies of war had been anticipated, labor and other nonspecific resources would not have been "locked up" in them for such lengthy periods of time.[22]

Similar to business-cycle crises, war-mobilization crises will also feature certain secondary, although highly visible, financial and monetary aspects. Many highly leveraged firms in higher-stage industries, confronted by slumping output prices, will attempt to fend off the prospect of defaulting on their debts by undertaking a "scramble for liquidity," which drives up short-term interest rates, raises the demand for money, and sharply lowers the prices of commodities that are dumped on the market for quick

---

[21]On this process of imputation, see Rothbard, *Man, Economy, and State*, pp. 483–84; and Mises, *Human Action*, pp. 294–300.

[22]According to Mises, some capital goods "can be employed for the new process without any alteration; but if it had been known at the time they were produced that they would be used in the new way, it would have been possible to manufacture at smaller cost other goods which could render the same service," *Human Action*, p. 503.

cash. This will precipitate a general fall in prices, which will then intensify and extend the liquidity scramble. Actual and threatened defaults on bank loans and other securities also will begin to erode confidence in the soundness of the financial system. Even if the fractional-reserve banking system bears up under the strain, sparing the economy a collapse of the money supply and a "secondary depression," the conspicuous bankruptcies of banks and business firms, reinforced by the sharp decline in private-financial wealth and after-tax incomes, will quickly disabuse the populace of any notion that war breeds prosperity.

The government will be unable to avoid, and may even exacerbate, the mobilization crisis by substituting borrowing for higher tax levies. The reason is that, in contrast to taxes, which must be paid out of present income and monetary assets and therefore reduce both private consumption and saving (in accordance with taxpayers' time preferences), government borrowing directly taps saving. When selling securities, the government competes with business for the public's saved funds, and, because it is capable of bidding up the interest rate it is willing to pay practically without limit, it is in the position to obtain all the funds it needs. As Rothbard concludes, "Public borrowing strikes at individual *savings* more effectively even than taxation, for it specifically lures away *savings* rather than taxing income in general."[23]

With a qualification to be mentioned shortly, by thus "crowding out" private investment to acquire the funds for war financing, government borrowing insures that the entire burden of adjustment to a war economy is borne solely by the capital goods industries. The adjustment is now exclusively vertical, because consumption is not diminished, obviating any horizontal reallocation of resources. Mises thus compares government borrowing to a kind of tax on accumulated capital in its devastating effect on the capital structure: "If current expenditure, however beneficial it may be considered, is financed by taking away by inheritance taxes those parts of higher incomes which would have been employed for investment, or by borrowing, the government becomes a factor making for capital consumption."[24]

Because it brings about capital consumption beyond that of tax financing, government borrowing promotes a more severe crisis. Thus, for example, on the eve of the outbreak of World War I, between July 23 and July 31, and before the would-be belligerent

---

[23]Rothbard, *Man, Economy, and State*, p. 881.
[24]Mises, *Human Action*, p. 850. For an analysis of the inheritance tax as a pure tax on capital, see Rothbard, *Power and Market*, pp. 84–85.

States had "gone off" the gold standard and began inflating their respective national money supplies, panic selling forced the closing of all major stock exchanges from St. Petersburg and Vienna to Toronto and New York. Certainly, this broad decline in the market value of stocks was partially attributable to general uncertainty of the future and an increased demand for liquidity.[25] But it also represented a response to expectations of heavy government borrowing to finance war mobilization under the non-inflationary conditions of the gold standard.

The British economist Ralph G. Hawtrey aptly described the initial stages of this mobilization crisis and the frantic attempts of government to suppress it by swift resort to legal-debt moratoria and bank-credit inflation:

> The prospect of forced borrowing by the Government on a large scale will stifle the demand for existing stock exchange securities, and stock exchange operators and underwriters will find themselves loaded up with securities which are saleable, if at all, only at a great sacrifice. The disorganization of business may be so great that an almost universal bankruptcy can only be staved off by special measures for suspending the obligations of debtors, like the crop of moratorium statutes with which Europe blossomed out in 1914.
>
> A Government, indeed, faced with a great war, cannot afford to let half the business of the country slip into bankruptcy, and . . . the embarrassed traders are propped up, either by lavish advances granted them by arrangement, or by a special statutory moratorium.[26]

As noted, there is an important qualification to our conclusion that the substitution of government borrowing for taxation will exacerbate the mobilization crisis. Even if the monetary costs of war are paid for entirely by borrowing, the resulting adjustment of the real economy will not be entirely vertical, because the supply of savings is more or less "elastic" or sensitive with respect to changes in the interest rate. Consequently, as the government's fiscal agent bids up interest rates, some members of the public will be induced to voluntarily reduce their present consumption, to a greater or lesser extent, in order to take advantage of the increased premium in terms of the enhanced future consumption per dollar of foregone present consumption promised by the higher-yielding securities. In fact, if the public's structure of time preferences makes

[25]Benjamin M. Anderson, *Economics and the Public Welfare: A Financial and Economic History of the United States, 1914–1946* (Indianapolis, Ind.: Liberty Press, [1949] 1979), pp. 28–29.

[26]Ralph G. Hawtrey, *Currency and Credit* (New York: Arno Press, [1919] 1979), pp. 210–11.

them sufficiently sensitive to rising interest rates in determining their own consumption-saving ratio, the consumer-good industries may even come to bear a larger burden of adjustment than they would under tax financing.

In any case, we conclude that, when undistorted by monetary inflation, regardless of the fiscal technique or combination of techniques employed, economic calculation clearly and immediately reveals to market participants, individually and in the aggregate, the enormous destruction of real wealth and decline in real income entailed in mobilizing for a large-scale war. What insures this result is monetary calculation based on genuine market prices. Indeed, as Mises points out, "The market economy is real because it can calculate. . . . Among the main tasks of economic calculation are those of establishing the magnitudes of income, saving, and capital consumption."[27]

Individual capital goods, even so-called fixed capital equipment, wear out in production and, in a world of unceasing change, must be replaced by physically different goods. The capital structure is thus undergoing a physical transformation at every instant of time. This means that capitalist-entrepreneurs, who must continually adjust the production processes under their control to changing consumer preferences, technical innovations, and resource availabilities must have recourse to a common denominator in order to determine the outcome of their past production decisions and to assess the resulting quantity of productive resources they currently can dispose of as a starting point for future decisions.

In other words, only the market's pricing process provides the meaningful cardinal numbers needed by entrepreneurs to calculate their costs, revenues, profits, and quantity of capital. Given the continual change in market conditions that impels constant adjustment of the real capital structure and given the vast physical heterogeneity of the complementary capital goods that constitute this structure, in the absence of monetary calculation utilizing genuine market prices, it becomes impossible for a producer not only to quantitatively appraise his capital and income, but to meaningfully conceive a distinction between them. Thus, without the guidance of capital accounting, there would be no telling how much of the gross receipts from his business the entrepreneur could allocate to his present consumption without dissipating his capital and therefore his ability to provide for future wants.[28]

[27]Mises, *Human Action*, p. 261.

[28]Mises writes, "Economic calculation is either an estimate of the expected outcome of future action or the establishment of the outcome of past action. But the latter

As we have learned from the socialist-calculation debate, in the absence of monetary calculation using genuine market prices, rational allocation of resources is impossible. By proscribing private property in the so-called "means of production," socialist central planning effectively eradicates markets and prices for capital goods, thereby bringing about the abolition of monetary calculation and the inevitable destruction of the existing capital structure.[29] While the effects of monetary inflation on economic calculation are not as manifestly devastating as outright socialization, at least initially, it nonetheless operates insidiously to falsify profit and capital calculations. One of the main reasons why inflation distorts monetary calculation is because accounting must assume a stability of the value of money which does not exist in reality. Nonetheless, where fluctuations in the purchasing power of money are minor, as is the case with market-based commodity moneys represented historically especially by the gold standard, this assumption does not practically affect the monetary calculations and appraisements of entrepreneurs. A mighty and complex structure of capital goods was built up under the 19th-century gold standard using precisely such methods of calculation.

However, when government operating through a central bank deliberately orchestrates a significant fiat money inflation to pay for a war or for any other purpose, matters are much different. The resulting large decrease in the purchasing power of money, to the extent that it is not recognized and immediately adapted to in accounting procedures, will inescapably falsify business calculations. Moreover, prices in general do not adjust instantaneously upward in response to the increase in the money supply; rather, the fall in the overall purchasing power of money is the final outcome of a time-consuming, sequential adjustment process involving a distortion of relative prices, including the interest rate or the price ratio

---

does not serve merely historical and didactic aims. Its practical meaning is to show how much one is free to consume without impairing the future capacity to produce. It is with regard to this problem that the fundamental notions of economic calculation—capital and income, profit and loss, spending and saving, cost and yield—are developed," *Human Action*, pp. 210–11. See also pp. 230, 260–62, 491, and 514–15.

[29]For recent views of the socialist-calculation debate that emphasize Mises's original thesis that socialism is "impossible" precisely because it lacks the means of economic calculation, see Joseph T. Salerno, "Ludwig von Mises as Social Rationalist," *Review of Austrian Economics* 4 (1990): 36–49; also idem, "Why a Socialist Economy Is 'Impossible,'" Postscript to Ludwig von Mises, *Economic Calculation in the Socialist Commonwealth*,. S. Adler, trans. (Auburn, Ala.: Praxeology Press, 1990); idem, Reply to Leland B. Yeager on "Mises and Hayek on Calculation and Knowledge," *Review of Austrian Economics* 7, no. 2 (1994): 111–25; and Murray N. Rothbard, "The End of Socialism and the Calculation Debate Revisited," *Review of Austrian Economics* 5, no. 2 (1991): 51–76.

between present and future goods.[30] Both of these effects operate to conceal the process of capital consumption during its early stages.

Under modern conditions, inflationary finance of war involves a government "monetizing" its debt by selling securities, directly or indirectly, to the central bank. The funds thus obtained are then spent on the items necessary to equip and sustain the armed forces of the nation. The result is a sudden expansion of demand for the products of the military and consumer-good industries, with no reduction in the monetary demand for the products of the capital-good industries. A boom is consequently precipitated, featuring rising prices, profits, and stock values in the former industries. The boom is particularly intense and dazzling in these industries because, during an inflation, prices rise in temporal sequence. Thus, prices and nominal incomes initially increase only for those sellers who receive the new money in the first round of spending and, therefore, before the prices of the productive inputs and consumer goods they themselves regularly purchase have had a chance to rise. As Mises concludes, "The war suppliers . . . have therefore gained not only from enjoying good business in the ordinary sense of the word but also from the fact that the additional quantity of money flowed first to them. The price rise of the goods and services that they brought to market was a double one, it was caused first by the increased demand for their labor, but then too by the increased supply of money."[31]

Because the increase in the demand for credit represented by the Treasury's issuance of securities is met by newly-created bank credit, on the one hand, market interest rates do not initially rise. On the other hand, the higher prices for consumer and war goods eventually spread up the ladder of the structure of production and result in higher prices for the capital-good inputs produced by the higher-stage firms. With their higher prospective earnings discounted by an unchanged interest rate, equity values increase for these firms also. War appears to breed universal prosperity.

Nonetheless, capital consumption is proceeding apace, with aggregate real losses being suffered especially by higher-order firms. The reason why these firms do not discern their losses and progressive decapitalization is because of their accounting practices, which served them so well during the prewar period of roughly stable prices. Thus, despite the depreciating monetary

---

[30]On the long-run non-neutrality of the monetary-adjustment process, see Ludwig von Mises, *The Theory of Money and Credit*, H.E. Batson, trans., 3rd ed. (Indianapolis, Ind.: Liberty Classics, 1981), pp. 160–68; also Joseph Salerno, "Ludwig von Mises on Inflation and Expectation," *Advances in Austrian Economics* 2b (1995): 297–325.

[31]Mises, *Nation, State, and Economy*, p. 158.

unit, they continue to carry their fixed capital equipment on their books at historical cost, calculating their depreciation quotas accordingly. Even though some of their costs, especially wage rates, are continually driven up by the inflation-fueled bidding of the producers of military and selected consumer goods, capital-good firms, nevertheless, appear to be earning profits as their output prices continue ever upward with a lag. It is only when it comes to replacing their plant and machinery—possibly years down the road—at the much higher "replacement cost" reflecting monetary depreciation that their decline in capital will at last become evident. Moreover, in many cases, the entrepreneurs will then discover that they themselves inadvertently exacerbated this capital consumption by spending their illusory pecuniary profits, which were actually part of their depreciation quotas, on high living and other forms of present consumption.

The Austrian economist, Fritz Machlup, illustrates this process of consumption of working capital with a striking example drawn from the Austrian inflation initiated during World War I:

> A dealer bought a thousand tons of copper. He sold them, as prices rose, with considerable profit. He consumed only half of the profit and saved the other half. He invested again in copper and got several hundred tons. Prices rose and rose. The dealer's profit was enormous; he could afford to travel and to buy cars, country houses, and what not. He also saved and invested again in copper. His money capital was now a high multiple of his initial one. After repeated transactions—he always could afford to live a luxurious life—he invested his whole capital, grown to an astronomical amount, in a few pounds of copper. While he and the public considered him a profiteer of the highest income, he had in reality eaten up his capital.[32]

WAR INFLATION AND THE ROAD TO ECONOMIC FASCISM

Even after the monetary inflation manifests itself in a general rise in prices, the public can still be misled into believing that these price increases are the result of temporary shortages of essential materials or the machinations of unscrupulous war profiteers and price-gougers. It is only a matter of time, however, before workers and investors outside the military–industrial complex come to recognize that a depreciating monetary unit is a permanent feature of the war economy and their eroding real wages and illusory profits are brought clearly and painfully into focus. To postpone the day of accurate reckoning of the costs of war yet again, the

[32]Fritz Machlup, "The Consumption of Capital in Austria," *Review of Economic Statistics* 17 (January 1935): 16.

government implements price controls. As a result of the inevitable shortages and inefficiencies generated by price controls, the government frantically institutes and then rapidly expands controls over production, distribution, and labor, until very little is left of the market economy and its capital structure. The final outcome of this process is an economy in which, although productive resources are still nominally privately owned, the State has effectively arrogated to itself the power to make all crucial production decisions. The all-encompassing war economy is, ultimately and inescapably, a fascist economy.[33]

Guenter Reiman has fittingly entitled his book on the fascist economic system of Nazi Germany, *The Vampire Economy*, because, as a permanent war economy, it systematically and madly consumes the capital, the very lifeblood, of the host capitalist economy. And to enforce the compliance of its citizens in this painfully self-destructive course, an all-powerful state is indispensable. As Reiman puts it: "[I]t is impossible to foretell when a military system will collapse as a result of a deficiency in foodstuffs, raw materials or other economic factors. As long as the state machine is in order, it has the power to cut down the consumption of the general public and to reduce—almost to eliminate—expenditures for the renewal of the industrial machine. . . . It is possible to increase production of arms and ammunition even with reduced supplies of raw materials. This can be done by drastically limiting production of consumption goods, by putting the population on starvation rations, and by letting vast sectors of the economy decay."[34] In Germany, for example, despite the fact that total production had increased from prewar levels as a result of the plundering of the

[33]As Charlotte Twight perceptively argues, "Fascism is unique among collectivist systems in selecting capitalism as its nominal economic mate, but capitalism is turned inside out in this unlikely union. . . . [F]ascism tolerates the *form* of private ownership at the government's pleasure, but it eliminates any meaningful right of private property. . . . Fascist capitalism is 'regulated' capitalism; it is government intervention in the economy on a massive scale," Charlotte Twight, *America's Emerging Fascist Economy* (New Rochelle, N.Y.: Arlington House Publishers, 1975), pp. 16–17. Avraham Barkai characterizes the Nazi economy in similar terms: "The market still existed but was not a free market, and most decisions taken by the owners of enterprise were not free, either. The term 'organized capitalism' suits this economic method, subject only to the reservation that organization was imposed from above by extraeconomic, that is, political factors; it was these factors that were responsible for directing the economy in accordance with basically noneconomic considerations. It was therefore a capitalist economy in which capitalists, like all other citizens, were not free even though they enjoyed a privileged status, had a limited measure of freedom in their activities, and were able to accumulate huge profits as long as they accepted the primacy of politics," Avraham Barkai, *Nazi Economics: Ideology, Theory, and Policy*, Ruth Hadass-Vashitz, trans. (New Haven, Conn.: Yale University Press, 1990), p. 248.

[34]Guenter Reiman, *The Vampire Economy: Doing Business under Fascism* (New York: Vanguard Press, 1939), p. xi.

386 Salerno – War and the Money Machine

productive wealth of conquered nations and the relocation and forced labor of conquered peoples, by 1944 the output of the vital construction industries had shrunk to 25 percent of its prewar level while consumer goods output had declined by only 15 percent.[35] The capital consumption that inflation brings about surreptitiously in the beginning, a repressive fascist State is required to sustain over the long run in the service of the war effort.

The American journalist John T. Flynn wrote that "A bad fascism is a fascist regime which is against us in the war. A good fascist regime is one that is on our side."[36] But, to repeat, all war economies are and must be in the end fascist economies. Higgs vividly characterizes the process by which, in an effort to conceal the costs of World War II from its citizens, the U.S. government was driven by the iron logic of economic theory to blunder into draconian fascist economic planning:

> Huge military and naval forces required correspondingly large amounts of equipment, supplies, subsistence, and transportation. When the government's procurement officers, their pockets bulging with newly created purchasing power, set in motion a bidding war that could have driven prices up to spectacular levels—thereby revealing the full costs of the government's program and provoking political reaction and resistance—the government moved to conceal the costs by price controls. . . . But price controls on goods and services could not be effectively enforced while wages remained free to rise. Hence controls of labor compensation followed in due course. The market economy, a vast and delicately interdependent system of transactions, invariably surprised and confounded the administrators of partial controls. In response the government progressively expanded and tightened the command system until, during the final two years of the war, a thoroughgoing garrison economy had been brought into operation. Fundamentally the authorities, not the market, determined what, how, and for whom the economy would produce under this regime.[37]

It is clear, then, that monetary inflation is the crucial first step in the process by which government seeks to conceal from its citizen-subjects the enormous costs associated with war, particularly the progressive destruction of the nation's productive wealth. Specifically, the inflationary process is indispensable for masking the capital decumulation crisis precipitated by war mobilization, which would otherwise be swiftly revealed to one and all by monetary calculation. In the absence of the veil cast over real economic

---

[35]Barkai, *Nazi Economics*, p. 238.

[36]John T. Flynn, *As We Go Marching* (Garden City, N.Y.: Doubleday, Doran, 1944), p. 165.

[37]Higgs, *Crisis and Leviathan*, pp. 234–35.

processes by inflation, skyrocketing interest rates, plummeting stock and bond markets, and pandemic business bankruptcies and bank runs—not to mention the levying of confiscatory kinds and levels of taxation—would serve to rapidly and significantly dampen the public's enthusiasm for the alleged glories of war. Ironically it is not money itself that is a "veil"—as classical economists used to claim and many contemporary quantity theorists still affirm—because it is precisely monetary calculation that permits market participants to meaningfully assess their wealth and income and appraise the outcomes of alternative allocations of resources. Rather it is central bank manipulation of the money supply that falsifies the calculation of economic quantities and distorts the insight of capitalists and entrepreneurs into market processes.

Finally, it is worth emphasizing that the characterization of monetary inflation as a means for obscuring the real costs of war is an inference from strictly value-free economic theory and, as such, does not logically imply the value judgment that war ought to be financed by non-inflationary fiscal methods. How a war should be financed and whether it should even be waged are questions that can only be resolved in light of a politico-ethical theory. Of course, this is not to deny that such a theory should be "consequentialist" in a broad sense and take into account in its formulation the positive conclusions of relevant sciences regarding the economics as well as of all other outcomes of various government policies. Indeed, given the conclusions of Austrian economic theory that the very concept of a "public good" is untenable and that national defense can and will be supplied most efficiently by the market, like any other desired good, the road has been cleared for the construction of a politico-ethical argument that defense of person and property from local criminals as well as from foreign invaders should be left to the free market.[38]

---

[38]For Austrian critiques of the concept of public good, see, for example, Rothbard, *Man, Economy, and State*, pp. 883–890; see also Hans-Hermann Hoppe, *A Theory of Socialism and Capitalism: Economics, Politics, and Ethics* (Boston: Kluwer Academic Publishers, 1989), pp. 187–210. For the classic article defending the competitive production of defense services by private enterprise, originally penned in 1848 by a leading economist of the French liberal school, see Gustave de Molinari, *The Production of Security*, J. Huston McCulloch, trans. (New York: Center for Libertarian Studies, 1977). For more recent expositions of how the free market would work to provide defense and other public goods, see Morris and Linda Tannehill, *The Market for Liberty* (Lansing, Mich.: Morris and Linda Tannehill, 1970); Murray N. Rothbard, *For a New Liberty: The Libertarian Manifesto*, 2nd ed. (New York: Collier Books, 1978), pp. 215–41; Rothbard, *Power and Market*, pp. 1–7; Jeffrey Rogers Hummel, "National Goods Versus Public Goods: Defense, Disarmament, and Free Riders," *Review of Austrian Economics* 4 (1990): 88–122; and Jeffrey Rogers Hummel and Don Lavoie, "National Defense and the Public-Goods Problem," *Journal des Economistes at des Etudes Humaines* (June/September 1994): 353–77.

18
TIME PREFERENCE, GOVERNMENT, AND THE PROCESS OF DE-CIVILIZATION: FROM MONARCHY TO DEMOCRACY

Hans-Hermann Hoppe

TIME PREFERENCE

I n acting, an actor invariably aims to substitute a more satisfactory for a less satisfactory state of affairs and thus demonstrates a preference for more rather than fewer goods. Moreover, he invariably considers when in the future his goals will be reached, i.e., the time necessary to accomplish them, as well as a good's duration of serviceability. Thus, he also demonstrates a universal preference for earlier over later goods, and for more over less durable ones. This is the phenomenon of time preference.[1]

Every actor requires some amount of time to attain his goal, and since man must always consume something and cannot entirely stop consuming while he is alive, time is always scarce. Thus, *ceteris paribus*, present or earlier goods are, and must invariably be, valued more highly than future or later ones. In fact, if man were not constrained by time preference and if the only constraint operating on him were that of preferring more over less, he would invariably choose those production processes which yielded the largest output per input, regardless of the length of time needed for these methods to bear fruit. He would always save and never consume. For instance, instead of building a fishing net first, Crusoe would have immediately begun constructing a fishing trawler—as it is the economically most efficient method of catching fish. That no one, including Crusoe, could act in this way makes it evident that man cannot but "value fractions of time of the same length in a different way according as they are nearer or remoter from the instant of the actor's decision." "What restricts the amount of saving and investment is time preference."[2]

---

[1]See on the following in particular Ludwig von Mises, *Human Action: A Treatise on Economics* (Chicago: Henry Regnery, 1966), chaps. 18, 19; also William Stanley Jevons, *Theory of Political Economy* (New York: Augustus M. Kelley, 1965); Eugen von Böhm-Bawerk, *Capital and Interest*, 3 vols. (South Holland, Ill.: Libertarian Press, 1959); Richard von Strigl, *Kapital und Produktion* (Vienna: J. Springer, 1934); Frank Fetter, *Capital, Interest, and Rent* (Kansas City: Sheed Andrews and McMeel, 1977); Murray N. Rothbard, *Man, Economy, and State* (Los Angeles: Nash, 1970).

[2]Mises, *Human Action*, p. 483, 491.

Constrained by time preference, man will only exchange a present good for a future one if he anticipates thereby increasing his amount of future goods. The rate of time preference, which is (and can be) different from person to person and from one point in time to the next, but which can never be anything but positive for everyone, simultaneously determines the height of the premium which present goods command over future ones as well as the amount of savings and investment. The market rate of interest is the aggregate sum of all individual time-preference rates reflecting the social rate of time preference and equilibrating social savings (i.e., the supply of present goods offered for exchange against future goods) and social investment (i.e., the demand for present goods thought capable of yielding future returns).

No supply of Loanable Funds can exist without previous savings, i.e., without abstaining from a possible consumption of present goods (an excess of current production over current consumption). And no demand for loanable funds would exist if no one perceived an opportunity to employ present goods productively, i.e., to invest them so as to produce a future output that would exceed current input. Indeed, if all present goods were consumed and none invested in time-consuming production methods, the interest rate would be infinitely high, which, anywhere outside of the Garden of Eden, would be tantamount to leading a mere animal existence, i.e., eking out a primitive subsistence living by encountering reality with nothing but one's bare hands and a desire for instant gratification.

A supply of and a demand for loanable funds only arise—and this is the human condition—if it is recognized first that indirect (more roundabout, lengthier) production processes yield a larger or better output per input than direct and short ones.[3] Second, it must be possible, by means of savings, to accumulate the amount of present (consumption) goods needed to provide for all those wants whose satisfaction during the prolonged waiting time is deemed more urgent than the increment in future well-being expected from the adoption of a more time-consuming production process.

So long as these conditions are fulfilled, capital formation and accumulation will set in and continue. Land and labor (the originary factors of production), instead of being supported by and

---

[3]To be sure, not all lengthier production processes are more productive than shorter ones, but under the assumption that man, constrained by time preference, will invariably (and at all times) select the shortest conceivable methods of producing some given output, any increase in output then can—praxeologically—only be achieved if the production process is lengthened, given constant technology.

engaged in instantaneously gratifying production processes, are supported by an excess of production over consumption and employed in the production of capital goods. Capital goods have no value except as intermediate products in the process of turning out final (consumer) goods later, and insofar as the production of final products is more productive with than without them, or, what amounts to the same thing, insofar as he who possesses and can produce with the aid of capital goods is nearer in time to the completion of his ultimate goal than he who must do without them. The excess in value (price) of a capital good over the sum expended on the complementary originary factors required for its production is due to this time difference and the universal fact of time preference. It is the price paid for buying time, for moving closer to the completion of one's ultimate goal rather than having to start at the very beginning. For the same reason, the value of the final output must exceed the sum spent on its factors of production (the price paid for the capital good and all complementary labor services).

The lower the time-preference rate, the earlier the onset of the process of capital formation, and the faster the roundabout structure of production will be lengthened. Any increase in the accumulation of capital goods and the roundaboutness of the production structure in turn raises the marginal productivity of labor. This leads to either increased employment or wage rates, or even if the labor supply curve should become backward sloping with increased wage rates, to a higher wage total. Supplied with an increased amount of capital goods, a better paid population of wage earners will produce an overall increased—future—social product, thus also raising the real incomes of the owners of capital and land.

FACTORS INFLUENCING TIME PREFERENCE AND THE PROCESS OF CIVILIZATION

Among the factors influencing time preference one can distinguish between external, biological, personal, and social or institutional ones.

External factors are events in an actor's physical environment whose outcome he can neither directly nor indirectly control. Such events affect time preference only if and insofar as they are expected. They can be of two kinds. If a positive event such as manna falling from heaven is expected to happen at some future date, the marginal utility of future goods will fall relative to that of present ones. The time-preference rate will rise and consumption will be stimulated. Once the expected event has occured and the larger supply of future goods has become a larger supply of present goods, the reverse will happen. The time-preference rate will fall, and savings will increase.

On the other hand, if a negative event such as a flood is expected, the marginal utility of future goods rises. The time-preference rate will fall and savings will increase. After the event, with a reduced supply of present goods, the time-preference rate will rise.[4]

Biological processes are technically within an actor's reach, but for all practical purposes and in the foreseeable future they too must be regarded as a given by an actor, similar to external events.

It is a given that man is born as a child, that he grows up to be an adult, that he is capable of procreation during part of his life, and that he ages and dies. These biological facts have a direct bearing on time preference. Due to biological constraints on their cognitive development, children have an extremely high time-preference rate. They do not possess a clear concept of a personal life expectancy extending over an extended period of time, and they lack a full comprehension of production as a mode of indirect consumption. Accordingly, present goods and immediate gratification are highly preferred to future goods and delayed gratification. Savings-investment activities are rare, and the periods of production and provision seldom extend beyond the most immediate future. Children live from day to day and from one immediate gratification to the next.

In the course of becoming an adult, an actor's initially extremely high time-preference rate tends to fall. With the recognition of one's life expectancy and the potentialities of production as a means of indirect consumption, the marginal utility of future goods rises. Saving and investment are stimulated, and the periods of production and provision are lengthened.

Finally, becoming old and approaching the end of one's life, one's time-preference rate tends to rise. The marginal utility of future goods falls because there is less of a future left. Savings and investments will decrease, and consumption—including the non-replacement of capital and durable consumer goods—will increase. This old-age effect may be counteracted and suspended, however. Owing to the biological fact of procreation, an actor may

---

[4]If it is expected that nothing at all can be done about the impending losses of future goods such that no present attempt to mitigate these losses through compensatory savings (or insurance) appears possible because such savings would be destroyed as well, the time-preference rate will immediately rise, and it will remain high after the event.

extend his period of provision beyond the duration of his own life. If and insofar as this is the case, his time-preference rate can remain at its adult-level until his death.

Within the constraints imposed by external and biological factors, an actor sets his time-preference rate in accordance with his subjective evaluations. How high or low this rate is and what changes it will undergo in the course of his lifetime depend on personal psychological factors. One man may not care about anything but the present and the most immediate future. Like a child, he may only be interested in instant or minimally delayed gratification. In accordance with his high time preference, he may want to be a vagabond, a drifter, a drunkard, a junkie, a daydreamer, or simply a happy-go-lucky kind of guy who likes to work as little as possible in order to enjoy each and every day to the fullest. Another man may worry about his and his offspring's future constantly and, by means of savings, may want to build up a steadily growing stock of capital and durable consumer goods in order to provide for an increasingly larger supply of future goods and an ever longer period of provision. A third person may feel a degree of time preference somewhere in between these extremes, or he may feel different degrees at different times and therefore choose still another lifestyle-career.[5]

---

[5]In contrast to the widespread recognition of the phenomenon of time preference by economists, in particular those of the "Austrian School," amazingly little attention has been paid to it by sociologists and political scientists. For a notable exception see Edward Banfield, *The Unheavenly City Revisited* (Boston: Little, Brown, 1974), esp. chap. 3. Banfield identifies time preference as the underlying cause for the persistent distinction between social classes and cultures, in particular between the "upper class" and the "lower class." Whereas members of the former are characterized by future-orientation, self-discipline, and a willingness to forego present gratification in exchange for a better future, members of the "lower class" are characterized by their present-orientation and hedonism.

> If (the lower class individual) has any awareness of the future, it is of something fixed, fated, beyond his control: things happen to him, he does not make them happen. Impulse governs his behavior, either because he cannot discipline himself to sacrifice a present for a future satisfaction or because he has no sense of the future. He is therefore radically improvident . . . He works only as he must to stay alive, and drifts from one unskilled job to another, taking no interest in his work. . . . He is careless with his things . . . and, even when nearly new, they are likely to be permanently out of order for lack of minor repairs. His body, too, is a thing "to be worked out but not repaired." (pp. 61–62)

Phenomena typically associated with the "lower class," such as family breakdown, promiscuity, venereal disease, alcoholism, drug addiction, violence, crime, high infant mortality, and low life expectancy, all have a common cause in high time preference. Their cause is not unemployment or low income. Rather, notes Banfield, causation is, if anything, the other way around: lasting unemployment and persistently low incomes likewise are the effects of an underlying high time preference.

However, no matter what a person's original time-preference rate or what the original distribution of such rates within a given population, once it is low enough to allow for any savings and capital or durable consumer-goods formation at all, a tendency toward a fall in the rate of time preference is set in motion, accompanied by a "process of civilization."[6]

The saver exchanges present (consumer) goods for future (capital) goods with the expectation that these will help produce a larger supply of present goods in the future. If he expected otherwise he would not save. If these expectations prove correct, *and if everything else remains the same*, the marginal utility of present goods relative to that of future ones will fall. His time-preference rate will be lower. He will save and invest more than in the past, and his future income will be still higher, leading to yet another reduction in his time-preference rate. Step by step, the time-preference rate approaches zero—without ever reaching it. In a monetary economy, as a result of his surrender of present money, a saver expects to receive a higher real-money income later. With a higher income, the marginal utility of present money falls relative to future money, the savings proportion rises, and future monetary income will be even higher.

Moreover, in an exchange economy, the saver-investor also contributes to a lowering of the time-preference rate of non-savers. With the accumulation of capital goods, the relative scarcity of labor services increases, and wage rates, *ceteris paribus*, will rise. Higher wage rates imply a rising supply of present goods for previous non-savers. Thus, even those individuals who were previously non-savers will see their personal time-preference rates fall.

In addition, as an indirect result of the increased real incomes brought about through savings, nutrition and health care improve, and the life expectancy tends to rise. In a development similar to the transformation from childhood to adulthood, with a higher life expectancy more distant goals are added to an individual's present value scale. The marginal utility of future goods relative to that of present ones increases, and the time-preference rate further declines.[7]

As another important exception to the general neglect of the phenomenon of time preference at the hands of non-economists see T. Alexander Smith, *Time and Public Policy* (Knoxville: University of Tennessee Press, 1988).

[6]For a detailed empirical, socio-psychological description of the phenomenon of the "process of civilization" see also N. Elias, *Über den Prozess der Zivilisation* (Frankfurt/M., 1968); English Edition *The Civilizing Process: A History of Manners* (New York: Urizen Books, 1978).

[7]To avoid any misunderstanding, it must be made clear that the mere fact of a longer life has no impact on time preference. Rather, it is only the personal

Simultaneously, the saver-investor initiates a "process of civilization." In generating a tendency toward a fall in the rate of time preference, he successively raises himself—and everyone directly or indirectly connected to him through a network of exchanges—from barbarism to civilization and from human childhood to adulthood.

In building up an expanding structure of capital and durable consumer goods, the saver-investor also steadily expands the range and horizon of his plans. The number of variables under his control that are taken into account in his present actions increases. Accordingly, this increases the number and time horizons of his predictions concerning future events. Hence, the saver-investor is interested in acquiring and steadily improving upon his knowledge concerning an increasing number of variables and their interrelationships. Yet once he has acquired or improved his own knowledge and verbalized or displayed it in action, such knowledge becomes a "free good," available for imitation and utilization by others for their own purposes. Thus, by virtue of the saver's saving, even the most present-oriented person will be gradually transformed from a barbarian to a civilized man. His life ceases to be brutish, nasty, and short, and becomes longer, increasingly refined, and comfortable.

Figure 1 provides a graphic illustration of the phenomena of time preference and the process of civilization. It relates individual time-preference rates (the height of the premium of a specified present good over the same good at a specified later date which induces a given individual to engage in intertemporal exchange) on the vertical axis to the individual's *real* money income (his supply of present money) on the horizontal. In accordance with the law of marginal utility, each individual time-preference curve, such as T_1 or T_2, slopes downward as the supply of present money increases. The process of civilization is depicted by a movement from point 11—with a time preference rate of t_{11}—to point 22—with a time preference rate of t_{22}. This movement is the composite result of two interrelated changes. On the one hand, it involves a movement along T_1 from point 11 to 12, representing the fall in the time-preference rate that results if an individual with a *given* personality possesses a larger supply of present goods. On the other hand, there is a movement from point 12 to 22. This change from a higher to a lower time-preference curve—with real income assumed to be given—represents the *changes* in personality as they occur during the transition from childhood to adulthood, in the course

___

knowledge—the subjective expectation—of this fact, that leads to a fall in a person's degree of time preference.

of rising life-expectancies, or as the result of an advancement of knowledge.

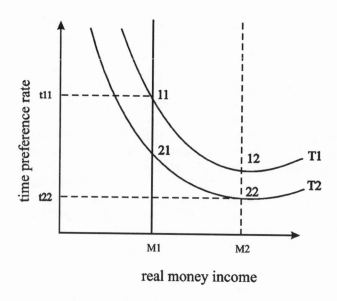

real money income

Figure 1: Time Preference and the Process of Civilization

TIME PREFERENCE, PROPERTY, CRIME, AND GOVERNMENT

The actual amount of present goods allocated to the production of future goods depends on the one hand on a person's technical knowledge. For instance, without the knowledge of how to build a fishing net, Crusoe obviously could not even have begun to exchange present goods for future ones, that is, to save and invest. On the other hand, *given* a person's technical knowledge, the amount of saving depends solely on his supply of present goods and his time-preference schedule. The smaller his supply of present goods and the higher his time-preference schedule, the higher his effective time-preference rate and the lower his actual savings will be.

In the beginning of humanity, there was only "land" (nature-given resources and obstacles) and "labor" (human bodies). Strictly speaking, the only *given* supply of any good is that of body-time. The supply of all other goods—be they perishable or durable consumer goods such as berries or caves, or indirectly useful goods (production factors), such as berry bushes and their surrounding land—is not "given." It is the result of someone's prior action; of the appropriation (homesteading) of nature by a specific individual. The facts and laws of nature and human biology are "givens," of course, and nature as such may be generous or skimpy. But only through an individual's act of appropriation is nature turned into a supply of goods. It is even more obvious that the supply of all *produced* goods is not "given." Be they consumer goods, which have been stored, conserved or made more durable, or produced factors of production (capital goods), they are all the outcome of the activities of specific individuals. Finally, technical knowledge is also not a "given." That one potato saved today can yield ten potatoes one year from now may be a fact of nature, but one must first have a potato. Yet even if one did and one were perfectly willing to invest it for this return or an even lower one, such a fact would be irrelevant unless the person in question knew the laws of potato growing.

Thus, neither the supply of present goods nor technology then is given or fixed. Rather, they are artifacts, created with the intention of improving their appropriator–producer's well-being. These expectations can turn out right or wrong, and rather than securing a profit for the actor, his actions may result in a loss. But one would not spend any time picking berries unless he originally expected berries to be eatable. No one would appropriate a berry bush unless he thought that this would enhance his berry harvest. No one would want to learn anything about any fact or law of nature unless he anticipated that such knowledge would help him improve his circumstances.

In a social context, an individual's supply of appropriated and produced goods, his time-preference schedule, and hence his effective time-preference rate may also be affected by the actions—and the expectations regarding these actions—of others.[8]

The tendency toward a fall in the time-preference rate and the accompanying process of civilization will proceed so long—as has

[8]See on the following Rothbard, *Man, Economy, and State*, pp. 147–59; see also Murray N. Rothbard, *Power and Market* (Kansas City: Sheed Andrews and McMeel, 1977); Hans-Hermann Hoppe, *A Theory of Socialism and Capitalism* (Boston: Kluwer, 1989); Hans-Hermann Hoppe, *The Economics and Ethics of Private Property* (Boston: Kluwer, 1993).

so far been tacitly assumed to be the case—as no one interferes with another's acts of nature-appropriation and production. So long as this is the case and each person is respected by everyone else as the owner of his supply of body-time and whatever goods he has appropriated and produced such that everyone may enjoy, unmolested by others, all present and future benefits to be derived from these goods, the existence of more than one person either leaves the tendency toward a fall in the time-preference rate unchanged, or it even accelerates and reinforces the very process. The former is the case if and insofar as A appropriates a previously unowned, nature-given good, or if he transforms such a good into a different one without causing any physical damage to the goods owned by another person B. A's supply of present goods, or the value of such goods for A, is increased, and hence, *ceteris paribus*, his time-preference rate will fall. Because A's acts have no impact on the supply of goods owned by B, B's time-preference rate remains unaffected. Furthermore, the tendency will actually be accelerated insofar as A and B, based on the mutual recognition of each other's property, engage in voluntary trade or cooperation and even without any such exchange insofar as they merely observe each other's activities and copy each other's knowledge. For any voluntary trade or cooperation between A and B increases—*ex ante*—the supply and/or the value attached to the supply of the goods of *both* parties (otherwise it would not take place), and hence the time-preference rate of both A *and* B will fall. Moreover, by learning facts and laws from one another, such as that there are potatoes, that potatoes can be eaten, or that one's present potato may yield ten future ones, the tendency toward a fall in the rate of time preference spreads from one person to another.

However, if violations of property rights occur and the goods appropriated or produced by A are stolen, damaged or expropriated by B, or if B restricts the uses that A is permitted to make of his goods in any way (apart from not being allowed to cause any physical damage to the property of B), then the tendency toward a fall in the rate of time preference will be disturbed, halted or even reversed.

The violations of property rights—and the effect they have on the process of civilization—can be of two kinds. They can take the form of criminal activities (including negligent behavior), or they can take the form of institutional or governmental interference.

The characteristic mark of criminal invasions of property rights is that such activities are considered illegitimate or unjust not only by the victim, but by property owners in general (and possibly even by the criminal himself). Hence, the victim is considered to be entitled to defend himself if need be by retaliatory force, and he may punish and/or exact compensation from the offender.

The impact of crime is twofold. On the one hand, criminal activity reduces the supply of the goods of the victimized appropriator–producer–exchanger, thereby raising his effective time-preference rate (his time-preference schedule being given). On the other hand, insofar as individuals perceive a risk of future victimization they will accordingly re-allocate their resources. They will build walls and fences, install locks and alarm systems, design or buy weapons, and purchase protection and insurance services. The existence of crime thus implies a setback in the process toward a fall in the rate of time preference as far as actual victims are concerned, and it leads to expenditures—by actual *and* potential victims—which would be considered wasteful without the existence of crime.[9]

Therefore, crime or a change in its rate has the same type of effect on time preference as the occurrence or a changed frequency of "natural" disasters. Floods, storms, heat waves, and earthquakes also reduce their victims' supplies of present goods and thus raise their effective time-preference rate. And the perceived risk/ change of natural disasters also leads to resource realloca-tions and expense-adjustments—such as the construction of dams, irrigation systems, dikes, shelters, or earthquake insurance—which would be unnecessary absent these natural risks.

More importantly, however, because actual and potential victims are permitted to defend, protect, and insure themselves against both social disasters such as crime as well as natural ones, the effect of these on time preference is only temporary and unsystematic. Actual victims will save or invest a smaller amount of goods because they are poorer. And the altered risk perceptions among actual and potential victims shape the *direction* of their future actions. But so long as physical protection and defense are permitted, the existence neither of social nor of natural disasters implies that the time-preference *degree* of actual or potential victims—their degree of *future*-orientation—will be systematically changed.[10] After taking account of the damage and redirecting

---

[9]See also Gordon Tullock, "The Welfare Costs of Tariffs, Monopolies, and Theft," *Western Economic Journal* 5 (1967).

[10]In terms of Figure 1 above: Social and natural disasters alike imply a movement upward and to the left on a given time-preference curve—insofar as actual victims

one's activities, the tendency toward a fall in the rate of time preference and the attending process of civilization will resume on its previous path. In its course, both the protection against crime as well as that against natural disasters can be expected to undergo continual improvement.[11]

Matters fundamentally change and the process of civilization is permanently derailed whenever property-rights violations take the form of government interference, however. The distinctive mark of government violations of private property rights is that contrary to criminal activities, they are considered legitimate not only by the government agents who engage in them, but by the general public as well (and in rare instances possibly even by the victim). Hence, in these cases a victim may *not* legitimately defend himself against such violations.[12]

The imposition of a government tax on property or income violates a property- or income-producer's rights as much as theft does. In both cases the appropriator–producer's supply of goods is diminished against his will and without his consent. Government money or "liquidity" creation involves no less a fraudulent expropriation of private-property owners than the operations of a criminal counterfeiter gang. Moreover, any government regulation as to what an owner may or may not do with his property—beyond

---

are concerned. But they do not imply a change in a person's character structure, i.e., a shift from a lower to a higher time-preference curve. Such a shift occurs in the presence of government-disasters, however.

[11]On the evolution and efficiency of systems of competitive law courts and privately provided defense and law enforcement see Gustave de Molinari, *The Production of Security* (New York: Center for Libertarian Studies, 1977); William C. Wooldridge, *Uncle Sam the Monopoly Man* (New Rochelle, N.Y.: Arlington House, 1970); Murray N. Rothbard, *For A New Liberty* (New York: Macmillan, 1978); Hoppe, *Economics and Ethics of Private Property*; Morris and Linda Tannehill, *The Market for Liberty* (New York: Laissez Faire Books, 1984); Terry Anderson and P.J. Hill, "The American Experiment in Anarcho-Capitalism: The Not So Wild, Wild West," *Journal of Libertarian Studies* (1980); Bruce L. Benson, "Guns for Protection, and other Private Sector Responses to the Government's Failure to Control Crime," *Journal of Libertarian Studies* (1986); Bruce L. Benson, *The Enterprise of Law: Justice Without the State* (San Francisco: Pacific Research Institute, 1990); Roger D. McGrath, *Gunfighters, Highwaymen and Vigilantes. Violence on the Frontier* (Berkeley: University of California Press, 1984); idem, "Treat Them to a Good Dose of Lead," *Chronicles* (January 1994).

[12]On the theory of the state see besides the works cited in footnote 9 above Franz Oppenheimer, *The State* (New York: Vanguard Press, 1914); Franz Oppenheimer, *System der Soziologie, Vol. 2: Der Staat* (Stuttgart: Gustav Fischer, 1964); Alexander Rüstow, *Freedom and Domination* (Princeton, N.J.: Princeton University Press, 1980); Charles Tilly, "War Making and State Making as Organized Crime," in *Bringing the State Back In*, Peter B. Evans, Dietrich Rueschemeyer and Theda Skocpol, eds. (Cambridge: Cambridge University Press, 1985); Richard Epstein, *Takings: Private Property and the Power of Eminent Domain* (Cambridge, Mass.: Harvard University Press, 1985).

the rule that no one may physically damage the property of others and that all exchange and trade with others must be voluntary and contractual—implies a "taking" of somebody's property on a par with acts of extortion, robbery, or destruction. But taxation, the government's provision of liquidity, and government regulations—unlike their criminal counterparts—are considered legitimate, and the victim of government interference—unlike the victim of a crime—is *not* entitled to physical defense and protection of his property.

Because of their legitimacy, then, government violations of property rights affect individual time preferences in a fashion which is systematically different and much more profound than are effects caused by crime. Like crime, any government interference with private-property rights reduces someone's supply of present goods and thus raises his effective time-preference rate. Yet government offenses—unlike crime—simultaneously raise the time-preference *degree* of actual and potential victims because they also imply a reduction in the supply of *future* goods (a reduced rate of return on investment). Crime, because it is illegitimate, occurs only intermittently—the robber disappears from the scene with his loot and leaves his victim alone. Thus, crime can be dealt with by increasing one's demand for protective goods and services (relative to that for non-protection goods) so as to restore or even increase one's future rate of investment return and make it less likely that the same or a different robber will succeed a second time with the same or a different victim. In contrast, because they are legitimate, governmental property-rights violations are continual. The offender does not disappear into hiding but stays around, and the victim does not "arm" himself but must (at least he is generally expected to) remain defenseless.[13] Consequently

[13]Lysander Spooner, *No Treason: The Constitution of No Authority* (Larkspur, Colo.: Pine Tree Press, 1966), p. 17, writes:

> The government does not, indeed, waylay a man in a lonely place, spring upon him from the roadside, and holding a pistol to his head, proceed to rifle his pockets. But the robbery is none the less a robbery on that account; and it is far more dastardly and shameful.
>
> The highwayman takes solely upon himself the responsibility, danger, and crime of his own act. He does not pretend that he has a rightful claim to your money, or that he intends to use it for your own benefit. He does not pretend to be anything but a robber. He has not acquired impudence enough to profess to be merely a "protector," and that he takes men's money against their will, merely to enable him to "protect" those infatuated travellers, who feel perfectly able to protect themselves, or do not appreciate his peculiar system of protection. He is too sensible a man to make such professions as these. Furthermore, having taken your money, he leaves you, as you wish him to do. He does not persist in following you on the road, against your will; assuming to be your rightful "sover-

future property-rights violations, rather than becoming less frequent, become institutionalized. The rate, regularity and duration of future victimization increases instead of decreasing. Instead of by improved "protection," the actual and potential victims of government property-rights violations—as demonstrated by their continued defenselessness *vis-à-vis* their offenders—respond by associating a permanently higher risk with all future production and systematically adjusting their expectations concerning the rate of return on all future investment downward.

Competing with the tendency toward a falling rate of time preference, another opposing tendency comes into operation with the existence of government. By simultaneously reducing the supply of present *and* (expected) future goods, governmental property rights violations not only raise time-preference rates (with given schedules) but also time-preference schedules. Because appropriator–producers are (and see themselves as) defenseless against future victimization by government agents, their expected rate of return on productive, future-oriented actions is reduced all-around, and accordingly all actual and potential victims become more present-oriented.

As will be explained in the course of the following section, if government property-rights violations take their course and grow extensive enough, the natural tendency of humanity to build an expanding stock of capital and durable consumer goods and to become increasingly more farsighted and provide for ever-more distant goals may not only come to a standstill, but may be reversed by a tendency toward de-civilization: formerly provident providers will be turned into drunks or daydreamers, adults into children, civilized men into barbarians, and producers into criminals.

GOVERNMENT, GOVERNMENT GROWTH, AND THE PROCESS OF DECIVILIZATION: FROM MONARCHY TO DEMOCRACY

Every government—every agency that engages in continual, institutionalized property-rights violations (expropriations)—is by

---

eign," on account of the "protection" he affords you. He does not keep "protecting" you, by commanding you to bow down and serve him; by requiring you to do this, and forbidding you to do that; by robbing you out of more money as often as he finds it for his interest or pleasure to do so; and by branding you as a rebel, a traitor, and an enemy to your country, and shooting you down without mercy, if you dispute his authority, or resist his demands. He is too much of a gentleman to be guilty of such impostures, and insults, and villainies as these. In short, he does not, in addition to robbing you, attempt to make you either his dupe or his slave.

its nature a territorial monopolist. There can be no "free entry" into the business of expropriations, because otherwise soon nothing would be left that could still be expropriated, and any form of *institutionalized* expropriation would thus become impossible. Under the assumption of self-interest, every government will use this monopoly of expropriation to its own advantage—in order to maximize its wealth and income. Hence every government should be expected to have an inherent tendency toward growth. And in maximizing its own wealth and income by means of expropriation, every government then represents a constant threat to the process of civilization—of falling time preferences and increasingly wider and longer provision—and an expanding source of decivilizing forces.

However, not every government prospers equally and produces decivilizing forces of the same strength. Different forms of government lead to different degrees of decivilization. Nor is every form of government, and every sequence of government forms, equally probable.

Given that all expropriation creates victims and victims cannot be relied upon to cooperate while being victimized, an agency that *institutionalizes* expropriation must possess legitimacy. A majority of the non-governmental public must regard the government's actions as just or at least as fair enough not to be resisted so as to render the victim defenseless.[14] Yet to acquire legitimacy is not an easy task. For this reason, it is not likely, for instance, that a single world government could initially arise. Instead, all governments must begin territorially small. Nor is it likely, even for as small a population as that of a clan, a tribe, a village or a town, that a government will initially be democratic, for who would not rather

---

[14]On the fundamental importance of favorable public opinion for the exercise of government power see the classic treatment by Étienne de la Boetie, *The Politics of Obedience: The Discourse of Voluntary Servitude* (New York: Free Life Editions, 1975), with an introduction by Murray N. Rothbard; see also David Hume, "The First Principles of Government" in *Essays: Moral, Political and Literary* (Oxford: Oxford University Press, 1971). Thus, Hume writes (p. 19): "Nothing appears more surprising to those who consider human affairs with a philosophical eye, than the easiness with which the many are governed by the few, and the implicit submission, with which men resign their own sentiments and passions to those of their rulers. When we inquire by what means this wonder is effected we shall find, that as Force is always on the side of the governed, the governors have nothing to support them but opinion. It is, therefore, on opinion only that government is founded, and this maxim extends to the most despotic and most military governments, as well as to the most free and popular. The sultan of Egypt, or the emperor of Rome, might drive his harmless subjects, like brute beasts, against their sentiment and inclination. But he must, at least, have led his mamalukes or praetorian bands, like men, by their opinions." See also Mises, *Human Action*, pp. 863–64.

trust a specific known individual—especially in as sensitive a matter as that of a territorial monopoly of expropriation—than an anonymous, democratically elected person?! Having to begin small, the originary form of government is typically that of *personal* rule: of *private* ownership of the governmental apparatus of compulsion (monarchy).[15]

In every society of any degree of complexity, specific individuals quickly acquire the status of an elite as a result of having diverse talents. Owing to achievements of superior wealth, wisdom, bravery, or a combination thereof, particular individuals command respect, and their opinions and judgments possess natural authority. As an outgrowth of this authority, members of the elite are most likely to succeed, typically via the monopolization of judicial services (courts and legislation) and law enforcement (police), in establishing a legitimate territorial monopoly of compulsion.[16] And because they owe their privileged position to their personal elitist character and achievements, they will consider themselves and be regarded by their fellows as the monopoly's *personal owner*. Democratic rule—where the government apparatus is considered "public" property administered by regularly elected officials who do *not* personally own and are not viewed as owning the government but as its temporary *caretakers* or *trustees*—typically only follows personal rule and private government ownership. Because masses or majorities cannot possibly possess any natural

---

[15]On the lengthy historical process of the acquisition of government power, and the primacy of monarchical rule, see Bertrand de Jouvenel, *Sovereignty: An Inquiry into the Political Good* (Chicago: University of Chicago Press, 1957), esp. chap. 10; idem, *On Power: The Natural History of its Growth* (New York: Viking, 1949); idem, "The Principate" in idem, *The Nature of Politics* (New York: Schocken Books, 1987); Rüstow, *Freedom and Domination*, esp. pp. 101–5.

[16]On the ubiquity of natural authority see de Jouvenel, *Sovereignty*, chap. 2. "All that was needed (for the formation of associations) was that some one man should feel within him a natural ascendancy and should then inspire others with trust in himself. . . .when we can see every day associations forming all around us, why should we imagine them forming in the distant past in some different way? What makes leaders, now as always, is natural ascendancy—authority as such. We see them arising under our very eyes whenever there is a rescue to organize or a fire to put out." (pp. 31–32)

And on the transition from authority to power, de Jouvenel goes on to say:

> Power, however, is something very different from authority. The distinguishing mark of the latter is that it is exercised only over those who voluntarily accept it: if the rulers have authority over only a part of their subjects, they may receive from that part a strength sufficient to subject the others to their power. . . . Authority ends where voluntary assent ends. There is in every state a margin of obedience which is won only by the use of force or the threat of force: it is this margin which breaches liberty and demonstrates the failure of authority. Among free peoples it is a very small margin, because there authority is very great. (pp. 32–33)

authority (this being a personal, individual trait), democratic governments can acquire legitimacy only unnaturally—most typically through war or revolution. Only in activities such as war and revolution do masses act in concert and do victory and defeat depend on mass effort. And only under exceptional circumstances such as these can mass majorities gain the legitimacy needed to transform government into *public* property.

These two forms of government—private or public ownership of government (monarchy or democracy)—have systematically different effects on social time preference and the attending process of civilization, and with the transition from personal (monarchical) to democratic (public) rule in particular, contrary to conventional wisdom, the de-civilizing forces inherent in any form of government are systematically strengthened.[17]

The defining characteristic of private government ownership and the reason for a personal ruler's relatively lower degree of time preference (as compared to criminals and democratic governments) is that the expropriated resources and the monopoly privilege of future expropriation are individually *owned*. The expropriated resources are added to the ruler's private estate and treated as if they were a part of it, and the monopoly privilege of future expropriation is attached as a title to this estate and leads to an instant increase in its present value ("capitalization" of monopoly profit). Most importantly, as the private owner of the government estate, the ruler is entitled to pass his possessions on to his personal heir. He may sell, rent, or give away part or all of his privileged estate (and privately pocket the receipts from the sale or rental), and he may personally appoint or dismiss every administrator and employee of his estate.[18]

[17]See on the following also the literature on the "tragedy of the commons," e.g. *Managing The Commons*, Garrett Hardin and John Baden, eds. (San Francisco: W.H. Freeman, 1977). See also Mancur Olson, "Dictatorship, Democracy, and Development," *American Political Science Review* 87, no. 3 (1993).

[18]According to this characterization of monarchy, present-day "monarchies" such as Great Britain, the Netherlands, Belgium, Sweden, Norway, Denmark, or Spain are clearly monarchies in name only. In fact, they represent examples of what is here and in the following referred to as democracies. The term "monarchy," as here defined, applies instead most appropriately to the form of government that characterized Europe through the end of the 18th century: the "ancien regime"— whence, stimulated by the American and in particular the French Revolution and in a process that was not completed until after the end of World War I, monarchies were gradually transformed into democracies.

Indeed, monarchy and democracy can be conceived of analytically as representing the two endpoints of a continuum, with various possible forms of government located at greater or lesser distances from one or the other extreme. Elective monarchies as they existed for periods of time in Poland, Bohemia, and Hungary, for instance, are obviously less monarchic than are hereditary monarchies. Likewise, "constitutional" monarchies are less monarchic than

The institution of private government ownership systematically shapes the incentive structure confronting the ruler and distinct-
ly influences his conduct of government affairs. Assuming no
more than self-interest, the ruler tries to maximize his total wealth,
i.e., the present value of his estate *and* his current income. He
would *not* want to increase current income at the expense of a
more than proportional drop in the present value of his assets.
And because acts of current income acquisition invariably have repercussions on present asset values (reflecting the value of all future expected asset earnings discounted by the rate of time preference), private ownership in and of itself leads to economic calculation and thus promotes farsightedness.

While this is true of private ownership generally, in the special
case of private ownership of *government* it implies a distinct moderation with respect to the ruler's drive to exploit his monopoly
privilege of expropriation. For acts of expropriation are by their
nature parasitic upon prior acts of production by the non-governmental public. Where nothing has first been produced, nothing
can be expropriated, and where everything has been expropriated,
all future production will come to a shrieking halt. Hence, a private owner of government (a king) would want to avoid taxing his
subjects so heavily as to reduce his future earning potential to the
extent that the present value of his estate (his kingdom) actually
fell, for instance. Instead, to preserve or even enhance the value of
his personal property, he would want to systematically restrain
himself in his taxing policies. For the lower the degree of taxation,
the more productive the subject population will be, and the more
productive the population, the higher the value of the ruler's parasitic monopoly of expropriation will be. He will use his monopolistic privilege, of course. He will not *not* tax. But as the government's private owner, it is in his interest to draw—parasitically—
on a growing, increasingly productive and prosperous non-government economy, as this would—always and without any effort

---

pre-constitutional ones. And "parliamentary" monarchies may well have to be
placed closer to a democracy than to a monarchy, or, with universal suffrage, they
may be no monarchy at all. On the other hand, while a republican form of
government implies by definition that the government apparatus is not privately
but publicly owned (by "the people"), and a republic thus possesses an inherent
tendency to gravitate toward the adoption of universal suffrage, i.e., democratic
republicanism, not all republics are in fact equally close to democracy. For
example, an aristocratic "republic" such as that of the Dutch United Provinces
before 1673 (when William of Orange was elected hereditary stadtholder) may
actually have to be classified as a quasi-monarchy rather than a democracy.

On the distinction between monarchy, republic, and democracy and their various historical manifestations see Erik von Kuehnelt-Leddihn, *Leftism Revisited:
From de Sade and Marx to Hitler and Pol Pot* (Washington, D.C.: Regnery Gateway,
1990).

on his part—also increase his own wealth and prosperity. Tax rates would thus tend to be low.[19]

Further, it is in a personal ruler's interest to use his monopoly of law (courts) and order (police) for the enforcement of the pre-established private property law. With the sole exception of himself (for the non-government public and all of its internal dealings, that is), he will want to enforce the principle that all property and income should be acquired productively and/or contractually, and accordingly, he will want to threaten all private-rule transgressions as crime with punishment. The less *private* crime there is, the more private wealth there will be and the higher will be the value of the *ruler's* monopoly of taxation and expropriation. In fact, a private ruler will not want to lean exclusively on *tax* revenue to finance his own expenditures. Rather, he will also want to rely on productive activities and allocate part of his estate to the production and provision of "normal" goods and services, with the purpose of earning its owner a "normal" (market) *sales* revenue.[20]

[19]Carlo M. Cipolla, *Before the Industrial Revolution: European Society and Economy, 1000-1700* (New York: W.W. Norton, 1980), p. 48, concludes: "All in all, one must admit that the portion of income drawn by the public sector most certainly increased from the eleventh century onward all over Europe, but it is difficult to imagine that, apart from particular times and places, the public power ever managed to draw more than 5 to 8 percent of national income." He notes further that this portion was not systematically exceeded until the second half of the 19th century. See also the two following notes.

[20]On the recognition of the pre-existing private-property law by monarchs see de Jouvenel, *Sovereignty*, esp. chaps. 10 and 11.

> The attitude of the sovereign toward rights is expressed in the oath of the first French kings: "I will honour and preserve each one of you, and I will maintain for each the law and justice pertaining to him." When the king was called "debtor for justice," it was no empty phrase. If his duty was *suum cuique tribuere*, the *suum* was a fixed datum. It was not the case of rendering to each what, in the plenitude of his knowledge, he thought would be best for him, but what belonged to him according to custom. Subjective rights were not held on the precarious tenure of grant but were freehold possessions. The sovereign's right also was a freehold. It was a subjective right as much as the other rights, though of a more elevated dignity, but it could not take the other rights away. (pp. 172–73)

de Jouvenel later goes on to say:

> The much-cited anecdote of Frederick the Great and the miller of Sans-Souci faithfully represents the ancient state of affairs. The king's rights have incomparably greater scope than those of the miller; but as far as the miller's right goes it is as good as the king's; on his own ground, the miller is entitled to hold off the king. Indeed there was a deep-seated feeling that all positive rights stood or fell together; if the king disregarded the miller's title to his land, so might the king's title to his throne be disregarded. The profound if obscure concept of legitimacy established the solidarity of all rights. (p. 189)

And on the funding of kings, de Jouvenel notes that:

Moreover, private ownership of government implies moderation for yet another systematic reason. All private property is by definition exclusive property. He who owns property is entitled to exclude everyone else from its use and enjoyment, and he is at liberty to choose with whom, if anyone, he is willing to share in its usage. Typically, a private-property owner will include his family and exclude all others. The property becomes family property with him as the head of the family, and every non-family person will be excluded from using family property, except as invited guests or as paid employees or contractors. In the case of government, this exclusive character of private property takes on a special meaning. In this case it implies that everyone but the ruler and his family is excluded from benefiting from non-productively acquired property and income. Only the ruling family—and to a minor extent its friends, employees, and business partners—shares in the enjoyment of tax revenues and can lead a parasitic life. The position as head of government—and of the government estate—is typically passed on within the ruling family, such that no one outside the king's family can realistically hope to become the next king. While entrance into the ruling family might not be closed entirely, it is highly restrictive. It might be possible to become a family member through marriage. However, the larger the ruling family, the smaller each member's share in the government's total confiscations will be. Hence, marriage typically will be restricted to members of the ruler's extended family. Only in exceptional cases will a member of the ruling family marry a complete "outsider"; and even if this occurs, a family member by marriage will not normally become the head of the ruling family.

Owing to these restrictions regarding entrance into government and the exclusive status of the individual ruler and his family (as king and nobles), private-government ownership (monarchism) stimulates the development of a clear "class consciousness"

> State expenditures, as we now call them, were thought of in feudal times as the king's own expenditures, which he incurred by virtue of his station. When he came into his station, he simultaneously came into an "estate" (in the modern sense of the word); i.e., he found himself endowed with property rights ensuring an income adequate to "the king's needs." It is somewhat as if a government of our own times were expected to cover its ordinary expenditures from the proceeds of state-owned industries. (p. 178)

However, it remains worth emphasizing that any monopolization of law and order still implies higher prices and/or lower product quality than those prevailing under competitive conditions, and that even a king will still employ his monopoly of punishment to his own advantage: by shifting increasingly from the principle of restituting and compensating the victim of a rights violation to that of compensating himself, the king. See on this Bruce L. Benson, "The Development of Criminal Law and Its Enforcement," *Journal des Economistes et des Etudes Humaines* 3 (1992).

on the part of the governed public and promotes opposition and resistance to any expansion of the government's power to tax. A clear-cut distinction between the few rulers and the many ruled exists, and there is little or no risk or chance of a person's moving from one class to the other. Confronted with an almost insurmountable barrier to "upward" mobility, solidarity among the ruled—their mutual identification as actual or potential victims of government violations of property rights—is strengthened, and the ruling class's risk of losing its legitimacy as a result of increased taxation is accordingly heightened.[21]

In fact, the class consciousness among the ruled exerts a moderating effect not only on the government's internal policies, but also on its conduct of external affairs. Every government must be expected to pursue an expansionist foreign policy. The larger the territory and the greater the population over which a monopoly of confiscation extends, the better off those in charge of this monopoly will be. Because only one monopoly of expropriation can exist in any given territory, this expansionary tendency must be expected to go hand in hand with a tendency toward centralization (with ultimately only one, world-wide government remaining). Moreover, because centralization implies reduced opportunities for interterritorial migration—of voting with one's feet against one's

[21]de Jouvenel writes: "A man of our time cannot conceive the lack of real power which characterized the medieval king, from which it naturally followed that in order to secure the execution of a decision he needed to involve other leaders whose say-so reinforced his own." Bertrand de Jouvenel, "On the Evolution of Forms of Government" in idem, *The Nature of Politics*, p. 113. Elsewhere, de Jouvenel noted:

> The king could not exact contributions, he could only solicit "subsidies." It was stressed that his loyal subjects granted him help of their free will, and they often seized this occasion to stipulate conditions. For instance, they granted subsidies to John the Good (of France), subject to the condition that he should henceforth refrain from minting money which was defective in weight. In order to replenish his Treasury, the king might go on a begging tour from town to town, expounding his requirements and obtaining local grants, as was done on the eve of the Hundred Years' War; or he might assemble from all parts of the country those whose financial support he craved. It is a serious mistake to confuse such an assembly with a modern sitting of parliament, though the latter phenomenon has arisen from the former. The Parliament is sovereign and may exact contributions. The older assemblies should rather be thought of as a gathering of modern company directors agreeing to turn over to the Exchequer a part of their profits, with some trade union leaders present agreeing to part with some of their unions' dues for public purposes. Each group was called on for a grant, and each was thus well placed to make conditions. A modern parliament could not be treated like that, but would impose its will by majority vote. (de Jouvenel, *Sovereignty*, pp. 178–79)

See also Douglas C. North and Robert P. Thomas, *The Rise of the Western World: A New Economic History* (Cambridge: Cambridge University Press, 1973), p. 96.

government and in favor of another—the process of intergovern-
mental competition, of expansive elimination, should be expected
to generate simultaneous tendencies toward increasingly higher
rates of government expropriation and taxation.[22]

However, a privately-owned government significantly affects
the form and pace of this process. Owing to its exclusive character
and the correspondingly developed class consciousness of the
ruled, government attempts at territorial expansion tend to be
viewed by the public as the ruler's private business, to be financed
and carried out with his own personal funds. The added territory
is the king's, and so he, not the public, should pay for it. Consequently, of the two possible methods of enlarging his realm, war
and military conquest or contractual acquisition, a private ruler
tends to prefer the latter. It must not be assumed that he is opposed to war, for he may well employ military means if presented
with an opportunity. But war typically requires extraordinary resources, and since higher taxes and/or increased conscription to
fund a war perceived by the public as somebody else's will encounter immediate popular resistance and thus pose a threat to the
government's internal legitimacy, a personal ruler will have to
bear all or most of the costs of a military venture himself. Accordingly, he will generally prefer the second, peaceful option as the
less costly one. Instead of through conquest, he will want to advance his expansionist desires through land purchases or, even
less costly and still better, through a policy of inter-marriage between members of different ruling families. For a monarchical
ruler, then, foreign policy is in large measure family and marriage
policy, and territorial expansion typically proceeds via the contractual conjunction of originally independent kingdoms.[23]

---

[22]On political decentralization—"political anarchy"—as a constraint on government power and a fundamental reason for the evolution of markets and capitalism,
as well as on the tendency toward political centralization—expansive elimination—
and the accompanying tendency toward an increase in governments' taxing and
regulatory powers see J. Baechler, *The Origins of Capitalism* (New York: St. Martin's
Press, 1976), esp. chap. 7; Hoppe, *Economics and Ethics*, esp. chaps. 3 and 4; Hans-
Hermann Hoppe, "Migrazione, centralismo e secessione nell'Europa contempo-
ranea," *biblioteca della liberta*, no. 118, 1992; Hans-Hermann Hoppe, "Nationalism
and Secession," *Chronicles* (November 1993); also Nathan Rosenberg and Luther E.
Birdzell, *How the West Grew Rich* (New York: Basic Books, 1986).

[23]As a prominent example of this type of foreign policy, the case of the Hapsburgs
of Austria may be cited, whose conduct has been characterized by the motto "*bella
gerunt alii; tu, felix Austria, nubes.*" Maximilian I (1493–1519)

> married the heiress of the dukes of Burgundy, who, over the past
> century, had acquired a number of provinces in the western extrem-
> eties of the [Holy Roman] Empire—the Netherlands and the Free
> County of Burgundy, which bordered upon France. Maximilian by
> this marriage had a son Philip, whom he married to Joanna, heiress

In contrast to the internal and external moderation of a monarchy, a democratic (publicly owned) government implies increased excess, and the transition from a world of kings to one of democratically-elected presidents must be expected to lead to a systematic increase in the intensity and extension of government power and a significantly strengthened tendency toward de-civilization.

A democratic ruler can use the government apparatus to his personal advantage, but he does not own it. He cannot sell government resources and privately pocket the receipts from such sales, nor can he pass government possessions on to his personal heir. He owns the *current use* of government resources, but not their capital value. In distinct contrast to a king, a president will want to maximize not total government wealth (capital values and current income) but current income (regardless and at the expense of capital values). Indeed, even if he wished to act differently, he *could not*, for as public property, government resources are unsaleable, and without market prices economic calculation is *impossible*. Accordingly, it must be regarded as unavoidable that public-government ownership results in continual capital consumption. Instead of maintaining or even enhancing the value of the government estate, as a king would do, a president (the government's temporary caretaker or trustee) will use up as much of the government resources as quickly as possible, for what he does not consume *now*, he may *never* be able to consume. In particular, a president (as distinct from a king) has no interest in not ruining his country. For why would he *not* want to increase his confiscations if the advantage of a policy of moderation—the resulting higher capital value of the government estate—can*not* be reaped privately, while the advantage of the opposite policy of higher taxes—a higher current income—*can* be so reaped? For a president, other than for a king, moderation offers only disadvantages.[24]

---

to Ferdinand and Isabella of Spain. Philip and Joanna produced a son Charles. Charles combined the inheritances of his four grandparents: Austria from Maximilian, the Netherlands and Free County from Mary of Burgundy, Castile and Spanish America from Isabella, Aragon and its Mediterranean and Italian possessions from Ferdinand. In addition, in 1519, he was elected Holy Roman Emperor and so became the symbolic head of all Germany. (Robert R. Palmer and Joel Colton, *A History of the Modern World* [New York: Alfred Knopf, 1992], p. 74).

On the limited and moderate character of monarchical wars see the discussion on democratic warfare below.

[24]On the nature of public ownership and its inherent irrationality see also Rothbard, *Power and Market*, pp. 172–84; Hoppe, *Socialism and Capitalism*, chap. 9.

Moreover, with public instead of private government owner-ship the second reason for moderation is also gone: the clear and developed class-consciousness of the ruled. There can always be only one supreme ruler, whether king or president. Yet while en-trance into the position of king and a promotion to the rank of no-bility is systematically restricted under a monarchy, in a publicly owned government, anyone, in theory, can become a member of the ruling class—or even president. The distinction between the rulers and the ruled is blurred, and the class-consciousness of the ruled becomes fuzzy. The illusion even arises that such a distinc-tion no longer exists: that with a democratic government no one is ruled by anyone but everyone instead rules himself. Indeed, it is largely due to this illusion that the transition from monarchy to

---

The fundamental difference between private ownership of government (and low time preference) and public ownership of government (and high time preference) may be further illustrated by considering the institution of slavery, and contrasting the case of private slave ownership, as it existed for instance in ante-bellum America, with that of public slave ownership, as it existed for instance in the former Soviet Union and its Eastern European empire.

Just as privately owned slaves were threatened with punishment if they tried to escape, in all of the former Soviet empire emigration was outlawed and pun-ished as a criminal offense, if necessary, by shooting those who tried to run away. Moreover, anti-loafing laws existed everywhere, and governments could assign any task and all rewards and punishments to any citizen. Hence the classification of the Soviet system as slavery. Unlike a private slave owner, however, Eastern-European slave owners—from Lenin to Gorbachev—could not sell or rent their subjects in a labor market and privately appropriate the receipts from the sale or rental of their "human capital." Hence the system's classification as public (or so-cialist) slavery.

Without markets for slaves and slave labor, matters are worse, not better, for the slave, for without prices for slaves and their labor, a slave owner can no longer rationally allocate his "human capital." He cannot determine the scarcity value of his various, heterogeneous pieces of human capital, and he can neither determine the opportunity-cost of using this capital in any given employment, nor compare it to the corresponding revenue. Accordingly, permanent misallocation, waste, and "consumption" of human capital results.

The empirical evidence indicates as much. While it occasionally happened that a private slave owner killed his slave, which is the ultimate "consumption" of human capital, the socialist slavery of Eastern Europe resulted in millions of murdered civilians. Under private slave ownership the health and life expectancy of slaves generally increased. In the Soviet Empire health-care standards steadily deteriorated and life expectancies actually declined in recent decades. The level of practical training and education of private slaves generally rose. That of socialist slaves fell. The rate of reproduction among privately-owned slaves was positive. Among the slave populations of Eastern Europe it was generally negative. The rates of suicide, self-incapacitation, family breakups, promiscuity, 'illegitimate' births, birth defects, venereal disease, abortion, alcoholism, and dull or brutish behavior among private slaves were high. But all such rates of "human capital consumption" were higher still for the socialist slaves of the former Soviet Empire. Similarly, while morally senseless and violent behavior among privately owned slaves occured after their emancipation, the brutalization of social life in the aftermath of the abolition of socialist slavery has been far worse, revealing an even greater degree of moral degeneration. See also Hans-Hermann Hoppe's "Note on Socialism and Slavery" in *Chronicles* (August 1993): 6.

democracy could be interpreted as progress and, hence, as deserving public support. Accordingly, public resistance against government power is systematically weakened. While expropriation and taxation before may have appeared clearly oppressive and evil to the public, they seem much less so, mankind being what it is, once anyone may freely enter the ranks of those who are at the receiving end.

Consequently, taxes will increase, be it directly in the form of higher tax rates or indirectly in that of increased governmental money "creation" (inflation). Likewise, government employment and the ratio of government employees ("public servants") to private employees tends to rise, attracting and promoting individuals with high degrees of time preference and low and limited farsightedness.[25]

[25]As de Jouvenel explains:

> From the twelfth to the eighteenth century governmental authority grew continuously. The process was understood by all who saw it happening; it stirred them into incessant protest and to violent reaction. In later times its growth has continued at an accelerated pace, and its extension has brought a corresponding extension of war. And now we no longer understand the process, we no longer protest, we no longer react. The quiescence of ours is a new thing, for which Power has to thank the smoke-screen in which it has wrapped itself. Formerly it could be seen, manifest in the person of the king, who did not disclaim being the master he was, and in whom human passions were discernible. Now, masked in anonymity, it claims to have no existence of its own, and to be but the impersonal and passionless instrument of the general will—but that is clearly a fiction—today as always Power is in the hands of a group of men who control the power house. All that has changed is that it has now been made easy for the ruled to change the personnel of the leading wielders of Power. Viewed from one angle, this weakens Power, because the wills which control a society's life can, at the society's pleasure, be replaced by other wills, in which it feels more confidence. But by opening the prospect of Power to all the ambitious talents, this arrangement makes the extension of Power much easier. Under the 'ancien regime,' society's moving spirits, who had, as they knew, no chance of a share in Power, were quick to denounce its smallest encroachment. Now, on the other hand, when everyone is potentially a minister, no one is concerned to cut down an office to which he aspires one day himself, or to put sand in a machine which he means to use himself when his turn comes. Hence it is that there is in the political circles of a modern society a wide complicity in the extension of power. (*On Power*, pp. 9–10)

In fact, during the entire monarchical age until the second half of the 19th century, which represents the turning point in the historical process of demonarchization and democratization beginning with the French Revolution and ending with World War I, the tax burden rarely exceeded 5 percent of national product (see also footnote 20 above). Since then it has constantly increased. In Western Europe it stood at 15 to 20 percent of national product after World War I, and in the meantime it has risen to around 50 percent. Likewise, during the entire monarchical age, until the latter half of the 19th century, government employment rarely exceeded 2 percent of the labor force. Since then it has steadily increased,

The combination of these interrelated factors—"public" ownership of the government plus free entry into it—significantly alters a government's conduct of both its internal and its external affairs. Internally, the government is likely to exhibit an increased tendency to incur debt. While a king is by no means opposed to debt, he is constrained in this "natural" inclination by the fact that as the government's private owner, he and his heirs are considered personally liable for the payment of all government debts (he can literally go bankrupt, or be forced by creditors to liquidate government assets). In distinct contrast, a presidential government caretaker is not held liable for debts incurred during his tenure of office. Rather, his debts are considered "public," to be repaid by future (equally non-liable) governments. If one is not held personally liable for one's debts, however, the debt load will rise, and present government consumption will be expanded at the expense of future government consumption. In order to repay a rising public debt, the level of future taxes (or monetary inflation) imposed on a future public will have to increase. And with the expectation of a higher future-tax burden, the non-government public also becomes affected by the incubus of rising time-preference degrees, for with higher future-tax rates, present consumption and short-term investment are rendered relatively more attractive as compared to saving and long-term investment.[26]

---

and today it typically makes up 15 to 20 percent. See for details Peter Flora, *State, Economy, and Society in Western Europe 1815–1975: A Data Handbook* (London: Macmillan Press, 1983), 1, chaps. 5 and 8.

[26]The difficulties encountered by monarchical rulers in securing loans are notorious (see also footnote 24 above); and kings typically had to pay above-average rates of interest reflecting their comparatively high default risk. See on this North and Thomas, *The Rise of the Western World*, p. 96. In contrast, democratic governments, as they came into full bloom with the end of World War I, have indeed demonstrated a constant tendency toward deficit-financing and increasing debts. Today, the "national debts" in Western Europe and the "Western World" rarely amount to less than 30 percent of national product and frequently exceed 100 percent.

Likewise, and directly related, the monarchical world was generally characterized by the existence of a commodity money—typically gold or silver—and with the establishment of a single, integrated world market in the course of the 17th and 18th centuries, by an international gold standard. A commodity money standard makes it difficult for a government to inflate the money supply. By monopolizing the mint and engaging in systematic "coin clipping" (currency depreciation), kings did their best to enrich themselves at the expense of the public. But as much as they tried, they did not succeed in establishing monopolies of pure fiat currencies: of irredeemable national paper monies that can be created virtually out of thin air, at practically no cost. No particular individual, not even a king, could be trusted with an extraordinary monopoly such as this! Instead, it was only under conditions of democratic republicanism in the aftermath of World War I that the gold standard was abolished and at long last replaced with a world-wide system of irredeemable national paper monies in 1971. Since then, the supply of money and credit has increased dramatically. A seemingly permanent "secular" tendency toward inflation and currency depreciation has come into existence.

More importantly still, the government's conduct as the monopolist of law and order will undergo a systematic change. As explained above, a king will want to enforce the pre-existing private property law, and notwithstanding his own exceptional status *vis-à-vis* some of its key provisions, he, too, will assume and accept private property notions for himself and his possessions (at least insofar as *international* king-to-king relations are concerned). He does not create new law but merely occupies a privileged position within an existing, all-encompassing system of private law. In contrast, with a "publicly" owned and administered government a new type of "law" emerges: "public" law, which exempts government agents from personal liability and withholds "publicly owned" resources from economic management. With the establishment of "public law" (including constitutional and administrative law) not merely as law but as a "higher" law, a gradual erosion of private law ensues; that is, there is an increasing subordination and displacement of private law by and through public law.[27]

Government deficit financing has turned into a mere banking technicality, and interest rates—as an indicator for the social rate of time preference—which had continuously declined for centuries and by the end of the 19th century had fallen to around 2 percent, have since exhibited a systematic upward tendency.

See also Murray N. Rothbard, *What Has Government Done to Our Money?* (Auburn, Ala.: Ludwig von Mises Institute, 1992); Murray N. Rothbard, *The Mystery of Banking* (New York: Richardson and Snyder, 1983); on the history of interest rates Sidney Homer and Richard Sylla, *A History of Interest Rates* (New Brunswick, N.J.: Rutgers University Press, 1991), esp. chap. 23, pp. 553–58.

[27]In fact, although undermined by the Renaissance and the Protestant Revolutions, throughout the monarchical age the notion prevailed that kings and their subjects were ruled by a single, universal law—"a code of rules anterior to and co-existent with the sovereign—rules which were intangible and fixed," (de Jouvenel, *Sovereignty*, p. 193). Law was considered something to be discovered and recognized as eternally "given," not something to be "made." It was held "that law could not be legislated, but only applied as something that had always existed," (B. Rehfeld, *Die Wurzeln des Rechts* [Berlin 1951], p. 67). Indeed, as late as the beginning of the 20th century, Albert V. Dicey (*Lectures on the Relation between Law and Public Opinion in England during the Nineteenth Century* [London: Macmillan, 1903]) could still maintain that as for Great Britain, public or administrative law, as distinct from private law, did not exist: government agents, in their relationship with private citizens, were still regarded as bound by the same rules and subject to the same laws as any private citizen. It is again only after World War I, under democratic republicanism, that public agents achieve "immunity" from the provisions of private law, and that a view such as the leading socialist legal-theorist Gustav Radbruch's found general acceptance: that "for an individualistic order of public law, the state, is only the narrow protective belt surrounding private law and private property. In contrast, for a social (democratic republican) order of law private law is to be regarded only as a provisional and constantly decreasing range of private initiative, temporarily spared within the all-comprehensive sphere of public law," (*Der Mensch im Recht* [Göttingen: Vandenhoeck, 1957], p. 40). In the meantime, "in our own day we are used to having our rights modified by the sovereign decisions of legislators. A landlord no longer feels surprised at being compelled to keep a tenant; an employer is no less used to having to raise the wages of his employees in virtue of the decrees of Power. Nowadays it is understood that our subjective rights are precarious and at the good pleasure of authority," (de Jouvenel, *Sovereignty*, p. 189).

Rather than upholding private law among the non-government public and exploiting its legal monopoly solely for the purpose of redistributing wealth and income from civil society onto itself, a government "ruled" by public law will also employ its power increasingly for the purpose of legislation, i.e., for the creation of new, "positive" civil law, with the intent of redistributing wealth and income *within* civil society. For as a government's caretaker (not owner) it is of little or no concern to him that any such redistribution can only reduce future productivity. Confronted with popular elections and free entry into government, however, the advocacy and adoption of redistributive policies is predestined to become the very prerequisite for anyone wanting to attain or retain a government caretaker position. Accordingly, rather than representing a "consumption state" (as the typical monarchy does), with public government ownership, complementing and reinforcing the overall tendency toward rising taxes (and/or inflation), government employment and debt, the state will become increasingly transformed into a "welfare state."[28] And contrary to its typical portrayal as a "progressive" development, with this transformation the virus of rising degrees of time preference will be planted in the midst of civil society, and a self-accelerating process of decivilization will be set in motion.[29]

On the distinction between law and legislation see also Bruno Leoni, *Freedom and the Law* (Princeton, N.J.: Van Nostrand, 1961); F.A. Hayek, *Law, Legislation, and Liberty* (Chicago: University of Chicago Press, 1973), 1, chaps. 4 and 6.

[28]Until the end of the 19th century, the bulk of public spending—often more than 50 percent—typically went to financing the army (which, assuming government expenditures to be 5 percent of national product, amounted to military expenditures of 2.5 percent of national product). The rest went to government administration. Welfare spending or "public charity" played almost no role. In contrast, under democratic republicanism military expenditures have typically risen to 5–10 percent of national product. But with public expenditures making up 50 percent of national product, military expenditures now only represent 10 to 20 percent of total government spending. The bulk of public spending, typically more than 50 percent of total expenditures—and 25 percent of the national product—now is eaten up by public-welfare spending. See also Cipolla, *Before the Industrial Revolution*, pp. 54–55; Flora, *State, Economy, and Society in Western Europe*, chap. 8.

[29]Most important among the policies affecting social time preference is the introduction of "social security" legislation, as it was introduced during the 1880s in Bismarck's Germany and then became universal throughout the Western world in the aftermath of World War I. By relieving an individual of the task of having to provide for his own old age, the range and the temporal horizon of private provisionary action will be reduced. In particular, the value of marriage, family, and children will fall because they are less needed if one can fall back on "public" assistance. Indeed, since the onset of the democratic–republican age, all indicators of "family dysfunction" have exhibited a systematic upward tendency: the number of children has declined, the size of the endogenous population has stagnated or even fallen, and the rates of divorce, illegitimacy, single parenting, singledom, and abortion have risen. Moreover, personal-savings rates have begun to stagnate or even decline rather than rise proportionally or even over-proportionally with rising

The legislatively-enacted redistribution of income and wealth within civil society can essentially take on three forms. It can take the form of simple transfer payments, in which income and/or wealth is taken from Peter (the "haves") and doled out to Paul (the "have-nots"). It can take the form of "free" or below-cost provision of goods and services (such as education, health care, or infrastructure) by government, in which income and/or wealth is confiscated from one group of individuals—the taxpayers—and handed out to another, non-identical one—the users of the respective goods and services. Or it can take the form of business and/or consumer regulations or "protection laws" (such as price controls, tariffs, or licensing requirements), whereby the wealth of the members of one group of businessmen or consumers is increased at the expense of a corresponding loss for those of another "competing" group (by imposing legal restrictions on the uses which the latter are permitted to make of their private properties).

Regardless of its specific form, however, any such redistribution has a two-fold effect on civil society. First, the mere fact of legislation—of democratic lawmaking—increases the degree of uncertainty. Rather than being immutable and hence predictable, law becomes increasingly flexible and unpredictable. What is right and wrong today may not be so tomorrow. The future is thus rendered more haphazard. Consequently, all-around time-preference degrees will rise, consumption and short-term orientation will be stimulated, and at the same time the respect for all laws will be systematically undermined and crime promoted (for if there is no immutable standard of "right," then there is also no firm definition of "crime").[30]

<hr/>

incomes. See Allan C. Carlson, *Family Questions. Reflections on the American Social Crises* (New Brunswick, N.J.: Transaction Publishers, 1992); Allan C. Carlson, "What Has Government Done to Our Families?" *Essays in Political Economy*, no. 13 (Auburn, Ala.: Ludwig von Mises Institute, 1991); Bryce J. Christensen, "The Family vs. the State," *Essays in Political Economy*, no. 14 (Auburn, Ala.: Ludwig von Mises Institute, 1992); also Joseph A. Schumpeter, *Capitalism, Socialism, and Democracy* (New York: Harper, 1942), chap. 14.

[30]On the relationship between time preference and crime see James Q. Wilson and Richard J. Herrnstein, *Crime and Human Nature* (New York: Simon and Schuster, 1985), pp. 49–56 and 416–22; Banfield, *The Unheavenly City Revisited*; Edward C. Banfield, "Present-Orientedness and Crime," in *Assessing the Criminal. Restitution, Retribution, and the Legal Process*, Randy E. Barnett and John Hagel, eds. (Cambridge, Mass.: Ballinger, 1977). While high time preference is by no means equivalent with crime—it also may find expression in such perfectly legal forms as personal recklessness, insensitivity, rudeness, unreliability, or untrustworthiness— a systematic relationship between them still exists, for in order to earn a market income a certain minimum of planning, patience, and sacrifice is required: one must first work for a while before one gets paid. In contrast, specific criminal activities such as murder, assault, rape, robbery, theft, and burglary require no such discipline: the reward for the aggressor is tangible and immediate whereas the sacrifice—possible punishment—lies in the future and is uncertain.

Secondly, any income or wealth redistribution within civil society implies that the recipients are made economically better off without having produced either more or better goods or services, while others are made worse off without their having produced quantitatively or qualitatively less. Not producing, not producing anything worthwhile, or not correctly predicting the future and

---

Accordingly, if the degree of social time preference is increased, it can be expected that the frequency of aggressive activities will rise. As Banfield explaines (ibid., pp. 140–41):

> The threat of punishment at the hands of the law is unlikely to deter the present-oriented person. The gains that he expects from the illegal act are very near to the present, whereas the punishment that he would suffer—in the unlikely event of his being both caught and punished—lies in a future too distant for him to take into account. For the normal person there are of course risks other than the legal penalty that are strong deterrents: disgrace, loss of job, hardship for wife and children if one is sent to prison, and so on. The present-oriented person does not run such risks. In his circle it is taken for granted that one gets "in trouble" with the police now and then; he need not fear losing his job since he works intermittently or not at all, and as for his wife and children, he contributes little or nothing to their support and they may well be better off without him.

On the magnitude of the increase in criminal activity brought about by the operation of democratic republicanism in the course of the last hundred years as a consequence of steadily increased legislation and an ever-expanding range of "social," as opposed to private, responsibilities—see McGrath, *Gunfighters, Highwaymen, and Vigilantes*, esp. chap. 13. Comparing crime in some of the wildest places of the American "Wild West" (two frontier towns and mining camps in California and Nevada) to that of some of the wilder places of the present age, McGrath ("Treat Them to a Good Dose of Lead," pp. 17–18) sums up thus by stating that the frontier towns of

> Bodie and Aurora actually suffered rarely from robbery . . . today's cities, such as Detroit, New York, and Miami, have 20 times as much robbery per capita. The United States as a whole averages three times as much robbery per capita as Bodie and Aurora. Burglary and theft were also of infrequent occurrence in the mining towns. Most American cities today average 30 or 40 times as much burglary and theft per capita as Bodie and Aurora. The national rate is ten times higher. . . .There were no reported cases of rape in either Aurora or Bodie. . . . Today, a rape occurs every five minutes . . . . More than 4,100 of them occur in Los Angeles county alone. . . . The rape rate in the United States per 100,000 inhabitants is 42. . . . [Violence, including homicide, was frequent in Bodie and Aurora] but the men involved were both young, healthy, armed, and willing. . . . Yes, men (and some women) went about armed and male combatants killed each other, mostly in fights where there were somewhat "even chances." On the other hand, the young, the old, the female, and those who chose not to drink in saloons and display reckless bravado were rarely the victims of crime or violence. Moreover, dirty, low-down scoundrels got their just dessert. . . . In the early 1950s the city of Los Angeles averaged about 70 murders a year. Today the city averages more than 90 murders a month. . . . In 1952 there were 572 rapes reported to the LAPD. In 1992 there were 2,030 reported. During the same years robbery increased from a reported total of 2,566 to 39,508, and auto theft from 6,241 to 68,783.

the future exchange-demand for one's products thus becomes relatively more attractive (or less prohibitive) as compared to producing something of value and predicting the future exchange-demand correctly. Consequently—and regardless of the specific legislative intent, be it to "help" or "protect" the poor, the unemployed, the sick, the young or the old, the uneducated or the stupid, the farmers, steelworkers or truckers, the uninsured, the homeless, whites or blacks, the married or unmarried, those with children or those without, etc.,—there will be more people producing less and displaying poor foresight, and fewer people producing more and predicting well. For if individuals possess even the slightest control over the criteria that "entitle" a person to be either on the receiving or on the "giving" end of the redistribution, they increasingly will shift out of the latter roles and into the former. There will be more poor, unemployed, uninsured, uncompetitive, homeless, and so on, than otherwise. Even if such a shift is not possible, as in the case of sex-, race-, or age-based income or wealth redistribution, the incentive to be productive and farsighted will still be reduced. There may not be more men or women, or whites or blacks, at least not immediately. However, because the members of the privileged sex, race, or age group are awarded an unearned income, they have less of an incentive to earn one in the future, and because the members of the discriminated sex, race, or age group are punished for possessing wealth or having produced an income, they, too, will be less productive in the future. In any case, there will be less productive activity, self-reliance and future-orientation, and more consumption, parasitism, dependency and shortsightedness. That is, the very problem that the redistribution was supposed to cure will have grown even bigger. Accordingly, the cost of maintaining the existing level of welfare distribution will be higher now than before, and in order to finance it, even higher taxes and more wealth confiscation must be imposed on the remaining producers. The tendency to shift from production to non-production activities will be further strengthened, leading to continuously rising time-preference rates and a progressive de-civilization—infantilization and demoralization—of civil society.[31]

In addition, with public ownership and free entry into a democratic–republican government, the foreign policy changes as well.

---

[31]On the "logic" of government interventionism—its counterproductivity, inherent instability, and "progressive" character—see Ludwig von Mises, *Critique of Interventionism* (New Rochelle, N.Y.: Arlington House, 1977); see also Mises, *Human Action*, pt. 6.

For empirical illustrations of the decivilizing and demoralizing effects of redistributive policies see Banfield, *The Unheavenly City Revisited*; Charles Murray, *Losing Ground* (New York: Basic Books, 1984).

All governments are expected to be expansionary, as ex-plained above, and there is no reason to assume that a president's expansionary desires will be any less than a king's. However, while a king may satisfy this desire through marriage, this route is essentially precluded for a president. He does not own the government controlled territory; hence, he cannot contractually combine separate territories. And even if he concluded inter-government treaties, these would not possess the status of contracts but constitute at best only temporary pacts or alliances, because as agreements concerning publicly-owned resources, they could be revoked at any time by other future governments. If a democratic ruler and a democratically elected ruling elite want to expand their territory and hence their tax base, then no option but a military one of conquest and domination is open to them. Hence, the likelihood of war will be significantly increased.[32]

Moreover, apart from its likelihood, the form of war will change, too. Kings have to fund their wars largely out of private funds because of a clear and developed class consciousness among the ruled, and their wars thus tend to be limited. The public views monarchical wars generally as private conflicts between different

[32]Prior to and long after the onset of the democratic–republican transformation of Europe with the French (and the American) Revolution, most prominent social philosophers—from Montesquieu, Rousseau, Kant, Say, to J.S. Mill—had essentially contended "That it was only the ruling classes [the king, the nobility] who wanted war, and that 'the people,' if only they were allowed to speak for themselves, would opt enthusiastically for peace." Michael Howard, *War and the Liberal Conscience* (New Brunswick, N.J.: Rutgers University Press, 1978), chaps. 1 and 2, p. 45. Indeed, Immanuel Kant, in his *Perpetual Peace of 1795*, claimed a republican constitution to be the prerequisite for perpetual peace. For under a republican constitution,

> when the consent of the citizens is necessary to decide whether there shall be war or not, nothing is more natural than that, since they would have to decide on imposing all of the hardships of war onto themselves, they will be very hesitant to begin such an evil adventure. In contrast, under a constitution where the subject is not a citizen, which is thus not republican, it is the easiest thing in the world, because the sovereign is not a citizen of the state but its owner, his dining, hunting, castles, parties, etc., will not suffer in the least from the war, and he can thus go to war for meaningless reasons, as if it were a pleasure trip. (*Gesammelte Werke in zwölf Bänden*, W. Weischedel, ed. [Frankfurt/M.: Suhrkamp, 1964], 11, pp. 205f)

In fact the opposite is true: the substitution of a republic for a monarchy does not imply less government power, or even self-rule. It implies the replacement of bad private-government administration by worse public-government administration. On the illusionary character of Kant's and others' views to the contrary and the "positive" historical correlation between democracy and increased militarization and war, see Michael Howard *War in European History* (New York: Oxford University Press, 1976); John F. Fuller, *War and Western Civilization 1832–1932* (Freeport, N.Y.: Books for Libraries, 1969); John F. Fuller, *The Conduct of War, 1789–1961* (New York: Da Capo Press, 1992); also E. Krippendorff, *Staat und Krieg* (Frankfurt/M.: Suhrkamp, 1985). See also footnote 35 below.

ruling families, and kings are thus compelled to recognize a distinction between combatants and non-combatants and to target their war efforts specifically against each other and their respective private properties. In contrast, democratic wars tend to be total wars. In blurring the distinction between the rulers and the ruled, a democratic republic strengthens the identification of the public with a particular state. Indeed, while dynastic rule promotes the identification with one's own family and community and the development of a "cosmopolitan" outlook and attitude,[33] democratic republicanism inevitably leads to nationalism, i.e., the emotional identification of the public with large, anonymous groups of people, characterized in terms of a common language, history, religion and/or culture and in contradistinction to other, foreign nations. Interstate wars thus turn into national wars. Rather than representing "merely" violent dynastic property disputes, which may be "resolved" through acts of territorial occupation, they become battles between different ways of life, which can only be "resolved" through cultural, linguistic or religious domination and subjugation (or extermination). It will be more and more difficult for members of the public to remain neutral or to extricate themselves from all personal involvement. Resistance against higher taxes to fund a war is increasingly considered to be

---

[33] As the result of marriages, bequests, inheritances, etc., royal territories were often discontiguous, and kings frequently came to rule linguistically and culturally distinct populations. Accordingly, they found it in their interest to speak several languages: universal ones such as Latin, and then French, as well as local ones such as English, German, Italian, Russian, Dutch, Czech, etc. (See M. Vale, "Civilization of Courts and Cities in the North, 1200–1500," in *Oxford History of Medieval Europe*, George Holmes, ed. [Oxford: Oxford University Press, 1988], pp. 322–23). Likewise the small social and intellectual elites were usually proficient in several languages and thereby demonstrated their simultaneously local and supra-local, or cosmopolitan–intellectual orientation. This cosmopolitan outlook came to bear in the fact that throughout the monarchical age until 1914, Europe was characterized by a nearly complete freedom of migration. "A man could travel across the length and breadth of the Continent without a passport until he reached the frontiers of Russia and the Ottoman Empire. He could settle in a foreign country for work or leisure without formalities except, occasionally, some health requirements. Every currency was as good as gold." A.J.P. Taylor, *From Sarajevo to Potsdam* (New York: Harcourt, Brace and World, 1966), p. 7. In contrast, today in the age of democratic republicanism, it has become unthinkable that one might be ruled by a "foreigner," or that states could be anything but contiguously extended territories. States are defined by their citizens, and citizens in turn are defined by their state passports. International migration is strictly regulated and controlled. Political rulers and the intellectual elite, far more numerous now, are increasingly ignorant of foreign languages. It is no coincidence that of all the members of the European Parliament, only Otto von Hapsburg, the current family head of the former Hapsburg rulers, speaks all of the parliament's official business languages.

For a prominent, highly apologetic historical treatment of the transition from cosmopolitanism to nationalism in 19th-century Germany, see Friedrich Meinecke, *Cosmopolitanism and the National State* (Princeton, N.J.: Princeton University Press, 1970).

treachery or treason. Conscription becomes the rule, rather than the exception. And with mass armies of cheap and hence easily disposable conscripts fighting for national supremacy (or against national suppression) backed by the economic resources of the entire nation, all distinctions between combatants and non-combatants will fall by the wayside, and wars will become increasingly brutal.[34]

RETROSPECTIVES AND PROSPECTS

The process of civilization set in motion by individual saving, investment, and the accumulation of durable consumer goods and

---

[34]Thus concludes Fuller (*War and Western Civilization*, pp. 26–27):

> The influence of the spirit of nationality, that is of democracy, on war was profound, . . . (it) emotionalized war and, consequently, brutalized it; . . . In the eighteenth century wars were largely the occupation of kings, courtiers and gentlemen. Armies lived on their depots, they interfered as little as possible with the people, and as soldiers were paid out of the king's privy purse they were too costly to be thrown away lightly on massed attacks. The change came about with the French Revolution, sans culottism replaced courtiership, and as armies became more and more the instruments of the people, not only did they grow in size but in ferocity. National armies fight nations, royal armies fight their like, the first obey a mob— always demented, the second a king—generally sane. . . . All this developed out of the French Revolution, which also gave to the world conscription—herd warfare, and the herd coupling with finance and commerce has begotten new realms of war. For when once the whole nation fights, then is the whole national credit available for the purposes of war.

Monarchical wars, Fuller (*The Conduct of War*, p. 23) quotes Daniel Defoe, often had "armies of fifty thousand men of a side stand at bay within view of one another, and spend a whole campaign in dodging, or, as it is genteely called, observing one another, and then march off into winter quarters." Similarly comments Sir John Fontescue (quoted in ibid., p. 25): "To force an enemy to consume his own supplies was much, to compel him to supply his opponents was more, to take up winter-quarters in his territory was very much more. Thus to enter an enemy's borders and keep him marching backwards and forwards for weeks without giving him a chance of striking a blow, was in itself no small success."

In contrast, with republicanism and democracy comes conscription. Formerly it had been argued that since one had no vote in the state, one should not be forced to fight its wars. Now the argument was reversed. Because one had the right to vote, one was compelled to fight.

> Conscription changed the basis of warfare. Hitherto soldiers had been costly, now they were cheap; battles had been avoided, now they were sought, and however heavy were the losses, they could rapidly be made good by the muster-roll. . . . From August [of 1793, when the parliament of the French republic decreed universal compulsory military service] onward, not only was war to become more and more unlimited, but finally total. In the fourth decade of the twentieth century life was held so cheaply that the massacre of civilian populations on wholesale lines became as accepted a strategic aim as battles were in previous wars. In 150 years conscription had led the world back to tribal barbarism. (Fuller, *The Conduct of War*, pp. 33 and 35)

capital goods—of gradually falling time preferences and an ever widening and lengthening range and horizon of private provisions—may be temporarily upset by crime. But because a person is permitted to defend himself against crime, the existence of criminal activities does not alter the direction of the process. It merely leads to more defense spending and less non-defense spending.

Instead, a change in direction—stagnating or even rising time preferences—can be brought about only if property-rights violations become *institutionalized*; i.e., in the environment of a government. Yet whereas all governments must be assumed to have a tendency toward internal growth as well as territorial expansion (political centralization), not all forms of government can be expected to be equally successful in their endeavors. If the government is privately owned (under monarchical rule), the incentive structure facing the ruler is such that it is in his self-interest to be relatively farsighted and only engage in moderate taxation and warfare. The speed of the process of civilization will be slowed down systematically. However, the decivilizing forces arising from monarchical rule may be expected to be insufficiently strong to overcome the fundamental, countervailing tendency toward falling time-preference rates and ever expanding ranges of private provisions. Rather, it is only when a government is *publicly* owned (under democratic–republican rule) that the decivilizing effects of government can be expected to grow strong enough to actually halt the civilizing process, or even to alter its direction and bring about an opposite tendency toward de-civilization: capital consumption, shrinking planning horizons and provisions, and a progressive infantilization and brutalization of social life.

Retrospectively, in light of these theoretical conclusions much of modern European and Western history can be rationally reconstructed and understood. In the course of one and a half centuries—beginning with the American and French Revolutions and ending with the end of World War I and continuing to the present—Europe, and in its wake the entire western world, underwent an epochal transformation. Everywhere, monarchical rule and sovereign kings were replaced by democratic–republican rule and sovereign "peoples."[35]

[35]On the historical significance and the revolutionary character of this transformation see G. Ferrero, *Peace and War* (Freeport, N.Y.: Books for Libraries, 1933/69), esp. pp. 155ff; idem, *Macht* (Bern: A. Francke, 1944); Palmer and Colton, *A History of the Modern World*, esp. chaps. 14 and 18; also Reinhard Bendix, *Kings or People* (Berkeley: University of California Press, 1978).

On the intellectual debate on the idea of popular sovereignty, and universal suffrage, in particular in Great Britain, see Elie Halevy, *The Growth of Philosophical Radicalism* (Boston: Beacon Press, 1955), esp. pp. 120–50.

The first direct attack by republicanism and popular sovereignty on the monarchical principle was repelled with the military defeat of Napoleon and the restoration of the Bourbon rule in France. As a result of the Napoleonic experience, during much of the 19th-century republicanism was widely discredited. "Republicanism was still thought to be violent—bellicose in its foreign policy, turbulent in its political workings, unfriendly to the church, and socialistic or at least equalitarian in its view of property and private wealth."[36] Still, the democratic–republican spirit of the French Revolution left a permanent imprint. From the restoration of the monarchical order in 1815 until the outbreak of World War I in 1914, popular political participation and representation was systematically expanded all across Europe. Everywhere the franchise was successively widened, and the powers of popularly elected parliaments were gradually increased.[37]

Nonetheless, although increasingly emasculated, the principle of monarchical government remained dominant until the cataclysmic events of World War I. Before the war only two republics existed in Europe: Switzerland and France. Only four years later, after the United States government had entered the European war and decisively determined its outcome, monarchies had all but disappeared, and Europe had turned to democratic-republicanism. With the involvement of the U.S., the war took on a new dimension. Rather than an old-fashioned territorial dispute, as was the case before 1917, it turned into an ideological war. The U.S. had been founded as a republic, and the democratic principle in particular, inherent in the idea of a republic, had only recently been carried to victory as the result of the violent defeat and devastation of the secessionist Confederacy by the centralist Union government. At the time of World War I, this triumphant ideology of an expansionist democratic–republicanism had found its very personification in then-U.S. President Woodrow Wilson. Under Wilson's administration the European war became an ideological mission—to make the world safe for democracy and free of dynastic rulers.[38] Hence, the defeated Romanovs, Hohenzollerns, and Hapsburgs had to abdicate or resign, and Russia, Germany, and Austria became democratic republics with universal—male and

---

[36]Palmer and Colton, *A History of the Modern World*, p. 606.

[37]For the details of this process see Flora, *State, Economy, and Society in Western Europe*, chap. 3.

[38]On the U.S. war involvement see Fuller, *The Conduct of War*, chap. 9; on the role of Woodrow Wilson in particular, see Murray N. Rothbard, "World War I as Fulfillment: Power and the Intellectuals," *Journal of Libertarian Studies* 9, no. 1 (1989); Paul Gottfried, "Wilsonianism: The Legacy that Won't Die," *Journal of Libertarian Studies* 9, no. 2 (1990).

female—suffrage and parliamentary governments. Likewise, all of the newly created successor states—Poland, Finland, Estonia, Latvia, Lithuania, Hungary, and Czechoslovakia, with the exception only of Yugoslavia—adopted democratic–republican constitutions. In Turkey and Greece, the monarchies were overthrown. And even where monarchies remained in existence, as in Great Britain, Italy, Spain, Belgium, the Netherlands, and the Scandinavian countries, monarchs no longer exercised any governmental power. Everywhere, universal adult suffrage was introduced, and all government power was invested in parliaments and "public" officials.[39] A new era—the democratic–republican age under the aegis of a dominating U.S. government—had begun.

From the perspective of economic theory, the end of World War I can be identified as the point in time at which private-government ownership was completely replaced by public-government ownership, and from which a tendency toward rising degrees of social time preference, government growth, and an attending process of decivilization should be expected to have taken off. Indeed, as indicated in detail above, such has been the grand underlying theme of 20th century Western history.[40] Since 1918, practically all indicators of high or rising time preferences have exhibited a systematic upward tendency: as far as government is concerned, democratic republicanism produced communism (and with this public slavery and government sponsored mass murder even in peacetime), fascism, national socialism and, lastly and most enduringly, social democracy ("liberalism").[41] Compulsory military service has become almost universal, foreign and civil wars have increased in frequency and in brutality, and the process of political centralization has advanced further than ever before. Internally, democratic republicanism has led to permanently rising taxes, debts, and public employment. It has led to the destruction of the gold standard, unparalleled paper-money inflation, and increased protectionism and migration controls. Even the most fundamental private law provisions have been perverted by an

[39]Interestingly, the Swiss republic, which was the first country to firmly establish the institution of universal suffrage for males above the age of 20 (1848), was the last to expand the suffrage also to women (1971).

[40]On the world-wide growth of statism since World War I see Paul Johnson, *Modern Times: The World from the Twenties to the Eighties* (New York: Harper and Row, 1983); on U.S. government growth, and its relation to war, see Robert Higgs, *Crisis and Leviathan: Critical Episodes in the Growth of American Government* (New York: Oxford University Press, 1987).

[41]On the common historical roots of Soviet communism, and of fascism and national socialism as "tyrannies" (literally: "arbitrary powers, the holders of which claim to use it for the people and in fact appeal to the people, for support")—in World War I, and on the "primary" character of the former and the "derivative" of the latter, see Elie Halevy, *The Era of Tyrannies* (Garden City: Anchor Books, 1965).

unabating flood of legislation and regulation. Simultaneously, as regards civil society, the institutions of marriage and family have been increasingly weakened, the number of children has declined, and the rates of divorce, illegitimacy, single parenthood, single-dom, and abortion have increased. Rather than rising with rising incomes, savings rates have been stagnating or even falling. In comparison to the 19th century, the cognitive prowess of the political and intellectual elites and the quality of public education have declined. And the rates of crime, structural unemployment, welfare dependency, parasitism, negligence, recklessness, incivility, psychopathy, and hedonism have increased.

Today, at the end of the 20th century, democratic-republican-ism in the U.S. and all across the Western world has apparently exhausted the reserve fund that was inherited from the past. For decades, real incomes have stagnated or even fallen.[42] The public debt and the cost of the existing social-security systems have brought on the prospect of an imminent economic meltdown. At the same time, social conflict and societal breakdown have risen to dangerous heights. Thus, at long last, the question arises: Can anything be done to prevent the process of de-civilization from running its full course to an outright economic and social catas-trophe?

Above all, the idea of democracy and democratic rule must be delegitimized! Ultimately, the course of human history is deter-mined by *ideas*, be they true or false. Just as kings could not exer-cise their rule unless a majority of public opinion accepted such rule as legitimate, so democratic rulers cannot last without ideo-logical support in public opinion. Likewise, the *transition* from monarchical to democratic rule has to be explained as fundamen-tally nothing but a *change* in public opinion: Until the end of World War I, the overwhelming majority of the public in Europe accepted monarchical rule as legitimate.[43] Today, hardly anyone would do so. Indeed, the idea of monarchical government is con-sidered laughable. Accordingly, a *return* to the "ancien regime" has to be regarded as impossible. The legitimacy of monarchical rule appears to have been irretrievably lost. Nor would such a re-turn be a genuine solution. Rather, the idea of democratic republi-can rule must be rendered equally if not more laughable (not the

---

[42]For an analysis of U.S. data see Robert Batemarco, "GNP, PPR, and the Standard of Living," *Review of Austrian Economics* 1 (1987).

[43]As late as 1871, for instance, with universal male suffrage, the National Assembly of the French republic contained only about 200 republicans out of more than 600 deputies. And the restoration of a monarchy was only prevented because the supporters of the Bourbons and the Orleans checkmated each other.

least by identifying it as the source of the ongoing process of de-civilization). It must be made clear that it is not government (monarchical *or* democratic), but private property, and the recognition and defense of private-property rights, which is the ultimate source of human civilization. And strategically—in order to promote the delegitimation of democracy and at the same time advance the supreme legitimacy of private property, contractualism, and individual responsibility—ideological support should be given to all decentralizing or even secessionist social forces. For a territorially smaller government makes for moderation, and only in small regional communities does it become possible for elites to emerge whose "natural (voluntarily acknowledged) authority" can lend legitimacy to the idea and institution of an "anarchic" private-law society as the answer to monarchy *and* democracy.

ADDITIONAL RECOMMENDED READING

Barnes, Harry Elmer. [1926] 1980. *Revisionism: A Key to Peace and Other Essays*. San Francisco: Cato Institute.

———. [1926] 1970. *The Genesis of World War*. New York: Howard Fertig.

Beard, Charles A. 1948. *President Roosevelt and the Coming of the War, 1941*. New Haven, Conn.: Yale University Press.

Chamberlin, William H. 1962. *America's Second Crusade*. Colorado Springs, Colo.: Ralph Myles.

Childs, Roy A., Jr. 1994. "Big Business and the Rise of American Statism." In Joan Kennedy Taylor, ed., *Liberty Against Power*. San Francisco: Fox and Wilkes.

Cochran, M. H. 1972. *Germany Not Guilty in 1914*. Colorado Springs, Colo.: Ralph Myles.

Cole, Wayne S. 1974. *Charles A. Lindbergh and the Battle Against American Intervention in World War II*. New York: Harcourt Brace Jovanovich.

———. 1983. *Roosevelt and The Isolationists*. Omaha: University of Nebraska Press.

Doenecke, Justus D. 1972. *The Literature of Isolationism: A Guide to Non-interventionist Scholarship, 1930–1972*. Colorado Springs, Colo.: Ralph Myles.

Eggleston, George T. 1979. *Roosevelt, Churchill, and the World War II Opposition*. Old Greenwich, Conn.: Devin-Adair.

Ekirch, Arthur A., Jr. 1969. *The Decline of American Liberalism*. New York: Atheneum.

Ely, John Hart. 1993. *War and Responsibility: Constitutional Lessons of Vietnam and its Aftermath*. Princeton, N.J.: Princeton University Press.

Epstein, Julius. 1973. *Operation Keelhaul: The Story of Forced Repatriation*. Old Greenwich, Conn.: Devin-Adair.

Flynn, John T. 1973. *As We Go Marching*. New York: Free Life.

Fussell, Paul. 1975. *The Great War and Modern Memory*. New York: Oxford University Press.

———. 1989. *Wartime: Understanding and Behavior in the Second World War*. New York: Oxford University Press.

Gaddis, John L. 1972. *The United States and the Origins of the Cold War, 1941–1947*. New York: Columbia University Press.

Garrett, Garet. 1953. "Rise of Empire." In *The People's Pottage*. Caldwell, Idaho: Caxton.

Higgs, Robert. 1987. *Crisis and Leviathan: Critical Episodes in the Growth of American Government*. New York: Oxford University Press.

Hughes, Jonathan R. T. 1991. *The Governmental Habit Redux: Economic Controls from Colonial Times to the Present*. Princeton, N.J.: Princeton University Press.

Hummel, Jeffrey Rogers. 1996. *Emancipating Slaves, Enslaving Free Men: A History of the American Civil War*. Chicago and LaSalle, Ill.: Open Court.

Kolko, Gabriel. 1968. *The Politics of War: The World and United States Foreign Policy, 1943–1945*. New York: Random House.

——. 1963. *The Triumph of Conservatism: A Reinterpretation of American History, 1900–1916*. Chicago: Quadrangle Paperbacks.

Kwitny, Jonathan. 1984. *Endless Enemies*. New York: Congdon and Weed.

Liggio, Leonard P. 1978. *Why the Futile Crusade?* New York: Center for Libertarian Studies.

——, and James J. Martin, eds. 1976. *Watershed of Empire: Essays on New Deal Foreign Policy*. Colorado Springs, Colo.: Ralph Myles.

Martin, James J. 1963. *American Liberalism and World Politics*. Old Greenwich, Conn.: Devin-Adair.

——. 1971. *Revisionist Viewpoints: Essays in a Dissident Historical Tradition*. Colorado Springs, Colo.: Ralph Myles.

Morgenstern, George. 1947. *Pearl Harbor: The Story of the Secret War*. Old Greenwich, Conn.: Devin-Adair.

Morley, Felix. 1951. *The Foreign Policy of the United States*. New York: Alfred A. Knopf.

Neilson, Frances. 1915. *How Diplomats Make War*. San Francisco: Cobden Press.

Opitz, Edmund A., ed. 1995. *Leviathan at War*. Irvington-on-Hudson, N.Y.: Foundation for Economic Education.

Radosh, Ronald. 1975. *Prophets on the Right: Conservative Critics of American Globalism*. New York: Simon and Schuster.

——, and Murray N. Rothbard, eds. 1972. *A New History of Leviathan: Essays on the Rise of the American Corporate State.* New York: E.P. Dutton.

Raimondo, Justin. 1993. *Reclaiming the American Right.* Burlingame, Calif.: Center for Libertarian Studies.

Ravenal, Earl C. 1978. *Never Again: Learning from America's Foreign Policy Failures.* Philadelphia: Temple University Press.

Ross, Bill D. 1991. *Peleliu: Tragic Triumph.* New York: Random House.

Rothbard, Murray N. 1995. *Wall Street, Banks, and American Foreign Policy.* Burlingame, Calif.: Center for Libertarian Studies.

——. 1974. "War, Peace and the State." In *Egalitarianism as a Revolt Against Nature and Other Essays.* Washington, D.C.: Libertarian Review Press.

Rusbridger, James and Nave, Eric. 1991. *Betrayal at Pearl Harbor: How Churchill Lured Roosevelt into World War II.* New York: Summit Books.

Russett, Bruce M. 1972. *No Clear and Present Danger: A Skeptical View of the United States Entry into World War II.* New York: Harper and Row.

Stein, Arthur A. 1980. *The Nation at War.* Baltimore, Maryland: Johns Hopkins University Press.

Stenehjem, Michele Flynn. 1976. *An American First: John T. Flynn and the American First Committee.* New Rochelle, N.Y.: Arlington House.

Taft, Robert. 1951. *A Foreign Policy for Americans.* Garden City, N.Y.: Doubleday.

Tansill, Charles C. [1938] 1963. *America Goes to War.* Gloucester, Mass.: Peter Smith.

——. 1952. *Back Door to War: The Roosevelt Foreign Policy, 1933–1941.* Chicago: Regnery.

Taylor, A. J. P. 1961. *The Origins of the Second World War,* 2nd ed. Greenwich, Conn.: Fawcett Premier Book.

Toland, John. 1982. *Infamy: Pearl Harbor and Its Aftermath.* Garden City, N.Y.: Doubleday.

Williams, William A. 1972. *The Tragedy of American Diplomacy.* New York: Dell.

Wilson, Edmund. 1962. *Patriotic Gore: Studies in the Literature of the American Civil War.* New York: Oxford University Press.

ABOUT THE CONTRIBUTORS

Allan Carlson is president of the Rockford Institute.

John V. Denson is an attorney in Opelika, Alabama.

Richard Gamble is assistant professor of history at Palm Beach Atlantic College.

Paul Gottfried is professor of political philosophy at Elizabethtown College.

Robert Higgs is research director of the Independent Institute.

Hans-Hermann Hoppe is professor of economics at the University of Nevada, Las Vegas, and coeditor of *The Review of Austrian Economics*.

Thomas Fleming is editor of *Chronicles: A Magazine of American Culture*.

Samuel Francis is a syndicated columnist and publishes *The Samuel Francis Newsletter*.

Paul Fussell is the Donald T. Regan professor of English literature at the University of Pennsylvania and a veteran of World War II.

Bill Kauffman is an author in Genesee County, New York.

Ralph Raico is professor of history at the State University College at Buffalo, New York.

Justin Raimondo is writer-in-residence at the Center for Libertarian Studies.

Murray N. Rothbard (1926–1995) was S. J. Hall distinguished professor of economics at the University of Nevada, Las Vegas, and academic vice president at the Ludwig von Mises Institute.

Joseph T. Salerno is professor of economics at Pace University and co-editor of *The Review of Austrian Economics*.

Eugene B. Sledge is professor *emeritus* of biology at the University of Montevallo and a former U.S. Marine.

Historian Joseph R. Stromberg is an adjunct scholar of the Center for Libertarian Studies.

Clyde N. Wilson is professor of history at the University of South Carolina and editor of *The Papers of John C. Calhoun*.

INDEX